Lecture Notes in Artificial Intelligence 9060

Subseries of Lecture Notes in Computer Science

T0234081

Thomas Eiter   Hannes Strass
Mirosław Truszczyński   Stefan Woltran (Eds.)

Advances in Knowledge Representation, Logic Programming, and Abstract Argumentation

Essays Dedicated to Gerhard Brewka
on the Occasion of His 60th Birthday

 Springer

Volume Editors

Thomas Eiter
Technische Universität Wien, Institut für Informationssysteme 184/3
Abteilung für Wissensbasierte Systeme
Favoritenstraße 9-11, 1040 Wien, Austria
E-mail: eiter@kr.tuwien.ac.at

Hannes Strass
Universität Leipzig, Institut für Informatik, Abteilung Intelligente Systeme
PF 100920, 04009 Leipzig, Germany
E-mail: strass@informatik.uni-leipzig.de

Mirosław Truszczyński
University of Kentucky, Department of Computer Science
329 Rose Street, Lexington, KY 40506-0633, USA
E-mail: mirek@cs.uky.edu

Stefan Woltran
Technische Universität Wien, Institut für Informationssysteme 184/2
Abteilung für Datenbanken und Artificial Intelligence
Favoritenstraße 9-11, 1040 Wien, Austria
E-mail: woltran@dbai.tuwien.ac.at

ISSN 0302-9743   e-ISSN 1611-3349
ISBN 978-3-319-14725-3   e-ISBN 978-3-319-14726-0
DOI 10.1007/978-3-319-14726-0
Springer Cham Heidelberg New York Dordrecht London

Library of Congress Control Number: 2014958453

LNCS Sublibrary: SL 7 – Artificial Intelligence

Typesetting: Camera-ready by author, data conversion by Scientific Publishing Services, Chennai, India

Printed on acid-free paper

Springer is part of Springer Science+Business Media (www.springer.com)

Gerhard Brewka

Preface

Gerhard Brewka has made a distinct mark on the field of artificial intelligence through his pioneering research ideas and fruitful collaborations. The present volume is a Festschrift in his honor on the occasion of his 60th birthday and covers the scientific fields Gerd contributed to. The articles address recent research in areas such as actions and agents, nonmonotonic and human reasoning, preferences, and argumentation. The Festschrift is complemented by a summary of Gerd Brewka's contributions compiled by the editors of this volume, a reflection on the current and future challenges within the field of knowledge representation by Wolfgang Bibel, and a personal account by Tom Gordon.

We would like to thank all authors who contributed to this Festschrift and the colleagues who acted as peer-reviewers.

A special thanks goes to Anni, Alena, and Janna Brewka for providing us with some photos from times when telephones and cameras were quite different things.

We finally thank Gerd's group in Leipzig, who have been of great help in making this Festschrift a reality.

November 2014

Thomas Eiter
Hannes Strass
Mirosław Truszczyński
Stefan Woltran

Organization

Program Committee

Pietro Baroni	University of Brescia, Italy
Ringo Baumann	Leipzig University, Germany
Richard Booth	University of Luxembourg, Luxembourg
Pedro Cabalar	University of Corunna, Spain
Jürgen Dix	Clausthal University of Technology, Germany
Wolfgang Dvořák	University of Vienna, Austria
Thomas Eiter	Vienna University of Technology, Austria
Stefan Ellmauthaler	Leipzig University, Germany
Michael Fink	Vienna University of Technology, Austria
Sarah Alice Gaggl	Technische Universität Dresden, Germany
Tomi Janhunen	Aalto University, Finland
Ulrich Junker	Biot, France
Gabriele Kern-Isberner	Technische Universität Dortmund, Germany
Jérôme Lang	LAMSADE
Thomas Linsbichler	Vienna University of Technology, Austria
Jörg Pührer	Leipzig University, Germany
Sebastian Rudolph	Technische Universität Dresden, Germany
Torsten Schaub	University of Potsdam, Germany
Tran Cao Son	New Mexico State University, USA
Hannes Strass	Leipzig University, Germany
Michael Thielscher	The University of New South Wales, Australia
Mirosław Truszczyński	University of Kentucky, USA
Johannes Peter Wallner	Vienna University of Technology, Austria
Stefan Woltran	Vienna University of Technology, Austria

Additional Reviewer

Bloch, Isabelle

Table of Contents

Preferences

Abstract Argumentation

Reflections on Knowledge Representation

Epilogue

A Glimpse on Gerhard Brewka's Contributions to Artificial Intelligence

Thomas Eiter[1], Hannes Strass[2], Mirosław Truszczyński[3], and Stefan Woltran[4]

[1] Knowledge-Based Systems Group, Vienna University of Technology,
Vienna, Austria
[2] Computer Science Institute, Leipzig University, Leipzig, Germany
[3] Department of Computer Science, University of Kentucky, Lexington, KY, USA
[4] Database and Artificial Intelligence Group, Vienna University of Technology,
Vienna, Austria

Abstract. Gerhard Brewka has made a remarkable impact on artificial intelligence, especially in the area of knowledge representation, through his ideas, collaborations and mentoring, always amazing those close to him with his ability to inspire. This short paper offers a glimpse into four areas of research where Gerd's imprint has been particularly distinct, intertwined with personal recollections of the authors, and with comments on those of Gerd's personal characteristics that make his research perspectives so appealing to others.

1 Introduction

"To continue in one path is to go backward." – Igor Stravinsky

Gerhard Brewka has made a distinct mark on the field of artificial intelligence through his pioneering research ideas, fruitful collaborations with many colleagues, deep influence on his students, and dedicated service to the broad AI community in high visibility and high impact roles. This article will provide an overview of Gerd's professional contributions, focusing on his research. But along the lines we will comment on those characteristics of Gerd that make him an inspiring colleague, friend and mentor. The four of us have been beneficiaries of Gerd's ideas, enthusiasm and friendship. By writing this article and editing this volume we hope in some small way to show our gratitude and appreciation.

Gerd's research covers a spectrum of problems central to AI that concern knowledge representation and reasoning. All of his endeavors addressed problems that were both fundamental and in urgent need of solutions. Importantly, he was able to connect disjoint ideas, for instance developing an integrated perspective on preferences and nonmonotonic reasoning, or proposing nonmonotonic multi-context systems. And throughout his career, Gerd's cutting-edge research has always been a source of inspiration for many researchers and students.

In order to reflect the multitude of Gerd's influential work, this paper is grouped into four sections corresponding roughly to those research areas where his ideas and contributions were felt the most. We start by reviewing Gerd's work

T. Eiter et al. (Eds.): Brewka Festschrift, LNAI 9060, pp. 1–16, 2015.

in the area of reasoning about actions and change (done by Hannes) and follow that with an account of his work in argumentation (naturally, done by Stefan). Section 4 gives an account of Gerd's record in the field of nonmonotonic reasoning (by Thomas). Gerd's ideas and contributions to the topic of preferences in AI (recollected by Mirek) concludes that brief tour. We must emphasize, however, that this tour is not an encyclopedic enshrinement of Gerd's contributions and achievements; rather it stops at some of the many pieces of a beautiful gallery, subjectively chosen and with personal commentaries and memories – doing it differently would have been very difficult if not impossible.

2   Reasoning about Actions and Change

An early, yet influential, work of Gerd was the article "How to Do Things with Worlds" in the *Journal of Logic and Computation* that he wrote together with Joachim Hertzberg [37]. The work started out with a critique of previous approaches to model the changes induced by actions proposed by Ginsberg and Smith [57] and Winslett [86]. Gerd and Joachim Hertzberg managed to show that the approach of Ginsberg and Smith was syntax-dependent, and that Winslett's method of measuring the distance between worlds incorporated no notion of causality and thereby allowed for unintuitive conclusions. In the paper, they put the possible-models approach on a firm semantic basis that is insensitive to syntactic variants of specifications. They also provided an early treatment of indeterminate effects (indeterminate like that of tossing a coin, where the result is either heads or tails, but it is outside of the scope of the specification to say which) that had at that time only just begun to be recognized as problematic [62]. Most significantly, that paper was one of the first works in reasoning about actions to incorporate causality. It was quickly picked up by a number of researchers [67,2,85] and remains among Gerd's most cited papers to this date.

But Gerd did not just contribute to the field of reasoning about actions, he also showed how reasoning about actions can benefit other sub-fields of AI. For instance, he employed a widely used reasoning about actions formalism, Reiter's version of the situation calculus [77], to model dynamic argumentation scenarios, such as discussions or court cases [20]. There, speech acts of single agents constitute the actions that influence the state of the world, that is, the current state of the dynamic argumentation scenario. Gerd explicitly formalized rules of order, and also allowed meta-argumentation about these rules (and meta-meta-argumentation up to arbitrary depth).

Together with Steven Shapiro, Gerd also investigated dynamic interactions between goals and beliefs [78]. It was standard practice in the agent/planning literature that an achievement goal (a goal to make a formula true) should be dropped when the agent comes to believe that the goal cannot be achieved any more. Gerd and Steven Shapiro extended this to an approach where, if at some point in time the beliefs of the agent change such that the goal becomes achievable again, then the agent can readopt the goal.

While reasoning about actions was probably not Gerd's main research area, he still made significant contributions and helped shape the field. In 2008, Gerd and my PhD supervisor Michael Thielscher (who was then at Dresden University of Technology) started a joint DFG[1] project on defaults and preferences in action formalisms. I was employed as a research associate in Dresden by that project and so came to know Gerd as our project partner. Due to the topic of my dissertation (default reasoning in action theories), it quickly became clear that Gerd would be the second supervisor of my PhD. After the conclusion of the project (culminating in a joint KR paper [5]), he offered me a position as a (post)doctoral researcher in Leipzig, which I gladly accepted and have held since. *So happy birthday Gerd, and thanks for everything!*

3   Argumentation

Formal Argumentation has been one of the success stories in the the recent history of Artificial Intelligence (AI) [8] and is nowadays a vibrant field at the intersection of computer science, philosophy, linguistics, and several application domains the most prominent of which certainly is legal reasoning [7]. Within AI, several subfields are particularly relevant to – and benefit from – studies of argumentation, in particular knowledge representation, nonmonotonic reasoning, and multi-agent systems. Argumentation studies how to model arguments and their relationships, as well as the necessary conflict resolution in the presence of diverging opinions, thus providing a general and formal treatment of several fundamental questions arising in various applications. A particular branch of argumentation is called abstract argumentation (or Dung's argumentation named after the inventor of abstract argumentation frameworks [50]), where the conflict between arguments is resolved by abstracting away from the arguments' contents, yielding a simple yet powerful framework for reasoning.

Taking Gerd's manifold interests in AI and knowledge representation into account, it is not at all surprising that he also contributed to argumentation. In fact, Gerd's most cited article [12] on preferred subtheories is referred to in many argumentation papers, since it explicitly deals with issues highly relevant to the field, namely inconsistency management in the light of preferences.[2] Another relevant paper is the one on dynamic argument systems [20], which has been already discussed above. Finally, also directly related to argumentation is a novel proposal to combine argumentation and multi-context systems [31].[3]

In what follows, I will focus on Gerd's contributions to the field of argumentation in the last five years, a period wherein I had the pleasure to work jointly with Gerd.

Abstract Frameworks become Dialectical. During a Dagstuhl meeting on Belief Change in 2009, Gerd and I recognized that we share some thoughts about how to generalize Dung's abstract argumentation frameworks. Indeed, several such

---

[1] Deutsche Forschungsgemeinschaft, the main national agency to fund basic research in Germany.

[2] More comments on that paper are in Section 5.

[3] Multi-context systems in Gerd's work are discussed in Section 4.

generalizations were already around that time (bipolar frameworks or set-attack frameworks to mention just two prominent ones, see also the survey paper [42]), but we had the joint feeling that there should be a more uniform and simple way to express these generalizations within a single formalism. Although my memories are a bit vague, I remember that we mainly thought about employing hypergraphs for argumentation frameworks.

A few months later – I was visiting Gerd in Leipzig for three months in winter 2009 – Gerd already came up with an alternative and strikingly elegant idea for our purpose. In a nutshell, arguments come with their own acceptance conditions which explicitly state when to accept an argument depending on the status of its neighbour arguments. This not only generalizes Dung's frameworks ("accept an argument if all parents are not accepted"), but also allows to express relations which mix supporting and attacking relations. During my visit we fine-tuned the idea and came up with generalizations of all standard Dung semantics for this new framework. Typical for Gerd, he thought that he lacks background in argumentation in order to publish and sell our ideas to the community. Hence, he organized what was called Argumentation Christmas Meeting (ACM) inviting experts from the field including Henry Prakken, Tom Gordon, Tony Hunter and Leila Amgoud. The meeting was an inspiring one, with many ideas proposed. To Gerd and me it had also yet another significant outcome. The name we proposed for our formalism raised some well founded objections. Fortunately, a better one was proposed too (thanks to Tom Gordon and Tony Hunter). And so we renamed our deliberation frameworks into abstract dialectical frameworks [24,46] and the name stuck. ACM 2009 was a great event where both Gerd and I strongly benefited from the talks and fruitful discussions in the course of the meeting. Moreover, all participants enjoyed the nice atmosphere of this informal workshop and the social program including a visit to a performance of Stravinsky's *Le sacre du printemps* in the Leipzig Opera House.

Dialectical Frameworks become Mature. In the next years, some further papers on abstract dialectical frameworks (ADFs) were published including joint work with Paul Dunne [27], where we investigated how ADFs can be translated back to Dungian frameworks, Gerd's work with Tom Gordon on an embedding of Carneades in ADF [35], and several system papers [49,51,52,53].

However, it was our students, in particular Johannes Wallner (who was visiting Gerd in spring 2012) and Stefan Ellmauthaler who have found some examples where the generalizations of the semantics we have proposed do not yield intuitive results. In the meantime also Hannes Strass was working on a unifying theory of argumentation semantics [80] based on approximating operators, a technique going back to a general operator-based theory of nonmonotonic reasoning developed in [48]. All this led to a correction of semantics which has been published at IJCAI 2013 [34]. Basically, the main difference is that we switched from a purely two-valued definition of the semantics to a three-valued approach making use of a uniform characteristic operator as initially suggested by Hannes Strass. Further semantics for ADFs have recently been proposed by Sylwia Polberg [73] and by Sarah Gaggl and Hannes Strass [54].

The years 2010–2013 also witnessed growing groups in Leipzig and Vienna working on Argumentation. While Ringo Baumann and Gerd did several works on enforcing in argumentation [3] and splitting [6] including a joint paper with Vienna [4], Hannes Strass joined the Leipzig group in 2011. In 2012, Gerd and I decided to apply for a bilateral FWF-DFG project for further pursuing the development of ADFs[4]. The project was launched in Summer 2013, giving us the opportunity to continue the work on the concept of ADFs and its applications, in collaboration with our second generation of PhD students.

The much Gerd and I enjoyed the excitement and commitment our students and local colleagues showed to further develop ADFs (see e.g., [74,65,81,82,83]) we still were slightly disappointed that ADFs – although cited quite often – were not used by other scientists from the field. One possible explanation is that due to the abstract notion of ADFs, tailored instantiations techniques are required to show their potential. During my second visit in Leipzig in winter term 2013, we thus have worked on a higher-level interface to formalize acceptance patterns (for instance, "accept argument a if more supporting arguments for a are accepted than arguments attacking a"). These abstract patterns are then associated to arguments and finally "compiled down" automatically taking the actual structure of the ADF into account. As a result, the rather technical notion of acceptance condition is thus hidden from the user who now directly works with a general semantical framework for assigning a precise meaning to labelled argument graphs. These ideas were first presented by Gerd's invited talk "Abstract Dialectical Frameworks and Their Potential for Legal Argumentation" at JURIX 2013 and have then been published at ECAI 2014 [47].

My second visit to Leipzig also allowed me to attend Ringo Baumann's PhD defense. As Pietro Baroni (as a neutral outsider) will agree, the party afterwards is something one should not have missed indeed! Seriously speaking, Ringo's thesis on various aspects of abstract argumentation and the fact that it received a honorable mention for the ECCAI Artificial Intelligence Dissertation Award in 2014 underlines that Gerd is not only a world-wide renowned researcher but also a great advisor and teacher.

Conclusion. Besides all the enjoyment during our scientific achievements, I will always remember the hospitality Gerd and his family offered; especially our joint visits to the stadiums of Borussia Dortmund and 1. FC Köln are memories that will never be forgotten. *Danke für alles und die besten Wünsche!*

4 Nonmonotonic Reasoning

Nonmonotonic reasoning became an exciting and hot research area in the mid 1980s, after the seminal works of Ray Reiter [76], McDermott and Doyle [70], and McCarthy [68] had been published in 1980, the *Annus Mirabilis* of the field.[5]

---

[4] See http://www.dbai.tuwien.ac.at/research/project/adf/.

[5] Cf. the Annus Mirabilis in Physics (1905) owing to several fundamental works of A. Einstein.

The need for nonmonotonic reasoning capabilities had been widely recognized, and a whole range of research issues opened up, with lots of challenges and opportunities for a young researcher. After joining in 1984 the *Gesellschaft für Mathematik und Datenverarbeitung (GMD)* in St. Augustin, a major research facility on Applied Mathematics and Computer Science in Germany at that time, Gerd thus started working in this field and published first papers [10,11], followed soon by further papers on different subjects.

In this early period of Gerd's work on nonmonotonic reasoning, there are two outstanding and influential contributions, namely his preferred subtheories [12] and his cumulative default logic [13]. Preferred subtheories are a simple yet powerful approach to cater for nonmonotonic reasoning on top of "classical" knowledge bases. An account of the latter is left to Section 5, where first-hand experience and reactions to the presentation of the paper are reported; we focus here on cumulative default logic.

In his critical analysis of Reiter's work, Gerd noticed that the way in which Reiter's approach arrives at conclusions (which, as Reiter explained to us in personal communication was well deliberated) had a weakness, in that assumptions (in technical terminology, justifications) that are made to apply default rules are local and not necessarily respected later in the proof (i.e., derivation) of a consequence from a default theory; this permits one to make contradictory assumptions at different steps of a derivation. To even this out, Gerd proposed a refinement of default logic which keeps track of assumptions in derivations. Notably, the resulting logic satisfies the following property: if from a stock K of knowledge we can infer x, then we can infer y from K if and only if we can infer it from $K \cup \{x\}$, i.e., a "lemma" x can be added without affecting derivability of y. This property, known as *cumulativity*, is missed by Reiter's formalization, and it was Gerd to term his approach *cumulative default logic (CDL)*. Among the many variants and refinements that default logic has seen over time, CDL is still the most striking and important.

A milestone in Nonmonotonic Reasoning was Gerd's book *Nonmonotonic Reasoning: Logical Foundations of Commonsense* [14] which was based on his PhD thesis, that he successfully defended in 1989. This was in fact among the first books in the field presenting the "classical" approaches to nonmonotonic reasoning coherently in one text,[6] and it enriched them with Gerd's contributions on CDL, preferred subtheories and further results. It also included inheritance networks, which were popular at this time, as well as a brief glimpse on conditional logic; and typically for Gerd, the book was closed by a critical chapter reflecting on the achievements and issues to be addressed, well-thought.

Fueled by the interest in Gerd's work, he was invited to the *International Computer Science Institute (ICSI)* in Berkeley, California, where he spent a year from 1991 to 1992 with his family; he there had the opportunity to exchange ideas with people in the Bay Area and US researchers who were working at the very frontier of this field, and to turn to new subjects. In the sequel he developed an interest to branch out in formalisms and inference methods, and in particular to

---

[6] The book [66] appeared slightly earlier.

non-monotonic logic programming and abductive reasoning [15,37,38], belief revision [87], actions and change [37] (see Section 2) but also towards argumentation [18]; furthermore, in the use of preferences in nonmonotonic logic [16,17].

I remember well when I met Gerd for the first time, which was in 1992 in Vienna, where he was visiting and gave talks at our department. He presented nonmonotonic reasoning in a superb lecture to the faculty and in a further talk his work on preferred subtheories to the specialists, which was inspiring for our research. Already on this first encounter, I could experience some features of Gerd which he has proven later many times: first, that he is an excellent communicator capable of conveying difficult results and material well to a broad audience; many talks and papers witness this. Second, that he is a good listener and open to comments, reflecting on them to improve his work. And third, that vice versa Gerd is concerned with providing useful comments on the work of others, to question and deepen it for the best of scientific progress. As an episode of the latter, I remember well that Gerd asked Georg Gottlob, who presented in a seminar during Gerd's stay in 1992 a translation of Reiter's default logic to Moore's autoepistemic logic [71], whether it could be modified to achieve modularity; indeed, this led Georg to come up with a proof that this is in fact impossible [60], using a smart proof technique which was used as a blueprint then by others for establishing similar impossibility results.

Notably, our faculty at Vienna University of Technology was impressed with Gerd's work and the rector offered him the newly created chair of knowledge-based systems, which he took over in 1995; for personal reasons, however, he could regretfully stay only a short time in Vienna before he moved 1996 to Leipzig, where he still works at the University.

Gerd's line of work in nonmonotonic reasoning continues with important contributions on well-founded semantics, already in combination with preference information [19,36]. The issue of preference handling for nonmonotonic formalisms, and in particular for logic programs had gained increased importance for him and he devoted much time and efforts thinking about it. An episode in that period which nicely exemplifies Gerd's reflection on the comments of others is our joint work on preferences [28,29]. It were some review comments on his idea to capture preferences on rules of an answer set program which made Gerd think about addressing the problem at a more systematic level and to present, in the spirit of the AGM Theory in belief revision [1], principles that any semantics for preferences on non-monotonic logic programs should satisfy. These principles and the way of looking at the problem had a major impact, and it led to a number of follow up works; only most recently, a PhD on this subject has been completed in which the study of principles has been advanced, reconfirming the value of the idea and of certain principles in the seminal paper [79].

Over the years, Gerd's interest and work on preferences has then further intensified such that a whole section (Section 5) ought to be designated to this stream of work. Furthermore, he also revived his interest in argumentation [20,43] which later has grown into a stream of contributions in this field that is also considered separately (see Section 3). Clearly, nonmonotonic behavior was always an issue there, as well as with other problems which Gerd studied.

In the past decade, Gerd's work includes one line that should be highlighted here, viz. his important contributions on multi-context systems. Rooted in seminal work of McCarthy on contexts [69], the Trento School around Fausto Giunchiglia and Luciano Serafini had developed a formalism to combine local knowledge bases called "contexts" in a global system interlinked with special bridge rules [56,58]. Later Serafini and colleagues aimed at allowing negation in bridge rules, and it was Gerd who helped them to get this right [44]. Intrigued by the idea he then proposed to develop a more abstract framework of multi-context systems [30] that allows for heterogeneous contexts with possible nonmonotonic semantics, modeled by families of belief sets, and bridge rules with nonmonotonic negation; the global semantics is defined strikingly simple in terms of an equilibrium over local states, akin to (but different from) notions in game theory. Our group in Vienna has followed up on this framework in research projects, in this course of which several joint works with Gerd have been published [31,32,33,25]. Most recent work on supported MCS [84] and evolving MCSs [59] shows the interest of other groups to develop this notion further.

Talking to Gerd has always been a pleasure, and I have enjoyed the privilege to work with him very much, be it on research or any other matters. Furthermore, it was always great fun to be out with Gerd or to meet him at home; he and Anni are perfect hosts and they served the greatest and most memorable asparagus soup of my life!

Thank you so much for all this Gerd, and on behalf of all who are in Nonmonotonic Reasoning and related topics, the very best wishes on your 60th birthday, and remember: you can't always get what you want, but if you try sometime you get what you need. . .

5   Preferences

In 1989 Gerd wrote a paper with the title *Preferred Subtheories: An Extended Logical Framework for Default Reasoning* [12].[7] The main goal of that paper was to introduce a new formalism for nonmonotonic reasoning. The formalism was striking because of its simplicity, on the one hand, and its generality, on the other. A theory in this formalism was a sequence of sets of gradually less and less *preferred* formulas. The theory imposed on interpretations a certain total preorder and those interpretations that were maximal with respect to this preorder were regarded as intended (or preferred) models of the theory. Despite its natural simplicity, the formalism turned out to be quite powerful, generalizing several other nonmonotonic logics, most notably the THEORIST by Poole [75].

---

[7] The paper was presented at IJCAI 1989 in Detroit. I attended the presentation and later talked to Gerd. That was when we first met. At that time I did not realize that our paths will intersect so many times and so closely in the future.

While a milestone in nonmonotonic reasoning, we mention the formalism here as it marks Gerd's first foray into the area of preference reasoning, an area that became one of his major fields of interest.

Gerd's original interest in preferences was driven by a strong sense of deep and multifaceted connections between nonmonotonicity and preferences. First, at the most basic level, nonmonotonicity arises in commonsense reasoning because we view some models as unlikely and restrict attention only to some, for instance, to minimal ones as in circumscription [68]. Any preference relation on models, derived in some way from the knowledge we have at our disposal or simply decided upon by the reasoner, gives rise to a nonmonotonic entailment relation. Thus, nonmonotonicity can be studied through preference relations. Second, in the context of specific reasoning systems, with default logic [76] being a prime example, we often face the problem of multiple extensions. These extensions result from choices about the order in which defaults are to be applied or, to put it differently, from priorities assigned to them. As before, these priorities can be inferred, for instance, by means of the specificity principle [72,64,63], or they can be selected by the reasoner.

Much of Gerd's research on preferences in nonmonotonic reasoning focused on this latter approach. His 1991 paper, written jointly with Ulrich Junker, introduced the prioritized default theories in which defaults were explicitly ordered, and proposed the notion of an extension for such theories [61]. Later papers [16,17] expanded these ideas and, in particular, led to generalizations which allow one to reason about default priorities [17]. The beauty of this work by Gerd stems again from the simplicity of the formalisms proposed. Gerd argues that since non-normal defaults are seen as a means to resolve conflicts (impose priorities), in formalisms that explicitly incorporate preferences it is justified to restrict attention to the case of normal defaults only! That "design choice" led Gerd to strong results and an elegant theory.

Nevertheless, in some settings, for instance in logic programming and extended logic programming [55] non-normal defaults are essential. Around the mid-1990s, Gerd turned his attention to these formalisms and considered extensions in which program rules were ordered. The goal was to propose formalisms in which preferences could be expressed directly in the language and could be derived dynamically. His first paper on this topic was concerned with extended logic programs under the well-founded semantics [19]. Gerd described there an extension of the language of extended logic programs to accommodate preferences, and defined a modification of the well-founded semantics extending the original one by taking preference information into account. He then illustrated the effectiveness of the formalism in the domain of legal reasoning. A natural next step was to develop a similar treatment for extended logic programs under the answer-set semantics. Gerd undertook this project jointly with Thomas Eiter. The resulting paper [28] is one of the milestones in the study of preferences in nonmonotonic formalisms. It gives a comprehensive analysis of the problem and presents a particular way to treat preferences on program rules. However, its most important contribution is to cast the problem in terms of general and abstract postulates any satisfactory treatment of preferences should satisfy. Gerd and Thomas formulated two such natural postulates and showed that, unlike earlier attempts at formalizing preferences in nonmonotonic formalisms, their proposal satisfied both.

The advent of the new millennium marked the emergence of new directions in Gerd's study of preferences. The first of them was based on an observation that multiple models (extensions) of (nonmonotonic) logic theories are often caused by the use of disjunction. If that disjunction was "ordered" to indicate the preferred disjunct (the preferred way in which to satisfy the disjunction), it would lead to the notion of a preferred model. Working with Salem Benferhat and Daniel Le Berre, Gerd built on this idea to introduce the *qualitative choice logic* [26] and described the precise semantics of statements involving *ordered disjunction*. Since disjunctions in the heads of logic programs are also responsible for multiple answer sets, the idea of an ordered disjunction also applies there. Gerd, later joined by Ilkka Niemelä and Tommi Syrjänen, proposed and studied the corresponding version of logic programming called logic programming with ordered disjunction [21,39].

The second direction was concerned with the design of modular and flexible languages to represent constraints and preferences. The first such modular language of *answer-set optimization* programs was proposed by Gerd in a joint work with Ilkka Niemelä and me [40]. It started in 2002, with a talk on preferences Gerd gave at the Dagstuhl Seminar dedicated to answer-set programming. Both Ilkka and I had commented upon it. Gerd saw a way to incorporate our comments into his way of thinking and proposed a collaboration. The basic idea was simple. Standard logic programs (or propositional theories) representing hard constraints were extended by rules modeling soft constraints in terms of some conditional preference statements. In answer-set optimization programs, preference statements are used to select preferred answer sets (models) from among those that satisfy all hard constraints. Continuing that line of research, Gerd, Ilkka and I generalized these ideas in the formalism of *prioritized component systems* [41] by incorporating some ideas from CP-nets [9]. Both formalisms were quite specific. Gerd felt a more general treatment of the issue of preference language design is needed. Consequently, he suggested and offered a compelling motivation for a general template of a preference description language [23,22]. Finally, in yet another related effort, in a joint work with Stefan Woltran and me, Gerd proposed a general language to describe preference orders on subsets of some ordered domain [45].

This brief account of Gerd's work on preferences can hardly do justice to the impact it had on the field. I hope at the very least it shows the breadth of scope and the depth of the insight. I feel fortunate to have had a chance to work with Gerd. To use a phrase that Gerd may recognize, this cooperation has been something I would not want to miss! Even more, I very much hope for more. *Best wishes, on your 60th birthday, Gerd.*

6   Conclusion

In this paper, we gave a brief account of Gerd's contributions to AI. While clearly subjective and of necessity non-encyclopedic, our overview nevertheless showcases Gerd's manifold contributions in several diverse areas he studied.

As we already have said earlier, Gerd is a great listener while, on the other hand, his comments and opinions are highly valued by his peers. He has a strong social attitude and is concerned with enabling scientific exchange and collaboration. It is thus not surprising that Gerd has served the scientific community throughout his career in many ways. Even in an early stage and as a young researcher with little institutional support, he was lecturing in the 1980s on Nonmonotonic Reasoning at the KIFS, the German Spring School on AI, he organized the (German open) Nonmonotonic Reasoning Workshop in Bonn in 1989, very well attended by international researchers, and pushed the Dutch-German Nonmonotonic Reasoning Workshop series. Furthermore he founded and was heading the German special interest group (SIG) in Nonmonotonic Reasoning. Gerd later expanded his service to the emerging KR community, and then all of AI in roles such as a chair of many meetings, including KI, LPNMR, KR, and ECAI, with ICJAI 2016 being next in row. He has also served as a member of review and advisory boards, and as head of major organizations in the field, including assignments as President of ECCAI and President of KR, Inc. This service makes him a research facilitator and adds to his scientific merits.

We very much hope that he continues this success story – *all the best, Gerd!*

References

1. Alchourrón, C., Gärdenfors, P., Makinson, D.: On the logic of theory change: Partial meet contraction and revision functions. Journal of Symbolic Logic 50, 510–530 (1985)
2. Baral, C.: Reasoning about actions: Non-deterministic effects, constraints, and qualification. In: Proceedings of the Fourteenth International Joint Conference on Artificial Intelligence (IJCAI), pp. 2017–2023. Morgan Kaufmann (1995)
3. Baumann, R., Brewka, G.: Expanding argumentation frameworks: Enforcing and monotonicity results. In: Baroni, P., Cerutti, F., Giacomin, M., Simari, G.R. (eds.) Proceedings of the 3rd Conference on Computational Models of Argument (COMMA 2010). Frontiers in Artificial Intelligence and Applications, vol. 216, pp. 75–86. IOS Press (2010)
4. Baumann, R., Brewka, G., Dvořák, W., Woltran, S.: Parameterized splitting: A simple modification-based approach. In: Erdem, E., Lee, J., Lierler, Y., Pearce, D. (eds.) Correct Reasoning. LNCS, vol. 7265, pp. 57–71. Springer, Heidelberg (2012)
5. Baumann, R., Brewka, G., Strass, H., Thielscher, M., Zaslawski, V.: State defaults and ramifications in the unifying action calculus. In: Lin, F., Sattler, U., Truszczyński, M. (eds.) Proceedings of the 12th International Conference on Principles of Knowledge Representation and Reasoning (KR 2010), pp. 435–444. AAAI Press (2010)
6. Baumann, R., Brewka, G., Wong, R.: Splitting argumentation frameworks: An empirical evaluation. In: Modgil, S., Oren, N., Toni, F. (eds.) TAFA 2011. LNCS, vol. 7132, pp. 17–31. Springer, Heidelberg (2012)

7. Bench-Capon, T.J.M., Dunne, P.E.: Argumentation in AI and Law: Editors' Introduction. Artif. Intell. Law 13(1), 1–8 (2005)
8. Bench-Capon, T.J.M., Dunne, P.E.: Argumentation in Artificial Intelligence. Artificial Intelligence 171(10-15), 619–641 (2007)
9. Boutilier, C., Brafman, R., Domshlak, C., Hoos, H., Poole, D.: CP-nets: A tool for representing and reasoning with conditional ceteris paribus preference statements. Journal of Artificial Intelligence Research 21, 135–191 (2003)
10. Brewka, G.: Tweety - still flying: Some remarks on abnormal birds applicable rules and a default prover. In: Kehler, T. (ed.) Proceedings of the 5th National Conference on Artificial Intelligence, Philadelphia, pp. 8–12. Morgan Kaufmann (1986)
11. Brewka, G.: The logic of inheritance in frame systems. In: McDermott, J.P. (ed.) Proceedings of the 10th International Joint Conference on Artificial Intelligence, pp. 483–488. Morgan Kaufmann (1987)
12. Brewka, G.: Preferred subtheories: An extended logical framework for default reasoning. In: Sridharan, N.S. (ed.) Proceedings of the 11th International Joint Conference on Artificial Intelligence, IJCAI 1989, pp. 1043–1048. Morgan Kaufmann (1989)
13. Brewka, G.: Cumulative default logic: In defense of nonmonotonic inference rules. Artificial Intelligence 50(2), 183–205 (1991)
14. Brewka, G.: Nonmonotonic Reasoning: Logical Foundations of Commonsense. Cambridge Tracts in Theoretical Computer Science, vol. 12, Cambridge Univ. Press (1991)
15. Brewka, G.: An abductive framework for generalized logic programs. In: Pereira, L.M., Nerode, A. (eds.) Proceedings of the Second International Workshop on Logic Programming and Non-monotonic Reasoning, pp. 349–564. MIT Press (1993)
16. Brewka, G.: Adding priorities and specificity to default logic. In: MacNish, C., Moniz Pereira, L., Pearce, D.J. (eds.) JELIA 1994. LNCS, vol. 838, pp. 247–260. Springer, Heidelberg (1994)
17. Brewka, G.: Reasoning about priorities in default logic. In: AAAI 1994: Proceedings of the Twelfth National Conference on Artificial Intelligence, vol. 2, pp. 940–945. American Association for Artificial Intelligence (1994)
18. Brewka, G.: A reconstruction of Rescher' s Theory of Formal Disputation based on default logic. In: Cohn, A.G. (ed.) Proceedings of the Eleventh European Conference on Artificial Intelligence, pp. 366–370 (1994)
19. Brewka, G.: Well-founded semantics for extended logic programs with dynamic preferences. Journal of Artificial Intelligence Research 4, 19–36 (1996)
20. Brewka, G.: Dynamic argument systems: A formal model of argumentation processes based on situation calculus. Journal of Logic and Computation 11(2), 257–282 (2001)
21. Brewka, G.: Logic programming with ordered disjunction. In: Dechter, R., Sutton, R.S. (eds.) Proceedings of the 18th National Conference on Artificial Intelligence and the 14th Conference on Innovative Applications of Artificial Intelligence, AAAI/IAAI-2002, pp. 100–105. AAAI Press (2002)
22. Brewka, G.: Complex preferences for answer set optimization. In: Dubois, D., Welty, C.A., Williams, M.-A. (eds.) Proceedings of the 9th International Conference on Principles of Knowledge Representation and Reasoning, KR-2004, pp. 213–223. AAAI Press (2004)
23. Brewka, G.: A rank based description language for qualitative preferences. In: de Mántaras, R.L., Saitta, L. (eds.) Proceedings of the 16th Eureopean Conference on Artificial Intelligence, ECAI-2004, pp. 303–307. IOS Press (2004)

24. Brewka, G.: Nonmonotonic tools for argumentation. In: Janhunen, T., Niemelä, I. (eds.) JELIA 2010. LNCS, vol. 6341, pp. 1–6. Springer, Heidelberg (2010)

25. Brewka, G.: Towards reactive multi-context systems. In: Cabalar, P., Son, T.C. (eds.) LPNMR 2013. LNCS, vol. 8148, pp. 1–10. Springer, Heidelberg (2013)

26. Brewka, G., Benferhat, S., Le Berre, D.: Qualitative choice logic. Artificial Intelligence 157(1-2), 203–237 (2004)

27. Brewka, G., Dunne, P.E., Woltran, S.: Relating the Semantics of Abstract Dialectical Frameworks and Standard AFs. In: Walsh, T. (ed.) Proceedings of the 22nd International Joint Conference on Artificial Intelligence (IJCAI 2011), pp. 780–785. AAAI Press (2011)

28. Brewka, G., Eiter, T.: Preferred answer sets for extended logic programs. Artificial Intelligence 109(1-2), 297–356 (1999)

29. Brewka, G., Eiter, T.: Prioritizing default logic. In: Hölldobler, S. (ed.) Intellectics and Computational Logic (to Wolfgang Bibel on the occasion of his 60th birthday). Applied Logic Series, vol. 19, pp. 27–45. Kluwer (2000)

30. Brewka, G., Eiter, T.: Equilibria in heterogeneous nonmonotonic multi-context systems. In: Proceedings of the Twenty-Second AAAI Conference on Artificial Intelligence, pp. 385–390. AAAI Press (2007)

31. Brewka, G., Eiter, T.: Argumentation context systems: A framework for abstract group argumentation. In: Erdem, E., Lin, F., Schaub, T. (eds.) LPNMR 2009. LNCS, vol. 5753, pp. 44–57. Springer, Heidelberg (2009)

32. Brewka, G., Eiter, T., Fink, M.: Nonmonotonic multi-context systems: A flexible approach for integrating heterogeneous knowledge sources. In: Balduccini, M., Son, T.C. (eds.) Logic Programming, Knowledge Representation, and Nonmonotonic Reasoning. LNCS, vol. 6565, pp. 233–258. Springer, Heidelberg (2011)

33. Brewka, G., Eiter, T., Fink, M., Weinzierl, A.: Managed multi-context systems. In: Walsh, T. (ed.) Proceedings of the 22nd International Joint Conference on Artificial Intelligence (IJCAI 2011), pp. 786–791. AAAI Press (2011)

34. Brewka, G., Ellmauthaler, S., Strass, H., Wallner, J.P., Woltran, S.: Abstract dialectical frameworks revisited. In: Rossi, F. (ed.) Proceedings of the 23rd International Joint Conference on Artificial Intelligence (IJCAI 2013), pp. 803–809. IJCAI/AAAI (2013)

35. Brewka, G., Gordon, T.F.: Carneades and abstract dialectical frameworks: A reconstruction. In: Baroni, P., Cerutti, F., Giacomin, M., Simari, G.R. (eds.) Proceedings of the 3rd Conference on Computational Models of Argument (COMMA 2010). Frontiers in Artificial Intelligence and Applications, vol. 216, pp. 3–12. IOS Press (2010)

36. Brewka, G., Gottlob, G.: Well-founded semantics for default logic. Fundam. Inform. 31(3/4), 221–236 (1997)

37. Brewka, G., Hertzberg, J.: How to do things with worlds: On formalizing actions and plans. Journal of Logic and Computation 3(5), 517–532 (1993)

38. Brewka, G., Konolige, K.: An abductive framework for general logic programs and other nonmonotonic systems. In: Bajcsy, R. (ed.) Proceedings of the 13th International Joint Conference on Artificial Intelligence, pp. 9–17. Morgan Kaufmann (1993)

39. Brewka, G., Niemelä, I., Syrjänen, T.: Logic programs with ordered disjunction. Computational Intelligence 20(2), 335–357 (2004)

40. Brewka, G., Niemelä, I., Truszczynski, M.: Answer set optimization. In: Gottlob, G., Walsh, T. (eds.) Proceedings of the 18th International Joint Conference on Artificial Intelligence, IJCAI-2003, pp. 867–872. Morgan Kaufmann (2003)

41. Brewka, G., Niemelä, I., Truszczynski, M.: Prioritized component systems. In: Veloso, M.M., Kambhampati, S. (eds.) Proceedings of the 20th National Conference on Artificial Intelligence and the 17th Conference on Innovative Applications of Artificial Intelligence, AAAI/IAAI-2005, pp. 596–601. AAAI Press (2005)
42. Brewka, G., Polberg, S., Woltran, S.: Generalizations of dung frameworks and their role in formal argumentation. IEEE Intelligent Systems 29(1), 30–38 (2014)
43. Brewka, G., Prakken, H., Vreeswijk, G.: Special issue on computational dialectics: an introduction. Journal of Logic and Computation 13(3), 317–318 (2003)
44. Brewka, G., Roelofsen, F., Serafini, L.: Contextual default reasoning. In: Veloso, M.M. (ed.) IJCAI 2007, Proceedings of the 20th International Joint Conference on Artificial Intelligence, pp. 268–273 (2007)
45. Brewka, G., Truszczynski, M., Woltran, S.: Representing preferences among sets. In: Fox, M., Poole, D. (eds.) Proceedings of the 24th AAAI Conference on Artificial Intelligence, AAAI-2010, pp. 273–278. AAAI Press (2010)
46. Brewka, G., Woltran, S.: Abstract dialectical frameworks. In: Lin, F., Sattler, U., Truszczyński, M. (eds.) Proceedings of the 12th International Conference on Principles of Knowledge Representation and Reasoning (KR 2010), pp. 780–785. AAAI Press (2010)
47. Brewka, G., Woltran, S.: GRAPPA: A semantical framework for graph-based argument processing. In: Schaub, T., Friedrich, G., O'Sullivan, B. (eds.) ECAI 2014 - 21st European Conference on Artificial Intelligence. Frontiers in Artificial Intelligence and Applications, vol. 263, pp. 153–158. IOS Press (2014)
48. Denecker, M., Marek, V.W., Truszczyński, M.: Ultimate approximation and its application in nonmonotonic knowledge representation systems. Inf. Comput. 192(1), 84–121 (2004)
49. Diller, M., Wallner, J.P., Woltran, S.: Reasoning in abstract dialectical frameworks using quantified boolean formulas. In: Parsons, S., Oren, N., Reed, C., Cerutti, F. (eds.) Computational Models of Argument - Proceedings of COMMA 2014. Frontiers in Artificial Intelligence and Applications, vol. 266, pp. 241–252. IOS Press (2014)
50. Dung, P.M.: On the acceptability of arguments and its fundamental role in nonmonotonic reasoning, logic programming and n-person games. Artificial Intelligence 77(2), 321–358 (1995)
51. Ellmauthaler, S., Strass, H.: The diamond system for argumentation: Preliminary report. CoRR, abs/1312.6140 (2013)
52. Ellmauthaler, S., Strass, H.: The DIAMOND system for computing with abstract dialectical frameworks. In: Parsons, S., Oren, N., Reed, C., Cerutti, F. (eds.) Computational Models of Argument - Proceedings of COMMA 2014. Frontiers in Artificial Intelligence and Applications, vol. 266, pp. 233–240. IOS Press (2014)
53. Ellmauthaler, S., Wallner, J.P.: Evaluating abstract dialectical frameworks with asp. In: Verheij, B., Szeider, S., Woltran, S. (eds.) Computational Models of Argument - Proceedings of COMMA 2012. Frontiers in Artificial Intelligence and Applications, vol. 245, pp. 505–506. IOS Press (2012)
54. Gaggl, S.A., Strass, H.: Decomposing Abstract Dialectical Frameworks. In: Parsons, S., Oren, N., Reed, C., Cerutti, F. (eds.) Computational Models of Argument - Proceedings of COMMA 2014. Frontiers in Artificial Intelligence and Applications, vol. 266, pp. 281–292. IOS Press (2014)
55. Gelfond, M., Lifschitz, V.: Classical negation in logic programs and disjunctive databases. New Generation Computing 9, 365–385 (1991)
56. Ghidini, C., Giunchiglia, F.: Local models semantics, or contextual reasoning = locality + compatibility. Artificial Intelligence 127(2), 221–259 (2001)

57. Ginsberg, M.L., Smith, D.E.: Reasoning about action I: A possible worlds approach. Artificial Intelligence 35, 233–258 (1987)
58. Giunchiglia, F., Serafini, L.: Multilanguage hierarchical logics or: How we can do without modal logics. Artificial Intelligence 65(1), 29–70 (1994)
59. Goncalves, R., Knorr, M., Leite, J.: Evolving multi-context systems. In: Schaub, T., Friedrich, G., O'Sullivan, B. (eds.) Proceedings of the 21st Eureopean Conference on Artificial Intelligence, ECAI 2014. Frontiers in Artificial Intelligence and Applications, vol. 263, pp. 225–230. IOS Press (2014)
60. Gottlob, G.: Translating default logic into standard autoepistemic logic. J. ACM 42(4), 711–740 (1995)
61. Junker, U., Brewka, G.: Handling partially ordered defaults in TMS. In: Kruse, R., Siegel, P. (eds.) ECSQAU 1991 and ECSQARU 1991. LNCS, vol. 548, pp. 211–218. Springer, Heidelberg (1991)
62. Kartha, G.N.: Two counterexamples related to Baker's approach to the frame problem. Artificial Intelligence 69(1-2), 379–391 (1994)
63. Kraus, S., Lehmann, D., Magidor, M.: Nonmonotonic reasoning, preferential models and cumulative logics. Artificial Intelligence 44, 167–207 (1990)
64. Lehmann, D., Magidor, M.: What does a conditional knowledge base entail? Artificial Intelligence 55, 1–60 (1992)
65. Linsbichler, T.: Splitting abstract dialectical frameworks. In: Parsons, S., Oren, N., Reed, C., Cerutti, F. (eds.) Computational Models of Argument - Proceedings of COMMA 2014. Frontiers in Artificial Intelligence and Applications, vol. 266, pp. 357–368. IOS Press (2014)
66. Lukaszewicz, W.: Non-Monotonic Reasoning - Formalization of Commonsense Reasoning. Ellis Horwood (1990)
67. McCain, N., Turner, H.: A causal theory of ramifications and qualifications. In: Proceedings of the Fourteenth International Joint Conference on Artificial Intelligence (IJCAI), pp. 1978–1984. Morgan Kaufmann (1995)
68. McCarthy, J.: Circumscription — a form of non-monotonic reasoning. Artificial Intelligence 13(1-2), 27–39 (1980)
69. McCarthy, J.: Notes on formalizing context. In: Bajcsy, R. (ed.) Proceedings of the 13th International Joint Conference on Artificial Intelligence, pp. 555–562. Morgan Kaufmann (1993)
70. McDermott, D., Doyle, J.: Non-monotonic logic I. Artificial Intelligence 13, 41–72 (1980)
71. Moore, R.: Semantical considerations on nonmonotonic logics. Artificial Intelligence 25, 75–94 (1985)
72. Pearl, J.: System Z: A natural ordering of defaults with tractable applications to nonmonotonic reasoning. In: Proceedings of the 3rd Conference on Theoretical Aspects of Reasoning about Knowledge, TARK 1990, pp. 121–135. Morgan Kaufmann (1990)
73. Polberg, S.: Extension-based semantics of abstract dialectical frameworks. CoRR, abs/1405.0406 (2014)
74. Polberg, S., Doder, D.: Probabilistic abstract dialectical frameworks. In: Fermé, E., Leite, J. (eds.) JELIA 2014. LNCS, vol. 8761, pp. 591–599. Springer, Heidelberg (2014)
75. Poole, D.: A logical framework for default reasoning. Artificial Intelligence 36(1), 27–47 (1988)
76. Reiter, R.: A logic for default reasoning. Artificial Intelligence 13(1-2), 81–132 (1980)

77. Reiter, R.: Knowledge in Action: Logical Foundations for Specifying and Implementing Dynamical Systems. The MIT Press (2001)
78. Shapiro, S., Brewka, G.: Dynamic interactions between goals and beliefs. In: IJCAI 2007: Proceedings of the 20th International Joint Conference on Artifical intelligence, pp. 2625–2630. Morgan Kaufmann Publishers Inc. (2007)
79. Šimko, A.: Logic Programming with Preferences on Rules. PhD thesis, Faculty of Mathematics, Physics and Informatics, Comenius University in Bratislava, Slovakia (2014)
80. Strass, H.: Approximating operators and semantics for abstract dialectical frameworks. Artificial Intelligence 205, 39–70 (2013)
81. Strass, H.: Instantiating Knowledge Bases in Abstract Dialectical Frameworks. In: Leite, J., Son, T.C., Torroni, P., van der Torre, L., Woltran, S. (eds.) CLIMA XIV 2013. LNCS, vol. 8143, pp. 86–101. Springer, Heidelberg (2013)
82. Strass, H.: On the relative expressiveness of argumentation frameworks, normal logic programs and abstract dialectical frameworks. In: Konieczny, S., Tompits, H. (eds.) Proceedings of the Fifteenth International Workshop on Non-Monotonic Reasoning (NMR) (2014)
83. Strass, H., Wallner, J.P.: Analyzing the Computational Complexity of Abstract Dialectical Frameworks via Approximation Fixpoint Theory. In: Proceedings of the Fourteenth International Conference on the Principles of Knowledge Representation and Reasoning (KR), pp. 101–110. AAAI Press (2014)
84. Tasharrofi, S., Ternovska, E.: Generalized multi-context systems. In: Baral, C., Giacomo, G.D., Eiter, T. (eds.) Proceedings of the Fourteenth International Conference on the Principles of Knowledge Representation and Reasoning (KR), pp. 368–377. AAAI Press (2014)
85. Thielscher, M.: Ramification and causality. Artificial Intelligence 89(1-2), 317–364 (1997)
86. Winslett, M.: Reasoning about action using a possible models approach. In: Proceedings of the Seventh National Conference on Artificial Intelligence (AAAI 1988), pp. 89–93 (1988)
87. Witteveen, C., Brewka, G.: Skeptical reason maintenance and belief revision. Artificial Intelligence 61(1), 1–36 (1993)

Ricochet Robots Reloaded:
A Case-Study in Multi-shot ASP Solving

Martin Gebser[1,2], Roland Kaminski[2], Philipp Obermeier[2], and Torsten Schaub[2,3,*]

[1] Aalto University, Finland
[2] University of Potsdam, Germany
[3] Inria Rennes, France

Abstract. Nonmonotonic reasoning is about drawing conclusions in the absence of (complete) information. Hence, whenever new information arrives, one may have to withdraw previously drawn conclusions. In fact, Answer Set Programming is nowadays regarded as the computational embodiment of nonmonotonic reasoning. However, traditional answer set solvers do not account for changing information. Rather they are designed as one-shot solvers that take a logic program and compute its stable models, basta! When new information arrives the program is extended and the solving process is started from scratch once more. Hence the dynamics giving rise to nonmonotonicity is not reflected by such solvers and left to the user. This shortcoming is addressed by multi-shot solvers that embrace the dynamicity of nonmonotonic reasoning by allowing a reactive procedure to loop on solving while acquiring changes in the problem specification.

In this paper, we provide a hands-on introduction to multi-shot solving with *clingo* 4 by modeling the popular board game of *Ricochet Robots*. Our particular focus lies on capturing the underlying turn based playing through the procedural-declarative interplay offered by the Python-ASP integration of *clingo* 4. From a technical perspective, we provide semantic underpinnings for multi-shot solving with *clingo* 4 by means of a simple stateful semantics along with operations reflecting *clingo* 4 functionalities.

1 Introduction

Nonmonotonic reasoning [1,2] is about drawing conclusions in the absence of (complete) information. Hence, whenever new information arrives, one may have to withdraw previously drawn conclusions. In fact, Answer Set Programming (ASP; [3,4]) can nowadays be regarded as the computational embodiment of nonmonotonic reasoning. However, traditional ASP solvers do not account for changing information. Rather they are designed as one-shot solvers that take a logic program and compute its stable models, basta! When new information arrives the program is extended and the solving process is re-started from scratch again. Hence, the dynamics giving rise to nonmonotonicity is not reflected by such solvers and left to the user. Turning towards the future, ASP is and will be an under-the-hood technology. Hence, in practice, ASP solvers are

---

* Affiliated with the School of Computing Science at Simon Fraser University, Burnaby, Canada, and the Institute for Integrated and Intelligent Systems at Griffith University, Brisbane, Australia.

T. Eiter et al. (Eds.): Brewka Festschrift, LNAI 9060, pp. 17–32, 2015.

embedded in encompassing software environments and thus have to interact with them in an easy way. Again, such interactions are not accounted for by traditional ASP solvers and once more left to the user.

This shortcoming is addressed by multi-shot solvers like *clingo* 4 that embrace the dynamicity of nonmonotonic reasoning by allowing a reactive procedure to loop on solving while acquiring changes in the problem specification. Given that this is accomplished by complementing the declarative approach of ASP with procedural means, like Python or Lua, one also gets a handle on communication with an environment. In what follows, we want to illustrate these aspects by providing a hands-on introduction to multi-shot solving with *clingo* 4 through modeling the popular board game of *Ricochet Robots*. Our particular focus lies on capturing the underlying round playing through the procedural-declarative interplay offered by the Python-ASP integration of *clingo* 4.

Ricochet Robots is a board game for multiple players designed by Alex Randolph.[1] A board consists of 16×16 fields arranged in a grid structure having barriers between various neighboring fields (see Figure 1 and 2). Four differently colored robots roam across the board along either horizontally or vertically accessible fields, respectively. In principle, each robot can thus move in four directions. A robot cannot stop its move until it either hits a barrier or another robot. The goal is to place a designated robot on a target location with a shortest sequence of moves. Often this involves moving several robots to establish temporary barriers. In fact, the game is played in rounds. At each round, a chip with a colored symbol indicating the target location is drawn. Then, the specific goal is to move the robot with the same color on this location. The player who reaches the goal with the fewest number of robot moves wins the chip. The next round is then played from the end configuration of the previous round. At the end, the player with most chips wins the game.

Ricochet Robots has been studied from the viewpoint of human problem solving [5] and analyzed from a theoretical perspective [6,7,8]. Moreover, it has a large community providing various resources on the web. Among them, there is a collection of fifty-six extensions of the game.[2] We also studied alternative ASP encodings of the game in [9], and used them to compare various ASP solving techniques. More disparate encodings resulted from the ASP competition in 2013, where *Ricochet Robots* was included in the modeling track. ASP encodings and instances of *Ricochet Robots* are available at [10].

2   Multi-shot Solving with *clingo* 4

clingo 4 offers high-level constructs for realizing complex reasoning processes that tolerate evolving problem specifications, either because data or constraints are added, deleted, or replaced. This is achieved within a single integrated ASP grounding and solving process in order to avoid redundancies in relaunching grounder and solver programs and to benefit from the learning capacities of modern ASP solvers. As detailed in [11], *clingo* 4 complements ASP's declarative input language by control capacities expressed via the (embedded) scripting languages Lua and Python. On the declarative

---

[1] http://en.wikipedia.org/wiki/Ricochet_Robot
[2] http://www.boardgamegeek.com/boardgame/51/ricochet-robots

side, *clingo* 4 offers a new directive `#program` that allows for structuring logic programs into named and parametrizable subprograms. The grounding and integration of these subprograms into the solving process is completely modular and fully controllable from the procedural side, viz. the scripting languages embedded via the `#script` directive. For exercising control, the latter benefit from a dedicated *clingo* library that does not only furnish grounding and solving instructions but moreover allows for continuously assembling the solver's program in combination with the directive `#external`.

While [11] details the partition and composition of logic programs as well as the use of Python as an embedded scripting language, we focus here on the usage of externally defined atoms along with the *clingo* 4 Python library. Hence, we refer the interested reader to [11] for more details on `#program` and `#script` directives; the semantical underpinnings of program composition in terms of module theory are given in [12]. Here, it is just important to note that base is a dedicated subprogram that gathers all rules not preceded by a `#program` directive. Since we do not use any `#program` directives, all rules belong to the base program.

As detailed in the following, the `#external` directive of *clingo* 4 allows for a flexible handling of yet undefined atoms. Moreover, the (external) manipulation of their truth values provides an easy mechanism to activate or deactivate ground rules on demand. This allows for continuously assembling ground rules evolving at different stages of a reasoning process. To be more precise, `#external` directives declare atoms that may still be defined by rules added later on. As detailed in [11], in terms of modules, such atoms correspond to inputs, which must not be simplified by fixing their truth value to false. In order to facilitate the declaration of input atoms, *clingo* 4 supports schematic `#external` directives that are instantiated along with the rules of their respective subprograms. To this end, a directive like '`#external p(X,Y) : q(X,Z), r(Z,Y).`' is treated similar to a rule '`p(X,Y) :- q(X,Z), r(Z,Y).`' during grounding. However, the head atoms of the resulting ground instances are merely collected as inputs, whereas the ground rules as such are discarded.

We define a (non-ground) logic program P' as *extensible*, if it contains some (non-ground) *external declaration* of the form

$$\#\text{external } a : B \tag{1}$$

where a is an atom and B a rule body. For grounding an external declaration as in (1), it is treated as a rule $a \leftarrow B, \varepsilon$ where ε is a distinguished ground atom marking rules from `#external` declarations. Formally, given an extensible program P', we define the collection D of rules corresponding to `#external` declarations as follows.

$$D = \{a \leftarrow B, \varepsilon \mid (\#\text{external } a : B) \in P'\}$$

With it, the ground instantiation of the extensible logic program P' is defined as the ground logic program P associated with the set E of ground atoms, where[3]

$$P = \{r \in grd(P' \cup (D \cup \{\{\varepsilon\} \leftarrow\})) \setminus \{\{\varepsilon\} \leftarrow\} \mid \varepsilon \notin B(r)\} \tag{2}$$

$$E = \{h(r) \mid r \in grd(P' \cup (D \cup \{\{\varepsilon\} \leftarrow\})), \varepsilon \in B(r)\} \tag{3}$$

---

[3] We use $h(r)$ and $B(r)$ to denote the head and body of a rule r, respectively, and $grd(P)$ to denote the set of all ground instances of rules in P.

For simplicity, we refer to P and E as a *logic program with externals*, and drop the reference to P' whenever clear from the context. Note that the choice rule '$\{\varepsilon\} \leftarrow$' is added above to cope with $grd(P' \cup (D \cup \{\{\varepsilon\} \leftarrow\}))$, understood as the outcome of grounding (including simplifications); in particular, the construction in (2) and (3) makes sure that neither ε nor '$\{\varepsilon\} \leftarrow$' appear in P or E, respectively.

As an example, consider the following extensible program, R':

```
1  #external e(X) : f(X), X < 2.
2  f(1..2).
3  a(X) :- e(X), f(X).
4  b(X) :- not e(X), f(X).
```

Grounding R' yields the below program R with externals $F = \{e(1)\}$.

```
1  f(1). f(2).
2  a(1) :- e(1).
3  b(1) :- not e(1).
4  b(2).
```

Note how externals influence the result of grounding. While e(1) remains untouched, the atom e(2) is set to false, followed by cascading simplifications.

For capturing the stable models of such logic programs with externals, we need the following definitions. A (partial) assignment i over a set $A \subseteq \mathcal{A}$ of atoms is a function: $i : A \rightarrow \{t, f, u\}$, where $\mathcal{A}$ is the set of given atoms. With this, we define $A^t = \{a \in A \mid i(a) = t\}$, $A^f = \{a \in A \mid i(a) = f\}$, and $A^u = \{a \in A \mid i(a) = u\}$. In what follows, we represent partial assignments either by $\langle A^t, A^f \rangle$ or $\langle A^t, A^u \rangle$ by leaving the respective default value implicit.

Given a program P with externals E, we define the set $I = E \setminus H(P)$ as input atoms of P.[4] That is, input atoms are externals that are not overridden by rules in P. Given a partial assignment $\langle I^t, I^u \rangle$ over I, we define $P_{\langle I^t, I^u \rangle} = P \cup (\{a \leftarrow \ \mid a \in I^t\} \cup \{\{a\} \leftarrow \ \mid a \in I^u\})$ to capture the extension of P with respect to an (external) truth assignment to the input I. In addition, *clingo* considers another partial assignment $\langle A^t, A^f \rangle$ over $A \subseteq \mathcal{A}$ for filtering stable models, and refers to them as assumptions.[5] Then, X is a stable model of a program P with externals E filtered by $\langle A^t, A^f \rangle$, if X is a stable model of $P_{\langle I^t, I^u \rangle}$ such that $A^t \subseteq X$ and $A^f \cap X = \emptyset$. This amounts to a semantical characterization of one-shot solving of programs with externals in *clingo* 4.

Note the difference among input atoms and (filtering) assumptions. While a true input atom amounts to a fact, a true assumption acts as an integrity constraint. Also, undefined input atoms are regarded as false, while undefined assumptions remain neutral. Finally, at the solver level, input atoms are a transient part of the representation, while assumptions only affect the assignment of a single search process.

For capturing multi-shot solving, we must account for sequences of system states, involving information about the programs kept within the grounder and the solver. To this end, we define a simple operational semantics based on system states and appropriate operations. A *clingo state* is a triple $\langle Q, P, I \rangle$ where

---

[4] We use $H(P) = \{h(r) \mid r \in P\}$ to denote all head atoms in P.

[5] In *clingo*, or more precisely in *clasp*, such assumptions are the principal parameter to the underlying solve function (see below). The term assumption traces back to [13,14].

- Q is a (non-ground) logic program,
- P is a ground logic program,
- I is a set of input atoms along with an implicit partial assignment $\langle I^t, I^u \rangle$ over I.

Such states can be modified by the following operations.

- $create() : \mapsto \langle \emptyset, \emptyset, \emptyset \rangle$

- $add(R) : \langle Q, P, I \rangle \mapsto \langle Q \cup R, P, I \rangle$ where R is a (non-ground) logic program

- $ground : \langle Q, P_1, I_1 \rangle \mapsto \langle \emptyset, P_2, I_2 \rangle$ where[6]
  - $(P, E) = grd_{P_1, I_1}(Q)$
  - $P_2 = P_1 \cup P$
  - $I_2 = (I_1 \cup E) \setminus H(P_2)$
    - $I_2^t = \{a \in I_2 \mid I_1(a) = t\}$
    - $I_2^u = \{a \in I_2 \mid I_1(a) = u\}$

- $assignExternal(a, t) : \langle Q, P, I_1 \rangle \mapsto \langle Q, P, I_2 \rangle$ where
  - $I_2 = I_1$
    - $I_2^t = I_1^t \cup \{a\}$ if $a \in I_1$, and $I_2^t = I_1^t$ otherwise
    - $I_2^u = I_1^u \setminus \{a\}$

  $assignExternal(a, u) : \langle Q, P, I_1 \rangle \mapsto \langle Q, P, I_2 \rangle$ where
  - $I_2 = I_1$
    - $I_2^t = I_1^t \setminus \{a\}$
    - $I_2^u = I_1^u \cup \{a\}$ if $a \in I_1$, and $I_2^u = I_1^u$ otherwise

  $assignExternal(a, f) : \langle Q, P, I_1 \rangle \mapsto \langle Q, P, I_2 \rangle$ where
  - $I_2 = I_1$
    - $I_2^t = I_1^t \setminus \{a\}$
    - $I_2^u = I_1^u \setminus \{a\}$

- $releaseExternal(a) : \langle Q, P_1, I_1 \rangle \mapsto \langle Q, P_2, I_2 \rangle$ where
  - $P_2 = P_1 \cup \{a \leftarrow a, \sim a\}$ if $a \in I_1$, and $P_2 = P_1$ otherwise
  - $I_2 = I_1 \setminus \{a\}$
    - $I_2^t = I_1^t \setminus \{a\}$
    - $I_2^u = I_1^u \setminus \{a\}$

- $solve(\langle A^t, A^f \rangle) : \langle Q, P, I \rangle \mapsto \langle Q, P, I \rangle$ outputs the set $\mathcal{X}_{P,I}$ defined as

$$\{X \mid X \text{ is a stable model of } P_{\langle I^t, I^u \rangle} \text{ such that } A^t \subseteq X \text{ and } A^f \cap X = \emptyset\} \quad (4)$$

For simplicity, we dropped the condition '$I_2^f = I_2 \setminus (I_2^t \cup I_2^u)$' from all transitions of I_1 to I_2 because undefined input atoms are regarded to be false. Note also that the above semantic account abstracts from the partition and composition of logic programs, dealt with in [12,11]. Rather it relies on a single (base) program whose addition complies with modularity (in terms of [15]).

---

[6] We use $grd_{P,I}(Q)$ to denote the (ground) logic program with externals obtained by instantiating the extensible program Q as defined in (2) and (3), respectively. We add the subscript P, I to indicate the context of the instantiation.

A central role is played by the *ground* function. First, programs like Q are always grounded in the context of P_1 and I_1 since they delineate the Herbrand base and universe. Second, one may also add new externals via E, provided they are not yet defined. The function *assignExternal* allows us to manipulate the truth values of input atoms. While their default value is false, making them undefined results in a choice. If an atom is not external, then *assignExternal* has no effect. On the contrary, *releaseExternal* removes the external status from an atom and sets it permanently to false, otherwise this function has no effect. Finally, *solve* leaves the *clingo* state intact and outputs the filtered set $\mathcal{X}_{P,I}$ of stable models of the logic program with externals comprised in the current state. This set is general enough to define all basic reasoning modes of *clingo*. On a technical note, the addition of $a \leftarrow a, \sim a$ does not offer any derivation for a but adds a to the head atoms, $H(P)$, so that it can neither be re-added as an external nor via a rule (since the latter would violate modularity [12]).

For illustration, reconsider the above extensible program R'. Adding and grounding R' in an initial state results in the *clingo* state[7] $ground(add(R')(create())) = \langle \emptyset, R, F^f \rangle$ where R and F are as given above. Applying *solve*() to $\langle \emptyset, R, F^f \rangle$ leaves the state unaffected and results in a single stable model containing b(1). Unlike this, the state $assignExternal(\text{e}(1), u)(\langle \emptyset, R, F^f \rangle)$ induces two models, one with a(1) and another with b(1), while $assignExternal(\text{e}(1), t)(\langle \emptyset, R, F^f \rangle)$ yields only the one with a(1).

From the viewpoint of operational semantics, the multi-shot solving process of a *clingo* object can be associated with the sequence of executed *clingo*-specific operations $\langle o_k \rangle_{k \in K}$ which in turn induce a sequence $\langle Q_k, P_k, I_k \rangle_{k \in K}$ of *clingo* states such that

1. $o_0 = create()$ and $o_k \neq create()$ for $k > 0$
2. $\langle Q_0, P_0, I_0 \rangle = create()$
3. $\langle Q_k, P_k, I_k \rangle = o_k(\langle Q_{k-1}, P_{k-1}, I_{k-1} \rangle)$ for $k > 0$

For capturing the result of the multi-shot solving process in terms of stable models, we consider the sequence of sets of stable models obtained at each solving step. More precisely, given a sequence of *clingo* operations and states as above, the multi-shot solving process can be associated with the sequence $\langle \mathcal{X}_{P_j, I_j} \rangle_{j \in K, o_j = solve(\langle A_j^t, A_j^f \rangle)}$ of sets of stable models defined in (4).

All of the above state operations have almost literal counterparts in *clingo*'s Python (and Lua) module, namely __init__ of *clingo*'s Control class, add, ground, assign_external, release_external, and solve.[8] However, as mentioned, the above semantic account abstracts from the partition and composition of logic programs. In fact, add as well as ground associate rules with subprograms. Moreover, subprograms are usually parametrized and thus grounded several times with different instantiations of the parameters. This is not reflected by *ground* (where Q is emptied). Also, our account disregards module composition, which is enforced by *clingo* (cf. [12]).[9]

---

[7] We use the informal notation F^f to indicate that the members of F are false.

[8] For a complete listing of functions and classes available in the gringo module,
see http://potassco.sourceforge.net/gringo.html

[9] Among others, this prevents redefining ground atoms.

Finally, it is worth mentioning that several *clingo* objects can be created and run in a multi-threaded yet independent fashion.

3   Encoding *Ricochet Robots*

The following encoding and fact formats follow the ones given in [9],[10] except that we use below the input language of *clingo* 4 that includes the ASP language standard *ASP-Core-2* [18].

An authentic board configuration of *Ricochet Robots* is shown in Figure 1 and represented as facts in Listing 1.1. The dimension of the board is fixed to 16 in Line 1. As put

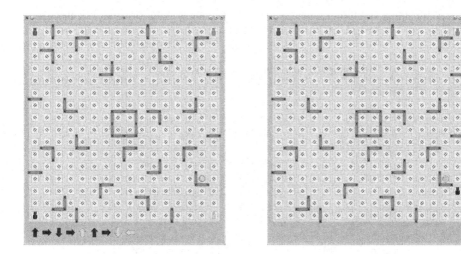

Fig. 1. Visualization of solving `goal(13)` from initially cornered robots

forward in [9], barriers are indicated by atoms with predicate `barrier/4`. The first two arguments give the field position and the last two the orientation of the barrier, which is mostly east (1,0) or south (0,1).[11] For instance, the atom `barrier(2,1,1,0)` in Line 3 represents the vertical wall between the fields (2,1) and (3,1), and `barrier(5,1,0,1)` stands for the horizontal wall separating (5,1) from (5,2).

Listing 1.1. The Board (`board.lp`)

```
1    dim(1..16).

3    barrier( 2,  1,  1,0).    barrier(13,11,  1,0).    barrier( 9, 7,0,  1).
4    barrier(10,  1,  1,0).    barrier(11,12,  1,0).    barrier(11, 7,0,  1).
5    barrier( 4,  2,  1,0).    barrier(14,13,  1,0).    barrier(14, 7,0,  1).
6    barrier(14,  2,  1,0).    barrier( 6,14,  1,0).    barrier(16, 9,0,  1).
7    barrier( 2,  3,  1,0).    barrier( 3,15,  1,0).    barrier( 2,10,0,  1).
8    barrier(11,  3,  1,0).    barrier(10,15,  1,0).    barrier( 5,10,0,  1).
```

---

[10] The encodings in [9] rely on the input language of *clingo* 3 [16,17].

[11] Symmetric barriers are handled by predicate `stop/4` in Line 4 and 5 of Listing 1.3.

```
9    barrier( 7, 4,  1,0).  barrier( 4,16,  1,0).  barrier( 8,10,0,-1).
10   barrier( 3, 7,  1,0).  barrier(12,16,  1,0).  barrier( 9,10,0,-1).
11   barrier(14, 7,  1,0).  barrier( 5, 1,0,  1).  barrier( 9,10,0,  1).
12   barrier( 7, 8,  1,0).  barrier(15, 1,0,  1).  barrier(14,10,0,  1).
13   barrier(10, 8,-1,0).  barrier( 2, 2,0,  1).  barrier( 1,12,0,  1).
14   barrier(11, 8,  1,0).  barrier(12, 3,0,  1).  barrier(11,12,0,  1).
15   barrier( 7, 9,  1,0).  barrier( 7, 4,0,  1).  barrier( 7,13,0,  1).
16   barrier(10, 9,-1,0).  barrier(16, 4,0,  1).  barrier(15,13,0,  1).
17   barrier( 4,10,  1,0).  barrier( 1, 6,0,  1).  barrier(10,14,0,  1).
18   barrier( 2,11,  1,0).  barrier( 4, 7,0,  1).  barrier( 3,15,0,  1).
19   barrier( 8,11,  1,0).  barrier( 8, 7,0,  1).
```

Listing 1.2 gives the sixteen possible target locations printed on the game's carton board (cf. Line 3 to 18). Each robot has four possible target locations, expressed by the ternary predicate `target`. Such a target is put in place via the unary predicate `goal` that associates a number with each location. The external declaration in Line 1 paves the way for fixing the target location from outside the solving process. For instance, setting `goal(13)` to true makes position `(15,13)` a target location for the `yellow` robot.

Listing 1.2. Robots and targets (`targets.lp`)

```
1   #external goal(1..16).

3   target(red,      5,  2)  :- goal(1).   % red moon
4   target(red,     15,  2)  :- goal(2).   % red triangle
5   target(green,    2,  3)  :- goal(3).   % green triangle
6   target(blue,    12,  3)  :- goal(4).   % blue star
7   target(yellow,   7,  4)  :- goal(5).   % yellow star
8   target(blue,     4,  7)  :- goal(6).   % blue saturn
9   target(green,   14,  7)  :- goal(7).   % green moon
10  target(yellow, 11,  8)  :- goal(8).   % yellow saturn
11  target(yellow,  5, 10)  :- goal(9).   % yellow moon
12  target(green,    2, 11)  :- goal(10).  % green star
13  target(red,     14, 11)  :- goal(11).  % red star
14  target(green,   11, 12)  :- goal(12).  % green saturn
15  target(yellow, 15, 13)  :- goal(13).  % yellow star
16  target(blue,     7, 14)  :- goal(14).  % blue star
17  target(red,      3, 15)  :- goal(15).  % red saturn
18  target(blue,    10, 15)  :- goal(16).  % blue moon

20  robot(red;green;blue;yellow).
21  #external pos((red;green;blue;yellow),1..16,1..16).
```

Similarly, the initial robot positions can be set externally, as declared in Line 21. That is, each robot can be put at 256 different locations. On the left hand side of Figure 1, we cornered all robots by setting `pos(red,1,1)`, `pos(blue,1,16)`, `pos(green,16,1)`, and `pos(yellow,16,16)` to true.

Finally, the encoding in Listing 1.3 follows the plain encoding of ricocheting robots given in [9, Listing 2], yet upgraded to the input language of *clingo* 4.

Listing 1.3. Simple encoding for *Ricochet Robots* (`ricochet.lp`)

```
1    time ( 1 .. horizon ).
2    dir ( − 1 ,0;1 ,0;0 , − 1;0 ,1).

4    stop( DX, DY,X,    Y   ) :− barrier (X,Y,DX,DY).
5    stop(−DX,−DY,X+DX,Y+DY) :− stop (DX,DY,X,Y).

7    pos (R,X,Y,0) :− pos (R,X,Y).

9    1 { move(R,DX,DY,T) : robot (R), dir (DX,DY) } 1 :− time (T).
10   move(R,T) :− move (R,_,_,T).

12   halt (DX,DY,X−DX,Y−DY,T) :− pos (_,X,Y,T), dir (DX,DY), dim (X−DX;Y−DY),
13                              not stop(−DX,−DY,X,Y), T < horizon .

15   goto (R,DX,DY,X,Y,T) :− pos (R,X,Y,T), dir (DX,DY), T < horizon .
16   goto (R,DX,DY,X+DX,Y+DY,T) :− goto (R,DX,DY,X,Y,T), dim (X+DX;Y+DY),
17                              not stop (DX,DY,X,Y), not halt (DX,DY,X,Y,T).

19   pos (R,X,Y,T) :− move (R,DX,DY,T), goto (R,DX,DY,X,Y,T−1),
20                   not goto (R,DX,DY,X+DX,Y+DY,T−1).
21   pos (R,X,Y,T) :− pos (R,X,Y,T−1), time (T), not move (R,T).

23   :− target (R,X,Y), not pos (R,X,Y,horizon ).

25   #show  move /4.
```

Following the description in [9], the first lines in Listing 1.3 furnish domain definitions, fixing the sequence of time steps (`time/1`)[12] and two-dimensional representations of the four possible directions (`dir/2`). The constant `horizon` is expected to be provided via *clingo* option `-c` (eg. '`-c horizon=20`'). Predicate `stop/4` is the symmetric version of `barrier/4` from above and identifies all blocked field transitions. The initial robot positions are fixed in Line 7 (in view of external input).

At each time step, some robot is moved in a direction (cf. Line 9). Such a `move` can be regarded as the composition of successive field transitions, captured by predicate `goto/6` (in Line 15–17). To this end, predicate `halt/5` provides temporary barriers due to robots' positions before the move. To be more precise, a robot moving in direction (`DX,DY`) must halt at field (`X-DX,Y-DY`) when some (other) robot is located at (`X,Y`), and an instance of `halt(DX,DY,X-DX,Y-DY,T)` may provide information relevant to the move at step `T+1` if there is no barrier between (`X-DX,Y-DY`) and (`X,Y`). Given this, the definition of `goto/6` starts at a robot's position (in Line 15) and continues in direction (`DX,DY`) (in Line 16–17) unless a barrier, a robot, or the board's border is encountered. As this definition tolerates board traversals of length zero, `goto/6` is guaranteed to yield a successor position for any `move` of a robot `R` in direction (`DX,DY`), so that the rule in Line 19–20 captures the effect of `move(R,DX,DY,T)`. Moreover, the frame axiom in Line 21 preserves the positions of unmoved robots, relying on the projection `move/2` (cf. Line 10).

Finally, we stipulate in Line 23 that a robot `R` must be at its target position (`X,Y`) at the last time point `horizon`. Adding directive '`#show move/4.`' further allows for projecting stable models onto the extension of the `move/4` predicate.

The encoding in Listing 1.3 allows us to decide whether a plan of length `horizon` exists. For computing a shortest plan, we may augment our decision encoding with an optimization directive. This can be accomplished by adding the part in Listing 1.4.

---

[12] The initial time point 0 is handled explicitly.

Listing 1.4. Encoding part for optimization (`optimization.lp`)

```
27   goon(T) :- target(R,X,Y), T = 0..horizon, not pos(R,X,Y,T).

29   :- move(R,DX,DY,T-1), time(T), not goon(T-1), not move(R,DX,DY,T).

31   #minimize{ 1,T : goon(T) }.
```

The rule in Line 27 indicates whether some goal condition is (not) established at a time point. Once the goal is established, the additional integrity constraint in Line 29 ensures that it remains satisfied by enforcing that the goal-achieving move is repeated at later steps (without altering robots' positions). Note that the `#minimize` directive in Line 31 aims at few instances of `goon/1`, corresponding to an early establishment of the goal, while further repetitions of the goal-achieving move are ignored. Our extended encoding allows for computing a shortest plan of length bounded by `horizon`. If there is no such plan, the problem can be posed again with an enlarged `horizon`. For computing a shortest plan in an unbounded fashion, we can take advantage of incremental ASP solving, as detailed in [9].[13]

Apart from the two external directives that allow us to vary initial robot and target positions, the four programs constitute an ordinary ASP formalization of a *Ricochet Robots* instance. To illustrate this, let us override the external directives by adding facts accounting for the robot and target positions on the left hand side of Figure 1. The corresponding call of *clingo* 4 is shown in Listing 1.5.[14]

Listing 1.5. One-shot solving with *clingo* 4

```
1   $ clingo-4 board.lp targets.lp ricochet.lp optimization.lp   \
2               -c horizon=10                                       \
3               <(echo "pos(red,1,1).    pos(green,16,1).    \
4                       pos(blue,1,16).  pos(yellow,16,16).  \
5                       goal(13)."                               )
```

Listing 1.6. Stable model projected onto the extension of the move/4 predicate

```
1   move(blue,0,-1,1)    move(blue,1,0,2)     move(blue,0,1,3)    \
2   move(blue,1,0,4)     move(yellow,0,-1,5)  move(blue,0,-1,6)   \
3   move(blue,1,0,7)     move(yellow,0,1,8)   move(yellow,-1,0,9) \
4   move(yellow,-1,0,10)
```

The resulting one-shot solving process yields a(n optimal) stable model containing the extension of the `move/4` predicate given in Listing 1.6. The `move` atoms in Line 1–4 of Listing 1.6 correspond to the plan indicated by the colored arrows at the bottom of the left hand side of Figure 1. That is, the blue robot starts by going north, east, south, and east, then the yellow one goes north, the blue one resumes and goes north and east, before finally the yellow robot goes south (bouncing off the blue one) and lands on the target by going west. This leads to the situation depicted on the right hand side of Figure 1. Note that the tenth move (in Line 4) is redundant since it merely replicates the previous one because the goal was already reached after nine steps.

---

[13] Note that [9] uses *iclingo* [14] for incremental solving. This functionality is now part of *clingo* 4 and makes *iclingo* obsolete. See [11] for details.

[14] Note that rather than using input redirection, we also could have passed the five facts via a file.

4   Playing in Rounds

Ricochet Robots is played in rounds. Hence, the next goal must be reached with robots placed at the positions resulting from the previous round. For example, when pursuing goal(4) in the next round, the robots must start from the end positions given on the right hand side of Figure 1. The resulting configuration is shown on the left hand side of Figure 2. For one-shot solving, we would re-launch *clingo* 4 from scratch as shown

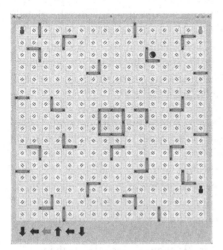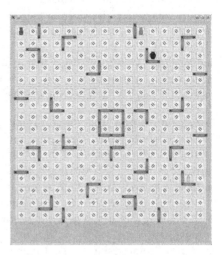

Fig. 2. Visualization of solving goal(4) from robot positions after having solved goal(13)

in Listing 1.5, yet by accounting for the new target and robot positions by replacing Line 3–5 of Listing 1.5 by the following ones.

```
3          <(echo "pos(red,1,1).    pos(green,16,1).     \
4                  pos(blue,16,10). pos(yellow,15,13). \
5                  goal(4)."                             )
```

Unlike this, our multi-shot approach to playing in rounds relies upon a single[15] operational *clingo* control object that we use in a simple loop:

1. Create an operational control object (containing a grounder and a solver object)
2. Load and ground the programs in Listing 1.1, 1.2, 1.3, and optionally 1.4 (relative to some fixed horizon) within the control object
3. While there is a goal, do the following
   (a) Enforce the initial robot positions
   (b) Enforce the current goal
   (c) Solve the logic program contained in the control object

---

[15] In general, multiple such control objects can be created and made to interact via Python.

The control loop is implemented in Python and relies on *clingo*'s Python module accompanying *clingo* 4.4. This module provides grounding and solving functionalities. An analogous module is available for Lua. As mentioned in Section 2, both modules support (almost) literal counterparts to 'Create', 'Load', 'Ground', and 'Solve'. The "enforcement" of robot and target positions is more complex, as it involves changing the truth values of externally controlled atoms (mimicking the insertion and deletion of atoms, respectively).

The resulting Python program is given in Listing 1.7. This program as well as its Lua counterpart are available at [10]. Line 1 shows how to import the `gringo` module.[16] We are only using three classes from the module,[17] which we directly pull into the global namespace to avoid qualification with "`gringo.`" and so to keep the code compact.

Line 3–34 show the `Player` class. This class encapsulates all state information including *clingo*'s `Control` object that in turn holds the state of the underlying grounder and solver. In the `Player`'s `__init__` function (similar to a constructor in other object-oriented languages) the following member variables are initialized:

`last_positions` This variable is initialized upon construction with the starting positions of the robots. During the progression of the game, this variable holds the initial starting positions of the robots for each turn.

`last_solution` This variable holds the last solution of a search call.

`undo_external` We want to successively solve a sequence of goals. In each step, a goal has to be reached from different starting positions. This variable holds a list containing the current goal and starting positions that have to be cleared upon the next step.

`horizon` We are using a bounded encoding. This (Python) variable holds the maximum number of moves to find a solution for a given step.

`ctl` This variable holds the actual object providing an interface to the grounder and solver. It holds all state information necessary for multi-shot solving along with heuristic information gathered during solving.

As shown in Line 4–13, the constructor takes the `horizon`, initial robot `positions`, and the `files` containing the various logic programs. *clingo*'s `Control` object is created in Line 9–10 by passing the option `-c` to replace the logic program constant `horizon` by the value of the Python variable `horizon` during grounding. Finally, the constructor loads all `files` and grounds the entire logic program in Line 11–13. Recall from Section 2 that all rules outside the scope of `#program` directives belong to the `base` program. Note also that this is the only time grounding happens because the encoding is bounded. All following solving steps are configured exclusively via manipulating external atoms.

The `solve` method in Line 15–24 starts with initializing the search for the solution to the new `goal`. To this end, it first undos in Line 16–17 the previous goal and starting positions stored in `undo_external` by assigning `False` to the respective atoms. In

---

[16] For historical reasons, it is called `gringo` in *clingo* 4.4 but it will be renamed to `clingo` with the next release.

[17] For a complete listing of functions and classes available in the `gringo` module, see `http://potassco.sourceforge.net/gringo.html`

Listing 1.7. The Ricochet Robot Player (`ricochet.py`)

```
1   from gringo import Control, Model, Fun

3   class Player:
4       def __init__(self, horizon, positions, files):
5           self.last_positions = positions
6           self.last_solution = None
7           self.undo_external = []
8           self.horizon = horizon
9           self.ctl = Control(
10              ['-c', 'horizon={0}'.format(self.horizon)])
11          for x in files:
12              self.ctl.load(x)
13          self.ctl.ground([("base", [])])

15      def solve(self, goal):
16          for x in self.undo_external:
17              self.ctl.assign_external(x, False)
18          self.undo_external = []
19          for x in self.last_positions + [goal]:
20              self.ctl.assign_external(x, True)
21              self.undo_external.append(x)
22          self.last_solution = None
23          self.ctl.solve(on_model=self.on_model)
24          return self.last_solution

26      def on_model(self, model):
27          self.last_solution = model.atoms()
28          self.last_positions = []
29          for atom in model.atoms(Model.ATOMS):
30              if (atom.name() == "pos" and
31                  len(atom.args()) == 4 and
32                  atom.args()[3] == self.horizon):
33                  self.last_positions.append(
34                      Fun("pos", atom.args()[:-1]))

36  horizon   = 15
37  encodings = ["board.lp", "targets.lp", "ricochet.lp", "optimization.lp"]
38  positions = [Fun("pos", [Fun("red"),     1,  1]),
39               Fun("pos", [Fun("blue"),    1, 16]),
40               Fun("pos", [Fun("green"),  16,  1]),
41               Fun("pos", [Fun("yellow"), 16, 16])]
42  sequence  = [Fun("goal", [13]),
43               Fun("goal", [4]),
44               Fun("goal", [7])]

46  player = Player(horizon, positions, encodings)
47  for goal in sequence:
48      print player.solve(goal)
```

the following lines 19 to 21, the next step is initialized by assigning `True` to the current `goal` along with the last robot positions; these are also stored in `undo_external` so that they can be taken back afterwards. Finally, the `solve` method calls *clingo*'s `ctl.solve` to initiate the search. The result is captured in variable `last_solution`. Note that the call to `ctl.solve` takes `ctl.on_model` as (keyword) argument, which is called whenever a model is found. In other words, `on_model` acts as a callback for intercepting models. Finally, variable `last_solution` is returned at the end of the method.

The last function of the `Player` class is the `on_model` callback. As mentioned, it intercepts the (final) `model`s computed by the solver, which can then be inspected via the functions of the `Model` class. At first, it stores the shown atoms in variable `last_solution` in Line 27.[18] The remainder of the `on_model` callback extracts the final robot positions from the stable model. For that, it loops in Line 29–34 over the full set of atoms in the `model` and checks whether their signatures match. That is, if an atom is formed from predicate `pos/4` and its fourth argument equals the `horizon`, then it is appended to the list of `last_positions` after stripping its time step from its arguments.

As an example, consider `pos(yellow,15,13,20)`, say the final position of the yellow robot on the right hand side of Figure 1 at an `horizon` of 20. This leads to the addition of `pos(yellow,15,13)` to the `last_positions`. Note that `pos(yellow,15,13)` is declared an external atom in Line 21 of Listing 1.2. For playing the next round, we can thus make it `True` in Line 20 of Listing 1.7. And when solving, the rule in Line 7 of Listing 1.3 allows us to derive `pos(yellow,15,13,0)` and makes it the new starting position of the yellow robot, as shown on the left hand side of Figure 2.

Line 36–44 show the code for configuring the player. They set the search `horizon`, the `encodings` to solve with, and the initial `positions` in form of *gringo* terms. Furthermore, we fix a `sequence` of goals in Line 42–44. In a more realistic setting, either some user interaction or a random sequence might be generated to emulate arbitrary draws.

Listing 1.8. Multi-shot solving with *clingo* 4's Python module

```
1    $ python ricochet.py
2    [move(red ,0 ,1 ,1),  move(red ,1 ,0 ,2),  move(red ,0 ,1 ,3),  ...]
3    [move(blue ,0 ,−1 ,1),  move(blue ,1 ,0 ,2),  move(blue ,0 ,1 ,3),  ...]
4    [move(green ,0 ,1 ,1),  move(green ,1 ,0 ,2),  move(green ,1 ,0 ,3),  ...]
```

Finally, Line 46–48 implement the search for sequences of moves that solve the configuration given above. For each `goal` in the `sequence`, a solution is plainly printed, as engaged in Line 48. The three lists in Listing 1.8 represent solutions to the three goals in Line 42–44. The *clingo* library does not foresee any output, which must thus be handled by the scripting language. Note also that the first list represents an alternative solution to the one given in Listing 1.6.

---

[18] In view of '`#show move/4.`' in Listing 1.3, this only involves instances of `move/4`, while all true atoms are included via the argument `Model.ATOMS` in Line 29.

5   Discussion

Multi-shot ASP solving is about successive yet operational grounding and solving of changing logic programs due to the addition, deletion, or replacement of facts or rules. Special cases include incremental, reactive, and window-based solving. For addressing such complex reasoning processes, *clingo* 4 complements ASP's declarative input language by control capacities expressed via the scripting languages Lua and Python. We elaborated upon *clingo*'s high-level constructs supporting multi-shot solving in several ways. First, we provided an operational semantics based on the concepts of *clingo* states and associated operations. These operations reflect the major functionalities offered by *clingo*'s Lua and Python library. A particular focus lay on the instantiation of extensible non-ground programs leading to ground programs with externals. Such externals are the primary means for changing problem specifications. Second, we provided a hands-on introduction to multi-shot solving with *clingo* 4 by modeling the popular board game of *Ricochet Robots*. In particular, we showed how *clingo*'s Python library allows for modeling turn playing by manipulating externals. Finally, we hope that our ASP-based implementation helps Gerd to win more often at *Ricochet Robots*.

Acknowledgments. This work was partially funded by German Science Foundation (DFG) under grant SCHA 550/9-1.

References

1. Bobrow, D. (ed.): Special issue on nonmonotonic logic, vol. 13. Artificial Intelligence (1980)
2. Brewka, G.: Nonmonotonic Reasoning: From Theoretical Foundation to Efficient Computation. Dissertation, Universität Hamburg (1989), revised version appeared as: Cambridge Tracts in Theoretical Computer Science. Cambridge University Press (1990)
3. Baral, C.: Knowledge Representation, Reasoning and Declarative Problem Solving. Cambridge University Press (2003)
4. Brewka, G., Eiter, T., Truszczyński, M.: Answer set programming at a glance. Communications of the ACM 54(12), 92–103 (2011)
5. Butko, N., Lehmann, K., Ramenzoni, V.: Ricochet Robots — a case study for human complex problem solving. In: Proceedings of the Annual Santa Fe Institute Summer School on Complex Systems (CSSS 2005) (2005)
6. Engels, B., Kamphans, T.: On the complexity of Randolph's robot game. Research Report 005, Institut für Informatik, Universität Bonn (2005)
7. Engels, B., Kamphans, T.: Randolph's robot game is NP-hard? Electronic Notes in Discrete Mathematics 25, 49–53 (2006)
8. Engels, B., Kamphans, T.: Randolph's robot game is NP-complete? In: Proceedings of the Twenty-second European Workshop on Computational Geometry (EWCG 2006), pp. 157–160 (2006)
9. Gebser, M., Jost, H., Kaminski, R., Obermeier, P., Sabuncu, O., Schaub, T., Schneider, M.: Ricochet robots: A transverse ASP benchmark. In: Cabalar, P., Son, T.C. (eds.) LPNMR 2013. LNCS, vol. 8148, pp. 348–360. Springer, Heidelberg (2013)
10. http://potassco.sourceforge.net/apps.html

11. Gebser, M., Kaminski, R., Kaufmann, B., Schaub, T.: *Clingo* = ASP + control: Preliminary report. In: Leuschel, M., Schrijvers, T. (eds.) Technical Communications of the Thirtieth International Conference on Logic Programming (ICLP 2014). Theory and Practice of Logic Programming, Online Supplement (2014) see also arXiv:1405.3694v1
12. Gebser, M., Kaminski, R., Kaufmann, B., Schaub, T.: *Clingo* = ASP + control: Extended report (2014), http://www.cs.uni-potsdam.de/wv/pdfformat/gekakasc14a.pdf
13. Eén, N., Sörensson, N.: Temporal induction by incremental SAT solving. Electronic Notes in Theoretical Computer Science 89(4) (2003)
14. Gebser, M., Kaminski, R., Kaufmann, B., Ostrowski, M., Schaub, T., Thiele, S.: Engineering an incremental ASP solver. In: Garcia de la Banda, M., Pontelli, E. (eds.) ICLP 2008. LNCS, vol. 5366, pp. 190–205. Springer, Heidelberg (2008)
15. Oikarinen, E., Janhunen, T.: Modular equivalence for normal logic programs. In: Brewka, G., Coradeschi, S., Perini, A., Traverso, P. (eds.) Proceedings of the Seventeenth European Conference on Artificial Intelligence (ECAI 2006), pp. 412–416. IOS Press (2006)
16. Gebser, M., Kaminski, R., König, A., Schaub, T.: Advances in *gringo* series 3. In: Delgrande, J.P., Faber, W. (eds.) LPNMR 2011. LNCS, vol. 6645, pp. 345–351. Springer, Heidelberg (2011)
17. Gebser, M., Kaminski, R., Kaufmann, B., Ostrowski, M., Schaub, T., Thiele, S.: A user's guide to gringo, clasp, clingo, and iclingo. (2010) http://sourceforge.net/projects/potassco/files/potassco_guide/2010-10-04/guide.pdf
18. Calimeri, F., Faber, W., Gebser, M., Ianni, G., Kaminski, R., Krennwallner, T., Leone, N., Ricca, F., Schaub, T.: ASP-Core-2: Input language format (2012), https://www.mat.unical.it/aspcomp2013/files/ASP-CORE-2.03b.pdf

Simulation of Action Theories and an Application to General Game-Playing Robots

Michael Thielscher

School of Computer Science and Engineering
The University of New South Wales
Sydney, NSW 2052, Australia
mit@cse.unsw.edu.au

Abstract. We consider the problem of verifying whether one action theory can *simulate* a second one. Action theories provide modular descriptions of state machines, and simulation means that all possible sequences of actions in one transition system can be matched by the other. We show how Answer Set Programming can be used to automatically prove simulation by induction from an axiomatisation of two action theories and a projection function between them. Our interest in simulation of action theories comes from general game-playing robots as systems that can understand the rules of new games and learn to play them effectively in a physical environment. A crucial property of such games is their *playability*, that is, each legal play sequence in the abstract game must be executable in the real environment.

1 Introduction

Simulation, and bisimulation, of state transition systems is an important and well researched concept in theoretical computer science and formal logic [30,3] but has not been applied in the context of action languages that provide logic-based, compact descriptions of state machines [5,14,29,32]. We consider the problem of automatically proving whether the transition system represented by one action theory can simulate the system described by another theory.

Our interest in simulation of action theories comes from an open problem in *general game-playing robotics*, which is concerned with the design of autonomous systems that can understand descriptions of new games and learn to play them in a physical game environment [28]. This is an attempt to create a new generation of AI systems that can understand the rules of new games and then learn to play these games without human intervention [16]. Unlike specialised game-playing systems such as the chess program Deep Blue [19], a general game player cannot rely on algorithms that have been designed in advance for specific games. Rather, it requires a form of general intelligence that enables the player to autonomously adapt to new and possibly radically different problems. General game playing programs therefore are a quintessential example of a new generation of systems that end users can customise for their own specific tasks and special needs [15],

T. Eiter et al. (Eds.): Brewka Festschrift, LNAI 9060, pp. 33–46, 2015.

Fig. 1. A physical game environment

and general game-playing robots extend this capability to AI systems that play games in the real world [28].

In general game playing, games are represented using a special-purpose action description language [16]. These game descriptions must satisfy a few basic requirements to ensure that a game is effectively playable; for example, there should always be at least one legal move in every nonterminal position [17]. In bringing gameplay from mere virtual into physical environments, general game-playing robots require an additional property that concern the manifestation of the game rules in the real world. Notably, a suitable game description requires all moves deemed legal by the rules of the abstract game to be executable in the real world [28].

As an example, consider the robotic environment shown in Fig. 1. It features a 4×4 chess-like board with an additional row of 4 marked positions on the right. Tin cans are the only type of objects and can be moved between the marked position (but cannot be stacked). This game environment can be interpreted in countless ways as physical manifestations of a game, including all kinds of mini chess-like games but also, say, single-player games like the 15-puzzle, where individual cans represent numbered tiles that need to be brought in the right order [28]. In fact, any abstract game is *playable* in this environment provided that all legal play sequences can be executed by the robot.

In order to prove the playability of a game, we consider its rules and those that govern the robotic environment as formal descriptions of state transition systems. This allows us to reduce the problem of verifying that a game is playable to the problem of proving that an action theory describing the environment can simulate the action theory that encodes the game. As a general technique, we will show how Answer Set Programming can be used to automatically prove the simulation of action theories based on their axiomatisation along with a projection function between the states of the two systems.

The remainder of the paper is organised as follows. Section 2 introduces a basic action description language that we will use for our analysis and which derives from the general game description language GDL [16]. In Section 3, we formally define the concept of simulation for action theories. The use of Answer Set Programming to automatically prove this property by induction are given in Section 4, and in Section 5 we show how the result can be applied to proving the playability of abstract games in physical environments. We conclude in Section 6.

2   Action Theories

A variety of knowledge representation languages exist for describing actions and change, including first-order formalisms such as the classical Situation Calculus and its variants [26,20,33], special-purpose action description languages [14,29], planning formalisms [8,11] or the general game description language [16]. While they are all subtly different, action languages invariably share the following standard elements:

- *fluents*, which describe atomic, variable properties of states;
- *actions*, whose execution triggers state transitions;
- *action preconditions*, defining conditions on states for an action to be executable;
- *effect specifications*, defining the result of actions;
- *initial state* description.

For the purpose of this paper, we will use a simple and generic specification language for basic action theories that uses Answer Set Programming (ASP) syntax to describe all of these basic elements. Many of the aforementioned action formalisms have straightforward translations into ASP, e.g. [21,6,2,12,34]. Hence, while our language borrows its five pre-defined predicates from the game description language GDL [16] in view of our motivating application, our definitions and results can be easily adapted to similar action representation formalisms.

Example. Before providing the formal language definition, let us consider the example of a 4×4 sliding puzzle, which is formally described by the action theory given in Fig. 2. The rules use the fluent $cell(x, y, z)$ to indicate the current state of position (x, y) as either occupied by tile z or being empty, where $x, y \in \{1, \ldots, 4\}$ and $z \in \{1, \ldots, 15, empty\}$. A second fluent $step(x)$ counts the number of moves, which has been limited to $x \in \{1, \ldots, 80\}$. The only action in this domain is $move(u, v, x, y)$, denoting the move of sliding the tile in (u, v) into position (x, y), where $u, v, x, y \in \{1, \ldots, 4\}$. Intuitively, the description can be understood as follows:

- Facts 1–17 completely describe the *initial state* as depicted.
- The *precondition axioms* 19–22 say that a tile can be slid into the adjacent empty cell.
- The *result* of sliding the tile in (u, v) into position (x, y) is that

```
1 init(cell(1,1,  9)).
2 init(cell(2,1,  2)).
3 init(cell(3,1,  8)).
4 init(cell(4,1,12)).
5 init(cell(1,2,11)).
6 init(cell(2,2,  3)).
7 init(cell(3,2,15)).
8 init(cell(4,2,10)).
9 init(cell(1,3,  6)).
10 init(cell(2,3,empty)).
11 init(cell(3,3,13)).
12 init(cell(4,3,  5)).
13 init(cell(1,4,14)).
14 init(cell(2,4,  4)).
15 init(cell(3,4,  1)).
16 init(cell(4,4,  7)).
17 init(step(1)).
18
19 legal(move(U,Y,X,Y)) :- true(cell(X,Y,empty)), succ(U,X), true(cell(U,Y,Z)).
20 legal(move(U,Y,X,Y)) :- true(cell(X,Y,empty)), succ(X,U), true(cell(U,Y,Z)).
21 legal(move(X,V,X,Y)) :- true(cell(X,Y,empty)), succ(V,Y), true(cell(X,V,Z)).
22 legal(move(X,V,X,Y)) :- true(cell(X,Y,empty)), succ(Y,V), true(cell(X,V,Z)).
23
24 next(cell(U,V,empty)) :- does(move(U,V,X,Y)).
25 next(cell(X,Y,Z))      :- does(move(U,V,X,Y)), true(cell(U,V,Z)).
26
27 next(cell(R,S,Z)) :- true(cell(R,S,Z)), does(move(U,V,X,Y)), R != U, R != X.
28 next(cell(R,S,Z)) :- true(cell(R,S,Z)), does(move(U,V,X,Y)), R != U, S != Y.
29 next(cell(R,S,Z)) :- true(cell(R,S,Z)), does(move(U,V,X,Y)), S != V, R != X.
30 next(cell(R,S,Z)) :- true(cell(R,S,Z)), does(move(U,V,X,Y)), S != V, S != Y.
31
32 next(step(Y)) :- true(step(X)), succ(X,Y).
33
34 succ(1,2).    succ(2,3).   ...   succ(79,80).
```

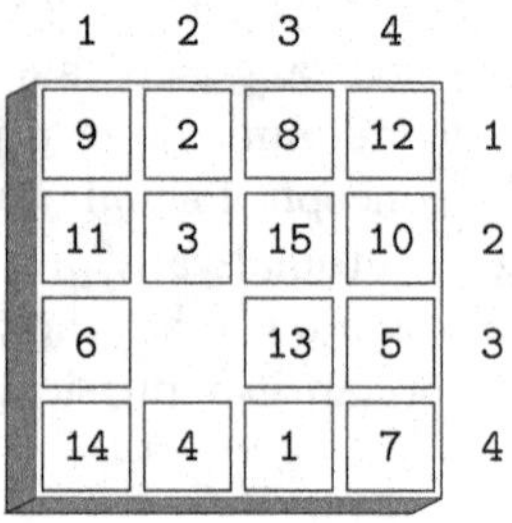

	1	2	3	4	
	9	2	8	12	1
	11	3	15	10	2
	6		13	5	3
	14	4	1	7	4

Fig. 2. The 15-puzzle described by an action theory

- cell (u, v) becomes empty while the tile is now in (x, y) (clauses 24, 25);
- all other cells retain their tiles (clauses 27–30);
- the step counter is incremented (clause 25).

As can be seen from this example, our action theory uses the following unary predicates as pre-defined keywords:

- init(f), to define fluent f to be true initially;
- true(f), denoting the condition that f is true in a state;
- does(a), denoting the condition that a is performed in a state;
- legal(a), meaning that action a is possible;
- next(f), to define the fluents that are true after an action is performed.

For the formal definition of the syntax of the action specification language, we assume that the reader is familiar with basic concepts of logic programs [23] and Answer Set Programming [4]. Our action theories are normal logic programs that have to satisfy a few syntactic restrictions borrowed from GDL [17] in order to ensure that they admit a unique and finite interpretation.

Definition 1. *Consider an alphabet that includes the unary predicates* init*,* legal*,* next*,* true *and* does*. An* action theory *is a normal logic program* P *such that*

1. P is stratified, *that is, its dependency graph has no cycles with a negative edge [1];*
2. P is allowed, *that is, each variable in a clause occurs in a positive atom of the body of that clause [24];*
3. P satisfies the following restrictions on the pre-defined predicates:
   (a) init *occurs only in the head of clauses and does not depend on any of the other special keywords;*
   (b) legal *occurs only in the head of clauses and does not depend on* does *;*
   (c) next *occurs only in the head of clauses;*
   (d) true *and* does *occur only in the body of clauses.*
4. P obeys the following *recursion restriction to ensure finite groundings: If predicates p and q occur in a cycle in the dependency graph of P, or if $p = \text{true}$ and $q = \text{next}$, and P contains a clause*

$$p(s_1, \ldots, s_m) :- b_1(t_1), \ldots, q(v_1, \ldots, v_k), \ldots, b_n(t_n)$$

then for every $i \in \{1, \ldots, k\}$,
   - *v_i is variable-free, or*
   - *v_i is one of $s_1, \ldots, s_m$, or*
   - *v_i occurs in some t_j $(1 \leq j \leq n)$ such that b_j does not occur in a cycle with p in the dependency graph of P.*

It is straightforward to verify that the action theory in Fig. 2 satisfies this definition of a proper action theory.

3   Simulation of Action Theories

The concept of simulation for action theories needs to be defined on the state transition systems that they describe, where generally states are identified by the fluents that hold and state transitions are triggered by actions [14,29,32]. In case of the action description language of Definition 1, this interpretation is obtained with the help of the stable models [13] of Answer Set Programs. Below, $\text{SM}[P]$ denotes the unique stable model of a stratified, finitely groundable program P.

Definition 2. *Let P be an action theory in the language of Definition 1 with ground fluents $\mathcal{F}$ and ground actions $\mathcal{A}$. P determines a* finite state machine $(\mathcal{A}, S, s_0, \delta)$ *as follows:*

1. $S = 2^{\mathcal{F}}$ *are the* states;
2. $s_0 = \{f \in \mathcal{F} : \text{init}(f) \in \text{SM}[P]\}$ *is the* initial state;
3. $\delta(a, s) = \{f \in \mathcal{F} : \text{next}(f) \in \text{SM}[P \cup \text{does}(a) \cup \text{true}|_s]\}$ *is the* transition function, *where*
   - $a \in \mathcal{A}$
   - $s \in S$
   - $\text{true}|_s = \{\text{true}(f) : f \in s\}$
   - $\text{legal}(a) \in \text{SM}[P \cup \text{true}|_s]$ *(that is, a is possible in s).*

A state $s \in S$ is called reachable *if there is a finite sequence of actions $a_1, \ldots, a_k$ such that $s = \delta(a_k, \ldots, \delta(a_1, s_0) \ldots)$.*

Put in words,

- states are sets of ground fluents;
- the initial state is given by all derivable instances of $\texttt{init}(f)$;
- to determine if an action is legal in a state s, this state s has to be encoded using facts $\texttt{true}(f)$, and then a is possible if $\texttt{legal}(a)$ can be derived;
- likewise, to determine the effects of an action a in a state s, the action and the state have to be encoded using facts $\texttt{does}(a)$ and $\texttt{true}(f)$, respectively, and then the resulting state is given by all derivable instances of $\texttt{next}(f)$.

Example. Recall the action theory in Fig. 2 describing the 15-puzzle. It is easy to see that the initial state is

$$s_0 = \{cell(1, 1, 9), \ldots, cell(1, 3, 6), cell(2, 3, empty), \ldots, step(1)\} \qquad (1)$$

It is straightforward to verify that the action $move(1, 3, 2, 3)$ is possible in this state: After adding each of the facts in $\texttt{true}|_{s_0}$, the unique stable model of the resulting program includes $\texttt{true}(cell(2, 3, empty))$, $\texttt{true}(cell(1, 3, 6))$ and $succ(1, 2)$, hence also $\texttt{legal}(move(1, 3, 2, 3))$ according to clause 19. From Definition 2 and the clauses 24–32 it follows that

$$\delta(move(1, 3, 2, 3), s_0) = \\ \{cell(1, 1, 9), \ldots, cell(1, 3, empty), cell(2, 3, 6), \ldots, step(2)\}$$

Given two state transition systems, the standard definition of a simulation requires that one matches all actions in the other. In case of two action theories P_1 and P_2, this requires that the actions and states of the simulated domain, P_1, can be projected onto actions and states in the simulating domain, P_2, such that

- the initial state of P_1 projects onto the initial state of P_2;
- if an action is possible in P_2, then the corresponding action is possible in the corresponding state in P_2 and the resulting states correspond, too.

This is formally captured by the following definition.

Definition 3. *Let P_1 and P_2 be two action theories, which describe finite state machines $(\mathcal{A}, S, s_0, \delta)$ and $(\mathcal{B}, T, t_0, \varepsilon)$, respectively. A* projection *of P_1 onto P_2 is a function π such that*

- *$\pi(a) \in \mathcal{B}$ for all $a \in \mathcal{A}$*
- *$\pi(s) \in T$ for all $s \in S$*

A projection π is a simulation *of P_1 by P_2 if*

1. *$\pi(s_0) = t_0$ and*
2. *for all $a \in \mathcal{A}$ and all reachable $s \in S$,*
   (a) if a is possible in s then $\pi(a)$ is possible in $\pi(s)$
   (b) $\pi(\delta(a, s)) = \varepsilon(\pi(a), \pi(s))$

```
1  init(piece(a,1)).
2  init(piece(b,1)).
3  init(piece(c,1)).
4  init(piece(d,1)).
5  init(piece(a,2)).
6  init(piece(c,2)).
7  init(piece(d,2)).
8  init(piece(a,3)).
9  init(piece(b,3)).
10 init(piece(c,3)).
11 init(piece(d,3)).
12 init(piece(a,4)).
13 init(piece(b,4)).
14 init(piece(c,4)).
15 init(piece(d,4)).
16
17 legal(put(U,V,X,Y)) :- true(piece(U,V)), coord(X,Y), not true(piece(X,Y)).
18
19 next(piece(X,Y)) :- does(put(U,V,X,Y)).
20 next(piece(X,Y)) :- true(piece(X,Y)), not moved(X,Y).
21
22 moved(X,Y) :- does(put(X,Y,U,V)).
23 coord(a,1).   coord(a,2).   coord(a,3).   coord(a,4).
24 ...
25 coord(x,1).   coord(x,2).   coord(x,3).   coord(x,4).
```

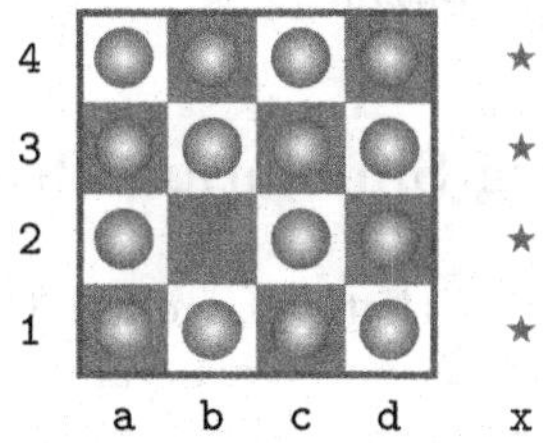

Fig. 3. An action theory describing the physical environment of the robot in Fig. 1

Example. The action theory in Fig. 3 describes the physical environment of the robot in Fig. 1 with the help of a single fluent, $piece(i,j)$, indicating whether a can has been placed at (i,j) where $i \in \{a,b,c,x\}$ and $j \in \{1,2,3\}$; and the action $put(i,j,k,l)$ of lifting the object at location (i,j) and putting it down at location (k,l).

The following projection function maps every action and state in the 15-puzzle to an action and state in the robotic game environment:

1. $\pi(move(u,v,x,y)) = put(\overline{u}, 5-v, \overline{x}, 5-y)$,
   where $\overline{1} = a, \ldots, \overline{4} = d$ (to account for the different coordinate systems);
2. $\pi(s) = \{piece(\overline{x}, 5-y) : cell(x,y,z) \in s, \ z \neq empty\}$.

It is easy to see that under this function, initial state (1) of the 15-puzzle projects onto the initial state of the action theory for the robotic environment. Indeed, the projection provides a simulation of the 15-puzzle in the physical robot domain: According to the rules in Fig. 2, the possible actions in the 15-puzzle are to move from a cell (u,v) to an adjacent and empty cell (x,y). This implies that there is no piece in the corresponding location $(\overline{x}, 5-y)$ on the physical board and also that there is a piece at $(\overline{u}, 5-v)$ since there can be no more than one empty cell in any reachable state of the game. Hence, the corresponding put action in the robotic environment is possible in the projected state according to clause 17 in Fig. 3. Moreover, the result of sliding a tile is that the tile and the empty location swap places, which corresponds to the effect of moving the respective tin can.

It is worth noting that the reverse does not hold: The robot can of course move any of the pieces into a non-adjacent, empty location, including the 4 marked positions to the right of the board. None of these actions can be matched by a legal move in the 15-puzzle.

4   Automating Simulation Proofs

An automated proof that one action theory indeed simulates a second one through a given projection, in general needs to inspect all action sequences possible in the simulated transition system. A viable and sound but incomplete alternative is to use induction proofs—a technique that has been successfully applied to automatically proving state constraints in action theories [18,22]. Indeed, the required properties of a simulation according to Definition 3 can be considered as state constraints over the combined action theories. In the following, we adapt the existing ASP-based proof technique for state constraints in general games [18] to solve the problem of automatically proving simulation of two action theories by induction.

Consider two action theories P_1 and P_2. We combine these into a single answer set program $P_1 \cup P_2$, which is then augmented as follows:

1. An encoding of a given projection function π from P_1 to P_2 by:
   (a) Clauses

   ```
   1  isimulation_error  :-  ¬Π[init].
   2  tsimulation_error  :-  ¬Π[true].
   3  nsimulation_error  :-  ¬Π[next].
   ```

   Here, Π stands for an ASP encoding of the conditions (on the fluents in the two action theories) under which a state from P_1 projects onto a state from P_2 according to π. The expression $\Pi[\text{init}]$ etc. means to replace every occurrence of a fluent f in Π by $\text{init}(f)$ etc.[1]
   (b) Clauses

   ```
   4  does(π(a))  :-  does(a).
   ```

   for actions a from P_1.
2. An encoding of the induction hypothesis as

   ```
   5  { true(F)  :  fluent(F) }.
   6  1 { does(A)  :  action(A) } 1.
   7  :-  action(A), does(A), not legal(A).
   8  :-  tsimulation_error.
   ```

   where the auxiliary predicate fluent ranges over all fluents in either P_1 or P_2 while action ranges over the actions of P_1 only.
3. The negation of the base case and of the induction step as

---

[1] For example, if the projection function requires that there be no empty cell (x, y) in the abstract game that houses a piece in the physical environment, then $\neg\Pi$ could be $(\exists x, y)\, cell(x, y, empty) \land piece(x, y)$, in which case $\neg\Pi[\text{init}]$ is $(\exists x, y)\, \text{init}(cell(x, y, empty)) \land \text{init}(piece(x, y))$.

```
 9  counterexample  :-  isimulation_error .
10  counterexample  :-  does(A), not legal(A).
11  counterexample  :-  nsimulation_error .
12  :- not counterexample .
```

If the resulting ASP admits *no* stable models, then this proves the projection function to be a simulation of P_1 by P_2: Clause 12 excludes solutions without a counter-example, which according to clauses 9–11 is obtained when

1. the initial state does not project, which corresponds to condition 1 in Definition 3;
2. an action exists (clause 6) that is legal (clause 7) but whose projection is not possible, which corresponds to condition 2(a) in Definition 3;
3. a state, i.e. a set of fluents, exists (clause 5) so that the result of a state transition does not project, which corresponds to condition 2(b) in Definition 3.

We have thus obtained at a technique for automating simulation proofs that is correct and also very viable in practice as it avoids inspecting all possible action sequences of the simulated state transition system, as a variety of systematic experiments with similar inductive proof techniques have demonstrated in the past [18].

While sound, these induction proofs are in general incomplete as can be shown with our two example action theories for the 15-puzzle and the robotic environment as given in Fig. 2 and 3, respectively.

Example. Using the same schema as the generic clauses 1–4 above, the projection function defined for our example in Section 3 can be encoded thus (where for the sake of clarity we assume that the two coordinate systems were identical):

```
does (put(U,V,X,Y))  :-  does(move(U,V,X,Y)).

isimulation_error  :-  init(piece(X,Y)), not icell_tile(X,Y).
isimulation_error  :-  not init(piece(X,Y)), icell_tile(X,Y).
tsimulation_error  :-  true(piece(X,Y)), not tcell_tile(X,Y).
tsimulation_error  :-  not true(piece(X,Y)), tcell_tile(X,Y).
nsimulation_error  :-  next(piece(X,Y)), not ncell_tile(X,Y).
nsimulation_error  :-  not next(piece(X,Y)), ncell_tile(X,Y).

icell_tile(X,Y)  :-  init(cell(X,Y,Z)), Z != empty.
tcell_tile(X,Y)  :-  true(cell(X,Y,Z)), Z != empty.
ncell_tile(X,Y)  :-  next(cell(X,Y,Z)), Z != empty.
```

Put in words, a projected state requires a tin can at location (x, y) if, and only if, the corresponding cell in the 15-puzzle exists and is not empty. Combined with the action theories of Fig. 2 and 3 and augmented by the general clauses 5–12 from above, the resulting ASP *does* admit stable models. For instance, one model of the ASP includes

$$\mathbf{true}(cell(1, 1, empty)), \ \mathbf{true}(cell(1, 2, empty)), \ \mathbf{legal}(move(1, 1, 1, 2))$$

Indeed, the action theory in Fig. 2 sanctions the move from one empty cell to a neighbouring empty cell while this is not possible in the robot domain, where only pieces can be moved. Another model of the ASP includes

$$\text{true}(cell(1,1,1)), \ \text{true}(cell(1,2,empty)), \ \text{legal}(move(1,1,1,2))$$
$$\text{true}(cell(1,2,2)), \ \text{true}(piece(1,2))$$

Indeed, the action theory in Fig. 2 sanctions the move into a cell with a numbered tile, here $(1,2)$, if the fluent is also true that says that this cell is empty. Again this is not possible in the robot domain, where a tin can cannot be put down at a location already occupied by an object.

Clearly, both these generated counter-examples refer to unreachable states in the 15-puzzle, hence their existence does not disprove our projection to provide a simulation of this game by the robot. In fact, we can enhance the capability of any ASP for proving simulation by adding state constraints of the simulated action theory that help to exclude unreachable states from being considered as counter-examples. Specifically, the 15-puzzle satisfies these state constraints:

```
inconsistent :-
   true(cell(U,V,empty)), true(cell(X,Y,empty)), U != X.
inconsistent :-
   true(cell(U,V,empty)), true(cell(X,Y,empty)), V != Y.
inconsistent :-
   true(cell(X,Y,empty)), true(cell(X,Y,Z)), Z != empty.
:- inconsistent.
```

Put in words, no consistent state contains two different cells that are both empty, or a cell that is both empty and occupied by a numbered tile. These constraints themselves can be automatically proved from the underlying action theory of Fig. 2 using existing methods [18,22]. Once they are added, the ASP for proving that the robotic domain can simulate the 15-puzzle admits no stable model, which establishes the intended result.

5 General Game-Playing Robots and the Playability of Games

The annual AAAI GGP Competition [16] defines a general game player as a system that understands the formal Game Description Language (GDL) [25] and is able to play effectively any game described therein. Since the first contest in 2005, General Game Playing has evolved into a thriving AI research area. Established methods include Monte Carlo tree search [9], the automatic generation of heuristic evaluation functions [7,31], and learning [10].

General game-playing robots extend this capability to AI systems that play games in the real world [28]. In bringing gameplay from mere virtual into physical environments, this adds a new requirement for suitable game descriptions, which concerns the manifestation of the game rules in the real world: An abstract game described in GDL can be played in a real robotic environment only if all moves deemed legal by the rules are actually possible in the physical world.

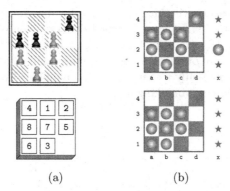

(a)   (b)

Fig. 4. (a) Different games and (b) their projections onto the game environment of Fig. 1

When we use a physical environment to play a game, the real objects become representatives of entities in the abstract game. A pawn in chess, for instance, is typically manifested by an actual wooden piece of a certain shape and colour. But any other physical object, including a tin can, can serve the same purpose. Conversely, any game environment like the $4 \times 4(+4)$ board with cans depicted in Fig. 1 can be interpreted in countless ways as physical manifestation of a game. For example, Fig. 4(a) shows two positions from two different games, a mini chess-like game and the 8-puzzle as a smaller variant of the standard sliding tile game. We can view the states depicted to the left of each position (Fig. 4(b)) as their projection onto our example physical game environment, in which the extra row can be used to park captured pieces (in chess-like games) or where gameplay is confined to a subregion of the board (for the 8-puzzle). Note that this manifestation abstracts away possible differences in the type of cans such as their colour or shape (or contents for that matter). Hence, it is only through a projection function that the robotic player knows whether a can stands for a white or a black pawn, say. The same holds for the sliding puzzles, where the goal position (with all tiles in ascending order) actually projects onto the very same abstract environment state as the starting position—the distinction lies entirely in the meaning attached to individual cans in regard to which number they represent. It is noteworthy that a similar feature is found in many games humans play, where also the physical manifestation of a game position is often an incomplete representation; for example, the pieces on a chessboard alone are not telling us whose move it is or which side still has castling rights [27].

The manifestation of a game in a physical environment can be mathematically captured by *projecting* the positions from the abstract game onto actual states of the game environment, and then a game is *playable* if all actions in the abstract game can be matched by actions in the projected environment [28]. The language GDL, which is commonly used to describe games in general game playing and which supports the description of any finite n-player game ($n \geq 1$), includes elements for the specifications of different players and goals [16]. Since these are irrelevant for the question whether a game is playable and because our action language of Definition 1 is in fact a stripped-down version of GDL, the formal concept of simulation of action theories, along with our proof technique, can be employed for the purpose of automatically proving that a game is playable in a robotic environment. The only requirement is to symbolically describe the latter by an action theory in the same language.

6   Conclusion

In this paper we have defined the concept of one action theory being able to simulate a second one. We have shown how Answer Set Programming can be used to automatically prove simulation by induction from an axiomatisation of the two action theories and a projection function between them. We have motivated and applied these results in the context of systems that draw together two topical yet disparate areas of artificial intelligence research: general game playing and robotics.

Our definition of simulation in action theories follows the standard one in theoretical computer science and formal logic, in that actions always need to be matched by single actions. In practice, this requires a similar level of abstraction in both models. But our notion of projection in Definition 3 can be straightforwardly generalised to allow for different degrees of abstraction in that an action in one model corresponds to a *sequence* of actions in the other one. A single move in the abstract 15-puzzle, for example, could then be mapped onto a complex movement of the robot arm in the physical environment: move above the can, open the fingers, go down, close the fingers, move to the target location, open the fingers, raise above the can, close the fingers and return back to the home position. The automation of simulation proofs then needs to be suitably extended by incorporating sequences of state updates in one action theory [18] and aligning them with a single state transition in the simulated system.

Acknowledgement. This article, like so many before (and hopefully after!), may very well have never been written had I not met Gerhard Brewka when I was still an undergraduate at Wolfgang Bibel's research group in Darmstadt. I very well remember that first research project meeting I ever attended, where I gave the first scientific talk in my life, hopelessly nervous of course, but then to my greatest surprise caught the attention of the most prominent scientist present. His words of encouragement, after a lot of sweat, tears and the journey of writing, eventually led to my first article in a journal, and a decent one at that, marking the beginning of my life as a scientist. Gerd may not remember, but over the years we have collaborated in research projects, co-authored papers and jointly supervised students, and a lifelong friendship ensued.

References

1. Apt, K., Blair, H., Walker, A.: Towards a theory of declarative knowledge. In: Minker, J. (ed.) Foundations of Deductive Databases and Logic Programming, ch. 2, pp. 89–148. Morgan Kaufmann (1987)
2. Babb, J., Lee, J.: CPLUS2ASP: Computing action language $\mathcal{C}+$ in answer set programming. In: Cabalar, P., Son, T.C. (eds.) LPNMR 2013. LNCS, vol. 8148, pp. 122–134. Springer, Heidelberg (2013)
3. van Benthem, J.: Logic in Games. MIT Press (2014)
4. Brewka, G., Eiter, T., Truszczynski, M.: Answer set programming at a glance. Communications of the ACM 54(12), 92–103 (2011)
5. Brewka, G., Hertzberg, J.: How to do things with worlds: on formalizing actions and plans. Journal of Logic and Computation 3(5), 517–532 (1993)
6. Cerexhe, T., Gebser, M., Thielscher, M.: Online agent logic programming with oClingo. In: Pham, D.-N., Park, S.-B. (eds.) PRICAI 2014. LNCS, vol. 8862, pp. 945–957. Springer, Heidelberg (2014)
7. Clune, J.: Heuristic evaluation functions for general game playing. In: Proceedings of the AAAI Conference on Artificial Intelligence, pp. 1134–1139. AAAI Press, Vancouver (2007)
8. Fikes, R., Nilsson, N.: STRIPS: A new approach to the application of theorem proving to problem solving. Artificial Intelligence 2, 189–208 (1971)
9. Finnsson, H., Björnsson, Y.: Simulation-based approach to general game playing. In: Proceedings of the AAAI Conference on Artificial Intelligence, pp. 259–264. AAAI Press, Chicago (2008)
10. Finnsson, H., Björnsson, Y.: Learning simulation control in general game-playing agents. In: Proceedings of the AAAI Conference on Artificial Intelligence, pp. 954–959. AAAI Press, Atlanta (2010)
11. Fox, M., Long, D.: PDDL2.1: an extension to PDDL for expressing temporal planning domains. Journal of Artificial Intelligence Research 20, 61–124 (2003)
12. Gebser, M., Kaminski, R., Knecht, M., Schaub, T.: plasp: A prototype for PDDL-based planning in ASP. In: Delgrande, J.P., Faber, W. (eds.) LPNMR 2011. LNCS, vol. 6645, pp. 358–363. Springer, Heidelberg (2011)
13. Gelfond, M.: Answer sets. In: van Harmelen, F., Lifschitz, V., Porter, B. (eds.) Handbook of Knowledge Representation, pp. 285–316. Elsevier (2008)
14. Gelfond, M., Lifschitz, V.: Representing action and change by logic programs. Journal of Logic Programming 17, 301–321 (1993)
15. Genesereth, M., Björnsson, Y.: The international general game playing competition. AI Magazine 34(2), 107–111 (2013)
16. Genesereth, M., Love, N., Pell, B.: General game playing: Overview of the AAAI competition. AI Magazine 26(2), 62–72 (2005)
17. Genesereth, M., Thielscher, M.: General Game Playing. Synthesis Lectures on Artificial Intelligence and Machine Learning. Morgan & Claypool (2014)
18. Haufe, S., Schiffel, S., Thielscher, M.: Automated verification of state sequence invariants in general game playing. Artificial Intelligence, 187–188, 1–30 (2012)
19. Hsu, F.H.: Behind Deep Blue: Building the Computer that Defeated the World Chess Champion. Princeton University Press (2002)
20. Kowalski, R.: Database updates in the event calculus. Journal of Logic Programming 12, 121–146 (1992)
21. Lee, J.: Reformulating the situation calculus and the event calculus in the general theory of stable models and in answer set programming. Journal of Artificial Intelligence Research 43, 571–620 (2012)

22. Li, N., Fan, Y., Liu, Y.: Reasoning about state constraints in the situation calculus. In: Proceedings of the International Joint Conference on Artificial Intelligence (IJCAI), Beijing, China (August 2013)
23. Lloyd, J.: Foundations of Logic Programming, 2nd extended edn. Series Symbolic Computation. Springer (1987)
24. Lloyd, J., Topor, R.: A basis for deductive database systems II. Journal of Logic Programming 3(1), 55–67 (1986)
25. Love, N., Hinrichs, T., Haley, D., Schkufza, E., Genesereth, M.: General Game Playing: Game Description Language Specification. Tech. Rep. LG–2006–01, Stanford Logic Group, Computer Science Department, Stanford University, 353 Serra Mall, Stanford, CA 94305 (2006), `games.stanford.edu`
26. McCarthy, J.: Situations and Actions and Causal Laws. Stanford Artificial Intelligence Project, Memo 2, Stanford University, CA (1963)
27. Pritchard, D.: The Encycolpedia of Chess Variants. Godalming (1994)
28. Rajaratnam, D., Thielscher, M.: Towards general game-playing robots: Models, architecture and game controller. In: Cranefield, S., Nayak, A. (eds.) AI 2013. LNCS, vol. 8272, pp. 271–276. Springer, Heidelberg (2013)
29. Sandewall, E.: Features and Fluents. The Representation of Knowledge about Dynamical Systems. Oxford University Press (1994)
30. Sangiorgi, D.: Introduction to Bisumlation and Coinduction. Cambridge University Press (2011)
31. Schiffel, S., Thielscher, M.: Fluxplayer: A successful general game player. In: Proceedings of the AAAI Conference on Artificial Intelligence, pp. 1191–1196. AAAI Press, Vancouver (2007)
32. Schiffel, S., Thielscher, M.: A multiagent semantics for the game description language. In: Filipe, J., Fred, A., Sharp, B. (eds.) ICAART 2009. CCIS, vol. 67, pp. 44–55. Springer, Heidelberg (2010)
33. Thielscher, M.: From situation calculus to fluent calculus: State update axioms as a solution to the inferential frame problem. Artificial Intelligence 111(1-2), 277–299 (1999)
34. Thielscher, M.: Answer set programming for single-player games in general game playing. In: Hill, P.M., Warren, D.S. (eds.) ICLP 2009. LNCS, vol. 5649, pp. 327–341. Springer, Heidelberg (2009)

From Testing Agent Systems
to a Scalable Simulation Platform

Tobias Ahlbrecht, Jürgen Dix*, and Federico Schlesinger

Department of Informatics
Clausthal University of Technology
Julius-Albert-Straße 4
38678 Clausthal-Zellerfeld, Germany
{tobias.ahlbrecht,dix,federico.schlesinger}@tu-clausthal.de

Abstract. Since 10 years our group in Clausthal is organizing the Multi-Agent Programming Contest, an international contest providing a flexible testbed for evaluating prototypical implementations of agent systems. We describe in this paper how the scenarios developed over time, which lessons we learned, and how this endeavour finally led to the idea of a scalable multiagent simulation platform. The important conclusion we draw is the need to move from academic prototypes to more seriously engineered software systems in order to support the uptake of academic research in industry.

1 Introduction

The year 1980 marks an important date in knowledge representation and reasoning. *Artificial Intelligence* published a special issue containing three of the most important papers starting a completely new field: *nonmonotonic reasoning.* Our dear colleague, Gerhard Brewka, is working in this area since the mid 80's and helped forming the field.

The first two decades have seen an enourmous amount of research which shed light on the relations and formal properties of many variants of nonmonotonic logics. The second author worked for many years on the relation between logic programming semantics and nonmonotonic reasoning. Two of the most prevailing goals have always been the following: *(1) Define a computable and efficient formalism to handle commonsense reasoning. (2) Develop an engineering methodology to apply this formalism to real-world problems.*

The gap between theory and practice has been huge in the beginning (it still is large). While the first goal initiated an impressive amount of work over the years, the second goal was not taken up with the same devotion.

Interestingly, one of the main researchers in nonmonotonic reasoning, Yoav Shoham, was also one of the influential people to start in the 90's another line of

---

* I would like to express my gratitude for working with Gerd Brewka in the late 80's and 90's, when I started my own research. It was a terrific time!

T. Eiter et al. (Eds.): Brewka Festschrift, LNAI 9060, pp. 47–62, 2015.

research, which led to the ever flourishing area of *agent systems* (his seminal paper on agent-oriented programming was also published in *Artificial Intelligence* in 1993).

The notion of an *intelligent agent* is perhaps the most important idea in artificial intelligence in the last four decades and turned out to be extremely influential in many areas (as evidenced by the recent textbook [10], the AAMAS conference series and many associated workshops, eg. ProMAS, EMAS, CLIMA, DALT, AOSE). The question *How does an agent take its decisions?* is closely related to classical knowledge representation and reasoning mechanisms: It is indeed a nonmonotonic procedure. Agents need to reconsider their intentions, revise their belief in the light of new information, and thus act in a nonmonotonic fashion.

An important feature is that agents always act in an environment with many other agents: they are not alone. This led to the introduction of *agent programming languages*. Most of these languages were still in their infancy at the beginning of this millenium. They were often developed within a PhD or in similar smaller projects, based on some sort of *computational logic*. Such implementations were proofs-of-concept, rather than seriously designed software systems.

In 2004, during one of the CLIMA conferences, the following idea (suggested by Paolo Torroni and Francesca Toni) came up: to organize an annual international event as an attempt to stimulate research in the field of programming multiagent systems by 1) identifying key problems, 2) collecting suitable benchmarks, and 3) gathering test cases which require and enforce coordinated action that can serve as milestones for testing multi-agent programming languages, platforms and tools. In 2014 the competition was organized and held for the tenth time.

Similar contests, competitions and challenges have taken place in the past few years. Among them are *Google's AI challenge*[1], the *AI-MAS Winter Olympics*[2], the *Starcraft AI Competition*[3], the *Mario AI Championship*[4], the *ORTS competition*[5], the *Planning Competition*[6], and the *General Game Playing Competition*[7].

The plan for this paper is as follows. In Section 2 we describe our Contest in more detail. In Section 3 we discuss the lessons we learned. Section 4 (which is based on joint work published in [2,3]) develops the idea of a scalable multi-agent simulation platform *MASeRaTi* that evolved out of (1) our work on the Contest, and (2) work on traffic simulation of the group led by our colleague in Clausthal, Jörg Müller. Finally we draw some conclusions and look into the future.

---

[1] http://aichallenge.org/
[2] http://www.aiolympics.ro/
[3] http://eis.ucsc.edu/StarCraftAICompetition
[4] http://www.marioai.org/
[5] http://skatgame.net/mburo/orts/
[6] http://ipc.icaps-conference.org/
[7] http://games.stanford.edu/

2 The Multi-Agent Programming Contest

The Contest is an international annual event that first took place in 2005. Over the years, the contest went through well defined episodes, characterized by the scenarios in which the agents perform and compete. Originally it was designed for problem solving approaches that are based on formal approaches and computational logics. But this was never a requirement. Indeed in the last few years we have seen participating teams which programmed entirely in Java or Python.

The trend in the design of the scenarios has been to increase the complexity; instead of a clever algorithm that solves the scenario (perfect algorithm), we wanted scenarios in which intelligent agents can and should make use of capabilities such as autonomy, coordination, flexibility, proactiveness and reactiveness, etc., features that the multi-agent programming paradigm aims to facilitate. We wanted to evaluate the underlying languages/systems by checking whether they support such capabilities.

Even though the contest has inspired some interest from other research communities and individuals, the core of the participants belongs to the multi-agent programming research community, and most of them are designers of multi-agent languages and platforms, who find in the Contest an excellent test-bed and benchmark for their own developments.

For this purpose the scenarios are adapted to the state of the art in multi-agent programming, and do not increase in complexity arbitrarily. Some desired features for the environments, such as a greater degree of uncertainty (e.g. by means of actions failing with higher probability, so that learning or nonmonotonic formalisms are useful), have been put off. While we could certainly put more emphasis on evaluating such knowledge representation issues in the future, the available languages currently do not provide enough constructs to deal with these problems.

2.1 The Underlying Platform

The first edition of the Contest presented a relatively simple scenario that had to be implemented in its totality by each participant and delivered as an executable for evaluation by the organizers. For the second edition, the *MASSim* infrastructure was introduced. *MASSim* is an extensible simulation server that provides the environment facilities. Agent programs can connect through the network to a *MASSim* server and control simulation level agents; this allowed the Multi-Agent Programming Contest to be run in a different way: the competitors should only focus on the agents' design and implementation; agents are run in the competitors' own computer infrastructure and connect to a *MASSim* instance running in the contest organizer's infrastructure, in which the scenario is implemented.

Besides freeing the competitors from dealing with the implementation of the environment, another key factor provided by *MASSim* is that agent programs from different locations can connect to the same simulation, thus enabling competitive scenarios. Since the introduction of *MASSim* in the 2006 edition, the format of the

Contest has been that of two teams competing against each other for performance in each simulation, and the overall winner of the contest defined by summing up the points after all participants have competed in simulations against each other, in a regular sports' tournament fashion.

All simulations are run in a step-by-step manner. In each step all agents execute their actions simultaneously from the point of view of the server, and there is a time limit within which agents must choose an action (otherwise they are regarded as a `no-op`). In the beginning of each step's cycle, the server sends each agent its current percepts of the environment, and waits for the response that specifies the action to execute. When the responses from all agents are received or when the timeout limit is reached, all received actions are executed in *MASSim*, and the agents' percepts for the next step are calculated. This cycle is repeated for a fixed number of steps, and then a winner is decided according to scenario-specific criteria.

MASSim is fully implemented in Java, and the information exchange with the agent programs is made through XML messages. It follows a plugin architecture for the simulations, which makes it easy to design new scenarios on top of it, as has been the case during the evolution of the Contest. Figure 1 describes this architecture. The addition of new scenarios does not imply the replacement of the previous one. Many different scenarios can convive within a single instance of *MASSim*, and they can be activated by choosing or modifying configuration files accordingly.

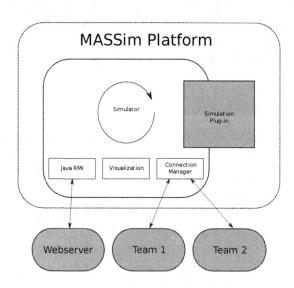

Fig. 1. The massim infraestructure

The *MASSim* package is fully open-source and openly available (`https://multiagentcontest.org/downloads`). It is not only used for the Contest, but has also proved useful both for researchers testing their advancements in the field, and in several classrooms, aiding the teaching of the multi-agent programming paradigm (https://multiagentcontest.org/massim-in-teaching).

To further ease the development of agents, the *MASSim* package includes EIS (http://sf.net/projects/apleis/), which is a proposed standard for agent-environment interaction. It maps the communication between *MASSim* and the agents (sending and receiving XML-messages to Java-method-calls and call-backs). On top of that it automatically establishes and maintains connections to a specified *MASSim*.

2.2 Previous Scenarios

The scenario used for the first edition of the Contest (2005) consisted in a simple grid in which agents could move to empty adjacent spaces. Food units would appear randomly through the simulation, and the objective was to collect these units and carry them to a storage location. This rather simplistic scenario had to be implemented in its totality by the participants.

The idea was refined for the second edition: *Gold Miners*. Now the agents were to collect gold in a competitive environment against other team, and some obstacles were introduced in the grid to add some navigation complexity. This scenario, which was also used in the third edition of the contest, was still very simplistic, and agents acted independently of their teammates, in the solutions proposed.

For the 2008 edition, a new scenario was designed to enforce coordination of agents: *Cows and Cowboys* (Figure 2). Still using a grid as the underlying map, the goal for this scenario was to lead a group to a particular area of the map, representing the team's own "corral", while preventing the opponent team from doing the same. The cows were animated entities that reacted to the agents' positions by trying to avoid them, so solving the map required agents coordinating their positions in order to lead big groups of cows into the corrals, whereas a single agent would in most cases disperse the group of cows and fail to lead them in the desired direction.

The "Cows and Cowboys" scenario was used also in the following two editions (2009 and 2010), with further refinemets such as the addition of gates that required explicit coordination: one agent had to stand in a particular position to keep the gate open while a teammate passed through.

2.3 The Agents on Mars Scenario

The Agents on Mars scenario introduced in 2011 and still in use for the 2014 edition was an important step in the contest's evolution, as it introduced many innovative features and increased the game's complexity. The map now takes the form a weighted graph representing the surface of Mars. The agents represent *All Terrain Vehicles* of different kinds, and their goal in the game is to discover the best water wells by exploring the map and then to keep control of as many wells as possible, by placing themselves in specific formations that ensure a covering

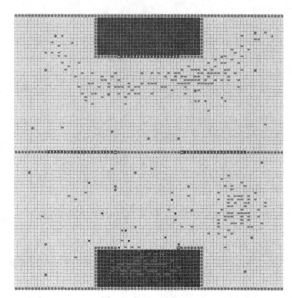

Fig. 2. The Cows and Cowboys scenario

of an area containing the wells while keeping rival agents aside. Figure 3 shows a screenshot of this scenario.

The agents in this scenario assume different complementing roles, promoting both autonomy and coordination. For example, *Explorers* are in charge of discovering the water wells, while *Saboteurs* can attack agents of the opposing team to temporarily disable some of their capabilities. *Repairers* are responsible for restoring its teammates capabilities when they have been attacked, in a coordinated manner. All roles must collaborate to produce the best map coverings.

These agents are much more complex entities than in the previous scenarios. They have now a rich set of actions to choose from, in contrast with only moving around the map. Furthermore, they count with a set of internal parameters that can vary through the simulation—*Energy*, *Visibility Range*, *Health* and *Strength*—that can affect the choice of available actions: almost every action that an agent can perform has an associated energy cost; once an agent's energy level reaches 0, the only action it can successfully execute is the *recharge* action. If an agent is attacked by a rival saboteur, it becomes *disabled* and cannot execute its role-specific actions until it is repaired.

Another important feature that was introduced with the Agents on Mars scenario is the concept of *Achievements*. By reaching certain predefined milestones (e.g. controlling an area is worth a certain amount of points), teams earn *Achievement points*. These can be used in two different ways: either they are kept to directly contribute to the team's score, or they can be used as currency to exchange for improvements to the agent's internals.

The evolution in the complexity of the scenario has remained on a par with the evolution of multi-agent programming technologies used by the participating

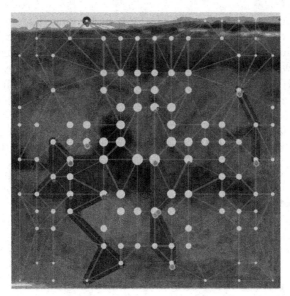

Fig. 3. The "agents on Mars" scenario

teams. A good quality of the teams has been reached, that ensured interesting games. Unlike previous scenarios, a strategy that works against every rival has proven harder to find, and thus the winners are not unbeatable.

2.4   The Next Scenario

While the 2014 edition on the Multi Agent Programming Contest has just taken place once again using the Agents on Mars scenario, we are already considering ideas for a completely new scenario for the next edition in 2015. A very promising possibility, for which some research has been made in other projects, is a traffic-simulation kind of scenario, we intend to use map information from real cities. The actual game to be played in this map is still to be refined.

3   Lessons Learned

In this section we will take a deeper look at some observations that we realised during ten times of hosting the Multi-Agent Programming Contest [5,4]. Most of them led to improvements of the contest platform or the employed scenario. Many lessons we learned are related to *engineering* issues (as opposed to *scientific* ones). For example, collecting statistical data or visualizations turned out to be as important as the choice of the scenarios.

3.1   From Gold Miners to Herding Cows

The first lesson we had to learn reaches back all the way to the first Contest in 2005. The agent implementations had to be submitted as an executable system and were run locally on the Contest platform. It became clear that a standard technical infrastructure had to be provided in order to ensure a fair and objective evaluation of the agent systems and to relieve the participating teams from having to deal with low-level implementation details. Instead they should focus on the internal logic of their agents. This finally led to a separation of the scenario and the agent implementation platform, further trying not to impose unnecessary constraints on the participants systems.

As already mentioned, we wanted to see agents make use of their distinct capabilities. It became clear that those features had to be explixitly elicited. Of those, the two most important were the following:

Cooperation: Clearly, a multiagent platform or framework should be unrivalled in providing cooperating entities. While it was first believed that agents would cooperate automatically in order to achieve better results, the first editions of the Contest proved the contrary. The food gathering and gold mining scenarios were quite simple and easy to handle by individual agents. Thus, the subsequent scenarios were designed to *enforce* rather than just encourage cooperation, by making it impossible for the agents to win without seriously coordinating their actions.

Autonomy: Another feature that was not especially required in the first editions was the autonomy of the agents. It was very much possible to have a central agent deciding and coordinating the actions of all the other agents by itself. This, of course, contradicts an agent's basic characteristics. This shortcoming has been alleviated to some degree by increasing the number of agents and the size of the respective scenario, which made it less feasible (or almost imossible) for one single agent to handle all the information by itself.

From a more technical viewpoint, the Contest has clearly shown that tools for debugging and testing agent platforms are very important during development. Indeed, the participants of the first editions of the Contest were more concerned with debugging rather than with devising good strategies. This became clear to the participating teams and the agent programming community in general, making it possible and inviting to put more effort into simplifying those tasks.

Lastly, we realised that the visualization and playability of the respective scenario is a key to reaching a broader audience, especially students, e.g. when *MASSim* is used in teaching in various courses all over the world.

3.2   Mars Scenario

Employing the Mars setting, we were again able to obtain a multitude of results and observations, mostly regarding (1) the usage of multiagent platforms, (2) the scenario, and (3) several technical issues.

Additionally, we now learned a lot from *interviewing the participants*, and *gathering statistical data*.

Usage of Multiagent Platforms. Employing the Mars domain, we noted an increasing application of multiagent platforms, i.e. starting with 33% in 2011 and up to 80% in 2013. Also, this scenario has always been won by a dedicated agent platform and those dedicated platforms seemingly outperform "ad-hoc" solutions. The presented agent solutions get better from year to year, although the complexity of the scenario is ever increasing. On the one hand, this can be attributed to some teams taking part repeatedly, but it also points to an increasing maturitiy and ease of use concerning multiagent platforms.

Scenario. We saw more coordination within the respective agent teams and of course more interaction with the opponent teams, which tells us again that the scenario has to be clearly designed to enforce cooperation and interaction.

Technical Issues. As identified earlier, debugging is a key problem in multiagent programming. Thus, in the second and third edition of this scenario, we had to work on our side of the Contest as well and improve the visualization and feedback that was sent to the agents. This made it easier to at least grasp what was going on in a simulation, maybe hinting where to start the debugging of the agents.

Asking the Participants. By requiring the participants to answer a predefined questionnaire [1], we tried to learn not only about the final agent platforms and the results they produced, but about the whole development process. For example, we learned why teams participated in the first place. For many, the motivation was to learn about multiagent systems or to refine their programming skills concerning them. A lot of teams furthermore shared our goal of evaluating multiagent frameworks and platforms. Regarding their structure, teams were composed of students as well as researchers with their background mostly in MAS or at least artificial intelligence in general.

We also asked the teams how difficult it was and how much effort had to be put into getting to a point where their system behaved as it finally did. We got very diverse results, reaching from 150 to 840 person hours and 1000 to 11000 lines of code that had to be written, tested and debugged. This clearly hints at varying levels of usability concerning different agent platforms.

Furthermore, teams noted that they not only debugged their agents but found and fixed bugs in the agent framework or platform they used as well, which shows that the Contest plays an important role concerning the development and evaluation of different platforms. Nevertheless, the teams are still not satisfied with the state-of-the-art debugging tools, since it still requires a lot of effort to debug even 20 agents, each with its own individual mindset.

Not always apparent from the simulation results, we further learned

- which strategies the participants intended to use,
- how they employed different frameworks, and
- how they implemented different features of agent-based systems.

Also, the teams were able to tell us which development tools they used to which extent. The most time-consuming task in development still was debugging, or, if that worked out rather well, coming up with a good strategy.

Gathering Statistical Data. Lastly, we implemented a new module for the Mars scenario that allowed us to collect a multitude of statistical data for better and faster analysing a simulation once it was completed. Using these data, we can easily retrace a whole simulation's progress by looking at the automatically generated charts instead of watching the whole replay, which can be quite tedious at times. The charts mainly focused on scenario-specific data, like the development of the score or stability of dominated zones. Furthermore, we were finally able to directly and easily compare different simulation runs without having to keep a lot of details in mind. This showed that better tools for analysing on our side of the Contest were as important as better debugging tools for the participants.

For example, in Figure 4, the zone scores of the teams UFSC-SMADAS and LTI-USP from their third simulation in the 2013 edition of the Contest are given. One can see that both teams overall managed to increase the size of their zones. Starting at around step 200, it seems that the USFC team (depicted in green, having a spike there) gained control of a zone that was formerly dominated by LTI-USP which suffered a setback with the same size of the spike of USFC. However, the exchange of control seemingly did not last long, since both scores quickly return to their original values. One can now easily confirm such an assumption by directly jumping to the right point of the replay.

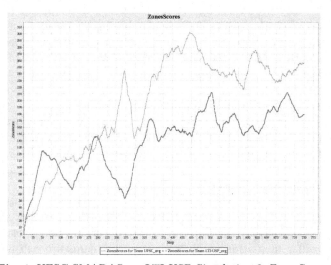

Fig. 4. UFSC-SMADAS vs. LTI-USP Simulation 3: Zone Scores

As we have seen, the Mars scenario follows the tradition and improved further on well-tried concepts while confirming observations made in earlier contests.

3.3   The *MASSim* Platform

Our platform served well over the course of many years in evaluating different agent platforms and solutions. Especially, developing the EIS standard and accompanying EISMASSim implementation [6,9] helped in easily introducing agent platforms to the *MASSim* platform.

However, the platform showed certain shortcomings as well. For one point, it is completely implemented in Java, which is known not to have the performance of e.g. C++. Additionally, it is difficult, if not impossible, to efficiently parallelize it and run it on a high performance cluster.

Another bottleneck can be found in the network traffic with its relatively high communication overhead. This was even a problem for some participants with less favorable internet connections.

From the point of view of the organizers, decoupling scenario and agent implementation made possible to exchange scenarios much more easily. However, the scenario is still hard-coded in Java and hard-wired to the simulation platform, which, again, makes implementing a new scenario a rather time-consuming task.

All in all, our long-term goal is to evolve *MASSim* into a platform that overcomes all these drawbacks. Creating a high performance platform would allow us to finally analyse and compare agent platforms with respect to their scalability. One step to reach the goal could be to establish a standard, e.g. in the spririt of EISMASSim, that enables all agents, and thus the whole Contest, to be run once again locally on our server. This would certainly free the participants from having to restart crashed agents during a simulation. It would also introduce robustness as a new and important requirement for multiagent systems in order to participate.

4   Large-Scale Simulation: Maserati

We have seen in the last few years that *MASSim* is a stable platform able to coordinate up to a hundred agents quite efficiently (and remotely over the net). Unfortunately, for reasons that we discuss below, it is not possible to extend *MASSim* to handle tens of thousands of agents (or even more). However, in massive simulations, eg. in traffic, energy or logistics, such numbers of agents are easily reached. *Scaling a microsimulation approach (like MASSim) to large scenarios is still a challenge.*

Nowadays massive simulations, eg. in traffic simulation, are undertaken with classical analytical models. These models only allow to deal with global properties, like the throughput or flow-rate. An example is the commercial traffic simulation platform *AIMSuN*.

Why can't we simply integrate *AIMSuN* with an agent programming platform? This has been undertaken in [7] where it was tried to integrate *AIMSuN* with the well-known agent platform *JADE*. However, experience showed that this is extremely difficult and does not work without having access to the source code of the commercial software product (which is not available in most cases).

So we are left with two extreme approaches:

Micro-view: a massive multiagent based simulation, where each entity is an agent, or

Macro-view: a commercial product based on analytical models and describing global properties of the system.

The idea of *MASeRaTi* is to develop a simulation platform which is inbetween: it supports both a *micro-view* as well as a *macro-view*. Ideally, the designer should be able to *zoom in* and turn particular parts of the system into agents (if such a detailed view is needed), or to rely on global parameters for other parts (there are some similarities to the notion of a view in databases). Often there are questions where the additional overhead to deal with a micro-view is not needed. Thus it would be appropriate not to be forced to deal with it.

MASeRaTi, currently being developed in the DeSIM project[8] at TU Clausthal, is a *distributed MABS platform* that aims at high scalability for *networked* simulations of *systems-of-systems*, e.g. in traffic and transport. It will be capable of running simulations containing a vast number of software agents.

This section should give the reader a bird's eye view of *MASeRaTi*. For details we refer to [3] and [2] (where parts of this section were taken from).

The *MASeRaTi* platform combines several promising features from different areas in one integrated system.

Architecture: Its architecture, in particular communication and the simulation cycles, are inspired by the architectures of massively multiplayer online role-playing games (MMORPG): All simulation objects are split into two disjoint sets, synchronized and non-synchronized objects. Synchronized objects are for instance the simulation world (also called area) or objects situated within, because these objects must be consistent over all nodes of the HPC. Other objects, e.g. agents, are defined as non-sychronized objects, allowing to be transferred to other nodes.

Scalability: We use high-performance computing algorithms with the message-passing-interface (MPI), so that we can use scalable structure with a high performance datalink between the cluster nodes (in the future, a P2P overlay can be used). Scalability is achieved by splitting the simulation objects into disjoint sets, so that we can design a distributed system with an optimization process for calculation.

Lua: We define an abstract agent model for an agent programming interface in Lua[9], which can be extended or fully redefined by the programmer.

The overall *MASeRaTi* architecture consists of three layers, see Fig. 5:

Micro-kernel (MK): Written in C++, this layer facilitates parallelization over a HPC using structure, scheduler, scaling and optimization features of the message passing interface (MPI) library. A plug-in interface allows to replace MPI by alternative communication technologies like BitTorrent.

Agent model layer (AML): The agent model layer defines an object-oriented model of a multiagent based simulation. Micro-kernel classes and objects are mapped into this layer, extending the existing structures. Lua is used as a modeling language because of its flexibility (imperative, object-oriented and functional programming) and its property of being interpreted at runtime.

---

[8] http://simzentrum.de/en/projects/desim
[9] http://www.lua.org/

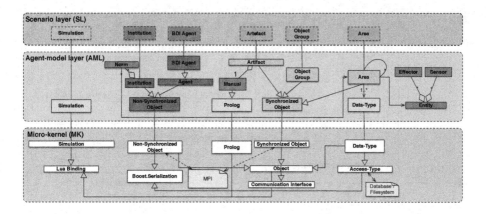

Fig. 5. Overview of the *MASeRaTi* architecture

Scenario layer (SL): This layer defines instances of an AML, adding domain-specific entities and behavioural models, e.g., for traffic simulation.

The reason for using Lua as the modeling language in the AML is twofold: Firstly, it has a very small interpreter (around 100kByte) written in native C. Secondly, C/C++ data structures can be pushed into the Lua interpreter at runtime with a native pointer structure, so we can easily extend Lua. The linkage between MK and AML is defined by Lua binding frameworks, e.g. Lua Bridge[10].

Finally, the simulation layer implements a simulation as an instance of the AML. A native Prolog interpreter is provided for reasoning tasks (e.g., for the belief base). One can also store Lua functions in it. Area structures like graph or grid systems can be added with the `Data-Type` interface. Such a data type models a certain structure (like a grid, a graph etc.) and implements the corresponding search algorithms such as Dijkstra's, $A^\star$ and $D^\star$.

The process of engineering (i.e., modeling and running) a simulation is geared to exploit the structure of the *MASeRaTi* platform. The platform itself runs on a HPC system enabling large sets of experiments. The steps of the process are illustrated in Fig. 6.

After each iteration, the developer should be able to test her prototype by creating a request for computation (Step 4). The HPC system instantiates this task, creates child processes and calculates the outcome. While the simulation is running, one can create another instance or a completely new scenario and add the task to the queue. Finally, in Step 5 and 6 the evaluation data of a simulation is processed by the client and additional analyses are made.

Due to the revision control system of the database, a scenario can run with different parameters and input data and the resulting datasets can be compared. The architecture is split into client and server parts, which communicate via the database. The database stores all scenario data into a repository, so the full

---

[10] `https://github.com/vinniefalco/LuaBridge`

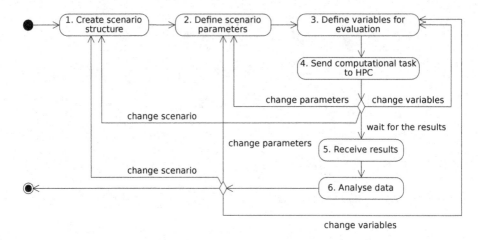

Fig. 6. Simulation engineering process

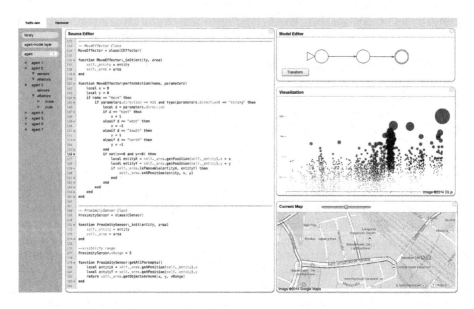

Fig. 7. UI Wireframe

developing process is being logged. A task can be seen as a current state of a repository with fixed parameters and input data. This mechanism enables the possibility to supervise and summarize the results of different tests.

Figure 7 sketches a user interface to support the simulation engineering process. The interface will be realised by techniques used in today's web browsers, so that each user can add modeling or analysing features to the system. The client, which can run small simulations, uses Qt QML [11] to create a browser interface.

---

[11] http://qt-project.org/doc/qt-5.0/qtqml/qtqml-index.html

We plan to add components for visualization like **Data-Driven Documents**[12] or **Chart.js**[13].

5   Conclusions

An important outcome, or rather insight, of the second author's work on logic programming and knowledge representation in the 90'ies is the following. While basic research flourished and produced many important results on the relation between various formal systems and on the complexity and expressivity of many semantical systems, it did not account for developing a methodology to apply these systems to the real world (or at least to nontrivial applications). The reason is simply that such methodologies are by many considered not *scientifically valuable* and thus it is difficult to get publications out of such work. The *engineering component*, which is invaluable for a potential serious implementation of a running system, is time-consuming yet the scientific content is low (given that the original theoretical results have already been published).

But the uptake of basic research in industry heavily depends on well-developed methodologies and seriously crafted software systems (as opposed to prototypes developed within PhD projects). Building such systems requires many person years and is almost never done within an academic environment.

The shift from logic programming semantics to *answer set programming*, seen as a paradigm to encode problems on the second level of the polynomial hierarchy and solve them with appropriate solvers, was of utmost importance. But without applications and ASP systems developed and improved along such applications it would have been nothing but an academic toy.

There are some similarities to the area of agent programming. As mentioned above, in the first few years agent programming languages developed in academia did only have premature (if any) debugging tools (and many more classical software tools were missing). The Multi-Agent Programming Contest helped, on a modest level, to improve some of the languages. But it addressed only relatively small problems/scenarios. As in the case of ASP, we need more *engineering* and we must take scalability seriously. This is what we have tried to do with *MASeRaTi*.

With an initial version of *MASeRaTi* including first scalability tests being available [3], future work in DeSIM will focus on optimizing the platform and increasing its runtime performance, e.g. by a more flexible distribution model, and by more sophisticated agent scheduling algorithms.

A key activity in this respect would be supporting collaborative modeling done by distributed teams of modelers including appropriate methodologies, tools, modeling abstractions, and libraries.

---

[12] http://d3js.org/

[13] http://www.chartjs.org/

References

1. Ahlbrecht, T., et al.: Multi-agent programming contest 2013: The teams and the design of their systems. In: Cossentino, et al. (eds.) [8], pp. 366–390
2. Ahlbrecht, T., Dix, J., Köster, M., Kraus, P., Müller, J.P.: A scalable runtime platform for multiagent-based simulation. In: Dalpaiz, F., Dix, J., van Riemsdijk, B. (eds.) EMAS 2014. LNCS, vol. 8758, pp. 81–102. Springer, Heidelberg (2014)
3. Ahlbrecht, T., Dix, J., Köster, M., Kraus, P., Müller, J.P.: A scalable runtime platform for multiagent-based simulation. Technical Report IfI-14-02, TU Clausthal (February 2014)
4. Ahlbrecht, T., Dix, J., Köster, M., Schlesinger, F.: Multi-agent programming contest 2013. In: Cossentino, et al. (eds.) [8], pp. 292–318
5. Behrens, T.M., Dastani, M., Dix, J., Köster, M., Novàk, P.: The multi-agent programming contest from 2005-2010 - from gold collecting to herding cows. Ann. Math. Artif. Intell. 59(3-4), 277–311 (2010)
6. Behrens, T.M., Hindriks, K.V., Dix, J.: Towards an environment interface standard for agent platforms. Ann. Math. Artif. Intell. 61(4), 261–295 (2011)
7. Chu, V.-H., Görmer, J., Müller, J.P.: ATSim: Combining AIMSUN and Jade for agent-based traffic simulation. In: Proc. 14th Conference of the Spanish Association for Artificial Intelligence (CAEPIA). Electronic Proceedings, vol. 1, AEPIA (2011)
8. Cossentino, M., Fallah-Seghrouchni, A.E., Winikoff, M.: EMAS 2013. LNCS, vol. 8245. Springer, Heidelberg (2013)
9. Hindriks, K., Dix, J.: Goal: A multi-agent programming language applied to an exploration game. In: Shehory, O., Sturm, A. (eds.) Research Directions Agent-Oriented Software Engineering, pp. 112–136. Springer (2013)
10. Weiss, G.: Multiagent Systems. The MIT Press (2013)

Deontic Logic for Human Reasoning

Ulrich Furbach and Claudia Schon*

Universität Koblenz-Landau, Germany
{uli,schon}@uni-koblenz.de

Abstract. Deontic logic is shown to be applicable for modelling human reasoning. For this the Wason selection task and the suppression task are discussed in detail. Different versions of modelling norms with deontic logic are introduced and in the case of the Wason selection task it is demonstrated how differences in the performance of humans in the abstract and in the social contract case can be explained. Furthermore, it is shown that an automated theorem prover can be used as a reasoning tool for deontic logic.

1 Introduction

Human reasoning and in particular conditional reasoning has been researched in various disciplines. In cognitive psychology a lot of experimental data is collected and there are numerous different modelling approaches. In philosophy rationality and normative reasoning is a topic with increasing interest. In artificial intelligence research the aim is to model human rational reasoning within artificial systems.

Recently, there are some papers from automated reasoning which try to model experiments from cognitive psychology; in particular the experiments involving the Wason selection and the suppression tasks are discussed in the literature ([13,12]).

In this paper we want to contribute to this discussion by advocating deontic logic to this end. We are well aware that this is not the first paper proposing deontic logic for conditional reasoning. However, our aim is not only to use this logic to model the settings and the result of these experiments, moreover, we want to use an *automated reasoning system* to solve the tasks. There are only few automated theorem provers specially dedicated for deontic logic and used by deontic logicians (see [1,2]). Nonetheless, several approaches to translate modal logic into (decidable fragments of) first-order predicate logics are stated in the literature. A nice overview including many relevant references is given in [20]. We will use the first order predicate logic prover Hyper for deontic logic, which is possible because we translate the latter into the description logic $\mathcal{ALC}$. This again can be translated into DL-clauses, for which Hyper is a decision procedure.

---

* Work supported by DFG FU 263/15-1 'Ratiolog'.

T. Eiter et al. (Eds.): Brewka Festschrift, LNAI 9060, pp. 63–80, 2015.

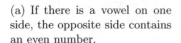

(a) If there is a vowel on one side, the opposite side contains an even number.

(b) If a person is less than 21 years old, she is not allowed to drink beer.

Fig. 1. The Wason Selection Task

The Wason selection task (WST) was first presented by the psychologist Peter C Wason in [24] and is one of the most carefully researched experiments in the area of human rational reasoning. The abstract case of the task is shown in part (a) of Fig. 1. In the task, four different cards are presented to a test person. The test person is told that each card contains a letter on one side and a number on the opposite side. Furthermore, a statement like "If there is a vowel on one side of the card, the opposite side contains an even number" is given. Now the test person is asked to verify/falsify this statement by turning a minimum number of cards. In this abstract task, less then 25 % of the test persons were able to find the solution. In [21] the WST and related experiments are discussed in deep detail. There also is a collection of different approaches using various logics for modelling the selection task in a way that the results from the experiments are captured. Very many experiments have shown that humans have problems to perform this inference properly. If context is added to the problem, people solve the problem with a much higher correctness rate. By adding additional context, the problem can be a social contract problem or a precaution problem. One example for a social contract context, as addressed in part (b) of Figure 1, is a setting in which one side of the cards shows a beverage, namely beer or lemonade and the other side the age of the person who drinks this beverage. The rule is "If a person is less than 21 years old, she is not allowed to drink beer". In this case 75 % of the subjects gave the correct solution.

A different class of contexts can be formulated by a so-called "precaution rule", e.g., rules of the form "If you agree in a hazardous activity, then you must take the precaution". In this case, like in the social contract context, people perform dramatically better compared to the abstract case.

Besides the WST there is a class of experiments called *suppression task*, where different sequences of conditional statements together with related questions are presented to test persons. We also discuss modelling of these tasks by deontic logic.

In the following section we discuss several logical approaches to model the WST. In Section 3 we introduce our approach using deontic logic. Section 4 models the suppression task and in Section 5 we show how our approach can be used to check the consistency of normative systems automatically. For a conclusion we briefly comment on attempts to formulate a kind of 'robot ethics'.

2   Logical Models for the WST

Since the WST is dealing with conditional reasoning, it seems to be natural to use predicate logic for modeling the task and to use existing logical inference mechanisms to model human reasoning. A very careful discussion of various logics to this end can be found in [21]; in particular all these investigation into logics are nicely combined with findings about the psychology of human reasoning. One of these logics, multi-valued logic, seems to be very likely in the case of the WST, where the invisible side of a card can easily be modeled by the truth value "unknown". Several authors apply multi-valued logic to model human reasoning, e.g., [13] uses a Lukaswiewicz logic together with logic programs. In [12] this approach is combined with the concept of abduction, which is proposed in [15] and it is also used for modeling human reasoning in [16].

All these approaches use logic programming for modeling human reasoning. However, one should have in mind that logic programming languages and its semantics have been designed for *programming*. There are at least three main issues of logic programs as used in the cited approaches:

- The language is restricted to definite clauses, i.e. clauses of the form $A \leftarrow B_1 \wedge \cdots \wedge B_n$, where the left-hand side, the head, contains only one atom and the right-hand side, the body, contains a conjunction of literals. This special form does not allow the representation of a disjunction like $A \vee B$. This is not a problem for programming purposes because one can easily show that every Turing computable function can be represented by definite clause programs. However, for the modeling of human reasoning it should be possible to express disjunctions.[1]
- The right hand side of a clause can contain literals, i.e. the negation of atoms. This negation, however, is not a logical negation. It is a non-monotonic negation, which usually is based on a closed-world assumption.
- The semantics of logic programs with non-monotonic negation involves either so-called completion mechanisms or interesting fixed-point operations to construct models. For all of these model construction mechanisms it turns out that they involve much more complex reasoning compared to the monoton case. Furthermore, we doubt that those constructions are easily accessible to humans and their inference mechanisms.

The extension of logic programs with abduction turns the clauses, the logical rules, into licences for conditionals using abnormality predicates: $A \leftarrow B_1 \wedge \cdots \wedge B_n \wedge \neg ab$, with the reading "If nothing abnormal is known and all the B_i hold, then A holds". Note that the negation symbol in front of the ab atom is the non-monotonic negation as mentioned before. We propose to model this distinction of normal from abnormal behaviour by introducing an explicit operator instead of coding it into the clauses; just use deontic logic.

---

[1] In Artificial Intelligence we very well remember the relapse in the development of artificial neural networks, when the observation that perceptrons cannot compute a disjunctive or was spread.

3   Deontic Logic and the WST

The difference in behavior between the abstract case of the WST, the social contract and the precaution problem leads immediately to a distinction between descriptive and deontic conditionals. A deontic interpretation of the rules from the WST leads to a description of a *norm*; hence the rule makes a statement about how the world *ought to be*.

There is an ongoing discussion about the use of deontic logic. In [21] the authors explicitly discuss deontic logic as a modal propositional logic for the WST. They construct models for a specification of the selection task, but they do not discuss the representation of the task itself in deontic logic. Another detailed investigation of deontic logic can be found in [9], where the authors give an overview from a psychological and neurobiological point of view. They further discuss the deontic nature of the selection task in various contexts. There is the purely declarative version, which corresponds in our example to the vowel–consonant version, and a social contract version, e.g., the beer–age version. Cosmides et al further argue that there is also the class of the precaution rules as introduced above. The different nature of these contexts causes the authors in [9] to conclude that there cannot be a general deontic logic for capturing human reasoning about conditionals. Indeed, there is strong evidence that humans have different reasoning mechanisms available depending on the nature of the reasoning task. There is the case of a patient, R.M., reported in [22], who had a severe accident and suffered from severe retrograde amnesia. The damage of his brain was in different areas of the cortex such that both sides of the amylgada were disconnected. The authors made extensive reasoning experiments with R.M. using 65 reasoning tasks based on the WST. It turned out that R.M.'s performance on the abstract reasoning problems (16,7 %) and on the precaution rules was comparable to controls (70 %), whereas the score on social contract problems was 31 percent points lower. This clearly indicates that there are different reasoning mechanisms for those contexts. In [9] the conclusion from these findings is that there is no general deontic logic applicable for the modeling of this behavior. We support this hypothesis and at the end of Section 3.4 we discuss a multi modal logic which very well is able to model these diverse kinds of reasoning.

Another observation discussed in [9] is that the WST in general can be seen as a cheat detection task. In different social contexts humans may apply different inference systems for cheat detection.

In the following deontic logic as a modal logic is introduced and used to formalize the WST.

3.1   Deontic Logic as Modal KD

Deontic logic is a well studied modal logic very suitable to model human reasoning. It corresponds to the modal logic K together with a seriality axiom D:

$$\text{D:} \quad \Box \Phi \rightarrow \Diamond \Phi$$

In contrast to K, the □-operator is interpreted as 'it is obligatory that' and the ◊ as 'it is permitted that'.

In modal logic, semantics are given by so called Kripke structures consisting of a set of *possible worlds* connected by a reachability function. Each world is labeled by the set of formulae which are true in the respective world. A formula of the form $\Box F$ is read as "F is true in every reachable world". Hence if w is a world we have

$$w \models \Box \Phi \quad \text{iff} \quad \forall v : R(w,v) \to v \models \Phi$$

A formula F is called satisfiable if there is a Kripke structure and a world in which F is true. This Kripke structure is called a *model* for F. The above mentioned seriality axiom states the following: if a formula holds in all reachable worlds, then there exists such a world. With the deontic reading of □ and ◊ this means whenever the formula Φ ought to be, then there exists a world where it holds. I.e. there is always a world in which the norms formulated by 'the ought to be'-operator hold.

To formalize the WST in deontic logic, we transform the statement about the cards into the following conditional:

> If there is a vowel on one side, it ought to be that the opposite side shows an even number.

As discussed in [10] and [18], there are different types of conditionals. It is distinguished for example between definitional, logical or causal conditionals. Since the above conditional is not truth functional, it can not be formalized by a material implication $P \to Q$ in classical logic using abbreviations P and Q. Formalizing the conditional as $P \to \Box Q$ using deontic logic is preferable. Oberserving a card with a vowel on one side and an odd number on the other side of the card does not make the formula of this formalization false. In this case, the observed world just does not correspond to the perfect normative world. Formalizing the conditional as $P \to \Box Q$ ensures the property that if we observe P, i.e. a card with a vowel on the upper side, due to the seriality axiom we know that there is a world in which the deontic conditional holds, hence Q holds. In other words there is a world where the opposite side of the card contains an even number.

Note that it would also be possible to formalize the statement as: $\Box(P \to Q)$. In [23] there is a careful discussion which of these two formalizations should be used for conditional norms. The latter one has severe disadvantages, which is why we prefer the first method. In Section 5 we demonstrate that the alternative very easily results in an inconsistent normative system.

Assume for simplicity that the letters on the cards can only be A or K, the numbers only 4 or 7, and that we consider only one card. We represent the card by atoms of the form $c(l, A)$, $c(l, K)$, $c(n, 4)$ and $c(n, 7)$. An l in the first position denotes the letter side and an n denotes the number side of a card. We further have formulae describing the way the card is constructed:

$$\top \to c(l, A) \vee c(l, K). \tag{1}$$
$$c(l, A) \wedge c(l, K) \to \bot. \tag{2}$$
$$\top \to c(n, 4) \vee c(n, 7). \tag{3}$$
$$c(n, 4) \wedge c(n, 7) \to \bot. \tag{4}$$

Formula (1) states that the letter side of the card contains an A or a K, formula (2) states, that there is only one letter on the letter side of the card. Formulae (3) and (4) describe the number side of the card respectively.

The rule expressing the normative conditional reads in this simplified example as

$$c(l, A) \to \Box c(n, 4) \tag{5}$$

Note that all the above formulae are propositional, although atoms like $c(l, A)$ seem to have a structure; logically, they are propositional variables being either *true* or *false*.

3.2 The WST Task

Until now, we formalized the knowledge and the observation; we did not address a logical representation of the task itself. Then we want to use an automated reasoning system in order to solve the task and hence it is mandatory to query the system in a logical way. To the best of our knowledge, we are not aware of such a formalization in the literature. Let's focus first on the abstract case without social or precaution context.

Usually, in logic based automated reasoning, a knowledge base KB together with a query Q is given and we want to know if Q is a logical consequence of KB, i.e. $KB \models Q$. In the WST the question is different since it corresponds to a cheat detection task:

> Given the knowledge KB, including the knowledge about norms, how can we detect cheating, or, which cards do we have to turn to detect a violation against the norm?

In the sequel, we use a standard tableau method for generating models. We assume the reader to be familiar with tableaux as introduced in [5]. We don't use indexing of worlds because we treat the $\Box$-operator as a literal and do not expand it. In the examples of this paper this works because we never have nested $\Box$-operators.

Thesis 1. *Boxed literals occurring in open branches can be used for cheat detection: If for example an open branch contains literals $\Box F$ and $\Box G$ this branch tells us to check if the current world fulfills both F and G.*

Note that the information provided by an open branch are not necessarily minimal. Therefore, in order to find a minimal set of actions required for cheat detection, it is necessary to construct all open branches and to compare the set of boxed literals contained in the respective branches. Only those branches containing a minimal (w.r.t. set inclusion) set of boxed literals provide a minimal set of actions required for cheat detection. For the WST this thesis leads to the following interpretation of open branches:

- If there is an open branch not containing any boxed literals, the observed situation does not require to check the hidden side of the card.
- If all open branches contain the same boxed literal e.g $\Box F$, we have to check the hidden side of the card (in the example we have to check if F is fulfilled).
- If all open branches contain boxed literals but not all open branches contain the same boxed literals, we have to compare the open branches with respect to the set of boxed literals. Those branches containing a minimal (w.r.t. set inclusion) set of boxed literals tell us what we have to check in order to make sure that the given norms are fulfilled.

Thesis 2. *From a model-theoretic point of view turning a card to do cheat detection corresponds to the question, if there is a model for the set of formulae with a world fulfilling the observed situation which is a successor of itself.*

This "self loop" ensures that F has to be fulfilled in the observed world, whenever a boxed formula $\Box F$ is true in the observed world. Intuitively this means that this world corresponds to the observed situation and fulfills everything that "ought to be". If there is no such model, it is obvious that the observed situation can only be caused by cheating.

Next we discuss two formalizations of the WST.

Naive Formalization. The first formalization of the WST we present consists of the set of formulae given in (1) to (4) together with the formula representing the norm given in formula (5). As an example, we add the observation of letter A on the card. In the sequel, $\mathcal{B}$ denotes the set of formulae consisting of formula (1) to (4) together with the observation and letter $\mathcal{N}$ denotes formula (5).

In Figure 2(a) we give a tableau for the resulting set of formulae $\mathcal{B} \cup \mathcal{N}$ (as mentioned above, we do not expand the boxed formulae in the tableau). This tableau has two open branches:

$$B_1 = \{c(l, A), \Box c(n, 4), c(n, 4)\} \qquad B_2 = \{c(l, A), \Box c(n, 4), c(n, 7)\}$$

Both open branches contain the same boxed literal $\Box c(n, 4)$. According to Thesis 1, this tells us to check, if the number side of the card depicts 4.

Taking a closer look at the open branches reveals that branch B_1 contains $c(n, 4)$ and $\Box c(n, 4)$. In B_1 the number side of the card depicts 4 and it ought to be the case that the number side of the card depicts 4, meaning that B_1 fulfills the norm. Contrary to that, B_2 contains $c(n, 7)$ and $\Box c(n, 4)$. In B_2 the number side of the card depicts 7 even though it ought to be the case that the number side of the card depicts 4. So B_2 violates the norm. Hence only from B_1 a model in form of a Kripke structure containing a world fulfilling $\mathcal{B} \cup \mathcal{N}$ which has a "self loop" can be constructed.

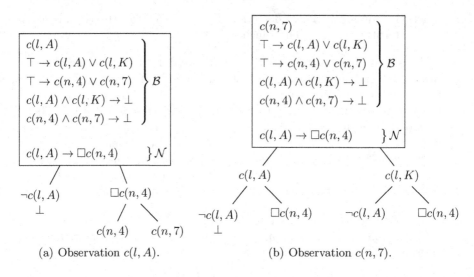

(a) Observation $c(l, A)$.   (b) Observation $c(n, 7)$.

Fig. 2. Tableaux for the simplified 1-card WST with naive formalization. $\mathcal{B}$ denotes the knowledge of the observer and $\mathcal{N}$ the normative system.

However this formalization of the WST does not always work as desired. Let us consider another example, where 7 is observed on the number side of the card. The tableau for this example is given in Figure 2(b). This tableau has three open branches:

$$B_1' = \{c(n,7), c(l,A), \Box c(n,4)\} \qquad B_2' = \{c(n,7), c(l,K), \neg c(l,A)\}$$
$$B_3' = \{c(n,7), c(l,K), \Box c(n,4)\}$$

In the case of observing 7 on the number side of the card, the desired conclusion is that there has to be a K on the letter side of the card. Hence we would expect to see $\Box c(l, K)$ in every open branch. However none of the open branches contains $\Box c(l, K)$. Taking a closer look at $\mathcal{B} \cup \mathcal{N}$ reveals that it is not possible to deduce $\Box c(l, K)$ from this set. What makes that even worse is that it is not possible to deduce information on what ought to be depicted on the letter side of a card!

The reason for this is well known in the literature about deontic conditionals. With a classical implication $c(l, A) \to c(n, 4)$ we can equivalently formulate the contrapositive $\neg c(n, 4) \to \neg c(l, A)$ expressing, if there is not a 4 on the number side, there is no A on the letter side. In deontic logic, however, the norm is represented by $c(l, A) \to \Box c(n, 4)$. The respective contrapositive is $\neg \Box c(n, 4) \to \neg c(l, A)$ or equivalently, $\Diamond \neg c(n, 4) \to \neg c(l, A)$. However, what we want to state is: if we don't see a 4 on the number side, then there ought to be no A on the letter side. This would be formalized as $\neg c(n, 4) \to \Box \neg c(l, A)$. Unfortunately this is not included in the naive formalization. Therefore we need to find a different formalization of the problem.

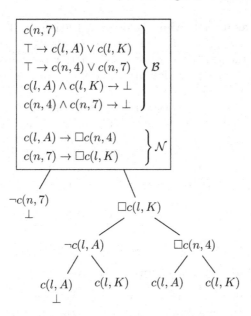

Fig. 3. Tableau for the simplified 1-card WST with for the formalization using the pseudo-contrapositive. $\mathcal{B}$ denotes the knowledge of the observer and $\mathcal{N}$ the normative system.

Formalization Using Pseudo-Contraposition. The drawback of the naive formalization of the WST is the fact that it is not possible to deduce what ought to be the case for the letter side of the card. To remedy this situation, we use a second norm called *pseudo-contrapositive*:

$$\neg c(n, 4) \rightarrow \Box \neg c(l, A)$$

which can be transformed into: $c(n, 7) \rightarrow \Box c(l, K)$

We add this norm to the naive formalization resulting in the new normative system:

$$c(l, A) \rightarrow \Box c(n, 4)$$
$$c(n, 7) \rightarrow \Box c(l, K)$$

With the help of the pseudo-contrapositive, we are now able to calculate a solution for the previous example. Again, we observe card $c(n, 7)$. Fig. 3 shows the tableau for the resulting set of formulae. This tableau has three open branches:

$B_1'' = \{c(n, 7), \Box c(l, K), \neg c(l, A), c(l, K)\}$ $B_2'' = \{c(n, 7), \Box c(l, K), \Box c(n, 4), c(l, A)\}$
$B_3'' = \{c(n, 7), \Box c(l, K), \Box c(n, 4), c(l, K)\}$

All three branches contain $\Box c(l, K)$. Therefore, we can deduce that the letter side of the card ought to show a K.

Reducing the Wason Selection Task to a Satisfiability Test. As mentioned before, the question in the WST is to detect cheating or to find out which cards have to be turned in order to detect a violation of the norm. The formalization using Pseudo-Contraposition presented in 3.2 can be used to detect if a card has to be turned.

Next we will transform this question into a satisfiability test: If a card has to be turned, this information is contained in all models. Given e.g. the observation $c(n, 7)$, all models constructed contained $\Box c(l, K)$, meaning that the letter side of the card ought to show K. Assuming that the set of formulae under consideration is satisfiable, another possibility would be to add $\neg\Box c(l, K) = \Diamond c(l, A)$ to the set of formulae and show that the resulting set of formulae is unsatisfiable.

In the next section, we will use an automated theorem prover to solve this satisfiability test. This leads us to an automated solution of the question of the WST.

3.3   WST and Automated Theorem Proving

Standard deontic logic (SDL) can be translated into decidable fragments of first order logic. See [20] for details. Hence practically any first order theorem prover could be used to reason in SDL.

Hyper [25] is a theorem prover for first order logic with equality. It is the implementation of the E-hypertableau calculus [3] which extends the hypertableau calculus with superposition based equality handling. Hyper has been successfully used in various AI-related applications like intelligent interactive books or natural language query answering. One of the advantages of the hyper tableau calculus is the avoidance of unnecessary or-branching. This is one reason why we decided to use Hyper to reason in SDL. Another reason is the fact that recently the E-hypertableau calculus and its implementation have been extended to deal with knowledge bases given in the description logic $\mathcal{SHIQ}$ [4]. There is a strong connection between modal logic and description logic. As shown in [19], the description logic $\mathcal{ALC}$ is a notational variant of the modal logic $\mathcal{K}_n$. Therefore any formula given in the modal logic $\mathcal{K}_n$ can be translated into an $\mathcal{ALC}$ concept and vice versa. When using Hyper as a theorem prover for SDL, it is not necessary to translate the SDL formulae into first order logic. It is sufficient to translate them to description logic which is more closely related to SDL than first order logic. Since we are only considering a modal logic as opposed to a multimodal logic, we will omit the part of the translation handling the multimodal part of the logic. Table 1 gives the inductive definition of a mapping ϕ from modal logic $\mathcal{K}$ formulae to $\mathcal{ALC}$ concepts.

Mapping ϕ can be used to translate the deontic logic formulae into the description logic $\mathcal{ALC}$ as well. The result of the translation of all formulae is shown in Table 2. For readability reasons we decided to keep the arguments of a ground atom e.g. we translate atoms like $c(l, A)$ into atomic concepts $c(l, A)$. In this very restricted scenario, with just one card, two letters and two numbers, it may be counterintuitive that $c(l, A)$ is a concept. This concept $c(l, A)$ represents the class of all cards with an A on the letter side. Considering an actual instance of

Table 1. Translation of modal logic $\mathcal{K}$ formulae into $\mathcal{ALC}$ concepts

$$\phi(\top) = \top \qquad\qquad \phi(\bot) = \bot$$
$$\phi(a) = a \qquad\qquad \phi(\neg c) = \neg\phi(c)$$
$$\phi(c \wedge d) = \phi(c) \sqcap \phi(d) \qquad \phi(c \vee d) = \phi(c) \sqcup \phi(d)$$
$$\phi(\Box c) = \forall r.\phi(c) \qquad\qquad \phi(\Diamond c) = \exists r.\phi(c)$$

Table 2. Translation of formulae given in the framed part of Figure 3 into $\mathcal{ALC}$

Deontic Logic	$\mathcal{ALC}$	
$\top \rightarrow c(n,7)$	$c(n,7)$	(1)
$\top \rightarrow c(l,A) \vee c(l,K)$	$c(l,A) \sqcup c(l,K)$	(2)
$c(l,A) \wedge c(l,K) \rightarrow \bot$	$\neg c(l,A) \sqcup \neg c(l,K)$	(3)
$\top \rightarrow c(n,4) \vee c(n,7)$	$c(n,4) \sqcup c(n,7)$	(4)
$c(n,4) \wedge c(n,7) \rightarrow \bot$	$\neg c(n,4) \sqcup \neg c(n,7)$	(5)
$\top \rightarrow \Box(c(l,A) \vee c(l,K))$	$\forall r.(c(l,A) \sqcup c(l,K))$	(6)
$\Box(c(l,A) \wedge c(l,K)) \rightarrow \bot$	$\forall r.(\neg c(l,A) \sqcup \neg c(l,K))$	(7)
$\top \rightarrow \Box(c(n,4) \vee c(n,7))$	$\forall r.(c(n,4) \sqcup c(n,7))$	(8)
$\Box(c(n,4) \wedge c(n,7)) \rightarrow \bot$	$\forall r.(\neg c(n,4) \sqcup \neg c(n,7))$	(9)
$c(l,A) \rightarrow \Box(c(n,4))$	$\neg c(l,A) \sqcup \forall r.(c(n,4))$	(10)
$c(n,7) \rightarrow \Box(c(l,K))$	$\neg c(n,7) \sqcup \forall r.(c(l,K))$	(11)
$\Box\Phi \rightarrow \Diamond\Phi$	$\top \sqsubseteq \exists r.\top$	(12)

a card is done by introducing an individual: $c(l,A)(a)$ states that individual a belongs to the concept $c(l,A)$, meaning that the card a shows an A at the letter side. If more then one card is considered, several individuals are introduced and the letters or numbers shown on these cards are represented by memberships to the respective concepts.

Note that line (1) of Table 2 describes the world we observe. Further line (2) to (5) describe the way the cards are constructed. The construction of the cards should be effective for all reachable worlds. This is why we add the formulae given in line (6) to (9). The conjunction of those formulae are denoted by $\mathcal{B}$. $\phi(\mathcal{B})$ denotes the result of the translation into an $\mathcal{ALC}$ concept. Line (10) and (11) describe the norm $\mathcal{N}$. Line (11) presents the translation of the seriality axiom, where r is a role introduced to represent the reachability relation. Note that the translation of the seriality axiom is put into the TBox later which will be denoted by $\mathcal{T}$.

Now the theorem prover Hyper is used to calculate if the card has to be turned in order to find out, if the observed situation obeys the given normative system. For this, the $\mathcal{ALC}$ concepts given in the right column of Table 2 are translated into DL-clauses, which is the input language of Hyper. We denote this transformation by Ξ. During the transformation into DL-clauses many auxiliary concepts are introduced, which makes the resulting set of DL-clauses complicated to read. Since the DL-clauses are not important to understand our example, we refrain from presenting them. See [17] for details on DL-clauses. In order to check if we have to turn the card in our example where the number side of the card shows 7, an individual a representing the card is introduced and we add the information that individual a belongs to the concepts obtained from translating $\mathcal{B}$ and $\mathcal{N}$ into $\mathcal{ALC}$. This is represented by the assertions $\phi(\mathcal{B}(a))$ and $\phi(\mathcal{N}(a))$. Furthermore, the assertion $\neg\forall r.c(l, K)(a)$ added. All these assertions together with the translation of the seriality axiom are transformed into DL-clauses and afterwards Hyper is used to check the satisfiability of the resulting set. According to Hyper, the resulting set of DL-clauses

$$\Xi(\phi(\mathcal{B})(a) \cup \phi(\mathcal{N})(a) \cup \mathcal{T} \cup \{\neg\forall r.c(l, K)(a)\})$$

is unsatisfiable. Hence, we know that we have to turn the card.

Since there is no TBox in deontic logic, the translation of the formulae given in Table 2 lead to a description logic concept together with one TBox axiom for the seriality axiom. The seriality axiom has to be added to the TBox because it is supposed to be true for every word. Another possibility to formalize the WST would be to directly use description logic and to use the TBox not only for the seriality axiom. The formulae describing the way the cards are constructed are also supposed to be true in every reachable world. Hence it makes sense to add the translation of those formulae into the TBox. This leads to the following TBox:

$$\mathcal{T} = \{\top \sqsubseteq \exists r.\top,$$
$$\top \sqsubseteq c(l, A) \sqcup c(l, K),$$
$$\top \sqsubseteq \neg c(l, A) \sqcup \neg c(l, K),$$
$$\top \sqsubseteq c(n, 4) \sqcup c(n, 7),$$
$$\top \sqsubseteq \neg c(n, 4) \sqcup \neg c(n, 7)\}$$

Note that, since the TBox is true in all worlds, we do not have to add formulae corresponding to line (6) to (9) of Table 2 to the TBox.

3.4   Abstract vs Context WST

We modeled the WST in deontic logic and discussed the use of an automated theorem prover to compute cheat detection. Next we address how the differences of the performance of humans in the abstract and in the context case of the WST can be modeled with the help of our approach.

We argued in Section 3.2 that the formalization of the task resulted in a check whether the open branches all contain the same boxed literal, as it was the case in the branches B_1 and B_2 on page 69. Such an occurrence of an 'ought-to'-literal tells us that it has to be checked.

Solving the WST in this abstract case more or less makes it necessary to involve a logical calculus as done by Hyper in order to construct the models and

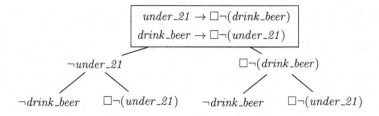

Fig. 4. Tableau for the two norms for the social contract version of the WST

to check it with respect to the boxed literals – obviously humans are not good at constructing models out of the given specification.

In the case of a context, we follow the hypothesis that humans have the appropriate models explicitly in their mind. They have been constructed by prior experience or even by evolution. This is very much in accordance with the mental model theory from Johnson-Laird, which is elaborated for the case of conditional reasoning in [14]. There the authors assume that there is a mental representation of models for conditionals as they are used in the WST. It is argued that the form and nature of the representation heavily influences the performance of people solving WST.

Thesis 3. *In the case of a social contract or a precaution rule, humans have the models of a world in which the norms hold in form of an explicit mental representation ready at hand. There is no need to construct them like it was necessary in the abstract case. – They just have to compare the observations in the WST with their mental model.*

To sum up, in both the abstract and the context version of the WST we have a *model checking task*. In the abstract case the model is given only implicitly by the rules for the norm — before comparing it, it has to be constructed. This can be done by a logical calculus as we demonstrated with the Hyper-prover. If all models from the result of the prover still contain the same boxed literal, we have to check it. This construction obviously is error prone if carried out by humans.

In the remainder of this section we will work this out in detail with the help of the experiment given in part (b) of Figure 1. The social contract rule for this example could be

$$under\_21 \rightarrow \Box \neg drink\_beer$$

We add the pseudo-contrapositive to this formalization

$$drink\_beer \rightarrow \Box \neg under\_21$$

resulting in the two formulae of the framed part in Figure 4. This tableau has four open branches:

$$B_1 = \{\neg under\_21, \neg drink\_beer\} \qquad B_2 = \{\neg under\_21, \Box \neg under\_21\}$$
$$B_3 = \{\Box \neg drink\_beer, \neg drink\_beer\} \qquad B_4 = \{\Box \neg drink\_beer, \Box \neg under\_21\}$$

Branches B_1 and B_2 represent those cases in which the observed persons age is over 21. Both models do not contain a boxed literal concerning the beverage. Therefore, whenever we observe a person of age clearly over 21, we instantly know that we do not have to take a closer look at the beverage. This is totally different as soon as the observed person is younger than 21. This case contradicts B_1 and B_2. This is why we have to consider B_3 and B_4 in this case. Both B_3 and B_4 contain $\Box \neg drink\_beer$ stating that the observed person is not allowed to drink beer. Therefore, we know that we have to check the beverage.

We argued above that in the social contract case the models are already at hand and just have to be compared with the open branches. Those four branches are already constructed as mental models in our brain. When we are confronted with the social contract version of the selection task, we don't have to perform the error prone construction of those models. We can use the mental models we have at hand and therefore we are able to perform the social contract version of the WST much better then the abstract version.

In the other case, where we observe a person drinking beer, the two branches which remain are B_2 and B_4 indicating that we have to make sure that $\Box \neg under\_21$ holds. Or to put it differently, we have learned that the only cases where we have to test are those where the premises of our norm and its pseudo-contrapositive holds.

Our approach using deontic logic can be easily extended to handle the effect of the patient from [9]. This person had a severe brain damage such that he was able to solve the precaution task very well, but in the task with the social contract he performed as badly as in the abstract case. It seems as if the mental representation of a model for the norms concerning precaution rules still exist, while the model of the social contract norm disappeared. It has to be constructed very much like in the abstract case.

To model such a behavior, we only have to switch to multi-modal logic; instead of one ought-to operator $\Box$ we simple introduce an operator $\Box_{sc}$ for social contract norms and another $\Box_{pr}$ for precaution rules. Such a mult-modal logic is very well investigated and in particular it is the core of description logics. Here we formulate conditionals with different contexts with different modal operators: The social contract rule from our example in Figure 1 could be

$$under\_21 \rightarrow \Box_{sc} \neg (drink\_beer)$$

whereas a precaution rule could be

$$driving\_a\_car \rightarrow \Box_{pr} (fasten\_seatbelt)$$

With such a multi-modal logic it could be the case that a reasoner has an explicit representation of a norm expressed with one operator, while for the other operator it has to compute the model before solving the task, just the same way as in the abstract case.

We suggested above to use the Hyper theorem prover for reasoning in deontic logic. Hyper is able to handle knowledge bases given in the description logic $\mathcal{SHIQ}$, which is the description logic $\mathcal{ALC}$ extended with transitive roles, role hierarchies, qualified number restrictions and inverse roles. Since $\mathcal{SHIQ}$ allows the usage of more than one role, Hyper can be used to reason in multi-deontic logic as well.

4   Deontic Logic and the Suppression Task

Another well researched phenomenon is the *suppression task*. In [7] a series of experiments are reported, which demonstrate that human reasoning is non-monotonic in a certain sense. Given the following two statements:

> If she has an essay to write, she will study late in the library.
> She has an essay to write.

In an experiment persons are asked to draw a valid conclusion out of these premises. It turned out that 98% of the test persons conclude correctly that

> She will study late in the library.

This shows that in such a setting modus ponens a is very natural rule of deduction. If an additional statement is given, namely

> If she has some textbooks to read, she will study late in the library.

this does not change the percentage of correct answers. Obviously this additional conditional is understood as an alternative. And indeed, we can transform the two conditionals

$$essay\_to\_write \rightarrow study\_late$$
$$textbooks\_to\_read \rightarrow study\_late$$

equivalently into a single one, where the premise is an disjunction:

$$essay\_to\_write \vee textbooks\_to\_read \rightarrow study\_late$$

If however as an additional premiss

> If the library stays open, she will study late in the library.

or as a formula $library\_open \rightarrow study\_late$ is added, only 38% draw the correct conclusion, although modus ponens is applicable in this case as well. People are understanding this additional conditional not as an alternative but as an additional premiss.

We propose the same method as applied in the case of the WST. The conditional $library\_open \rightarrow study\_late$ is not just additional knowledge, moreover it can be understood as trigger of additional knowledge about the world. We know that usually to study late in the library, the library is open $study\_late \rightarrow library\_open$.

If we assume this additional formula as a *norm*; which can be formulated with the help of the deontic ought-to-operator $\Box$, this leads to the following:

Table 3. Contrary-to-duty obligation together with the formalization in deontic logic

Natural Language	Normative System $\mathcal{N}'$
a ought not steal.	$\Box\neg s$
a steals.	s
If a steals, he ought to be punished for stealing.	$s \rightarrow \Box p$
If a does not steal, he ought not be punished for stealing.	$\Box(\neg s \rightarrow \neg p)$

$$essay\_to\_write \rightarrow study\_late \qquad (6)$$
$$library\_open \rightarrow study\_late$$
$$study\_late \rightarrow \Box library\_open \qquad (7)$$
$$essay\_to\_write \qquad (8)$$

The question $study\_late$ can easily be answered positively by using formulae (6) and (8). If, however, the norm (7) is taken into account, the questions corresponds to a model checking task as discussed in Section 3.2. We can easily find a model

$$M = \{essay\_to\_write, study\_late, \Box library\_open\}$$

by constructing a tableau similar to the one in Figure 3. However we are not able to check – in contrast to the WST – whether $\Box library\_open$ holds, it *ought to be the case*. This explains why much lesser persons are answering the question whether she is studying late positively.

5   Consistency Testing of Normative Systems

In the philosophical literature deontic logic is also used to formulate entire normative systems (e.g. [23]). In practice such normative systems can be rather complex. This makes it difficult for the creator of a normative system to see if a normative system is consistent. We will show that it is helpful to be able to check consistency of normative systems automatically. We will use the Hyper theorem prover for this task.

As an example, we consider the well-known problem of *contrary-to-duty obligations* introduced in [8]. In Table 3 the problem is given in natural language together with formalization in deontic logic discussed in [23]. As shown in [23], the normative system given in Table 3 is inconsistent. We will use Hyper to show this inconsistency. For this, we first transform $\mathcal{N}'$ into $\mathcal{ALC}$. The result of this transformation is given in Table 4.

Checking the consistency of the normative system $\mathcal{N}'$ corresponds to checking the consistency of $\phi(\mathcal{N}')$ w.r.t. the TBox $\mathcal{T} = \{\top \sqsubseteq \exists R.\top\}$, where $\phi(\mathcal{N}')$ is the conjunction of the concepts given in the right column of Table 4. We transform $\phi(\mathcal{N}')$ into DL-clauses, which is the input language of Hyper. We will not give the result of this transformation and refer to [17] for details. Hyper constructs a hypertableau for the resulting set of DL-clauses. This hypertableau is closed and therefore we can conclude that the set of DL-clauses is unsatisfiable. This tells us that the above formalized normative system $\mathcal{N}'$ is inconsistent.

Table 4. Translation of the normative system $\mathcal{N}'$ into $\mathcal{ALC}$

Deontic Logic	$\mathcal{ALC}$
$\Box \Phi \to \Diamond \Phi$	$\top \sqsubseteq \exists R.\top$
$\Box \neg s$	$\forall R.\neg S$
s	S
$s \to \Box p$	$\neg S \sqcup \forall R.P$
$\Box(\neg s \to \neg p)$	$\forall R.(S \sqcup \neg P)$

6 Conclusion

The goal of this paper was twofold: on one side we wanted to show that deontic logic can be very well used to model various phenomena in human reasoning. The different performance of humans in different contexts could be explained be combining deontic logic with mental model theory from cognitive science. And secondly, we wanted to demonstrate that an automated theorem proving system, like Hyper, can be used to decide deontic logic by transforming it into description logic and in DL-clauses.

To conclude this paper, we want to briefly comment a new area of research, namely the formalization of 'robot ethics'. In multi-agents systems and in robotics one is aiming at defining formal rules for the behavior of agents. As an example consider Asimov's laws, which aim at controlling the relation between robots and humans. In [6] the authors depict a small example of two surgery robots, which have to deal with ethical codes to perform there work. These codes are given with the help of deontic logic very much the same as we defined the normative systems in this paper. In [11] we show how to use Hyper to resolve conflicts in multi-agent systems.

References

1. Artosi, A., Cattabriga, P., Governatori, G.: Ked: A deontic theorem prover. In: On Legal Application of Logic Programming, ICLP 1994, pp. 60–76 (1994)
2. Bassiliades, N., Kontopoulos, E., Governatori, G., Antoniou, G.: A modal defeasible reasoner of deontic logic for the semantic web. Int. J. Semant. Web Inf. Syst. 7(1), 18–43 (2011)
3. Baumgartner, P., Furbach, U., Pelzer, B.: Hyper tableaux with equality. In: Pfenning, F. (ed.) CADE 2007. LNCS (LNAI), vol. 4603, pp. 492–507. Springer, Heidelberg (2007)
4. Bender, M., Pelzer, B., Schon, C.: Systm description: E-kRHyper 1.4. In: Bonacina, M.P. (ed.) CADE 2013. LNCS, vol. 7898, pp. 126–134. Springer, Heidelberg (2013)
5. Blackburn, P., van Benthem, J., Wolter, F. (eds.): Handbook of Modal Logic. Studies in Logic and Practical Reasoning, vol. 3. Elsevier Science (December 2006)
6. Bringsjord, S., Arkoudas, K., Bello, P.: Toward a general logicist methodology for engineering ethically correct robots. IEEE Intelligent Systems 21(4), 38–44 (2006)

7. Byrne, R.M.: Suppressing valid inferences with conditionals. Cognition 31(1), 61–83 (1989)
8. Chisolm, R.M.: Contrary-to-duty imperatives and deontic logic. Analysis 23, 33–36 (1963)
9. Cosmides, L., Tooby, J.: Can a general deontic logic capture the facts of human moral reasoning? How the mind interprets social exchange rules and detects cheaters. Moral Psychology 1, 53–120 (2008)
10. Edgington, D.: Conditionals. In: Zalta, E.N. (ed.) The Stanford Encyclopedia of Philosophy, Winter 2008 edn. (2008)
11. Furbach, U., Schon, C., Stolzenberg, F.: Automated reasoning in deontic logic. In: Proceedings of the KIK 2014 Workshop. CEUR Workshop Proceedings (2014)
12. Hölldobler, S., Philipp, T., Wernhard, C.: An abductive model for human reasoning. In: AAAI Spring Symposium: Logical Formalizations of Commonsense Reasoning (2011)
13. Hölldobler, S., Kencana Ramli, C.D.P.: Logic programs under three-valued Lukasiewicz semantics. In: Hill, P.M., Warren, D.S. (eds.) ICLP 2009. LNCS, vol. 5649, pp. 464–478. Springer, Heidelberg (2009)
14. Johnson-Laird, P.N., Byrne, R.M.: Conditionals: a theory of meaning, pragmatics, and inference. Psychological Review 109(4), 646 (2002)
15. Kakas, A.C., Kowalski, R.A., Toni, F.: Abductive logic programming. Journal of Logic and Computation 2(6), 719–770 (1992)
16. Kowalski, R.: Computational logic and human thinking: how to be artificially intelligent. Cambridge University Press (2011)
17. Motik, B., Shearer, R., Horrocks, I.: Optimized Reasoning in Description Logics Using Hypertableaux. In: Pfenning, F. (ed.) CADE 2007. LNCS (LNAI), vol. 4603, pp. 67–83. Springer, Heidelberg (2007)
18. Sanford, D.: If P, then Q: Conditionals and the Foundations of Reasoning. Routledge (1989)
19. Schild, K.: A correspondence theory for terminological logics: Preliminary report. In: Proc. of IJCAI-91, pp. 466–471 (1991)
20. Schmidt, R.A., Hustadt, U.: First-order resolution methods for modal logics. In: Voronkov, A., Weidenbach, C. (eds.) Programming Logics. LNCS, vol. 7797, pp. 345–391. Springer, Heidelberg (2013)
21. Stenning, K., Van Lambalgen, M.: Human reasoning and cognitive science. MIT Press (2008)
22. Stone, V.E., Cosmides, L., Tooby, J., Kroll, N., Knight, R.T.: Selective impairment of reasoning about social exchange in a patient with bilateral limbic system damage. Proceedings of the National Academy of Sciences 99(17), 11531–11536 (2002)
23. von Kutschera, F.: Einführung in die Logik der Normen, Werte und Entscheidungen. In: Alber (1973)
24. Wason, P.C.: Reasoning about a rule. The Quarterly Journal of Experimental Psychology 20(3), 273–281 (1968)
25. Pelzer, B., Wernhard, C.: System description: E- kRHyper. In: Pfenning, F. (ed.) CADE 2007. LNCS (LNAI), vol. 4603, pp. 508–513. Springer, Heidelberg (2007)

A System Z-like Approach
for First-Order Default Reasoning

Gabriele Kern-Isberner[1] and Christoph Beierle[2]

[1] Department of Computer Science, TU Dortmund, Germany
[2] Department of Computer Science, University of Hagen, Germany

Abstract. Default rules of the form "If A then (usually, probably) B" can be represented conveniently by conditionals. To every consistent knowledge base $\mathcal{R}$ with such qualitative conditionals over a propositional language, system Z assigns a unique minimal model that accepts every conditional in $\mathcal{R}$ and that is therefore a model of $\mathcal{R}$ inductively completing the explicitly given knowledge. In this paper, we propose a generalization of system Z for a first-order setting. For a first-order conditional knowledge base $\mathcal{R}$ over unary predicates, we present the definition of a system Z-like ranking function, prove that it yields a model of $\mathcal{R}$, and illustrate its construction by a detailed example.

1 Introduction

Reasoning with default rules, i.e., rules that allow for exceptions and so for a nonmonotonic reasoning behaviour, is a core topic of nonmonotonic logics. In many approaches, conditionals are used as representations of such rules, see e. g. [10]. A conditional has the form $(B \mid A)$ and represents the (defeasible) rule "If A then (usually, probably) B". Employing conditionals instead of material implications goes beyond the limits of classical logics which are deemed to be too strict for defeasible reasoning since conditionals are inherently three-valued, their semantics relying on verification, falsification, and a neutral behaviour in case the antecedent A is not satisfied [7]. Ordinal conditional functions (OCF, also called ranking functions) [16,17] provide a popular and convenient semantical framework for interpreting conditionals by associating degrees of (im)plausibility with possible worlds and formulas. According to a given OCF, a conditional $(B \mid A)$ is accepted if its verification $A \wedge B$ is more plausible than its refutation $A \wedge \neg B$. Within this framework, system Z [15,10] is a prominent approach to default reasoning which features a method for OCF-based inductive reasoning from conditional knowledge bases. To each (consistent [1]) conditional knowledge base, system Z assigns an OCF that accepts each conditional of the knowledge base and allows for further inductive reasoning from this OCF-model. In more qualitative frameworks, system Z corresponds to rational closure [14]. The popularity of system Z relies on three features [10]: First, its OCF semantics is straightforward and intuitive, and it allows for high quality, expressive inferences. Second, there are obvious algorithms to compute system Z. Finally, the OCF chosen by system Z is most cautious in that it does not restrict the plausibility of worlds unnecessarily.

However, as most approaches to default reasoning except for approaches that make use of logic programming [8], default logics are propositional, only few advances have

T. Eiter et al. (Eds.): Brewka Festschrift, LNAI 9060, pp. 81–95, 2015.

been made to build on first-order logics, or fragments thereof. In [6], Delgrande presents a first-order conditional logic that allows for the representation of information both on classes and on individuals in the same framework. Several approaches to first-order default reasoning focus particularly on applications for description logics, aiming at making subsumptions defeasible so that typical, but not strict relationships can be expressed [3,5,9]. Many of these approaches rely on modal logics. In [13], a first-order conditional semantics was proposed that is based on OCF, extending well-known properties of OCF in propositional frameworks to first-order settings. As a proof of concept, that paper presents a model-based inductive reasoning method from first-order conditional knowledge bases that is based on c-representations [11] and that is known to be similar to (but different from) system Z in propositional settings [12]. An obvious question is whether also system Z can be transferred to the first-order case within the same semantical framework.

In this paper, we show that the first-order conditional semantics from [13] which is based on OCF and extends seamlessly propositional OCF semantics for conditionals also allows a generalization of system Z for first-order settings. As a crucial feature, we focus on conditionals making use of unary predicates only, as this is a straightforward extension of the rationale behind system Z to the first-order case.

Example 1 (Penguins and super-penguins). Following the long tradition in knowledge representation and nonmonotonic logic of using scenarios involving birds and abnormal birds for illustration (e.g. [4]), here we assume that we have *penguins (P), birds (B)*, and *super-penguins (S)* as well as *winged things (W)* and *flying things (F)*. Then the four conditionals

$$r_1 : \ (F(x) \,|\, B(x))$$
$$r_2 : \ (W(x) \,|\, B(x))$$
$$r_3 : \ (\overline{F}(x) \,|\, P(x))$$
$$r_4 : \ (F(x) \,|\, S(x))$$

express that birds usually fly (r_1) and have wings (r_2), and that penguins usually do not fly (r_3), but super-penguins usually fly (r_4).

Thus, propositional conditionals $(B|A)$ are now encoded by $(B(x)|A(x))$, allowing us to consider the uncertain relationship between A and B for different instances $x = a$, but nevertheless being able to express a general behaviour within a population that justifies the acceptance of $(B(x)|A(x))$. For this, particularly strong instances via so-called representatives are necessary for which the conditional is not only accepted but which surpass other individuals with respect to different criteria in terms of OCF-measured plausibility. Our approach features a kind of tolerance partitioning of the conditionals that is crucial for the propositional system Z [10] which comes along with a partitioning of the domain elements. In this way, a relation on the domain elements is set up which is a basic component of many other approaches to first-order default reasoning. In our approach, this relation can be determined by the interactions among the conditionals in the knowledge base. We also allow factual knowledge on individuals to be given, and these facts are taken into account when defining a system Z-like OCF that is a model of the (factual and conditional) knowledge base.

The rest of this paper is organized as follows. We continue with introducing the syntax of first-order conditional logic (Section 2) and describe our ranking semantics for first-order conditionals afterwards (Section 3). In Section 4, we present the construction of a system Z-like ranking function from a knowledge base with given corresponding partitionings of the conditionals and the domain elements, and prove that this construction yields an OCF accepting the knowledge base. The construction is illustrated by a detailed example in Section 5. Finally, in Section 6 we conclude with a brief summary and discussion of future work.

2 Syntax of First-Order Conditionals

Let Σ be a first-order signature consisting of a finite set of predicates P_Σ and a finite set of constant symbols D_Σ but without function symbols of arity > 0. An *atom* is a predicate of arity n together with a list of n constants and/or variables. A *literal* is an atom or a negated atom. Formulas are built on atoms using conjunction ($\land$), disjunction ($\lor$), negation ($\neg$), and quantification ($\forall, \exists$). We abbreviate conjunctions by juxtaposition and negations usually by overlining, e. g. AB means $A \land B$ and $\overline{A}$ means $\neg A$. A *ground* formula contains no variables. In a *closed* formula, all variables (if they occur) are bound by quantifiers, otherwise, the formula is *open*, and the variables that occur outside of the range of quantifiers are called *free*. If a formula A contains free variables we also use the notation $A(\boldsymbol{x})$ where $\boldsymbol{x} = (x_1, \ldots, x_n)$ contains all free variables in A. If $\boldsymbol{c}$ is a vector of the same length as $\boldsymbol{x}$ then $A(\boldsymbol{c})$ is meant to denote the instantiation of A with $\boldsymbol{c}$. A formula $\forall \boldsymbol{x} A(\boldsymbol{x})$ ($\exists \boldsymbol{x} A(\boldsymbol{x})$) is *universal* (*existential*) if A involves no further quantification. Let $\mathcal{L}_\Sigma$ be the first-order language that allows no nested quantification, i.e., all quantified formulas are either universal or existential formulas.

$\mathcal{L}_\Sigma$ is extended by a conditional operator "$|$" to a conditional language $(\mathcal{L}_\Sigma \mid \mathcal{L}_\Sigma)$ containing first-order conditionals $(B \mid A)$ with $A, B \in \mathcal{L}_\Sigma$, and (universally or existentially) quantified conditionals $\forall \boldsymbol{x}(B \mid A), \exists \boldsymbol{x}(B \mid A)$[1]. When writing $(B(\boldsymbol{x}) \mid A(\boldsymbol{x}))$, we assume $\boldsymbol{x}$ to contain all free variables occurring in either A or B. For $r = (B \mid A) \in (\mathcal{L}_\Sigma \mid \mathcal{L}_\Sigma)$ (without outer quantification), we set $\overline{r} = (\overline{B} \mid A)$. Conditionals cannot be nested. When the signature is clear from context, we will also omit the subscript Σ. To exemplify the syntax, consider the rules r_1, r_2, r_3, r_4 from Example 1 in the introduction which are open first-order conditionals.

A *first-order conditional knowledge base* $\mathcal{R}$ is a (finite) set of (conditional) formulas from $\mathcal{L}_\Sigma \cup (\mathcal{L}_\Sigma \mid \mathcal{L}_\Sigma)$ with the restriction that no existential (outer) quantification of conditionals may occur. A *first-order knowledge base* $\mathcal{KB} = \langle \mathcal{F}, \mathcal{R} \rangle$ consists of a first-order conditional knowledge base $\mathcal{R}$, together with a set $\mathcal{F}$ of closed formulas from $\mathcal{L}_\Sigma$, called *facts*.

3 OCF-Based Semantics

In propositional settings, *ordinal conditional functions* (OCF, [17]), also called *ranking functions* are a well-known framework for nonmonotonic reasoning and belief revision. We recall very briefly the basic details of this approach here before widening the scope for first-order challenges. So first, let $\mathcal{L}_\Sigma$ be a purely propositional language over a set

---

[1] These quantifications will often be distinguished as *outer* quantifications in the paper.

Σ of propositional atoms. Let Ω denote the set of possible worlds over $\mathcal{L}$; Ω will be taken simply as the set of all propositional interpretations over $\mathcal{L}$ and can be identified with the set of all complete conjunctions over Σ. For $\omega \in \Omega$, $\omega \models A$ means that the propositional formula $A \in \mathcal{L}_\Sigma$ holds in the possible world ω. A (propositional) conditional $(B|A)$ is an object of a three-valued nature, partitioning the set of worlds Ω in three parts: those worlds satisfying AB, thus *verifying* the conditional, those worlds satisfying $A\overline{B}$, thus *falsifying* the conditional, and those worlds not fulfilling the premise A and so which the conditional may not be applied to at all.

An *ordinal conditional function* is a function $\kappa : \Omega \to \mathbb{N} \cup \{\infty\}$ with $\kappa^{-1}(0) \neq \emptyset$ which maps each world $\omega \in \Omega$ to a degree of implausibility $\kappa(\omega)$; ranks of formulas $A \in \mathcal{L}_\Sigma$ are defined by $\kappa(A) = \min\{\kappa(\omega) \mid \omega \models A\}$. An OCF κ *accepts* a conditional $(B|A)$, in symbols $\kappa \models (B|A)$, if and only if $\kappa(AB) < \kappa(A\overline{B})$, that is, if and only if the conditional's verification AB is more plausible than its falsification $A\overline{B}$. In this case, we call κ a (ranking) model of $(B|A)$, and κ is (ranking) model of a conditional knowledge base $\mathcal{R}$ if it is a model of each of the conditionals in $\mathcal{R}$.

For a given conditional knowledge base $\mathcal{R} = \{(B_1|A_1), \ldots, (B_n|A_n)\}$, the system Z approach by Pearl [15,10] defines an OCF κ_z that is a model of $\mathcal{R}$ and that is unique among all such models in that it restricts the plausibility of worlds in a minimal way. System Z is based on a notion of tolerance: A conditional $(B|A)$ is *tolerated* by $\mathcal{R}$ if and only if there is a world $\omega \in \Omega$ such that $\omega \models AB$ and $\omega \models A_i \Rightarrow B_i$ for every $1 \leqslant i \leqslant n$. Now, system Z is set up by first partitioning $\mathcal{R} = \mathcal{R}_0 \cup \ldots \cup \mathcal{R}_m$ into maximal sets $\mathcal{R}_j$ such that each conditional in $\mathcal{R}_j$ is tolerated by $\cup_{i \geqslant j} \mathcal{R}_i$. Then the function $Z : \mathcal{R} \to \mathbb{N}$ is defined by $Z(B|A) = k$ iff $(B|A) \in \mathcal{R}_k$, and finally, κ_z is given by

$$\kappa_z(\omega) = \begin{cases} 0, & \text{iff } \omega \models (A_i \Rightarrow B_i) \text{ for all } 1 \leqslant i \leqslant n \\ \max_{1 \leqslant i \leqslant n} \{Z(B_i|A_i) \mid \omega \models A_i\overline{B_i}\} + 1, & \text{otherwise.} \end{cases}$$

We will now focus on the first-order case. For classical interpretation of first-order aspects we use the Herbrand semantics. The *Herbrand base* $\mathcal{H}^\Sigma$ of a first-order signature Σ is the set of all ground atoms of Σ. A *possible world* ω is any subset of $\mathcal{H}^\Sigma$. Analogously to the propositional case, a possible world can be concisely represented as a *complete conjunction* or *minterm*, i.e. a conjunction of literals where every atom of $\mathcal{H}^\Sigma$ appears either in positive or in negated form. Also as in the propositional case, we denote the set of all possible worlds of Σ by Ω_Σ, and $\models$ denotes the classical satisfaction relation between possible worlds and first-order formulas from $\mathcal{L}_\Sigma$.

For an open conditional $r = (B(\boldsymbol{x}) \mid A(\boldsymbol{x})) \in (\mathcal{L}_\Sigma \mid \mathcal{L}_\Sigma)$ let $\mathcal{H}^{(B(\boldsymbol{x}) \mid A(\boldsymbol{x}))}$ denote the set of all constant vectors $\boldsymbol{a}$ used for proper groundings of $(B(\boldsymbol{x}) \mid A(\boldsymbol{x}))$ from the Herbrand universe $\mathcal{H}^\Sigma$, i.e. $\mathcal{H}^{(B(\boldsymbol{x}) \mid A(\boldsymbol{x}))} = D_\Sigma^{|\boldsymbol{x}|}$ where $|\boldsymbol{x}|$ is the length of $\boldsymbol{x}$. For $\boldsymbol{a} \in \mathcal{H}^{(B(\boldsymbol{x}) \mid A(\boldsymbol{x}))}$, let $r(\boldsymbol{a}) = (B(\boldsymbol{a}) \mid A(\boldsymbol{a}))$ denote the instantiation of r by $\boldsymbol{a}$.

Just as in the propositional case, the set Ω_Σ of possible worlds can be ranked by an ordinal conditional function that assigns degrees of (im)plausibility resp. disbelief to possible worlds and statements. For a concise and complete introduction of ranking semantics for first-order settings and to make the seamless generalization from the propositional case explicit, we present the adjusted definitions in full detail.

Definition 1. *An ordinal conditional function (OCF) κ on Ω_Σ is a function $\kappa : \Omega_\Sigma \to \mathbb{N} \cup \{\infty\}$ with $\kappa^{-1}(0) \neq \emptyset$.*

We can now make use of the possible world semantics to assign degrees of disbelief also to formulas. In the following, let $A, B \in \mathcal{L}_\Sigma$ denote closed formulas, and let $A(x), B(x) \in \mathcal{L}_\Sigma$ denote open formulas.

Definition 2. *Let κ be an OCF. The κ-ranks of closed formulas are defined via*

$$\kappa(A) = \min_{\omega \models A} \kappa(\omega)$$

Furthermore, we define the κ-ranks for open formulas by evaluating most plausible instances:

$$\kappa(A(x)) = \min_{a \in \mathcal{H}^{A(x)}} \kappa(A(a))$$

The ranks of first-order formulas are coherently based on the usage of OCFs for propositional formulas. Just as in the propositional case, these degrees of beliefs are used to specify when a formula from $(\mathcal{L}_\Sigma \mid \mathcal{L}_\Sigma)$ is accepted, i. e. deemed highly plausible, by a ranking function κ (where acceptance is denoted by $\models$). We will first consider the acceptance of closed (conditional) formulas.

Definition 3. *Let κ be an OCF. The acceptance relation between κ and formulas from $\mathcal{L}_\Sigma$ and $(\mathcal{L}_\Sigma \mid \mathcal{L}_\Sigma)$ is defined as follows:*

– for closed formulas:
  - $\kappa \models A$ *iff for all $\omega \in \Omega$ with $\kappa(\omega) = 0$, it holds that $\omega \models A$.*
  - $\kappa \models (B \mid A)$ *iff $\kappa(AB) < \kappa(A\overline{B})$.*
– for universal/existential conditionals:
  - $\kappa \models \forall x(B(x) \mid A(x))$ *iff $\kappa \models (B(a) \mid A(a))$ for all $a \in \mathcal{H}^{(B(x) \mid A(x))}$.*
  - $\kappa \models \exists x(B(x) \mid A(x))$ *iff there is $a \in \mathcal{H}^{(B(x) \mid A(x))}$ such that $\kappa \models (B(a) \mid A(a))$.*

Acceptance of a sentence by a ranking function is the same as in the propositional case for ground sentences, and interprets the classical quantifiers in a straightforward way. Note that no classical relations hold between universal and existential formulas, as acceptance by ranking functions is three-valued.

The treatment of acceptance of open formulas is more intricate, as such formulas will be used to express default statements, like in "A is plausible", or in "usually, if A holds, then B also holds". The basic idea here is that such (conditional) open statements hold if there are individuals that provide most convincing instances of the respective conditional. These so-called *representatives* should, of course, allow for the acceptance of the instantiated conditional (as in Definition 3) while most plausibly verifying the conditional (i. e. satisfying A and B). Moreover, representatives are expected to be least exceptional with respect to falsifying the conditional. The following definition makes use of the κ-ranks of Definition 2 to formalize this precisely.

Definition 4. *Let* $r = (B(\boldsymbol{x}) \mid A(\boldsymbol{x})) \in (\mathcal{L}_\Sigma \mid \mathcal{L}_\Sigma)$ *be a non-quantified conditional in-volving open formulas from* $\mathcal{L}_\Sigma$. *We say that* $\boldsymbol{a} \in \mathcal{H}^{(B(\boldsymbol{x}) \mid A(\boldsymbol{x}))}$ *is a weak representative of* r *iff it satisfies the following conditions:*

$$\kappa(A(\boldsymbol{a})B(\boldsymbol{a})) = \kappa(A(\boldsymbol{x})B(\boldsymbol{x})) \tag{1}$$

$$\kappa(A(\boldsymbol{a})B(\boldsymbol{a})) < \kappa(A(\boldsymbol{a})\overline{B}(\boldsymbol{a})) \tag{2}$$

The set of weak representatives of r *is denoted by* $WRep(r)$. *We say that* $\boldsymbol{a} \in \mathcal{H}^{(B(\boldsymbol{x}) \mid A(\boldsymbol{x}))}$ *is a* (strong) *representative of* r *iff it is a weak representative of* r *and*

$$\kappa(A(\boldsymbol{a})\overline{B}(\boldsymbol{a})) = \min_{\boldsymbol{b} \in WRep(r)} \kappa(A(\boldsymbol{b})\overline{B}(\boldsymbol{b})). \tag{3}$$

The set of all representatives of r *is denoted by* $Rep(r)$.

(Weak) Representatives of a conditional are characterized by being most general and least exceptional. This is expressed by condition (1) that postulates that representatives are most normal with respect to A's being also B's, and also by condition (3) that demands that representative individuals should be least specific with respect to violating the link between A and B; otherwise, this violation might be caused by extraordinary attributes. This can be easily exemplified in the popular penguin scenario. Consider a scenario where we have birds, penguins, and super-penguins. Birds usually fly, whereas penguins are expected not to fly while super-penguins are famous for flying. What is a representative (flying) bird here? It is definitely not a penguin since penguins usually do not fly (violating condition (2)). While we might more strongly believe that super-penguins fly than care about the non-specified bird next to us (super-penguins are famous!), super-penguins are too specific to serve as good representatives. Representatives should be general, covering as many species of flying birds as possible. But, due to this generality, we would also be more willing to accept an exception here than for more specific subclasses. Superpenguins might be able to fly because they are equipped with motorized wings, and their failure of flying might be caused by a motor problem, an explanation that certainly does not apply to the failure of flying of a normal bird. This motivates condition (3). Note that (weak) representatives are only *conditional representatives*, i. e., representatives for the respective conditional relationship, as we do not postulate that representatives (certainly or plausibly) satisfy the premise of the conditional. It might well be the case that individuals may serve as representatives for different conditionals. Now we can base our definition of acceptance of open conditionals on the notion of representatives as follows.

Definition 5. *Let* κ *be an* OCF *and* $r = (B(\boldsymbol{x}) \mid A(\boldsymbol{x}))$ *an open (non-quantified) conditional. Then* κ *accepts* r, *denoted by* $\kappa \models r$, *iff* $Rep(r) \neq \emptyset$, *and one of the two following (exclusive) conditions is satisfied:*

(Acc-1) *it holds that*

$$\kappa(A(\boldsymbol{x})B(\boldsymbol{x})) < \kappa(A(\boldsymbol{x})\overline{B}(\boldsymbol{x})); \tag{4}$$

(Acc-2) $\kappa(A(x)B(x)) = \kappa(A(x)\overline{B}(x))$, *and for all* $a_1 \in Rep((B(x) \mid A(x)))$ *and for all* $a_2 \in Rep((\overline{B}(x) \mid A(x)))$, *it holds that*

$$\kappa(A(a_1)\overline{B}(a_1)) < \kappa(A(a_2)B(a_2)). \tag{5}$$

The acceptance of an open conditional is based on the existence of a suitable a satisfying (2), i. e., on the acceptance of the propositional conditional $(B(a) \mid A(a))$ (note that $Rep((B(x) \mid A(x))) \neq \emptyset$ iff $WRep((B(x) \mid A(x))) \neq \emptyset$). However, conditions (1) and (2) alone are too weak to justify the acceptance of $(B(x) \mid A(x))$ since it might well be the case that there are a and b fulfilling (1) and (2) for $(B(x) \mid A(x))$ and $(\overline{B}(x) \mid A(x))$, respectively. This means that κ might accept both $(B(x) \mid A(x))$ and $(\overline{B}(x) \mid A(x))$, which would be counterintuitive. Hence, we need to make acceptance unambiguous by giving preference to one of the two conditionals. This can be done either by postulating (4) or (5). Condition (4) looks like a natural prerequisite for the acceptance of $(B(x) \mid A(x))$. However, in the birds scenario with penguins and super-penguins, equalities like $\kappa(A(x)B(x)) = \kappa(A(x)\overline{B}(x))$ quite naturally arise since penguins are as normal non-flying birds as doves are normal flying birds (see Example 2 below). In this case, (5) again uses the idea of least exceptionality for specifying proper representatives; it makes $(B(x) \mid A(x))$ acceptable, as opposed to $(\overline{B}(x) \mid A(x))$, if the representatives of the first conditional less exceptionally violate the respective conditional than the representatives of the latter conditional. Note that (5) holds vacuously in case that $Rep((\overline{B}(x) \mid A(x)))$ is empty. Furthermore, Definition 5 nicely extends the definition of acceptance in the propositional case, i. e., $\kappa \models (B(a) \mid A(a))$ iff $\kappa(A(a)B(a)) < \kappa(A(a)\overline{B}(a))$.

Definitions 4 and 5 can be used to define acceptance of open non-conditional formulas $A(x)$ by considering them as conditionals with tautological antecedents, i.e., as $(A(x) \mid \top)$. However, it is crucial to remark here that $(A(x) \mid \top)$ mandatorily demands for a default reading like "being A is plausible", as opposed to "A certainly holds". This distinction is made in our approach by distinguishing between certain knowledge $\mathcal{F}$ (all elements here are closed formulas of $\mathcal{L}_\Sigma$) and default (conditional) beliefs in $\mathcal{R}$ which may involve both closed and open formulas (well-formed according to our syntax definitions). Formally, this is handled by giving different semantics to the two parts of our knowledge bases.

Definition 6. *Let* $\mathcal{KB} = \langle \mathcal{F}, \mathcal{R} \rangle$ *be a first-order knowledge base, and let* κ *be an OCF.*

1. κ *accepts* $\mathcal{R}$, *denoted by* $\kappa \models \mathcal{R}$, *iff* $\kappa \models \varphi$ *for all* $\varphi \in \mathcal{R}$.
2. κ *accepts* $\mathcal{KB}$, *denoted by* $\kappa \models \mathcal{KB}$, *iff* $\kappa(\omega) = \infty$ *for all* $\omega \not\models \mathcal{F}$, *and* $\kappa \models \mathcal{R}$.

If $\kappa \models \mathcal{KB}$ *then we also say that* κ *is a* model *of* $\mathcal{KB}$. *If there is no* κ *with* $\kappa \models \mathcal{KB}$ *then* $\mathcal{KB}$ *is* inconsistent.

In this way, we can accurately distinguish between the statements "A certainly holds for all individuals" ($\forall x A(x) \in \mathcal{F}$), "it is plausible that A holds for all individuals" ($\forall x A(x) \in \mathcal{R}$, treated as $(\forall x A(x) \mid \top)$), and "$A$ is plausible" ($A(x) \in \mathcal{R}$, treated as $(A(x) \mid \top)$). In general, having a classical (i. e., unconditional) formula A in $\mathcal{F}$ expresses "A is certain" while A in $\mathcal{R}$ means "A is plausible". Before illustrating the first-order semantics defined above, we first carry over the idea of (propositional) c-representations [11] to the first-order case. This will endow us with the possibility of constructing proper OCF-models of knowledge bases in an easy way.

4 System Z for First-Order Conditionals

In this section, we present the construction of a system Z-like ranking function from a first-order conditional knowledge base. We assume given partitionings of the conditionals and the domain elements satisfying some contraints inspired by the notion of tolerance used in system Z. We present a theorem stating that our construction yields an OCF accepting the given knowledge base.

Let $\mathcal{R} = \{(B_1(\boldsymbol{x}_1) \,|\, A_1(\boldsymbol{x}_1)), \dots, (B_n(\boldsymbol{x}_n) \,|\, A_n(\boldsymbol{x}_n))\}$ be a finite set of first-order conditionals. These conditionals can either involve open or closed formulas; we may omit the (outer) quantification of conditionals, as no existential conditional may occur, and all universal conditionals can be replaced by the set of all instantiations, according to Definition 3. Moreover, all formulas in $\mathcal{R}$ can be assumed to have a conditional form, according to the remarks around Definition 6 at the end of the preceding section.

We focus on conditionals over languages $\mathcal{L}_\Sigma$ whose signature consists only of constants and unary predicates. Given a knowledge base $\mathcal{KB}$ over $\mathcal{L}_\Sigma$ that fulfills certain prerequisites, we set up a ranking function κ_z that transfers the main ideas of system Z [10] into the first-order environment and that we prove to be a model of $\mathcal{KB}$.

Theorem 1. *Let $\mathcal{KB} = \langle \mathcal{F}, \mathcal{R} \rangle$ be a first-order knowledge base over a language $\mathcal{L}_\Sigma$ the signature of which consists only of constants and unary predicates that satisfies the following conditions:*

(C1) $\mathcal{F}$ is consistent, and no formula in $\mathcal{F}$ or $\mathcal{R}$ mentions more than one constant or variable.

(C2) There are partitionings $\mathcal{R} = \mathcal{R}_0 \cup \dots \cup \mathcal{R}_m$ and $D = D_0 \cup \dots \cup D_m$ such that for all i, for all $r \in \mathcal{R}_i$, there is $a \in D_i$ and $\omega \in \Omega, \omega \models \mathcal{F}$, such that ω verifies $r(a)$ and ω does not falsify $r'(a')$ for all $r' \in \cup_{j \geqslant i} \mathcal{R}_j$ and all $a' \in D_i$.

For $\omega \in \Omega, \omega \models \mathcal{F}$, and for $0 \leqslant i \leqslant m$, define

$$\lambda_i(\omega) = \begin{cases} 0, & \text{if } r(a) \text{ is not falsified in } \omega \; \forall a \in D_i, \forall r \in \mathcal{R} \\ \max_{a \in D_i} \max_{r \in \mathcal{R}} \{j \mid r \in \mathcal{R}_j \text{ and } r(a) \text{ is falsified in } \omega\} + 1, & \text{otherwise} \end{cases}$$

Then the OCF κ_z defined by $\kappa_z(\omega) = \infty$ for $\omega \not\models \mathcal{F}$, and

$$\kappa_z(\omega) = \sum_{i=0}^{m} (m+2)^i \lambda_i(\omega) - \kappa_0$$

$$\kappa_0 = \min_{\omega \in \Omega} \sum_{i=0}^{m} (m+2)^i \lambda_i(\omega)$$

(6)

for $\omega \models \mathcal{F}$, is a model of $\mathcal{KB}$.

Proof. Since $\mathcal{F}$ is consistent so that there is $\omega \in \Omega$ with $\omega \models \mathcal{F}$, it is clear that κ_z is an OCF since κ_0 normalizes κ_z to ensure that $0 = \min_{\omega \in \Omega} \kappa_z(\omega)$. Since κ_0 is the same for all ω in $\kappa_z(\omega)$ in (6), for the proof we can focus on the sum in $\kappa_z(\omega)$ since minimization and inequalities between different $\kappa_z(\omega)$ only depend upon the summation part. Furthermore, all $\lambda_i(\omega)$ are natural numbers between 0 and $m + 1$. This allows for exactly $m + 2$ different values. This means that we can associate with each $\kappa_z(\omega)$ resp. its summation part a vector $(\lambda_0(\omega), \ldots, \lambda_m(\omega))$,

$$\kappa_z(\omega) \sim (\lambda_0(\omega), \ldots, \lambda_m(\omega)),$$

such that $\kappa_z(\omega) = \sum_{i=0}^{m}(m + 2)^i \lambda_i(\omega) - \kappa_0$. Then for two $\omega, \omega' \models \mathcal{F}$, the following holds:

- $\kappa_z(\omega) \quad < \quad \kappa_z(\omega')$ iff $\kappa_z(\omega) \quad \sim \quad (\lambda_0(\omega), \ldots, \lambda_m(\omega)), \kappa_z(\omega') \quad \sim$ $(\lambda_0(\omega'), \ldots, \lambda_m(\omega'))$ and there is $j, 0 \leqslant j \leqslant m$ such that $\lambda_j(\omega) < \lambda_j(\omega')$ and $\lambda_i(\omega) = \lambda_i(\omega')$ for all $i > j$;
- $\kappa_z(\omega) \quad = \quad \kappa_z(\omega')$ iff $\kappa_z(\omega) \quad \sim \quad (\lambda_0(\omega), \ldots, \lambda_m(\omega)), \kappa_z(\omega') \quad \sim$ $(\lambda_0(\omega'), \ldots, \lambda_m(\omega'))$ and $\lambda_i(\omega) = \lambda_i(\omega')$ for all $0 \leqslant i \leqslant m$.

In particular, this means that $\kappa_z(\omega)$ is minimal (with respect to given conditions) if all components $\lambda_i(\omega)$ are (respectively) minimal.

Since the language contains only unary predicates, and due to prerequisite *(C1)* in the theorem, each possible world ω can be written as a conjunction of independent components $\omega(a)$ that contain all literals for one $a \in D$. So, for each (open) conditional r, $r(a)$ is verified resp. falsified by ω iff it is verified resp. falsified by $\omega(a)$. We write $\omega(D_i)$ for the conjunction of all $\omega(a)$ for $a \in D_i$. Since λ_i considers only the falsifications within D_i, we have $\lambda_i(\omega) = \lambda_i(\omega(D_i))$.

We have to prove that $\kappa_z \models r$ for all $r \in \mathcal{R}$. More precisely, we have to prove that $Rep(r) \neq \emptyset$ (which is the case iff $WRep(r) \neq \emptyset$) and to verify the conditions of Definition 5. So let $r = (B(x)|A(x)) \in \mathcal{R}$. Then there is $i, 0 \leqslant i \leqslant m$, such that $r \in \mathcal{R}_i$. Due to prerequisite *(C2)*, there is $a \in D_i$ and $\omega_a \in \Omega, \omega_a \models \mathcal{F}$, such that $\omega_a \models A(a)B(a)$ and ω_a does not falsify $r'(a')$ for all $r' \in \cup_{j \geqslant i}\mathcal{R}_j$ and all $a' \in D_i$. This implies that $\lambda_i(\omega_a) = \lambda_i(\omega_a(D_i)) \leqslant (i - 1) + 1 = i$. Choose $a \in D_i$ with appertaining ω_a in such a way that $\lambda_i(\omega_a)$ is minimal; we can even choose ω_a such that $\lambda_j(\omega_a)$ is (overall) minimal for $j \neq i$ since for $j \neq i$, $\omega_a(D_j)$ is independent from $\omega_a(D_i)$.

We will show that $a \in WRep(r)$. First, $\kappa_z(A(a)B(a)) = \kappa_z(\omega_a)$ because ω_a is minimal in all λ_j-components with respect to $\omega \models A(a)B(a)$, and even more, we also have $\kappa_z(A(a)B(a)) = \kappa_z(A(x)B(x))$: For, assume there were $c \in D$ such that $\kappa_z(A(c)B(c)) < \kappa_z(A(a)B(a))$, $\kappa_z(A(c)B(c)) = \kappa_z(\omega_c)$. Then there is a last k such that $\lambda_k(\omega_c) < \lambda_k(\omega_a)$ and $\lambda_j(\omega_c) = \lambda_j(\omega_a)$ for all $j > k$. Since for all $j \neq i$, $\lambda_j(\omega_a)$ was chosen overall minimal, we must have $k = i$. But within D_i, a was chosen in such a way to make $\lambda_i(\omega_a)$ minimal among all $\lambda_i(\omega)$ such that $\omega \models \mathcal{F}$, $\omega \models A(d)B(d)$ for some $d \in D_i$, and ω does not falsify $r'(a')$ for all $r' \in \cup_{j \geqslant i}\mathcal{R}_j$ and all $a' \in D_i$. We have $\omega_c \models \mathcal{F}$, and $\omega_c \models A(c)B(c)$, so if ω_c would falsify any $r'(a')$ for some $r' \in \cup_{j \geqslant i}\mathcal{R}_j$ and some $a' \in D_i$, then $\lambda_i(\omega_c) > i \geqslant \lambda_i(\omega_a)$ which contradicts the assumption $\kappa_z(A(c)B(c)) < \kappa_z(A(a)B(a))$. Therefore, (1) from Definition 4 holds for a, and now, we show (2) from Definition 4 for a. Let $\kappa_z(A(a)\overline{B}(a)) = \kappa_z(\omega'_a)$, i.e., ω'_a is minimal with respect to falsifying $(B(a)|A(a))$. For all components $\omega'_a(D_j)$ with $j \neq i$, $\lambda_j(\omega'_a) = \lambda_j(\omega_a)$, since both are overall minimal. But for i, we have $\lambda_i(\omega'_a) \geq i + 1 > i$, since ω'_a falsifies $r(a)$ and $a \in D_i$. Therefore, we have $\kappa_z(\omega'_a) > \kappa_z(\omega_a)$ and hence $\kappa_z(A(a)B(a)) < \kappa_z(A(a)\overline{B}(a))$, so (2) holds as well. Summarizing our results obtained so far, a is a weak representative of r, and we may also assume in the following, that a is a representative of r. In particular, $Rep(r) \neq \emptyset$.

Next, we turn to check the conditions of Definition 5 in order to show that κ_z accepts $r = (B(x)|A(x)) \in \mathcal{R}$. If $\kappa_z(A(x)B(x)) < \kappa_z(A(x)\overline{B}(x))$, then *(Acc-1)* holds and we are done. Otherwise, we have $\kappa_z(A(x)\overline{B}(x)) \leq \kappa_z(A(x)B(x))$. Let $\kappa_z(A(x)\overline{B}(x)) = \kappa_z(A(b)\overline{B}(b))$ with $b \in D_k$, and choose $\omega_b \models A(b)\overline{B}(b)$ such that $\kappa_z(A(b)\overline{B}(b)) = \kappa_z(\omega_b)$. First, we observe that b cannot be in D_i because otherwise we would have $\lambda_i(\omega_b) \geq i + 1$ due to ω_b falsifying $r(b)$ and $b \in D_i$. But this would imply $\lambda_i(\omega_a) < \lambda_i(\omega_b)$ and $\lambda_j(\omega_a) \leq \lambda_j(\omega_b)$ for $j \neq i$ since $\lambda_j(\omega_a)$ is minimal. Hence, we would have $\kappa_z(A(x)B(x)) = \kappa_z(A(a)B(a)) < \kappa_z(A(b)\overline{B}(b)) = \kappa_z(A(x)\overline{B}(x))$ which contradicts the assumption of the considered case. So, $b \in D_k$ with $k \neq i$.

Because $\kappa_z(\omega_b)$ is minimal among all $\kappa_z(\omega)$ with $\omega \models A(b)\overline{B}(b)$, it is clear that also $\lambda_k(\omega_b)$ must be minimal with respect to ω falsifying $r(b)$, and $\lambda_j(\omega_b)$ must be minimal overall for $j \neq k$. Since $k \neq i$, we can find ω_{ab} such that $\omega_{ab}(D_i) = \omega_a(D_i), \omega_{ab}(D_k) = \omega_b(D_k)$, and for $j \notin \{i, k\}$, $\omega_{ab}(D_j)$ is chosen to make $\lambda_j(\omega_{ab})$ minimal. Then $\omega_{ab} \models A(a)B(a)$ and $\omega_{ab} \models A(b)\overline{B}(b)$, $\lambda_i(\omega_{ab}) = \lambda_i(\omega_a)$ and $\lambda_k(\omega_{ab}) = \lambda_k(\omega_b)$ so that ω_{ab} is minimal both with respect to verifying and falsifying r, and hence we must have $\kappa_z(A(x)\overline{B}(x)) = \kappa_z(A(x)B(x))$.

If $Rep(\overline{r}) = \emptyset$, then $\kappa \models r$, and we are done. Otherwise, let $b \in Rep(\overline{r})$ (we have already presupposed that $a \in Rep(r)$) with $b \in D_k$. It remains to be shown that $\kappa_z(A(a)\overline{B}(a)) < \kappa_z(A(b)B(b))$. Note that all details that we proved above for b still hold, in particular, from the above, we have $k \neq i$. Due to presupposition (2), there is $\nu_b \in \Omega, \nu_b \models \mathcal{F}$, such that ν_b does not falsify $r'(b')$ for all $r' \in \cup_{j \geq k} \mathcal{R}_j$ for all $b' \in D_k$ (including b). Hence $\lambda_k(\nu_b) \leq (k - 1) + 1 = k$. W.l.o.g. we may assume that $\lambda_k(\nu_b)$ is minimal. Let us first assume that $k < i$. Then $\lambda_k(\nu_b) < i$. Choose ν_{ab} in such a way that $\nu_{ab}(D_i) = \omega_a(D_i), \nu_{ab}(D_k) = \nu_b(D_k)$, and for $j \notin \{i, k\}$, $\nu_{ab}(D_j)$ is chosen to make $\lambda_j(\nu_{ab})$ minimal. Then $\lambda_i(\nu_{ab}) = \lambda_i(\omega_a)$ and $\lambda_k(\nu_{ab}) = \lambda_k(\nu_b) < i$, all other $\lambda_j(\nu_{ab})$ being minimal. Since $\nu_{ab} \models A(a)B(a)$, we have $\kappa_z(A(a)B(a)) \leq \kappa_z(\nu_{ab}) \leq \kappa_z(\omega_a)$ due to the construction of ω_a and ν_{ab}, hence $\kappa_z(A(a)B(a)) = \kappa_z(\nu_{ab}) = \kappa_z(\omega_a)$. But now, recall that $\kappa_z(A(a)B(a)) = \kappa_z(\omega_a) = \kappa_z(\omega_b) = \kappa_z(A(b)\overline{B}(b))$, due to $\kappa_z(A(x)\overline{B}(x)) = \kappa_z(A(x)B(x))$. This means that all λ_j-components of ω_a and ω_b must be the same. However, we have $\lambda_k(\omega_a) = \lambda_k(\nu_{ab}) = \lambda_k(\nu_b) < i$, whereas for ω_b, we have $\lambda_k(\omega_b) > i$ since $r(b)$ is falsified for $b \in D_k$. So, we must have $i < k$. Let ω'_b be chosen minimal with respect to $\omega \models \mathcal{F}, \omega \models A(b)B(b)$, in particular, $\kappa_z(A(b)B(b)) = \kappa_z(\omega'_b)$. In the first part of the proof, we already chose ω'_a with $\kappa_z(A(a)\overline{B}(a)) = \kappa_z(\omega'_a)$. Now, we have to show $\kappa_z(\omega'_a) < \kappa_z(\omega'_b)$ to complete the proof. Altogether, we have (in the considered case)

$$\kappa_z(\omega_a) = \kappa_z(A(a)B(a)) = \kappa_z(A(x)B(x))$$
$$= \kappa_z(A(x)\overline{B}(x)) = \kappa_z(A(b)\overline{B}(b)) = \kappa_z(\omega_b),$$
$$\kappa_z(\omega'_a) = \kappa_z(A(a)\overline{B}(a)) > \kappa_z(A(a)B(a)) = \kappa_z(\omega_a),$$
$$\kappa_z(\omega'_b) = \kappa_z(A(b)B(b)) > \kappa_z(A(b)\overline{B}(b)) = \kappa_z(\omega_b),$$

where ω_a and ω'_a differ only in the D_i-component with $\lambda_i(\omega_a) < \lambda_i(\omega'_a)$ and all other λ_j-components chosen minimal, while ω_b and ω'_b differ only in the D_k-component with $\lambda_k(\omega_b) < \lambda_k(\omega'_b)$ and all other λ_j-components chosen minimal. For all $j > k (> i)$, we have $\lambda_j(\omega'_a) = \lambda_j(\omega'_b)$, since both components were chosen minimal. For the kth component, we have $\lambda_k(\omega'_a) = \lambda_k(\omega_a) = \lambda_k(\omega_b) < \lambda_k(\omega'_b)$. Hence $\kappa_z(\omega'_a) < \kappa_z(\omega'_b)$ which shows inequality (5) from condition *(Acc-2)* in Definition 5. Therefore, $\kappa_z \models r$.

□

Note that condition *(C2)* of Theorem 1 transfers the idea of tolerance on which system Z is based to the first-order setting. Since we do not give an algorithm how to construct the partitionings of Theorem 1, several κ_z-models of $\mathcal{R}$ are possible. Providing such an algorithm and determining a unique κ_z-model of $\mathcal{R}$, maybe equipped with properties that characterize it among all models of $\mathcal{R}$, as in the propositional case, is left for future work.

5 Examples

We demonstrate the κ_z construction introduced in the previous section by a well-known example (see also [13]).

Fig. 1. Illustration of possibly flying penguins (by Silja Isberner in [2, page 259])

Example 2 (Penguins and super-penguins (cont'd)). We extend Example 1 where we introduced *penguins (P), birds (B)* and also *(flying) super-penguins (S)* as well as *winged things (W)* and *flying things (F)*. Our universe consists of the following objects resp. constants $D = \{p, t, s\}$ with $t = $ *Tweety*, $p = $ *Polly*, $s = $ *Supertweety*. The knowledge base $\mathcal{KB}_{tweety} = \langle \mathcal{F}, \mathcal{R} \rangle$ consists of the facts

$$\mathcal{F} = \{B(p), P(t), S(s), \forall x S(x) \Rightarrow P(x), \forall x P(x) \Rightarrow B(x)\},$$

and the conditional knowledge base $\mathcal{R} = \{r_1, r_2, r_3, r_4\}$ containing four open first-order conditionals already given in Example 1:

$$
\begin{aligned}
r_1 &: \ (F(x) \mid B(x)) \\
r_2 &: \ (W(x) \mid B(x)) \\
r_3 &: \ (\overline{F}(x) \mid P(x)) \\
r_4 &: \ (F(x) \mid S(x))
\end{aligned}
$$

Precondition *(C1)* of Theorem 1 is clearly satisfied for this knowledge base.

The set Ω of possible worlds consists of all ω of the form

$$\omega = \underbrace{B(p)\dot{F}(p)\dot{P}(p)\dot{S}(p)\dot{W}(p)}_{\omega(p)} \underbrace{B(t)\dot{F}(t)P(t)\dot{S}(t)\dot{W}(t)}_{\omega(t)} \underbrace{B(s)\dot{F}(s)P(s)S(s)\dot{W}(s)}_{\omega(s)},$$

where the dotted predicates indicate that both verification and falsification of the respective atom is possible. Let partitionings of $\mathcal{R}$ and D be given as follows:

$$
\begin{aligned}
\mathcal{R}_0 &= \{r_1, r_2\}, \quad D_0 = \{p\}, \\
\mathcal{R}_1 &= \{r_3\}, \qquad D_1 = \{t\}, \\
\mathcal{R}_2 &= \{r_4\}, \qquad D_2 = \{s\}.
\end{aligned}
$$

Consider the world

$$\omega_0 = \underbrace{B(p)F(p)\overline{P}(p)\overline{S}(p)W(p)}_{\omega_0(p)} \underbrace{B(t)\overline{F}(t)P(t)\overline{S}(t)W(t)}_{\omega_0(t)} \underbrace{B(s)F(s)P(s)S(s)W(s)}_{\omega_0(s)}.$$

We can easily check that precondition *(C2)* of Theorem 1 holds by choosing ω_0 for each conditional. For r_1 and r_2 which are both in R_0, we then have to check that ω_0 verifies $(F(p) \mid B(p))$ and $(W(p) \mid B(p))$ and that it does not falsify $(F(p) \mid B(p))$, $(W(p) \mid B(p))$, $(\overline{F}(p) \mid P(p))$, or $(F(p) \mid S(p))$, which obviously holds. For $r_3 \in R_1$, we observe that ω_0 verifies $(\overline{F}(t) \mid P(t))$ and that it does not falsify $(\overline{F}(t) \mid P(t))$ or $(F(t) \mid S(t))$. For $r_4 \in R_2$, we observe that ω_0 verifies $(F(s) \mid S(s))$ and that it does not falsify $(F(s) \mid S(s))$.

Since in ω_0, no p-instance of a conditional in $\mathcal{R}$ is falsified we get $\lambda_0(\omega_o) = 0$. Since $(F(t) \mid B(t))$ is falsified by ω_0 and $(F(x) \mid B(x)) \in R_0$ and since no other t-instance of a conditional in $\mathcal{R}$ is falsified by ω_0 we get $\lambda_1(\omega_o) = 1$. Finally, since $(F(s) \mid P(s))$ is falsified by ω_0 and $(\overline{F}(x) \mid P(x)) \in R_1$ and since no other s-instance of a conditional in $\mathcal{R}$ is falsified by ω_0 we get $\lambda_2(\omega_o) = 2$.

Since $m = 2$, κ_z is defined by

$$\kappa_z(\omega) = \sum_{i=0}^{2} 4^i \lambda_i(\omega) - \kappa_0, \quad \kappa_0 = \min_{\omega \in \Omega} \sum_{i=0}^{2} 4^i \lambda_i(\omega).$$

Given that all ω have to satisfy $\mathcal{F}$, i.e., all ω have to satisfy $B(p)B(t)P(t)B(s)P(s)S(s)$, it is clear that ω_0 minimizes the sum in the expression defining κ_0, so we get $\kappa_0 = \sum_{i=0}^{2} 4^i \lambda_i(\omega_0) = 36$ since $\kappa_z(\omega_0) \sim (0, 1, 2)$.

To verify that indeed $\kappa_z \models \mathcal{R}$ according to the semantics defined in Section 3, the following table lists all relevant ground formulas ϕ for each conditional $r_i \in \mathcal{R}$. For each ϕ, the λ_i-components of its minimal models and the resulting κ_z value for ϕ is given:

	ϕ	$(\lambda_0, \lambda_1, \lambda_2)$	$\kappa_z(\phi)$
$r_1:$	$B(p)F(p)$	$(0, 1, 2)$	0
	$B(t)F(t)$	$(0, 2, 2)$	4
	$B(s)F(s)$	$(0, 1, 2)$	0
	$B(p)\overline{F}(p)$	$(1, 1, 2)$	1
	$B(t)\overline{F}(t)$	$(0, 1, 2)$	0
	$B(s)\overline{F}(s)$	$(0, 1, 3)$	16
$r_2:$	$B(p)W(p)$	$(0, 1, 2)$	0
	$B(t)W(t)$	$(0, 1, 2)$	0
	$B(s)W(s)$	$(0, 1, 2)$	0
	$B(p)\overline{W}(p)$	$(1, 1, 2)$	1
	$B(t)\overline{W}(t)$	$(0, 1, 2)$	0
	$B(s)\overline{W}(s)$	$(0, 1, 2)$	0
$r_3:$	$P(p)\overline{F}(p)$	$(1, 1, 2)$	1
	$P(t)\overline{F}(t)$	$(0, 1, 2)$	0
	$P(s)\overline{F}(s)$	$(0, 1, 3)$	16
	$P(p)F(p)$	$(2, 1, 2)$	2
	$P(t)F(t)$	$(0, 2, 2)$	4
	$P(s)F(s)$	$(0, 1, 2)$	0
$r_4:$	$S(p)F(p)$	$(2, 1, 2)$	2
	$S(t)F(t)$	$(0, 2, 2)$	4
	$S(s)F(s)$	$(0, 1, 2)$	0
	$S(p)\overline{F}(p)$	$(3, 1, 2)$	3
	$S(t)\overline{F}(t)$	$(0, 3, 2)$	8
	$S(s)\overline{F}(s)$	$(0, 1, 3)$	16

From this table, we find

- for r_1, that $\kappa_z(B(x)F(x)) = \kappa_z(B(x)\overline{F}(x)) = 0$ with $WRep(r_1) = \{p, s\}$ but $Rep(r_1) = \{p\}$, and $WRep(\overline{r_1}) = \{t\} = Rep(\overline{r_1})$ and hence $\kappa_z \models r_1$ since $\kappa_z(B(p)\overline{F}(p)) = 1 < 4 = \kappa_z(B(t)F(t))$;
- for r_2, that $\kappa_z(B(x)W(x)) = \kappa_z(B(x)\overline{W}(x)) = 0$ with $WRep(r_2) = \{p\} = Rep(r_2)$, but $WRep(\overline{r_2}) = Rep(\overline{r_2}) = \emptyset$, so condition *(Acc-2)* from Definition 5 is satisfied trivially, and $\kappa_z \models r_2$;

- for r_3, that $\kappa_z(P(x)\overline{F}(x)) = \kappa_z(P(x)F(x)) = 0$ with $WRep(r_3) = \{t\} = Rep(r_3)$ and $WRep(\overline{r_3}) = \{s\} = Rep(\overline{r_3})$, furthermore $\kappa_z(P(t)F(t)) = 4 < 16 = \kappa_z(P(s)\overline{F}(s))$ and so $\kappa_z \models r_3$;
- for r_4, that $\kappa_z(S(x)F(x)) = 0 < 3 = \kappa_z(S(x)\overline{F}(x))$ and hence immediately $\kappa_z \models r_4$.

Finally, it is interesting to check whether κ_z allows us to find out if penguins have wings. For in the propositional case, system Z is known to suffer from the so-called *drowning problem* [10]: as penguins are exceptional birds, the propositional system Z cannot decide whether penguins have wings or not. So, let us consider the conditional $r_5 = (W(x)|P(x))$. Here, we find that $\kappa_z(P(p)W(p)) = \kappa_z(P(p)\overline{W}(p)) = 1$ (with λ_i-vector $(1, 1, 2)$, and for both t and s, we compute $\kappa_z(P(t)W(t)) = \kappa_z(P(t)\overline{W}(t)) = 0 = \kappa_z(P(s)W(s)) = \kappa_z(P(s)\overline{W}(s))$. So, there is not even a single instance such that the conditional can be verified or falsified, i.e., κ_z is completely undecided with respect to penguins having wings. Note that in [13] it was shown that the approach of c-representations is able to overcome this problem, same as for the propositional case.

6   Conclusions and Future Work

For knowledge bases consisting of propositional default rules in the form of qualitative conditionals, system Z [15,10] provides a popular and attractive method for inductive reasoning. Thus, when moving from propositional to first-order conditionals, it is worthwhile to investigate whether the advantages of system Z can also be revealed in such an extended setting. In this paper, we argued that for the case of unary predicates, the conditional semantics proposed in [13] allows for a system Z-like approach to first-order default reasoning. In addition to a knowledge base with facts and open conditionals we assume that a set of constants is given. Using the notion of a representative for a conditional, we showed how a ranking function in the spirit of system Z can be constructed, and we proved that this construction indead yields a model of the knowledge base.

In the propositional case of system Z, the notion of tolerance induces both a criterion for the consistency of a knowledge base and a unique partitioning of the conditionals which is used in the computation of the ranking function. In the extended first-order setting of this paper, we assume that corresponding partitionings of the conditionals in $\mathcal{R}$ and of the domain elements are given. According to Theorem 1, the existence of such a pair of partitionings implies the consistency of $\mathcal{R}$.

While for the situation given in Example 2, the considered pair of partitionings seems to be unique, in general, there may be several different such partitionings, possibly leading to different ranking functions. For instance, after removing the specific knowledge about *Tweety*, *Polly*, and *Supertweety* from the knowledge base $\mathcal{KB}_{tweety}$ in Example 2, the three constants t, p and s are pairwise exchangeable; hence, different partitionings leading to different ranking functions can be obtained. Our current work includes the development of criteria for the existence of a pair of partitionings fulfilling condition *(C2)* of Theorem 1, and the design of an algorithm computing such pairs. A further open problem is how the possibly different ranking functions obtained from different partitionings of the conditionals and the domain elements may be ordered by a preference relation, and whether such a preference ordering will lead to a unique ranking function for $\mathcal{R}$.

Acknowledgements. We would like to thank the anonymous referees of this paper for their helpful comments and valuable suggestions.

References

1. Adams, E.: Probability and the logic of conditionals. In: Hintikka, J., Suppes, P. (eds.) Aspects of Inductive Logic, pp. 265–316. North-Holland, Amsterdam (1966)
2. Beierle, C., Kern-Isberner, G.: Methoden wissensbasierter Systeme - Grundlagen, Algorithmen, Anwendungen, 5th, revised and extended edn. Springer, Wiesbaden (2014)
3. Bonatti, P., Faella, M., Sauro, L.: Defeasible inclusions in low-complexity DLs. Journal of Artificial Intelligence Research 42, 719–764 (2011)
4. Brewka, G.: Tweety - still flying: Some remarks on abnormal birds applicable rules and a default prover. In: Kehler, T. (ed.) Proceedings of the 5th National Conference on Artificial Intelligence, Philadelphia, PA, August 11-15. Science, vol. 1, pp. 8–12. Morgan Kaufmann (1986)
5. Britz, K., Heidema, J., Meyer, T.: Semantic preferential subsumption. In: Proceedings of KR-2008. pp. 476–484. AAAI Press/MIT Press (2008)
6. Delgrande, J.: On first-order conditional logics. Artificial Intelligence 105, 105–137 (1998)
7. de Finetti, B.: La prévision, ses lois logiques et ses sources subjectives. Ann. Inst. H. Poincaré 7 (1937), English translation in Kyburg, H., Smokler, H.E.: Studies in Subjective Probability, pp. 93-158. Wiley, New York (1964)
8. Gelfond, M., Leone, N.: Logic programming and knowledge representation – the A-prolog perspective. Artificial Intelligence 138, 3–38 (2002)
9. Giordano, L., Gliozzi, V., Olivetti, N.: Minimal model semantics and rational closure in description logics. In: Proceedings of DL-2013 (2013)
10. Goldszmidt, M., Pearl, J.: Qualitative probabilities for default reasoning, belief revision, and causal modeling. Artificial Intelligence 84, 57–112 (1996)
11. Kern-Isberner, G.: A thorough axiomatization of a principle of conditional preservation in belief revision. Annals of Mathematics and Artificial Intelligence 40(1-2), 127–164 (2004)
12. Kern-Isberner, G., Eichhorn, C.: Structural inference from conditional knowledge bases. Studia Logica, Special Issue Logic and Probability: Reasoning in Uncertain Environments 102(4) (2014)
13. Kern-Isberner, G., Thimm, M.: A ranking semantics for first-order conditionals. In: De Raedt, L., Bessiere, C., Dubois, D., Doherty, P., Frasconi, P., Heintz, F., Lucas, P. (eds.) Proceedings 20th European Conference on Artificial Intelligence, ECAI-2012. Frontiers in Artificial Intelligence and Applications, vol. 242, pp. 456–461. IOS Press (2012)
14. Lehmann, D., Magidor, M.: What does a conditional knowledge base entail? Artificial Intelligence 55, 1–60 (1992)
15. Pearl, J.: System Z: A natural ordering of defaults with tractable applications to nonmonotonic reasoning. In: Proc. of the 3rd Conf. on Theor. Asp. of Reasoning about Knowledge, TARK 1990, pp. 121–135. Morgan Kaufmann Publishers Inc., San Francisco (1990)
16. Spohn, W.: Ordinal conditional functions: a dynamic theory of epistemic states. In: Harper, W., Skyrms, B. (eds.) Causation in Decision, Belief Change, and Statistics, II, pp. 105–134. Kluwer Academic Publishers (1988)
17. Spohn, W.: The Laws of Belief: Ranking Theory and Its Philosophical Applications. Oxford University Press (2012)

Cumulativity Tailored for Nonmonotonic Reasoning*

Tomi Janhunen and Ilkka Niemelä

Helsinki Institute for Information Technology HIIT
Department of Information and Computer Science
Aalto University, 00076 AALTO, Finland
{Tomi.Janhunen,Ilkka.Niemela}@aalto.fi

Abstract. In nonmonotonic reasoning, conclusions can be retracted when new pieces of information are incorporated into premises. This contrasts with classical reasoning which is monotonic, i.e., new premises can only increase the set of conclusions that can be drawn. Slightly weaker properties, such as cumulativity and rationality, seem reasonable counterparts of such a monotonicity property for nonmonotonic reasoning but intriguingly it turned out that some major nonmonotonic logics failed to be cumulative. These observations led to the study of variants in hope of restoring cumulativity but not losing other essential properties. In this paper, we take a fresh view on cumulativity by starting from a notion of rule entailment in the context of answer set programs. It turns out that cumulativity can be revived if the expressive precision of rules subject to answer set semantics is fully exploited when new premises are being incorporated. Even stronger properties can be established and we illustrate how the approach can be generalized for major nonmonotonic logics.

1 Introduction

Nonmonotonicity is a frequently appearing phenomenon, e.g., in commonsense reasoning, reasoning by default, diagnostic reasoning, etc. The typical pattern is that earlier conclusions may have to be retracted upon the incorporation of new premises, typically emerging from new observations about the domain of interest. This contrasts with the *monotonicity*[1] of classical logic and indicates that classical logic is as such insufficient for certain applications. The study of nonmonotonicity was put forth by the introduction of *nonmonotonic logics* [19,21,24] as well as nonmonotonic classes of logic programs [9,10,17]. The abstract properties of nonmonotonic formalisms were of interest and soon *cumulativity* [15] was proposed as a desired property of nonmonotonic reasoning once monotonicity was being renounced. Cumulativity can be understood as a combination of two principles called *cautious monotony* and *cut*. They are formulated below for a prototypical consequence relation $\mathrel{|\!\sim}$, a set of premises Σ, and sentences φ and χ.

Cautious monotony: If $\Sigma \mathrel{|\!\sim} \varphi$ and $\Sigma \mathrel{|\!\sim} \chi$, then $\Sigma \cup \{\varphi\} \mathrel{|\!\sim} \chi$.
Cut: If $\Sigma \mathrel{|\!\sim} \varphi$ and $\Sigma \cup \{\varphi\} \mathrel{|\!\sim} \chi$, then $\Sigma \mathrel{|\!\sim} \chi$.

---

* The support from the Finnish Centre of Excellence in Computational Inference Research (COIN) funded by the Academy of Finland (under grant #251170) is gratefully acknowledged.
[1] Formally, $\Sigma \vdash \varphi$ and $\Sigma \subseteq \Gamma$ imply $\Gamma \vdash \varphi$.

T. Eiter et al. (Eds.): Brewka Festschrift, LNAI 9060, pp. 96–111, 2015.

The classical consequence relation $\vdash$ is cumulative besides being monotonic. By defining the set of consequences $\mathrm{Cn}(\Sigma) = \{\chi \in \mathcal{L} \mid \Sigma \vdash \chi\}$, cumulativity is expressed by the equation $\mathrm{Cn}(\Sigma) = \mathrm{Cn}(\Sigma \cup \{\varphi\})$ for every sentence φ such that $\Sigma \vdash \varphi$. In words, if $\Sigma \vdash \varphi$, then φ is *redundant* in view of adding it to Σ as the set of consequences $\mathrm{Cn}(\Sigma)$ remains unchanged. Thus, adding φ does not seem reasonable for the sake of compact representation, but φ could also act as a *lemma* boosting further inference from Σ.

The KLM postulates [15] led to a vivid study of cumulativity in the context of non-monotonic logics and logic programs (see, e.g., [1,2,3,4,5,12,14]). Unfortunately, only few positive results were established: McCarthy's *circumscription* [19], logic programs under the *well-founded semantics* [8], and *stratified* nonmonotonic inference [2] turned out to be cumulative. But otherwise, nonmonotonic formalisms failed to be cumulative and typically this was due to lack of cautious monotony. Our first example provides a counter-example in the case of logic programs subject to stable model semantics [9], but the example was first illustrated in the context of *truth maintenance systems*.

Example 1 (Brewka et al. [2]). Consider a logic program P having the following rules:

$$a \leftarrow {\sim}b. \qquad c \leftarrow a. \qquad b \leftarrow c, {\sim}a.$$

The program has a unique stable model $M = \{a, c\}$, which makes a and c *cautious* consequences of P. If, however, we add c as a fact to P, we obtain another stable model $\{b, c\}$ and thus a is not a *cautious consequence* of $P \cup \{c \leftarrow\}$ (cf. Definition 2 for a standard definition of cautious consequence). ∎

Analogous counter-examples can be devised, e.g., for Reiter's *default logic* [24] and Moore's *autoepistemic logic* [21]. Consequently, many variants of nonmonotonic formalisms were devised, aiming to restore cumulativity in a way or another. For instance, new cumulative semantics were proposed but no clear solution was found because other desirable properties of reasoning were sacrificed. Tackling the failure of cautious monotony at meta level typically increased the computational time complexity of main reasoning problems. Brewka [1] pointed out the role of witnessing justifications and he managed to restore cumulativity in a variant of default logic where justifications are incorporated into premises in addition to actual consequences.

In this paper, we take a fresh view on cumulativity and study it from the perspective of *rule entailment*, which is based on the idea of *redundancy* [13] as discussed above in the case of classical (monotonic) logic. More formally, a rule r is *entailed* by a program P, denoted by $P \mapsto r$, if and only if r is *redundant* in the context of P, i.e., programs P and $P \cup \{r\}$ have exactly the same stable models [9]. The resulting notion of entailment is inherently different from classical entailment. According to a characterization to be presented later, $P \mapsto r$ *implies* that r is satisfied by every stable model of P but, in general, $P \mapsto r$ is a stronger relation than satisfaction under stable models. Rule entailment from P and the gap with respect to satisfaction under the stable models of P are illustrated by the following example.

Example 2. The rule $a \leftarrow c, {\sim}d$ is entailed by a program P_1 having the rules[2] $a \leftarrow b$; $b \leftarrow c$; and $c \leftarrow {\sim}d$ because both P_1 and $P_1 \cup \{a \leftarrow c, {\sim}d\}$ have a unique stable

---

[2] From time to time, we use ";" as a rule separator to avoid confusion with "," in rule bodies.

model $\{a, b, c\}$. The fact $a \leftarrow$ is not entailed by a program P_2 having a single rule $a \leftarrow \sim a$, because P_2 has no stable models and $P_2 \cup \{a \leftarrow\}$ has a unique stable model $\{a\}$. But $a \leftarrow$ is trivially satisfied in every stable model of P since there are none. ∎

The second program in Example 2 demonstrates an interesting special case, i.e., the entailment $P \mapsto a \leftarrow$ of a fact $a \leftarrow$ for an atom $a \in \text{At}(P)$ of interest. This particular example shows that being a cautious consequence, denoted by $P \mathrel{\vert\!\sim_c} a$, does not necessarily imply $P \mapsto a \leftarrow$. The key observation is that $P \mathrel{\vert\!\sim_c} a$ does not entitle us to add a fact $a \leftarrow$ in a program. Doing so may affect stable models as it is clear by the second program of Example 2. Our hypothesis is that the failure of cumulativity for stable semantics goes back to this mismatch. In other words, adding a fact $a \leftarrow$ in the face of $P \mathrel{\vert\!\sim_c} a$ does not take into account the potential defeasibilty of the conclusion a and thus can be considered as a misinterpretation of KLM postulates in the context of logic programs subject to stable semantics. In this paper, we will establish that $P \mathrel{\vert\!\sim_c} a$ coincides with the rule entailment $P \mapsto a \leftarrow \sim a$ and suggest that a cautious consequence $P \mathrel{\vert\!\sim_c} a$ should be recorded as a rule $a \leftarrow \sim a$ rather than a fact $a \leftarrow$. This observation allows us to rewrite the principles of *cautious monotony* and *cut* as follows:

Restricted cautious monotony: If $P \mathrel{\vert\!\sim_c} a$ and $P \mathrel{\vert\!\sim_c} b$, then $P \cup \{a \leftarrow \sim a\} \mathrel{\vert\!\sim_c} b$.
Restricted cut: If $P \mathrel{\vert\!\sim_c} a$ and $P \cup \{a \leftarrow \sim a\} \mathrel{\vert\!\sim_c} b$, then $P \mathrel{\vert\!\sim_c} b$.

This is to say that stable semantics is cumulative if the respective KLM rules are interpreted in the right way. Actually, much stronger abstract properties can be established if cautious consequences are incorporated into the underlying logic program in the way described above. In this paper, we investigate this idea further as follows. First, we introduce a simple class of logic programs in Section 2 and review the basic notions of stable model semantics. The notion of rule entailment is recalled and elaborated for the purposes of this paper in Section 3. The cautious entailment based on stable models is then characterized in a number of ways using rule entailment in Section 4. The emphasis, however, is on positive consequences whereas the negative ones are covered in Section 5. As a result, both positive and negative consequences can be incorporated into programs in a systematic and symmetric way. The connection to search procedures for stable models is also worked out using the tableau method as the conceptual model. Potential generalizations for other forms of nonmonotonic reasoning are considered in Section 6. Related work is briefly addressed in Section 7. Finally, the conclusions of the paper are presented in Section 8.

2   Preliminaries

The goal of this section is to introduce the class of logic programs of interest in the propositional case. We aim at a minimal generalization of *normal programs* that is still sufficient for characterization results to be presented in Section 4 and leave other classes of programs to be addressed in Section 6. Our rules of interest are of three forms

$$a \leftarrow b_1, \ldots, b_m, \sim c_1, \ldots, \sim c_n. \tag{1}$$
$$\{a_1, \ldots, a_l\} \leftarrow b_1, \ldots, b_m, \sim c_1, \ldots, \sim c_n. \tag{2}$$
$$\leftarrow b_1, \ldots, b_m, \sim c_1, \ldots, \sim c_n. \tag{3}$$

where a, a_i's, b_j's, and c_k's are *propositional atoms*, or *atoms* for short. Atoms are also called *positive literals* whereas their negations formed in terms of $\sim$ are *negative literals*. Rules of the form (1) are called *normal* and they allow the derivation of the *head* a in case that the *body* of the rule is satisfied, i.e., $b_1, \ldots, b_m$ are derivable by other rules and none of $c_1, \ldots, c_n$ are derivable. A normal rule is *positive*, if $n = 0$, and a *fact*, if $m = n = 0$. A *choice rule* of the form (2) is similar except that any subset of the head atoms $a_1, \ldots, a_l$ can be derived upon the satisfaction of the rule body. An integrity constraint (3) with an empty head, denoting contradiction, essentially states that its body is never satisfied. We call logic programs consisting of the rule types above *normal choice-constraint* programs, or NCC programs for short.

The meaning of NCC programs depends on the context and to make that precise, we proceed to the definition of *stable models* first introduced for normal programs [9]. The *signature* of a logic program P is denoted by $\mathrm{At}(P)$ and it is assumed that the rules of P contain atoms from this set only. An *interpretation* I of P is any subset of $\mathrm{At}(P)$ determining which atoms a are true ($a \in I$) and which false ($a \notin I$). A negative literal $\sim c$ is satisfied in I, denoted $I \models \sim c$, iff $c \notin I$. A normal rule (1) is satisfied by I iff $\{b_1, \ldots, b_m\} \subseteq I$ and $\{c_1, \ldots, c_n\} \cap I = \emptyset$ imply $a \in I$. A choice rule (2) is always satisfied by I. An integrity constraint (3) is satisfied by I iff $\{b_1, \ldots, b_m\} \not\subseteq I$ or $\{c_1, \ldots, c_n\} \cap I \neq \emptyset$. An interpretation $M \subseteq \mathrm{At}(P)$ is a *model* of a program P, denoted $M \models P$, iff $M \models r$ for every rule $r \in P$. A model $M \models P$ is *minimal* iff there is no other model $N \models P$ such that $N \subset M$. Every *positive* program P solely consisting of positive rules of the form $a \leftarrow b_1, \ldots, b_m$ is guaranteed to have a unique minimal model, the *least* model of P, denoted by $\mathrm{LM}(P)$. Given a normal rule r of the form (1) and an interpretation $I \subseteq \mathrm{At}(P)$, the Gelfond-Lifschitz reduct r^I of r with respect to I is the program containing the single positive rule $a \leftarrow b_1, \ldots, b_m$ iff $\{c_1, \ldots, c_n\} \cap I = \emptyset$, and $\emptyset$ otherwise. For a choice rule r of the form (2), the reduct r^I contains a positive rule $a_i \leftarrow b_1, \ldots, b_m$ iff $I \models a_i$ and $\{c_1, \ldots, c_n\} \cap I = \emptyset$. The reduct r^I of an integrity constraint r of the form (3) is always $\emptyset$. For an entire NCC program P, the reduct P^I of P with respect to I is defined as the union $\bigcup_{r \in P} r^I$.

Definition 1 (Stable Models [9,26]). *An interpretation $M \subseteq \mathrm{At}(P)$ is a stable model of an NCC program P iff $M \models P$ and $M = \mathrm{LM}(P^M)$.*

The number of stable models may vary in general and hence we denote the set of stable models of a program P by $\mathrm{SM}(P)$.

Definition 2. *Given a logic program P, a literal l based on $\mathrm{At}(P)$ is*

1. *cautious consequence of P iff $M \models l$ for every stable model $M \in \mathrm{SM}(P)$, and*
2. *brave consequence of P iff $M \models l$ for some stable model $M \in \mathrm{SM}(P)$.*

We use notations $P \mathrel{|\!\sim_c} l$ and $P \mathrel{|\!\sim_b} l$, respectively, to denote that a literal l is a cautious/brave consequence of a program P. Deciding whether a literal l is a cautious/brave consequence of a finite normal program P forms a coNP/NP-complete decision problem. This is the case for NCC programs, too, based on the complexity results concerning SMODELS programs [26]. The effects of choice rules are illustrated next.

Example 3. The program P consisting of a single choice rule $\{a\} \leftarrow$ has two stable models $M_1 = \emptyset$ and $M_2 = \{a\}$ justified by $P^{M_1} = \emptyset$ and $P^{M_2} = \{a \leftarrow\}$. ∎

Example 3 shows how one can express *choices* under stable model semantics. The atom a can be either true or false which is exceptional under stable model semantics which assigns atoms *false by default*. Given the choice rule $\{a\} \leftarrow$, the atom a behaves classically as there is no longer asymmetry between its truth values. This feature can be exploited, e.g., when reducing instances of the Boolean satisfiability (SAT) problem into NCC programs. Such a rule would then be introduced for each atom involved in the clauses or, alternatively, all atoms $a_1, \ldots, a_l$ occuring in the clauses could be incorporated into one global choice rule (2) with an empty body, i.e., $m = n = 0$. A further by-product of choice rules is that the *antichain* property of stable models is lost. Indeed, Example 3 illustrates two stable models in a proper subset relation. Such a setting cannot arise in the case of pure normal programs.

When NCC programs or logic programs in general are compared with each other, two natural notions of equivalence arise from stable model semantics. Programs P and Q are considered to be *weakly equivalent* if and only if $\mathrm{SM}(P) = \mathrm{SM}(Q)$. The notion of *strong equivalence* [16] introduces an arbitrary context program R in this setting: programs P and R are strongly equivalent if and only if $\mathrm{SM}(P \cup R) = \mathrm{SM}(Q \cup R)$ for any R. Strong equivalence (SE) can be characterized in terms of *SE-models* [27,28] that generalize for NCC programs given the definitions presented so far. A pair of interpretations $\langle X, Y \rangle$ where $X \subseteq Y \subseteq \mathrm{At}(P)$ is an SE-model of a program P iff $Y \models P$ and $X \models P^Y$. This is a generalization of classical models, since for each $X \models P$ we have $\langle X, X \rangle \models P$. By Turner's results [27,28], we know that P and Q are strongly equivalent iff they have exactly the same SE-models. It is also possible to define a notion of entailment based on SE-models. For an atom $a \in \mathrm{At}(P)$, $P \models_{\mathrm{se}} a$ iff $a \in X$ for every SE-model $\langle X, Y \rangle \models P$. Generalizing for a rule r such that $\mathrm{At}(r) \subseteq \mathrm{At}(P)$, $\langle X, Y \rangle \models_{\mathrm{se}} r$ iff $Y \models r$ and $X \models r^Y$ for every SE-model $\langle X, Y \rangle \models P$.

3   Rule Entailment

As discussed in the introduction, the notion of rule entailment parallels that of *rule redundancy* [13] in analogy to classical logic. Our next goal is to present the respective notions for programs and rules and to characterize the resulting entailment relation $\mapsto$.

Definition 3. *A rule r is entailed by a program P, denoted by $P \mapsto r$, if and only if* $\mathrm{SM}(P) = \mathrm{SM}(P \cup \{r\})$.

Example 4. Consider a program P based on the following rules:

$$a \leftarrow \sim b. \qquad b \leftarrow \sim c. \qquad c \leftarrow d. \qquad d \leftarrow a.$$

The stable models of P are $M_1 = \{a, c, d\}$ and $M_2 = \{b\}$. The rule $a \leftarrow d$ is entailed by P because we have that $\mathrm{SM}(P) = \mathrm{SM}(P \cup \{a \leftarrow d\})$.   ∎

Lemma 1. *Let P be a positive program and r a positive rule such that $\mathrm{At}(r) \subseteq \mathrm{At}(P)$. Then $\mathrm{LM}(P) \models r$ if and only if $\mathrm{LM}(P) = \mathrm{LM}(P \cup \{r\})$.*

Proof. Let $M = \mathrm{LM}(P)$ which implies $M \models P$. ($\Longrightarrow$) Let $M \models r$ hold. Now $M \subseteq \mathrm{LM}(P \cup \{r\})$ follows by the monotonicity of $\mathrm{LM}(\cdot)$. Since $M \models P$ and $M \models r$ we have $\mathrm{LM}(P \cup \{r\}) \subseteq M$. ($\Longleftarrow$) Clearly, $M = \mathrm{LM}(P \cup \{r\})$ implies $M \models r$.   □

Proposition 1. *For a program P and a rule r such that* $\mathrm{At}(r) \subseteq \mathrm{At}(P)$, $P \mapsto r$ *iff*

1. $M \models r$ *for every* $M \in \mathrm{SM}(P)$ *and*
2. $\mathrm{LM}(P^M) \models r^M$ *for every* $M \in \mathrm{SM}(P \cup \{r\})$.

Proof. Given the characterization from [13], it is sufficient to establish that for every $M \in \mathrm{SM}(P \cup \{r\})$, $\mathrm{LM}(P^M) \models r^M$ if and only if $M = \mathrm{LM}(P^M)$. Since both P^M and r^M are positive and $\mathrm{At}(r^M) \subseteq \mathrm{At}(P^M)$, this relationship holds by Lemma 1.   □

Intuitively speaking, $P \mapsto r$ demands that r is satisfied in every stable model of P and, *in addition*, given any stable model M of $P \cup \{r\}$, the least model $\mathrm{LM}(P^M) \subseteq M$ is closed under r^M, i.e., $\mathrm{LM}(P^M) = M$. The second part essentially requires that P *without* r is able to simulate r in the very contexts created by stable models of $P \cup \{r\}$. For the program P_1 in Example 2, we note that $\mathrm{LM}(P_1^{\{a,b,c\}}) = \mathrm{LM}(\{a \leftarrow b;\ b \leftarrow c;\ c \leftarrow\}) = \{a, b, c\}$ is closed by $(a \leftarrow c, \sim d)^{\{a,b,c\}} = \{a \leftarrow c\}$.

As far as additions of rules are concerned, the relation $\mapsto$ is not (cautiously) monotonic in general, nor does it satisfy the cut property. Counter-examples for the abstract properties of interest are provided by the following example. The immediate observation is that $\mapsto$ in the raw does not provide us with a cumulative consequence relation.

Example 5. To illustrate the failure of cautious monotonicity, let us reconsider the program $P_2 = \{a \leftarrow \sim a\}$ from Example 1 under the assumption that $\mathrm{At}(P_2) = \{a, b\}$. It is clear that $P_2 \mapsto \{a\} \leftarrow b$ and $P_2 \mapsto b \leftarrow$, because adding either rule to P_2 will not affect its stable models, i.e., there are none. However, adding both rules to P_2 gives rise to a unique stable model $M = \{a, b\}$ justified by the rules $a \leftarrow b$ and $b \leftarrow$ in the reduct. Thus, we have symmetrically $P_2 \cup \{\{a\} \leftarrow b\} \not\mapsto b \leftarrow$ and $P_2 \cup \{b \leftarrow\} \not\mapsto \{a\} \leftarrow b$, indicating that $\mapsto$ is not cautiously monotone.

For the lack of the cut property, recall the program P from Example 1. Since $\mathrm{SM}(P) = \mathrm{SM}(P \cup \{a \leftarrow\}) = \mathrm{SM}(P \cup \{a \leftarrow, c \leftarrow\})$, we have $P \mapsto a \leftarrow$ and $P \cup \{a \leftarrow\} \mapsto c \leftarrow$. On the other hand, $\mathrm{SM}(P) \subset \mathrm{SM}(P \cup \{c \leftarrow\})$ so that $P \not\mapsto c \leftarrow$.   ∎

Proposition 2. *For a program P and a rule r such that* $\mathrm{At}(r) \subseteq \mathrm{At}(P)$, $P \models_{\mathrm{se}} r$ *implies* $P \mapsto r$ *but not necessarily vice versa.*

Proof. Let $P \models_{\mathrm{se}} r$ hold and assume that $P \not\mapsto r$, i.e., by Proposition 1 (i) $M \not\models r$ for some $M \in \mathrm{SM}(P)$ or (ii) $\mathrm{LM}(P^M) \not\models r^M$ for some $M \in \mathrm{SM}(P \cup \{r\})$.

In the case (i), $M \in \mathrm{SM}(P)$ implies $M \models P^M$ which makes $\langle M, M \rangle$ an SE-model of P. In addition, $M \not\models r$ implies $M \not\models r^M$ and $P \not\models_{\mathrm{se}} r$, a contradiction.

In the case (ii), $M \in \mathrm{SM}(P \cup \{r\})$ implies $M = \mathrm{LM}(P^M \cup r^M)$. The monotonicity of $\mathrm{LM}(\cdot)$ implies that $N = \mathrm{LM}(P^M) \subseteq M$ and since $N \not\models r^M$, it must be the case that $r^M \neq \emptyset$ and $N \subset M$. It follows that $\langle N, M \rangle \not\models_{\mathrm{se}} r$, a contradiction.

To see that the converse implication does not hold in general, recall the program P and the rule $a \leftarrow d$ from Example 4. We have $P \not\models_{\mathrm{se}} r$ witnessed, e.g., by a classical model $X = \{b, c, d\}$ of P such that $\langle X, X \rangle \not\models a \leftarrow d$.   □

It is clear by the preceding analysis that rule entailment is much more specific to the given program P than SE-entailment, which also covers potential extensions of P.

4   Characterizing Cautious Entailment

In this section, we characterize the cautious entailment relation $P \mathrel{\mid\!\sim_c} a$ in terms of rule entailment. The basic observation was already made for the program P_2 in Example 2, i.e., whether P entails the fact $a \leftarrow$ does not match with $P \mathrel{\mid\!\sim_c} a$. Actually, this relationship can be made more precise: the former implies the latter. Moreover, we are able to characterize the exact difference of these two entailment relations as follows.

Lemma 2. *For a program P and an atom $a \in \mathrm{At}(P)$,*

$$\mathrm{SM}(P \cup \{a \leftarrow \sim a\}) = \{M \in \mathrm{SM}(P) \mid a \in M\}. \tag{4}$$

Proof. For any interpretation $M \subseteq \mathrm{At}(P)$,

$$
\begin{aligned}
& M \in \mathrm{SM}(P \cup \{a \leftarrow \sim a\}) \\
\iff\ & M = \mathrm{LM}(P^M \cup \{a \leftarrow \sim a\}^M) \\
\iff\ & M = \mathrm{LM}(P^M) \text{ and } \{a \leftarrow \sim a\}^M = \emptyset \\
\iff\ & M \in \mathrm{SM}(P) \text{ and } a \in M. \qquad\qquad \square
\end{aligned}
$$

Corollary 1. *For a program P and an atom $a \in \mathrm{At}(P)$, $P \mathrel{\mid\!\sim_c} a$ iff $P \mathrel{\not\mapsto} a \leftarrow \sim a$.*

Lemma 3. *For a program P and an atom $a \in \mathrm{At}(P)$,*

$$\mathrm{SM}(P \cup \{\{a\} \leftarrow\}) = \mathrm{SM}(P \cup \{\leftarrow a\}) \cup \mathrm{SM}(P \cup \{a \leftarrow\}). \tag{5}$$

Proof. Consider any interpretation $M \subseteq \mathrm{At}(P)$.

1. If $a \notin M$, then $M \in \mathrm{SM}(P \cup \{\{a\} \leftarrow\}) \iff M = \mathrm{LM}(P^M) \iff M \in \mathrm{SM}(P) \iff M \in \mathrm{SM}(P \cup \{\leftarrow a\})$.
2. If $a \in M$, then $M \in \mathrm{SM}(P \cup \{\{a\} \leftarrow\}) \iff M = \mathrm{LM}(P^M \cup \{a \leftarrow\}) \iff M \in \mathrm{SM}(P \cup \{a \leftarrow\})$. $\qquad \square$

Theorem 1. *Given a program P and an atom $a \in \mathrm{At}(P)$, $P \mathrel{\not\mapsto} a \leftarrow$ if and only if $P \mathrel{\not\mapsto} a \leftarrow \sim a$ and $P \mathrel{\not\mapsto} \{a\} \leftarrow$.*

Proof. Given the definition of $\mapsto$, the goal is to establish that $\mathrm{SM}(P) = \mathrm{SM}(P \cup \{a \leftarrow\})$ iff $\mathrm{SM}(P) = \mathrm{SM}(P \cup \{a \leftarrow \sim a\})$ and $\mathrm{SM}(P) = \mathrm{SM}(P \cup \{\{a\} \leftarrow\})$.
  ($\Longrightarrow$) Assuming that $\mathrm{SM}(P) = \mathrm{SM}(P \cup \{a \leftarrow\})$ it is clear that $a \in M$ for every $M \in \mathrm{SM}(P)$. Thus, $\mathrm{SM}(P) = \mathrm{SM}(P \cup \{a \leftarrow \sim a\})$ by Lemma 2. Moreover, we have $\mathrm{SM}(P \cup \{\leftarrow a\}) = \emptyset$ so that $\mathrm{SM}(P) = \mathrm{SM}(P \cup \{\{a\} \leftarrow\})$ follows from (5).
  ($\Longleftarrow$) Suppose that $\mathrm{SM}(P \cup \{a \leftarrow \sim a\}) = \mathrm{SM}(P) = \mathrm{SM}(P \cup \{\{a\} \leftarrow\})$. It is clear by Lemma 2 that $a \in M$ for every $M \in \mathrm{SM}(P)$ which enforces $\mathrm{SM}(P \cup \{\leftarrow a\}) = \emptyset$. Thus, $\mathrm{SM}(P) = \mathrm{SM}(P \cup \{a \leftarrow\})$ follows from (5) in Lemma 3. $\qquad \square$

Since the rules $a \leftarrow \sim a$ and $\{a\} \leftarrow$ can be understood as weakened forms of the fact $a \leftarrow$, the only-if-direction of Theorem 1 is intuitively clear. For the other direction, we point to the theorem $\sim a \vee \sim\sim a$ of *equilibrium logic* [22] that characterizes stable models. Given this formula and implications $\sim a \rightarrow a$ and $\sim\sim a \rightarrow a$ corresponding to rules under consideration, we may derive a as a result of case analysis (disjunctive syllogism). On the other hand, it is well-known that $a \leftarrow a$ is an SE-consequence of any program P and we have $P \not\mapsto a \leftarrow a$ in general by Proposition 2. The formula $a \vee \sim a$ is not a theorem of equilibrium logic and thus we cannot derive a from the formulas $a \rightarrow a$ and $\sim a \rightarrow a$ by similar case analysis. Indeed, the model correspondence in (5) indicates that $P \not\mapsto a \leftarrow$ is still possible even if $P \mapsto a \leftarrow a$ and $P \mapsto a \leftarrow \sim a$.

In the following, we incorporate cautious consequences in programs in terms of constraints $a \leftarrow \sim a$ rather than facts $a \leftarrow$. This allows us to establish restricted cumulativity as sketched in the introduction, but actually we can establish similarly restricted versions of monotonicity and the cut rule for $\vdash_c$.

Theorem 2. *For a program P, an atom $a \in \mathrm{At}(P)$, and a literal l based on $\mathrm{At}(P)$:*

1. *If $P \vdash_c l$, then $P \cup \{a \leftarrow \sim a\} \vdash_c l$.*
2. *If $P \vdash_c a$ and $P \cup \{a \leftarrow \sim a\} \vdash_c l$, then $P \vdash_c l$.*

Proof. For the first, we note that $\mathrm{SM}(P \cup \{a \leftarrow \sim a\}) \subseteq \mathrm{SM}(P)$ by Lemma 2. It is clear by definition of $\vdash_c$ that if $M \models l$ for every $M \in \mathrm{SM}(P)$ this is also the case for every $M \in \mathrm{SM}(P \cup \{a \leftarrow \sim a\})$. For the second, $P \vdash_c a$ implies by Lemma 2 that $\mathrm{SM}(P \cup \{a \leftarrow \sim a\}) = \mathrm{SM}(P)$ and the rest follows again by the definition of $\vdash_c$. □

The respective restricted form of cautious monotonicity is obtained directly as a weakening of the first item of Theorem 2. Yet another abstract property is *rationality* [15] which strengthens cautious monotony by replacing a, the lemma for which $P \vdash_c a$ holds, by a *consistent conclusion* a, for which $P \not\vdash_c \sim a$ holds. It is clear by Theorem 2 that $P \vdash_c l$ and $P \not\vdash_c \sim a$ imply $P \cup \{a \leftarrow \sim a\} \vdash_c l$. However, there is a mismatch in the sense that $a \leftarrow \sim a$ does not properly encode the consistency of a.

5   Negative Cautious Consequences

In the previous section, we concentrated on recording *positive* cautious consequences of a program in the program itself. We change the perspective in this section by considering *negative* cautious consequences of programs. The main observation is that $P \vdash_c \sim a$ corresponds to adding to P an integrity constraint of the form $\leftarrow a$. This gives rise to a characterization similar to the one in Section 4 but technically in a much simpler way.

Lemma 4. *For a program P and an atom $a \in \mathrm{At}(P)$,*

$$\mathrm{SM}(P \cup \{\leftarrow a\}) = \{M \in \mathrm{SM}(P) \mid a \notin M\}. \tag{6}$$

Proof. This follows directly by the definition of stable models, i.e., Definition 1. □

Theorem 3. *For a program P, an atom $a \in \mathrm{At}(P)$, and a literal l based on $\mathrm{At}(P)$:*

1. *If $P \vdash_c l$, then $P \cup \{\leftarrow a\} \vdash_c l$.*
2. *If $P \vdash_c \sim a$ and $P \cup \{\leftarrow a\} \vdash_c l$, then $P \vdash_c l$.*

Proof. The proof is highly analogous to that of Theorem 2: the rule $a \leftarrow \sim a$ is simply replaced by the integrity constraint $\leftarrow a$ and Lemma 2 by Lemma 4. □

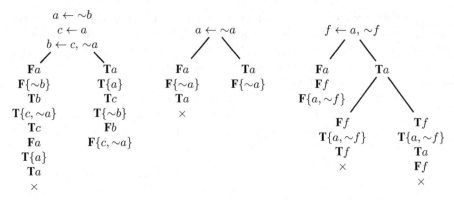

Fig. 1. Tableau proofs for the program in Example 1 as well as individual rules

It is highly interesting to put the results formalized by Theorems 2 and 3 together. Given a set of literals L we write $P \mathrel{\vdash_c} L$ to denote that $P \mathrel{\vdash_c} l$ for every $l \in L$. Overall, the reasoning mechanism underlying stable model semantics exhibits monotonicity and cumulativity up to restrictions imposed on recording consequences.

Corollary 2. *For a program P, a literal l, and a set of literals L based on* At(P):

1. *If $P \mathrel{\vdash_c} l$, then $P \cup \{a \leftarrow \sim a \mid a \in L\} \cup \{\leftarrow a \mid \sim a \in L\} \mathrel{\vdash_c} l$.*
2. *If $P \mathrel{\vdash_c} L$ and $P \cup \{a \leftarrow \sim a \mid a \in L\} \cup \{\leftarrow a \mid \sim a \in L\} \mathrel{\vdash_c} l$, then $P \mathrel{\vdash_c} l$.*

Corollary 2 illustrates how positive and negative consequences of a program can be incorporated as rules without affecting stable models. In fact, such assumptions have been used implicitly in algorithms implementing the search for stable models, such as the SMODELS procedure [26]. The difference is that assumptions about stable models being computed are stored in the respective data structures of algorithms rather than inserted as rules in the program. In what follows, we want to illustrate the effects of such additions on a higher level of abstraction provided by *semantic tableaux* and, in particular, when tailored to the case of normal programs [6].[3] An example follows.

Example 6. The leftmost tree in Figure 1 provides a tableau constructed for the normal program P from Example 1. Since the rules of the program act as premises they are listed in the root of the tableau. As usual, the branches of the tableau represent case analysis performed in order to determine the stable models of P. The two branches with assumptions **F**a and **T**a are first created by the application of the *cut* tableau rule.

Afterwards, the analysis on the left branch proceeds as follows. Since a should be false, the rules for a must have false bodies. This makes the only body literal $\sim b$ false and b true. This must be justified by the unique rule for b, making its body true. Thus, c must be true and a false. On the other hand, c must be justified by the unique rule defining it, which makes a true, a contradiction (also indicated by "×" at the end of the branch). Thus, P cannot have a stable model M such that $a \notin M$.

---

[3] The extended rules of the SMODELS system are covered by an extended tableau calculus [7].

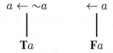

$$a \leftarrow \sim a \qquad \leftarrow a$$

$$\mathbf{T}a \qquad \mathbf{F}a$$

Fig. 2. Derived tableaux rules to handle rules of the forms $a \leftarrow \sim a$ and $\leftarrow a$

Reasoning taking place on the right branch is similar. In particular, the body of the only rule for b is falsified and thus b can be assumed to be false. The analysis is complete since the truth values of all atoms and rule bodies are consistently determined. Thus, the branch identifies the unique stable model $M = \{a, c\}$ of P. ∎

The second tableau in Figure 1 shows a partial case analysis in the presence of the rule $a \leftarrow \sim a$ that we would like to insert to P on the basis of Corollary 2 as $P \hspace{1pt} \vdash_{\mathrm{c}} a$ holds. The resulting tableau does not depend on other (potential) rules for a and thus we obtain a derived tableau rule given on the left side of Figure 2. The third tableau in Figure 1 concerns the case of an integrity constraint $\leftarrow a$ but encoded as a normal rule $f \leftarrow a, \sim f$ where f is supposed to be a globally new atom. Abstracting on the outcome yields a derived rule as illustrated in Figure 2 on the right. Thus, any positive and negative consequences, if encoded by the respective rules, can be immediately unwound as assumptions on stable models without creating unnecessary branches in the resulting tableau. Now, assuming that $a \leftarrow \sim a$ is inserted to the program P and to the root of the leftmost tableau in Figure 1, too, the application of this derived rule essentially yields a single-branch tableau having only the right branch of the original tableau as illustrated in Figure 3. Thus, the tableau proof is condensed and the rule $a \leftarrow \sim a$ acts as a *lemma* in the traditional sense.

Fig. 3. Condensed tableau

6 Generalizations for Nonmonotonic Reasoning

While the preceding sections concentrate on the case of NCC programs, the goal of this section is to take into consideration other nonmonotonic formalisms. Most notably, we will address other classes of logic programs as well as major nonmonotonic logics from literature. The outcome of the forthcoming analysis is that analogous results can be obtained. However, in certain cases, issues related to particular syntax and restricted expressive power may prohibit an expected generalization. For instance, the introduction of auxiliary atoms may pre-empt exact correspondences such as (5).

We begin with SMODELS programs which generalize normal programs with extended rule types such as choice, cardinality, and weight rules [25,26]. Thus, NCC programs are easily covered so that Theorem 1 and Corollary 2 transfer through the generalization of stable models for rule extensions. The case of disjunctive programs [10] is complicated by the fact that a choice rule $\{a\} \leftarrow$ is not available as such in the language. The choice can be expressed using a new *complementary* atom $\bar{a}$ and rules $a \leftarrow \sim\bar{a}$ and $\bar{a} \leftarrow \sim a$ but (5) could fail because $\bar{a}$ is true in stable models where a is not present. These rules could substitute $\{a\} \leftarrow$ in Theorem 1 under the assumption that $\bar{a} \notin \text{At}(P)$. On the other hand, Theorems 2 and 3 generalize as such. Nested programs [17] allow for a recursive rule structure where connectives $\leftarrow$ and $\sim$ may nest arbitrarily. Consequently, a choice rule $\{a\} \leftarrow$ can be systematically substituted by a rule $a \leftarrow \sim\sim a$. [4] Thus, the theorems under consideration lift in a straightforward way.

Next we turn out attention to nonmonotonic logics. McCarthy's *circumscription* [19] is based on $\subseteq$-minimal models of propositional theories. It is an exceptional nonmonotonic logic because it features cumulative inference. Given a set of sentences Σ in a propositional language $\mathcal{L}$, a model $M \models \Sigma$ is $\subseteq$-minimal iff there is no other model $N \subset M$ such that $N \models \Sigma$. Let $\text{MM}(\Sigma)$ denote the set of minimal models of Σ. A *classical* literal l is a cautious consequence of Σ subject to circumscription iff $M \models l$ for every $M \in \text{MM}(\Sigma)$. Adding such a literal to Σ will not affect minimal models, which makes cautious circumscriptive inference cumulatively monotonic. However, adding arbitrary literals do not correspond to *selection* of minimal models in general, e.g., in view of restricted monotonicity established as the first parts of Theorems 2 and 3.

Example 7. Consider the propositional theory $\Sigma = \{a \vee b,\ c \rightarrow a,\ c \rightarrow b\}$ having two minimal models $M_1 = \{a\}$ and $M_2 = \{b\}$. Thus, $\neg c$ is a cautious consequence of Σ subject to minimal models and it is easy to see that $\text{MM}(\Sigma \cup \{\neg c\}) = \{M_1, M_2\}$. But, adding a non-consequence c will result in a unique minimal model $M = \{a, b, c\}$. ∎

The example above can be encoded as a disjunctive logic program P consisting of rules

$$a \mid b. \qquad a \leftarrow c. \qquad b \leftarrow c.$$

The stable models are M_1 and M_2 from above. Applying the first half of Theorem 2, the literal c can be added as a rule $c \leftarrow \sim c$. In contrast with $\Sigma \cup \{c\}$ above, the resulting program will have no stable models and hence the restricted monotonicity property is not jeopardized. Indeed, adding c to Σ amounts to adding the fact $c \leftarrow$ to P.

Moore's *autoepistemic logic* [21] is based on a modality $\mathbf{B}$ for *beliefs* and the respective modal (propositional) language $\mathcal{L}_{\mathbf{B}}$. Given the initial assumptions $\Sigma \subseteq \mathcal{L}_{\mathbf{B}}$ of an agent, its beliefs are determined by *stable expansions* Δ of Σ satisfying the fixed point condition $\Delta = \text{Cn}(\Sigma \cup \mathbf{B}\Delta \cup \neg\mathbf{B}\overline{\Delta})$ where $\mathbf{B}\Delta = \{\mathbf{B}\varphi \mid \varphi \in \Delta\}$ and $\neg\mathbf{B}\overline{\Delta} = \{\neg\mathbf{B}\varphi \mid \varphi \in \mathcal{L}_{\mathbf{B}} \setminus \Delta\}$. We write $\text{Exp}(\Sigma)$ for the set of stable expansions of Σ. A sentence $\varphi \in \mathcal{L}_{\mathbf{B}}$ is a cautious consequence of Σ, denoted $\Sigma \mathrel{\vdash_c} \varphi$, if and only if $\varphi \in \Delta$ for every $\Delta \in \text{Exp}(\Sigma)$. Moreover, it is possible to define $\Sigma \mathrel{\mapsto} \varphi$ if and only if $\text{Exp}(\Sigma) = \text{Exp}(\Sigma \cup \{\varphi\})$, i.e., φ is redundant given Σ. The difference of these relations can be illustrated, e.g., using $\Sigma = \{\neg\mathbf{B}b \rightarrow a,\ a \rightarrow c,\ \neg\mathbf{B}a \wedge c \rightarrow b\}$ derived from the program P in Example 1. Now $\Sigma \mathrel{\vdash_c} c$ but $\Sigma \mathrel{\not\mapsto} c$ as adding c gives rise to new expansions. To work out further connections, we point out autoepistemic formulas which can be introduced as counterparts to rules $a \leftarrow;\ a \leftarrow \sim a;\ a \leftarrow \sim\sim a;$ and $\leftarrow a$ addressed before. The respective formulas are φ, $\neg\mathbf{B}\varphi \rightarrow \varphi$, $\mathbf{B}\varphi \rightarrow \varphi$, and $\mathbf{B}\varphi \wedge \neg\mathbf{B}\neg\varphi \rightarrow \neg\varphi$. In particular, we have $\Sigma \mathrel{\vdash_c} \varphi$ iff $\Sigma \mathrel{\mapsto} \neg\mathbf{B}\varphi \rightarrow \varphi$, which is clear by the first item of Lemma 5 collecting analogs of Lemmas 2–4. The second item reveals that an autoepistemic theory may have an inconsistent expansion $\Delta = \mathcal{L}_{\mathbf{B}}$.

---

[4] Rules $\{a\} \leftarrow$ and $a \leftarrow \sim\sim a$ are unconditionally satisfied and always yield the same reduct.

Lemma 5. *For an autoepistemic theory* $\Sigma \subseteq \mathcal{L}_\mathbf{B}$ *and a sentence* $\varphi \in \mathcal{L}_\mathbf{B}$:

1. $\mathrm{Exp}(\Sigma \cup \{\neg\mathbf{B}\varphi \to \varphi\}) = \{\Delta \in \mathrm{Exp}(\Sigma) \mid \varphi \in \Delta\}$.
2. $\mathrm{Exp}(\Sigma \cup \{\mathbf{B}\varphi \wedge \neg\mathbf{B}\neg\varphi \to \neg\varphi\}) =$

$$\{\Delta \in \mathrm{Exp}(\Sigma) \mid \varphi \notin \Delta\} \cup \{\mathcal{L}_\mathbf{B} \mid \mathcal{L}_\mathbf{B} \in \mathrm{Exp}(\Sigma)\}.$$

3. $\mathrm{Exp}(\Sigma \cup \{\mathbf{B}\varphi \to \varphi\}) = \mathrm{Exp}(\Sigma \cup \{\mathbf{B}\varphi \wedge \neg\mathbf{B}\neg\varphi \to \neg\varphi\}) \cup \mathrm{Exp}(\Sigma \cup \{\varphi\})$.

Proof. Item *1*. For ($\subseteq$), let $\Delta \in \mathrm{Exp}(\Sigma \cup \{\neg\mathbf{B}\varphi \to \varphi\})$. Assuming $\varphi \notin \Delta$ implies $\neg\mathbf{B}\varphi \in \neg\mathbf{B}\overline{\Delta}$ and $\varphi \in \Delta$, a contradiction. Thus, $\varphi \in \Delta$ and $\Sigma \cup \mathbf{B}\Delta \cup \neg\mathbf{B}\overline{\Delta} \models \neg\mathbf{B}\varphi \to \varphi$, so that $\Delta \in \mathrm{Exp}(\Sigma)$. To show ($\supseteq$), let $\Delta \in \mathrm{Exp}(\Sigma)$ and $\varphi \in \Delta$. It follows that $\mathbf{B}\varphi \in \mathbf{B}\Delta$ and $\Sigma\cup\mathbf{B}\Delta\cup\neg\mathbf{B}\overline{\Delta} \models \neg\mathbf{B}\varphi \to \varphi$. Thus, $\Delta \in \mathrm{Exp}(\Sigma\cup\{\neg\mathbf{B}\varphi \to \varphi\})$.

Item *2*. To show inclusion ($\subseteq$), consider $\Delta \in \mathrm{Exp}(\Sigma \cup \{\mathbf{B}\varphi \wedge \neg\mathbf{B}\neg\varphi \to \neg\varphi\})$. First, if Δ is consistent, assuming $\varphi \in \Delta$ implies that $\neg\varphi \notin \Delta$, $\mathbf{B}\varphi \in \mathbf{B}\Delta$, $\neg\mathbf{B}\neg\varphi \in \neg\mathbf{B}\overline{\Delta}$, and $\neg\varphi \in \Delta$, a contradiction. Therefore $\varphi \notin \Delta$ is necessary and $\neg\mathbf{B}\varphi \in \neg\mathbf{B}\overline{\Delta}$. Thus, $\Sigma \cup \mathbf{B}\Delta \cup \neg\mathbf{B}\overline{\Delta}$ entails $\mathbf{B}\varphi \wedge \neg\mathbf{B}\neg\varphi \to \neg\varphi$, and we obtain $\Delta \in \mathrm{Exp}(\Sigma)$ in addition to $\varphi \notin \Delta$. Second, if $\Delta = \mathcal{L}_\mathbf{B}$, then $\neg\mathbf{B}\overline{\Delta} = \emptyset$ and we obtain $\Sigma \cup \mathbf{B}\Delta \models \mathbf{B}\varphi \wedge \neg\mathbf{B}\neg\varphi \to \neg\varphi$ since $\mathbf{B}\neg\varphi \in \mathbf{B}\Delta$. Thus, $\Delta = \mathrm{Cn}(\Sigma \cup \mathbf{B}\Delta)$, so that $\Delta \in \mathrm{Exp}(\Sigma)$. For ($\supseteq$), similar cases arise. If $\Delta \in \mathrm{Exp}(\Sigma)$ is inconsistent, augmenting Σ by $\mathbf{B}\varphi \wedge \neg\mathbf{B}\neg\varphi \to \neg\varphi$ is redundant and $\Delta \in \mathrm{Exp}(\Sigma \cup \{\mathbf{B}\varphi \wedge \neg\mathbf{B}\neg\varphi \to \neg\varphi\})$ follows. The same can be concluded, if $\Delta \in \mathrm{Exp}(\Sigma)$ is consistent and $\varphi \notin \Delta$, since the latter implies that $\neg\mathbf{B}\varphi \in \neg\mathbf{B}\overline{\Delta}$ and $\Sigma \cup \mathbf{B}\Delta \cup \neg\mathbf{B}\overline{\Delta} \models \mathbf{B}\varphi \wedge \neg\mathbf{B}\neg\varphi \to \neg\varphi$.

Item *3*. Consider any *stable theory*[5] Δ such that $\varphi \in \Delta$. Now $\mathbf{B}\varphi \in \mathbf{B}\Delta$, enforcing $\Sigma \cup \{\mathbf{B}\varphi \to \varphi\} \cup \mathbf{B}\Delta \cup \neg\mathbf{B}\overline{\Delta}$ and $\Sigma \cup \{\varphi\} \cup \mathbf{B}\Delta \cup \neg\mathbf{B}\overline{\Delta}$ logically equivalent. Thus, $\Delta \in \mathrm{Exp}(\Sigma \cup \{\mathbf{B}\varphi \to \varphi\})$ iff $\Delta \in \mathrm{Exp}(\Sigma \cup \{\varphi\})$. Secondly, let $\varphi \notin \Delta$ for a stable theory Δ. It follows that Δ is consistent and $\neg\mathbf{B}\varphi \in \neg\mathbf{B}\overline{\Delta}$. Then $\Sigma\cup\mathbf{B}\Delta\cup\neg\mathbf{B}\overline{\Delta}$ entails both $\mathbf{B}\varphi \to \varphi$ and $\mathbf{B}\varphi \wedge \neg\mathbf{B}\neg\varphi \to \neg\varphi$. It follows that $\Delta \in \mathrm{Exp}(\Sigma \cup \{\mathbf{B}\varphi \to \varphi\})$ iff $\Delta \in \mathrm{Exp}(\Sigma)$ iff $\Delta \in \mathrm{Exp}(\Sigma \cup \{\mathbf{B}\varphi \wedge \neg\mathbf{B}\neg\varphi \to \neg\varphi\})$ by Item 2, since $\varphi \notin \Delta$.   □

The second item of Lemma 5 illustrates the fact that an inconsistent expansion possessed by an autoepistemic theory cannot be filtered out by adding formulas. However, inconsistent expansions do not affect cautious reasoning and thus our results from previous sections can be naturally generalized without additional consistency requirements.

Theorem 4. *Given an autoepistemic theory* $\Sigma \subseteq \mathcal{L}_\mathbf{B}$ *and a sentence* $\varphi \in \mathcal{L}_\mathbf{B}$, $\Sigma \hspace{0.5mm}\mid\!\sim\hspace{0.5mm} \varphi$ *if and only if* $\Sigma \hspace{0.5mm}\mid\!\sim\hspace{0.5mm} \neg\mathbf{B}\varphi \to \varphi$ *and* $\Sigma \hspace{0.5mm}\mid\!\sim\hspace{0.5mm} \mathbf{B}\varphi \to \varphi$.

Proof. ($\Longrightarrow$) Assuming that $\Sigma \hspace{0.5mm}\mid\!\sim\hspace{0.5mm} \varphi$, we obtain $\mathrm{Exp}(\Sigma) = \mathrm{Exp}(\Sigma \cup \{\varphi\})$ and that $\varphi \in \Delta$ for each $\Delta \in \mathrm{Exp}(\Sigma)$. In particular, if $\Delta = \mathcal{L}_\mathbf{B} \in \mathrm{Exp}(\Sigma)$, then $\varphi \in \Delta$ and $\Delta \in \mathrm{Exp}(\Sigma \cup \{\varphi\})$, too. Thus, $\mathrm{Exp}(\Sigma) = \mathrm{Exp}(\Sigma \cup \{\mathbf{B}\varphi \to \varphi\})$ and $\mathrm{Exp}(\Sigma) = \mathrm{Exp}(\Sigma \cup \{\neg\mathbf{B}\varphi \to \varphi\})$ by Lemma 5 so that $\Sigma \hspace{0.5mm}\mid\!\sim\hspace{0.5mm} \neg\mathbf{B}\varphi \to \varphi$ and $\Sigma \hspace{0.5mm}\mid\!\sim\hspace{0.5mm} \mathbf{B}\varphi \to \varphi$.

($\Longleftarrow$) Using the definition of $\hspace{0.5mm}\mid\!\sim\hspace{0.5mm}$, we obtain $\mathrm{Exp}(\Sigma) = \mathrm{Exp}(\Sigma \cup \{\neg\mathbf{B}\varphi \to \varphi\})$ and $\mathrm{Exp}(\Sigma) = \mathrm{Exp}(\Sigma \cup \{\mathbf{B}\varphi \to \varphi\})$. The former implies $\Sigma \hspace{0.5mm}\mid\!\sim_\mathrm{c}\hspace{0.5mm} \varphi$ so that $\mathrm{Exp}(\Sigma \cup \{\mathbf{B}\varphi \wedge \neg\mathbf{B}\neg\varphi \to \neg\varphi\})$ can include $\Delta = \mathcal{L}_\mathbf{B}$ only if $\mathrm{Exp}(\Sigma)$ does. Thus, the equality $\mathrm{Exp}(\Sigma) = \mathrm{Exp}(\Sigma\cup\{\varphi\})$ follows from $\mathrm{Exp}(\Sigma) = \mathrm{Exp}(\Sigma\cup\{\mathbf{B}\varphi \to \varphi\})$ by Lemma 5 and we may conclude that $\Sigma \hspace{0.5mm}\mid\!\sim\hspace{0.5mm} \varphi$.   □

---

[5] A stable theory $\Delta \subseteq \mathcal{L}_\mathbf{B}$ contains (i) $\varphi \in \mathcal{L}_\mathbf{B}$ whenever $\Delta \models \varphi$, (ii) $\mathbf{B}\varphi$ whenever $\varphi \in \Delta$, and (iii) $\neg\mathbf{B}\varphi$ whenever $\varphi \in \mathcal{L}_\mathbf{B} \setminus \Delta$. Stable expansions of Σ are stable theories including Σ.

The following result incorporates two sets of *positive* and *negative* assumptions Γ and Υ, respectively, which can be arbitrary sentences of $\mathcal{L}_\mathbf{B}$.

Theorem 5. *Given an autoepistemic theory $\Sigma \subseteq \mathcal{L}_\mathbf{B}$ and two subsets Γ and Υ of $\mathcal{L}_\mathbf{B}$:*

1. *If $\Sigma \mathrel{\vert\!\sim_c} \varphi$, then $\Sigma \cup \{\neg\mathbf{B}\chi \to \chi \mid \chi \in \Gamma\} \cup \{\mathbf{B}\chi \wedge \neg\mathbf{B}\neg\chi \to \neg\chi \mid \chi \in \Upsilon\} \mathrel{\vert\!\sim_c} \varphi$.*
2. *If $\Sigma \mathrel{\vert\!\sim_c} \chi$ for each $\chi \in \Gamma$, $\Sigma \mathrel{\vert\!\sim_c} \neg\mathbf{B}\chi$ for each $\chi \in \Upsilon$, and $\Sigma \cup \{\neg\mathbf{B}\chi \to \chi \mid \chi \in \Gamma\} \cup \{\mathbf{B}\chi \wedge \neg\mathbf{B}\neg\chi \to \neg\chi \mid \chi \in \Upsilon\} \mathrel{\vert\!\sim_c} \varphi$, then $\Sigma \mathrel{\vert\!\sim_c} \varphi$.*

Proof. Let Σ' extend Σ by $\{\neg\mathbf{B}\chi \to \chi \mid \chi \in \Gamma\}$ and $\{\mathbf{B}\chi \wedge \neg\mathbf{B}\neg\chi \to \neg\chi \mid \chi \in \Upsilon\}$. By the repeated application of the first two items of Lemma 5, we have $\Delta \in \mathrm{Exp}(\Sigma')$ iff (i) $\Delta \in \mathrm{Exp}(\Sigma)$, $\Gamma \subseteq \Delta$, and $\Upsilon \cap \Delta = \emptyset$, or (ii) $\Delta = \mathcal{L}_\mathbf{B} \in \mathrm{Exp}(\Sigma)$. Thus, $\mathrm{Exp}(\Sigma') \subseteq \mathrm{Exp}(\Sigma)$. For the first item, it is then clear that $\Sigma \mathrel{\vert\!\sim_c} \varphi$ implies $\Sigma' \mathrel{\vert\!\sim_c} \varphi$.

For the second item, let $\Delta \in \mathrm{Exp}(\Sigma)$. If $\Delta = \mathcal{L}_\mathbf{B}$, then $\Delta \in \mathrm{Exp}(\Sigma')$ is immediate by (ii). Otherwise, Δ is consistent and $\Sigma \mathrel{\vert\!\sim_c} \chi$ implies $\chi \in \Delta$ for any $\chi \in \Gamma$. Thus, $\Gamma \subseteq \Delta$. Then consider any $\chi \in \Upsilon$ for which $\Sigma \mathrel{\vert\!\sim_c} \neg\mathbf{B}\chi$ implies $\neg\mathbf{B}\chi \in \Delta$. Assuming that $\chi \in \Delta$ implies $\mathbf{B}\chi \in \Delta$ indicating the inconsistency of Δ. Thus, $\Upsilon \cap \Delta = \emptyset$ and we have shown that $\Delta \in \mathrm{Exp}(\Sigma')$ by (i). $\qquad\square$

Reiter's default logic [24] is based on default rules, or simply *defaults*, of the form $\frac{\alpha:\beta_1,\ldots,\beta_n}{\gamma}$. Such an inference rule allows the derivation of γ upon the derivation of α if, in addition, each one of justifications $\beta_1,\ldots,\beta_n$ can be consistently assumed. A default theory is a pair $\langle D, W \rangle$ where D is a set of defaults and W is a propositional theory in some propositional language $\mathcal{L}$. The semantics of $\langle D, W \rangle$ is determined by its *extensions* $E \subseteq \mathcal{L}$ which are defined in [18] as the *least* theories that contain W and are closed under propositional consequence and the set of ordinary *inference rules*

$$D^E = \{\frac{\alpha}{\gamma} \mid \frac{\alpha : \beta_1,\ldots,\beta_n}{\gamma} \in D \text{ and each } \beta_i \text{ is consistent with } E\}. \qquad (7)$$

We write $\mathrm{Ext}(D, W)$ for the set of extensions of $\langle D, E \rangle$. *Disjunctive defaults* [11] generalize defaults by allowing disjunctive consequents $\gamma_1 \mid \ldots \mid \gamma_k$. Such disjunctions turn closures under D^E non-unique and hence extensions E are required to be *minimal* theories containing W and being closed under propositional consequence and D^E.

However, even disjunctive defaults lack expressive precision in view of our purposes and hence we resort to *nested defaults* [27]. Such defaults are written in the form of inference rules but connectives $\mid$ and $\sim$ may be used recursively in propositional formulas. The reduct of a nested rule $\frac{\alpha}{\gamma}$ with respect to a theory $E \subseteq \mathcal{L}$ is obtained by replacing any maximal occurrence of the form $\sim\beta$ in α or γ by $\bot$, if $\beta \in E$, and $\top$ otherwise. In view of the results to be established, the following nested defaults will form the counterparts of rules that were used in the context of nested programs:

$$\frac{\top}{\varphi}, \qquad \frac{\sim\varphi}{\varphi}, \qquad \frac{\sim\sim\varphi}{\varphi}, \qquad \frac{\top}{\sim\varphi}.$$

For instance, the reduct of $\frac{\sim\sim\varphi}{\varphi}$ is $\frac{\top}{\varphi}$, if $\varphi \in E$, and $\frac{\bot}{\varphi}$ otherwise, assuming that φ is negation-free. This demonstrates how the *choice* about φ can be realized in analogy to Example 3. We write D^E for the reduct of a set of defaults D with respect to $E \subseteq \mathcal{L}$.

In the case of nested default logic, the background theory W can be incorporated as inference rules $\frac{\top}{\varphi}$ for $\varphi \in W$. Thus, we write $\mathrm{Ext}(D)$ for a set D of nested defaults and omit W altogether. A propositional sentence φ is a cautious consequence of D, denoted $D \mathrel{\vrule height 1.2ex\hskip0.2em\sim}_{\mathrm{c}} \varphi$, iff $\varphi \in E$ for every $E \in \mathrm{Ext}(D)$. Similarly, we write $D \mathrel{\vrule height 1.2ex\hskip0.2em\sim}_{\mathrm{c}} \sim\varphi$ to indicate that $\varphi \notin E$ for every $E \in \mathrm{Ext}(D)$. To define rule entailment for any nested rule $\frac{\alpha}{\gamma}$, let $D \mapsto \frac{\alpha}{\gamma}$ hold iff $\mathrm{Ext}(D) = \mathrm{Ext}(D \cup \{\frac{\alpha}{\gamma}\})$ in analogy to our previous notions.

Lemma 6. *For a set of nested defaults D based on $\mathcal{L}$ and a sentence $\varphi \in \mathcal{L}$:*

1. $\mathrm{Ext}(D \cup \{\frac{\sim\varphi}{\varphi}\}) = \{E \in \mathrm{Ext}(D) \mid \varphi \in E\}$.
2. $\mathrm{Ext}(D \cup \{\frac{\top}{\sim\varphi}\}) = \{E \in \mathrm{Ext}(D) \mid \varphi \notin E\} \cup \{\mathcal{L} \mid \mathcal{L} \in \mathrm{Ext}(D)\}$.
3. $\mathrm{Ext}(D \cup \{\frac{\sim\sim\varphi}{\varphi}\}) = \mathrm{Ext}(D \cup \{\frac{\top}{\sim\varphi}\}) \cup \mathrm{Ext}(D \cup \{\frac{\top}{\varphi}\})$.

Proof. Let $E \subseteq \mathcal{L}$ be a propositionally closed theory.

Item *1.* The reduct of $\frac{\sim\varphi}{\varphi}$ with respect to E is $\frac{\bot}{\varphi}$, if $\varphi \in E$, and $\frac{\top}{\varphi}$, if $\varphi \notin E$. Thus, $E \in \mathrm{Ext}(D \cup \{\frac{\sim\varphi}{\varphi}\})$ implies $\varphi \in E$. But then $E \in \mathrm{Ext}(D \cup \{\frac{\sim\varphi}{\varphi}\})$ iff $E \in \mathrm{Ext}(D)$.

Item *2.* The reduct of $\frac{\top}{\sim\varphi}$ with respect to E is $\frac{\top}{\top}$, if $\varphi \in E$, and $\frac{\top}{\bot}$, if $\varphi \notin E$. Thus, if $E = \mathcal{L}$, then $E \in \mathrm{Ext}(D \cup \{\frac{\top}{\sim\varphi}\})$ iff $E \in \mathrm{Ext}(D)$. Otherwise, E is consistent. If additionally $E \in \mathrm{Ext}(D \cup \{\frac{\top}{\sim\varphi}\})$, then $\varphi \notin E$ is necessary because $\varphi \in E$ would insert $\frac{\top}{\bot}$ to the reduct. So, whenever $\varphi \notin E$, $E \in \mathrm{Ext}(D \cup \{\frac{\top}{\sim\varphi}\})$ iff $E \in \mathrm{Ext}(D)$.

Item *3.* Recall that the reduct of $\frac{\sim\sim\varphi}{\varphi}$ with respect to E is $\frac{\top}{\varphi}$, if $\varphi \in E$, and $\frac{\bot}{\varphi}$, if $\varphi \notin E$. Now, assuming that $\varphi \in E$, we have that $E \in \mathrm{Ext}(D \cup \{\frac{\sim\sim\varphi}{\varphi}\})$ iff $E \in \mathrm{Ext}(D \cup \{\frac{\top}{\varphi}\})$. On the other hand, if $\varphi \notin E$, then E is consistent and $E \in \mathrm{Ext}(D \cup \{\frac{\sim\sim\varphi}{\varphi}\})$ iff $E \in \mathrm{Ext}(D)$ iff $E \in \mathrm{Ext}(D \cup \{\frac{\top}{\sim\varphi}\})$ by Item 2. $\qquad\square$

Theorem 6. *Given a set of nested defaults D based on $\mathcal{L}$ and a sentence $\varphi \in \mathcal{L}$: $D \mapsto \frac{\top}{\varphi}$ if and only if $D \mapsto \frac{\sim\varphi}{\varphi}$ and $D \mapsto \frac{\sim\sim\varphi}{\varphi}$.*

Proof. The proof is perfectly analogous to that of Theorem 4 where the respective defaults replace autoepistemic formulas and Lemma 6 takes the role of Lemma 5. $\qquad\square$

The generalization of restricted monotonicity and cut involve sets of positive and negative assumptions, viz. P and N, now encoded in terms of defaults.

Theorem 7. *Given a set of nested defaults D based on $\mathcal{L}$, two sets of sentences $P \subseteq \mathcal{L}$ and $N \subseteq \mathcal{L}$, and a sentence $\varphi \in \mathcal{L}$:*

1. *If $D \mathrel{\vrule height 1.2ex\hskip0.2em\sim}_{\mathrm{c}} \varphi$, then $D \cup \{\frac{\sim\chi}{\chi} \mid \chi \in P\} \cup \{\frac{\top}{\sim\chi} \mid \chi \in N\} \mathrel{\vrule height 1.2ex\hskip0.2em\sim}_{\mathrm{c}} \varphi$.*
2. *If $D \mathrel{\vrule height 1.2ex\hskip0.2em\sim}_{\mathrm{c}} \chi$ for each $\chi \in P$, $D \mathrel{\vrule height 1.2ex\hskip0.2em\sim}_{\mathrm{c}} \sim\chi$ for each $\chi \in N$, and $D \cup \{\frac{\sim\chi}{\chi} \mid \chi \in P\} \cup \{\frac{\top}{\sim\chi} \mid \chi \in N\} \mathrel{\vrule height 1.2ex\hskip0.2em\sim}_{\mathrm{c}} \varphi$, then $D \mathrel{\vrule height 1.2ex\hskip0.2em\sim}_{\mathrm{c}} \varphi$.*

Proof. The proof is obtained in the same way as for Theorem 6. $\qquad\square$

7 Related Work

As recalled in the introduction, the study of cumulativity led to the introduction of non-monotonic formalisms with non-standard syntax or semantics. Due to limited space, we mention only a few representative examples. For instance, *rational default logic* [20] modifies the semantics of defaults. Our results suggest that this is not necessary in view of obtaining restricted cumulativity. On the other hand, cumulative default logic [1] extends the language so that justifications for conclusions drawn can be incorporated. Theorems 6 and 7 suggest that this is not necessary if the full expressive power and preciseness of nested defaults is available. Interestingly, this was not the case in the early 90:s when [1] was published. Similar attempts were done in the realm of logic programming. The *revised* stable models of [23] achieve cumulativity but sacrifice other abstract properties. For instance, the existence of stable models, i.e., *coherence* is presumed. Coherence is problematic from the point of view of applications: non-existence of stable models typically captures the non-existence of solutions to the problem of interest. In contrast, no such requirement is needed in our approach. Stable models remain intact and additional constraints of the forms $a \leftarrow \sim a$ and $\leftarrow a$ can be freely used to constrain them as done by the search procedures designed for stable models, too.

8 Conclusions

In this paper, we re-evaluate the grounds for the cumulativity of nonmonotonic reasoning from a new perspective. The starting point for the study was the notion of rule entailment based on rule redundancy, which was first analyzed to remove redundancy from logic programs. Although rule entailment is not cumulative per se, it provided the necessary insight into understanding the failure of cumulativity in major nonmonotonic formalisms. The key observation is that cautious consequences have traditionally been incorporated into premises too firmly as facts in view of obtaining cumulativity. Our conclusion is that it is crucial to respect the defeasibilty of nonmonotonic conclusions in general and to take advantage of the expressive precision of nonmonotonic languages. Consequently, a *restricted* form of cumulativity and even monotonicity can be established. Our results indicate that this can be achieved in a broad spectrum for central formalisms, such as major classes of nonmonotonic logic programs, default logic, and autoepistemic logic. Interestingly, the underlying formalisms and their semantics require no changes if cumulativity is understood in its restricted form proposed in this paper and thus the computational complexity of the main reasoning tasks is not affected.

References

1. Brewka, G.: Cumulative default logic: In defense of nonmonotonic inference rules. Artificial Intelligence 50(2), 183–205 (1991)
2. Brewka, G., Makinson, D., Schlechta, K.: Cumulative inference relations for JTMS and logic programming. In: Dix, J., Schmitt, P.H., Jantke, K.P. (eds.) NIL 1990. LNCS, vol. 543, pp. 1–12. Springer, Heidelberg (1991)
3. Dix, J.: Default theories of poole-type and a method for constructing cumulative versions of default logic. In: Proceedings of ECAI 1992, pp. 289–293 (1992)
4. Dix, J.: Cumulativity and rationality in semantics of normal logic programs. In: Dix, J., Schmitt, P.H., Jantke, K.P. (eds.) NIL 1990. LNCS, vol. 543, pp. 13–37. Springer, Heidelberg (1991)

5. Dix, J.: Classifying semantics of disjunctive logic programs. In: Proceedings of JICSLP 1992, pp. 798–812. MIT Press (1992)
6. Gebser, M., Schaub, T.: Tableau calculi for answer set programming. In: Etalle, S., Truszczyński, M. (eds.) ICLP 2006. LNCS, vol. 4079, pp. 11–25. Springer, Heidelberg (2006)
7. Gebser, M., Schaub, T.: Generic tableaux for answer set programming. In: Dahl, V., Niemelä, I. (eds.) ICLP 2007. LNCS, vol. 4670, pp. 119–133. Springer, Heidelberg (2007)
8. Gelder, A.V., Ross, K., Schlipf, J.: The well-founded semantics for general logic programs. Journal of the ACM 38(3), 620–650 (1991)
9. Gelfond, M., Lifschitz, V.: The stable model semantics for logic programming. In: Proceedings of ICLP 1988, pp. 1070–1080 (1988)
10. Gelfond, M., Lifschitz, V.: Classical negation in logic programs and disjunctive databases. New Generation Computing 9, 365–385 (1991)
11. Gelfond, M., Przymusinska, H., Lifschitz, V., Truszczynski, M.: Disjunctive defaults. In: Proceedings of KR 1991, pp. 230–237. Morgan Kaufmann (1991)
12. Gottlob, G., Mingyi, Z.: Cumulative default logic: Finite characterization, algorithms, and complexity. Artificial Intelligence 69(1-2), 329–345 (1994)
13. Janhunen, T.: Removing redundancy from answer set programs. In: Garcia de la Banda, M., Pontelli, E. (eds.) ICLP 2008. LNCS, vol. 5366, pp. 729–733. Springer, Heidelberg (2008)
14. Janhunen, T., Niemelä, I.: A scheme for weakened negative introspection in autoepistemic reasoning. In: Mundici, D., Gottlob, G., Leitsch, A. (eds.) KGC 1993. LNCS, vol. 713, pp. 211–222. Springer, Heidelberg (1993)
15. Kraus, S., Lehmann, D., Magidor, M.: Nonmonotonic reasoning, preferential models and cumulative logics. Artificial Intelligence 44(1-2), 167–207 (1990)
16. Lifschitz, V., Pearce, D., Valverde, A.: Strongly equivalent logic programs. ACM Transactions on Computational Logic 2(4), 526–541 (2001)
17. Lifschitz, V., Tang, L., Turner, H.: Nested expressions in logic programs. Annals of Mathematics and Artificial Intelligence 25(3-4), 369–389 (1999)
18. Marek, W., Truszczyński, M.: Nonmonotonic Logic: Context-Dependent Reasoning. Springer, Berlin (1993)
19. McCarthy, J.: Applications of circumscription to formalizing commonsense knowledge. Artificial Intelligence 28, 89–116 (1986)
20. Mikitiuk, A., Truszczynski, M.: Constrained and rational default logics. In: Proceedings of IJCAI 1995, pp. 1509–1517. Morgan Kaufmann (1995)
21. Moore, R.: Semantical consideration on nonmonotonic logic. Artificial Intelligence 25(1), 234–252 (1985)
22. Pearce, D.: Equilibrium logic. Annals of Mathematics and Artificial Intelligence 47(1-2), 3–41 (2006)
23. Moniz Pereira, L., Pinto, A.M.: Revised stable models – A semantics for logic programs. In: Bento, C., Cardoso, A., Dias, G. (eds.) EPIA 2005. LNCS (LNAI), vol. 3808, pp. 29–42. Springer, Heidelberg (2005)
24. Reiter, R.: A logic for default reasoning. Artificial Intelligence 13, 81–132 (1980)
25. Simons, P.: Extending the stable model semantics with more expressive rules. In: Gelfond, M., Leone, N., Pfeifer, G. (eds.) LPNMR 1999. LNCS (LNAI), vol. 1730, pp. 305–316. Springer, Heidelberg (1999)
26. Simons, P., Niemelä, I., Soininen, T.: Extending and implementing the stable model semantics. Artificial Intelligence 138(1-2), 181–234 (2002)
27. Turner, H.: Strong equivalence for logic programs and default theories (Made easy). In: Eiter, T., Faber, W., Truszczyński, M. (eds.) LPNMR 2001. LNCS (LNAI), vol. 2173, pp. 81–92. Springer, Heidelberg (2001)
28. Turner, H.: Strong equivalence made easy: nested expressions and weight constraints. Theory and Practice of Logic Programming 3(4-5), 609–622 (2003)

Decidability of Circumscribed Description Logics Revisited

Piero Bonatti[1], Marco Faella[1], Carsten Lutz[2], Luigi Sauro[1], and Frank Wolter[3]

[1] Dept. of Electrical Engineering and Information Technologies,
University of Naples, Italy
[2] Dept. of Computer Science, University of Bremen, Germany
[3] Dept. of Computer Science, University of Liverpool, UK

Abstract. We revisit non-monotonic description logics based on circumscription (with preferences) and prove several decidability results for their satisfiability problem. In particular, we consider circumscribed description logics without the finite model property (DL-Lite$_\mathcal{F}$ and $\mathcal{ALCFI}$) and with fixed roles (DL-Lite$_\mathcal{F}$ and a fragment of DL-Lite$_\mathcal{R}$), improving upon previous decidability results that are limited to logics which have the finite model property and do not allow to fix roles during minimization.

1 Introduction

During the evolution from frame systems to description logics (DLs), nonmonotonic inferences and constructs (such as those supported by the LOOM system in the 1990s) have disappeared from the mainstream. However, a range of knowledge engineering requirements kept interest in nonmonotonic DLs alive, see e.g. [21,23,5] for more details. In fact, along the years all of the major non-monotonic semantics have been adapted to DLs, including the integration of default rules and DLs [2,12,20,16,17], circumscription [7,22], and variations of autoepistemic logics, preferential semantics and rational closure [8,11,14,15,10]. In this paper, we focus on circumscription, which was first applied in the DL context by Gerd Brewka to whom this volume is dedicated [7]. The general idea of circumscription is to select a subclass of the classical models of the knowledge base by minimizing the extension of some selected predicates that represent abnormal situations. During minimization, the interpretation of the other predicates can be fixed or vary freely. To achieve a faithful modeling, in addition it is often necessary to allow a preference order on the minimized predicates, that is, if P_1 is preferred to P_2, then we allow the interpretation of P_2 to become larger (or change in an orthogonal way) if this allows the interpretation of P_1 to become smaller.

All these aspects of circumscription are incorporated in the *circumscription patterns* studied in [6,5], where a range of (un)decidability results for circumscribed DLs based on circumscription patterns has been obtained. The positive results are mostly obtained by using a filtration type of construction as known from modal logic [4], which is limited to logics that enjoy the finite model property. The negative results show that a main cause of undecidability is to allow

T. Eiter et al. (Eds.): Brewka Festschrift, LNAI 9060, pp. 112–124, 2015.

role names (binary relations) to be minimized or fixed during minimization instead of minimizing/fixing only concept names (unary relations). However, many popular description logics such as those underlying the OWL ontology language recommended by the W3C do not enjoy the finite model property; moreover, minimizing/fixing roles would be useful as a modeling tool for applications.

In this paper, we contribute to a better understanding of the computational properties of circumscribed DLs without the finite model property and with fixed role names. Regarding the former, we deviate from the filtration approach and prove decidability by reduction to the (decidable) first-order theory of set systems with a binary predicate expressing that two sets have the same cardinality [13]. The reduction is inspired by reductions of inseparability problems for DL TBoxes to BAPA (Boolean Algebra with Presburger Arithmetic) from [19]. We note that the surprisingly close relationship between inseparability (and conservative extensions) of DL TBoxes and circumscribed DLs has been exploited to prove results in both areas before: complexity results for circumscribed DLs have been used to investigate the complexity of deciding inseparability and conservative extensions in [18]. Conversely, undecidability results for inseparability proved in [18] have been used in [5] to prove undecidability results for circumscribed $\mathcal{EL}$ TBoxes. Regarding fixed roles, we show that decidability results can be obtained for members of the DL-Lite family of inexpressive DLs. Considering two such members, we show that decidability results can be both obtained by reduction to the afore mentioned theory of set systems and by the original filtration-style method from [5].

In detail, our results are as follows (all referring to concept satisfiability relative to circumscribed knowledge bases as introduced in Section 2):

1. Circumscribed $\mathcal{ALCFI}$ without minimized roles and fixed roles is decidable where $\mathcal{ALCFI}$ is the basic DL $\mathcal{ALC}$ extended with functional and inverse roles. This extends the previous decidability results for DLs such as $\mathcal{ALCI}$ and $\mathcal{ALCQ}$ which enjoy the finite model property [6].
2. Circumscribed DL-Lite$_{bool}^{\mathcal{F}}$ with fixed roles (but no minimized roles) is decidable where DL-Lite$_{bool}^{\mathcal{F}}$ is DL-Lite with boolean concept connectives and functional roles. Note that, in addition, DL-Lite$_{bool}^{\mathcal{F}}$ is another example of a decidable circumscribed DL without the finite model property.
3. Circumscribed DL-Lite$_{bool}^{\mathcal{R}}$ with fixed roles (but no minimized roles) is decidable if it is additionally assumed that no minimized or fixed role is subsumed by a varying role, where DL-Lite$_{bool}^{\mathcal{R}}$ is DL-Lite with boolean concept connectives and role inclusions.

2   Preliminaries

The alphabet of description logics (DLs) consists of three (pairwise disjoint) sets: a set N_I of *individual names*, denoted $a, b, \ldots$, a set N_C of *concept names*, denoted $A, B, \ldots$, and a set N_R of *role names*, denoted P. A *role*, denoted R, is either a role name or an *inverse role*, that is, an expression of the form P^-. As a convention, we set $R^- = P$ if $R = P^-$. We consider two members of the DL-Lite family of DLs [9,1]. The *concepts* C of DL-Lite$_{bool}^{\mathcal{F}}$ are defined inductively as follows:

$$B ::= \bot \quad | \quad \top \quad | \quad A_i \quad | \quad \exists R,$$
$$C ::= B \quad | \quad \neg C \quad | \quad C_1 \sqcap C_2.$$

The concepts of the form B are called *basic*. A *concept inclusion* in DL-Lite$_{bool}^{\mathcal{F}}$ is of the form $C_1 \sqsubseteq C_2$, where C_1 and C_2 are DL-Lite$_{bool}^{\mathcal{F}}$ concepts. A TBox $\mathcal{T}$ in DL-Lite$_{bool}^{\mathcal{F}}$ is a finite set of concept inclusions in DL-Lite$_{bool}^{\mathcal{F}}$ and *functionality assertions* func(R), where R is a role.

Concept inclusions in DL-Lite$_{bool}^{\mathcal{R}}$ are defined in the same way as concept inclusions in DL-Lite$_{bool}^{\mathcal{F}}$. A TBox $\mathcal{T}$ in DL-Lite$_{bool}^{\mathcal{R}}$ is a finite set of concept inclusions in DL-Lite$_{bool}^{\mathcal{R}}$ and *role inclusions* $R_1 \sqsubseteq R_2$, where R_1 and R_2 are roles.

The concepts C of the DL $\mathcal{ALCFI}$ are defined inductively as follows:

$$C \quad ::= \quad \bot \quad | \quad \top \quad | \quad A_i \quad | \neg C \quad | \quad C_1 \sqcap C_2 \quad | \quad \exists R.C.$$

Concept inclusions and TBoxes $\mathcal{T}$ in $\mathcal{ALCFI}$ are defined in the same way as TBoxes in DL-Lite$_{bool}^{\mathcal{F}}$, where concepts in DL-Lite$_{bool}^{\mathcal{F}}$ are replaced by concepts in $\mathcal{ALCFI}$.

An *ABox* $\mathcal{A}$ is a finite set of assertions of the form $A(a)$ and $P(a,b)$. We use $P^-(a,b)$ to denote the assertion $P(b,a)$. By $\mathsf{Ind}(\mathcal{A})$ we denote the set of individual names in $\mathcal{A}$. A *knowledge base* (KB, for short) is a pair $\mathcal{K} = (\mathcal{T}, \mathcal{A})$ with a TBox $\mathcal{T}$ and an ABox $\mathcal{A}$.

The semantics of DL knowledge bases is defined as usual, see [3] for details. An interpretation $\mathcal{I} = (\Delta^{\mathcal{I}}, \cdot^{\mathcal{I}})$ is given by its domain $\Delta^{\mathcal{I}}$ and an interpretation function that associates with every concept name A a set $A^{\mathcal{I}} \subseteq \Delta^{\mathcal{I}}$, with every role name P a relation $P^{\mathcal{I}} \subseteq \Delta^{\mathcal{I}} \times \Delta^{\mathcal{I}}$, and with every individual name a an element $a^{\mathcal{I}} \in \Delta^{\mathcal{I}}$. We make the unique name assumption ($a^{\mathcal{I}} \neq b^{\mathcal{I}}$ if $a \neq b$). We denote by $C^{\mathcal{I}} \subseteq \Delta^{\mathcal{I}}$ the interpretation of a (complex) concept C in $\mathcal{I}$ and say that an interpretation $\mathcal{I}$ is *a model of a KB* $\mathcal{K} = (\mathcal{T}, \mathcal{A})$ if

- $C^{\mathcal{I}} \subseteq D^{\mathcal{I}}$, for all $C \sqsubseteq D \in \mathcal{T}$;
- $R^{\mathcal{I}} \subseteq S^{\mathcal{I}}$, for all $R \sqsubseteq S \in \mathcal{T}$;
- $R^{\mathcal{I}}$ is a partial function, for all func(R) $\in \mathcal{T}$;
- $a^{\mathcal{I}} \in A^{\mathcal{I}}$, for all $A(a) \in \mathcal{A}$;
- $(a^{\mathcal{I}}, b^{\mathcal{I}}) \in P^{\mathcal{I}}$, for all $R(a,b) \in \mathcal{A}$.

Given a DL $\mathcal{L}$, *concept satisfiability relative to $\mathcal{L}$ KBs* is the following problem: given a concept C in $\mathcal{L}$ and a KB $\mathcal{K}$ in $\mathcal{L}$, decide whether there exists a model $\mathcal{I}$ of $\mathcal{K}$ such that $C^{\mathcal{I}} \neq \emptyset$. Concept satisfiability is NP-complete for DL-Lite$_{bool}^{\mathcal{F}}$ and DL-Lite$_{bool}^{\mathcal{R}}$, and ExpTime-complete for $\mathcal{ALCFI}$.

To define DLs with circumscription, we start by introducing circumscription patterns. Such a pattern describes how individual predicates are treated during minimization.

Definition 1 (Circumscription pattern, $<_{\mathsf{CP}}$). *A circumscription pattern is a tuple* CP *of the form* $(\prec, M, F, V)$, *where* $\prec$ *is a strict partial order over* M, *and M, F, and V are mutually disjoint and exhaustive subsets of $\mathsf{N_C} \cup \mathsf{N_R}$, the minimized, fixed, and varying predicates, respectively. By $\preceq$, we denote the reflexive closure of $\prec$. Define a preference relation $<_{\mathsf{CP}}$ on interpretations by setting $\mathcal{I} <_{\mathsf{CP}} \mathcal{J}$ iff the following conditions hold:*

1. *$\Delta^{\mathcal{I}} = \Delta^{\mathcal{J}}$ and, for all $a \in \mathsf{N_I}$, $a^{\mathcal{I}} = a^{\mathcal{J}}$,*
2. *for all $p \in F$, $p^{\mathcal{I}} = p^{\mathcal{J}}$,*
3. *for all $p \in M$, if $p^{\mathcal{I}} \not\subseteq p^{\mathcal{J}}$ then there exists $q \in M$, $q \prec p$, such that $q^{\mathcal{I}} \subset q^{\mathcal{J}}$,*
4. *there exists $p \in M$ such that $p^{\mathcal{I}} \subset p^{\mathcal{J}}$ and for all $q \in M$ such that $q \prec p$, $q^{\mathcal{I}} = q^{\mathcal{J}}$.*

A circumscribed knowledge base with circumscription pattern $\mathsf{CP} = (\prec, M, F, V)$ and KB $\mathcal{K}$ is denoted by $\mathsf{Circ}_{\mathsf{CP}}(\mathcal{K})$. An interpretation $\mathcal{I}$ is a *model* of $\mathsf{Circ}_{\mathsf{CP}}(\mathcal{K})$ if it is a model of $\mathcal{K}$ and no $\mathcal{J} <_{\mathsf{CP}} \mathcal{I}$ is a model of $\mathcal{K}$.

In this paper, we consider the decidability and complexity of *concept satisfiability relative to circumscibed KBs*: a concept C is *satisfiable* relative to a circumscribed KB $\mathsf{Circ}_{\mathsf{CP}}(\mathcal{T}, \mathcal{A})$ if some model $\mathcal{I}$ of $\mathsf{Circ}_{\mathsf{CP}}(\mathcal{T}, \mathcal{A})$ satisfies $C^{\mathcal{I}} \neq \emptyset$. By (concept) satisfiability problem relative circumscribed KBs we mean the problem to decide whether a given concept C is satisfiable relative to a given circumscribed KB. Other reasoning problems such as subsumption and instance checking relative to circumscribed KBs can be reduced to concept satisfiability relative to circumscribed KBs [6].

3   Decidability for DL-Lite$_{bool}^{\mathcal{F}}$

We show decidability of concept satisfiability relative to circumscribed DL-Lite$_{bool}^{\mathcal{F}}$ KBs with fixed roles and without minimized roles. Note that fixed roles easily lead to undecidability of concept satisfiability relative to circumscribed KBs, such as for the circumscribed version of the popular lightweight (and tractable) DL $\mathcal{EL}$ [5]. Also note that DL-Lite$_{bool}^{\mathcal{F}}$ does not have the finite model property. An example showing this is given by the KB $\mathcal{K} = (\mathcal{T}, \mathcal{A})$, where

$$\mathcal{T} = \{A \sqsubseteq \exists P, \exists P^- \sqsubseteq \exists P, A \sqsubseteq \neg \exists P^-, \mathsf{func}(P^-)\}, \quad \mathcal{A} = \{A(a)\}.$$

It is easy to see that $\mathcal{K}$ is satisfiable but has no finite model. Thus, approaches to reasoning in circumscribed DLs that are based on filtration [6] cannot be employed in this case.

We prove decidability by reduction to the first-order theory of set systems with a binary predicate expressing that two sets have the same cardinality, which is decidable [13]. Formally, the language SC of set systems with cardinality is defined as follows. Its *terms* are constructed from variables $X_1, X_2, \ldots$ (interpreted as sets) and constants $\mathbf{0}$ (the empty set) and $\mathbf{1}$ (the whole set) using the binary function symbols $\cap$ (intersection), $\cup$ (union), and the unary function symbol $^-$ (complement). As usual, we prefer the infix notation for the binary function symbols and write, e.g., $X \cap Y$ instead of $\cap(X, Y)$. *Atomic SC formulas* are of the form

- $B_1 = B_2$ and $B_1 \subseteq B_2$, where B_1 and B_2 are terms;
- $|B_1| = |B_2|$ and $|B_1| \leq |B_2|$, where B_1 and B_2 are terms.

SC formulas are now constructed in the standard way using quantification, conjunction and negation. We are interested in the satisfiability of SC sentences in structures of the form $\mathfrak{A} = (2^{\Delta}, \cap, \cup, \bar{}, \emptyset, \Delta)$, where Δ is a non-empty set. We call such structures *SC structures*. An *SC model* $\mathfrak{M}$ consists of an SC structure $\mathfrak{A}$ and an *interpretation function* $X_i^{\mathfrak{M}} \subseteq \Delta$ of the variables X_i in $\mathfrak{A}$. The truth of SC sentences in an SC model is defined in the obvious way, for example,

- $\mathfrak{M} \models B_1 = B_2$ if $B_1^{\mathfrak{M}} = B_2^{\mathfrak{M}}$;
- $\mathfrak{M} \models |B_1| = |B_2|$ if $|B_1^{\mathfrak{M}}| = |B_2^{\mathfrak{M}}|$.

Decidability of satisfiability of SC sentences in SC models is proved in [13]:

Theorem 1. *Satisfiability of SC sentences is decidable.*

Suppose that a KB $\mathcal{K} = (\mathcal{T}, \mathcal{A})$, a circumscription pattern $\mathsf{CP} = (\prec, M, F, V)$, and a concept C_0 are given such that no role name is minimized in CP (that is, M contains no role names). We encode satisfiability of C_0 relative to $\mathsf{Circ}_{\mathsf{CP}}(\mathcal{K})$ as a satisfiability problem for SC sentences.

Take for every concept name B in $\mathcal{K} \cup \{C_0\}$ and any B of the form $\exists P$ or $\exists P^-$ such that P occurs in $\mathcal{K} \cup \{C_0\}$, an SC variable X_B. Then define inductively for every subconcept C of $\mathcal{K} \cup \{C_0\}$ an SC term C^s:

$$B^s = X_B, \qquad\qquad \perp^s = \mathbf{0}, \qquad\qquad \top^s = \mathbf{1},$$
$$(\neg C)^s = \overline{C^s}, \qquad\qquad (C_1 \sqcap C_2)^s = C_1^s \cap C_2^s.$$

We also set

$$\mathcal{T}^s = \{C_1^s \subseteq C_2^s \mid C_1 \sqsubseteq C_2 \in \mathcal{T}\}.$$

If $\mathcal{T}$ and C_0 do not contain roles, then clearly C_0 is satisfiable relative to (uncircumscribed) $\mathcal{T}$ iff the SC sentence $\exists \boldsymbol{X} \left(\neg(C_0^s = \mathbf{0}) \wedge \bigwedge_{\alpha \in \mathcal{T}^s} \alpha\right)$ is satisfiable where $\boldsymbol{X}$ is the sequence of variables occurring in $\mathcal{T}^s$ or C_0^s. To extend this to an encoding of satisfiability of C_0 relative to (uncircumscribed) $\mathcal{T}$ with roles, it is sufficient to state that $X_{\exists P}$ is empty iff $X_{\exists P^-}$ is empty for every role name P and to state for functional roles R that the cardinality of $X_{\exists R}$ is not smaller that the cardinality of $X_{\exists R^-}$. Thus, we extend $\mathcal{T}^s$ to $\mathcal{T}^{s,e}$ by adding the following SC formulas to $\mathcal{T}^s$:

$$(\neg(X_{\exists P} = \mathbf{0}) \leftrightarrow \neg(X_{\exists P^-} = \mathbf{0})),$$

for every role name P in $\mathcal{K} \cup \{C_0\}$, and

$$|X_{\exists R}| \geq |X_{\exists R^-}|$$

for every role R with $\mathsf{func}(R) \in \mathcal{T}$. We prove that C_0 is satisfiable relative to $\mathcal{T}$ iff the SC formula $\varphi = \exists \boldsymbol{X} \left(\neg(C_0^s = \mathbf{0}) \wedge \bigwedge_{\alpha \in \mathcal{T}^{s,e}} \alpha\right)$ is satisfiable. First let $\mathcal{I}$ be a model of $\mathcal{T}$ such that $C_0^{\mathcal{I}} \neq \emptyset$. Define an SC structure $\mathfrak{M}$ based on $\mathfrak{A} = (2^{\Delta}, \cap, \cup, \bar{}, \emptyset, \Delta)$ by setting $\Delta = \Delta^{\mathcal{I}}$, $X_A^{\mathfrak{M}} = A^{\mathcal{I}}$ for all concept names A, and $X_{\exists R}^{\mathfrak{M}} = \{d \in \Delta \mid \exists d' \, (d, d') \in R^{\mathcal{I}}\}$ for all roles R. It is readily checked that $\mathfrak{M}$ satisfies φ. Conversely, assume that a model $\mathfrak{M}$ based on $\mathfrak{A} = (2^{\Delta}, \cap, \cup, \bar{}, \emptyset, \Delta)$ satisfies φ. Define $\mathcal{I}$ by setting $\Delta^{\mathcal{I}} = \Delta$,

- $A^{\mathcal{I}} = X_A^{\mathfrak{M}}$ for all concept names A;
- $P^{\mathcal{I}} = X_{\exists P}^{\mathfrak{M}} \times X_{\exists P^-}^{\mathfrak{M}}$ for all roles P with neither func(P) nor func(P^-) in $\mathcal{T}$;
- and defining $R^{\mathcal{I}}$ as a surjective function with domain $X_{\exists R}^{\mathfrak{M}}$ and range $X_{\exists R^-}^{\mathfrak{M}}$ if func$(R) \in \mathcal{T}$ (such a function exists since $|X_{\exists R}^{\mathfrak{M}}| \geq |X_{\exists R^-}^{\mathfrak{M}}|$ for every role R with func$(R) \in \mathcal{T}$).

One can check that $\mathcal{I}$ satisfies $\mathcal{T}$ and that $C_0^{\mathcal{I}} \neq \emptyset$.

To encode circumscription, we define a second translation C^m of every sub-concept C in $\mathcal{K} \cup \{C_0\}$. C^m is defined in exactly the same way as C^s except that we use fresh SC variables Y_B instead of the SC variables X_B used in the translation C^s. We define $\mathcal{T}^m$ and $\mathcal{T}^{m,e}$ in exactly the same way as $\mathcal{T}^s$ and $\mathcal{T}^{s,e}$ with X_B replaced by Y_B.

Assume now that the ABox $\mathcal{A}$ is empty. Then we can encode satisfiability of C_0 relative to $\mathsf{Circ}_{\mathsf{CP}}(\mathcal{K})$ in a straightforward way by considering satisfiability of the SC sentence

$$\exists \boldsymbol{X} \left(\neg(C_0^s = \boldsymbol{0}) \wedge \bigwedge_{\alpha \in \mathcal{T}^{s,e}} \alpha \ \wedge \ \forall \boldsymbol{Y}(\boldsymbol{Y} <_{\mathsf{CP}} \boldsymbol{X} \to \neg \bigwedge_{\alpha \in \mathcal{T}^{m,e}} \alpha) \right) \tag{1}$$

where $\boldsymbol{X}$ is as above, $\boldsymbol{Y}$ is the sequence of variables occuring in $\mathcal{T}^m$ and $\boldsymbol{Y} <_{\mathsf{CP}} \boldsymbol{X}$ stands for the conjunction of

$$X_B = Y_B,$$

for each concept name B in F and B of the form $\exists P$ or $\exists P^-$ with $P \in F$,

$$\bigwedge_{A \in M} ((Y_A \not\subseteq X_A) \to \bigvee_{B \in M, B \prec A} (Y_B \subset X_A)),$$

and

$$\bigvee_{A \in M} ((Y_A \subset X_A) \wedge \bigwedge_{B \in M, B \prec A} (Y_B = X_B)).$$

We now extend the encoding above to KBs with non-empty ABox $\mathcal{A}$. To encode the ABox, take for every individual name $a \in \mathsf{Ind}(\mathcal{A})$ an SC variable X_a and define the set of SC formulas $\mathcal{A}^s$ as follows:

(A1) $|X_a| = 1$ for all $a \in \mathsf{Ind}(\mathcal{A})$, where $|X_a| = 1$ abbreviates the conjunction of $|X_a| > |\boldsymbol{0}|$ and $\forall X((X \subset X_a) \to (X = \boldsymbol{0}))$.

(A2) $X_a \cap X_b = \boldsymbol{0}$ for $a \neq b$ and $a, b \in \mathsf{Ind}(\mathcal{A})$. These formulas encode the unique name assumption.

(A3) $X_a \subseteq X_A$ if $A(a) \in \mathcal{A}$ for $a \in \mathsf{Ind}(\mathcal{A})$.

(A4) $X_a \subseteq X_{\exists P}$ if $P(a, b) \in \mathcal{A}$ for some b.

(A5) $X_a \subseteq X_{\exists P^-}$ if $P(b, a) \in \mathcal{A}$ for some b.

(A6) $\boldsymbol{0} = \boldsymbol{1}$ if there exists a role R with func$(R) \in \mathcal{T}$ and a, b, b' with $b \neq b'$ such that $R(a, b), R(a, b') \in \mathcal{A}$.

(A7) If func$(R) \in \mathcal{T}$ and func$(R^-) \notin \mathcal{T}$, then let $\mathcal{X}_R$ be the set of $a \in \mathsf{Ind}(\mathcal{A})$ such that there exists b with $R(a, b) \in \mathcal{A}$ and let $\mathcal{Y}_R$ be the set of $b \in \mathsf{Ind}(\mathcal{A})$ such that there exists a with $R(a, b) \in \mathcal{A}$. Include

$$|X_{\exists R} \setminus (\bigcup_{a \in \mathcal{X}_R} X_a)| \geq |X_{\exists R^-} \setminus (\bigcup_{a \in \mathcal{Y}_R} X_a)|$$

in $\mathcal{A}^s$. (Note that for such R we can remove from $\mathcal{T}^s$ the formulas $|X_{\exists R}| \geq |X_{\exists R^-}|$ since they are implied.)

Define $\mathcal{A}^m$ analogously to $\mathcal{A}^s$ with X_B replaced by Y_B (note that we do *not* introduce fresh variables Y_a since the interpretation of individual names is fixed). Set $\mathcal{K}^s = (\mathcal{T}^{s,e}, \mathcal{A}^s)$ and $\mathcal{K}^m = (\mathcal{T}^{m,e}, \mathcal{A}^m)$. Now, it is readily checked that C_0 is satisfiable relative to $\mathsf{Circ}_{\mathsf{CP}}(\mathcal{K})$ if the following SC sentence is satisfiable:

$$\exists \boldsymbol{X} \left(\neg(C_0^s = \boldsymbol{0}) \wedge \bigwedge_{\alpha \in \mathcal{K}^s} \alpha \;\wedge\; \forall \boldsymbol{Y} \left(\boldsymbol{Y} <_{\mathsf{CP}} \boldsymbol{X} \to \neg \bigwedge_{\alpha \in \mathcal{K}^m} \alpha \right) \right) \tag{2}$$

We have proved the following result:

Theorem 2. *Satisfiability of concepts relative to circumscribed DL-Lite$_{bool}^{\mathcal{F}}$ KBs without minimized roles is decidable.*

4   Decidability for $\mathcal{ALCFI}$

We show decidability of concept satisfiability for circumscribed $\mathcal{ALCFI}$ KBs without minimized and fixed roles. The proof is again by reduction to the theory of set systems with a binary predicate expressing that two sets have the same cardinality. Note that decidability of concept satisfiability for circumscribed KBs without minimized and fixed roles has been proved using filtration in [6] for DLs with the finite model property such as $\mathcal{ALCI}$ and $\mathcal{ALCF}$. As an extension of DL-Lite$_{bool}^{\mathcal{F}}$, $\mathcal{ALCFI}$ does not have the finite model property.

Consider a circumscribe $\mathcal{ALCFI}$ KB $\mathcal{K} = \mathsf{Circ}_{\mathsf{CP}}(\mathcal{T}, \mathcal{A})$ where the pattern $\mathsf{CP} = (\prec, M, F, V)$ has no minimized or fixed role names, and a $\mathcal{ALCFI}$-concept C_0. We encode satisfiability of C_0 relative to $\mathsf{Circ}_{\mathsf{CP}}(\mathcal{K})$ as a satisfiability problem for an SC sentence.

Take for every concept name B in $\mathcal{K} \cup \{C_0\}$ and any concept B of the form $\exists P.C$ or $\exists P^-.C$ which occurs in $\mathcal{K} \cup \{C_0\}$, an SC variable X_B. Then define inductively for every subconcept C of $\mathcal{K} \cup \{C_0\}$ an SC term C^s as before:

$$B^s = X_B, \qquad\qquad \bot^s = \boldsymbol{0}, \qquad\qquad\qquad \top^s = \boldsymbol{1},$$
$$(\neg C)^s = \overline{C^s}, \qquad (C_1 \sqcap C_2)^s = C_1^s \sqcap C_2^s.$$

By $\mathsf{sub}(\mathcal{K} \cup \{C_0\})$ we denote the closure under single negation of the subconcepts that occur in $\mathcal{K} \cup \{C_0\}$. A *type* $\mathbf{t}$ is a subset of $\mathsf{sub}(\mathcal{K} \cup \{C_0\})$ such that

- $\bot \notin \mathbf{t}$ and $\top \in \mathbf{t}$;
- $\neg C \in \mathbf{t}$ iff $C \notin \mathbf{t}$, for all $\neg C \in \mathsf{sub}(\mathcal{K} \cup \{C_0\})$;
- $C_1 \sqcap C_2 \in \mathbf{t}$ iff $C_1, C_2 \in \mathbf{t}$, for all $C_1 \sqcap C_2 \in \mathsf{sub}(\mathcal{K} \cup \{C_0\})$.

We use $\mathbf{t}^s$ as an abbreviation for the SC term $\bigcap_{C \in \mathbf{t}} C^s$. To encode the behavior of roles we, intuitively, decompose roles R into roles $R_{\mathbf{t},\mathbf{t}'}$ such that two individuals d, d' are in relation $R_{\mathbf{t},\mathbf{t}'}$ iff they are in relation R and d is in $\mathbf{t}$ and d' is in $\mathbf{t}'$.

We cannot directly talk about $R_{\mathbf{t},\mathbf{t}'}$ in SC and so we introduce variables denoting the domain and range of $R_{\mathbf{t},\mathbf{t}'}$, respectively: for any pair $\mathbf{t}, \mathbf{t}'$ of types and any role R introduce an SC variable $X_{R,\mathbf{t},\mathbf{t}'}$. Intuitively $X_{R,\mathbf{t},\mathbf{t}'}$ stands for all individuals which are in $\mathbf{t}$ and which are in the relation R to an individual in $\mathbf{t}'$. Define $\mathcal{T}^r$ as the union of $\{C_1^s \subseteq C_2^s \mid C_1 \sqsubseteq C_2 \in \mathcal{T}\}$ and the following SC formulas:

(a) $\mathbf{t}^s \cap X_{R,\mathbf{t}',\mathbf{t}''} = \mathbf{0}$ if $\mathbf{t} \neq \mathbf{t}'$, for all types $\mathbf{t}, \mathbf{t}'$. These formulas state that an individual in $\mathbf{t}$ cannot be in the domain of $R_{\mathbf{t}',\mathbf{t}''}$ for $\mathbf{t} \neq \mathbf{t}'$.
(b) $\mathbf{t}^s \subseteq \bigcup_{C \in \mathbf{t}'} X_{R,\mathbf{t},\mathbf{t}'}$ if $\exists R.C \in \mathbf{t}$. These formulas state that if d is in $\mathbf{t}$ and $\mathbf{t}$ contains some $\exists R.C$, then d must be in relation R to some d' in $\mathbf{t}'$ with $C \in \mathbf{t}'$.
(c) $\mathbf{t}^s \cap X_{R,\mathbf{t},\mathbf{t}'} = \mathbf{0}$ if $\neg \exists R.C \in \mathbf{t}$ and $C \in \mathbf{t}'$.
(d) $X_{R,\mathbf{t},\mathbf{t}'} \cap X_{R,\mathbf{t},\mathbf{t}''} = \mathbf{0}$ if R is functional and $\mathbf{t}' \neq \mathbf{t}''$.

Now we extend $\mathcal{T}^r$ to $\mathcal{T}^{r,e}$ by adding the following SC formulas to $\mathcal{T}^r$:

$$(\neg(X_{P,\mathbf{t},\mathbf{t}'} = \mathbf{0}) \leftrightarrow \neg(X_{P^-,\mathbf{t}',\mathbf{t}} = \mathbf{0})),$$

for every role name P in $\mathcal{K} \cup \{C_0\}$, and

$$|X_{R,\mathbf{t},\mathbf{t}'}| \geq |X_{R^-,\mathbf{t}',\mathbf{t}}|$$

for every role R with $\mathsf{func}(R) \in \mathcal{T}$. We show that C_0 is satisfiable relative to $\mathcal{T}$ iff the SC sentence $\exists \mathbf{X} \left(\neg(C_0^s = \mathbf{0}) \wedge \bigwedge_{\alpha \in \mathcal{T}^{r,e}} \alpha \right)$ is satisfiable where $\mathbf{X}$ is the sequence of variables occurring in $\mathcal{T}^{r,e}$ or C_0^s.

First let $\mathcal{I}$ be a model of $\mathcal{T}$ such that $C_0^{\mathcal{I}} \neq \emptyset$. Define an SC model $\mathfrak{M}$ based on $\mathfrak{A} = (2^{\Delta}, \cap, \cup, \dot{-}, \emptyset, \Delta)$ by setting $\Delta = \Delta^{\mathcal{I}}$, $X_A^{\mathfrak{M}} = A^{\mathcal{I}}$ for all concept names A, $X_{\exists R.C}^{\mathfrak{M}} = \{d \in \Delta \mid \exists d' \in C^{\mathcal{I}} \text{ and } (d,d') \in R^{\mathcal{I}}\}$ for all $\exists R.C \in \mathsf{sub}(\mathcal{K}, \cup\{C_0\})$, and

$$X_{R,\mathbf{t},\mathbf{t}'}^{\mathfrak{M}} = \{d \in (\mathbf{t}^s)^{\mathfrak{M}} \mid \exists d' \in (\mathbf{t}'^s)^{\mathfrak{M}} \text{ and } (d,d') \in R^{\mathcal{I}}\},$$

for all roles R and types $\mathbf{t}, \mathbf{t}'$. It is readily checked that $\mathfrak{M}$ satisfies φ. Conversely, assume that a model $\mathfrak{M}$ based on $\mathfrak{A} = (2^{\Delta}, \cap, \cup, \dot{-}, \emptyset, \Delta)$ satisfies φ. Define $\mathcal{I}$ by setting $\Delta^{\mathcal{I}} = \Delta$,

 - $A^{\mathcal{I}} = X_A^{\mathfrak{M}}$ for all concept names A;
 - $P^{\mathcal{I}} = \bigcup_{\mathbf{t},\mathbf{t}'} X_{P,\mathbf{t}',\mathbf{t}}^{\mathfrak{M}} \times X_{P^-,\mathbf{t},\mathbf{t}'}^{\mathfrak{M}}$ for all roles P with $\mathsf{func}(P), \mathsf{func}(P^-) \notin \mathcal{T}$;
 - $R^{\mathcal{I}}$ is the union of surjective functions $f_{\mathbf{t},\mathbf{t}'}$ with domain $X_{R,\mathbf{t},\mathbf{t}'}^{\mathfrak{M}}$ and range $X_{R^-,\mathbf{t}',\mathbf{t}}^{\mathfrak{M}}$ if $\mathsf{func}(R) \in \mathcal{T}$ (where $\mathbf{t}, \mathbf{t}'$ range over all types).

One can check that $\mathcal{I}$ satisfies $\mathcal{T}$ and that $C_0^{\mathcal{I}} \neq \emptyset$.

To encode circumscription, we again define a second translation C^n of every subconcept C in $\mathcal{K} \cup \{C_0\}$. C^n is defined in exactly the same way as C^s except that we use fresh SC variables Y_B instead of the SC variables X_B used in the translation C^s. We also introduce fresh SC variables $Y_{R,\mathbf{t},\mathbf{t}'}$ for every role R and types $\mathbf{t}, \mathbf{t}'$. Now define $\mathcal{T}^n$ and $\mathcal{T}^{n,e}$ in exactly the same way as $\mathcal{T}^r$ and $\mathcal{T}^{r,e}$, where the variables X are replaced by the corresponding variables Y.

Assume again that the ABox $\mathcal{A}$ is empty. Then we can encode satisfiability of C_0 relative to $\mathsf{Circ_{CP}}(\mathcal{K})$ in a straightforward way by considering satisfiability of the SC sentence

$$\exists \boldsymbol{X} \left(\neg(C_0^s = \boldsymbol{0}) \wedge \bigwedge_{\alpha \in \mathcal{T}^{r,e}} \alpha \ \wedge \ \forall \boldsymbol{Y}(\boldsymbol{Y} <_{\mathsf{CP}}^a \boldsymbol{X} \to \neg \bigwedge_{\alpha \in \mathcal{T}^{n,e}} \alpha) \right) \tag{3}$$

where $\boldsymbol{X}$ is as above, $\boldsymbol{Y}$ is the sequence of variables occuring in $\mathcal{T}^m$ and now $\boldsymbol{Y} <_{\mathsf{CP}}^a \boldsymbol{X}$ is obtained from $\boldsymbol{Y} <_{\mathsf{CP}} \boldsymbol{X}$ by taking the equations $X_A = Y_A$ for concept names $A \in F$ only. (The remaining equations involving $X_{\exists R}$ do not make sense here.)

We extend the encoding above to KBs with non-empty ABox $\mathcal{A}$. Take again for every individual name $a \in \mathsf{Ind}(\mathcal{A})$ an SC variable X_a and define a set $\mathcal{A}^r$ of SC formulas by taking the formulas in (A1), (A2), (A3), and (A6) from above as well as the following:

- for all $R(a,b) \in \mathcal{A}$ and all types $\mathbf{t}_1, \mathbf{t}_2$ include

$$(X_a \subseteq \mathbf{t}_1^s) \wedge (X_b \subseteq \mathbf{t}_2^s) \to (X_a \subseteq X_{R,\mathbf{t}_1,\mathbf{t}_2}),$$

into $\mathcal{A}^r$.
- Assume, as in (A7), that $\mathsf{func}(R) \in \mathcal{T}$ and $\mathsf{func}(R^-) \notin \mathcal{T}$. Let $\mathcal{X}_R$ be the set of $a \in \mathsf{Ind}(\mathcal{A})$ such that there exists b with $R(a,b) \in \mathcal{A}$ and let $\mathcal{Y}_R$ be the set of $b \in \mathsf{Ind}(\mathcal{A})$ such that there exists a with $R(a,b) \in \mathcal{A}$. Include for all types $\mathbf{t}, \mathbf{t}'$ the formula

$$|X_{R,\mathbf{t},\mathbf{t}'} \setminus (\bigcup_{a \in \mathcal{X}_R} X_a)| \geq |X_{R^-,\mathbf{t}',\mathbf{t}} \setminus (\bigcup_{a \in \mathcal{Y}_R} X_a)|$$

into $\mathcal{A}^r$.

Define $\mathcal{A}^n$ analogously to $\mathcal{A}^r$ with variables X replaced by the corresponding variables Y. Set $\mathcal{K}^r = (\mathcal{T}^{r,e}, \mathcal{A}^r)$ and $\mathcal{K}^n = (\mathcal{T}^{n,e}, \mathcal{A}^n)$. Now, it is readily checked that C_0 is satisfiable relative to $\mathsf{Circ_{CP}}(\mathcal{K})$ if the following SC sentence is satisfiable:

$$\exists \boldsymbol{X} \left(\neg(C_0^s = \boldsymbol{0}) \wedge \bigwedge_{\alpha \in \mathcal{K}^r} \alpha \ \wedge \ \forall \boldsymbol{Y}(\boldsymbol{Y} <_{\mathsf{CP}}^a \boldsymbol{X} \to \neg \bigwedge_{\alpha \in \mathcal{K}^n} \alpha) \right) \tag{4}$$

We have proved the following result:

Theorem 3. *Satisfiability of concepts relative to circumscribed $\mathcal{ALCFI}$ KBs without minimized and fixed roles is decidable.*

5   Decidability for DL-Lite$_{bool}^{\mathcal{R}}$

We prove decidability of concept satisfiability relative to circumscribed DL-Lite$_{bool}^{\mathcal{R}}$ knowledge bases with fixed roles and without minimized roles under the additional assumption that no varying role is subsumed by a fixed role. In contrast to the previous two sections, our approach is to use a filtration-style technique to establish a finite (in fact, single exponential) model property. To capture the mentioned syntactic restriction, we call a circumscribed KB $\mathsf{Circ}_{\mathsf{CP}}(\mathcal{T},\mathcal{A})$ in DL-Lite$_{bool}^{\mathcal{R}}$ *role-layered* if for each role inclusion $R \sqsubseteq S \in \mathcal{T}$ either $R \in F$ or $S \in V$.

For a concept C_0, ABox $\mathcal{A}$, and TBox $\mathcal{T}$, we denote by $\mathsf{cl}(C_0,\mathcal{T},\mathcal{A})$ the set of subconcepts of concepts in C_0, $\mathcal{A}$, and $\mathcal{T}$. The *concept-size* of C_0 and a KB $(\mathcal{T},\mathcal{A})$ is the cardinality of $\mathsf{cl}(C_0,\mathcal{T},\mathcal{A})$.

Lemma 1. *Let C_0 be a concept in DL-Lite$_{bool}^{\mathcal{R}}$ and $\mathsf{Circ}_{\mathsf{CP}}(\mathcal{T},\mathcal{A})$ a KB in DL-Lite$_{bool}^{\mathcal{R}}$ that is role-layered and does not contain minimized roles. If C_0 is satisfiable relative to $\mathsf{Circ}_{\mathsf{CP}}(\mathcal{T},\mathcal{A})$, then it is satisfied in a model $\mathcal{J}$ of $\mathsf{Circ}_{\mathsf{CP}}(\mathcal{T},\mathcal{A})$ with $|\Delta^{\mathcal{J}}| \leq 2^n + |\mathsf{Ind}(\mathcal{A})|$, where n is the concept size of C_0 and $(\mathcal{T},\mathcal{A})$.*

Proof. Let $\mathcal{I}$ be a model of $\mathsf{Circ}_{\mathsf{CP}}(\mathcal{T},\mathcal{A})$ satisfying C_0. Set $\mathsf{Ind}^{\mathcal{I}}(\mathcal{A}) = \{a^{\mathcal{I}} \mid a \in \mathsf{Ind}(\mathcal{A})\}$. Define on $\Delta^{\mathcal{I}}$ the equivalence relation $\sim$ by setting $d \sim d'$ iff

$$\{C \in \mathsf{cl}(C_0,\mathcal{T},\mathcal{A}) \mid d \in C^{\mathcal{I}}\} = \{C \in \mathsf{cl}(C_0,\mathcal{T},\mathcal{A}) \mid d' \in C^{\mathcal{I}}\}$$

and $d,d' \notin \mathsf{Ind}^{\mathcal{I}}(\mathcal{A})$ or $d = d'$ (this is needed to respect the unique name assumption). We use $[d]$ to denote the equivalence class of d w.r.t. $\sim$. Let $\mathcal{J}$ be the following interpretation:

$$\begin{aligned}
\Delta^{\mathcal{J}} &= \{[d] \mid d \in \Delta^{\mathcal{I}}\} \\
A^{\mathcal{J}} &= \{[d] \mid d \in A^{\mathcal{I}}\} \\
P^{\mathcal{J}} &= \{([d_1],[d_2]) \mid \exists d \in [d_1], d' \in [d_2] \text{ s.t. } (d,d') \in P^{\mathcal{I}}\} \\
a^{\mathcal{J}} &= [a^{\mathcal{I}}].
\end{aligned}$$

We show that $\mathcal{J}$ is a model of $\mathsf{Circ}_{\mathsf{CP}}(\mathcal{T},\mathcal{A})$ that satisfies C_0. It is standard to show the following by induction on C:

Claim 1. *For all $d \in \Delta^{\mathcal{I}}$ and $C \in \mathsf{cl}(C_0,\mathcal{T},\mathcal{A})$: $d \in C^{\mathcal{I}}$ iff $[d] \in C^{\mathcal{J}}$.*

Claim 1 implies that $\mathcal{J}$ satisfies C_0 and is a model of the KB $(\mathcal{T},\mathcal{A})$. To prove that $\mathcal{J}$ is a model of $\mathsf{Circ}_{\mathsf{CP}}(\mathcal{T},\mathcal{A})$, it thus remains to show that $\mathcal{J}$ is minimal w.r.t. $<_{\mathsf{CP}}$. Assume for a proof by contradiction that there exists a model $\mathcal{J}'$ of $\mathcal{T}$ and $\mathcal{A}$ such that $\mathcal{J}' <_{\mathsf{CP}} \mathcal{J}$. Define $\mathcal{I}'$ as follows:

$$\begin{aligned}
\Delta^{\mathcal{I}'} &= \Delta^{\mathcal{I}} \\
A^{\mathcal{I}'} &= \bigcup_{[d] \in A^{\mathcal{J}'}} [d] \\
P^{\mathcal{I}'} &= \bigcup_{([d_1],[d_2]) \in P^{\mathcal{J}'}} [d_1] \times [d_2] \text{ if } P \in V \\
P^{\mathcal{I}'} &= P^{\mathcal{I}} \text{ if } P \in F \\
a^{\mathcal{I}'} &= a^{\mathcal{I}}.
\end{aligned}$$

Observe that, by construction, each fixed concept name A has the same interpretation in $\mathcal{I}$ and $\mathcal{I}'$.

Claim 2. Let $d, d' \in \Delta^{\mathcal{I}'}$ and let R be a role occurring in $\mathcal{T}$. Then

1. if $R \in V$, then $(d, d') \in R^{\mathcal{I}'}$ iff $([d], [d']) \in R^{\mathcal{J}'}$;
2. if $R \in F$, then $(d, d') \in R^{\mathcal{I}'}$ implies $([d], [d']) \in R^{\mathcal{J}'}$.

For Point 1, assume first that $R \in V$. Let $(d, d') \in R^{\mathcal{I}'}$. By construction $(d, d') \in [d_1] \times [d_2]$, for some $([d_1], [d_2]) \in R^{\mathcal{J}'}$. Clearly, $[d_1] = [d]$ and $[d_2] = [d']$. The converse direction is by construction. For Point 2, assume $R \in F$ and let $(d, d') \in R^{\mathcal{I}'}$. Then $(d, d') \in R^{\mathcal{I}}$. By construction $([d], [d']) \in R^{\mathcal{J}}$. Then, using $R \in F$ and the semantics it follows that $([d], [d']) \in R^{\mathcal{J}'}$.

Claim 3: For all $d \in \Delta^{\mathcal{I}'}$ and $C \in \mathsf{cl}(C_0, \mathcal{T}, \mathcal{A})$: $d \in C^{\mathcal{I}'}$ iff $[d] \in C^{\mathcal{J}'}$.

The proof is by induction on the structure of C, where the interesting case is $C = \exists R$. If $R \in V$, Claim 3 follows directly from Point 1 of Claim 2. Assume that $R \in F$. By Point 2 of Claim 2, $d \in (\exists R)^{\mathcal{I}'}$ implies $[d] \in (\exists R)^{\mathcal{J}'}$. Conversely, assume that $[d] \in (\exists R)^{\mathcal{J}'}$. Clearly, we have that $([d], [d']) \in R^{\mathcal{J}'}$, for some $[d'] \in \Delta^{\mathcal{J}'}$. Since $R \in F$, $([d], [d']) \in R^{\mathcal{J}}$, i.e. $[d] \in (\exists R)^{\mathcal{J}}$. By Claim 1, $d \in (\exists R)^{\mathcal{I}}$ and using that $R \in F$ we obtain that $d \in (\exists R)^{\mathcal{I}'}$.

We now prove that $\mathcal{I}'$ is a model of $\mathcal{T}$ and $\mathcal{A}$. Indeed, if $d \in C_1^{\mathcal{I}'} \setminus C_2^{\mathcal{I}'}$ for some $C_1 \sqsubseteq C_2 \in \mathcal{T}$, then, by Claim 3, $[d] \in C_1^{\mathcal{J}'} \setminus C_2^{\mathcal{J}'}$ which contradicts the assumption that $\mathcal{J}'$ is a model of $\mathcal{T}$. Let $R \sqsubseteq S \in \mathcal{T}$ and assume that $(d, d') \in R^{\mathcal{I}'} \setminus S^{\mathcal{I}'}$. If R and S are varying, by Point 2 of Claim 2 we obtain that $([d], [d']) \in R^{\mathcal{J}'} \setminus S^{\mathcal{J}'}$ in contradiction to $\mathcal{J}'$ being a model of $\mathcal{T}$. If R and S are fixed, then $(d, d') \in R^{\mathcal{I}} \setminus S^{\mathcal{I}}$ in contradiction to $\mathcal{I}$ being a model of $\mathcal{T}$. Finally, if R is fixed and S varying, by Point 2 of Claim 2, $([d], [d']) \in R^{\mathcal{J}'}$ and Point 1 implies that $([d], [d']) \notin S^{\mathcal{J}'}$, again a contradiction. These three cases are exhaustive since our circumscribed knowledge base is role-layered. Therefore, $\mathcal{I}'$ is a model of $\mathcal{T}$. That $\mathcal{I}'$ is a model of $\mathcal{A}$ follows directly from the construction of $\mathcal{I}'$.

Finally, notice that for each $A \in \mathsf{N_C}$, $A^{\mathcal{I}} \odot A^{\mathcal{I}'}$ iff $A^{\mathcal{J}} \odot A^{\mathcal{J}'}$, where $\odot = \subseteq, \supseteq$. Consequently, since $M \subseteq \mathsf{N_C}$, $\mathcal{J}' <_{\mathsf{CP}} \mathcal{J}$ implies $\mathcal{I}' <_{\mathsf{CP}} \mathcal{I}$. Therefore, $\mathcal{I}$ is not a model of $\mathsf{Circ_{CP}}(\mathcal{T}, \mathcal{A})$ and we have derived a contradiction. □

The single exponential model property just proved implies the following decidability result.

Theorem 4. *Satisfiability of concepts relative to circumscribed role-layered DL-$\mathsf{Lite}_{bool}^{\mathcal{R}}$ KBs without minimized roles is decidable.*

Note that we also obtain a $\mathrm{NExp^{NP}}$-upper bound for checking concept satisfiability: given C_0 and $\mathsf{Circ_{CP}}(\mathcal{T}, \mathcal{A})$ guess a model $\mathcal{I}$ with $|\Delta^{\mathcal{I}}| \leq 2^n + |\mathsf{Ind}(\mathcal{A})|$, where n is the concept size of C_0 and $(\mathcal{T}, \mathcal{A})$ and then check using an NP-oracle whether $\mathcal{I}$ is a model of C_0 and $\mathsf{Circ_{CP}}(\mathcal{T}, \mathcal{A})$.

6   Open Problems

We briefly discuss some computational problems regarding DLs with circumscription that remain open.

- First note that we have not proved any new results for circumscription patterns with minimized roles. In particular, the decidability and complexity of circumscribed reasoning in DL-Lite$_{bool}^{\mathcal{F}}$ and DL-Lite$_{bool}^{\mathcal{R}}$ with minimized roles remains open.
- Our concern in this was paper was decidability of reasoning in circumscribed DLs without the finite model property and/or fixed roles instead of a detailed complexity analysis. Thus, the complexity of reasoning in circumscribed DL-Lite$_{bool}^{\mathcal{F}}$ KBs with fixed roles (and without minimized roles), the complexity of reasoning in circumscribed $\mathcal{ALCFI}$ KBs without fixed and minimized roles, and the complexity of reasoning in role-layered circumscribed DL-Lite$_{bool}^{\mathcal{R}}$ KBs without minimized roles remains open. For $\mathcal{ALCFI}$, we conjecture concept satisfiability to be NExp^{NP}-complete. Note that, in this case, hardness follows from the NExp^{NP}-lower bound for $\mathcal{ALC}$ established in [6].
- It remains open whether the condition of being role-layered is necessary for obtaining the finite model property/decidability result for DL-Lite$_{bool}^{\mathcal{R}}$.
- Finally, it would be of great interest to extend our results to more expressive ontology and query languages and, for example, to consider the decidability and complexity of conjunctive query answering relative to circumscribed KBs.

References

1. Artale, A., Calvanese, D., Kontchakov, R., Zakharyaschev, M.: The DL-lite family and relations. J. Artif. Intell. Res (JAIR) 36, 1–69 (2009)
2. Baader, F., Hollunder, B.: Embedding defaults into terminological knowledge representation formalisms. J. Autom. Reasoning 14(1), 149–180 (1995)
3. Baader, F., McGuiness, D.L., Nardi, D., Patel-Schneider, P.: The Description Logic Handbook: Theory, implementation and applications. Cambridge University Press (2003)
4. Blackburn, P., de Rijke, M., Venema, Y.: Modal Logic. Cambridge Tracts in Theoretical Computer Science, vol. 53. Cambridge University Press (2001)
5. Bonatti, P.A., Faella, M., Sauro, L.: Defeasible inclusions in low-complexity DLs. J. Artif. Intell. Res (JAIR) 42, 719–764 (2011)
6. Bonatti, P.A., Lutz, C., Wolter, F.: The complexity of circumscription in DLs. J. Artif. Intell. Res (JAIR) 35, 717–773 (2009)
7. Brewka, G.: The logic of inheritance in frame systems. In: Proceedings of the 10th International Joint Conference on Artificial Intelligence (IJCAI 1987), pp. 483–488. Morgan Kaufmann (1987)
8. Cadoli, M., Donini, F., Schaerf, M.: Closed world reasoning in hybrid systems. In: Proc. of ISMIS 1990, pp. 474–481. Elsevier (1990)
9. Calvanese, D., De Giacomo, G., Lembo, D., Lenzerini, M., Rosati, R.: DL-Lite: Tractable description logics for ontologies. In: Proc. of AAAI 2005, pp. 602–607 (2005)
10. Casini, G., Straccia, U.: Defeasible inheritance-based description logics. J. Artif. Intell. Res (JAIR) 48, 415–473 (2013)
11. Donini, F.M., Nardi, D., Rosati, R.: Description logics of minimal knowledge and negation as failure. ACM Trans. Comput. Log. 3(2), 177–225 (2002)
12. Eiter, T., Ianni, G., Lukasiewicz, T., Schindlauer, R., Tompits, H.: Combining answer set programming with description logics for the semantic web. Artificial Intelligence 172(12), 1495–1539 (2008)

13. Feferman, S., Vaught, R.L.: The first-order properties of algebraic systems. Fundamenta Mathematicae 47, 57–103 (1959)
14. Giordano, L., Gliozzi, V., Olivetti, N., Pozzato, G.L.: Preferential description logics. In: Dershowitz, N., Voronkov, A. (eds.) LPAR 2007. LNCS (LNAI), vol. 4790, pp. 257–272. Springer, Heidelberg (2007)
15. Giordano, L., Gliozzi, V., Olivetti, N., Pozzato, G.L.: A non-monotonic description logic for reasoning about typicality. Artif. Intell. 195, 165–202 (2013)
16. Gottlob, G., Hernich, A., Kupke, C., Lukasiewicz, T.: Equality-friendly well-founded semantics and applications to description logics. In: Description Logics (2012)
17. Gottlob, G., Hernich, A., Kupke, C., Lukasiewicz, T.: Stable model semantics for guarded existential rules and description logics. In: Principles of Knowledge Representation and Reasoning: Proceedings of the Fourteenth International Conference, KR 2014, Vienna, Austria, July 20-24 (2014)
18. Konev, B., Lutz, C., Walther, D., Wolter, F.: Model-theoretic inseparability and modularity of description logic ontologies. Artif. Intell. 203, 66–103 (2013)
19. Kontchakov, R., Wolter, F., Zakharyaschev, M.: Logic-based ontology comparison and module extraction, with an application to dl-lite. Artif. Intell. 174(15), 1093–1141 (2010)
20. Motik, B., Rosati, R.: Reconciling description logics and rules. Journal of the ACM (JACM) 57(5), 30 (2010)
21. Rector, A.L.: Defaults, context, and knowledge: Alternatives for OWL-indexed knowledge bases. In: Pacific Symposium on Biocomputing, pp. 226–237. World Scientific (2004)
22. Sengupta, K., Krisnadhi, A.A., Hitzler, P.: Local closed world semantics: Grounded circumscription for OWL. In: Aroyo, L., Welty, C., Alani, H., Taylor, J., Bernstein, A., Kagal, L., Noy, N., Blomqvist, E. (eds.) ISWC 2011, Part I. LNCS, vol. 7031, pp. 617–632. Springer, Heidelberg (2011)
23. Stevens, R., Aranguren, M.E., Wolstencroft, K., Sattler, U., Drummond, N., Horridge, M., Rector, A.L.: Using OWL to model biological knowledge. International Journal of Man-Machine Studies 65(7), 583–594 (2007)

Stability, Supportedness, Minimality and Kleene Answer Set Programs[*]

Patrick Doherty[1] and Andrzej Szałas[1,2]

[1] Dept. of Computer and Information Science
Linköping University, 581 83 Linköping, Sweden
patrick.doherty@liu.se
[2] Institute of Informatics, University of Warsaw
Banacha 2, 02-097 Warsaw, Poland
andrzej.szalas@{liu.se,mimuw.edu.pl}

Abstract. Answer Set Programming is a widely known knowledge representation framework based on the logic programming paradigm that has been extensively studied in the past decades. The semantic framework for Answer Set Programs is based on the use of stable model semantics. There are two characteristics intrinsically associated with the construction of stable models for answer set programs. Any member of an answer set is supported through facts and chains of rules and those members are in the answer set only if generated minimally in such a manner. These two characteristics, supportedness and minimality, provide the essence of stable models. Additionally, answer sets are implicitly partial and that partiality provides epistemic overtones to the interpretation of disjunctive rules and default negation. This paper is intended to shed light on these characteristics by defining a semantic framework for answer set programming based on an extended first-order Kleene logic with weak and strong negation. Additionally, a definition of strongly supported models is introduced, separate from the minimality assumption explicit in stable models. This is used to both clarify and generate alternative semantic interpretations for answer set programs with disjunctive rules in addition to answer set programs with constraint rules. An algorithm is provided for computing supported models and comparative complexity results between strongly supported and stable model generation are provided.

1 Introduction

Answer Set Programming (ASP) [2, 4–6, 16, 17] is a knowledge representation framework based on the logic programming paradigm that uses an answer set/stable model semantics for logic programs as its basis. There are a number of extensions to the language of ASP that provide increased expressivity relative to standard Prolog with negation as failure. ASP allows two kinds of negation, classical or "strong" negation and default or "weak" negation. Additionally, it is extended to allow disjunctive heads in rules.

[*] This work is partially supported by the Swedish Research Council (VR) Linnaeus Center CADICS, the ELLIIT network organization for Information and Communication Technology, the Swedish Foundation for Strategic Research (CUAS Project), the EU FP7 project SHERPA (grant agreement 600958), and Vinnova NFFP6 Project 2013-01206.

T. Eiter et al. (Eds.): Brewka Festschrift, LNAI 9060, pp. 125–140, 2015.

A very attractive feature of ASP is the use of an open world assumption as default in its semantic theory rather than the closed world assumption present in standard Prolog and most variants of Datalog. The open world assumption arises naturally in ASP since its semantic theory is intrinsically based on partial interpretations or models. Additionally, one can syntactically encode local closed world assumptions for particular relations in an answer set program in a fine-grained manner when needed.

ASP also includes constraint rules, rules whose heads are false. Constraint rules have been shown to be quite useful as a model filtering technique in various applications of ASP. Interestingly, the ASP semantics for constraint rules (and existing implementations) makes implicit use of a technique associated with filtered circumscription where answer sets are first generated for a subset of rules (non-constraint rules) in an answer set program and then these answer sets are filtered with the remaining constraint rules. There are other ways to interpret the semantics of constraint rules that are equally intuitive and will be considered.

In [16] the following informal principles that guide such a construction by a rational reasoner are pointed out. During the construction of an answer set S for an answer set program Π,

1. S must satisfy the rules of Π in the sense that any atom in S is in the head of a rule r of Π and the chain of rules used to satisfy the atom should be grounded in facts of Π;
2. the construction of S does not include any atoms that are not forced to be in S except through the explicit use of chains of rules grounded in facts.

The first principle describes a form of chained rule *support* for any atom in S while the second principle describes a *minimality* principle for any answer set S for an answer set program Π. In fact, a supported, minimal model for Π is a stable model for Π in the technical sense.

On the surface, both supportedness and the minimality principle make intuitive sense, especially in the context of normal answer set programs (those with non-disjunctive heads) and without constraint rules. When an answer set program is extended with either rules with disjunctive heads or constraint rules, or both, there are equally intuitive semantics that provide partial models for such programs that are not necessary minimal in the sense used for stable model semantics.

In order to explore these distinctions in the context of semantic alternatives for answer set programs which allow both rules with disjunctive heads and constraint rules, the underlying formalism has to be able to make a distinction between *supportedness* and *minimality*. Additionally, one would like the underlying semantic theory to elucidate the use of partial interpretations explicitly in the logical apparatus used. This implies the use of a multi-valued logic as a semantic basis for answer set programming.

The underlying logic used as a basis for a semantic theory for answer set programs that may include both classical and default negation, disjunctive heads in rules, and constraint rules will be a well known first-order three-valued logic proposed by Kleene. This logic uses the strong connectives for disjunction, conjunction. implication and (strong) negation and is denoted by $\mathcal{K}_3$. $\mathcal{K}_3$ is then extended with a nonmonotonic (weak) negation connective, *not*, in addition to a conditional connective that supports the intuitive reading of ASP rules. Rules are also generalized to include arbitrary first-order Kleene formulas in the bodies of rules.

Interestingly, this logic is sound for ASP programs with finite domains in the following sense. Let Π be an answer set program and $M_{asp}(\Pi)$ the stable models of Π using the stable model semantics. Additionally, let $M_{KL^*}(\Pi)$ be the partial models of Π using the modified Kleene logic and $Trans()$ a straightforward translation function that takes a partial model from $\mathcal{K}_3$ and returns an ASP model consisting of positive and (classically) negative literals. Then:

$$M_{asp}(\Pi) \subseteq \{m \mid m' \in M_{KL^*}(\Pi) \wedge m = Trans(m')\},$$

where:

$$Trans(m') \overset{\text{def}}{=} \{\ell \mid m'(\ell) = \text{T}\} \cup \{\neg\ell \mid m'(\ell) = \text{F}\}. \tag{1}$$

Given that this is the case, definitions will be provided that allow us to distinguish between strongly supported models for an ASP program Π and minimal, supported models for Π. For normal ASP's, supported models and stable models are equivalent. For ASPs with disjunctive rules, one can define a semantics in terms of only strongly supported models, or strongly supported, minimal models. In the latter case, equivalence is shown between the strongly supported, minimal models of an answer set program with disjunctive rules and its stable models.

An alternative semantics for ASPs is provided by simply appealing to the use of strongly supported models. The gain here is that the semantic intuitions are equally convincing, yet the complexity in constructing answer sets for ASPs with disjunctive rules is lower. An algorithm for generating strongly supported models for ASP's is also provided. Comparative complexity results are provided for stable models and supported models.

The paper concludes with a discussion of constraint rules and ASPs. Two alternative ways to generate answer sets for ASPs that include constraints are provided. In the first case, one simply generates the strongly supported, (minimal) models of the ASP using Kleene semantics and translates these into answer sets using the $Trans()$ function. In the other case, one partitions an ASP into two sets, C and NC, representing the constraint rules and other rules, respectively. One then generates the supported minimal models for NC using Kleene semantics and then filters these with the constraint rules in C leaving only those models that satisfy the constraints rules in C, too.

The latter case appears to provide the current semantics for ASPs with constraint rules and existing implementations of ASPs appear to follow this semantics. Interestingly, the former case is equally feasible and seems to make more sense in the context of ASPs that have an underlying Kleene semantics. A constraint rule is simply a rule like any other in an ASP and filtering is implicit in the model construction for the full ASP. These two approaches do not necessarily generate the same models for an ASP.

The paper is structured as follows. In Section 2 we define an extended first-order language and its modified Kleene three-valued semantics. In Section 3 we introduce ASP^K and define its semantics using strongly supported models. We also consider ASP^K_{min} admitting only minimal strongly supported models. Section 4 is devoted to alternative semantics for constraint rules. In Section 5 we discuss minimality and its effects in the context of standard ASP stable model semantics and ASP^K strongly supported model semantics. Section 6 presents an algorithm for computing strongly supported models and comparative complexity results between standard ASP, ASP^K and ASP^K_{min}. Finally, Section 7 concludes the paper.

2   First-Order Formulas with Default Negation

Answer set rules in the formalism to be introduced will be generalized to allow arbitrary first-order formulas with default negation in their bodies. In this section, the language of first-order formulas used is introduced. Additionally, the underlying semantics for this language will be a modified first-order three-valued Kleene logic $\mathcal{K}_3$ with weak and strong negation that is also described.

Let D be a finite set of constants, called the *domain*. In the current paper we deal with finite domains only and assume that these domains consist of constant symbols. We further assume that V is the set of individual variables and $\mathcal{R}$ is the set of relation symbols. The number of arguments of $r \in \mathcal{R}$ is denoted by $n(r)$.

Definition 1. By a *positive literal* (or an *atom*) we mean any expression of the form $r(a_1, \ldots, a_{n(r)})$, where $r \in \mathcal{R}$ and $a_1, \ldots, a_{n(r)} \in D \cup V$. A *negative literal* is an expression of the form $\neg\ell$, where ℓ is a positive literal. A *literal* is a positive or a negative literal. A *ground literal* is a literal without variables. A set of literals is *consistent* if it contains no literal ℓ together with its negation $\neg\ell$.[1]   ◁

Definition 2. By *Kleene first-order formulas*, KFOL, we understand formulas of first-order logic with an additional connective '*not*', called *default negation*:

$$\langle \text{KFOL} \rangle ::= \text{T} \mid \text{F} \mid \text{U} \mid \langle \textit{Atom} \rangle \mid \neg \langle \text{KFOL} \rangle \mid \textit{not} \langle \text{KFOL} \rangle \mid$$
$$\langle \text{KFOL} \rangle \vee \langle \text{KFOL} \rangle \mid \langle \text{KFOL} \rangle \wedge \langle \text{KFOL} \rangle \mid \langle \text{KFOL} \rangle \Rightarrow \langle \text{KFOL} \rangle$$
$$\exists \langle V \rangle \langle \text{KFOL} \rangle \mid \forall \langle V \rangle \langle \text{KFOL} \rangle \mid (\langle \text{KFOL} \rangle) \qquad ◁$$

The semantics of KFOL is three-valued, with the set of truth values $\{\text{T}, \text{F}, \text{U}\}$ ordered by '$<$' defined as follows:

$$\text{F} < \text{U} < \text{T}. \tag{2}$$

For the propositional connectives, we use the semantics of Kleene's system with strong connectives [18]. We denote the logic as $\mathcal{K}_3$.

Definition 3. For $u, w \in \{\text{T}, \text{F}, \text{U}\}$ we define:

$$u \vee w \stackrel{\text{def}}{=} \max\{u, w\}, \quad u \wedge w \stackrel{\text{def}}{=} \min\{u, w\}, \tag{3}$$

where max, min are maximum and minimum w.r.t. ordering (2).

Strong Kleene negation, $\neg$, is defined as:

$$\neg\text{F} \stackrel{\text{def}}{=} \text{T}, \quad \neg\text{U} \stackrel{\text{def}}{=} \text{U}, \quad \neg\text{T} \stackrel{\text{def}}{=} \text{F} \tag{4}$$

---

[1] We always remove double strong negations using $\neg(\neg\ell) \stackrel{\text{def}}{=} \ell$.

Implication $\Rightarrow$ is defined by:

$$u \Rightarrow w \stackrel{\text{def}}{=} \neg u \vee w. \tag{5}$$

$\triangleleft$

We then extend $\mathcal{K}_3$ logic with two additional *external* connectives for default negation and the implication connective used in rules.

Default negation will be defined as *weak* or *external* negation, '*not*':

$$not\ \text{F} \stackrel{\text{def}}{=} \text{T}, \quad not\ \text{U} \stackrel{\text{def}}{=} \text{T}, \quad not\ \text{T} \stackrel{\text{def}}{=} \text{F}. \tag{6}$$

Weak negation is a nonmonotonic connective with the intuitive reading *absence of truth*. Both types of negation have been used in the study of presupposition in natural language [12].

To define the semantics of rules we will also use another implication:

$$u \leftarrow w \stackrel{\text{def}}{=} \begin{cases} \text{F for } w = \text{T and } u \in \{\text{F}, \text{U}\}; \\ \text{T otherwise.} \end{cases} \tag{7}$$

This implication connective is also discussed in [23].

Remark 1.

– A similar logic has been considered in [22]. However, we use different implications here in addition to using two negation connectives. Also, our definition of satisfiability of rules (Definition 8) is different. There is a rich history of explicit use of partial interpretations and multi-valued logics as a basis for semantic theories for logic programs. Some related and additional representative examples are [8, 14, 15].
– In [21] the logic of here-and-there (HT) is used to define the semantics of ASP. HT can be defined by means of a five-valued logic, N_5, defined over two worlds: h (here) and t (there), where the set of literals associated with h is included in the set of literals associated with t. N_5 uses truth values $\{-2, -1, 0, 1, 2\}$, where the values $-1, 1$ characterize literals associated with h and not associated with t. On the other hand, for ASP models it is assumed that these sets are equal, so $-1, 1$ become redundant. Therefore, in the context of ASP one actually does not have to use full N_5 as it reduces to the three-valued logic of Kleene $\mathcal{K}_3$ with the additional implication (7) used in the current paper, with $-2, 0, 2$ of N_5 corresponding to F, U, T of $\mathcal{K}_3$, respectively. $\triangleleft$

Definition 4. For a given set of relation symbols $\mathcal{R}$ and a set of constants D, by an *interpretation* over $\mathcal{R}$ and D we mean any finite consistent set of ground literals (positive or negative) with relation symbols from $\mathcal{R}$ and constants from D. $\triangleleft$

Note that $Trans()$, defined in (1), allows us to easily switch between three-valued Kleene interpretations and interpretations in the sense of Definition 4.

Definition 5.

- Given a domain D, a *valuation of variables* (*valuation*, in short) is a mapping $v : V \longrightarrow D$.
- For $A \in$ KFOL and valuation v, by $v(A)$ we mean a formula obtained from A by replacing every free variable x in A by the constant $v(x)$.   ◁

Definition 6. For a given set of relation symbols $\mathcal{R}$, domain D, interpretation I over D, $\mathcal{R}$, and valuation v, the *value of a* KFOL *formula A w.r.t. I and v*, denoted by A_v^I, is defined as follows:

- for $t \in \{T, F, U\}$ we have $t_v^I \overset{\text{def}}{=} t$;
- $r(a_1, \dots, a_{n(r)})_v^I \overset{\text{def}}{=} \begin{cases} T \text{ when } r(a'_1, \dots, a'_{n(r)}) \in I, \\ \quad \text{where } a'_i = a_i \text{ for } a_i \in D \text{ and } a'_i = v(a_i) \text{ for } a_i \in V; \\ F \text{ when } \neg r(a'_1, \dots, a'_{n(r)}) \in I, \text{ where } a'_i \text{ are as above}; \\ U \text{ otherwise}; \end{cases}$
- for $A \circ B$ and $\circ A$, where $\circ$ is a propositional connective, we use definitions of connectives (3)–(7), respectively;
- $\exists x[A(x)] \overset{\text{def}}{=} \max_{a \in D}\{A(a)\}$, $\forall x[A(x)] \overset{\text{def}}{=} \min_{a \in D}\{A(a)\}$, where max, min are maximum and minimum w.r.t. ordering (2).   ◁

In the case of expressions without variables, in Definition 6 the valuation v becomes redundant, so we sometimes write A^I rather than A_v^I.

3   Kleene Answer Set Programs

Kleene answer set programs can now be defined as a set of rules where arbitrary first-order formulas are allowed in the bodies of rules.

Definition 7. A *Kleene answer set program* consists of a finite set of rules of the following form, where $\ell_1, \dots, \ell_k$ are (positive or negative) literals and A is a Kleene first-order formula or the empty symbol:

$$\ell_1 \vee \dots \vee \ell_k \leftarrow A. \tag{8}$$

The disjunction $\ell_1 \vee \dots \vee \ell_k$ is called the *head* and A is called the *body* of (8). Variables occurring in the head of a rule should also occur free in the rule's body.

The empty head evaluates to F. Rules with the empty head are called *constraints*. The empty body evaluates to T. Rules with the empty body are called *facts* and are written without the symbol '$\leftarrow$'.   ◁

Remark 2. Note that in Definition 7 we require a rather weak form of safety. Safety in the context of answer set programming is usually defined by requiring that in every rule each variable appearing in the rule appears in at least one positive literal in the body of that rule (see, e.g., [1, 3]). However, this notion of safety is rather restrictive as it disallows, e.g., important rules for closing the world locally, such as:

$$\neg p(X) \leftarrow not \ p(X). \tag{9}$$

When rules allow for more complex expressions, different versions of safety are considered [7]. On the other hand, when we fix domains as finite sets of constant symbols, the problems related to non-safety disappear. Namely, if D is the domain, whenever a rule uses a variable, the rule implicitly involves the "domain checking" atom for each variable. For example, (9), in fact, expresses:

$$\neg p(X) \leftarrow d(X) \wedge not\ p(X). \tag{10}$$

The positive atom $d(X)$ in (10) expresses the fact that the value of X is in D. If there are more variables, rules semantically behave as if such "domain checks" were added for each variable appearing in the rule.   ◁

Definition 8. An interpretation I is a *model* of (8) if for every valuation $v : V \longrightarrow D$,

$$\left((\ell_1 \vee \ldots \vee \ell_k) \leftarrow A\right)_v^I = \textsc{t}. \tag{11}$$

I is a model of an ASP^K program if it is a model of every rule of the program.   ◁

Definition 9. A model I of an ASP^K program Π is *minimal* if there is no model J of Π such that $J \subsetneq I$.   ◁

The following definitions generalize known definitions of well-supported models for standard normal logic programs with a two-valued semantics [10, 11] to the case of ASP^K programs. This generalization is called *strongly supported* models. Our formulation concentrates on derivability rather than on the existence of a certain well-founded ordering, as in [10, 11]. The intuition is that whenever a (positive or negative) literal belongs to a strongly supported model for a program Π then there should be a finite derivation of the literal starting from facts of Π and, if needed, using rules of Π. Of course, our definition can also be given in terms of well-founded relations as in [10, 11], but the definition used here simplifies presentation and proofs.

Let us start with a definition of the value of a formula w.r.t. two interpretations: the first one for evaluating formulas outside of the scope of '*not* ' and the second one for evaluating formulas of the form '*not C*'.

Definition 10. Given a domain D, interpretations I, N and a valuation v, the *value of a* KFOL *formula A w.r.t. D, I, N, v*, denoted by $A_v^{I,N}$, is defined as follows:[2]

$$A_v^{I,N} \overset{\mathrm{def}}{=} \mathbb{A}_v^I,$$

where $\mathbb{A}$ is obtained from A by substituting subformulas of the form '*not C*' by truth values $(not\ C_v^N)$.[3]   ◁

Strongly supported models can now be defined.

Definition 11. Let Π be an ASP^K program. A model N for Π is *strongly supported* provided that there is a sequence of interpretations I_i with $i = 0, \ldots, m$ for some $m \in \omega$, such that $N = \bigcup_{0 \leq i \leq m} I_i$, and:

---

[2] Recall that $\mathbb{A}_v^I$ is defined in Definition 6.
[3] Note that C_v^N is a truth value, so $(not\ C_v^N)$ is a truth value, too.

(i) for every fact of the form '$\ell_1 \vee \ldots \vee \ell_k$', at least one of literals of $\ell_1, \ldots, \ell_k$ is in I_0;

(ii) for every $0 < n \leq m$, every rule '$\ell_1 \vee \ldots \vee \ell_k \leftarrow A$' in Π and every valuation v, if $A_v^{\bigcup_{0 \leq j \leq n-1} I_j, N} = \text{T}$ then a (possibly empty) subset of $\{v(\ell_1), \ldots, v(\ell_k)\}$ is included in I_n;

(iii) for $i = 0, \ldots, m$, I_i can only contain literals obtained by applying points (i) and (ii) specified above.   ◁

The following examples illustrate various aspects of Definition 11.

Example 1. Let the domain be $D_1 = \{a, b\}$ and let Π_1 be the program:

$$r(X) \leftarrow p(X).$$
$$p(a).$$

Then, using the notation of Definition 11, we have that $I_0 = \{p(a)\}$, $I_1 = \{r(a)\}$. Of course, $N = I_0 \cup I_1 = \{p(a), r(a)\}$ is a model for Π_1 so it is a strongly supported model. On the other hand, $\{p(a), r(a), r(b)\}$ is a model of Π_1 but is not strongly supported.   ◁

Example 2. Let the domain be $D_2 = \{a, b\}$ and let Π_2 be the program:

$$r(X) \leftarrow \neg q(X) \wedge not\ p(X).$$
$$\neg q(a).$$
$$q(b).$$

Then $N = \{\neg q(a), q(b), r(a)\}$ is a strongly supported model for Π_2. Using again the notation of Definition 11, we have that $N = I_0 \cup I_1$, where $I_0 = \{\neg q(a), q(b)\}$, $I_1 = \{r(a)\}$. This follows from the fact that for $v(X) = a$:

$$\left(\neg q(X) \wedge not\ p(X)\right)_v^{I_0, N} = (\neg q(X))_v^{I_0} \wedge not\ p(X)_v^{N}$$
$$= \neg q(a)^{I_0} \wedge not\ p(a)^{N} = \text{T}.$$ ◁

Example 3. Let the domain be $D_3 = \emptyset$ and let Π_3 be the program:

$$p \leftarrow q.$$
$$q \leftarrow not\ p.$$
$$p \leftarrow not\ q.$$

Then the only strongly supported model for Π_3 is $N = \{p\}$. Here $N = I_0 \cup I_1$, where $I_0 = \emptyset$ (there are no facts) and $I_1 = \{p\}$ since for the third rule we have:

$$(not\ q)^{I_0, N} = (not\ q^{N}) = not\ \text{U} = \text{T}.$$

On the other hand, $N' = \{p, q\}$ is not strongly supported. Again, $I_0 = \emptyset$, so for the first rule we have $q^{I_0, N} = \text{U}$, for the second rule we have $(not\ p)^{I_0, N} = \text{F}$ and, for the third rule, $(not\ q)^{I_0, N} = \text{F}$. Therefore, no rule produces new results.   ◁

The following example shows that strongly supported models do not have to be minimal.

Example 4. Consider the following program Π_4 over domain $D_4 = \{a\}$:

$q(X) \leftarrow p(X)$.
$p(a) \vee q(a)$.

According to Definition 11, program Π_4 has two strongly supported models: $N = \{q(a)\}$ and $N' = \{p(a), q(a)\}$. Of course, N' is not minimal since $N \subsetneq N'$.   ◁

The following definitions and theorem show the relation between stable models and strongly supported models. For a discussion of stable models see [19].

Definition 12. An interpretation I for a Kleene answer set program Π is a *stable model* for Π provided that I is a minimal strongly supported model for Π.   ◁

We shall consider two versions of ASP.

Definition 13.

- By ASP^K we understand Kleene answer set programs with the semantics given by strongly supported models.
- By ASP^K_{min} we understand Kleene answer set programs with the semantics given by stable models.   ◁

Theorem 1.

1. For answer set programs with rules of the (traditional) form, where all ℓ_i are literals and $k > 0$:[4]

   $$\ell_1 \vee \ldots \vee \ell_k \leftarrow \ell_m, \ldots, \ell_n, not\ \ell_s, \ldots, not\ \ell_t,$$

   ASP^K_{min} coincides with answer set programming in the traditional sense (as presented, e.g., in [5, 16, 19]).
2. If rules of an ASP^K program Π are all of the form '$\ell \leftarrow A$.', where ℓ is a literal, then a model I for Π is stable iff I is strongly supported.

Proof.
1. Let I be a stable model in the sense of Definition 12. Then I is both strongly supported and minimal.

Observe that strongly supported models are constructed in such a way that all formulas of the form '$not\ C$' are evaluated in the context of the final interpretation N (see Definition 11) and, for a given valuation v, they have fixed truth values $(not\ C_v^N)$. By assumption, C is a literal. In the traditional definition of stable models [19], the notion of reduct corresponds to substituting '$not\ C$' by $(not\ C_v^N)$ and removing redundant literals and rules. Now minimality guarantees stability in the traditional sense.

2. Of course, by definition, stability implies strong supportedness.

To prove that strong supportedness implies stability, suppose that there are two strongly supported models, J and J' such that $J \subsetneq J'$. By the construction of strongly supported models, $J' = J \cup K$, where literals in K are obtained by point (ii). of Definition 11. However, that would mean that J was not a model of Π as literals are added in (ii) only when there is a rule with true body and head not being true. Such literals are uniquely determined (by assumption heads contain single literals).   ◁

---

[4] The case when $k = 0$ (constraints) is dealt with in Section 4.

4 Constraints

Given a standard ASP program Π, let $NC(\Pi)$ be the rules in Π that are not constraint rules and let $C(\Pi)$ be the rules in Π that are constraint rules, where $NC(\Pi) \cup C(\Pi) = \Pi$. There are at least two alternatives for providing a semantic theory for constraints.

- In the first, one first computes the stable models for $NC(\Pi)$ and then eliminates those models in $NC(\Pi)$ that do not satisfy the constraint rules in $C(\Pi)$.
- In the second, one simply computes the stable models of $NC(\Pi) \cup C(\Pi)$.

The first alternative is that used traditionally for standard ASP (see, e.g., [16]). It is the basis for many of the most prominent implementations of ASP in the literature and is in fact similar to filtered circumscriptive approaches. The second method, which appears to be as intuitive, is similar to non-filtered circumscriptive approaches. These methods apply equally well for strongly supported models and ASP^K. In Definition 11, the second alternative is used. However, one can easily adjust the definition to reflect the first alternative.

The following example shows that these approaches are not equivalent.

Example 5. Consider program Π_5 (see [2, Example 32]):

$$a \vee b \leftarrow . \tag{12}$$

$$a \vee c \leftarrow . \tag{13}$$

$$\leftarrow a \wedge (not\ b) \wedge (not\ c). \tag{14}$$

$$\leftarrow (not\ a) \wedge b \wedge c. \tag{15}$$

According to the standard ASP semantics which uses the first alternative, Π_5 has no stable models. This follows from the fact that stable models of Π_5 without constraints (i.e., with only rules (12), (13)) are $\{a\}$ and $\{b, c\}$, and these models do not satisfy the constraints (14), (15).

When using the second alternative, when all rules (12)–(15) participate in computing models, there are two stable models $\{a, b\}, \{a, c\}$, which are also strongly supported models. The explanation used in [2] is that these models are not minimal for Π_5 without constraints, so they should not be considered. On the other hand, these models are both minimal and strongly supported for the theory expressed by Π_5 (in which case $\{a\}, \{b, c\}$ are not models, so are not considered in checking minimality). Note also that $\{a, b, c\}$ is a strongly supported but non-minimal model when Π_5 is interpreted using ASP^K.   ◁

Remark 3.

- Theorem 1(ii) holds when we allow constraints with the traditional semantics, since one first computes models and later eliminates those not satisfying constraints. Strongly supported models are in this case minimal and remain so even after filtering out some of them.
- Theorem 1(ii) also holds for the case when constraints participate in finding models: the models are in this case minimal models satisfying the whole program consisting of rules and constraints.   ◁

5 Minimality Revisited

In this section, we consider some relationships between stability, minimality [13, 20], and strong supportedness. When focussing on normal ASPs that do not contain disjunctive rules or constraints, stable model construction naturally generates only minimal models due to the lack of choice in the iterated construction from base facts. On the other hand, when extending expressivity to include rules with disjunctive heads and constraint rules, choice in the iterated construction of models and the different alternatives that can be used in applying constraints, open up opportunities for making different semantic choices when interpreting ASPs.

These choices become very clear when one bases semantic theories for ASPs on an explicit three-valued logic together with distinguishing strong supportedness from minimality. As is often the case with semantic intuitions associated with nonmonotonic formalisms, due to the space of choices, one has a number of different alternatives to choose from. The approach taken in this paper is simply to clarify these choices in as lucid a manner as possible and provide mechanisms for leaving the choice up to the knowledge engineer.

In the case of enforcing minimality in ASP theories, there are a number of arguments, not against minimality in principle, but for enforcing strong supportedness instead. For the case of normal ASPs (no disjunctive heads), strong supportedness and minimality are equivalent. In the case of ASPs with disjunctive rules, there is a history in the nonmonotonic literature of viewing minimality assumptions applied to disjunctions with suspicion, both for intuitive and pragmatic reasons as some of the examples have shown.

One of the more interesting reasons for not only having the capability to distinguish between supportedness and minimality, but to also be able to only construct strongly supported models in isolation, is a complexity argument (see Theorem 2 in Section 6). Complexity for constructing strongly supported models in the case of ASPs with disjunctive rules is lower than the complexity of constructing minimal, strongly supported models. Additionally, since one has the capability of applying local closed world assumptions to specific relations due to the default open world assumption associated with the ASP framework, one seems to have the best of both worlds. In the following, a number of examples are provided to further clarify the subtle relationships between stability, minimality and supportedness.

The following example is from [19].

Example 6. Consider the domain $D_6 = \{a, b\}$ and program Π_6:

$r(X) \leftarrow p(X) \wedge not\ q(X).$

$p(a).\ p(b).\ q(a).$

Then Π_6 has two minimal models:

$$I_0 = \{p(a), p(b), q(a), r(b)\}, I_1 = \{p(a), p(b), q(a), q(b)\}.$$

According to [19], I_0 is a "good" model (an answer set) while I_1 is "bad" (not an answer set). The explanation given in [19] is related to an argument based on program completion. A more direct explanation is that the fact $q(b)$ appearing in I_1 is not supported (not being a conclusion of the rule of Π_6).   ◁

Example 7. Let the program domain be $D_7 = \{jack, john, xco\}$ and Π_7 consist of the following rule and facts:[5]

$$luckyBroker(X) \vee successfulBroker(X) \leftarrow \tag{16}$$
$$\forall Y(invests(X, Y) \Rightarrow makesProfit(X, Y)). \tag{17}$$
$$\neg luckyBroker(X) \leftarrow not\ \big(\forall Y(invests(X, Y) \Rightarrow makesProfit(X, Y))\big). \tag{18}$$
$$perfectBroker(X) \leftarrow successfulBroker(X) \wedge luckyBroker(X). \tag{19}$$
$$invests(jack, xco). \tag{20}$$
$$invests(john, xco). \tag{21}$$
$$makesProfit(jack, xco). \tag{22}$$

According to the ASP^K semantics, Π_7 has the following strongly supported models:

$$\{(20), (21), (22), luckyBroker(jack), \neg luckyBroker(john)\}, \tag{23}$$
$$\{(20), (21), (22), successfulBroker(jack), \neg luckyBroker(john)\}, \tag{24}$$
$$\{(20), (21), (22), luckyBroker(jack), successfulBroker(jack), \tag{25}$$
$$perfectBroker(jack), \neg luckyBroker(john)\}$$

According to the ASP^K_{min} semantics, Π_7 has only (stable) models (23) and (24). But model (25) makes perfect intuitive sense and it is questionable whether or not it should be omitted.   ◁

Recall that one can close the world locally, using rules of the form (9). However, such closures minimize relations in the classical sense (by minimizing their positive instances while maximizing negative ones). In Definition 9, minimality is defined w.r.t. both positive and negative instances. Since the rule (9) adds literals, in general such closures do not preserve the set of stable models nor strongly supported models and may seriously affect the result, as the following example shows.

Example 8. Let the domain be $D_8 = \{a\}$ and let Π_8 be the program:

$$r(X) \leftarrow not\ p(X).$$
$$s(X) \leftarrow \neg p(X).$$

The only strongly supported model for Π_8, being also its stable model, is $\{r(a)\}$.

By closing the relation p in Π_8 by rule (9), we obtain a program with the only strongly supported (and stable) model $\{\neg p(a), r(a), s(a)\}$.   ◁

---

[5] Observe that the right arrow $\Rightarrow$ is used in formulas in the antecedent of a rule according to the syntax of first-order formulas allowed in the antecedent to a rule, whereas the left arrow $\leftarrow$ is used to distinguish between the antecedent and consequent of a rule.

6   Computing Strongly Supported Models and Complexity Results

Algorithm 1 allows us to compute strongly supported models. The intuition is that we first guess a candidate for a strongly supported model and then we check whether the model is strongly supported (i.e., can be generated from facts, using rules).

Algorithm 1. Computing strongly supported models for ASP^K programs

---

Input: An ASP^K program Π with domain D, consisting of a set of rules S.
Output: A nondeterministically computed strongly supported model N for Π.

/ * For notation see Definition 10   */

1 **generate** nondeterministically an interpretation N with constants from D;
2 **if** there is $r \in S$ and a valuation v of variables in D with $r_v^N \neq$ T **then**
3   **reject** N;   / * N is not a model for P */
4   **stop**;

/ * otherwise N is a candidate for a strongly supported model.   */

/ * In the remaining part of the algorithm we verify whether N */
/ * is a strongly supported model by generating a supported interpretation I */
/ * and checking whether $N = I$.   */

/ * We use the fact that during computations I cannot decrease and always $I \subseteq N$.   */

5 set $I = \emptyset$;
6 **repeat**
7   set $W = \big\{ (r, v) \mid r \in S$ and v is valuation of variables in D with $r_v^{I,N} \neq$ T $\big\}$;
8   **foreach** $(r, v) \in W$ **do**
        / * Let $r =$ '$\ell_1 \vee \ldots \vee \ell_k \leftarrow A$.'   */
9   **if** $N \cap \{v(\ell_1), \ldots, v(\ell_k)\} = \emptyset$ **then reject** N; **stop**;
10   / * no subset of $\{v(\ell_1), \ldots, v(\ell_k)\}$, when added to I, can make $r_v^{I,N} =$ T   */
11   / * without violating the invariant $I \subseteq N$ */
12   **else set** $I = I \cup (N \cap \{v(\ell_1), \ldots, v(\ell_k)\})$;
13 **until** $W = \emptyset$;
14 **if** $N = I$ **then accept** N as a strongly supported model for Π
15 **else reject** N;

In the following theorem we consider data complexity. In the answer set programming literature, expression (program) complexity is more common, mainly due to the use of grounding. On the other hand, ASP^K is a database language (by restriction to finite domains) and we do not use grounding. Therefore data complexity is more relevant here.

Theorem 2.

1. Checking whether an ASP^K program has a strongly supported model is Σ_1^P-complete (i.e., NP-complete).
2. Checking whether an ASP_{min}^K program has a stable model is Σ_2^P-complete.

Proof.

1. To prove the first claim it suffices to observe that ASP^K is at least as expressive as ASP, so the considered problem is NP-hard. To show that it is in NP, we use Algorithm 1 which runs in time polynomial w.r.t. the size of the domain D (assuming the input program Π is fixed, so has size bounded by a constant).
2. To prove the second claim we first show hardness of the considered problem for Σ_2^P and then we show that the problem actually is in Σ_2^P.
   (a) By results of [9, Section 3],[6] checking whether an ASP_{min}^K program has a stable model is Σ_2^P-hard.
   (b) To show that checking whether an ASP_{min}^K program has a stable model is in Σ_2^P, we encode the problem by a second-order formula of the form:

$$\exists \bar{P} \forall \bar{R} \; A(\bar{P}, \bar{R}), \tag{26}$$

where $\exists \bar{P} \forall \bar{R}$ are all second-order quantifiers used.
To check whether an ASP^K program Π has a stable model we first guess the model and then check the model for minimality:
   - guessing the model can be expressed by using existential second-order quantifiers $\exists \bar{P}$, where $\bar{P}$ are all relations in Π;
   - checking the guessed model for minimality can be done in a manner similar to circumscription, where quantifiers $\forall \bar{R}$ are used – for details of how the suitable formula can look like see, e.g., [13].

As a result, one obtains a formula of the required form (26), meaning that the considered problem is indeed in Σ_2^P.   ◁

The above theorem shows that the minimality requirement raises complexity from NP (i.e., Σ_1^P) to Σ_2^P in terms of the polynomial hierarchy.

Remark 4. Note that Algorithm 1 treats rules and constraints uniformly.

The algorithm can be easily modified for the case when constraints are separated. Namely, S in the algorithm should consist of all rules with nonempty heads (not being constraints). After generating strongly supported models one should check whether such models satisfy the constraints and reject models not satisfying them.   ◁

7   Conclusions

This paper has explored the subtle relationship between stability, supportedness and minimality in the context of Answer Set Programming. This has been done by making a formal distinction between two characteristics of stable models, strong supportedness and minimality. This was done by introducing a modified first-order three-valued Kleene Logic used as the semantic basis for interpreting Kleene answer set programs in the language of ASP^K. Strongly supported models were then defined. It was shown that strongly supported models and stable models are equivalent in the context of normal answer set programs, where no constraint rules or disjunctive rules are allowed.

---

[6] With a suitable encoding allowing one to move from expression complexity to data complexity.

With the addition of disjunctive rules, use of strongly supported models as a semantic basis differs from stable models due in part to the separation of support and minimality. An argument is presented for using (strongly) supported models as a semantic interpretation of disjunctive answer set programs. The argument is not exclusive since one can combine minimality and supportedness if so desired. One of the advantages of not doing this is based on a complexity argument. Expressiveness of answer set programs can be extended to the use of arbitrary first-order formulas in the antecedents of rules without any modification to the underlying semantics. A non-deterministic algorithm for generating strongly supported models is also provided. Additionally, an analysis of constraint rules is provided with consideration of two alternative approaches to their application, leading to two different semantic interpretations of answer set programs with constraint rules.

References

1. Alviano, M., Faber, W., Leone, N., Perri, S., Pfeifer, G., Terracina, G.: The disjunctive datalog system DLV. In: de Moor, O., Gottlob, G., Furche, T., Sellers, A. (eds.) Datalog 2010. LNCS, vol. 6702, pp. 282–301. Springer, Heidelberg (2011)
2. Baral, C.: Knowledge Representation, Reasoning, and Declarative Problem Solving. Cambridge University Press (2003)
3. Bonatti, P., Calimeri, F., Leone, N., Ricca, F.: Answer set programming. In: Dovier, A., Pontelli, E. (eds.) GULP. LNCS, vol. 6125, pp. 159–182. Springer, Heidelberg (2010)
4. Brewka, G.: Preferences, contexts and answer sets. In: Dahl, V., Niemelä, I. (eds.) ICLP 2007. LNCS, vol. 4670, pp. 22–22. Springer, Heidelberg (2007)
5. Brewka, G., Eiter, T., Truszczynski, M.: Answer set programming at a glance. Commun. ACM 54(12), 92–103 (2011)
6. Brewka, G., Niemelä, I., Truszczynski, M.: Answer set optimization. In: Gottlob, G., Walsh, T. (eds.) Proc. 18th IJCAI, pp. 867–872. Morgan Kaufmann (2003)
7. Cabalar, P., Pearce, D., Valverde, A.: A revised concept of safety for general answer set programs. In: Erdem, E., Lin, F., Schaub, T. (eds.) LPNMR 2009. LNCS, vol. 5753, pp. 58–70. Springer, Heidelberg (2009)
8. Denecker, M., Marek, V., Truszczynski, M.: Stable operators, well-founded fixpoints and applications in nnonmonotonic reasoning. In: Minker, J. (ed.) Logic-based Artificial Intelligence, pp. 127–144. Kluwer Academic Pub. (2000)
9. Eiter, T., Gottlob, G.: Complexity results for disjunctive logic programming and application to nonmonotonic logics. In: Miller, D. (ed.) Proceedings of the 1993 International Symposium on Logic Programming, pp. 266–278 (1993)
10. Fages, F.: A new fixpoint sematics for general logic programs compared with the well-founded and stable model semantics. New Generation Computing 9, 425–443 (1991)
11. Fages, F.: Consistency of Clark's completion and existence of stable models. Methods of Logic in Computer Science 1, 51–60 (1994)
12. Fenstad, J.E.: Situations, Language and Logic. D. Reidel Publishing Company (1987)
13. Ferraris, P., Lifschitz, V.: On the minimality of stable models. In: Balduccini, M., Son, T.C. (eds.) Logic Programming, Knowledge Representation, and Nonmonotonic Reasoning. LNCS, vol. 6565, pp. 64–73. Springer, Heidelberg (2011)
14. Fitting, M.: A Kripke-Kleene semantics for logic programs. J. Logic Programming 2(4), 295–312 (1985)
15. Fitting, M.: The family of stable models. J. Logic Programming 17(2/3&4), 197–225 (1993)

16. Gelfond, M., Kahl, Y.: Knowledge Representation, Reasoning, and the Design of Intelligent Agents - The Answer-Set Programming Approach. Cambridge University Press (2014)
17. Gelfond, M., Lifschitz, V.: The stable model semantics for logic programming. In: Kowalski, R., Bowen, K. (eds.) Proc. of Int'l Logic Programming, pp. 1070–1080. MIT Press (1988)
18. Kleene, S.C.: On a notation for ordinal numbers. Symbolic Logic 3, 150–155 (1938)
19. Lifschitz, V.: Thirteen definitions of a stable model. In: Blass, A., Dershowitz, N., Reisig, W. (eds.) Fields of Logic and Computation. LNCS, vol. 6300, pp. 488–503. Springer, Heidelberg (2010)
20. Lonc, Z., Truszczynski, M.: Computing minimal models, stable models and answer sets. TPLP 6(4), 395–449 (2006)
21. Pearce, D.: Equilibrium logic. Annals of Mathematics and AI 47(1-2), 3–41 (2006)
22. Przymusinski, T.: Stable semantics for disjunctive programs. New Generation Comput. 9(3/4), 401–424 (1991)
23. Shepherdson, J.C.: A sound and complete semantics for a version of negation as failure. Theoretical Computer Science 65(3), 343–371 (1989)

Asynchronous Multi-Context Systems*

Stefan Ellmauthaler and Jörg Pührer

Institute of Computer Science, Leipzig University, Germany
{ellmauthaler,puehrer}@informatik.uni-leipzig.de

Abstract. We present *asynchronous multi-context systems* (aMCSs), a framework for loosely coupling different knowledge representation formalisms that allows for online reasoning in a dynamic environment. An aMCS interacts with the outside world via input and output streams and may therefore react to a continuous flow of external information. In contrast to recent proposals, contexts in an aMCS communicate with each other in an asynchronous way which fits the needs of many application domains and is beneficial for scalability. The federal semantics of aMCSs renders our framework an integration approach rather than a knowledge representation formalism itself. We illustrate the introduced concepts by means of an example scenario dealing with rescue services. In addition, we compare aMCSs to reactive multi-context systems and describe how to simulate the latter with our novel approach.

1 Introduction

The achievements in knowledge representation and reasoning (KR) have originated a vast amount of different languages and formats. Nowadays many of them (e.g., ontologies, triple-stores, modal logics, temporal logics, nonmonotonic logics, logic programs under nonmonotonic answer set semantics, ...) are utilised in diverse applications. Each formalism has its own specialised concepts to model knowledge and is often tailored towards a specific task. Due to this specialisation it would often be beneficial to combine different approaches when problems of multiple kinds have to be solved. However, exchanging information between different KR formalisms is not always a trivial task. Expressing all the knowledge usually represented in specifically tailored languages in a universal language would be too hard to achieve from the point of view of complexity as well as the troubles arising from the translation of the representations. Moreover, in a *"connected world"* it is desirable not to spread out all information over different applications but to have it available for every application if need be. Therefore, a framework seems desirable that integrates multiple existing formalisms in order to represent every piece of knowledge in the language that is most appropriate for it.

Another aspect that has received relatively little attention until recently in the development of KR formalisms (notable exceptions include, e.g., earlier work on evolving logic programs [1]) is that in a variety of applications, knowledge is provided in a constant flow of information and it is desired to reason over this knowledge in a continuous

---

* This work has been partially supported by the German Research Foundation (DFG) under grants BR-1817/7-1 and FOR 1513. An earlier version of this paper appeared in the proceedings of ReactKnow 2014 [11].

T. Eiter et al. (Eds.): Brewka Festschrift, LNAI 9060, pp. 141–156, 2015.

manner. Many formalisms operate in a one-shot fashion: given a knowledge base, the user triggers the computation of a result (e.g., the answer to a query). In this paper we aim at using KR formalisms in an *online* fashion as it has been done in recent works, e.g., on stream data processing and querying [17,15], stream reasoning with answer set programming [12], and forgetting [14,8].

To address the demand for an integration of heterogeneous knowledge representation formalisms together with the awareness of a continuous flow of knowledge over time, reactive multi-context systems (rMCSs) [6] and evolving multi-context systems (eMCSs) [13] where proposed. Both frameworks are based on the ideas of managed multi-context systems (mMCSs) [5] which combine multiple *contexts* which can be seen as representations of different formalisms. The semantics of rMCSs and eMCSs are based on the notion of an *equilibrium* which realises a tight semantical integration of the different context formalisms. Due to reasoning over all contexts, the whole computation is necessarily synchronous as the different contexts have to agree on common beliefs for establishing equilibria.

Many real world applications which utilise communication between different services use asynchronous communication protocols (e.g., web services) and compute as soon as they have appropriate information about the problem they have to address. Therefore, we introduce *asynchronous multi-context systems* (aMCSs), a framework for loosely coupled knowledge representation formalisms and services. It still provides the capabilities to express different knowledge representation languages and the translation of information from one formalism to another. In addition, aMCSs are also aware of continuous streams of information and provide ways to model the asynchronous exchange of information. To communicate with the environment, they utilise input and output streams.

We illustrate aMCSs using the example of a task planner for medical rescue units. Here, we assume a scenario where persons are calling an emergency response employee to report incidents. The employee needs to collect all relevant information about the case. Then, the case needs to be classified and available resources (e.g., free ambulances, ...) are assigned. In addition, current traffic data as well as the estimated time of arrival should be considered by another employee, the dispatcher. The aMCS we propose provides recommendations for the emergency response employee as well as for the dispatcher. It incorporates different contexts like a medical ontology, a database with the current state of the ambulances, and a navigation system which is connected to a traffic density reporter. We want to stress that in this application, allowing for asynchronous computation and communication is a great gain for the overall system, as it is not necessary for a context to wait for all other contexts (e.g., there is no need to wait for the recommendation of a plan for the dispatcher during the treatment of an emergency call).

The remainder of this paper is structured as follows. At first we will give a short background on concepts we need. In Section 3, we extend the basic ideas of MCSs to propose our new notion of aMCSs for modelling asynchronous interaction between coupled knowledge representation formalisms and formally characterise its behaviour over time. The subsequent section presents an example scenario, where asynchronous computation and a reactive response to different events is needed. Section 5 compares aMCSs to rMCSs and shows how the latter can be simulated by the former. Section 6 concludes this paper with a discussion including an outlook on future work.

2   Preliminaries

We base our approach on the underlying ideas of mMCSs [5] which extend heterogeneous multi-context systems (MCSs) [4] by a management layer. It allows for complex updates and revisions of knowledge bases and is realised by a management function that provides the updates for each equilibrium. Despite we build on mMCSs, they differ substantially in some aspects from the formalism we introduce in this work for reasons intrinsic to the asynchronous approach. We discuss these reasons and introduce rMCS that generalise mMCSs later in Section 5. Next, we define basic notions needed throughout the paper.

Like mMCS, aMCSs build on the notion of a *logic suite* which can be seen as an abstraction of different KR formalisms. A logic suite is a triple $\mathcal{LS} = \langle \mathcal{KB}, \mathcal{BS}, \mathcal{ACC} \rangle$, where $\mathcal{KB}$ is the set of admissible knowledge bases (KBs) of $\mathcal{LS}$. Each knowledge base is a set of formulas that we do not further specify. $\mathcal{BS}$ is the set of possible belief sets of $\mathcal{LS}$, whose elements are beliefs. A semantics for $\mathcal{LS}$ is a function $\mathrm{ACC} : \mathcal{KB} \to 2^{\mathcal{BS}}$ assigning to each KB a set of acceptable belief sets. Using a semantics with potentially more than one acceptable belief set allows for modelling non-determinism, where each belief set corresponds to an alternative solution. Finally, $\mathcal{ACC}$ is a set of semantics for $\mathcal{LS}$. For a given logic suite $\mathcal{LS} = \langle \mathcal{KB}, \mathcal{BS}, \mathcal{ACC} \rangle$, we denote $\mathcal{KB}, \mathcal{BS}$, respectively, $\mathcal{ACC}$, by $\mathcal{KB}_{\mathcal{LS}}, \mathcal{BS}_{\mathcal{LS}}$, respectively, $\mathcal{ACC}_{\mathcal{LS}}$.

The motivation behind having multiple semantics for one formalism is that in our framework, the semantics of a formalism can be changed over time. While it is probably rarely the case that one wants to switch between different families of semantics during a run, e.g., from the stable-model semantics to the well-founded semantics of logic programs, other switches of semantics are quite natural to many applications: we use different semantics to express different reasoning modes or to express different queries, i.e., ACC_1 returns belief sets answering a query q_1, whereas ACC_2 answers query q_2; ACC_3, in turn, could represent the computation of all solutions to a problem, whereas at some point in time one could be interested in using ACC_4 that only computes a single solution. For instance one that is optimal with respect to some criterion.

3   Asynchronous Multi-Context Systems

An aMCS is built up by multiple contexts which are defined next and which are used for representing reasoning units. We assume a set $\mathcal{N}$ of names that will serve as labels for sensors, contexts, and output streams.

Definition 1. *A context is a pair* $C = \langle \mathsf{n}, \mathcal{LS} \rangle$ *where* $\mathsf{n} \in \mathcal{N}$ *is the name of the context and* $\mathcal{LS}$ *is a logic suite.*

For a given context $C = \langle \mathsf{n}, \mathcal{LS} \rangle$ we denote n and $\mathcal{LS}$ by n_C and $\mathcal{LS}_C$, respectively.

Definition 2. *An aMCS (of length* n *with* m *output streams) is a pair* $M = \langle \mathsf{C}, \mathsf{O} \rangle$, *where* $\mathsf{C} = \langle C_1, \ldots, C_n \rangle$ *is an* n-*tuple of contexts and* $\mathsf{O} = \langle \mathsf{o}_1, \ldots, \mathsf{o}_m \rangle$ *with* $\mathsf{o}_j \in \mathcal{N}$ *for each* $1 \leq j \leq m$ *is a tuple containing the names of the output streams of* M.

By $\mathcal{N}(M)$ we denote the set $\{\mathsf{n}_{C_1}, \ldots, \mathsf{n}_{C_n}, \mathsf{o}_1, \ldots, \mathsf{o}_m\}$ of names of contexts and output streams of M.

A context in an aMCS communicates with other contexts and the outside world by means of streams of data. In particular, we assume that every context has an input stream on which information can be written from both external sources (we call them sensors) and internal sources (i.e., other contexts). For the data in the communication streams we assume a communication language $\mathcal{IL}$ where every $i \in \mathcal{IL}$ is an abstract *piece of information*. In our framework, the data in the input stream of a context and the data in output streams are modelled by information buffers that are defined in the following.

Definition 3. *A* data package *is a pair* $d = \langle s, I \rangle$, *where* $s \in \mathcal{N}$ *is either a context name or a sensor name, stating the* source *of* d, *and* $I \subseteq \mathcal{IL}$ *is a set of pieces of information. An* information buffer *is a sequence of data packages.*

As we assume that data is asynchronously passed to a context on its input stream, it is natural that not all information required for a computation is available at all times. Consequently, we need means to decide whether a computation should take place, depending on the current KB and the data currently available on the stream, or whether the context has to wait for more data. In our framework, this decision is made by a computation controller as defined next.

Definition 4. *Let* $C = \langle \mathsf{n}, \mathcal{LS} \rangle$ *be a context. A* computation controller *for* C *is a relation* cc *between a KB* $\mathrm{KB} \in \mathcal{KB}_{\mathcal{LS}}$ *and a finite information buffer.*

Thus, if $\langle \mathrm{KB}, \mathrm{ib} \rangle \in$ cc then a computation should take place, whereas $\langle \mathrm{KB}, \mathrm{ib} \rangle \notin$ cc means that further information is required before the next computation is triggered in the respective context.

In contrast to the original definition of multi-context systems [3] and extensions thereof, we do not make use of so-called *bridge rules* as a means to communicate: a bridge rule defines which information a context should obtain based on the results of all the contexts of a multi-context system. In the asynchronous approach, we do not have (synchronised) results of all contexts available in general. As a consequence we use another type of rules, called *output rules*, that define which information should be sent to another context or an output stream, based on a result of a single context.

Definition 5. *Let* $C = \langle \mathsf{n}, \mathcal{LS} \rangle$ *be a context. An* output rule r *for* C *is an expression of the form*

$$\langle \mathsf{n}, \mathsf{i} \rangle \leftarrow b_1, \ldots, b_j, \text{not } b_{j+1}, \ldots, \text{not } b_m, \tag{1}$$

such that $\mathsf{n} \in \mathcal{N}$ *is the name of a context or an output stream,* $\mathsf{i} \in \mathcal{IL}$ *is a piece of information, and every* b_ℓ $(1 \leq \ell \leq m)$ *is a belief for* C, *i.e.,* $b_\ell \in S$ *for some* $S \in \mathcal{BS}_{\mathcal{LS}}$.

We call n the *stakeholder* of r, $\langle \mathsf{n}, \mathsf{i} \rangle$ the head of r denoted by $hd(r)$, and $b_1, \ldots, b_j$, not $b_{j+1}, \ldots,$ not b_m the body $\mathrm{bd}(r)$ of r. Moreover, we say that r is active under S, denoted by $S \models \mathrm{bd}(r)$, if $\{b_1, \ldots, b_j\} \subseteq S$ and $\{b_{j+1}, \ldots, b_m\} \cap S = \emptyset$.

Intuitively, the stakeholder is a reference to the addressee of information i.

Definition 6. *Let* $C = \langle \mathsf{n}, \mathcal{LS} \rangle$ *be a context,* OR *a set of output rules for* C, $S \in \mathcal{BS}_{\mathcal{LS}}$ *a belief set, and* $\mathsf{n}' \in \mathcal{N}$ *a name. Then, the data package*

$$d_C(S, \mathrm{OR}, \mathsf{n}') = \langle \mathsf{n}, \{\mathsf{i} \mid r \in \mathrm{OR}, hd(r) = \langle \mathsf{n}', \mathsf{i} \rangle, S \models \mathrm{bd}(r)\} \rangle$$

is the output *of* C *with respect to* OR *under* S *relevant for* n.

Compared to previous notions of multi-context systems, contexts in our setting only specify which formalisms they use but they do not contain knowledge bases, the concrete semantics to use, and communication specifications. The reason is that for aMCSs these may change over time. Instead, we wrap concepts that are subject to change during runtime in the following notion of a *configuration*.

Definition 7. *Let $C = \langle n, \mathcal{LS} \rangle$ be a context. A* configuration *of C is a tuple $cf = \langle KB, ACC, ib, cm \rangle$, where $KB \in \mathcal{KB}_{\mathcal{LS}}$, $ACC \in \mathcal{ACC}_{\mathcal{LS}}$, ib is a finite information buffer, and cm is a* context management *for C which is a triple $cm = \langle cc, cu, OR \rangle$, where*

- *cc is a computation controller for C,*
- *OR is a set of output rules for C, and*
- *cu is a* context update function *for C which is a function that maps an information buffer $ib = d_1, \ldots, d_m$ and an admissible knowledge base of $\mathcal{LS}$ to a configuration $cf' = \langle KB', ACC', ib', cm' \rangle$ of C with $ib' = d_k, \ldots, d_m$ for some $k \geq 1$.*

We write cc_{cm}, cu_{cm}, and OR_{cm} to refer to the components of a given context management $cm = \langle cc, cu, OR \rangle$. The context management is the counterpart of a *management function* of an rMCS (see Section 5), that computes an update of the knowledge base of a context given the results of bridge rules of the context.

In Section 2 we already discussed why we want to change semantics over time. Allowing also for changes of output rules can be motivated with applications where it should be dynamically decided where to direct the output of a context. For example, if a particular sub-problem can be solved by two contexts C_1 and C_2 and it is known that some class of instances can be better solved by C_1 and others by C_2. Then a third context that provides an instance can choose whether C_1 or C_2 should carry out the computation by adapting its output rules. Dynamically changing output rules and semantics could require adjustments of the other components of the context management. Thus, it makes sense that also computation controllers and context update functions are subject to change for the sake of flexibility.

Definition 8. *Let $M = \langle \langle C_1, \ldots, C_n \rangle, \langle o_1, \ldots, o_m \rangle \rangle$ be an aMCS. A* configuration *of M is a pair*

$$Cf = \langle \langle cf_1, \ldots, cf_n \rangle, \langle ob_1, \ldots, ob_m \rangle \rangle,$$

where

- *for all $1 \leq i \leq n$ $cf_i = \langle KB, ACC, ib, cm \rangle$ is a configuration for C_i and for every output rule $r \in OR_{cm}$ we have $n \in \mathcal{N}(M)$ for $\langle n, i \rangle = hd(r)$, and*
- *For each $1 \leq j \leq m$, $ob_j = \ldots, d_{l-1}, d_l$ is an information buffer with a final element d_l such that for each $h \leq l$ with $d_h = \langle n, i \rangle$ we have $n = n_{C_i}$ for some $1 \leq i \leq n$.*

Intuitively, each information buffer ob_j corresponds to the data on the output stream named o_j. Figure 1 depicts an aMCS M with three contexts and a configuration for M.

We next characterise the dynamic behaviour of an aMCS. Our approach requires a discrete notion of time. This could be realised in an event-based fashion, where the availability of new information triggers a new logical point in time. In this paper, we stick to timestamps represented by integers for easier notation.

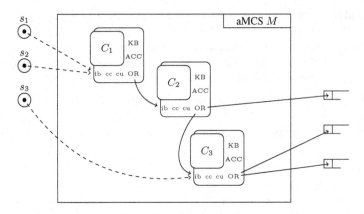

Fig. 1. An aMCS with three contexts, three sensors on the left side, and three output streams on the right side. A solid line represents a flow of information from a context to its stakeholder streams, whereas a dashed line indicates sensor data written to the input buffer of a context.

Definition 9. *Let* $M = \langle \langle C_1, \ldots, C_n \rangle, \langle o_1, \ldots, o_m \rangle \rangle$ *be an aMCS. A run structure for* M *is a sequence*

$$R = \ldots, Cf^t, Cf^{t+1}, Cf^{t+2}, \ldots \quad ,$$

where $t \in \mathbb{Z}$ *is a point in time, and every* $Cf^{t'}$ *in* R ($t' \in \mathbb{Z}$) *is a configuration of* M.

We will sometimes use cf_i^t to denote the configuration of a context i that appears at time t in a given run structure in the context of a given aMCS. Similarly, ob_j^t refers to the information buffer representing the data in the output stream named o_j. Moreover, we write KB_i^t, ACC_i^t, ib_i^t, and cm_i^t to refer to the components of $cf_i^t = \langle KB, ACC, ib, cm \rangle$. We say that context C_i is *waiting* at time t if $\langle KB_i^t, ib_i^t \rangle \notin cc_{cm_i^t}$.

In aMCSs we take into account that the computation of the semantics of a knowledge base needs time. Moreover, in a computation of our framework, different belief sets may become available at different times and verifying the non-existence of further belief sets can also take time after the final belief set has been computed. In order to model whether a context is busy with computing, we introduce a boolean variable $busy_i^t$ for each configuration cf_i^t in a run structure. Hence, context C_i is *busy* at time t if and only if $busy_i^t$ is true. While a context is busy, it does not read new information from its input stream until every belief set has been computed and it has concluded that no further belief set exists.

After the computation of a belief set, the output rules are applied in order to determine which data is passed on to stakeholder contexts or output streams. These are represented by *stakeholder buffers*: An information buffer b is the stakeholder buffer of C_i (for n) at time t if

- b = $ib_{i'}^t$ for some $1 \leq i' \leq n$ such that n = n_{C_i} is stakeholder of some output rule in $OR_{cm_i^t}$ or
- b = $ob_{j'}^t$ for some $1 \leq j' \leq m$ such that n = $o_{j'}$ is stakeholder of some output rule in $OR_{cm_i^t}$.

In order to indicate that a computation has finished we assume a dedicated symbol $\text{EOC} \in \mathcal{IL}$ that notifies a context's stakeholder buffers about the end of a computation.

The behaviour of aMCSs is characterised by the notion of a *run*. A run structure is a run if it adheres to five conditions that we describe next. In the following, let M be an aMCS of length n with m output streams, R a run structure for M, $1 \leq i \leq n$, and $1 \leq j \leq m$. Condition (i) describes the transition from an idle phase to an ongoing computation.

(i) if cf_i^t and cf_i^{t+1} are defined, C_i is neither busy nor waiting at time t, then
   - C_i is busy at time $t+1$,
   - $cf_i^{t+1} = \text{cu}_{cm_i^t}(\text{ib}_i^t, \text{KB}_i^t)$

We say that C_i *started a computation* for KB_i^{t+1} at time $t+1$. The end of such a computation is marked by an end of computation notification as introduced in Item (ii).

(ii) if C_i *started a computation* for KB at time t then
   - we say that this computation *ended at* time t', if t' is the earliest time point with $t' \geq t$ such that $\langle n_{C_i}, \text{EOC}\rangle$ is added to every stakeholder buffer b of C_i at t'; the addition of $\langle n_{C_i}, \text{EOC}\rangle$ to b is called an *end of computation notification*.
   - for all $t' > t$ such that $cf_i^{t'}$ is defined, C_i is busy at t' unless the computation ended at some time t'' with $t < t'' < t'$.
   - if the computation ended at time t' and $cf_i^{t'+1}$ is defined then C_i is not busy at $t'+1$.

Condition (iii) states that between the start and the end of a computation all belief sets are computed and stakeholders are notified.

(iii) if C_i *started a computation* for KB at time t that ended at time t' then for every belief set $S \in \text{ACC}_i^t$ there is some time t'' with $t \leq t'' \leq t'$ such that
   - $d_{C_i}(S, \text{OR}_{cm_i^{t''}}, \mathsf{n})$ is added to every stakeholder buffer b of C_i for n at t''.

We say that C_i *computed S* at time t''. The addition of $d_{C_i}(S, \text{OR}_{cm_i^{t''}}, \mathsf{n})$ to b is called a *belief set notification*. Finally, Conditions (iv) and (v) express how data is added to an output stream or to an input stream, respectively.

(iv) if ob_j^t and ob_j^{t+1} are defined and $ob_j^t = \ldots, d_{l-1}, d_l$ then $ob_j^{t+1} = \ldots, d_{l-1}$, $d_l, \ldots, d_{l'}$ for some $l' \geq l$. Moreover, every data package $d_{l''}$ with $l < l'' \leq l'$ that was added at time $t+1$ results from an end of computation notification or a belief set notification.

(v) if cf_i^t and cf_i^{t+1} are defined, C_i is busy or waiting at time t, and $\text{ib}_i^t = d_1, \ldots, d_l$ then we have $\text{ib}_i^{t+1} = d_1, \ldots, d_l, \ldots, d_{l'}$ for some $l' \geq l$. Moreover, every data package $d_{l''}$ with $l < l'' \leq l'$ that was added at time $t+1$ either results from an end of computation notification or a belief set notification or $\mathsf{n} \notin \mathcal{N}(M)$ (i.e., n is a sensor name) for $d_{l''} = \langle \mathsf{n}, \mathsf{i}\rangle$.

Note that in these conditions, sensors and the flow of information from sensors to the input buffers of contexts are implicit. That is, data packages from a sensor may appear at the end of input buffers at all times and the only reference to a particular sensor is its name appearing in a data package. We are now ready to define a run.

Definition 10. *Let M be an aMCS of length n with m output streams and R a run structure for M. R is a* run *for M if Conditions (i)-(v) hold for every $1 \leq i \leq n$ and every $1 \leq j \leq m$.*

Summarising the behaviour characterised by a run, whenever a context C is not busy, its context controller cc checks whether a new computation should take place, based on the knowledge base and the current input buffer of C. If yes, the current configuration of the context is replaced by a new one, computed by the context update function cu of C. Here, the new input buffer has to be a suffix of the old one and a new computation for the updated knowledge base starts. After an undefined period of time, belief sets are computed and based on the application of output rules of C, data packages are sent to stakeholder buffers. At some point in time, when all belief sets have been computed, an end of computation notification is sent to stakeholders, and the context is not busy anymore.

4 Scenario: Computer-Aided Emergency Team Management

Now we want to consider a scenario, where aMCSs may be used to describe the asynchronous information-exchange between different specialised reasoning systems. Our example deals with a system for the coordination and handling of ambulance assignments. Note that there are different commercial computer-aided dispatch and computer-aided call handling systems (for an overview see [9]). Our example has the purpose to illustrate aMCSs and thus we consider a simplified problem setting, providing a more meta-level centred point of view. Albeit our example is simplified, it still shares a similar structure to these commercial solutions. The suggested aMCS supports decisions in different stages of an emergency case. It gives assistance during the rescue call, helps in assigning priorities and rescue units to a case, and assists in the necessary communication among all involved parties. The suggestions given by the system are based on different specialised systems which react to sensor readings. Moreover, the system can tolerate and incorporate overriding solutions proposed by the user that it considers non-optimal.

Figure 2 depicts the example aMCS which models such a *Computer-Aided Emergency Team Management System* (CAET Management System). Note that interaction with a human (e.g., EM employee) is modelled as a pair containing an input stream and an output stream. The system consists of the following contexts:

Case Analyser (ca). This context implements a computer-aided call handling system which assists an emergency response employee (ER employee) during answering an emergency call. The system utilises reasoning methods to choose which questions need to be asked based on previous answers. In addition, it may check whether answers are inconsistent (e.g., amniotic sac bursts when the gender is male). For these purposes the case analyser context may also consult a medical ontology represented by another context. The communication with the ER employee is represented, on the one hand, as a sensor that reads the input of the employee and, on the other hand, by an output stream which prints the questions and results on a computer screen.

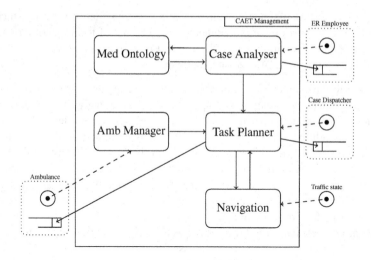

Fig. 2. The Computer-Aided Emergency Team Management aMCS

During the collection of all the important facts for this emergency case, the analyser computes the priority of the case and passes it to the task planner.

Med Ontology (mo). This medical ontology can be realised, e.g., by a description logic reasoner which handles requests from the case analyser and returns more specific knowledge about ongoing cases. This information may be used for the prioritisation of the importance of a case.

Task Planner (tp). This context keeps track of emergency cases. Based on the priority and age of a case and the availability and position of ambulances it suggests an efficient plan of action for the ambulances to the (human) case dispatcher (cd). The dispatcher may approve some of the suggestions or all of them. If the dispatcher has no faith in the given plan of action, she can also alter it at will. These decisions are reported back to the planning system such that it can react to the alterations and provide further suggestions. Based on the final plan, the task planner informs the ambulance about their new mission.

The knowledge base of the context is an answer-set program for reasoning about a suggested plan. It gets the availability and position of the ambulances by the ambulance manager. In addition, the cases with their priority are provided by the case analyser. With this information, the task planner gives the locations of the ambulances together with the target locations of the cases to a navigation system which provides the distances (i.e., the estimated time of arrival (ETA)) of all the ambulances to all the locations.

Amb Manager (am). The ambulance manager is a database, which keeps track of the status and location of ambulance units. Each ambulance team reports its status (e.g., to be on duty, waiting for new mission, . . .) to the database (modelled by the sensor "Ambulance" (amb)). Additionally, the car periodically sends GPS-coordinates to the database. These updates will be pushed to the task planner.

Navigation (na). This part of the aMCS gets traffic information (e.g., congestions, construction zones, roadblocks, . . .) to predict the travel time for each route as accurate as possible. The task planner may push a query to the navigation system, which consists of a list of locations of ambulance units and a list of locations of target areas. Based on all the given information this context will return a ranking for each target area, representing the ETAs for each ambulance.

Now we want to have a closer look on the instantiation details of some aspects of our example. At first we investigate the cc relation of the case analyser. It allows for the computation of new belief sets whenever the ER employee pushes new information to the analyser. In addition, it will also approve of a new computation if the medical ontology supplies some requested information. Recall that the case analyser also assigns a priority to each case and that we want to allow the employee to set the priority manually. Let us suppose that such a manual override occurs and that the case analyser has an ongoing query to the medical ontology. Due to the manual priority assignment, the requested information from the ontology is no longer needed. Therefore, it would be desirable that cc does not allow for a recomputation if all conclusions of the ontology are only related to the manually prioritised case. With the same argumentation in mind, the context update function cu will also ignore this information on the input stream. This kind of behaviour may need knowledge about past queries which can be provided by an additional output rule for the case analyser which feeds the relevant information back to the context.

Next, we will have a look at the task planner that is based on answer-set programming. We will only present parts of the program, to show how the mechanics are intended to work. To represent the incoming information on the input stream, the following predicates can be used:

case(caseid,loc,priority) represents an active case (with its location and priority) which needs to be assigned to an ambulance.

avail(amb,loc) states the location of an available ambulance.

eta(caseid,amb,value) provides the estimated time of arrival for a unit at the location of the target area of the case.

assign(amb,caseid) represents the assignment of an ambulance to a case by the dispatcher.

These predicates will be added by the context update function to the knowledge base if corresponding information is put on the input stream of the context. Based on this knowledge, the other components of the answer-set program will compute the belief sets (e.g., via the stable model semantics). Note that an already assigned ambulance or case will not be handled as an available ambulance or an active case, respectively. In addition, cu can (and should) also manage forgetting of no longer needed knowledge. For our scenario it may be suitable to remove all eta, avail and case predicates when the cases or the unit is assigned. The assign predicate can be removed when the ambulance manager reports that the assigned ambulance is available again.

The set OR of output rules of the task planner could contain the following rules:

$$\langle \text{cd,assign}(A, C) \rangle \leftarrow \text{sugassignment}(A, C)$$
$$\langle \text{na,queryA}(L) \rangle \leftarrow \text{avail}(A), \text{not assign}(A, \_), \text{loc}(A, L)$$
$$\langle \text{na,queryC}(L) \rangle \leftarrow \text{case}(C, P), \text{loc}(A, L), \text{not assign}(A, \_)$$
$$\langle \text{amb,assigned}(A, C) \rangle \leftarrow \text{assign}(A, C)$$

The first rule informs the case dispatcher (cd) about a suggested assignment that has been computed by the answer-set program. Rules two and three prepare lists of ambulances and cases for querying the navigation context. Recall that the latter needs a list of ambulance locations (generated by rule two) and a list of target area locations (generated by rule three). Also keep in mind that for each belief set a data package with all information for one context or output stream is constructed. So the whole list of current target areas and free ambulance units will be passed to the navigation context at once. The last rule notifies the ambulance team that it has been assigned to a specific case.

Related to this example we want to mention privacy aspects as a real world policy which is especially important to applications in public services and health care. As the multi-context system is a heterogeneous system with different contexts, a completely free exchange of data may be against privacy policies. This issue can be addressed by the adequate design of output rules, which can also be altered with respect to additional information in the input stream (e.g., some context gains the permission to receive real names instead of anonymous data). So each context may decide by its own which parts of the belief sets are shared and exchanged with other contexts.

Another interesting aspect about aMCSs is the possibility to easily join two aMCSs together, outsource a subset of contexts in a new aMCS, or to view an aMCS as an abstract context for another aMCS in a modular way. This can be achieved due to the abstract communication by means of streams. With respect to our scenario there could be some aMCS which does the management of resources for hospitals (e.g., free beds with their capabilities). The task planner might communicate with this system to take the needed services for a case into account (e.g., intensive care unit) and informs the hospital via these streams about incoming patients. It would be easy to join both aMCSs together to one big system or to outsource some contexts as input sensors paired with an output stream. In addition, one may also combine different contexts or a whole aMCS to one abstract context to provide a dynamic granularity of information about the system and to group different reasoning tasks together.

5   Relation to Reactive Multi-Context Systems

In this section we want to address differences and commonalities between aMCSs and rMCSs [6] as both are types of multi-context systems that work in an online fashion and can react to external information.

Next, we introduce rMCSs. For simplicity, as in [6], for each context in an rMCS (called r-context), we assume a single semantics. An r-context is of the form $C = \langle \mathcal{LS}, ops, mng \rangle$, where

- $\mathcal{LS}$ is a logic suite with $\mathcal{ACC}_{\mathcal{LS}} = \{ACC\}$,
- ops is a set of operations,
- $mng : 2^{ops} \times \mathcal{KB}_{\mathcal{LS}} \rightarrow \mathcal{KB}_{\mathcal{LS}}$ is a management function.

For an indexed r-context C_i we denote its components and ACC by $\mathcal{LS}_i$, ops_i, mng_i, and ACC_i.

External information is integrated in rMCSs by means of *sensors*. A sensor $\Pi = \langle L_\Pi, \pi \rangle$ is a device which is able to provide new information in a given language L_Π

specific to the sensor. At all times, the set $\pi \subseteq L_\Pi$ represents the current sensor reading. Given a tuple of sensors $\Pi = \langle \Pi_1, \ldots, \Pi_k \rangle$, an observation Obs for Π (Π-observation for short) consists of a sensor reading for each sensor, that is $Obs = \langle \pi_1, \ldots, \pi_k \rangle$ where for $1 \le i \le k$, $\pi_i \subseteq L_{\Pi_i}$.

Integrating sensor information and communication between r-contexts is realised by means of *bridge rules*. Let $C_r = \langle C_1, \ldots, C_n \rangle$ be a tuple of r-contexts and Π as above. A bridge rule for C_i ($1 \le i \le n$) over C_r and Π is of the form

$$\text{op} \leftarrow a_1, \ldots, a_j, \text{not } a_{j+1}, \ldots, \text{not } a_m, \qquad (2)$$

such that op $\in ops_i$ and every a_ℓ ($1 \le \ell \le m$) is either a *context atom* of form c:b where $c \in \{1, \ldots, n\}$, and b is a belief for C_c, i.e., b $\in S$ for some $S \in BS_{L_c}$, or a *sensor atom* of form o@s, where s is an index determining a sensor ($1 \le s \le k$) and o $\in L_{\Pi_s}$ is a piece of sensor data. For a bridge rule r, the operation $hd(r) = $ op is the *head* of r, while $\text{bd}(r) = \{a_1, \ldots, a_j, \text{not } a_{j+1}, \ldots, \text{not } a_m\}$ is the *body* of r.

Definition 11. *A* reactive multi-context system *(rMCS) over sensors* $\Pi = \langle \Pi_1, \ldots, \Pi_k \rangle$ *is a tuple* $M = \langle C_r, \text{BR}, \text{KB} \rangle$, *where* $C_r = \langle C_1, \ldots, C_n \rangle$ *is a tuple of r-contexts,* $\text{BR} = \langle br_1, \ldots, br_n \rangle$, *where each* br_i *is a set of bridge rules for* C_i *over* C_r *and* Π, *and* $\text{KB} = \langle kb_1, \ldots, kb_n \rangle$ *such that* $kb_i \in \mathcal{KB}_{\mathcal{L}S_i}$.

A belief state $S = \langle S_1, \ldots, S_n \rangle$ for a rMCS M consists of belief sets $S_i \in BS_{\mathcal{B}S_{\mathcal{L}S_i}}$, $1 \le i \le n$. A context atom c:p $\in \text{bd}(r)$ is satisfied by S if p $\in S_c$. Moreover, let Π be a tuple of sensors and $Obs = \langle \pi_1, \ldots, \pi_k \rangle$ a Π-observation. Then, a sensor atom o@s is *satisfied* by Obs if o $\in \pi_s$; a literal not o@s is *satisfied* by Obs if o $\notin \pi_s$.

A bridge rule r in BR is *applicable* with respect to S and Obs, symbolically $S \models_{Obs} \text{bd}(r)$, if every atom in $\text{bd}(r)$ is satisfied by S or Obs and every negated atom in $\text{bd}(r)$ is neither satisfied by S nor by Obs. For each r-context C_i in an rMCS, we collect the heads of applicable bridge rules in the set $app_i(S, Obs) = \{hd(r) \mid r \in br_i \wedge S \models_{Obs} \text{bd}(r)\}$.

Runs of rMCSs are based on equilibria which are collections of belief sets—one for each context—on which, intuitively, all of the contexts have to agree.

Definition 12. *Let* $M = \langle C_r, \text{BR}, \text{KB} \rangle$ *be an rMCS with sensors* Π *and* Obs *a* Π-*observation. A belief state* $S = \langle S_1, \ldots, S_n \rangle$ *for* M *is an* equilibrium *of* M *under* Obs *if, for* $1 \le i \le n$, $S_i \in ACC_i(mng_i(app_i(S, Obs), kb_i))$.

The tuple $\text{KB}^S = \langle mng_1(app_1(S, Obs), kb_1), \ldots, mng_n(app_n(S, Obs), kb_n) \rangle$ *contains all KBs generated by an equilibrium* S. *We call the pair* $\langle S, \text{KB}^S \rangle$ *a* full equilibrium *of* M *under* Obs.

We now introduce the notion of a run of an rMCS (called r-run) induced by a sequence of observations:

Definition 13. *Let* $M = \langle C_r, \text{BR}, \text{KB} \rangle$ *be an rMCS with sensors* Π *and* $O = (Obs^0, Obs^1, \ldots)$ *a sequence of* Π-*observations. An* r-run *of* M *induced by* O *is a sequence of pairs* $R = (\langle S^0, \text{KB}^0 \rangle, \langle S^1, \text{KB}^1 \rangle, \ldots)$ *such that*

- $\langle S^0, \text{KB}^0 \rangle$ *is a full equilibrium of* M *under* Obs^0,
- *for* $\langle S^i, \text{KB}^i \rangle$ *with* $i > 0$, $\langle S^i, \text{KB}^i \rangle$ *is a full equilibrium of* $\langle C, \text{BR}, \text{KB}^{i-1} \rangle$ *under* Obs^i.

Being based on equilibria, r-runs realise a tight integration approach in which the semantics of the individual contexts are interdependent. However, the high level of integration also comes at the price that the different contexts must wait for each other for the computation of each equilibrium, i.e., they are synchronised. In aMCSs, on the other hand, the coupling of the semantics is much looser—communication between contexts only works via data packages that are sent to another context after a computation and not via a higher-level common semantics for multiple contexts. But as a benefit, each context can run at its own pace which is useful in settings where there is a context that requires much more time for evaluating its semantics than others.

A further difference is the role of non-determinism in the semantics of aMCSs and rMCSs. An equilibrium in a rMCS consists of a single belief set for each context. Hence, as rMCSs also use a multiple belief set semantics, there may also be multiple equilibria as a source of non-determinism at each step in an r-run. For aMCSs, all belief sets of a context are computed in a consecutive way (we assume that if only a single belief set is desired than the semantics of the respective context should be adapted accordingly by the knowledge engineer). Nevertheless, there is also a source of non-determinism in the case of aMCSs caused by the undefined duration of computations.

Regarding the computational complexity of the two frameworks, the computation of an equilibrium requires guessing an equilibrium candidate before the semantics of the context is computed which is expensive regarding runtime when put to practice. In theory, this guess does not add extra complexity if the context semantics is already **NP**-hard (as shown in [6]) because it can be combined with the guesses required in the contexts. However, this trick cannot be used in implementations that uses black boxes for computing context semantics. On the other hand, aMCSs do not add substantial computational requirements to the effort needed for computing context semantics. In particular, aMCSs are scalable as adding a further context has no direct effect on how the semantics of the other contexts are computed but can only influence their input.

Both, aMCSs and rMCSs are very general frameworks that allow for simulating Turing machines and thus for performing multi-purpose computations even if only very simple context formalisms are used (if the length of a run is not restricted). In this sense the approaches are equally expressive. Moreover, when allowing for arbitrary contexts one could trivially simulate the other by including it as a context. Despite the existence of these straightforward translations, we next sketch how we simulate an rMCS with an aMCS using a more direct translation, as this gives further insight into the differences of the two frameworks. Moreover, it demonstrates a way to implement rMCSs by means of aMCSs. For every r-context C_i of a given rMCS M_r, we introduce three contexts in the aMCS M_a that simulates M_r:

- a context C_i^{kb} that stores the current knowledge base of the r-context,
- a context $C_i^{kb'}$ in which a candidate for an updated knowledge base can be written and its semantics is computed, and
- a context C_i^m that implements the bridge rules and the management function of C_i.

There are three further contexts:

- C^{obs} receives sensor data and distributes it to every context C_i^m where C_i depends on the respective sensor. The context is also responsible for synchronisation: for each sensor, new sensor data is only passed on after an equilibrium has been computed.

- C^{guess} guesses equilibrium candidates for M and passes them to the management contexts C_i^m. Based on that and the information from C^{obs}, C_i^m computes an update kb_i' of the knowledge base in C_i^{kb} and stores kb_i' in $C_i^{kb'}$. The latter r-context then computes the semantics of kb_i' and passes it to the final r-context
- C^{check} that compares every belief set it receives with the equilibrium candidate (that it also receives from C^{guess}). If a matching belief set has been found for each context of M_r, the candidate is an actual equilibrium. In this case C^{check} sends the equilibrium to an output stream and notifies the other contexts about the success.

In case of a success, every r-context C_i^m replaces the knowledge base in C_i^{kb} by kb_i' and a next iteration begins. In case no equilibrium was found but one of the $C_i^{kb'}$ contexts has finished its computation, C^{check} orders C^{guess} to guess another equilibrium candidate.

6   Related Work and Discussion

A concept similar to output-rules has been presented in the form of reactive bridge rules [10] for multi-context systems. There the flow of information is represented by rules which add knowledge to the input streams of other contexts. Which information is communicated to other contexts is also determined by the local belief set of each context.

Note that evolving multi-context systems [13] follow a quite similar approach as rMCSs and hence the relation of aMCSs to rMCSs sketched in the previous section also applies in essence to this approach.

The Dedalus language [2] allows for modelling distributed systems over time. A Dedalus program is a datalog program using a non-monotonic choice construct that adheres to certain syntactic restrictions. For modelling time, every predicate has a timestamp as its final attribute. Three types of rules are admitted that differ in the relation of the time variable $\mathcal{T}$ that their body literals refer to and the time variable $\mathcal{S}$ of their respective head atom. Head and body of so-called deductive rules refer to the same time instant, i.e., $\mathcal{T} = \mathcal{S}$. Inductive rules derive atoms for the next point in time, hence $\mathcal{T} + 1 = \mathcal{S}$. The network interaction between different systems is modelled by means of the third type of rules, so-called communication rules, where there is no given relation between $\mathcal{T}$ and $\mathcal{S}$. Instead, the value of $\mathcal{S}$ is guessed non-deterministically, for modelling asynchronous and unreliable network communication where data may be received in wrong order or not at all. Thus, communication rules play a similar role as output rules in our approach, namely dispatching information. Conceptually, context formalisms are incorporated in an aMCS, whereas in Dedalus, reasoning within individual nodes of a distributed system must be modelled using datalog or simulated by adding facts of extensional predicates to the Dedalus program. The individual contexts in our approach are meant to operate independently from each other, whereas in Dedalus the whole distributed system is represented in a single datalog program. Accordingly, a run of an aMCS emerges from communicating the results of the context semantics over time, whereas the semantics of a Dedalus program is given by its (infinite) perfect model.

Peer-to-peer systems [7] address the problem of data integration and distributed knowledge over so-called "peers". Similar to contexts in our settings, peers also act independently of each other. In difference to peer-to-peer systems, aMCSs are meant to incorporate heterogeneous contexts, while peers are usually understood as equally privileged and equipotent. In addition, peer-to-peer systems usually focus on query answering between different databases, while an aMCS is supposed to act as a generalised framework for exchanging arbitrary information between independent reasoners.

Also multi-agent systems [16] share some aspects with aMCSs. A multi-agent system comprises different interacting agents and their environment. Agents exchange information among each other, have means to perceive the environment, and may perform actions to manipulate the environment. As both, aMCSs and multi-agent systems are expressive frameworks, it is easy to view one in terms of the other when contexts are interpreted as agents or vice versa. Conceptually, contexts in aMCSs are intended to represent knowledge bases of different formalisms, whereas agents in a multi-agent system typically represent physical entities or beings of some kind.

The system `clingo` [12] is a reactive answer-set programming solver. It utilises TCP/IP ports for incoming input streams and does also report the resulting answer sets via such a port. It provides means to compute different semantics and can keep learned structures and knowledge from previous solving steps. Although there are no output rules or input stream pre-processing as in aMCSs, the system features embedded imperative programming languages which may be helpful to model some of the presented concepts.

In general, the tasks performed by a context management can be realised by different formalisms (e.g., imperative scripting languages or declarative programming). Here, it seems likely that different languages can be the most appropriate management language, depending on the type of context formalism and the concrete problem domain. A feature that is not modelled in our proposal but that is potentially useful and we intend to consider in the future is to allow for aborting computations. Moreover, we want to study modelling patterns and best practices for aMCSs design for typical application settings and compare different inter-context topologies and communication strategies.

As a next step we plan to implement a prototype of our framework that allows for integrating external knowledge sources as contexts and for specifying context managements. We want to analyse whether and how existing tools such as `clingo` can be used for the implementation. We are also interested in how reactive features of `clingo` (e.g., iterative computation, on-demand grounding, online-queries, ...) relate to aMCS concepts (e.g., cc, ib, ...) and whether they can be described in terms of an aMCS.

References

1. Alferes, J.J., Brogi, A., Leite, J., Moniz Pereira, L.: Evolving logic programs. In: Flesca, S., Greco, S., Leone, N., Ianni, G. (eds.) JELIA 2002. LNCS (LNAI), vol. 2424, pp. 50–61. Springer, Heidelberg (2002)
2. Alvaro, P., Marczak, W.R., Conway, N., Hellerstein, J.M., Maier, D., Sears, R.: Dedalus: Datalog in time and space. In: Proc. Datalog 2.0., pp. 262–281 (2011)
3. Brewka, G., Eiter, T.: Equilibria in heterogeneous nonmonotonic multi-context systems. In: AAAI 2007, pp. 385–390 (2007)

4. Brewka, G., Eiter, T., Fink, M.: Nonmonotonic multi-context systems: A flexible approach for integrating heterogeneous knowledge sources. In: Balduccini, M., Son, T.C. (eds.) Logic Programming, Knowledge Representation, and Nonmonotonic Reasoning. LNCS, vol. 6565, pp. 233–258. Springer, Heidelberg (2011)
5. Brewka, G., Eiter, T., Fink, M., Weinzierl, A.: Managed multi-context systems. In: IJCAI 2011, pp. 786–791 (2011)
6. Brewka, G., Ellmauthaler, S., Pührer, J.: Multi-context systems for reactive reasoning in dynamic environments. In: Proc. ECAI 2014, pp. 159–164 (2014)
7. Calvanese, D., De Giacomo, G., Lenzerini, M., Rosati, R.: Logical Foundations of Peer-To-Peer Data Integration. In: Beeri, C., Deutsch, A. (eds.) Proc. PODS 2004, pp. 241–251. ACM (2004)
8. Cheng, F.L., Eiter, T., Robinson, N., Sattar, A., Wang, K.: Lpforget: A system of forgetting in answer set programming. In: Proc. AUSAI 2006, pp. 1101–1105 (2006)
9. Dispatch Magazine On-Line: Computer-Aided Dispatch Resources (2014), https://www.911dispatch.com/computer-aided-dispatch-resources/
10. Ellmauthaler, S.: Generalizing multi-context systems for reactive stream reasoning applications. In: Proc. ICCSW 2013, pp. 17–24 (2013)
11. Ellmauthaler, S., Pührer, J.: Asynchronous Multi-Context Systems. In: Proc. ReactKnow 2014, pp. 31–37 (2014)
12. Gebser, M., Grote, T., Kaminski, R., Obermeier, P., Sabuncu, O., Schaub, T.: Stream reasoning with answer set programming: Preliminary report. In: Proc. KR 2012 (2012)
13. Gonçalves, R., Knorr, M., Leite, J.: Evolving multi-context systems. In: Proc. ECAI 2014, pp. 375–380 (2014)
14. Lang, J., Marquis, P.: Reasoning under inconsistency: A forgetting-based approach. Artif. Intell. 174, 799–823 (2010)
15. Le-Phuoc, D., Parreira, J.X., Hauswirth, M.: Linked stream data processing. In: Proc. RW 2012, pp. 245–289 (2012)
16. Wooldridge, M.J.: An Introduction to MultiAgent Systems (2nd edn.). Wiley (2009)
17. Zaniolo, C.: Logical foundations of continuous query languages for data streams. In: Proc. Datalog 2.0., pp. 177–189 (2012)

Twenty-Five Years of Preferred Subtheories

Jérôme Lang

CNRS-LAMSADE
Université Paris-Dauphine, France
lang@lamsade.dauphine.fr

Abstract. In the seminal paper [6], Gerd Brewka argued that ranking a set of default rules without prerequisites, and selecting extensions according to a lexicographic refinement of the inclusion ordering proves to be a natural, simple and efficient way of dealing with the multiple extension (or "subtheories") problem. This natural idea has been reused, discussed, revisited, reinvented, adapted many times in the AI community and beyond. Preferred subtheories do not only have an interest in default reasoning, but also in reasoning about time, reasoning by analogy, reasoning with compactly represented preferences, judgment aggregation, and voting. They have several variants (but arguably not so many). In this short paper I will say as much as I can about preferred subtheories in sixteen pages.

1   Prioritized Default Theories and Preferred Subtheories

Preferred subtheories were introduced in [6] as a way of representing and exploiting priorities between default rules. Their starting point was the THEORIST system [28] for default reasoning. In Poole's system – equivalent to the restriction of Reiter's default logic to normal defaults without prerequisites – a default theory is a set of facts F plus a set of hypotheses Δ (both composed of logical formulas) and an extension is the set of logical consequences of a set-inclusion maximal subset D of Δ such that $D \cup F$ is consistent. In spite of the (apparently drastic) restriction to normal defaults without prerequisites, this system is able to deal adequately with many of the standard default reasoning examples from the literature, but not all, because of the impossibility of expressing priorities between defaults. Let me reuse this example from [6], suggested to Gerd Brewka by Ulrich Junker.

> "Usually one has to go to a meeting.
> This rule does not apply if somebody is sick, unless he only has a cold.
> The rule is also not applicable if somebody is on vacation."

As shown by [6] (Section 3), given that the person is sick, the natural writing of this example in Poole's system generates two extensions: one where she has to attend the meeting and one where she does not. In order to avoid this, one would need to

> "(...) look down in the hierarchy of exceptions and block defaults lower in the hierarchy. (...) the number of defaults may increase heavily in cases where more exceptions and exceptions of exceptions are involved"

T. Eiter et al. (Eds.): Brewka Festschrift, LNAI 9060, pp. 157–172, 2015.

which is arguably unpleasant and inefficient. The core of the problem is the impossibility to express that a default has a priority over an other default – in this case, when an agent only has a cold and is on vacation, the rule that someone on vacation does not have to attend should have priority over the rule that someone who has only a cold has to attend. This inability to represent priorities in Poole's system was Brewka's motivation for generalizing it by introducing explicit priorities among defaults. By convention, degree 1 corresponds to the highest priority defaults.

Definition 0. *A ranked default theory T is a tuple $(T_1, \ldots, T_n)$ where each T_i is a set of classical first-order (possibly open) formulas. Without loss of generality, we assume that all formulas appearing in T are different.*[1]

The meeting example is expressed as

$$T_1 = \{ \quad cold \to sick, vacation \to \neg r_1, cold \to \neg r_2,$$
$$r_2 \wedge sick \to \neg r_1, r_1 \to meeting \qquad \}$$
$$T_2 = \{r_2\}$$
$$T_3 = \{r_1\}$$

while the classical Tweety story is expressed as

$$T_1 = \{bird(tweety), \forall x.penguin(x) \to bird(x)\}$$
$$T_2 = \{penguin(x) \to \neg flies(x)\}$$
$$T_3 = \{bird(x) \to flies(x)\}$$

Now, it remains to define the *preferred subtheories* of a ranked default theory. This beautiful yet simple notion has several equivalent characterizations, each of which can be used as a definition. Below we give no less than six definitions; two others will come in Section 2.

We first define a *subtheory* of T as a tuple $S = (S_1, \ldots, S_n)$ with $S_i \subseteq T_i$ for each i, and such that $\cup_i S_i$ is consistent. By abuse of language, we also consider S as a subset of T, that is, we sometimes note $\delta \in S$ for ($\delta \in S_i$ for some i). The first definition we give is Brewka's original definition [6]. In all definitions, $T = (T_1, \ldots, T_n)$ is a ranked default theory and $S = (S_1, \ldots, S_n)$ is a subtheory of T.

Definition 1 (preferred subtheories, first definition). *S is a preferred subtheory of T iff for all $k = 1, \ldots, n$, $S_1 \cup \ldots \cup S_k$ is a maximal consistent subset of $T_1 \cup \ldots \cup T_k$.*

To paraphrase the definition in the author's terms:

"(...) to obtain a preferred subtheory of T we have to start with any maximal consistent subset of T_1, add as many formulas from T_2 as consistently can be added (in any possible way), and continue this process for $T_3, \ldots, T_n$."

This explanation does not in fact correspond to Definition 1, but to the following equivalent, more constructive definition with a clear algorithmic flavour, which is also

---

[1] This is without loss of generality, because if a formula appears several times, all its occurrences except one can be rewritten into syntactically different, equivalent formulas. We could have chosen to allow some formulas to appear several times, but then each T_i should be defined as a multiset rather than a set, and this would be slightly more complicated.

the definition used for prioritized removal in prioritized base revision [25]. Given two sets of formulas F and G, we say that $G' \subseteq G$ is maximal F-consistent if $G' \cup F$ is consistent and for all G'' such that $G' \subset G'' \subseteq G$, $G'' \cup F$ is inconsistent.

Definition 2 (preferred subtheories, second definition). S *is a* preferred subtheory *of* T *iff for all* $i = 1, \ldots, n$, S_i *is a maximal* $(S_1 \cup \ldots S_{i-1})$-*consistent subset of* T_i.

In the meeting example, if we add the facts $F = \{cold, vacation\}$ to T_1, then *meeting* is not derived from the preferred subtheory $F \cup T_1$; but if we add only $F' = \{cold\}$, then the preferred subtheory is $F' \cup T_1 \cup \{r_1\}$, and *meeting* is derived, and if we don't add any fact, then the preferred subtheory is $T_1 \cup \{r_1, r_2\}$, and again, *meeting* is derived. In the Tweety example, the only preferred subtheory is $T_1 \cup T_2$ and allows to derive $\neg flies(Tweety)$.

Here is another example with more than one preferred subtheory: $T = T_1 \cup T_2 \cup T_3$ with $T_1 = \{a \vee b, a \to c\}$, $T_2 = \{\neg a, \neg b\}$, $T_3 = \{\neg c\}$. T has two preferred subtheories: $T_1 \cup \{\neg a, \neg c\}$ and $T_1 \cup \{\neg b\}$.

Two dual notions of provability from a default theory can be defined: given a default theory T, formula α is *strongly provable* from T if for every preferred subtheory S of T we have $S \models \alpha$, and *weakly provable* from T if for some preferred subtheory S of T we have $S \models \alpha$. These notions come back to Rescher [29] and have been used and discussed many times afterwards, under different names such as credulous and skeptical inferences, in various areas such as nonmonotonic reasoning, belief revision, inconsistency-tolerant reasoning, argumentation, and beyond (see, *e.g.*, [9,4]). In this short paper we focus on subtheories and won't discuss inference again.

The third definition is the basis of Brewka's second generalization of Poole's system [6], introduced for priority orders between defaults that are strict partial orders (see Section 2.1). It says that a preferred subtheory can be obtained by consistently adding formulas in any possible order that respects the priority relation. Given two defaults δ, δ' of T, let $r(\delta)$ be the integer i such that $\delta \in T_i$.[2] A ranking of T is a bijective mapping σ from $\{1, \ldots, |T|\}$ to T; for all $i \leq |T|$ we note $\sigma(i) = \delta_i$. We say that σ *respects* T iff for all $\delta_i, \delta_j \in T$, $r(\delta) < r(\delta')$ implies $i < j$.

Definition 3 (preferred subtheories, third definition). S *is a* preferred subtheory *of* T *if there is a ranking* σ *of* T *respecting* T, *such that* $S = S_\sigma$, *where* S_σ *is defined inductively by:*

$$\Sigma_0 = \emptyset$$
for $i = 1, \ldots, n$ **do**
  if $\Sigma_{i-1} \cup \{\delta_i\}$ *is consistent* **then**
    $\Sigma_i = \Sigma_{i-1} \cup \{\delta_i\}$
  else
    $\Sigma_i = \Sigma_{i-1}$
  end if
end for
return $S_\sigma = \Sigma$

---

[2] Recall that we assumed that $T_i \cap T_j = \emptyset$ for $i \neq j$.

The next definition is based on the "discrimin" order (the terminology comes from [16]); it appears under different forms in [21] (there the definition works also for partially ranked default theories), [11] (under the name "democratic"), and [19] (in the context of soft constraint satisfaction problems).

Definition 4 (preferred subtheories, fourth definition). *Let S and S' be two subtheories of T. Define $MinIndex(S \setminus S') = \min\{j | S_j \setminus S'_j \neq \emptyset\}$. We say that S is discrimin-preferred to S' with respect to T, denoted by $S \succ_T^{discrimin} S'$, if $MinIndex(S \setminus S') < MinIndex(S' \setminus S)$. Finally, S is a preferred subtheory of T if there is no consistent subtheory S' of T such that $S' \succ_T^{discrimin} S$.*

The next definition we give is from [17,3].

Definition 5 (preferred subtheories, fifth definition). *Let S and S' be two subtheories of T. We say that S is preferred to S' with respect to T, denoted by $S \succ_T S'$, if and only if there is some $k \leq n$ such that*

- *for all $i \leq k$, $S_i = S'_i$;*
- *$S_k \supset S'_k$.*

Finally, S is a preferred subtheory of T if there is no subtheory S' of T such that $S' \succ_T S$.

The last definition is semantical, as it is based on a preference relation over interpretations. Let PS be the set of propositional symbols on which the formulas of T are defined. Given an interpretation $I \in 2^{PS}$, and a default theory, we define $Sat(T_i, I) = \{\delta \in T_i \mid I \models \delta\}$ and $Sat(T, I) = (Sat(T_1, I), \ldots, Sat(T_n, I))$. Note that $Sat(T, I)$ is a subtheory of T.

Definition 6 (preferred subtheories, sixth definition). *Given two interpretations I, $I' \in 2^{PS}$, we say that I is preferred to I' with respect to T, denoted by $I \succ_T I'$, if and only if there is some $k \leq n$ such that*

- *for all $i \leq k$, $Sat(T_k, I) = Sat(T_k, I')$.*
- *$Sat(T_i, I) \supset Sat(T_i, I')$.*

Finally, I is a preferred model with respect to T iff there is no I' such that $I' \succ_T I$, and S is a preferred subtheory of T if there exists a preferred model I with respect to T such that $Sat(T, I) = S$.

Proposition 1. *Definitions 1, 2, 3, 4, 5 and 6 are equivalent.*

This result is more or less a "folklore" result[3], in the sense that most equivalences are already known without there being an well-identified reference for them. Still, some equivalences have been proven in [3,16] (and probably elsewhere, I apologize

---

[3] Ulrich Junker made me notice that "folklore" may be understood by some people in a pejorative way (*e.g.*, for unproven claims). It should be clear that the meaning I give here to this word is the same as there:
http://en.wikipedia.org/wiki/Mathematical_folklore

for missed references). I however give a proof (in Appendix), not only for the sake of completeness, but also because I cannot see a place where all these definitions are assembled and proven equivalent.

While the notion of preferred subtheory is based on set inclusion, there is a natural variant, defined in [3], based on cardinality. Our definition is a variant of the *second* definition of a preferred subtheory. If X and Y are two sets of formulas, a *maxcard* X-consistent subset of Y is a X-consistent subset Z of Y such that for all $Z' \subseteq Y$, Z' is X-consistent implies $|Z'| \leq |Z|$.

Definition 7 (cardinality-preferred subtheories, first definition). S *is a* C-preferred subtheory *of T iff for all $k = 1, \ldots, n$, S_i is a maxcard $(S_1 \cup \ldots S_{i-1})$-consistent subset of T_i.*

Again we have equivalent definitions, but less than for preferred subtheories. The second definition has been proposed by [17,3] under the name "lexicographic preferred subbases" and in [24] under the name "lexicographic closure".

Definition 8 (cardinality-preferred subtheories, second definition). S *is a C-preferred subtheory of T if there is no subtheory S' of T such that $S' \succ^C_T S$, where $S' \succ^C_T S$ if for some $k \leq n$ we have*

- *for all $i \leq k$, $|S_i| = |S'_i|$;*
- *$|S_k| > |S'_k|$.*

Definition 9 (cardinality-preferred subtheories, third definition). *Define $I' \succ^C_T I$ if and only if there is some $k \leq n$ such that*

- *for all $i \leq k$, $|Sat(T_i, I)| = |Sat(T_i, I')|$.*
- *$|Sat(T_k, I)| > |Sat(T_k, I')|$.*

Then S is a C-preferred subtheory of T if $S = Sat(T, I)$ for some C-preferred model I with respect to T, where I is C-preferred w.r.t. T if there is no I' such that $I' \succ^C_T I$.

Proposition 2. *Definitions 7, 8 and 9 are equivalent.*

This is again a "folklore" result. We omit the proof, which is similar to the proof of Proposition 1.

While Definitions 3 and 4 do not seem to be adaptable to cardinality-preferred subtheories, Definition 1 can, but interestingly, leads to a more conservative notion, based on first-order stochastic dominance:

Definition 10 (SD-preferred subtheories, first definition). S *is an SD-preferred subtheory of T iff for all $k = 1, \ldots, n$, $S_1 \cup \ldots \cup S_k$ is a maxcard consistent subset of $T_1 \cup \ldots \cup T_k$.*

Again is is possible to give two equivalent definitions (which we omit).

Let $PST(T)$ be the set of preferred subtheories of T, $CPST(T)$ be the set of C-preferred subtheories of T, and $SDPST(T)$ be the set of SD-preferred subtheories of T. Then we have these straightforward facts:

1. $PST(T) \supseteq CPST(T) \neq \emptyset$.
2. if $SDPST(T) \neq \emptyset$ then $CPST(T) = SDPST(T)$.

Sometimes the set of SD-preferred subtheories is empty. Let $T = (\{a \wedge b\}, \{\neg a, \neg b\})$. T has a single C-preferred subtheory, namely $S = (\{a \wedge b\}, \emptyset)$. However S is not a SD-preferred subtheory of T, because $\{a \wedge b\}$ is not a maxcard subset of $\{a \wedge b, \neg a, \neg b\}$.

2   What For? Where Do Priorities Come From?

One key question is, where do these priorities come from, what do they correspond to? As we will see below, there is not a single but a lot of different interpretations of priorities, in various domains of knowledge representation, reasoning, and decision making, which in turn correspond to various understandings of preferred subtheories. I will review here several such interpretations – no less then five, and I'm sure I forget some. Two of these interpretations will allow us to derive new equivalent characterizations of preferred subtheories, in case the reader would think we don't have enough with the six already stated.

2.1   Default Reasoning

The interpretation that Brewka had in mind in [6] was default reasoning. Priorities there correspond to a precedence order bearing on the application of default rules, and allowing to choose between multiple extensions. The examples he uses (two of which are quoted in Section 1) are of that kind: the rule that penguins do not fly has precedence over the rule that birds fly, in the sense that when both are "candidate for application", the first one should be applied first (which, here, implies that the second one will *not* be applied). While [6] deals with normal defaults without prerequisites, also called super-normal defaults, he goes further in [7] and extends the framework to normal defaults.

Brewka argues that there are two kinds of priorities: *explicit* and *implicit* priorities, that I'd prefer to call *exogeneous* and *endogeneous*. Quoting from [7]:

> A number of different techniques for handling priorities of defaults have been developed. Two main types of approaches can be distinguished:
> 1. approaches which handle explicit priority information that has to be specified by the user and is not part of the logical language (...)
> 2. approaches which handle implicit priority information based on the specificity of defaults (...).
>
> (...) For real world applications it seems unrealistic to assume that all relevant priorities can be specified by the user explicitly. On the other hand, specificity as the single preference criterion is (...) insufficient in many cases.

As a consequence, he argues that both types of priorities should be handled together in an homogeneous way.

Deriving priorities from specificity relations between default rules originates in the work on conditionals by [1] and was given more attention in a number of papers starting from Pearl's System Z [27]. This systematic construction of priorities from the expression of defaults is beautiful and elegant, but insufficient when the defaults are not ordered into a single specificity hierarchy: for instance, if Δ contains $\delta_1 =$ birds fly, δ_2 = birds that can be seen in Antarctica don't fly, δ_3 = birds that can be seen in Antarctica because they escaped from a ship fly, δ_4 = birds that can be seen in Antarctica because they escaped from a ship but had their wings broken during the trip don't fly, δ_5 = lions eat meat, δ_6 = vegetarian lions don't eat meat, then System-Z will produce the following ranking: $\delta_4 \sim \delta_6 > \delta_3 \sim \delta_5 > \delta_2 > \delta_1$. While it does make sense to order $\delta_4, \delta_3, \delta_2$ and δ_1 this way, and similarly, to rank δ_6 over δ_5, does it make sense to give δ_5 and δ_3 the same rank, and *a fortiori*, that δ_5 should have priority over δ_2? Of course not: either the order between $\{\delta_1, \delta_2, \delta_3, \delta_4\}$ and $\{\delta_5, \delta_6\}$ should be given exogeneously (by some expert in zoology, for instance), or there should be no order between them. For this, a generalization of preferred subtheories to partially ordered defaults is proposed in [6]. It is a generalization of Definition 3: instead of starting from a complete weak order over defaults, we start from a *partial order* $>$ between defaults and we say that a bijective mapping σ from $\{1, \ldots, |T|\}$ to T *respects* $(T, >)$ iff for all $\delta, \delta' \in T, \delta > \delta'$ implies $\sigma^{-1}(\delta) < \sigma^{-1}(\delta')$. The rest of the definition is unchanged.

2.2 Goal-Based Preference Representation

So far we considered a ranked base as being composed of *beliefs*; these beliefs may take the form of facts with some degree of reliability, facts that persist through time with some degree of certainty (see further), rules with possible exceptions, actions with normal and exceptional effects, and so on, but in all cases they deal with an agent's doxastic and epistemic state (her beliefs, her knowledge). Now, ranked bases can also be used with a totally different meaning, so as to express the *preferential state* of an agent, that is, her preferences, goals, desires. The difference between beliefs and preferences is paramount to decision theory – in standard decision theory, beliefs are expressed by probability distributions over states of the world whereas preferences are expressed by utility values over possible consequences of the acts.

Because of this, in this subsection we change the terminology – and notation. A *ranked goal base*, or *prioritized goal base*, is defined exactly as a stratified belief base: it is a tuple $(G_1, \ldots, G_n)$ where each G_i is a set of classical formulas, representing the agent's goals of priority degree i – with the convention that lower indexes correspond to more important goals.

Prioritized goals bases prove to be a very efficient way of representing succinctly preferences over *combinatorial* domains of solutions to a decision problem. Let me quote [8]:

> "By a solution we mean an assignment of a certain value d to each variable v in given set of variables V such that d is taken from the finite domain of v. (...) [In] the Boolean case where the values for each variable are true or false (...), solutions (...) correspond to interpretations in the sense of classical propositional logic. (...)
> We are (...) looking for ways of specifying preferences among such models in a concise yet flexible way. (...)

The number of models is exponential in the number of variables. For this reason it is, in general, impossible for a user to describe her preferences by enumerating all pairs of the preference relation among models. This is where logic comes into play."

Using prioritized bases for succinct preference representation has been discussed in a few papers that all appeared around the same time: [8] defines a general rank-based preference representation language (see further); [22] focuses on the complexity of the computational tasks; and [12] on the expressivity and the succinctness of these languages. Note that here we are no longer interested in preferred subtheories themselves, but in the preference relation between solutions: again quoting [8],

"Traditionally, logic is used for proving theorems. Here, we are not so much interested in logical consequence, we are interested in whether a model satisfies a formula or not."

Thus, the definition that makes most sense here is the sixth one, which we rewrite here into: $I \succ_G I'$ if and only if there is some $k \leq n$ such that $Sat(G_k, I) \supset Sat(G_k, I')$ and for all $i \leq k$, $Sat(G_i, I) = Sat(G_i, I')$. Moreover, $I \sim_G I'$ if and only if $Sat(G_i, I) = Sat(G_i, I')$ for all $i \leq n$, and $I \succeq_G I'$ if $I \succ_G I'$ or $I \sim_G I'$.

The two cardinality-based notions are now rewritten as follows:

- $I' \succ_T^C I$ if and only if there is some $k \leq n$ such that $|Sat(G_k, I)| > |Sat(G_k, I')|$ and for all $i \leq k$, $|Sat(G_i, I)| = |Sat(G_i, I')|$. Moreover, $I \sim_G^C I'$ if and only if for all $i \leq n$, $|Sat(G_i, I)| = |Sat(G_i, I')|$; and $I \succeq_G^C I'$ if $I \succ_G^C I'$ or $I \sim_G^C I'$.
- $I' \succeq_G^{SD} I$ if and only if for all $k \leq n$, $|Sat(G_1 \cup \ldots \cup G_k, I)| \geq |Sat(G_1 \cup \ldots \cup G_k, I')|$.

The following implications are parts of the "folklore": $I' \succeq_G^{SD} I$ implies $I' \succeq_G^C I$, and $I' \succeq_G I$ implies $I' \succeq_G^C I$. Note also that $\succeq_G^C$ is a complete weak order, whereas $\succeq_G$ and $\succeq_G^{SD}$ are partial orders.

These three ways of deriving a preference relation from a prioritized goal base can be characterized utility-theoretically. Given a goal base $G = (G_1, \ldots, G_n)$ with $G_i = \{g_i^j, j = 1, \ldots, m_i\}$, we say that $(u_i^j | i = 1, \ldots, n; j = 1, \ldots, m_i)$, where each u_i^j is a strictly positive real number, is a utility vector for G.

Given a utility vector $\boldsymbol{u}$ for G, and an interpretation I, define

$$u_G(I) = \sum \{u_i^j \mid i \leq n; j \leq m_i; I \models g_i^j\},$$

that is, each goal induces a fixed reward if it is satisfied by I, and 0 if not.

We now consider three restrictions on utility vectors. A utility vector $\boldsymbol{u}$ for G is

- *uniform* if for all $i \leq n$ and all $j, j' \leq m_i$, we have $u_i^j = u_i^{j'}$.
- *faithful* if for all $i < k \leq n$, $j \leq m_i$, $l \leq m_k$, we have $u_i^j > u_k^l$.
- *big-stepped* if for all $i \leq n$ and all $j \leq m_i$, we have $u_i^j > \sum_{k=i+1}^{n} \sum_{l=1}^{m_k} u_k^l$.

Note that any big-stepped vector is faithful.[4] The next result gives one more characterization of preferred subtheories and its two variants.

---

[4] The terminology "big-stepped" comes from [15].

Proposition 3. *Let G be a goal base and I, I' two interpretations.*

1. *$I \succ_G I'$ if and only if $u_G(I) > u_G(I')$ holds for all big-stepped vectors $\mathbf{u}$ for G.*
2. *$I \succ_G^C I'$ if and only if $u_G(I) > u_G(I')$ holds for all uniform and big-stepped vectors $\mathbf{u}$ for G.*
3. *$I \succ_G^{SD} I'$ if and only if $u_G(I) > u_G(I')$ holds for all uniform and faithful vectors $\mathbf{u}$ for G.*

Point 1 leads to a seventh definition of a preferred subtheory:

Definition 11 (preferred subtheories, seventh definition). *S is a* preferred subtheory *of T if and only if $S = Sat(T, I)$ for some interpretation I such that for all big-stepped vectors $\mathbf{u}$ for T, there is no I' such that $u_T(I') > u_T(I)$.*

Once these different semantics for defining a preference relation from a prioritized goal base are defined, they can be combined: [8] defines a language allowing to express Boolean combinations of prioritized goals bases, possibly with different semantics.

Since prioritized goal bases can be used for representing compactly preferences over combinatorial domains, they can be used efficiently in several domains where preference play a role and where domains are typically of this kind, such as planning [20], game theory [5] or voting [22].

2.3   Reliability

We now come back to the primary interpretation of ranked bases as *belief bases*. Perhaps the most obvious interpretation of a ranked belief base is that each formula is a piece of information that has been provided by some unreliable source. This is also the interpretation at work in prioritized merging [14], where preferred subtheories and C-preferred subtheories are used for defining prioritized merging operators. Let $B = (B_1, \ldots, B_n)$ where $B_i = \{b_i^j \mid j = 1, \ldots, m_i\}$. For every formula b_i^j in B_i we define a source σ_i^j with reliability degree $p_i^j \in (\frac{1}{2}, 1)$ for all i, j (sources have a bias towards reliability, and no source is perfectly reliable). The reliability of a source is the likelihood that it tells the truth about p_i^j, that is $p_i^j = Prob(\sigma_i^j : b_i^j \mid b_i^j) = Prob(\sigma_i^j : \neg b_i^j \mid \neg b_i^j)$, where $\sigma_i^j : \varphi$ is the event "σ_i^j says φ". Let $\sigma : B$ be the conjunction of all events $\sigma_i^j : b_i^j$: informally, B is observed if all sources give the formulas that are contained in B. Now, let $S = (S_1, \ldots, S_n)$ be a consistent subbase of B. The likelihood of observing B given that the "true" subbase of B (the one composed of the fomulas of T that are true in the actual world) is S is

$$Prob(\sigma : B \mid S) = \prod_{(i,j):b_i^j \in S} p_i^j \prod_{(i,j):b_i^j \notin S} (1 - p_i^j)$$

Now we have

$$\log Prob(s : B \mid S) = \sum_{(i,j):b_i^j \in S} \log p_i^j + \sum_{(i,j):b_i^j \notin S} \log(1 - p_i^j)$$
$$= \sum_{(i,j) \mid i \le n, j \le m_i} \log(1 - p_i^j) + \sum_{(i,j):b_i^j \in S} \log\left(\frac{p_i^j}{1 - p_i^j}\right)$$
$$= \alpha + \sum_{(i,j):b_i^j \in S} \log\left(\frac{p_i^j}{1 - p_i^j}\right)$$

where α is a constant, independent of S. Define $\succ_p$ as: $S \succ_p S'$ if and only if $Prob(\sigma :$

$B \mid S) \geq Prob(\sigma : B \mid S')$. Now, let $u_i^j = \log\left(\frac{p_i^j}{1-p_i^j}\right)$. We have that $S \succ_p S'$ if and only if $\sum_{(i,j):b_i^j \in S} u_i^j > \sum_{(i,j):b_i^j \in S'} u_i^j$; furthermore, if $S = Sat(T, I)$ and $S' = Sat(T, I')$, then $S \succ_p S'$ if and only if $u(I_S) > u(I_{S'})$. This correspondence allows to translate the conditions of Proposition 3 in probabilistic terms. Say that p is

- *uniform* if for all $i \leq n$ and all $j, j' \leq m_i$, we have $p_i^j = p_i^{j'}$.
- *faithful* if for all $i < k \leq n$, $j \leq m_i$, $l \leq m_k$, we have $p_i^j > p_k^l$.
- *big-stepped* if for all $i \leq n$ and all $j \leq m_i$, we have $\frac{p_i^j}{1-p_i^j} > \prod_{k=i+1}^{n} \prod_{l=1}^{m_k} \frac{p_k^l}{1-p_k^l}$.

Corollary 1. *Let B be a goal base and S, S' two subbases of B.*

1. *$S \succ_B S'$ if and only if $S \succ_p S'$ holds for all big-stepped vectors $\mathbf{p}$ for B.*
2. *$S \succ_B^C S'$ if and only if $S \succ_p S'$ holds for all uniform, big-stepped vectors $\mathbf{p}$ for B.*
3. *$S \succ_B^{SD} S'$ if and only if $S \succ_p S'$ holds for all uniform, faithful vectors $\mathbf{p}$ for B.*

Point 1 leads to an eighth definition of a preferred subtheory:

Definition 12 (preferred subtheories, eighth definition). *S is a preferred subtheory of T if there is no consistent subtheory S' of T such that $S \succ_p S'$ holds for all big-stepped vector $\mathbf{p}$ for B.*

2.4   Time, Space, Analogy

A context where prioritized defaults oocur in a natural way is that of *time-stamped data bases*: there, priorities correpond to recency, and a fact observed at time $t - 1$ is more likely to have persisted until t than a fact observed at time $t - 2$.

Example 1

$$now \quad\quad : a \vee b$$
$$now - 1 : a \rightarrow c$$
$$now - 2 : \neg a, \neg b$$
$$now - 3 : \neg c$$

If we focus on what holds now, then this scenario gives us the ranked default theory ($T_1 = \{a \vee b\}, T_2 = \{a \rightarrow c\}, T_3 = \{\neg a, \neg b\}, T_4 = \{\neg c\}$) – with two preferred subtheories $\{a \vee b, a \rightarrow c, \neg a, \neg c\}$ and $\{a \vee b, a \rightarrow c, \neg b\}$.. However, default persistence does not only work forward but also backward: if $a \vee b$ holds now, by default it holds also at $now - 1$, etc. If we focus on what holds at $now - 3$, we get the ranked default theory ($T_1 = \{\neg c\}, T_2 = \{\neg a, \neg b\}, T_3 = \{a \rightarrow c\}, T_4 = \{a \vee b\}$) with one preferred subtheory $T_1 \cup T_2 \cup T_3$. If we focus on what holds at $now - 1$, this becomes more complicated: should we have the ranked default theory ($T_1 = \{a \rightarrow c\}, T_2 = \{a \vee b, \neg a, \neg b\}, T_3 = \{\neg c\}$), that is, should the information at now and the information at $now - 2$ count equally, or should we rather have a partially ordered default theory $a \rightarrow c > a \vee b, a \rightarrow c > \neg a, \neg b > \neg c\}$, and apply the second generalization of [6]? (In both cases we get three preferred subtheories $\{a \rightarrow c, a \vee b, \neg a, \neg c\}$, $\{a \rightarrow c, a \vee b, \neg b\}$ and $\{a \rightarrow c, \neg a, \neg b, \neg c\}$.

Other natural examples involve reasoning about spatial observations, about case-labelled facts (reasoning by analogy, case-based reasoning), about ontologies. A more general framework where priorities come from distances between 'labels' (such as time points, points in space, cases, classes) and where observations are labelled, is described in [2].

2.5   Judgment Aggregation and Voting

Given a set of formulas $A = \{\alpha_1, \neg\alpha_1, \ldots, \alpha_m, \neg\alpha_m\}$ closed under negation (called the *agenda*), a *judgment set* is a consistent subset of A containing, for all i, either α_i or $\neg\alpha_i$, and a *profile* is a collection of n individual judgment sets. An *(irresolute) judgment aggregation rule* maps a profile into a set of collective judgment sets. As common in social choice, there is a tension between respecting majority and requiring consistency of the collective judgment sets.

An interesting family of judgment aggregation rules is composed of rules that are based on the *support* of a profile, that is, the vector containing, for each element of the agenda, the number of individual judgment sets that contain it. For instance, if $A = \{p, \neg p, q, \neg q, p \wedge q, \neg(p \wedge q)\}$, and $P = \langle J_1, J_2, J_3, J_4, J_5, J_6, J_7 \rangle$ where $J_1 = J_2 = J_3 = \{p, q, p \wedge q\}$, $J_4 = J_5 = \{\neg p, q, \neg(p \wedge q)\}$ and $J_6 = J_7 = \{p, \neg q, \neg(p \wedge q)\}$, the support vector associated with P is $s_P = \langle 5, 2, 5, 2, 3, 4 \rangle$. Now, define the prioritized base $T(P)$ where priorities correspond to strength of support: in our example, $T_1(P) = \{p, q\}$ (support 5), $T_2(P) = \{\neg(p \wedge q)\}$ (support 4), $T_3(P) = \{p \wedge q\}$ (support 3), and $T_4(P) = \{\neg p, \neg q\}$ (support 2). Given a profile P, Nehring et al. [26] define a *supermajority efficient judgment set* as (reformulated in my terms) a SD-undominated subtheory of $T(P)$, and define the so-called *leximin* judgment aggregation rule as the set of C-preferred subtheories of $T(P)$, while Lang et al. [23] define the so-called *ranked agenda* rule as the set of preferred subtheories of $T(P)$. See also [18] for a discussion on these rules.

These connections between judgment aggregation rules and preferred theories and their variants carry on to *voting rules*, which is not surprising given that preference aggregation can be see as a specific case of judgment aggregation. The *ranked pairs* voting rule [30] thus corresponds to the ranked agenda rule, when the agenda consists of propositions of the form xPy ("x is preferred to y"), where x and y range over a set of *candidates*, together with the transitivity constraint bearing on judgment sets. In other terms, this means that *the ranked pairs voting rule can be seen as a specific application of preferred subtheories.* This is is probably the first time that this connection between this well-known voting rule (and the corresponding judgment aggregation rule) is mentioned; interestingly, the ranked pairs rule and preferred subtheories have been invented roughly at the same time, in two research areas that were (at the time) totally disconnected from each other. Let me end up with an example.

Example 2. Let the set of candidates be $C = \{a, b, c, d\}$ and the 38-voter profile P consisting of 5 votes $abdc$ (with the usual convention that $abdc$ is a shorthand for $a \succ b \succ d \succ c$), 7 votes $cdab$, 8 votes $bcad$, 7 votes $dabc$, 4 votes $dcab$, 3 votes $cbda$, 2 votes $bacd$, 1 vote $dbca$ and 1 vote $acdb$. The pairwise majority matrix is

$$
\begin{array}{c c c c c}
 & a & b & c & d \\
a & - & 24 & 15 & 16 \\
b & 14 & - & 23 & 18 \\
c & 23 & 15 & - & 21 \\
d & 22 & 20 & 17 & -
\end{array}
$$

and the corresponding prioritized base is $T(P) = (T_1(P), T_2(P), \ldots, T_{11}(P)))$, where $T_1(P) = Trans$ is the transitivity constraint, $T_2(P) = \{aPb\}$, $T_3(P) = \{bPc, cPa\}$, $T_4(P) = \{dPa\}$, $T_5(P) = \{cPd\}$, $T_6(P) = \{dPb\}$) etc. The preferred subtheories of $T(P)$ are $\{Trans, aPb, bPc, dPa, dPb, aPc, dPc\}$, corresponding to the collective ranking $dabc$ and to the winner d, and $\{Trans, aPb, cPa, dPa, cPd, dPb, cPb\}$, corresponding to the collective ranking $cdab$ and to the winner c.

Note that taking C-preferred subtheories instead of preferred subtheories leads to a refinement of the ranked pairs rules (in our example, the sole winner for this rule is c).

3   Conclusion

We have seen that preferred subtheories and their extensions and variants have had a tremendous impact in the Artificial Intelligence literature and beyond, and are tightly connected to notions that have been developed independently in social choice. If I had more pages, I could talk for instance about the computation of preferred subtheories and inferences therefrom (e.g., [10,13]. A further question is, is logic really useful when defining preferred subtheories? We have seen at least one example (voting) where logic isn't necessary at all. After all, all we use from logic is the notion of *consistency*. When defining the ranked pairs voting rule, a weighted graph plays the role of the ranked base, and acyclicity plays the role of consistency. How can we define an abstract (logic-free) notion of preferred subtheory and what about other applications and/or connections?

Acknowledgements. Thanks to Richard Booth and Ulrich Junker for helpful comments on a previous version of this paper.

References

1. Adams, E.W.: The Logic of Conditionals. Reiter, Dordrecht (1975)
2. Asher, N., Lang, J.: When nonmonotonicity comes from distances. In: KI-94: Advances in Artificial Intelligence, Proceedings of the 18th Annual German Conference on Artificial Intelligence, Saarbrücken, Germany, September 18-23, pp. 308–318 (1994)
3. Benferhat, S., Cayrol, C., Dubois, D., Lang, J., Prade, H.: Inconsistency management and prioritized syntax-based entailment. In: Proceedings of the 13th International Joint Conference on Artificial Intelligence, Chambéry, France, August 28-September 3, pp. 640–647 (1993)
4. Benferhat, S., Dubois, D., Prade, H.: Some syntactic approaches to the handling of inconsistent knowledge bases: A comparative study. Part 2: The Prioritized Case 24, 473–511 (1998)
5. Bonzon, E., Lagasquie-Schiex, M.C., Lang, J.: Dependencies between players in boolean games. Int. J. Approx. Reasoning 50(6), 899–914 (2009)

6. Brewka, G.: Preferred subtheories: An extended logical framework for default reasoning. In: Proceedings of the 11th International Joint Conference on Artificial Intelligence, Detroit, MI, USA, pp. 1043–1048 (August 1989)
7. Brewka, G.: Reasoning about priorities in default logic. In: Proceedings of the 12th National Conference on Artificial Intelligence, Seattle, WA, USA, July 31-August 4, vol. 2, pp. 940–945 (1994)
8. Brewka, G.: A rank based description language for qualitative preferences. In: Proceedings of the 16th Eureopean Conference on Artificial Intelligence, ECAI 2004, including Prestigious Applicants of Intelligent Systems, PAIS 2004, Valencia, Spain, August 22-27, pp. 303–307 (2004)
9. Cayrol, C., Lagasquie-Schiex, M.: Non-monotonic syntax-based entailment: A classification of consequence relations. In: Froidevaux, C., Kohlas, J. (eds.) ECSQARU 1995. LNCS, vol. 946, pp. 107–114. Springer, Heidelberg (1995)
10. Cayrol, C., Lagasquie-Schiex, M., Schiex, T.: Nonmonotonic reasoning: From complexity to algorithms. Ann. Math. Artif. Intell. 22(3-4), 207–236 (1998)
11. Cayrol, C., Royer, V., Saurel, C.: Management of preferences in assumption-based reasoning. In: Valverde, L., Bouchon-Meunier, B., Yager, R.R. (eds.) IPMU 1992. LNCS, vol. 682, pp. 13–22. Springer, Heidelberg (1993)
12. Coste-Marquis, S., Lang, J., Liberatore, P., Marquis, P.: Expressive power and succinctness of propositional languages for preference representation. In: Principles of Knowledge Representation and Reasoning: Proceedings of the Ninth International Conference (KR 2004), Whistler, Canada, June 2-5, pp. 203–212 (2004)
13. Coste-Marquis, S., Marquis, P.: On stratified belief base compilation. Ann. Math. Artif. Intell. 42(4), 399–442 (2004)
14. Delgrande, J.P., Dubois, D., Lang, J.: Iterated revision as prioritized merging. In: Proceedings of the Tenth International Conference on Principles of Knowledge Representation and Reasoning, Lake District of the United Kingdom, June 2-5, pp. 210–220 (2006)
15. Dubois, D., Fargier, H.: A unified framework for order-of-magnitude confidence relations. In: Proceedings of the 20th Conference in Uncertainty in Artificial Intelligence, UAI 2004, Banff, Canada, July 7-11, pp. 138–145 (2004)
16. Dubois, D., Fargier, H., Prade, H.: Refinements of the maximin approach to decision-making in a fuzzy environment. Fuzzy Sets and Systems (1996)
17. Dubois, D., Lang, J., Prade, H.: Inconsistency in Possibilistic Knowledge Bases: To Live with It or Not Live with It. In: Fuzzy logic for the management of uncertainty, pp. 335–351. John Wiley & Sons, Inc. (1992)
18. Everaere, P., Konieczny, S., Marquis, P.: Counting votes for aggregating judgments. In: Proceedings of the 13th International Conference on Autonomous Agents and Multiagent Systems, AAMAS 2014, pp. 1177–1184 (2014)
19. Fargier, H., Lang, J., Schiex, T.: Selecting preferred solutions in Fuzzy Constraint Satisfaction Problems. In: Proc. of the 1st European Congress on Fuzzy and Intelligent Technologies (1993)
20. Feldmann, R., Brewka, G., Wenzel, S.: Planning with prioritized goals. In: Proceedings of the Tenth International Conference on Principles of Knowledge Representation and Reasoning, Lake District of the United Kingdom, June 2-5, pp. 503–514 (2006)
21. Geffner, H.: Default Reasoning: Causal and Conditional Theories. MIT Press, Cambridge (1992)
22. Lang, J.: Logical preference representation and combinatorial vote. Ann. Math. Artif. Intell. 42(1-3), 37–71 (2004)
23. Lang, J., Pigozzi, G., Slavkovik, M., van der Torre, L.: Judgment aggregation rules based on minimization. In: TARK, pp. 238–246 (2011)

24. Lehmann, D.: Another perspective on default reasoning. Annals of Mathematics and Artificial Intelligence 15(1), 61–82 (1995)
25. Nebel, B.: Belief revision and default reasoning: Syntax-based approaches. In: Proceedings of the 2nd International Conference on Principles of Knowledge Representation and Reasoning (KR 1991), Cambridge, MA, USA, April 22-25, pp. 417–428 (1991)
26. Nehring, K., Pivato, M.: Majority rule in the absence of a majority. MPRA Paper 46721, University Library of Munich, Germany (May 2013),
http://ideas.repec.org/p/pra//46721.html
27. Pearl, J.: System Z: A natural ordering of defaults with tractable applications to nonmonotonic reasoning. In: Proceedings of the 3rd Conference on Theoretical Aspects of Reasoning about Knowledge, Pacific Grove, CA, pp. 121–135 (March 1990)
28. Poole, D.: A logical framework for default reasoning. Artif. Intell. 36(1), 27–47 (1988)
29. Rescher, N.: Hypothetical Reasoning. Studies in Logic, North-Holland (1964)
30. Tideman, T.N.: Independence of clones as a criterion for voting rules. Social Choice and Welfare 4, 185–206 (1987)

Appendix

Proof of Proposition 1

Proof. Throughout the proof, we say that S is a i-PST of T (where $1 \leq i \leq 6$) if S is a preferred subtheory of T according to Definition i. Let S be a subtheory of T.

- $1 \Rightarrow 2$: Assume that S is not a 2-PST of T; then for some i there is $S_i' \supset S_i$ such that S_i' is $S_1 \cup \ldots \cup S_{i-1}$-consistent. Since $S_1 \cup \ldots \cup S_{i-1} \cup S_i'$ is consistent and $S_1 \cup \ldots \cup S_{i-1} \cup S_i \subset S_1 \cup \ldots \cup S_{i-1} \cup S_i'$, $S_1 \cup \ldots \cup S_i$ is not a maximal consistent subset of $T_1 \cup \ldots \cup T_i$, henceforth, not a 1-PST of T.

- $2 \Rightarrow 1$: Assume that S is not a 1-PST of T; then for some i, $S_1 \cup \ldots \cup S_i$ is not a maximal consistent subset of $T_1 \cup \ldots \cup T_i$. Let $S_1' \cup \ldots S_i' \supset S_1 \cup \ldots \cup S_i$ be a maximal consistent subset of $T_1 \cup \ldots \cup T_i$ and let $j = \min\{i, S_i \neq S_i'\}$. Then S_j' is a $S_1 \cup \ldots \cup S_{j-1}$ consistent subset of T_j, which implies that S_j is not, and that S is not a 2-PST of T.

- $4 \Rightarrow 2$: Assume that S is not a a 2-PST of T; then for some i there is $S_i' \supset S_i$ such that S_i' is $S_1 \cup \ldots \cup S_{i-1}$-consistent. Let $S' = S_1 \cup \ldots \cup S_{i-1} \cup S_i'$. S' is a subtheory of T and we have $MinIndex(S' \setminus S) = i$ and $MinIndex(S \setminus S') > i$, therefore S is not a a 4-PST of T.

- $5 \Rightarrow 4$: Assume that S is not a 4-PST of T; then for some S' we have $MinIndex (S' \setminus S) \leq MinIndex(S \setminus S')$. Since $MinIndex(S' \setminus S) = MinIndex(S \setminus S')$ is not possible, we must have $MinIndex(S' \setminus S) = k < MinIndex(S \setminus S')$. Now, for all $j < k$ we have $S_j = S_j'$ and $S_k' \supset S_k$, therefore S is not a 5-PST of T.

- $2 \Rightarrow 3$: assume S is a 2-PST of T. Let us construct σ this way: σ considers first formulas of S_1 (in any order), followed by formulas in $T_1 \setminus S_1$ (in any order), then S_2 then $T_2 \setminus S_2$, etc. until $T_n \setminus S_n$. We show by induction on i that after considering all formulas of T_i, we have $\Sigma_{t(i)} = S_1 \cup \ldots \cup S_i$, where $t(i) = |T_1 \cup \ldots \cup T_i|$. This is true for $i = 1$, because S_1 is maximal consistent. Assume it is true for i, i.e., $\Sigma_{t(i)} = S_1 \cup \ldots \cup S_i$. Because S is a 2-PST of T, S_{i+1} is $(S_1 \cup \ldots \cup S_i)$-consistent, therefore, all formulas of S_{i+1} are added, and because it is maximal $(S_1 \cup \ldots \cup S_i)$-consistent, none of the formulas of $T_{i+1} \setminus S_{i+1}$ are added. Therefore, at the end of step $t(i)$ $\Sigma_{t(i+1)} = S_1 \cup \ldots \cup S_{i+1}$. Applying the induction hypothesis to $i = n$ leads to $S_\sigma = \Sigma_{t(n)} = S$: S is a 3-PST of T.

- $3 \Rightarrow 6$: Let S be a 3-PST of T and let σ such that $S_\sigma = S$. Note that S is necessarily maximal consistent: if there was $\delta \in T \setminus S$ such that $S \cup \{\delta\}$ is consistent, then δ would have been added to Σ when considered; therefore, there exists I such that $Sat(T, I) = S$. Assume S is not a 6-PST of T: then there is $I' \succ_T I$, that is, for some k, we have that for all $i < k$, $Sat(T_i, I) = Sat(T_i, I')$, and $Sat(T_k, I) \subset Sat(T_k, I')$. But then, when the defaults of T_k are considered for addition to Σ, all formulas of $Sat(T_k, I') \setminus Sat(T_k, I)$ should have been added, which contradicts $S_\sigma = S$.

- $6 \Rightarrow 5$: Assume that S is a 6-PST of T: there is an I such that $Sat(T, I) = S$. Assume that S is not a 5-PST of T: then there is an S' such that $S' \succ_T S$. Because $S' \subset S'' \subseteq T$ implies $S' \succ_T S$, there is a maximal consistent subset S'' of T such that $S'' \succ_T S$. Let $S'' = Sat(T, I'')$: then $I'' \succ_T I$, which contradicts the assumption that S is a 6-PST of T.

Proof of Proposition 4

Proof. 1. Assume $I \succ_G I'$ and let k such that $Sat(G_j, I) = Sat(G_j, I')$ for all $j < k$, and $Sat(G_k, I) \supset Sat(G_k, I')$. Let $\mathbf{u}$ be a big-stepped vector for G. Let $A_i = \sum \{u_i^j \mid j \leq n_i; \; g_i^j \in Sat(G_i, I) \setminus Sat(G_i, I')\} - \sum \{u_i^j \mid j \leq n_i; \; g_i^j \in Sat(G_i, I') \setminus Sat(G_i, I)\}$. We have $u_G(I) - u_G(I') = \sum_{i \leq n} A_i$. Because $Sat(G_j, I) = Sat(G_j, I')$ for all $j < k$, we have (1) $A_i = 0$ for all $i < k$. Because $Sat(G_k, I) \supset Sat(G_k, I')$, there exists some $g_k^l \in Sat(G_k, I) \supset Sat(G_k, I')$. Because $\mathbf{u}$ is big-stepped, we have $u_k^l > \sum_{p=k+1}^{n} \sum_{q=1}^{m_p} u_p^q$, which implies (2) $u_k^l > \sum_{p=k+1}^{n} |A_p|$. Now, (1) and (2) imply $u_G(I) - u_G(I') = A_k + \sum_{i > k} A_i > 0$, that is, $u(I) > u(I')$.

Conversely, assume $I \not\succ_G I'$. If $I \sim_G I'$, then clearly $u(I) = u(I')$. If not, then there is a k such that $Sat(G_j, I) = Sat(G_j, I')$ for all $j < k$, and $Sat(G_k, I') \setminus Sat(G_k, I) \neq \emptyset$. Let $g_k^l \in Sat(G_k, I') \setminus Sat(G_k, I)$. Define $\mathbf{u}$ as follows: $u_k^l = |B_k|$; for all $l' \neq l$, $u_k^{l'} = 1$; and the other values u_i^j are defined in any way such that $\mathbf{u}$ is big-stepped (since we have put constraints on values concerning level k, this is obviously possible to do so). Let A_i be defined as above. Since $\mathbf{u}$ is big-stepped, we have, for all $l' \neq l$, $u_k^{l'} = 1 > \sum_{p=k+1}^{n} \sum_{q=1}^{m_p} u_k^l$, which implies $-1 < \sum_{p=k+1}^{n} A_k < 1$. Finally, $A_k \leq -|B_k| + \sum_{j \leq m_k, j \neq l} u_i^j \leq -1$, and $u(I) - u(I') = \sum_{i \leq n} A_i = A_k + \sum_{i > k} A_i < 0$, that is, $u(I) < u(I')$.

2. Assume $I \succ_G^C I'$ and let k such that $|Sat(G_j, I)| = |Sat(G_j, I')|$ for all $j < k$, and $|Sat(G_k, I)| > |Sat(G_k, I')|$. Let $\mathbf{u}$ be a uniform, big-stepped vector for G, and let $u_i^j = u_i$ for all $j \leq m_i$. Define A_i, for all $i \leq n$, as above. Then (1) for all $i < k$, $A_i = (2|Sat(G_i, I)| - m_i).u_i - (2|Sat(G_i, I')| - m_i).u_i = 0$, (2) $A_k = 2|Sat(G_k, I)| - m_k).u_k - (2|Sat(G_k, I')| - m_k).u_k = 2(Sat(G_k, I)| - |Sat(G_k, I')| > 2u_k$ and because $\mathbf{u}$ is big-stepped, (3) $u_k > \sum_{p=k+1}^{n} |A_p|$. (1), (2) and (3) imply $u_G(I) - u_G(I') > 0$, that is, $u(I) > u(I')$.

Conversely, assume $I \not\succ_G^C I'$. If $I \sim_G^C I'$, then clearly $u(I) = u(I')$. If not, then, because $\succ_G^C$ is total, we have $I' \succ_G^C I$, which using the first part of the proof, implies that for all uniform, big-stepped $\mathbf{u}$ for G, we have $u(I) < u(I')$.

3. Assume $I \succ_G^{SD} I'$. Then for all $i \leq n$, $\sum_{j \leq i} |Sat(G_j, I)| \geq \sum_{j \leq i} |Sat(G_j, I)$, and for some k, (1) $\sum_{j \leq k} |Sat(G_j, I)| > \sum_{j \leq k} |Sat(G_j, I)$. Let $\boldsymbol{u}$ be uniform and faithful. Let $\alpha_i = |\tilde{S}at(G_i, I)|$ and $\beta_i = [\tilde{S}at(G_i, I')|$. Let V (resp. W) be the multiset containing α_i (resp. β_i) occurrences of u_i for all i, and reorder V and W non-increasingly, that is, $V = \{v_{(1)}, \ldots, v_{(p)}\}$ and $W = \{w_{(1)}, \ldots, w_{(q)}\}$ with $v_{(1)} \geq \ldots \geq v_{(p)}$ and $w_{(1)} \geq \ldots \geq w_{(q)}$. $I \succ_G^{SD} I'$ and the faithfulness of u imply $p \geq q$ and for all i, $v_{(i)} \geq w_{(i)}$. Finally, together with (1) they imply that there is a j such that $v_{(i)} > w_{(i)}$. Now, $u(I) - u(I') = \sum_{i=1}^{q} (v_{(i)} - w_{(i)}) + \sum_{i=q+1}^{p} v_{(i)}$ is a sum of positive terms, with at least one strictly positive term, therefore, $u(I) > u(I')$.

Conversely, assume $I \not\succ_G^{SD} I'$. If $I \sim_G^{SD} I'$, then $I \sim_G^{C} I'$ and $u(I) = u(I')$. If not, then there is some k such that $\sum_{j \leq k} |\tilde{S}at(G_j, I)| < \sum_{j \leq k} |Sat(G_j, I)$. Define the uniform, faithful vector $\boldsymbol{u}$ as $u_i = i + (k - i)\epsilon$ for all $i \leq k$ and $u_i = (i - k).\epsilon$ for all $i > k$, where $\epsilon < \frac{1}{k|G|}$. Then $u(I') - u(I) > 1 - \sum_{i<k} |G_i|(k-1)\epsilon > 0$, therefore, $u(I) < u(I')$.

A Fuzzy Set Approach to Expressing Preferences in Spatial Reasoning

Hans W. Guesgen

Massey University, Palmerston North, New Zealand
h.w.guesgen@massey.ac.nz

Abstract. The way we use spatial descriptions in many everyday situations is of a qualitative nature. This is often achieved by specifying spatial relations between objects or regions. The advantage of using qualitative descriptions is that we can be less precise and thereby less prone to making an error. For example, it is often easier to decide whether an object is inside another object than to specify exactly where the first object is with respect to the second one. In artificial intelligence, a variety of formalisms have been developed that deal with space on the basis of relations between objects or regions that objects might occupy. One of these formalisms is the RCC theory, which is based on a primitive relation, called connectedness, and uses a set of topological relations, defined on the basis of connectedness, to provide a framework for reasoning about regions. This paper discusses an extension of the RCC theory based on fuzzy logic, which enables us to express preferences among spatial descriptions.

1 Introduction

The ability to reason about space plays a significant role in everyday life. There are many ways of dealing with spatial and temporal information, but it can be argued that humans often do so in qualitative way. It is therefore not a surprise that researchers in computer science, particularly artificial intelligence, have developed qualitative spatial reasoning methods to mimic how humans reason about space and time.

One of the early approaches [11] is based on Allen's temporal logic [1]. It extends this logic to the three dimensions of space by applying very simple methods for constructing higher-dimensional models. Other approaches to qualitative spatial reasoning followed and addressed aspects of space such as topology, direction, and distance. It is beyond the scope of this chapter to name them all or to even find a representative sample. We therefore rather refer the reader to Ligozat's book on spatial and temporal reasoning [16], which provides a good overview of the various approaches to reasoning about space and time.

The approach that this chapter is based on, the RCC theory, has gained particular interest in the research community in the past twenty years [17]. It is a first-order theory based on a primitive relation called connectedness. The theory uses a number of topological relations, defined on the basis of connectedness, to

T. Eiter et al. (Eds.): Brewka Festschrift, LNAI 9060, pp. 173–185, 2015.

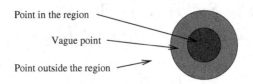

Point in the region

Vague point

Point outside the region

Fig. 1. A vague region represented by two crisp regions (the egg and the yolk)

provide a framework for reasoning about regions. Of particular interest is the RCC8 theory, which restricts the topological relations to eight jointly exhaustive and pairwise disjoint relations.

The original RCC theory assumes that regions are well defined, which is not always the case. For example, it is almost impossible to specify exactly the boundary of a forest region, or which part of a country counts as the northern part. In most cases, this is a matter of preference and might vary from observer to observer.

To address this issue, the RCC theory has been extended to cope with uncertainty in spatial representations, in particular vague or indeterminate boundaries [6]. The extension, called the egg-yolk theory, uses two crisp regions, the egg and the yolk, to characterise a vague region. All points within the yolk are considered to be in the region, whereas all points outside the egg are outside the region. The white characterises the points that may or may not belong to the region (see Figure 1).

When interpreting descriptions that contain elements of uncertainty, we are often confronted with the question of what the preferred interpretations are in a particular scenario. In the late eighties, Brewka [4] introduced a framework for expressing preferred subtheories in default logic. This work has been widely cited and has inspired similar approaches in other areas, including the one introduced in this chapter.

Our approach utilises the neighbourhood structure that is inherent in the RCC8 theory and defines fuzzy sets for the relations between regions based on this neighbourhood structure. Our approach is related to the one described in [19], which also introduces fuzzy sets into the RCC theory. However, they do not use the neighbourhood structure but replace the primitive relation of connectedness by a fuzzy relation. They then generalise the definitions of the other RCC relations accordingly. Our approach is to some degree also related to [8], which uses the concept of 9-intersection instead of the RCC theory as basis. They do not use fuzzy logic, but they utilise a structure similar to the RCC8 neighbourhood structure, called the closest topological relationship graph, to deal with indeterminate boundaries. There is also some overlap with the work described in [3], where fuzzy spatial relationships are used for image processing and interpretation.

The chapter is organized as follows. We start with a brief review of the RCC theory and its extension to regions with indeterminate boundaries. We then show a way of associating fuzzy sets with the relations in the RCC theory. This enables us to express preferences among the relations in situations where the boundaries

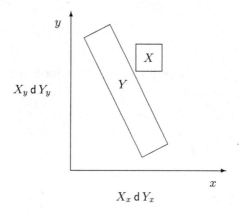

Fig. 2. The relations between two rectangles with respect to the x-axis and y-axis, where d denotes the Allen relation during, which is interpreted as inside in the spatial domain. The relations suggest that one rectangle is inside the other rectangle, which in fact is not the case.

of the regions are not precisely defined. After that, we sketch an algorithm to reason about these fuzzy sets. Finally, we demonstrate how the same approach can be used for reasoning in dynamic environments, i.e., environments where regions can move and change their shape. The aim here is to express preferences among the possible movements and deformations.

2   The RCC Theory Revisited

The idea of using relations to reason about spatial information dates back at least to the eighties [11], when Allen's temporal logic [1] was extended to three-dimensional space. The problem with this approach is that it often leads to counterintuitive results, in particular if rectangular objects are not aligned to the chosen axes (see Figure 2).

The RCC theory [17] avoids this problem by using topological properties to define the relation between two regions. The basis of the RCC theory is the connectedness relation, which is a reflexive and symmetric relation, satisfying the following axioms:

1. For each region X: $\mathsf{C}(X, X)$
2. For each pair of regions X, Y: $\mathsf{C}(X, Y) \to \mathsf{C}(Y, X)$

From this relation, additional relations can be derived, which include the eight jointly exhaustive and pairwise disjoint RCC8 relations shown in Figure 3:

$$\mathsf{RCC8} = \{\mathsf{DC}, \mathsf{EC}, \mathsf{PO}, \mathsf{EQ}, \mathsf{TPP}, \mathsf{TPPi}, \mathsf{NTPP}, \mathsf{NTPPi}\}$$

Relation/Interpretation	Illustration
DC(X,Y) X disconnected from Y	
EC(X,Y) X externally connected to Y	
PO(X,Y) X partially overlaps Y	
EQ(X,Y) X identical with Y	
TPP(X,Y) X tangential proper part of Y	
TPPi(X,Y) Y tangential proper part of X	
NTPP(X,Y) X nontangential proper part of Y	
NTPP(X,Y) Y nontangential proper part of X	

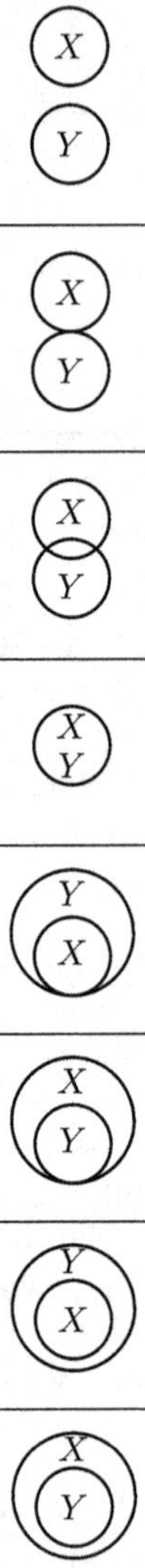

Fig. 3. An illustration of the RCC8 relations

Reasoning about space is achieved in the RCC theory by applying a composition table to pairs of relations, similar to the composition table in Allen's logic. Given the relation R_1 between the regions X and Y, and the relation R_2 between the regions Y and Z, the composition table determines the relation R_3 between the regions X and Z, i.e., $R_3 = R_1 \circ R_2$. In the case of a set of regions $\mathcal{X}$ with more than three regions, the composition table can be applied repeatedly to three-element subsets of $\mathcal{X}$ until no more relations can be updated, resulting in a set of relations that is locally consistent.

3   Expressing Preferences of Spatial Relations

Reasoning about space often has to deal with some form of uncertainty. For example, when we talk about a region like a forest, we usually do not know exactly where the boundary is for that region. Nevertheless, we are perfectly capable to reason about such a region: If we hear on the radio that a fire is spreading towards the forest, we can estimate when the fire "connects" with the forest, although we might not be able to decide with certainty whether the fire is still disconnected from (DC), externally connected to (EC), or already partially overlapping (PO) the forest. However, we usually prefer some relation over others when making such an estimate.

[15] introduces an extension to the RCC theory, called the egg-yolk theory, which deals with imprecision in spatial representations by using two crisp regions to characterise an imprecise region. One of these regions is called the yolk, the other one the egg. All points within the yolk are considered to be in the region, whereas all points outside the egg are outside the region. The white (i.e., the egg without the yolk) characterises the points that may or may not belong to the region.

The egg-yolk theory uses a set of five base relations, called RCC5, instead of the eight base relations in RCC8:

$$RCC5 = \{DR, PO, EQ, PP, PPi\}$$

Given two imprecise regions $\widetilde{X}$ and $\widetilde{Y}$, the RCC5 relations are used to describe the relationship between (1) the egg of $\widetilde{X}$ and the egg of $\widetilde{Y}$, (2) the yolk of $\widetilde{X}$ and the yolk of $\widetilde{Y}$, (3) the egg of $\widetilde{X}$ and the yolk of $\widetilde{Y}$, and (4) the yolk of $\widetilde{X}$ and the egg of $\widetilde{Y}$, resulting in 46 possible relationships between $\widetilde{X}$ and $\widetilde{Y}$.

As [15] points out, it is possible to use more than two regions to describe an imprecise region. We follow this idea here and combine it with an approach that we used before to introduce imprecise reasoning into Allen's logic. The approach is based on the concept of conceptual neighbourhoods, which was first introduced in [9] for Allen relations and later applied to the RCC theory [5,6]. An alternative would have been to use the lattice structure of the RCC relations, but this would have resulted in a more complex framework.

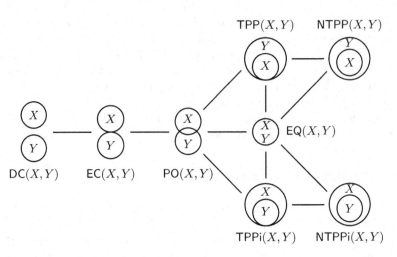

Fig. 4. The RCC8 relations arranged in a graphs showing the conceptual neighbours

4   Conceptual Neighbourhoods and Fuzzy Sets

Two relations on regions X and Y are conceptual neighbours if the shape of X or Y can be continuously deformed such that one relation is transformed into the other relation without passing through a third relation. Figure 4 shows the conceptual neighbours for the RCC8 relations.

The notion of conceptual neighbours can be used to introduce imprecision into reasoning about spatial relations [12]. For that purpose, we first represent each RCC8 relation by a characteristic function as follows:

$$\mu_R : RCC8 \longrightarrow \{0, 1\}$$

The function yields a value of 1 if and only if the argument is equal to the RCC8 relation denoted by the characteristic function:

$$\mu_R(R') = \begin{cases} 1, \text{ if } R' = R \\ 0, \text{ else} \end{cases}$$

The next step towards the introduction of imprecision is to transform the RCC8 relations into fuzzy sets. In general, a fuzzy set $\tilde{A}$ of a domain D is a set of ordered pairs, $(d, \mu_{\tilde{A}}(d))$, where d is an element of the underlying domain D and $\mu_{\tilde{A}} : D \to [0, 1]$ is the membership function of $\tilde{A}$. In other words, instead of specifying whether an element d belongs to a subset A of D or not, we assign a grade of membership to d. The membership function replaces the characteristic function of a classical subset of D.

In analogy to the intersection, union, and complement of crisp sets, we can define similar operations for fuzzy sets. [20] defines these as follows. Given two fuzzy sets $\tilde{A}_1$ and $\tilde{A}_2$ with membership functions $\mu_{\tilde{A}_1}(d)$ and $\mu_{\tilde{A}_2}(d)$, respectively, then the membership function of the intersection $\tilde{A}_3 = \tilde{A}_1 \cap \tilde{A}_2$ is pointwise defined by:

$$\mu_{\tilde{A}_3}(d) = \min\{\mu_{\tilde{A}_1}(d), \mu_{\tilde{A}_2}(d)\}$$

Analogously, the membership function of the union $\tilde{A}_3 = \tilde{A}_1 \cup \tilde{A}_2$ is pointwise defined by:

$$\mu_{\tilde{A}_3}(d) = \max\{\mu_{\tilde{A}_1}(d), \mu_{\tilde{A}_2}(d)\}$$

The membership grade for the complement of a fuzzy set $\tilde{A}$, denoted as $\neg\tilde{A}$, is defined in the same way as the complement in probability theory:

$$\mu_{\neg\tilde{A}}(d) = 1 - \mu_{\tilde{A}}(d)$$

[20] stresses that this is not the only scheme for defining intersection and union of fuzzy sets, and that it depends on the context which scheme is the most appropriate. While some of the schemes are based on empirical investigations, others are the result of theoretical considerations [7,14].

In the context of the RCC8 relations, this means that each RCC8 relation is represented as a set of pairs, each pair consisting of an element of RCC8 (which is the underlying domain) and the value of the characteristic function of the relation applied to that element. For example, if two regions X and Y are externally connected (i.e., $EC(X, Y)$), we use the characteristic function of the relation EC to convert this statement into the following:

$$\{(R, \mu_{EC}(R)) \mid R \in RCC8\}(X, Y) =$$
$$\{(EC, 1), (DC, 0), (PO, 0), \ldots\}(X, Y)$$

Instead of having two classes, one with the accepted relations where μ_{EC} results in 1 and another with the discarded relations where μ_{EC} results in 0, we now assign acceptance grades (or membership grades, to use the term from fuzzy set theory) to the relations. If the relation is EC, we assign a high membership grade, say $1 \geq \alpha_0 \geq 0$; if the relation is a neighbour of EC, we choose a membership grade α_1 with $\alpha_0 \geq \alpha_1 \geq 0$; if the relation is a neighbour of a neighbour of EC, we assign a grade α_2 with $\alpha_1 \geq \alpha_2 \geq 0$; and so on.

Since there is no general formula for determining $\alpha_0, \alpha_1, \alpha_2, \ldots,$, choosing the right grade for each degree of neighbourhood can be a problem. On the other hand, there are experiments showing that fuzzy membership grades are quite robust, which means that it is not necessary to have precise estimations of these grades [2]. The explanation given for this observation is twofold: first, fuzzy membership grades are used to describe imprecise information and therefore do not have to be precise, and second, each individual fuzzy membership grade plays only a minor role in the whole reasoning process, as it is usually combined with several other membership grades. If the membership grades are combined using the min/max combination scheme, as it is the case in the rest of this paper, we do not even need numeric values for the alphas. In this case, reasoning can be performed on symbolic values, provided that there is a total order on the alphas.

Non-atomic RCC8 relations (i.e., disjunctions of RCC8 relations) can be transformed into fuzzy RCC8 relations by using the same technique. A non-atomic

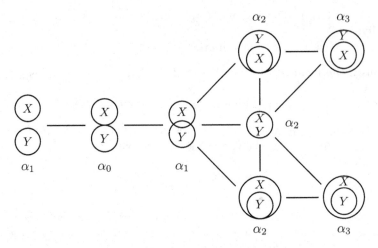

Fig. 5. The assignment of membership grades to the RCC8 relations with $EC(X, Y)$ as reference relation

RCC8 relation is given by a set of atomic RCC8 relations, which is interpreted in a disjunctive way. We therefore transform each atomic relation in the set into a fuzzy RCC8 relation and compute the fuzzy union of the resulting sets. There are different ways of computing the union of fuzzy sets. Here, we choose the one introduced in [20], which associates with each element in the resulting fuzzy set the maximum of the membership grades that the element has in the original fuzzy sets.

Formally, a fuzzy RCC8 relation $\widetilde{R}$ can be defined by using a function $\varDelta$ that denotes the conceptional distance between the relation R and a relation R', i.e., $\varDelta$ results in 1 if R is a neighbour of R', in 2 if R is a neighbour of a neighbour of R', and so on:

$$\varDelta : \text{RCC8} \times \text{RCC8} \longrightarrow \{0, 1, 2, \ldots\}$$

$\varDelta$ can be defined recursively as follows:

1. If $R = R'$, then
   $\varDelta(R, R') = 0$
2. Otherwise,
   $\varDelta(R, R') = \min\{\varDelta(R, R'') + 1 \mid R'' \text{ neighbour of } R'\}$

Given a sequence of membership grades, $1 \geq \alpha_0 \geq \alpha_1 \geq \alpha_2 \geq \cdots \geq 0$, the function $\varDelta$ can be used to associate RCC8 relations with membership grades, depending on some given RCC8 relation R (see Figure 5 for an example). In particular, we can define a membership function $\mu_{\widetilde{R}}$ as follows:

$$\mu_{\widetilde{R}} : \text{RCC8} \longrightarrow [0, 1]$$

$$\mu_{\widetilde{R}}(R') = \alpha_{\varDelta(R, R')}$$

With this definition, the fuzzy RCC8 relation $\tilde{R}$ of a relation $R \in RCC8$ is given by the following:

$$\tilde{R} = \{(R', \mu_{\tilde{R}}(R')) \mid R' \in RCC8\}$$

We now extend the formulation of RCC8 relations as characteristic functions to the composition of RCC8 relations, starting again with crisp relations and continuing with fuzzy relations. In the crisp case, the composition table can be represented as a set of characteristic functions of the following form:

$$\mu_{R_1 \circ R_2} : RCC8 \longrightarrow \{0, 1\}$$

The function yields a value of 1 for arguments that are elements of the corresponding entry in the composition table; otherwise, a value of 0:

$$\mu_{R_1 \circ R_2}(R) = \begin{cases} 1, \text{ if } R \subseteq R_1 \circ R_2 \\ 0, \text{ else} \end{cases}$$

For example, if $R_1 = EC$ and $R_2 = TPPi$, then the characteristic function of the relation $R_1 \circ R_2 = EC \circ TPPi = \{EC, DC\}$ is defined as follows:

$$\mu_{EC \circ TPPi}(R) = \begin{cases} 1, \text{ if } R \in \{EC, DC\} \\ 0, \text{ else} \end{cases}$$

Adopting the min/max combination scheme from fuzzy set theory, we can now define the fuzzy composition $\tilde{R}_1 \circ \tilde{R}_2$ of two fuzzy RCC8 relations $\tilde{R}_1$ and $\tilde{R}_2$ as the following fuzzy RCC8 relation:

$$\{(R, \mu_{\tilde{R}_1 \circ \tilde{R}_2}(r)) \mid R \in RCC8\}$$

where $\mu_{\tilde{R}_1 \circ \tilde{R}_2}$ is given by the following:

$$\mu_{\tilde{R}_1 \circ \tilde{R}_2}(r) = \max_{\substack{R'_1, R'_2 \in RCC8 \\ \mu_{R'_1 \circ R'_2}(r) = 1}} \{\min\{\mu_{\tilde{R}_1}(R'_1), \mu_{\tilde{R}_2}(R'_2)\}\}$$

The advantage of using the min/max combination scheme, rather than one of the other schemes proposed in the literature [7,14], is that we can use qualitative instead of numeric values for $\alpha_0, \alpha_1, \alpha_2 \ldots$

The fuzzy composition of relations plays a central role in a number of algorithms for reasoning about fuzzy RCC8 relations. One of these algorithms is an Allen-type algorithm for computing local consistency in networks of fuzzy RCC8 relations. Input to this algorithm is a set of regions and a set of (not necessarily atomic) fuzzy RCC8 relations. The aim of the algorithm is to transform the given relations into a set of relations that are consistent with each other. This is achieved through an iterative process that repeatedly looks at three regions X, Y, and Z, and their fuzzy relations $\tilde{R}_1(X, Y)$, $\tilde{R}_2(Y, Z)$, and $\tilde{R}_3(X, Z)$, computes the composition of two of the relations, and compares the result with the third relation:

$$\tilde{R}_3(X, Z) \leftarrow \tilde{R}_3(X, Z) \cap [\tilde{R}_1(X, Y) \circ \tilde{R}_2(Y, Z)]$$

Unlike Allen's original algorithm, the fuzzy version of the algorithm does not make a yes–no decision about whether a relation is admissible or not, but computes a new membership grade for that relation. The new membership grade is compared with the initial membership grade of the relation. If the new grade is smaller than the initial grade, the membership grade of the relation is updated with the new grade.

Figure 6 shows pseudocode for the extended algorithm. A more elaborate discussion of the algorithm can be found in [13].

Fuzzy RCC8 Algorithm

- Let $\widetilde{\mathcal{R}}$ be a set of fuzzy RCC8 relations between regions $\{X_1, X_2, \ldots, X_n\}$.
- While $\widetilde{\mathcal{R}}$ is not empty:
  1. Select a relation $\widetilde{R}(X_i, X_j) \in \widetilde{\mathcal{R}}$
  2. $\widetilde{\mathcal{R}} \leftarrow \widetilde{\mathcal{R}} - \{\widetilde{R}(X_i, X_j)\}$
  3. For $k \in \{1, \ldots, n\}$ with $k \neq i, j$:
     $\widetilde{R}(X_k, X_j) \leftarrow \widetilde{R}(X_k, X_j) \cap [\widetilde{R}(X_k, X_i) \circ \widetilde{R}(X_i, X_j)]$
     If $\widetilde{R}(X_k, X_j)$ changed, then $\widetilde{\mathcal{R}} \leftarrow \widetilde{\mathcal{R}} \cup \{\widetilde{R}(X_k, X_j)\}$
     $\widetilde{R}(X_i, X_k) \leftarrow \widetilde{R}(X_i, X_k) \cap [\widetilde{R}(X_i, X_j) \circ \widetilde{R}(X_j, X_k)]$
     If $\widetilde{R}(X_i, X_k)$ changed, then $\widetilde{\mathcal{R}} \leftarrow \widetilde{\mathcal{R}} \cup \{\widetilde{R}(X_i, X_k)\}$

Fig. 6. Fuzzy version of Allen's algorithm for the RCC8 relations. Without loss of generality, we assume that $\widetilde{R}(X_i, X_j)$ is defined for every $i, j \in \{1, 2, \ldots, n\}$ with $i \neq j$, possibly as universal relation $\{(\mathsf{DC}, 1), (\mathsf{EC}, 1), (\mathsf{PO}, 1), \ldots\}$.

Research in the area of spatio-temporal reasoning has shown that Allen's algorithm in general only computes local consistency. To obtain a globally consistent network of relations, additional methods have to be used, which usually involves some form of backtracking in the non-fuzzy case. In networks with fuzzy relations, we are seeking some level of optimality, which means that a plain backtracking algorithm is insufficient. Instead, the algorithm must continue after a consistent instantiation is found, if this instantiation is not 'good enough' (in terms of the membership grades of the instantiation). One way to achieve this goal is by applying an optimization technique like branch and bound [10], which operates in the same way as backtracking search with some variations:

1. The best instantiation so far is recorded.
2. A search path is abandoned when it is clear that it cannot lead to a better solution.
3. Search stops when all search paths have been either explored or abandoned, or when a perfect instantiation has been found.

5   From Static to Dynamic Spatial Environments

We will show now how the same approach can be used to model situations where regions are not static but can change over time. For example, a glacier usually changes its shape and size over time, or a river its width as the season changes. A fire, which previously had not spread over a residential area, might after some time overlap that area. These situations require the ability to model movement and deformation of regions and to express preferences among the possible movements and deformations.

Movement and deformation is closely related to the notion of direction. The idea of incorporating directions into a static spatial theory is not new. [18], for example, introduces the directed interval algebra, which uses 26 base relations to describe the relationship between two directed intervals. However, this approach cannot directly be applied to the RCC theory, because movement or deformation is not aligned to a particular axis in this theory (see Figure 7).

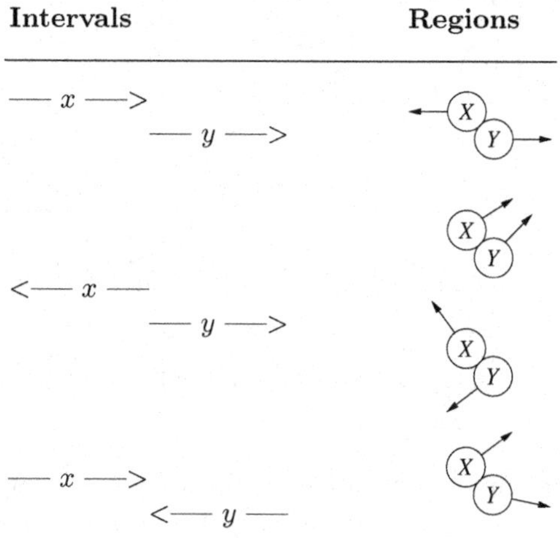

Fig. 7. All possible movements/deformations in the directed interval algebra for the meets relation as opposed to some examples of movements/deformations in the RCC theory for the EC relation

A purely qualitative approach to modeling movements or deformations of regions in the RCC theory, similar to the one used in the directed interval algebra, would lead to descriptions that are too coarse to make meaningful inferences. On the other hand, precise mathematical descriptions of movements or deformations are often too complex. In the following, we suggest a formalism that is more powerful than the analog of the directed interval algebra for regions and, at the same time, computationally less expensive than a precise mathematical one.

The approach taken here is again based on the notion of conceptual neighbours. Given a particular relation between two regions X and Y, this relation may change due to movement or deformation of the regions. However, it is likely that the new relation is a conceptual neighbour of the original relation, or if this it not the case, at least a neighbour of the neighbour of the original relation, and so on. To quantify this fact, we replace the original relation again with a fuzzy set, but this time take the expected movement or deformation into consideration.

For example, if two regions X and Y are externally connected (i.e., $\mathsf{EC}(X,Y)$) and moving towards each other, we would assume that neither $\mathsf{DC}(X,Y)$ nor $\mathsf{EC}(X,Y)$ can be observed in the next time instance, but all the other relations are plausible with decreasing membership grades $1 \geq \alpha_0 \geq \alpha_1 \geq \alpha_2 \cdots \geq 0$. Figure 8 illustrates this observation.

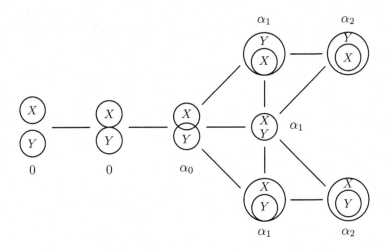

Fig. 8. The assignment of membership grades to the RCC8 relations with $\mathsf{EC}(X,Y)$ as reference relation

Once the preferred alpha values have been chosen, we can reason about the fuzzy sets by applying the same algorithm as in the previous section.

6   Conclusion

This chapter looked at a particular approach to qualitative spatial reasoning, namely the RCC theory, and showed how preferences can be expressed in this theory by utilising fuzzy set theory. The reason for looking at qualitative spatial reasoning is that qualitative descriptions can be less precise and thereby less prone to making errors. It can also be argued that qualitative descriptions are more adequate from the cognitive point of view, since the way humans use spatial descriptions in many everyday situations is of a qualitative nature.

The theory that we have looked at in this chapter focuses on topological relations among objects. Topology is only one aspect relevant in spatial reasoning; other aspects are orientation and distance. There are various theories for these, and it would be interesting to explore whether similar fuzzification techniques can be applied to them as well.

References

1. Allen, J.: Maintaining knowledge about temporal intervals. Commun. ACM 26, 832–843 (1983)
2. Bloch, I.: Spatial representation of spatial relationship knowledge. In: Proc. KR 2000, pp. 247–258. Breckenridge, Colorado (2000)
3. Bloch, I.: Fuzzy spatial relationships for image processing and interpretation: A review. Image and Vision Computing 23, 89–110 (2005)
4. Brewka, G.: Preferred subtheories: An extended logical framework for default reasoning. In: Proc. IJCAI 1989, pp. 1043–1048 (1989)
5. Cohn, A., Bennett, B., Gooday, J., Gotts, N.: Representing and reasoning with qualitative spatial relations about regions. In: Stock, O. (ed.) Spatial and Temporal Reasoning, pp. 97–134. Kluwer, Dordrecht (1997)
6. Cohn, A., Gotts, N.: The 'Egg-Yolk' representation of regions with indeterminate boundaries. In: Burrough, P., Frank, A. (eds.) Geographical Objects with Undetermined Boundaries. GISDATA Series, vol. 2, pp. 171–187. Taylor and Francis, London (1996)
7. Dubois, D., Prade, H.: Fuzzy Sets and Systems: Theory and Applications. Academic Press, London (1980)
8. Egenhofer, M., Al-Taha, K.: Reasoning about gradual changes of topological relationships. In: Frank, A.U., Campari, I., Formentini, U. (eds.) GIS 1992. LNCS, vol. 639, pp. 196–219. Springer, Heidelberg (1992)
9. Freksa, C.: Temporal reasoning based on semi-intervals. Artificial Intelligence 54, 199–227 (1992)
10. Freuder, E., Wallace, R.: Partial constraint satisfaction. Artificial Intelligence 58, 21–70 (1992)
11. Guesgen, H.: Spatial reasoning based on Allen's temporal logic. Technical Report TR-89-049, ICSI, Berkeley, California (1989)
12. Guesgen, H., Hertzberg, J.: Spatial persistence. Applied Intelligence (Special Issue on Spatial and Temporal Reasoning) 6, 11–28 (1996)
13. Guesgen, H., Hertzberg, J., Philpott, A.: Towards implementing fuzzy Allen relations. In: Proc. ECAI-94 Workshop on Spatial and Temporal Reasoning, Amsterdam, The Netherlands, pp. 49–55 (1994)
14. Klir, G., Folger, T.: Fuzzy Sets, Uncertainty, and Information. Prentice Hall, Englewood Cliffs (1988)
15. Lehmann, F., Cohn, A.: The EGG/YOLK reliability hierarchy: Semantic data integration using sorts with prototypes. In: Proc. 3rd International Conference on Information and Knowledge Management (CIKM 1994), pp. 272–279. Gaithersburg, Maryland (1994)
16. Ligozat, G. (ed.): Qualitative Spatial and Temporal Reasoning. Wiley-ISTE, Hoboken (2011)
17. Randell, D., Cui, Z., Cohn, A.: A spatial logic based on regions and connection. In: Proc. KR 1992, pp. 165–176. Cambridge, Massachusetts (1992)
18. Renz, J.: A spatial odyssey of the interval algebra: 1. directed intervals. In: Proc. IJCAI 2001, pp. 51–56. Seattle, Washington (2001)
19. Schockaert, S., De Cock, M., Cornelis, C., Kerre, E.: Fuzzy region connection calculus: Representing vague topological information. Journal of Approximate Reasoning 48, 314–331 (2008)
20. Zadeh, L.: Fuzzy sets. Information and Control 8, 338–353 (1965)

Upside-Down Preference Reversal: How to Override Ceteris-Paribus Preferences?*

Ulrich Junker

201, route des Clausonnes, 06410 Biot, France
uli.junker@free.fr

Abstract. Decision making may involve multiple viewpoints which are comparing the given options according to different preference relations. The paper studies questions that arise when multiple viewpoints are merged into a single one. It shows how more specific preference statements over the merged viewpoint can override ceteris-paribus preferences resulting from aggregating the preferences of the individual viewpoints.

1 Introduction

Preferences guide decision making and guarantee that choice behaviour is consistent in recurrent situations. Decision scientists use preference models to explain, predict, and improve human and organizational decision making. Those preference models include quantitative (cardinal) preferences such as numeric utilities as well as qualitative (ordinal) preferences such as complete preorders.

A preference model is based on basic principles (axioms). Examples are the transitivity of the preference order and the ceteris-paribus principle, which says that a preference over (a group of) attributes is valid as long as the values of other attributes remain the same. For example, if Chris prefers meat to fish, all else equal, then Chris will prefer meat with beer to fish with beer and Chris will prefer meat with wine to fish with wine.

The ceteris-paribus principle appears to be quite natural and not very restrictive. Combined with transitivity, it can nevertheless lead to strong results. Suppose that Chris and Pam want to have a dinner together while respecting their combined ceteris-paribus preferences. If Pam prefers beer to wine, all else equal, then Pam will prefer meat with beer to meat with wine and Pam will prefer fish with beer to fish with wine. By transitivity, Chris and Pam will prefer meat with beer to fish with wine. If a preference relation rigorously respects given axioms, it thus is possible to deduce new preferences from given ones.

But what if Chris and Pam don't agree to those conclusions? Perhaps they prefer meat to fish and beer to wine individually, but they prefer the combination of fish and wine to the combination of meat and beer. Is there a way to relax the ceteris-paribus principle in certain circumstances and to reverse its conclusions?

A previous work [6] studies the effects of discovering new criteria when constructing a preference relation and the effects of combining preference relations

---

* This paper is a fully revised version of an article of same title published in the AAAI Technical Report WS-07-10 and of which the author has retained the ownership.

T. Eiter et al. (Eds.): Brewka Festschrift, LNAI 9060, pp. 186–201, 2015.

over different sets of attributes. The ceteris-paribus principle is applied by default, but it may be reversed when a viewpoint is enlarged. Whereas [6] shows how to represent reversals in a compact form, the present paper investigates which ceteris-paribus preferences are overridden when more specific preference statements are added. For example, a specific preference of fish with wine to meat with beer will override some of the ceteris-paribus preferences that imply the preference of meat with beer to fish with wine since otherwise cyclic preferences are obtained. This leads to a preference revision problem.

Section 2 recalls the enlargement and merging of combinatorial viewpoints from [6], thus setting the context of the preference revision problem. Section 3 distinguishes derived and reduced preferences. Section 4 defines and characterizes preference revisions in terms of the reduced preferences. An arbitrary revision may relax all the original preferences. As this is not desired, Section 5 studies minimal revisions. After adding a preference of a desired outcome to an outcome that is optimal under ceteris-paribus preferences, this desired outcome should be optimal under the revised preferences. Minimality of revisions does not guarantee this property. However, Section 6 defines preferred revisions based on a universal meta-preference relation between preferences that have this desired property and that are uniquely defined in the considered scenario.

2   Enlargements of Combinatorial Viewpoints

Classic decision-making problems consist in choosing a single decision from a set of actions $\mathcal{A}$. A viewpoint constitutes an independent way to analyze the actions and to evaluate and compare the outcomes of the actions. We model the evaluation by a mapping of the actions to single outcomes and the comparison by a reflexive and transitive preference relation. We thus restrict our discussion to actions having deterministic outcomes, but allow incomplete preferences.

Definition 1. *A* viewpoint *v for a finite set of actions $\mathcal{A}$ is characterized by a finite outcome space Ω_v, a criterion $z_v : \mathcal{A} \to \Omega_v$ mapping actions to their outcomes, and a pre-order $\succsim_v$ over Ω_v defining weak preferences between outcomes.*

The preference order $\succsim_v$ can be split into a strict partial order $\succ_v$ expressing strict preferences and an equivalence relation $\sim_v$ expressing indifference. An outcome ω_1 is strictly preferred to an outcome ω_2 if ω_1 is weakly preferred to ω_2, but not vice versa. The outcomes ω_1 and ω_2 are indifferent if ω_1 is weakly preferred to ω_2 and ω_2 is weakly preferred to ω_1. Two outcomes ω_1 and ω_2 are called comparable if ω_1 is weakly preferred to ω_2 or ω_2 is weakly preferred to ω_1. A pre-order $\succsim_v$ is called complete if all pairs of outcomes are comparable. We also use the partial order $\succeq_v$ where $\omega_1 \succeq_v \omega_2$ if $\omega_1 \succ_v \omega_2$ or $\omega_1 = \omega_2$.

As an example, we formulate Chris' and Pam's viewpoints C and P over the sets of dishes $V_1 := \{m, f\}$ and drinks $V_2 := \{b, w\}$. The actions are the dinners $\mathcal{A} = V_1 \times V_2$ consisting of a dish and a drink. As Chris cares only about the dish, Ω_C is V_1 and z_C is the projection of a tuple to its first component. As Pam cares only about the drink, Ω_P is V_2 and z_P is the projection of a tuple to its second component. Their respective strict preferences are $m \succ_C f$ and $b \succ_P w$ and their indifference relations coincide with equality.

An *extension* w of a viewpoint v is a viewpoint having the same actions, outcome space, criterion, and indifference relation as v, but additional strict preferences, i.e. $\succ_w$ is a superset of $\succ_v$. An extension of a viewpoint is complete if its preorder $\succsim_w$ is complete. An action is an *optimal decision of a complete viewpoint* if its outcome is at least as preferred as the outcomes of all other actions of this viewpoint. An *action is an optimal decision of an incomplete viewpoint* if it is an optimal decision of a complete extension of this viewpoint. This is the case iff no other action has an outcome that is strictly preferred to the outcome of the considered action in the original viewpoint.

A viewpoint v is *combinatorial* if Ω_v is a vectorial space of n_v dimensions. Given an ordered set I of indices $\pi_1, \ldots, \pi_k$ from $N_v := \{1, \ldots, n_v\}$, we denote the projection of Ω_v to I by $\Omega_{v,I}$, the projection of z_v to I by $z_{v,I}$, and the projection of $\omega \in \Omega_v$ to I by $\omega_{v,I}$. Note that the projection X_I of X to I consists of the π_1-th, π_2-th, $\ldots$, π_k-th components of X.

As each non-combinatorial viewpoint can be transformed into a one-dimensional viewpoint, we define the following concepts only for combinatorial viewpoints. A combinatorial viewpoint w is an *enlargement* of a combinatorial viewpoint v under an ordered set I of indices from N_w if the viewpoints are defined for the same actions, the size of I is n_v, $\Omega_v = \Omega_{w,I}$ and $z_v = z_{w,I}$. A *default enlargement* is an enlargement under the ceteris-paribus semantics, i.e. $\alpha \succsim_w \beta$ holds if $\alpha_I \succsim_v \beta_I$ and $\alpha_{N_w - I} = \beta_{N_w - I}$ hold.

A viewpoint w is a *merge* of two viewpoints u, v under an ordered set I of indices from $N_w := \{1, \ldots, n_w\}$ if w is an enlargement of u under I and an enlargement of v under $N_w - I$. A *default merge* of two viewpoints is a merge under the ceteris-paribus semantics, which is the case if both enlargements are default enlargements of the respective viewpoints.

The smallest default merge CP of Chris' and Pam's viewpoints has the outcome space $\Omega_{CP} := V_1 \times V_2$ and the identity function as criterion z_{CP}. We abbreviate the elements of Ω_{CP} by mb, mw, fb, fw. The strict preferences of CP are $mb \succ_{CP} mw$, $fb \succ_{CP} fw$, $mb \succ_{CP} fb$, $mw \succ_{CP} fw$, $mb \succ_{CP} fw$ and its indifference relation is the equality. Its optimal decision is mb. Let us suppose that Chris' and Pam change their attitude when being together and prefer fw to mb. The viewpoint CP thus needs to be revised to accommodate to this change.

3   Reduced Preferences

Revisions of viewpoints are obtained when adding and removing preferences. In this section, we distinguish between derived and reduced preferences. These reduced preferences will permit us to define revisions of a viewpoint.

The *transitive closure* R^+ of a binary relation R is the smallest superset of R that is transitive. The *reflexive transitive closure* R^* of R is the smallest superset of R that is reflexive and transitive. A binary relation is *acyclic* if its transitive closure is irreflexive. In this paper, we say that a binary relation R is *irreducible* if $p \notin (R - \{p\})^+$ for all $p \in R$. Irreducibility implies anti-transitivity, but is stronger. A binary relation R is anti-transitive if $(a, b) \in R$ and $(b, c) \in R$ imply $(a, c) \notin R$. For example, $\{(a, b), (b, c), (c, d), (a, d)\}$ is anti-transitive, but not irreducible since $\{(a, d)\}$ is in the transitive closure of $\{(a, b), (b, c), (c, d)\}$. However, an irreducible acyclic binary relation satisfies the following property:

Lemma 1. *Let R be an irreducible acyclic binary relation. If $(\alpha, \beta) \in R^+$ and $(\beta, \gamma) \in R^+$ then $(\alpha, \gamma) \notin R$.*

Proof. Suppose $(\alpha, \beta) \in R^+$, $(\beta, \gamma) \in R^+$, and $(\alpha, \gamma) \in R$. Hence, there exists a chain $\gamma_1, \ldots, \gamma_k$ for $k \geq 2$ s.t. $(\alpha, \beta) = (\gamma_1, \gamma_k)$ and $(\gamma_i, \gamma_{i+1}) \in R$ for all $i = 1, \ldots, k - 1$ and a chain $\delta_1, \ldots, \delta_m$ for $m \geq 2$ s.t. $(\beta, \gamma) = (\delta_1, \delta_m)$ and $(\delta_i, \delta_{i+1}) \in R$ for all $i = 1, \ldots, m-1$. As $(\alpha, \gamma) \in R$ and R is irreducible, (α, γ) is equal to (γ_j, γ_{j+1}) for a $j \in \{1, \ldots, k-1\}$ or to (δ_j, δ_{j+1}) for a $j \in \{1, \ldots, m-1\}$. In the first case, $(\gamma, \beta) \in R^*$ holds. As $(\beta, \gamma) \in R^+$ holds as well, this implies $(\gamma, \gamma) \in R^+$. In the second case, $(\beta, \alpha) \in R^*$ holds. As $(\alpha, \beta) \in R^+$ holds as well, this implies $(\alpha, \alpha) \in R^+$. In both cases, R is not acyclic. $\square$

A *transitive reduction* of a finite binary relation R over Ω is a minimal relation R over Ω that has the same transitive closure as R [1]. Minimality implies that a transitive reduction is irreducible. A finite acyclic relation R has a unique transitive reduction R^- which is a subset of R. As noted in [1], it can be determined by removing all transitive links, i.e. by computing $R^- = R - \{p \in R \mid p \in (R - \{p\})^+\}$. However, multiple transitive reductions may be obtained for relations containing cycles. An example is a preorder $\succsim$ over $\{a, b, c\}$ such that $a \succsim b$, $b \succsim a$, $c \succsim a$, $c \succsim b$. This preorder has two transitive reductions, namely $\{(a, b), (b, a), (c, a)\}$ and $\{(a, b), (b, a), (c, b)\}$. As a strict partial order is acyclic, it has a unique transitive reduction which is irreducible and acyclic. Furthermore, the transitive closure of an irreducible and acyclic binary relation is a strict partial order. The transitive reduction of the transitive closure of such an irreducible and acyclic relation is equal to itself:

Lemma 2. *Let R be an irreducible and acyclic finite binary relation The transitive reduction of the transitive closure of R is equal to R.*

Proof. The transitive closure R^+ is acyclic and finite since R is acyclic and finite. Hence, it has a unique transitive reduction S. As S has the same transitive closure as R^+, S^+ is equal to R^+ since R^+ is already closed.

Suppose $(\alpha, \beta) \in R - S$. Hence, (α, β) is in R^+ and thus in S^+. There exists a chain $\gamma_1, \ldots, \gamma_k$ for $k \geq 2$ s.t. $(\alpha, \beta) = (\gamma_1, \gamma_k)$ and $(\gamma_i, \gamma_{i+1}) \in S$ for all $i = 1, \ldots, k - 1$. As (α, β) is not in S, k is at least 3. Consequently, (α, γ_2) and (γ_2, β) are both in S^+ and thus in R^+. Due to Lemma 1, R is not irreducible.

Suppose $(\alpha, \beta) \in S - R$. We can show in a similar way as above that S is not irreducible. Hence, there is a $p \in S$ s.t. $p \in (S - \{p\})^+$. Then $S^+ = (S - \{p\})^+$ and S is not a minimal relation having the same transitive closure as R. $\square$

As the preference order of a viewpoint is a preorder, it does not have a unique transitive reduction as explained above. In this paper, we consider only the transitive reduction of the strict part of the preference order and use it to define the reduced preferences of a viewpoint:

Definition 2. *The set $\succ_v^-$ of reduced preferences of a viewpoint v is the transitive reduction of the strict part of the preference order of the viewpoint.*

Strict preferences $\alpha \succ_v \beta$ that are not among the reduced preferences will be called *derived preferences* as they can be derived from a chain $\gamma_1 \succ_v^- \gamma_2, \gamma_2 \succ_v^- \gamma_3, \ldots, \gamma_{k-1} \succ_v^- \gamma_k$ of reduced preferences for some $k \geq 3$ where $(\alpha, \beta) = (\gamma_1, \gamma_k)$. In the example of Section 2, (mb, fw) is a derived preference and the other strict preferences are reduced preferences.

Whereas every acyclic and irreducible relation represents a strict preference order, namely its transitive closure, this preference order is not necessarily disjoint from a given indifference relation. Certain properties need to be satisfied to guarantee this. Firstly, we note that $\alpha \sim_v \beta$ and $\alpha \succ_v \gamma$ imply $\alpha \not\sim_v \gamma$ and thus $\beta \not\sim_v \gamma$ since $\sim_v$ is an equivalence relation. As $\alpha \sim_v \beta$ and $\alpha \succ_v \gamma$ imply $\beta \succsim_v \gamma$, they furthermore imply $\beta \succ_v \gamma$. Now we consider an indifference $\alpha \sim_v \beta$ and a reduced preference $\alpha \succ_v^- \gamma$. According to the property above, this implies a strict preference $\beta \succ_v \gamma$. If this were a derived preference, then there would exist a δ such that $\beta \succ_v \delta$ and $\delta \succ_v \gamma$. According to the property above, this would imply $\alpha \succ_v \delta$, meaning that $\alpha \succ_v^- \gamma$ does not hold.

Similar arguments hold for a reduced preference $\gamma \succ_v^- \alpha$ and an indifference $\alpha \sim_v \beta$. Hence reduced preferences are 'closed' under indifference:

1. If $\alpha \sim_v \beta$ and $\alpha \succ_v^- \gamma$ then $\beta \succ_v^- \gamma$.
2. If $\alpha \sim_v \beta$ and $\gamma \succ_v^- \alpha$ then $\gamma \succ_v^- \beta$.

Vice versa, an acyclic and irreducible relation needs to satisfy these properties if we want to combine it with a given indifference relation:

A binary relation R is *compatible* with an equivalence relation $\sim$ if R is disjoint from $\sim$ and R is closed under the indifference relation, i.e.

1. If $\alpha \sim \beta$ and $(\alpha, \gamma) \in R$ then $(\beta, \gamma) \in R$.
2. If $\alpha \sim \beta$ and $(\gamma, \alpha) \in R$ then $(\gamma, \beta) \in R$.

Given an acyclic and irreducible relation R that is compatible with $\sim$, the reflexive transitive closure of the union of these two relations is a preorder that has strict preferences represented by R and $\sim$ as indifference relation:

Proposition 1. *If an acyclic relation R is compatible with an equivalence relation $\sim$ then the strict part of the reflexive transitive closure of $R \cup \sim$ is equal to the transitive closure of R and the indifference relation of the reflexive transitive closure of $R \cup \sim$ is equal to $\sim$.*

Proof. Let (α, β) be an element of the reflexive transitive closure of $R \cup \sim$. Consider a shortert chain $\gamma_1, \ldots, \gamma_k$ for deriving (α, β) from $R \cup \sim$. This chain satisfies $(\alpha, \beta) = (\gamma_1, \gamma_k)$ and $(\gamma_i, \gamma_{i+1}) \in R \cup \sim$ for all $i = 1, \ldots, k-1$. If $k = 1$ then (α, β) is in $\sim$ since $\alpha = \beta$. If $k = 2$ then (α, β) is in $R^+ \cup \sim$ by definition.

If $k \geq 3$ and $(\gamma_i, \gamma_{i+1}) \in R$ for all $i = 1, \ldots, k-1$ then $(\alpha, \beta) \in R^+$. Now suppose that $k \geq 3$ and $\gamma_j \sim \gamma_{j+1}$ for a $j \in \{1, \ldots, k-1\}$. First consider the case where $j = 1$. If $\gamma_2 \sim \gamma_3$, then $\gamma_1 \sim \gamma_3$. Moreover, if $(\gamma_2, \gamma_3) \in R$, then $(\gamma_1, \gamma_3) \in R$ since R is compatible with $\sim$. In both cases, $\gamma_1, \gamma_3, \ldots, \gamma_k$ is a shorter chain for deriving (α, β) from $R \cup \sim$. Next consider the case where $j > 1$. If $\gamma_{j-1} \sim \gamma_j$, then $\gamma_{j-1} \sim \gamma_{j+1}$. Moreover, if $(\gamma_{j-1}, \gamma_j) \in R$, then $(\gamma_{j-1}, \gamma_{j+1}) \in R$ since R is compatible with $\sim$. In both cases, $\gamma_1, \ldots, \gamma_{j-1}, \gamma_{j+1} \ldots, \gamma_k$ is a shorter chain for deriving (α, β) from $R \cup \sim$. Therefore, (α, β) is in $R^+ \cup \sim$ in all cases. As a consequence, the reflexive transitive closure of $R \cup \sim$ is equal to $R^+ \cup \sim$.

Suppose $\alpha \sim \beta$ for an $(\alpha, \beta) \in R^+$. As R is disjoint from $\sim$, there is a γ s.t. $(\alpha, \gamma) \in R$ and $(\gamma, \beta) \in R^+$. As R is closed under $\sim$, $(\beta, \gamma) \in R$, meaning that R is not acyclic. Therefore, R^+ is disjoint from $\sim$. As a consequence, the strict part of $R^+ \cup \sim$ is R^+ and the indifference relation of $R^+ \cup \sim$ is $\sim$. $\square$

Hence, any acyclic, irreducible, and $\sim$-compatible relation can be extended to a strict preference order that is disjoint from the indifference relation $\sim$.

4   Preference Revisions

In this section, we revise the strict preferences of a viewpoint by adding new preferences while keeping the indifference relation unchanged. The added preferences may reverse existing preferences of the viewpoint, thus requiring a removal of some of those existing preferences. This corresponds to a revision problem similar to those studied by Gärdenfors [4] and his colleagues. The approach chosen in this paper formulates the revision in terms of reduced preferences. It is closer to Brewka's belief revision framework [3], which operates over underived beliefs.

When adding new preferences to a viewpoint, we require that the newly added preferences are reduced preferences of the revised viewpoint. Moreover, we require that all reduced preferences of the revised viewpoint that are not reduced preferences of the original viewpoint are among the newly added preferences.

Definition 3. *Let v be a viewpoint and Δ be an acyclic and irreducible set of preferences that is compatible with $\sim_v$. A revision of v under Δ is a viewpoint w of same outcome space, criterion, and indifference relation as v such that all elements of Δ are reduced preferences of w and all reduced preferences of w are reduced preferences of v or are elements of Δ.*

According to this definition, any viewpoint v can be transformed into any other viewpoint w of same outcome space, criterion, and indifference relation by adding all reduced preferences of w that are not reduced preferences of v and by removing all reduced preferences of v that are not reduced preferences of w. A revision may not only add or remove preferences, but also change the status of a preference. A reduced preference of v becomes a derived preference of a revision of v if it can be derived with help of the added preferences. Moreover, a derived preference of v becomes a reduced preference of a revision of v if it is explicitly added. However, adding a reduced preference of v has no effect.

The set of reduced preferences of a revision w of v under Δ is the union of Δ and a subset R of the reduced preferences of v. The complement of R is the set D of reduced preferences of v that are not reduced preferences of the revision w. This *set of reduced preferences of v removed in w* uniquely characterizes a revision under Δ:

Lemma 3. *If a viewpoint w is a revision of the viewpoint v under Δ and D is the set of reduced preferences of v removed in w then the preference order of w is the reflexive transitive closure of $\succ_v^- - D \cup \Delta \cup \sim_v$.*

Proof. By definition, the set of reduced preferences of w is a superset of Δ and a subset of $\succ_v^- \cup \Delta$. As all the reduced preferences of v that are not reduced preferences of w are in D, the set of reduced preferences of w is $\succ_v^- - D \cup \Delta$. Hence the strict part $\succ_w$ of the preferences of w is the transitive closure of $\succ_v^- - D \cup \Delta$. Then the preference order $\succsim_w$ of w is the union of $\sim_w$ and the transitive closure of $\succ_v^- - D \cup \Delta$. As $\succsim_w$ is a preorder, it is equal to its reflexive transitive closure, i.e. the reflexive transitive closure of the union of $\sim_w$ and the transitive closure of $\succ_v^- - D \cup \Delta$. It is thus equal to the reflexive transitive closure of the union of $\sim_w$ and $\succ_v^- - D \cup \Delta$. Finally, it should be noted that $\sim_w$ is equal to $\sim_v$. $\qquad\square$

We will now characterize the set D of reduced preferences to be removed from v in terms of constraints that guarantee the construction of a revision. These constraints state which preferences of v need to be broken:

A set D of preferences *breaks* a strict preference $\alpha \succ_v \beta$ if for each chain $\gamma_1, \ldots, \gamma_k$ satisfying $(\alpha, \beta) = (\gamma_1, \gamma_k)$ and $\gamma_i \succ_v^- \gamma_{i+1}$ for $i = 1, \ldots, k-1$ there exists a j s.t. $(\gamma_j, \gamma_{j+1}) \in D$. A set D of preferences *breaks* $\alpha \succsim_v \beta$ if $\alpha \succ_v \beta$ and D breaks $\alpha \succ_v \beta$. Note that a preference (α, β) can be derived from the reduced preferences in $\succ_v^- - D$ if $\alpha \succ_v \beta$ holds and D does not break $\alpha \succ_v \beta$.

Definition 4. *A set D of removed reduced preferences is a* diagnosis *for the revision of v under Δ if the following conditions are satisfied:*

1. *If there are $k \geq 1$ and $(\alpha_i, \beta_i) \in \Delta$ for $i = 1, \ldots, k$ such that $\beta_i \succsim_v \alpha_{(i \bmod k)+1}$ for $i = 1, \ldots, k$ then D breaks $\beta_i \succsim_v \alpha_{(i \bmod k)+1}$ for some $i = 1, \ldots, k$.*
2. *If there are $k \geq 1$ and $(\alpha_i, \beta_i) \in \Omega_v^2$ for $i = 1, \ldots, k$ such that $\beta_k \succ_v^- \alpha_k$ and $k \geq 2$ hold or (β_k, α_k) is in Δ, and (α_i, β_i) is in Δ and different to (β_k, α_k) for $i = 1, \ldots, k-1$, and $\beta_i \succsim_v \alpha_{(i \bmod k)+1}$ for $i = 1, \ldots, k$ then D breaks $\beta_i \succsim_v \alpha_{(i \bmod k)+1}$ for some $i = 1, \ldots, k$ or (β_k, α_k) is in D.*
3. *If $\alpha \sim_v \beta$ and $\alpha \succ_v^- \gamma$ then $(\alpha, \gamma) \in D$ iff $(\beta, \gamma) \in D$.*
4. *If $\alpha \sim_v \beta$ and $\gamma \succ_v^- \alpha$ then $(\gamma, \alpha) \in D$ iff $(\gamma, \beta) \in D$.*

The first condition ensures that D breaks all cycles involving preferences of v and Δ. The second condition ensures that D breaks all ways to derive preferences of Δ from other preferences of v and Δ. It also ensures that D breaks all ways to derive reduced preferences of v that are not elements of D from preferences of v and Δ. The third and fourth conditions ensure that revised preferences are closed under indifference. These four conditions indicate conflicting sets of preferences in v and impose constraints on a diagnosis D as D contains an element from each conflicting set. Note that if Δ contains a reduced preference of v then this preference will be a reduced preference of each revision of v under Δ and thus cannot be an element of any diagnosis for the revision of v under Δ.

A diagnosis necessarily exists. For example, the set of all reduced preferences of v that are not in Δ is a diagnosis for the revision of v under Δ. As it breaks all strict preferences of D that are not in Δ, it satisfies condition 1 since Δ is acyclic, condition 2 since Δ and $\succ_v^-$ are both irreducible, and conditions 3 and 4 since D contains all reduced preferences of v that are not in Δ and Δ is closed under $\sim_v$. The following lemma relates diagnoses to acyclic, irreducible, and $\sim$-compatible relations:

Lemma 4. D *is a diagnosis for the revision of a viewpoint* v *under* Δ *iff* $\succ_v^-$ $-D \cup \Delta$ *is acyclic, irreducible, and compatible with* $\sim_v$.

Proof. Suppose $\succ_v^- -D \cup \Delta$ is not acyclic. There is $n \geq 1$ and $\gamma_1, \ldots, \gamma_n$ such that $\gamma_n = \gamma_1$ and (γ_j, γ_{j+1}) is in $\succ_v^- -D \cup \Delta$ for $j = 1, \ldots, n-1$. Let J be the set of indices j such that (γ_j, γ_{j+1}) is not in $\succ_v^- -D$. As $\succ_v^- -D$ is acyclic, J contains at least one element. Let k be the cardinality of J and π_i be the i-th element of J. Then $k \geq 1$ and $(\gamma_{\pi_i}, \gamma_{\pi_i+1}) \in \Delta$ for $i = 1, \ldots, k$. Furthermore, γ_{π_i+1} is either equal to $\gamma_{\pi_{(i \bmod k)+1}}$ or the preference $(\gamma_{\pi_i+1}, \gamma_{\pi_{(i \bmod k)+1}})$ can be derived from preferences in $\succ_v^- -D$. Therefore, $\gamma_{\pi_i+1} \succeq_v \gamma_{\pi_{(i \bmod k)+1}}$ and D does not break $\gamma_{\pi_i+1} \succeq_v \gamma_{\pi_{(i \bmod k)+1}}$ for all $i = 1, \ldots, k$. Hence D is not a diagnosis.

Suppose $\succ_v^- -D \cup \Delta$ is not irreducible and contains a preference (α, β) that is in the transitive closure of $(\succ_v^- -D \cup \Delta) - \{(\alpha, \beta)\}$. Hence, there exists a chain $\gamma_1, \ldots, \gamma_n$ for an $n \geq 3$ such that $\alpha = \gamma_1$, $\beta = \gamma_n$ and (γ_j, γ_{j+1}) is in $(\succ_v^- -D \cup \Delta) - \{(\alpha, \beta)\}$ for $j = 1, \ldots, n-1$. Let J be the set of indices j s.t. (γ_j, γ_{j+1}) is not in $\succ_v^- -D$. As $\succ_v^-$ is irreducible, J contains at least one element or (α, β) is in $\Delta - \succ_v^-$. Let k be the cardinality of J plus 1 and π_i be the i-th element of J. Then $k \geq 1$ and $(\gamma_{\pi_i}, \gamma_{\pi_i+1})$ in Δ and different to (α, β) for $i = 1, \ldots, k-1$. Define γ_{n+1} as α and π_k as n. Then (α, β) is equal to $(\gamma_{\pi_k+1}, \gamma_{\pi_k})$ which is in $\succ_v^- \cup \Delta$ and not in D. Furthermore, γ_{π_i+1} is either equal to $\gamma_{\pi_{(i \bmod k)+1}}$ or the preference $(\gamma_{\pi_i+1}, \gamma_{\pi_{(i \bmod k)+1}})$ can be derived from $\succ_v^- -D$. Therefore, $\gamma_{\pi_i+1} \succeq_v \gamma_{\pi_{(i \bmod k)+1}}$ and D does not break $\gamma_{\pi_i+1} \succeq_v \gamma_{\pi_{(i \bmod k)+1}}$ for all $i = 1, \ldots, k$. Hence D is not a diagnosis.

Suppose $\succ_v^- -D \cup \Delta$ is not compatible with $\sim_v$. First suppose that there are $\alpha, \beta, \gamma \in \Omega_v$ such that $\alpha \sim \beta$ and (α, γ) is in $\succ_v^- -D \cup \Delta$ and (β, γ) is not in $\succ_v^- -D \cup \Delta$. If (α, γ) were in Δ, (β, γ) would be in Δ as well as Δ is closed under $\sim_v$, which contradicts the supposition. Hence, (α, γ) is not in Δ. As Δ is closed under $\sim_v$, (β, γ) is not in Δ either. Hence, (α, γ) is in $\succ_v^-$ and not in D. As the reduced preferences of v are closed under $\sim_v$, (β, γ) is in $\succ_v^-$ as well and consequently in D. Hence, D is not a diagnosis in that case. Next suppose that there are $\alpha, \beta, \gamma \in \Omega_v$ such that $\alpha \sim \beta$ and (γ, α) is in $\succ_v^- -D \cup \Delta$ and (γ, β) is not in $\succ_v^- -D \cup \Delta$. Again, it can be shown that D is not a diagnosis.

Suppose that $\succ_v^- -D \cup \Delta$ is acyclic, irreducible, and compatible with $\sim_v$ and that D is not a diagnosis. Hence any of the four conditions is violated: If the first condition is violated, there will be $k \geq 1$ and $(\alpha_i, \beta_i) \in \Delta$ for $i = 1, \ldots, k$ such that $\beta_i \succeq_v \alpha_{(i \bmod k)+1}$ for all $i = 1, \ldots, k$ and D does not break $\beta_i \succeq_v \alpha_{(i \bmod k)+1}$ for all $i = 1, \ldots, k$. Hence, $\succ_v^- - D \cup \Delta$ contains a cycle.

If the second condition is violated, then there will be a $k \geq 1$ and $(\alpha_i, \beta_i) \in \Omega_v^2$ for $i = 1, \ldots, k$ such that $\beta_k \succ_v^- \alpha_k$ and $k \geq 2$ hold or (β_k, α_k) is in Δ, and (α_i, β_i) is in Δ and different to (β_k, α_k) for $i = 1, \ldots, k-1$ and $\beta_i \succeq_v \alpha_{(i \bmod k)+1}$ for $i = 1, \ldots, k$ and D does not break $\beta_i \succeq_v \alpha_{(i \bmod k)+1}$ for all $i = 1, \ldots, k$ and $(\beta_k, \alpha_k) \notin D$. If $k = 1$ then $\beta_1 \succ_v^- \alpha_1$ does not hold. Hence, (β_1, α_1) is in $\Delta - \succ_v^-$ in that case. As Δ is acyclic, α_1 and β_1 need to be different. Hence, $\beta_1 \succ_v \alpha_1$. As $\beta_1 \succ_v^- \alpha_1$ does not hold, there is $\gamma \in \Omega_v$ such that $\beta_1 \succ_v \gamma$ and $\gamma \succ_v \alpha_1$ and D does not break $\beta_1 \succ_v \gamma$ and $\gamma \succ_v \alpha_1$. Hence, (β_1, γ) and (γ, α_1) are in the transitive closure of $\succ_v^- - D \cup \Delta$ and (β_1, α_1) is in $\succ_v^- - D \cup \Delta$. Therefore, $\succ_v^- - D \cup \Delta$ is not irreducible due to Lemma 1. If $k \geq 2$ then (α_1, β_1) is different to (β_k, α_k). Suppose that $\beta_k = \alpha_1$. Hence $\beta_1 \neq \alpha_k$ and (β_1, α_k) is in the transitive closure of $\succ_v^- - D \cup \Delta$. As (α_1, β_1), which is equal to (β_k, β_1), is also in this closure and (β_k, α_k) is in $\succ_v^- - D \cup \Delta$, the relation $\succ_v^- - D \cup \Delta$ is not irreducible due to Lemma 1. Now suppose $\beta_k \neq \alpha_1$. Then (β_k, α_1) is in the transitive closure of $\succ_v^- - D \cup \Delta$. Furthermore, (α_1, α_k) is in the transitive closure of $\succ_v^- - D \cup \Delta$. As (β_k, α_k) is in $\succ_v^- - D \cup \Delta$, this relation is not irreducible.

If the third condition is violated, there will be $\alpha \sim_v \beta$ and $\alpha \succ_v^- \gamma$ such that $(\alpha, \gamma) \in D$ and $(\beta, \gamma) \notin D$. As $\succ_v^-$ is closed under $\sim_v$, $\beta \succ_v^- \gamma$ holds. Hence, $\succ_v^- - D \cup \Delta$ contains (β, γ), but not (α, γ). Therefore, $\succ_v^- - D \cup \Delta$ is not closed under $\sim_v$ and thus not compatible with $\sim_v$. If the fourth condition is violated, similar arguments show that $\succ_v^- - D \cup \Delta$ is not compatible with $\sim_v$.   □

On the one hand, the reduced preferences of a viewpoint that are removed in a revision of this viewpoint form a diagnosis. On the other hand, each diagnosis D permits the construction of a revision v_D. Both results follow from Lemma 4:

Proposition 2. *Let w be a revision of the viewpoint v under Δ. Then the set D of reduced preferences of v removed in w is a diagnosis for the revision of v under Δ.*

Proof. By definition, $\succ_v^- - D \cup \Delta$ is the set of reduced preferences of w, meaning that it is acyclic and irreducible. As the set of the reduced preferences of w is disjoint from and closed under the indifference relation $\sim_w$, it is compatible with $\sim_w$ and thus with $\sim_v$. Hence, D is a diagnosis for the revision of v under Δ.   □

Proposition 3. *Let D be a diagnosis for the revision of a viewpoint v under Δ and let v_D be a viewpoint of same actions, outcome space, and criterion as v such that the reflexive transitive closure of $\succ_v^- - D \cup \Delta \cup \sim_v$ is the preference order of v_D. Then v_D is a revision of v under Δ.*

Proof. Due to Lemma 4, $\succ_v^- - D \cup \Delta$ is acyclic, irreducible, and $\sim_v$-compatible. As the preference order of v_D is the reflexive transitive closure of $\succ_v^- - D \cup \Delta \cup \sim_v$, its indifference relation is equal to $\sim_v$ and its strict part is equal to the transitive closure of $\succ_v^- - D \cup \Delta$ due to Proposition 1. The set of reduced preferences of v_D is equal to the transitive reduction of the transitive closure of $\succ_v^- - D \cup \Delta$, which is equal to $\succ_v^- - D \cup \Delta$ since this set is irreducible and acyclic. Hence, the set of reduced preferences of v_D is a superset of Δ and a subset of $\succ_v^- \cup \Delta$.   □

As a consequence, revisions of a viewpoint exist as diagnoses for this revision exist. The merged viewpoint of Chris and Pam even has nine revisions under (fw, mb) as each diagnosis contains at least one element of the conflicting preferences (mb, mw) and (mw, fw) and at least one element of the conflicting preferences (mb, fb) and (fb, fw). We therefore need a way to choose among those diagnoses.

5 Minimal Preference Revisions

Certain revisions may remove more preferences than others, meaning that the removal of these additional preferences is not necessary. Minimal revisions seek to preserve a maximal subset of the original preferences:

Definition 5. *A revision w of v under Δ is a* minimal revision *of v under Δ iff there is no other revision w^* of v under Δ such that the preference order of w^* is a proper superset of the preference order of w.*

It can be shown that a minimal revision leads to a minimal removal of reduced preferences. However, the inverse relationship does not hold as there are minimal diagnoses that lead to non-minimal revisions. An example is a viewpoint v with three possible outcomes a, b, c, an indifference relation that is the equality relation, and two reduced preferences (a, b) and (a, c). This viewpoint has three revisions w_1, w_2, w_3 under $\{(b, c)\}$. Diagnosis $D_1 := \{(a, b)\}$ leads to a revision w_1 that has the reduced preferences (a, c) and (b, c) and no derived preference. Diagnosis $D_2 := \{(a, c)\}$ leads to a revision w_2 that has the reduced preferences (a, b) and (b, c) and the derived preference (a, c). Diagnosis $D_3 := \{(a, b), (a, c)\}$ leads to a revision w_3 that has the reduced preference (b, c) and no derived preferences. Whereas D_2 is a minimal diagnosis that leads to the minimal revision w_2, the minimal diagnosis D_1 leads to a non-minimal revision w_1. The diagnosis D_1 is minimal as D_2 contains a derived preference of w_2.

We therefore exclude preferences of diagnoses that are derived preferences of the resulting revisions when comparing two diagnoses. The *core* $core(D)$ of a diagnosis D for the revision of v under Δ is the set of preferences of D that are not derived preferences of the revision v_D constructed from D. The elements of the core of a diagnosis D are neither reduced, nor derived preferences of the revision v_D. However, all reduced preferences of v that are not in the core of a diagnosis D are reduced or derived preferences of v_D. Moreover, all preferences that are elements of $\succ_v^- - core(D) \cup \Delta \cup \sim_v$, but not of its subset $\succ_v^- - D \cup \Delta \cup \sim_v$, are elements of D outside the core of D and can thus be derived from $\succ_v^- - D \cup \Delta \cup \sim_v$. As a consequence, the reflexive transitive closure of $\succ_v^- - D \cup \Delta \cup \sim_v$ is equal to the reflexive transitive closure of $\succ_v^- - core(D) \cup \Delta \cup \sim_v$. If the core of a diagnosis violates condition 1 or 2 of the definition of a diagnosis D for the case where $(\beta_k, \alpha_k) \in \Delta$, then the diagnosis also violates those conditions as we can replace derived preferences of D by chains of preferences from $core(D) \cup \Delta$.

We now define diagnoses having a minimal core and show that they characterize all minimal revisions and only minimal revisions:

Definition 6. A diagnosis D for the revision of v under Δ is a diagnosis of minimal core for the revision of v under Δ iff there is no other diagnosis D^* for the revision of v under Δ s.t. the core of D^* is a proper subset of the core of D.

Proposition 4. Let w be a revision of a viewpoint v under Δ and D be the set of reduced preferences of v removed in w. Then w is a minimal revision of v under Δ if and only if D is diagnosis of minimal core for the revision of v under Δ.

Proof. Suppose that w is a minimal revision of v under Δ, but that D is not a diagnosis of minimal core. Hence, there exists a diagnosis D^* for the revision of v under Δ such that $core(D^*) \subset core(D)$. Consequently, there is a reduced preference p of v that is in $core(D)$, but not in $core(D^*)$. As p is in $core(D)$, it is not among the preferences of w. Moreover, the reflexive transitive closure of $\succ_v^- - core(D^*) \cup \Delta \cup \sim_v$ is a superset of the reflexive transitive closure of $\succ_v^- - core(D) \cup \Delta \cup \sim_v$. According to the properties of cores, the reflexive transitive closure of $\succ_v^- - D^* \cup \Delta \cup \sim_v$ is a superset of the reflexive transitive closure of $\succ_v^- - D \cup \Delta \cup \sim_v$. The first closure is the preference order of the revision v_{D^*} and the second closure is the preference order of w. Hence, the first closure contains p, but not the second one, meaning that the preference order of v_{D^*} is a proper superset of that w. Hence, w is not a minimal revision.

Suppose that D is a diagnosis of minimal core for the revision of v under Δ, but that w is not a minimal revision of v under Δ. Hence, there exists a revision w^* of v under Δ such that the preference order of w^* is a proper superset of the preference order of w. Let D^* be the set of reduced preferences of v removed in w^*. Then D^* is a diagnosis for the revision of v under Δ and the transitive closure of $\succsim_v^- - D^* \cup \Delta \cup \sim_v$ is a proper superset of the transitive closure of $\succsim_v^- - D \cup \Delta \cup \sim_v$. According to the properties of the core of a diagnosis, the transitive closure of $\succsim_v^- - core(D^*) \cup \Delta \cup \sim_v$ is a proper superset of the transitive closure of $\succsim_v^- - core(D) \cup \Delta \cup \sim_v$. Since D is a diagnosis of minimal core, $core(D^*)$ cannot be a proper subset of $core(D)$ and it cannot be equal to $core(D)$ either since this implies that the two closures are equal. Hence, there exists a preference p in $core(D^*) - core(D)$. Since p is in $core(D^*)$, it is not a preference of w^*, but a reduced preference of v. As p is not in $core(D)$, p is a preference of w and thus of w^* since $\succsim_{w^*}$ is a superset of $\succsim_w$.   □

Chris' and Pam's merged viewpoint under (fw, mb) has four minimal revisions obtained by the following diagnoses of minimal core: $D_{CP,1} := \{(mb, mw), (mb, fb)\}$, $D_{CP,2} := \{(mb, mw), (fb, fw)\}$, $D_{CP,3} := \{(mw, fw), (mb, fb)\}$, $D_{CP,4} := \{(mw, fw), (fb, fw)\}$. In this example, each diagnosis is equal to its core.

6   Preferred Preference Revisions

Constructive approaches to decision making are able to accommodate a preference model to a situation where the decision maker did not follow a recommended decision, but made another decision. The model is extended by adding a preference between the chosen decision and the recommended decision, thus ensuring that the chosen decision becomes an optimal decision of the extended model.

This approach can also be applied to revisions of preferences. After adding a preference between a desired outcome and an optimal outcome of a viewpoint, the desired outcome should be optimal under the revised preferences. However, this property is not satisfied by every minimal revision. For example, fw is not an optimal outcome of the minimal revisions of Chris' and Pam's viewpoint under (fw, mb) that correspond to the diagnosis $D_{CP,1}$, $D_{CP,2}$, and $D_{CP,3}$.

When choosing a revision, it appears to be more important to keep preferences among preferred outcomes than to keep preferences among dispreferred outcomes. This idea can be expressed by a meta-preference relation between strict preferences. Given two strict preferences (α, β) and (γ, δ) of a base order $\succ$, (α, β) is *meta-preferred* to (γ, δ) under $\succ$ if $\beta \succeq \gamma$. This meta-preference relation is a strict partial order if the base order is a strict partial order. If a strict preference (α, β) were meta-preferred to itself then $\beta \succeq \alpha$ would hold, thus implying $\alpha \succ \alpha$, which contradicts the irreflexivity of $\succ$. Moreover, if a strict preference (α_1, β_1) is meta-preferred to a second strict preference (α_2, β_2) which is meta-preferred to a third strict preference (α_3, β_3), then $\beta_1 \succeq \alpha_2$ and $\beta_2 \succeq \alpha_3$ hold. As $\succ$ is transitive, $\beta_1 \succeq \alpha_3$ holds as well, meaning that (α_1, β_1) is meta-preferred to (α_3, β_3). This shows that the meta-preference relation is irreflexive and transitive. In the example, (mb, mw) is meta-preferred to (mw, fw) and (mb, fb) is meta-preferred to (fb, fw).

The meta-preference order over individual preferences can be lifted to a meta-preference order over preference relations by using a scheme studied in [5]. Consider two preference relations R_1 and R_2 that are subsets of the same base order $\succ$. R_1 is *meta-preferred* to R_2 under $\succ$ if R_1 is different to R_2 and for each preference $p \in R_2 - R_1$, there exists a preference $p^* \in R_1 - R_2$ that is meta-preferred to p under $\succ$. Similarly, R_1 is *meta-dispreferred* to R_2 under $\succ$ if R_1 is different to R_2 and for each preference $p \in R_1 - R_2$, there exists a preference $p^* \in R_2 - R_1$ that is meta-preferred to p under $\succ$. The latter relation is the inverse of the former relation.

We cannot compare the strict preference orders of different revisions of a viewpoint as those preference orders are not subsets of a common strict partial order. Consider a viewpoint v with three outcomes a, b, c, equality as indifference relation, and two reduced preferences (a, b) and (b, c). The viewpoint v has two minimal revisions under (c, a), where the first one has (c, a) and (a, b) as reduced preferences and the second one has (b, c) and (c, a) as reduced preferences. The union of these reduced preferences is not acyclic and there is no transitive relation that contains all these reduced preferences and that is irreflexive.

As diagnoses for a revision of a viewpoint are subsets of the strict preference order of this viewpoint, we can compare them under the meta-preference relation.

Definition 7. *A diagnosis D for the revision of v under Δ is a* dispreferred *diagnosis for the revision of v under Δ if there is no diagnosis D^* for the revision of v under Δ s.t. the core of D^* is meta-dispreferred to the core of D under $\succ_v$.*

Due to this definition, a dispreferred diagnosis is a diagnosis of minimal core. Now, consider a viewpoint v having the reduced preferences $(\gamma_1, \gamma_2), (\gamma_1, \gamma_2), \ldots (\gamma_{k-2}, \gamma_{k-1}), (\gamma_{k-1}, \gamma_k)$. A dispreferred diagnosis for the revision of v under $\{(\gamma_k, \gamma_1)\}$ seeks to exclude as many meta-preferred elements from its core as possible. It thus consists of the last element, namely (γ_{k-1}, γ_k).

The revision of Chris' and Pam's merged viewpoint under (fw, mb) has a single dispreferred diagnosis, namely $D_{CP,4}$ which contains the dispreferred element (mw, fw) among the conflicting preferences (mb, mw) and (mw, fw) and the dispreferred element (fb, fw) among the conflicting preferences (mb, fb) and (fb, fw). It leads to a revision having the reduced preferences (fw, mb), (mb, mw) and (mb, fb) and the derived preferences (fw, mw) and (fw, fb). None of the other diagnoses is meta-dispreferred to $D_{CP,4}$. Indeed, we even observe that each of the other diagnoses is meta-preferred to $D_{CP,4}$. For example, $D_{CP,2}$ is meta-preferred to $D_{CP,4}$ since $core(D_{CP,2}) - core(D_{CP,4})$ contains the preference (mb, mw) which is meta-preferred to the single element (mw, fw) of $core(D_{CP,4}) - core(D_{CP,2})$. Similar arguments hold for the other diagnoses.

It should be noted that $D_{CP,4}$ contains all preferences of the form (α, fw) and thus avoids that some other outcome is preferred to fw in the resulting revision. We can generalize this property for those cases where all preferences in Δ have the same preferred outcome. We say that Δ is *head-equal* under $\sim_v$ if $\alpha_1 \sim_v \alpha_2$ for all (α_1, β_1) and (α_2, β_2) in Δ. This leads to our main result:

Theorem 1. *If Δ is head-equal then there is a unique dispreferred diagnosis for the revision of v under Δ.*

Proof. Let C^* be the set of preferences (α, β) in $\succ_v^- - \Delta$ s.t. $\gamma \succeq_v \alpha$ for a $\gamma \in \Omega_v$ and (1) $(\beta, \gamma) \in \Delta$ or (2) $(\delta, \beta) \in \Delta$ and $(\delta, \gamma) \in \succ_v^- \cup \Delta$ for a $\delta \in \Omega_v$. Let v^* be a viewpoint having the same outcome space and criterion as v and the reflexive transitive closure of $\succ_v^- - C^* \cup \Delta \cup \sim_v$ as preference order. Let D^* be the set of reduced preferences of v that are not reduced preferences of v^*.

The set C^* is disjoint from Δ by definition and disjoint from $\sim_v$ since it is a subset of $\succ_v^-$. Hence, the preferences in C^* are not in $\succ_v^- - C^* \cup \Delta \cup \sim_v$ and can neither be reduced preferences of this set, nor reduced preferences of the reflexive transitive closure of this set, i.e. $\succeq_{v^*}$. Hence, the elements of C^* are reduced preference of v, but not of v^*. Consequently C^* is a subset of D^*.

Since Δ, $\succ_v^-$, and $\succ_v$ are all closed under $\sim_v$, it can be shown that C^* is compatible with $\sim_v$ and that $\succ_v^- - C^* \cup \Delta$ is compatible with $\sim_v$ as well.

Suppose that $\succ_v^- - C^* \cup \Delta$ is not acyclic. Consider a chain $\gamma_1, \ldots, \gamma_k$ of length $k \geq 2$ s.t. $(\gamma_i, \gamma_{i \bmod k+1})$ is a preference from $\succ_v^- - C^* \cup \Delta$ for $i = 1, \ldots, k$. As Δ is acyclic, the chain contains at least one element from $\succ_v^- - \Delta$. Without loss of generality, suppose (γ_1, γ_2) is in $\succ_v^- - \Delta$. Since $\succ_v^-$ is acyclic, the chain also contains at least one element from Δ. Let s and l be the smallest and largest index of those preferences from Δ. Note that $s \geq 2$, meaning that (γ_{s-1}, γ_s) is in $\succ_v^- -\Delta$. Furthermore, $\gamma_{l \bmod k+1} \succeq_v \gamma_{s-1}$ holds. As Δ is head-equal, $\gamma_s \sim_v \gamma_l$ holds. As Δ is closed under $\sim_v$, it also contains $(\gamma_s, \gamma_{l \bmod k+1})$. Hence, (γ_{s-1}, γ_s) is in C^*, which contradicts the fact that it is in $\succ_v^- -C^* \cup \Delta$. Therefore, $\succ_v^-$ $-C^* \cup \Delta$ is acyclic. Due to Proposition 1, the strict preference order of v^* is the transitive closure of $\succ_v^- -C^* \cup \Delta$ and its indifference relation is $\sim_v$.

Suppose that $p \in \Delta$ is a derived preference of $\succ_v^- -C^* \cup \Delta$. There exists a chain $\gamma_1, \ldots, \gamma_k$ of length $k \geq 3$ s.t. (γ_i, γ_{i+1}) is a preference from $\succ_v^- -C^* \cup \Delta$ for $i = 1, \ldots, k-1$ and p is equal to (γ_1, γ_k). As Δ is irreducible, at least one of these preference is in $\succ_v^- -\Delta$. Let l be the largest index s.t. (γ_l, γ_{l+1}) is in $\succ_v^- -\Delta$ and s be the largest index s.t. $s < l$ and (γ_s, γ_{s+1}) is in Δ or $s \leq 0$. Then $\gamma_{s+1} \succeq_v \gamma_l$ and $\gamma_{s+1} \succ_v \gamma_{l+1}$. If $l < k-1$ then Δ contains $(\gamma_{l+1}, \gamma_{l+2})$, which implies $\gamma_l \sim_v \gamma_{l+1}$ and $\gamma_l \not\succ_v \gamma_{l+1}$. Hence s cannot be 0 if $l < k-1$. If $s = 0$ and $l = k-1$ then (γ_1, γ_2) is in $\succ_v^-$ and $\gamma_2 \succeq_v \gamma_l$ holds and $(\gamma_1, \gamma_{l+1}) \in \Delta$. Hence, (γ_l, γ_{l+1}) is in C^* since it satisfies condition (2). If $s \geq 1$ then Δ contains (γ_s, γ_{s+1}) and also (γ_1, γ_{s+1}) since it is head-equal and closed under $\sim_v$. If $s \geq 1$ and $l = k-1$ hold, then (γ_l, γ_{l+1}) is in C^* since it satisfies condition (2). If $s \geq 1$ and $l < k-1$, then Δ contains $(\gamma_{l+1}, \gamma_{l+2})$ and also $(\gamma_{l+1}, \gamma_{s+1})$ since it is head-equal and closed under $\sim_v$. Then (γ_l, γ_{l+1}) is in C^* since it satisfies condition (1). However, as (γ_l, γ_{l+1}) is in $\succ_v^- -C^* \cup \Delta$, it cannot be in C^* in any of those cases. Therefore, all elements of Δ are reduced preferences of v^*. By definition, all reduced preferences of v^* are elements of $\succ_v^- -C^* \cup \Delta$ and thus of $\succ_v^- \cup \Delta$. As a consequence, v^* is a revision of v under Δ.

Suppose some preference p of D^* is not in C^*. As p is in D^*, it is a reduced preference of v, but not of v^*. Due to the definition of v^*, p is a preference of v^* since it is not in C^*. Consequently, p is a derived preference of v^* and cannot be in the core of D^*. Hence, the core of D^* is a subset of C^*.

Suppose there is a diagnosis D s.t. $core(D^*)$ is not dispreferred to $core(D)$. Hence, there is a preference (α, β) in $core(D^*) - core(D)$ s.t. no preference in $core(D) - core(D^*)$ is meta-preferred to (α, β) under $\succ_v$. As $core(D^*)$ is a subset of C^*, (α, β) is in C^* and there exists $\gamma \in \Omega_v$ s.t. $\gamma \succeq_v \alpha$ for a $\gamma \in \Omega_v$ and (1) $(\beta, \gamma) \in \Delta$ or (2) $(\delta, \beta) \in \Delta$ and $(\delta, \gamma) \in \succ_v^- \cup \Delta$ for a $\delta \in \Omega_v$. Consider a chain $\gamma_1, \ldots, \gamma_k$ of length $k \geq 1$ s.t. $\gamma_i \succ_v^- \gamma_{i+1}$ for $i = 1, \ldots, k-1$ and $(\gamma_1, \gamma_k) = (\gamma, \alpha)$. Let γ_0 be δ if condition (2) holds and γ otherwise. Let l be the largest index s.t. (γ_l, γ_{l+1}) is in C^* or not in $\succ_v^-$ or $l < 0$. Then $\gamma_{l+1} \succeq_v \alpha$ and $\gamma_{l+1} \succ_v \beta$ hold. Each of the reduced preferences (γ_i, γ_{i+1}) is meta-preferred to (α, β) for $i = l+1, \ldots, k-1$ and not in $core(D) - core(D^*)$. As these preferences are not in C^*, they are not in its subset $core(D^*)$ and thus not in $core(D)$. Hence, the core of D does not break $\gamma_{l+1} \succ_v \beta$. If $(\gamma_l, \gamma_{l+1}) \in C^*$, (γ_{l+1}, ω) or (ω, γ_{l+1}) are in Δ for some $\omega \in \Omega_v$. Consider the first case. If (β, γ) were in Δ, then $\gamma_{l+1} \sim_v \beta$ would hold, which contradicts $\gamma_{l+1} \succ_v \beta$. Hence, (δ, β) is in Δ, which implies $\delta \sim_v \gamma_{l+1}$ and $(\gamma_{l+1}, \beta) \in \Delta$, meaning that the core of D violates condition 2 of a diagnosis. In the second case, $\beta \sim_v \omega$ or $\delta \sim_v \omega$ hold and (β, γ_{l+1}) or (δ, γ_{l+1}) are in Δ, respectively. If $(\gamma_l, \gamma_{l+1}) \notin C^*$, this also holds or $\delta = \gamma_{l+1}$. In those cases, the core of D violates condition 1 or 2 of a diagnosis. It can be shown that D violates those conditions as well and cannot be a diagnosis. $\qquad\square$

We thus obtain a preference revision operator that maps a viewpoint and a suitable set of preferences to a uniquely defined *preferred revision*, i.e. the revision produced by the dispreferred diagnosis. Future work is needed to investigate which of Gärdenfors' postulates are satisfied by this operator.

The dispreferred diagnosis contains critical preferences of the form (γ, α^*) where α^* is the head of some preference in Δ. This allows us to show that α^* is an optimal outcome of the preferred revision if Δ contains preferences of the form (α^*, β) for all optimal outcomes β of the original viewpoint:

Proposition 5. *Let $\alpha^* \in \Omega_v$ be the outcome of an action in $\mathcal{A}$, but not of an optimal decision of v. Let Δ be the set of preferences (α, β) such that $\alpha^* \sim_v \alpha$ and β is the outcome of an optimal decision of v. Let D^* be a dispreferred diagnosis for the revision of v under Δ. The outcome ω^* of each optimal decision of w_{D^*} satisfies $\omega^* \sim_v \alpha^*$.*

Proof. By definition, Δ is head-equal and there is a unique dispreferred diagnosis D^* for the revision of v under Δ. Consider the outcome ω^* of an optimal decision of w_{D^*}. If it were the outcome of an optimal decision of v, then there would be the preference (α^*, ω^*) in Δ, which contradicts the optimality of ω^* in w_{D^*}. Hence, ω^* is not an optimal decision of v and there exists an outcome β^* of an optimal decision of v such that $\beta^* \succ_v \omega^*$. Then the preference (α^*, β^*) is in Δ. Consider a chain $\gamma_1, \ldots, \gamma_k$ of length $k \geq 2$ s.t. $\gamma_i \succ_v^- \gamma_{i+1}$ for $i = 1, \ldots, k-1$ and $(\gamma_1, \gamma_k) = (\beta^*, \omega^*)$. As ω^* is optimal in w_{D^*}, some of the reduced preferences $\gamma_i \succ_v^- \gamma_{i+1}$ is not a preference of w. Let l be the largest index s.t. $\gamma_l \succ_v^- \gamma_{l+1}$ is in the core of D^*. Then either (δ, γ_{l+1}) or (γ_{l+1}, δ) are in Δ for some $\delta \in \Omega_v$. In the first case, $\alpha^* \sim_v \delta$ holds and (α^*, γ_{l+1}) is in Δ. This implies $\alpha^* \succ_w \omega^*$ and contradicts the optimality of ω^* in w_{D^*}. In the second case, $\alpha^* \sim_v \gamma_{l+1}$ holds. This implies $\alpha^* \succsim_w \omega^*$ and thus $\alpha^* \sim_w \omega^*$ since ω^* is optimal in w_{D^*}. $\square$

It is thus possible to accommodate a viewpoint to a desired decision by adding preferences between the desired decision and the optimal decisions of the viewpoint. This gives a justification to the chosen meta-preference ordering and shows that the approach is able to override existing preferences in a desired way, including ceteris-paribus preferences. As a consequence, ceteris-paribus preferences are not universally valid, but only by default. This is similar to the work of Brafman and Dimopoulos who use the partial stable model semantics to relax ceteris-paribus preferences in presence of inconsistent CP-networks [2], but which do not give higher priority to more specific preferences.

Our approach also provides a new way to model conditional ceteris-paribus preferences: let us say that, by default, Jim prefers meat to fish all else equal, but that he prefers fish to meat if the drink is wine. The default enlargement of Jim's viewpoint has the reduced preferences (mb, fb) and (mw, fw), but its preferred revision under (fw, mw) has the reduced preferences (mb, fb) and (fw, mw), which express conditional ceteris-paribus preferences. Similarly, we can model trade-offs by adding preferences between incomparable outcomes. For example, the revision of Chris' and Pam's viewpoint under (fb, mw) extends the preference order of this viewpoint, but does not remove any element from it.

7 Conclusion

We introduced a mechanism for overriding aggregated preferences by more specific preferences. It results in preference orders that respect the ceteris-paribus semantics by default, but which remove certain ceteris-paribus preferences if they conflict with the more specific preferences. As there are different minimal revisions of the preference order, we prefer those that keep as many preferences between more preferred outcomes as possible, thus gaining several benefits. Firstly, there is a unique preferred revision that dominates all other ones under this universal meta-preference relation. Secondly, the revision mechanism permits an adaption of a preference model to situations where the recommended decision does not correspond to a desired decision. It is sufficient to add a preference between the desired decision and the recommended decision and the desired decision will become an optimal decision in the preferred revision.

Other approaches for relaxing ceteris-paribus preferences do not give higher priority to more specific preferences [2] or do not use a universal preference order to compare different revisions, but similarity measures [7].

Future work consists in studying which of Gärdenfors' postulates are satisfied by the preferred revision and in elaborating algorithms for computing the dispreferred diagnosis and using it for optimization and dominance checking.

Acknowledgements. The questions leading to this work arose from a long collaboration with Prof. Dr. Gerhard Brewka during the years 1987-1993. It was Gerd Brewka who introduced me to the research community of non monotonic reasoning and my research has strongly been influenced and shaped by these years of intellectual exchange. I therefore dedicate this article with much pleasure to his Festschrift.

References

1. Aho, A.V., Garey, M.R., Ullman, J.D.: The Transitive Reduction of a Directed Graph. SIAM Journal on Computing 1(2), 131–137 (1972)
2. Brafman, R.I., Dimopoulos, Y.: Extended Semantics and Optimization Algortihms for CP-Networks. Computational Intelligence 20(2), 218–245 (2004)
3. Brewka, G.: Belief revision in a framework for default reasoning. In: Fuhrmann, A., Morreau, M. (eds.) The Logic of Theory Change. LNCS, vol. 465, pp. 206–222. Springer, Heidelberg (1991)
4. Gärdenfors, P.: Knowledge in Flux: Modeling the Dynamics of Epistemic States. College Publications (2008)
5. Junker, U.: Relationships between Assumptions. Ph.D. thesis, University of Kaiserslautern, Kaiserslautern (1992)
6. Junker, U.: Preferences in an Open World. In: Rossi, F., Tsoukias, A. (eds.) ADT 2009. LNCS, vol. 5783, pp. 215–224. Springer, Heidelberg (2009)
7. Wicker, A.W., Doyle, J.: Comparing preferences expressed by CP-networks. In: AAAI Workshop on Advances in Preference Handling, pp. 128–133. AAAI (2008)

A Non-monotonic Goal Specification Language for Planning with Preferences

Tran Cao Son[1], Enrico Pontelli[1], and Chitta Baral[2]

[1] Department of Computer Science New Mexico State University,
Las Cruces, New Mexico, USA
{tson,epontell}@cs.nmsu.edu
[2] Department of Computer Science and Engineering,
Arizona State University, Tempe, Arizona, USA
chitta@asu.edu

Abstract. This paper introduces a default logic based approach to defining goal specification languages that can be non-monotonic and allow for the specification of inconsistencies and priorities among goals. The paper starts by presenting a basic goal specification language for planning with preferences. It then defines goal default theories (resp. with priorities) by embedding goal formulae into default logic (resp. prioritizing default logic). It is possible to show that the new language is general, as it can express several features of previously developed goal specification languages. The paper discusses how several other features can be subsumed by extending the basic goal specification language. Finally, we identify features that might be important in goal specification that cannot be expressed by our language.

1 Introduction

An important component of autonomous agent design is *goal specification*. In classical planning, goals deal with reaching one of a particular set of states. Nevertheless, goals of agents are not just about reaching a particular state; goals are often about satisfying desirable *conditions* imposed on the trajectory. For example, a person can have the following desire in preparing travel plans to conferences:

(*) *I prefer to fly to the conference site (since it is usually too far to drive).*

The user's preference restricts the means that can be used in achieving her goal of reaching the conference site, which leads to the selection of a plan that reaches the conference site by airplane, whenever possible. Ultimately, this affects what actions the person should take in order to achieve the goal.

These observations led to the development of languages for the specification of *soft goals* in planning, such as the language $\mathcal{PP}$, introduced in [13] and extended in [6]. In $\mathcal{PP}$, a *basic desire* is a temporal formula describing desirable properties of a trajectory. *Atomic* and *general preferences* are particular classes of formulae built over basic desires. A preference formula Φ defines a preference order $\prec_\Phi$ among the trajectories that achieve the *hard goal* of the problem, i.e., for every pair of trajectories α and β, $\alpha \prec_\Phi \beta$ indicates that α is preferable to β. $\prec_\Phi$ is often a partial order, built on a notion of satisfaction between trajectories and preference specifications. Similar ideas have been

T. Eiter et al. (Eds.): Brewka Festschrift, LNAI 9060, pp. 202–217, 2015.

considered in the planning community and led to extensions of the *Planning Domain Description Language (PDDL),* with features for representing classes of preferences over plans using temporal extended preferences (e.g., [10]).

In [4], the authors argue that a goal specification language should be *non-monotonic* for various reasons, such as elaboration tolerance and simplicity of goal specification. For example, the same traveler with the preference (*) would probably not mind driving at most three hours to the conference site if the only flight to the destination requires to travel the day before the conference starts. In this case, her preference becomes:

(**) *Normally, I prefer to fly to the conference site (since it is usually too far to drive). However, if there are no flights on the same day of the conference and the driving time is at most three hours, then I will drive.*

To address this issue, an extension of LTL [11], called N-LTL, has been proposed, allowing weak and strong exceptions to certain rules. A weakness of this language is that it requires the classification of weak and strong exceptions when a goal is specified. In [5], the language ER-LTL is introduced to address this limitation of N-LTL. Similarly to $\mathcal{PP}$, the semantics of N-LTL and ER-LTL rely on the notion of satisfaction between plans and N-LTL or ER-LTL specifications. Observe that the issue of non-monotonicity is dealt with in $\mathcal{PP}$ and in the extensions of PDDL by revising the soft goals, which is an approach that N-LTL specifically tries to avoid.

We observe that the focus of the work in [1, 4, 5, 6, 10] is on classical planning, i.e., the planning domains are deterministic and the initial state is complete, while the work in [13] considers non-deterministic domains and only discusses preferences among weak plans. In [2], it is argued that a plan for a non-deterministic domain should be a *policy* (i.e., a partial function from the set of states to the set of actions); this leads to the design of the language π-CTL* or specifying goals in non-deterministic domains. π-CTL* is an extension of CTL* [9] with two modalities A_π and E_π for considering all or some trajectories w.r.t. a given policy. In [3], the language π-CTL* is extended with quantifiers over policies to increase its expressiveness. Policies satisfying a goal specification are viewed as the solutions of a planning problem.

In this paper, we explore an approach based on prioritizing default logic for defining a goal specification language. The new language, called *goal default theories with priorities,* is a variation of prioritizing default logic, in which formulae occurring within a default can be temporally extended preference formulae. We show that the core of the new language subsumes several features from existing goal languages and can be extended to subsume several other features from other goal languages. Finally, we discuss the possible applications of the new language in the study of existing goal languages and the development of new ones.

2 Background

In this section, we briefly review the basic definitions of planning, linear temporal logic (LTL) and its extension for specifying preferences in planning.

2.1 LTL and Temporal Extended Preferences

Let $\mathcal{L}$ be a propositional language. By $\langle p \rangle$ we denote a propositional formula from $\mathcal{L}$. LTL-formulae $\langle f \rangle$ are defined by the following grammar:

$$\langle f \rangle ::= \langle p \rangle \mid \langle f \rangle \wedge \langle f \rangle \mid \langle f \rangle \vee \langle f \rangle \mid$$
$$\neg \langle f \rangle \mid \bigcirc \langle f \rangle \mid \square \langle f \rangle \mid \Diamond \langle f \rangle \mid \langle f \rangle \mathsf{U} \langle f \rangle \tag{1}$$

The semantics of LTL-formulae is defined with respect to sequences of interpretations of $\mathcal{L}$. For later use, we will refer to an interpretation of $\mathcal{L}$ as a *state* and a possibly infinite sequence of interpretations $s_0, s_1, \ldots$ of $\mathcal{L}$ as a *trajectory*. For a trajectory $\sigma = s_0, s_1, \ldots$, by σ_i we denote the suffix $s_i, s_{i+1}, \ldots$ of σ. A trajectory $\sigma = s_0, s_1, \ldots$ *satisfies* an LTL-formula f, denoted by $\sigma \models f$, if $\sigma_0 \models f$ where:[1]

- $\sigma_j \models p$ iff $s_j \models p$
- $\sigma_j \models \neg f$ iff $\sigma_j \not\models f$
- $\sigma_j \models f_1 \wedge f_2$ iff $\sigma_j \models f_1$ and $\sigma_j \models f_2$
- $\sigma_j \models f_1 \vee f_2$ iff $\sigma_j \models f_1$ or $\sigma_j \models f_2$
- $\sigma_j \models \bigcirc f$ iff $\sigma_{j+1} \models f$
- $\sigma_j \models \square f$ iff $\sigma_k \models f$, for all $k \geq j$
- $\sigma_j \models \Diamond f$ iff $\sigma_i \models f$ for some $i \geq j$
- $\sigma_j \models f_1 \mathsf{U} f_2$ iff there exists $k \geq j$ such that $\sigma_k \models f_2$ and for all $i, j \leq i < k, \sigma_i \models f_1$.

A finite trajectory $s_0, \ldots, s_n$ satisfies an LTL-formula f if its extension $s_0, \ldots, s_n, s_{n+1}, \ldots$ satisfies f, where $s_k = s_n$ for $k > n$. In order to deal with planning problems, LTL is extended with the following constructs

$$\texttt{at\_end}\ \langle p \rangle \mid \langle p \rangle\ \texttt{sometime\_before}\ \langle p \rangle \mid \langle p \rangle\ \texttt{sometime\_after}\ \langle p \rangle \tag{2}$$

Formulae of the extended LTL are referred to as *Temporal Extended Preferences (TEP)*. Note that the last two are syntactic sugar for LTL formulae. Temporal extended preferences are interpreted over finite trajectories. The notion of satisfaction for standard LTL-formulae is defined as above, while satisfaction of TEP formulae is as follows: given a finite trajectory $\sigma = s_0, \ldots, s_n$:

- $\sigma \models \texttt{at\_end}\ p$ iff $s_n \models p$;
- $\sigma \models p_1\ \texttt{sometime\_before}\ p_2$ iff for every $i, 0 \leq i \leq n$, if $\sigma_i \models p_1$ then $\sigma_j \models p_2$ for some $i \leq j \leq n$; and
- $\sigma_j \models p_1\ \texttt{sometime\_after}\ p_2$ iff for every $i, 0 \leq i \leq n$, if $\sigma_i \models p_1$ then $\sigma_j \models p_2$ for some $0 \leq j < i \leq n$.

2.2 Planning

We describe a *dynamic domain* as a labeled transition system $T = (F, A, S, L)$, where:

- F is a set of fluents (or propositions),
- A is a set of actions,
- S is a set of interpretations (or states) of F, and
- $L \subseteq S \times A \times S$.

---

[1] We will also use the other propositional connectives, e.g., $\Rightarrow$ with the expected meaning.

Each triple $\langle s_1, a, s_2 \rangle \in L$ indicates that the execution of the action a in the state s_1 might result in the state s_2. T is *deterministic* if for each state s and action a, L contains at most one triple $\langle s, a, s_2 \rangle$; otherwise, T is non-deterministic.

Given a transition system T, a finite or infinite sequence $s_0 a_0 s_1 a_1 \ldots s_n a_n s_{n+1} \ldots$ of alternate states and actions is called a *run* if $\langle s_i, a_i, s_{i+1} \rangle \in L$ for every $i = 0, \ldots$ A *policy* π in a transition system T is a partial function $\pi : S \to A$ from the set of states to the set of actions. A run $s_0 a_0 s_1 a_1 \ldots s_k a_k s_{k+1} \ldots$ is said to be induced by a policy π if $a_i = \pi(s_i)$ for every $i = 0, \ldots, k, \ldots$ With a slight abuse of terminology, we will refer to a *plan* as either a sequence of actions or a policy from a transition system T.

Definition 1. *A planning problem is a triple $\langle T, S_i, S_f \rangle$ where $T = (F, A, S, L)$ is a transition system, $S_i \subseteq S$ is the set of initial states, and $S_f \subseteq S$ is the set of final states.*

Intuitively, a planning problem asks for a *plan* which transforms the transition system from any state belonging to S_i to some state in S_f. In the rest of the discussion, we assume S_i and S_f to be finite sets. We distinguish two classes of planning problems:

- *Deterministic planning*: in this case, T is deterministic and a *solution* (or *plan*) of $\langle T, S_i, S_f \rangle$ is an action sequence $[a_0; \ldots; a_n]$ such that, for every $s_0 \in S_i$, $s_0 a_0 s_1 a_1 \ldots a_n s_{n+1}$ is a run in T and $s_{n+1} \in S_f$;
- *Non-deterministic planning*: T is non-deterministic and a solution (or plan) of $\langle T, S_i, S_f \rangle$ is a policy π such that, for every $s_0 \in S_i$ and every run induced by π in T, the run is finite and is of the form $s_0 a_0 s_1 a_1 \ldots s_k a_k s_{k+1}$ where $s_{k+1} \in S_f$.

In the following, whenever we refer to a possible plan in a transition system T, we mean a sequence of actions (resp. a policy) if T is deterministic (resp. non-deterministic) that can generate a correct run. Let us illustrate these basic definitions using the following simple example.

Example 1. Consider a transportation robot. There are different locations, say $l_1, \ldots, l_k$, whose connectivity is given by a graph and there might be different objects at each location. Let O be a set of objects. The robot can travel between two directly connected locations. It can pick up objects at a location, hold them, drop them, and carry them between locations. We assume that, for each pair of connected locations l_i and l_j, the robot has an action $a_{i,j}$ for traveling from l_i to l_j. The robot can hold only one object at a time. The domain can be represented by a transition system $T_1 = (F, A, S, L)$:[2]

- F contains the following types of propositions:
  - $at(i)$ denotes that the robot is at the location l_i;
  - $o\_at(o, i)$ denotes that the object o is at the location l_i;
  - $h(o)$ denotes that the robot is holding the object o.
- A contains of the following types of actions:
  - $a_{i,j}$ the robot moves from l_i to l_j;
  - $release(o)$ the robot drops the object o;
  - $pickup(o)$ the robot picks up the object o.

---

[2] We simplify the definitions of S and L for readability.

- S contains the interpretations of F which satisfy the basic constraints, such as the robot is at one location at a time, it holds only one object, etc.
- L contains transitions of the form $\langle s, a, s' \rangle$ such that s' is the result of the execution of a in s; for example, if $a = a_{i,j}$ and $at(i) \in s$ then $s' = s \setminus \{at(i)\} \cup \{at(j)\}$.

T_1 is a deterministic transition system. We will also refer to T_2 as the non-deterministic version of T_1 by defining $T_2 = (F, A, S, L')$ where $L' = L \cup \{\langle s_i, a_{i,j}, s_i \rangle \mid a_{i,j} \in A\}$ and $at(i) \in s$. Intuitively, T_2 encodes the fact that the action $a_{i,j}$ might fail and, when it does, the robot will remain in position l_i after the execution of $a_{i,j}$.

A planning problem P in this domain is given by specifying the initial location of the robot and of the objects and the final location of the robot and of the objects. It is deterministic (resp. non-deterministic) if T_1 (resp. T_2) is considered.

For example, $P_i = \langle T_i, \{\{at(1)\}\}, S_f \rangle$ where for each $s \in S_f$, $at(k) \in s$ is a planning problem for T_i. A solution for P_1 is a sequence $[a_{1,2}; \ldots; a_{k-1,k}]$. On the other hand, a solution for P_2 is a policy π defined by (for each $t < k$): $\pi(s) = a_{t,t+1}$ iff $at(t) \in s$.

3 A Basic Goal Specification Language for Planning with Preferences

In the literature, a planning problem with preferences is defined as a pair (P, Φ), where $P = \langle T, S_i, S_f \rangle$ is a planning problem, with $T = (F, A, S, L)$, and Φ is a preference formula in a goal specification language. A plan δ of P is called a *preferred plan* if it is a plan for P and satisfies Φ, where the notion of satisfaction of a preference formula by a plan is language dependent.

In general, we can characterize a goal specification language $\mathcal{G}$ over a transition system T by a set of preference formulae $\mathcal{F}$ and a satisfaction relation $\models_{\mathcal{G}}$ between the set of possible plans of T and formulae in $\mathcal{F}$. We will write $\delta \models_{\mathcal{G}} \Phi$ to denote that the plan δ satisfies the formula Φ under the language $\mathcal{G}$.

For later use, we will define a *basic goal specification language* for a transition system $T = (F, A, S, L)$, written as $\mathcal{G}_b = (\mathcal{F}_b, \models_{\mathcal{G}_b})$, as follows:

- The set of preference formulae $\mathcal{F}_b$ is the set of TEP-formulae over $F \cup A$, and
- The relation $\models_{\mathcal{G}_b}$ is defined as follows: for each planning problem $P = \langle T, S_i, S_f \rangle$
    - If T is deterministic, a plan $\delta = [a_0, \ldots, a_n]$ for P satisfies a formula Φ in $\mathcal{F}_b$ if for every $s_0 \in S_i$, $s_0 a_0 s_1 a_1 \ldots a_n s_{n+1}$ is a run in T and $(s_0 \cup \{a_0\}), \ldots, (s_n \cup \{a_n\}), s_{n+1}$ is a trajectory satisfying Φ (in the TEP-language over $F \cup A$);
    - If T is non-deterministic, a plan π for P satisfies a formula Φ in $\mathcal{F}_b$ if for every $s_0 \in S_i$ and every run $s_0 a_0 s_1 a_1 \ldots s_k a_k s_{k+1}$ in T induced by π, $(s_0 \cup \{a_0\}), \ldots, (s_n \cup \{a_n\}), s_{n+1}$ is a trajectory satisfying Φ (in the TEP-language over $F \cup A$).

In the following, we will assume that any goal specification language $\mathcal{G}$ is a conservative extension of $\mathcal{G}_b$, i.e., (*i*) $\mathcal{G}$ contains all formulae in $\mathcal{G}_b$; and (*ii*) for every planning problem P and a formula Φ in $\mathcal{G}$, if $\Phi \in \mathcal{G}_b$ and $\delta \models_{\mathcal{G}_b} \Phi$ then $\delta \models_{\mathcal{G}} \Phi$.

Example 2. Some preference formulae in $\mathcal{G}_b$ for the transition systems in Example 1:

- $\Diamond at(2)$: the robot should visit the location l_2 during the execution of the plan;
- $at(1) \wedge \Diamond at(2)$: the robot must (*i*) start in a state satisfying $at(1)$ (or the robot is at the location l_1 initially); and (*ii*) visit the location l_2 at some point during the execution of the plan;
- $\Box[at(2) \Rightarrow (\bigvee_{i \neq 2} a_{2,i})]$: whenever the robot visits l_2, it should leave that location immediately by executing an action going to one of its neighbors;
- $h(o) \Rightarrow \bigcirc \bigcirc \neg h(o)$: if the robot holds an object o in the initial state then it should release o after the execution of one action;
- $\Box[h(o) \Rightarrow \bigcirc \bigcirc \neg h(o)]$: whenever the robot holds an object o it should release o after the execution of an action;
- $h(o)$ sometime_before $at(5)$: whenever the robot holds the object o, it must visit the location l_5 thereafter before reaching the goal;
- at_end $[\bigwedge_{o \in O} \neg h(o)]$: at the end, the robot should not hold any object. $\Box$

With a slight abuse of notation, let us view a state s as a formula $\bigwedge_{s \models_f f} f \wedge \bigwedge_{s \models_f \neg f} \neg f$.
Let S_i and S_f be two sets of states and

$$
\Phi = \left[\underbrace{\bigvee_{s \in S_i} s}_{\Phi_1} \wedge \text{at\_end} \underbrace{[\bigvee_{s \in S_f} s]}_{\Phi_2} \right]
$$

It is easy to see that any plan satisfying Φ requires its execution to start from a state satisfying Φ_1, which is one of the states in S_i, and end in a state satisfying Φ_2, which is one of the states in S_f. For this reason, the description of the initial and final states can be folded into a preference formula. We will therefore define planning problems as follows.

Definition 2. *Given a transition system T and a goal specification language $\mathcal{G} = (\mathcal{F}, \models_{\mathcal{G}})$ over T, a goal formula Φ in $\mathcal{F}$ is called a* planning problem. *A* solution *of Φ is a plan δ in T such that $\delta \models_{\mathcal{G}} \Phi$.*

By Def. 2, a goal formula represents a planning problem. The literature is quite varied when a user faces two or more goal formulae which are contradictory with each other. For example, the formula $\Diamond at(2)$ is contradictory with $\Box \neg at(2)$; $\Box \neg (\bigwedge_{o \in O} h(o))$ conflicts with $\Diamond h(o_1)$; etc. A possibility is to consider a possible plan as solution if it satisfies some goal formulae. Another possibility is to rank the goal formulae and identify solutions as plans that satisfy the formula with the highest possible ranking. In the following, we will show that a uniform framework for dealing with conflicting goal formulae can be obtained by embedding goal formulae into Reiter's default logic.

4 Goal Default Theories

In this section, we will introduce a new goal specification language, called *goal default theory*. A goal default theory is a variation of Reiter's default theory [12], whose defaults can contain preference formulae. Goal default theories provide a possible treatment of planning with multiple goal formulae.

A goal default theory is defined over a transition system $T = (F, A, S, L)$ and a goal specification language $\mathcal{G} = (\mathcal{F}, \models_{\mathcal{G}})$ over T. We say that two formulae φ, ψ in $\mathcal{F}$ are equivalent w.r.t. $\models_{\mathcal{G}}$ if, for each plan δ of T, we have that $\delta \models_{\mathcal{G}} (\varphi \Leftrightarrow \psi)$.[3] We can easily extend this to define the notion of *logical consequence w.r.t.* $\models_{\mathcal{G}}$—if S is a set of formulae from $\mathcal{F}$ and f is another formula in $\mathcal{F}$, then $S \models_{\mathcal{G}} f$ if, for each plan δ of T, we have that $\delta \models_{\mathcal{G}} \bigwedge_{\varphi \in S} \varphi$ implies $\delta \models_{\mathcal{G}} f$. Given a set of formulae S from $\mathcal{F}$, we define $Decl(S) = \{\varphi \mid \varphi \in \mathcal{F}, S \models_{\mathcal{G}} \varphi\}$.

A *preference default* (or *p-default*) d over $\mathcal{G}$ is of the following form

$$\frac{\alpha \, : \, \beta}{\gamma} \tag{3}$$

where α, β, and γ are formulae in $\mathcal{F}$. We call α the *precondition*, β the *justification*, and γ the *consequence* of d, and we denote them with $prec(d)$, $just(d)$, and $cons(d)$, respectively. A default d is said to be

- *Normal* if its justification is equivalent to its conclusion;
- *Prerequisite-free* if its precondition is equivalent to *true*; and
- *Supernormal* if it is normal and prerequisite-free.

Given a set of formulae S from $\mathcal{F}$, a default d is said to be *defeated* in S if $S \models \neg just(d)$. Some preferences and their representation as p-defaults over $\mathcal{G}_b$ for the domain from Example 1 are given next.

Example 3. In these examples, o denotes a particular object in the domain.

- If there is no evidence that the robot is initially at location l_2, then it should eventually go to l_2:

$$\frac{\top \, : \, \neg at(2)}{\Diamond at(2)} \tag{4}$$

- Assume that objects might be defective, represented by the proposition *defective*. We can write

$$\frac{\top \, : \, \Box[\neg defective(o)]}{\Box[at(2) \Rightarrow h(o)]} \tag{5}$$

to indicate that, normally, we would like the robot to hold the object o whenever it is at location l_2. An exception to this rule is possible if the object o becomes defective.

- If the robot is not required to hold the object o in the final state and there is no evidence that it initially holds o, then it should not execute the action of picking up the object o:

$$\frac{\top \, : \, \text{at\_end}\,(\neg h(o)) \wedge \neg h(o)}{\Box[\neg pickup(o)]} \tag{6}$$

- If there is no evidence that the object o is initially in the wrong place then the robot should not start by executing the action of picking up the object o:

$$\frac{\text{at\_end}\,(o\_at(o, i)) \, : \, \bigwedge_{i \neq j} \neg o\_at(o, j)}{\neg pickup(o)} \tag{7}$$

---

[3] $\varphi \Leftrightarrow \psi$ is a shorthand for $(\varphi \wedge \psi) \vee (\neg \varphi \wedge \neg \psi)$.

- A stronger version of (7) is

$$\frac{\mathtt{at\_end}\,(o\_at(o,i))\ :\ \bigwedge_{i\neq j} \neg o\_at(o,j)}{\Box \neg pickup(o)} \tag{8}$$

indicates that the robot should never pick up the object o if o could already be in the desired final location.

- If there is the possibility that the robot might reach location l_2, then it must leave the location immediately after its arrival at l_2:

$$\frac{\top\ :\ \Diamond[at(2)]}{\Box[at(2) \Rightarrow \bigcirc \bigvee_{i\neq 2} a_{2,i}]} \tag{9}$$

- If there is no evidence that an object o will ever appear in location i then the robot should never go there.

$$\frac{\top\ :\ \Box[\neg o\_at(o,i)]}{\Box[\bigvee_{j\neq i} \neg a_{j,i}]} \tag{10}$$

In the following, we will refer to the p-defaults in (4)-(9) by $p_1, \ldots, p_6$, respectively. □

We next define the notion of a goal default theory.

Definition 3. *A goal default theory over a goal language* $\mathcal{G} = (\mathcal{F}, \models_{\mathcal{G}})$ *and a transition system* T *is a pair* $\Sigma = (D, W)$ *where* D *is a set of p-defaults over* $\mathcal{G}$ *and* $W \subseteq \mathcal{F}$.

Given a set of p-defaults D, we denote with $cons(D)$ the set $cons(D) = \{cons(d) \mid d \in D\}$. A p-default d is *applicable* w.r.t. a set of formulae S from $\mathcal{F}$ if $S \models_{\mathcal{G}} prec(d)$ and $S \not\models_{\mathcal{G}} \neg just(d)$. Let us denote with $\Pi_D(S)$ the set of p-defaults from D that are applicable w.r.t. S. The next definition is similar to the notion of extension in [12].

Definition 4. *Let* $\Sigma = (D, W)$ *be a goal default theory over* $\mathcal{G} = (\mathcal{F}, \models_{\mathcal{G}})$ *and* T. *An extension of* Σ *is a minimal set* $E \subseteq \mathcal{F}$ *that satisfies the condition* $E = Decl(W \cup Cons(\Pi_D(E)))$. *We say that* Σ *is* satisfiable *if it has at least one extension.*

From this definition, any default over the propositional language $F \cup A$ is a p-default, and any Reiter's default theory over the language $F \cup A$ is a goal default theory.

Definition 5. *Given a transition system* $T = (F, A, S, L)$ *and a goal specification language* $\mathcal{G} = (\mathcal{F}, \models_{\mathcal{G}})$ *over* T, *a* planning problem *over* T *and* $\mathcal{G}$ *is a goal default theory* $\Sigma = (D, W)$ *over* $\mathcal{G}$ *and* T.

The notion of a solution to a planning problem is modified as follows.

Definition 6. *Given a transition system* $T = (F, A, S, L)$, *a goal specification language* $\mathcal{G} = (\mathcal{F}, \models_{\mathcal{G}})$ *over* T, *and a planning problem* Σ *over* T *and* $\mathcal{G}$, *a* solution *of* Σ *is a plan* δ *in* T *such that* $\delta \models_{\mathcal{G}} E$ *for some extension* E *of* Σ.

Some planning problems over the transition systems in Example 1 and the language $\mathcal{G}_b$ are given in the next example.

Example 4 (Continuation of Example 3)

- Let $\Sigma_1 = (\{p_1\}, \{at(1), \mathtt{at\_end}\, at(5)\})$ where p_1 is the default (4). Intuitively, we have that Σ_1 identifies plans where the robot starts at location l_1, goes through the location l_2, and ends in location l_5.
- Let $\Sigma_2 = (\{p_6\}, \{at(1), \mathtt{at\_end}\, at(5)\})$ where p_6 is the default (9). This identifies plans where the robot starts at location l_1, ends in location l_5, and either *(i)* never goes through the location l_2; or *(ii)* never stays in the location l_2 within two consecutive steps.   □

The planning problems in Example 4 are simple, in that they are specified by goal default theories whose set of defaults is a singleton. Let us consider a more complicated example. Assume that we have two temporal formulae Φ and Ψ such that there exists no plan that can satisfy both Φ and Ψ. In this case, the use of goal default theory as a goal formula is convenient. Indeed, every solution of the planning problem expressed by the goal default theory

$$\Sigma_{\Phi, \Psi} = \left(\left\{ \frac{\top : \neg\Psi}{\Phi}, \frac{\top : \neg\Phi}{\Psi} \right\}, \emptyset \right) \tag{11}$$

satisfies either Φ or Ψ. The following result generalizes this observation—whose truth is a natural consequence of the notion of applicability; the sets Δ_δ are maximal subsets of Δ which are consistent.

Proposition 1. *Let $T = (F, A, S, L)$ be a transition system, $\mathcal{G} = (\mathcal{F}, \models_\mathcal{G})$ be a goal specification language, and $\Delta = \{\Phi_1, \ldots, \Phi_n\}$ be a set of preference formulae in $\mathcal{F}$. Furthermore, let*

$$\Sigma_\Delta = (\{ \tfrac{\top : \Psi}{\Psi} \mid \Psi \in \Delta \}, \emptyset) \tag{12}$$

For every solution δ to the problem Σ_Δ there exists a maximal (w.r.t. $\subseteq$) set of preferences $\Delta_\delta \subseteq \Delta$ such that $\delta \models_\mathcal{G} \bigwedge_{\Psi \in \Delta_\delta} \Psi$.

Proof. Since δ is a solution to the problem Σ_Δ, there exists an extension E of Σ_Δ such that $\delta \models_\mathcal{G} E$. We have that $\Delta_\delta = \{\Psi \mid \Psi \in \Delta, \Psi \in E\}$ is the set of preference formulae satisfying the condition of the proposition.   □

5   Goal Default Theories with Priorities

Proposition 1 shows that goal default theories can be used to specify planning problems with multiple preferences which might not be consistent with each other. For instance, consider a traveler from New York to San Francisco who has two preferences: reach the destination as fast as possible (Φ_1) and spend the least amount of money (Φ_2). In general, these two preferences cannot be satisfied at the same time. It is reasonable to assume that a plan satisfying one of the criteria is an acceptable solution. Thus, $\Sigma_{\{\Phi_1, \Phi_2\}}$ is a reasonable goal specification if the traveler is impartial about Φ_1 and Φ_2. On the other hand, if the traveler prefers Φ_1 over Φ_2 (or vice versa), we will need to change the goal specification or provide additional ways for the traveler to specify this priority. The literature offers several approaches for adding priorities to default theories

[7, 8], which can be easily adapted to goal default theories. We next define goal default theories with priorities by adapting the work of [7] to goal default theories.

Let us start by introducing *static priorities,* encoded by a well-ordering relation $\prec$ among p-defaults—i.e., $\prec$ is transitive, irreflexive, and each set of elements admits a least element in the ordering. We denote with $\min_\prec(X)$ the least element of X with respect to $\prec$. We define a goal default theory with priorities as follows.

Definition 7. *A goal default theory with priorities over a goal language $\mathcal{G} = (\mathcal{F}, \models_\mathcal{G})$ and a transition system T is a triple $(D, W, \prec)$ where D is a set of p-defaults over $\mathcal{G}$, $\prec$ is a well-ordering relation over D, and $W \subseteq \mathcal{F}$.*

Following the general design of prioritizing default theories [7], the notion of *preferred extension* can be defined by successively simplifying the structure of the defaults.

Let us define a construction of preferred extension through the application of defaults according to the ordering imposed by $\prec$. In the following, let $\Pi_D^*(S) = \{d \mid d \in \Pi_D(S), S \not\models cons(d)\}$. Let us introduce the $\mathcal{PR}$ operator which computes the next "preferred" set of goal formulae from an existing one:

- $\mathcal{PR}_\prec(S) = Decl(S \cup \{cons(d)\})$
  if $\Pi_D^*(S) \neq \emptyset \wedge d = \min_\prec(\{x \mid x \in \Pi_D^*(S)\})$;
- $\mathcal{PR}_\prec(S) = S$ if $\Pi_D^*(S) = \emptyset$

If the elements in D (for a goal default theory (D, W)) are supernormal, then it is possible to use $\mathcal{PR}_\prec$ to produce a monotone sequence of goal formulae, by setting $S_0 = Decl(W)$, $S_{i+1} = \mathcal{PR}_\prec(S_i)$ for any successor ordinal $i + 1$ and $S_i = Decl(\bigcup_{j<i} S_j)$ for any limit ordinal i. We will denote the result of this construction as $Pref_\prec(D, W) = \bigcup_{i \geq 0} S_i$.

The process of determining a preferred extension will apply $Pref_\prec$ on a reduced version of the theory, in a style similar to that used in the Gelfond-Lifschitz reduct. Following the model proposed in [7], the reduct of a goal default theory with priorities $(D, W, \prec)$ w.r.t. a set of goal formulae S, denoted $(D^S, W, \prec^S)$, is obtained as follows:

- Determine $D' = \{\frac{\top \,:\, just(d)}{cons(d)} \mid d \in D, S \models_\mathcal{G} prec(d)\}$
- Determine $D^S = \{d \in D' \mid cons(d) \notin S \text{ or } S \not\models_\mathcal{G} \neg just(d)\}$ and $\prec^S$ is such that $d_1' \prec^S d_2'$ if $d_1 \prec d_2$ and d_1 (d_2) is the $\prec$-least element that introduced d_1' (d_2') in D'.

We define preferred extensions as follows.

Definition 8. *Let $(D, W, \prec)$ be a goal default theory with priorities over $\mathcal{G} = (\mathcal{F}, \models_\mathcal{G})$ and T. A preferred extension E of $(D, W, \prec)$ is a set of goal formulae in $\mathcal{F}$ such that E is an extension of (D, W) and $E = Pref_{\prec^E}(D^E, W)$.*

Similar to [7], we can generalize the above definitions and define *(i)* A goal default theory with priorities as a triple $(D, W, \prec)$ where (D, W) is a goal default theory and $\prec$ is a partial order among defaults in D; and *(ii)* A set of formulae E is a preferred extension of $(D, W, \prec)$ if it is a preferred extension of some $(D, W, \prec_E)$ for some well-ordering $\prec_E$ which is an extension of $\prec$. For brevity, we omit the precise definitions. Definitions 5 and 6 can be extended in the obvious way: a planning problem is a goal default theory with priorities $(D, W, \prec)$ and its solutions are preferred extensions of $(D, W, \prec)$.

Example 5. Let us consider the domain in Example 1. Let us assume that, among the objects, there is a very valuable object o_1 and a dangerous object o_2. Furthermore, let us assume that the robot is equipped with actions that can detect the object o_2 whenever the robot is at the same location as o_2. However, the equipment might not be working. We will denote with *working* the fact that the equipment is working properly. Let us consider the two formulae:

- $\varphi := \Diamond h(o_1)$: the robot should try to get the object o_1
- $\psi := \Box[\bigwedge_{i \in \{1,\ldots,k\}} (o\_at(o_2, i) \Rightarrow \neg at(i))]$: the robot should not be at the same place with object o_2 at any time.

With these formulae, we can define the following p-defaults:

$$g_1 \equiv \frac{\top \;:\; working}{\psi \wedge \varphi} \qquad g_2 \equiv \frac{\top \;:\; \neg working}{\varphi}$$

g_1 indicates that if the equipment is initially working, then the robot will get o_1 while trying to avoid o_2. g_2 states that if the equipment is not working, then the robot will only worry about getting o_1. The theory $(\{g_1, g_2\}, \emptyset, \{g_1 \prec g_2\})$ states that we prefer that the robot tries to satisfy g_1 before trying to satisfy g_2.

6   Relationship to other Goal Languages

In this section, we relate a goal default theory with priorities to previously developed goal specification languages. In this section, for a plan δ and a formula Φ, we write $\delta \models \Phi$ to denote that δ satisfies Φ as defined in the other goal languages.

6.1   Temporal Extended Preferences

Temporal extended preferences (or TEP formulae) (Section 2) are defined as part of PDDL 3.0, and used to specify preferences over plans in deterministic domains. They are referred to as *constraints*. TEP formulae have been implemented in a heuristic search based planner in [1]. Given a set of TEP formulae $\Delta = \{\Phi_1, \ldots, \Phi_n\}$, a planning problem is an optimization problem that maximizes the rewards obtained by satisfying the preferences in Δ. Formally, the reward over a plan δ is

$$\Sigma_{\Phi_i \in \Delta, \delta \models \Phi_i} reward(\Phi_i) - \Sigma_{\Phi_i \in \Delta, \delta \not\models \Phi_i} penalty(\Phi_i)$$

where $reward(\Phi)$ and $penalty(\Phi)$ denote the reward and penalty for satisfying and not satisfying the preference Φ, respectively.

Observe that the basic goal specification language (Section 3) does not provide the means for selecting a plan based on such a reward function. Nevertheless, the planning problem can be expressed by a goal default theory with priorities as follows. Let S be a set of formulae, $S \subseteq \Delta$, and d_S be the default

$$\frac{\top \;:\; \bigwedge_{\Phi \in S} \Phi \wedge \bigwedge_{\Phi \in \Delta \setminus S} \neg \Phi}{\bigwedge_{\Phi \in S} \Phi \wedge \bigwedge_{\Phi \in \Delta \setminus S} \neg \Phi}$$

Let $D_\Delta = \{d_S \mid S \subseteq \Delta\}$ and $\prec_\Delta$ be the partial order over D_Δ where $d_S \prec_\Delta d_{S'}$ if

$$\Sigma_{\Phi_i \in S} reward(\Phi_i) - \Sigma_{\Phi_i \notin S} penalty(\Phi_i) \geq \Sigma_{\Phi_i \in S'} reward(\Phi_i) - \Sigma_{\Phi_i \notin S'} penalty(\Phi_i).$$

We can show that $(D_\Delta, \emptyset, \prec_\Delta)$ is a goal default theory with priorities representing the given planning problem, i.e., any preferred solution of $(D_\Delta, \emptyset, \prec_\Delta)$ is a solution of the original planning problem and vice versa.

6.2 $\mathcal{PP}$

The language $\mathcal{PP}$ introduced in [13] allows the specification of basic desires, atomic preferences, and general preferences. In [6], the language $\mathcal{PP}$ is modified and extended with aggregate formulae. The modification and extension are applied over general preferences. We discuss how basic desires and atomic preferences can be encoded as a goal default theory with priorities. We will also identify a difficulty in expressing a general preference as a goal default theory with priorities.

- *Basic desires*: a basic desire φ is a preference over a trajectory and, therefore, is a part of the basic goal language described in Section 3.
- *Atomic preferences*: an atomic preference is an ordering among basic desires $\Phi = \Phi_1 \lhd \Phi_2 \ldots \lhd \Phi_k$ and expresses that the preference Φ_i is more important than Φ_{i+1} for $1 \leq i < k-1$. The semantics of $\mathcal{PP}$ states that a plan δ is a solution of Φ if there exists no plan δ' such that there exists some i and *(i)* for every $j < i$, $\delta \models \Phi_j$ iff $\delta' \models \Phi_j$, and *(ii)* $\delta \not\models \Phi_i$ while $\delta' \models \Phi_i$. It is easy to see that an atomic preference Φ can be represented by the following goal default theory with priorities

$$\left(\left\{ \frac{\top : \Phi_i}{\Phi_i} \;\middle|\; i = 1, \ldots, k \right\}, \emptyset, \prec_\Phi \right)$$

  where $\prec_\Phi$ is defined by $\frac{\top : \Phi_i}{\Phi_i} \prec_\Phi \frac{\top : \Phi_j}{\Phi_j}$ for $1 \leq i < j \leq k$.
- *General preferences*: a general preference is either an atomic preference or a combination of general preferences such as $\Phi \& \Psi$, $\Phi | \Psi$, and $!\Phi$ where Φ and Ψ are general preferences. Intuitively, general preferences add finitely many levels to the specification of preferences and thus cannot be easily represented by goal default theories which assume ceteris paribus over the preferences. Adding priorities allows only an extra layer of comparison between preferences. We view this as a weakness of goal default theories and plan to further investigate this issue.

6.3   N-LTL and ER-LTL

N-LTL is defined in [4] and it allows the specification of weak and strong exceptions within goal formulae represented as LTL-formulae. An N-LTL theory consists of a set of rules of the form $\langle e : f \rangle$, where e is a label drawn from a set of labels R (which contains a distinct element g) and f is an LTL-formula over P (as defined in (1)) extended with the following constructs

$$\langle f \rangle ::= [\langle r \rangle](\langle f \rangle) \mid [[\langle r \rangle]](\langle f \rangle) \tag{13}$$

where $\langle r \rangle$ is a label in R. $[\langle r \rangle](\langle f \rangle)$ denotes that normally $\langle f \rangle$ is true with the weak exception denoted by $\langle r \rangle$, while $[[\langle r \rangle]](\langle f \rangle)$ denotes that normally $\langle f \rangle$ is true with the strong exception denoted by $\langle r \rangle$. A label a depends on a label b if b occurs in the body of a rule of the form $\langle a : f \rangle$. The notion of dependency between labels is extended by transitivity. A theory is said to be loop-free if there is no label r which depends on itself. In [4], the semantics of an N-LTL theory is defined for loop-free N-LTL theories by compiling away the extended constructs $[\langle r \rangle]$ and $[[\langle r \rangle]]$ to create a single LTL-formula. In this sense, $\mathcal{G}_b$ subsumes N-LTL.

ER-LTL [5] replaces the two constructs in (13) by the single construct

$$[\langle r \rangle](\langle f_1 \rangle \rightsquigarrow \langle f_2 \rangle) \tag{14}$$

which states that normally, if the precondition $\langle f_1 \rangle$ is satisfied then the consequence $\langle f_2 \rangle$ should be satisfied except for the exceptions indicated by $\langle r \rangle$. Again, the semantics of an ER-LTL theory is defined by a compilation process that creates an LTL-formula, and thus, we can conclude that $\mathcal{G}_b$ also subsumes ER-LTL.

Observe that the constructs in (13) or (14) are fairly close to default logic. We believe that interesting collections of N-LTL (ER-LTL) theories can be translated into goal default theories—which would provide a reasonable semantics for N-LTL (ER-LTL) theories with loops. For simple cases, there is a straightforward translation of N-LTL (ER-LTL) formulae to p-defaults. For example, if Φ and Ψ are LTL-formulae then the formula $[r]\Phi$ could be viewed as the p-default $\frac{\top \,:\, \neg ab_r}{\Phi}$ where ab_r denotes that the rule r is applicable; the formula $[r] : (\Phi \rightsquigarrow \Psi)$ can be represented by $\frac{\Phi \,:\, \neg ab_r}{\Psi}$. However, N-LTL (ER-LTL) formulae allow, for example, labels to be nested and this straightforward translation will not be sufficient. We leave this question of how to translate arbitrary N-LTL (ER-LTL) theories into goal default theories as future work.

Finally, we would like to note that $\mathcal{G}_b$ can be easily extended to consider N-LTL (ER-LTL) formulae by extending

- $\mathcal{F}_b$ with N-LTL (ER-LTL) formulae;
- $\models_{\mathcal{G}_b}$ to define that $\delta \models_{\mathcal{G}_b} S$ iff $\delta \models_{\mathcal{G}_b} c(S)$ where $c(S)$, a LTL formula, denotes the result of compiling S to an LTL formula as described in [4, 5].

6.4 π-CTL* and P-CTL*

With the exception of the language $\mathcal{PP}$, which considers non-deterministic domains, all other goal specification languages are defined only for deterministic systems. $\mathcal{PP}$, however, only deals with trajectories. In presence of non-deterministic actions, we need to expand the notion of a plan from a simple sequence of actions to a policy, i.e., a mapping from states to actions. As such, preferences should be defined over policies. The language π-CTL* [2], which is an extension of CTL*, is defined for expressing goals in non-deterministic domains, but does not allow for preferences among goals to be defined.

To relate our goal language with π-CTL* we need to review its basic definitions. There are two kinds of formulae in CTL*: state formulae and path formulae. Let $\langle p \rangle$ denote an atomic proposition, $\langle sf \rangle$ denotes state a formula, and $\langle pf \rangle$ denotes a path formula. The syntax of state and path formulae in π-CTL* is as follows.

$$\langle sf \rangle ::= \langle p \rangle \mid \langle sf \rangle \wedge \langle sf \rangle \mid \langle sf \rangle \vee \langle sf \rangle \mid \neg \langle sf \rangle \mid \mathsf{E} \langle pf \rangle \mid \mathsf{A} \langle pf \rangle \mid \mathsf{E}_\pi \langle pf \rangle \mid \mathsf{A}_\pi \langle pf \rangle$$
$$\langle pf \rangle ::= \langle sf \rangle \mid \langle pf \rangle \vee \langle pf \rangle \mid \neg \langle pf \rangle \mid \langle pf \rangle \wedge \langle pf \rangle \mid \langle pf \rangle \ \mathsf{U} \ \langle pf \rangle \mid \bigcirc \langle pf \rangle \mid \Diamond \langle pf \rangle \mid \Box \langle pf \rangle$$

Intuitively, state formulae are properties of states, while path formulae are properties of paths. Compared to CTL*, π-CTL* introduces two new constructs: E_π and A_π, whose intuitive readings are: there is a path (resp. for all paths) that is (are) consistent with respect to the policy π. These two constructs address the issues raised in [2].

Given a transition system T and a policy π, π-CTL* formulae are interpreted with respect a state s. For a run $\sigma = s_0 a_0 s_1 a_1 \ldots s_n a_n s_{n+1} \ldots$ in T, by $traj(\sigma)$ we denote the trajectory $s_0, s_1, \ldots, s_n, s_{n+1} \ldots$ obtained from σ by removing every occurrence of actions in σ. The entailment of a state formula φ with respect to a state s and a policy π, denoted by $(s, \pi) \models \varphi$, is defined as follows:

- $(s, \pi) \models p$ iff $s \models p$
- $(s, \pi) \models \neg f$ iff $(s, \pi) \not\models f$
- $(s, \pi) \models f \vee f'$ iff $(s, \pi) \models f$ or $(s, \pi) \models f'$
- $(s, \pi) \models f \wedge f'$ iff $(s, \pi) \models f$ and $(s, \pi) \models f'$
- $(s, \pi) \models \mathsf{E} \ pf$ iff there exists a run $\sigma = s_0 a_0 s_1 a_1 \ldots s_n a_n s_{n+1}$ in T such that $s_0 = s$ and $(traj(\sigma), \pi) \models pf$
- $(s, \pi) \models \mathsf{A} \ pf$ iff for every run $\sigma = s_0 a_0 s_1 a_1 \ldots s_n a_n s_{n+1}$ in T such that $s_0 = s$, we have that $(traj(\sigma), \pi) \models pf$
- $(s, \pi) \models \mathsf{E}_\pi \ pf$ iff there exists a run $\sigma = s_0 a_0 s_1 a_1 \ldots s_n a_n s_{n+1}$ induced by π in T such that $s_0 = s$ and $(traj(\sigma), \pi) \models pf$
- $(s, \pi) \models \mathsf{A}_\pi \ pf$ iff for every run $\sigma = s_0 a_0 s_1 a_1 \ldots s_n a_n s_{n+1}$ induced by π in T such that $s_0 = s$, we have that $((traj(\sigma), \pi) \models pf$

The entailment of a path formula φ is defined with respect to a trajectory $\sigma = s_0, s_1, \ldots$, and is denoted by $(\sigma, \pi) \models \varphi$ where:

- $(\sigma, \pi) \models sf$ iff $(s_0, \pi) \models sf$
- $(\sigma, \pi) \models \neg pf$ iff $(\sigma, \pi) \not\models pf$
- $(\sigma, \pi) \models pf_1 \wedge pf_2$ iff $(\sigma, \pi) \models pf_1$ and $(\sigma, \pi) \models pf_2$
- $(\sigma, \pi) \models pf_1 \vee pf_2$ iff $(\sigma, \pi) \models pf_1$ or $(\sigma, \pi) \models pf_2$
- $(\sigma, \pi) \models \bigcirc pf$ iff $(\sigma_1, \pi) \models pf$
- $(\sigma, \pi) \models \Box pf$ iff $(\sigma_i, \pi) \models pf$ for each $i \geq 0$
- $(\sigma, \pi) \models \Diamond pf$ iff $(\sigma_i, \pi) \models pf$ for some $i \geq 0$
- $(\sigma, \pi) \models pf_1 \mathsf{U} pf_2$ iff there is $k \geq 0$ such that $(\sigma_k, \pi) \models pf_2$ and for all $0 \leq i < k$ we have $(\sigma_i, \pi) \models pf_1$.

A planning problem is a triple $P = \langle T, \{s\}, \Phi \rangle$ where T is a transition system, s is a state, and Φ is a π-CTL* path formula. A policy π is a solution of P if $(traj(\sigma_s), \pi) \models \Phi$ where σ_s is the run induced by π with $s_0 = s$.

Observe that the set of formulae $\mathcal{F}_b$ contains path formulae of π-CTL* which do not contain the operators A, E, A_π, and E_π. Nevertheless, the definition of entailment $\models_{\mathcal{G}_b}$, as defined in Section 3, does take into consideration the policy in its definition. Indeed, we can show that if Φ is a π-CTL* formula, which belongs to $\mathcal{F}_b$, and s is a state then for every policy π, $(s, \pi) \models \Phi$ then π is a solution to the planning problem $\langle T, \{s\}, \Phi \rangle$. Thus, the CTL* part of π-CTL* can be expressed in $\mathcal{G}_b$. It is easy to see that $\mathcal{G}_b$ can be extended to allow formulae of π-CTL*.

π-CTL* was developed for specifying goals in non-deterministic systems. It does not provide means for specifying preferences between goals in π-CTL*. This is addressed in P-CTL* [3] by adding the two quantifiers $\mathcal{EP}$ and $\mathcal{AP}$ over state formulae. We observe that using goal default theories or goal default theories with priorities, we can easily introduce preferences into π-CTL* but the two new operators are not expressible in our goal language.

7 Conclusions and Future Work

In this paper, we describe a default logic based approach to defining non-monotonic goal specification languages. We start with a basic goal specification language and use default logic (or prioritizing default logic) to provide a natural way for dealing with inconsistency and priorities over goals. We show that the new language subsumes some goal languages in the literature and can describe several features from other goal languages. We identify desirable features that cannot be easily expressed by our goal language, among them is the multi-level of preferences between goals, which we intend to investigate in the near future. We also discuss possible applications of the proposed goal language.

Acknowledgments. The first two authors were partially supported by the NSF grants HRD-1345232 and DGE-0947465.

References

[1] Baier, J.A., Bacchus, F., McIlraith, S.A.: A heuristic search approach to planning with temporally extended preferences. Artif. Intell. 173(5-6), 593–618 (2009)

[2] Baral, C., Zhao, J.: Goal specification in presence of non-deterministic actions. In: de Mántaras, R.L., Saitta, L. (eds.) Proceedings of the 16th Eureopean Conference on Artificial Intelligence, ECAI 2004, including Prestigious Applicants of Intelligent Systems, PAIS 2004, Valencia, Spain, August 22-27, pp. 273–277. IOS Press (2004)

[3] Baral, C., Zhao, J.: Goal specification, non-determinism and quantifying over policies. In: Proceedings of the Twenty-First National Conference on Artificial Intelligence and the Eighteenth Innovative Applications of Artificial Intelligence Conference, July 16-20, AAAI Press, Boston (2006)

[4] Baral, C., Zhao, J.: Non-monotonic temporal logics for goal specification. In: Veloso, M.M. (ed.) IJCAI 2007, Proceedings of the 20th International Joint Conference on Artificial Intelligence, Hyderabad, India, January 6-12, pp. 236–242 (2007)

[5] Baral, C., Zhao, J.: Non-monotonic temporal logics that facilitate elaboration tolerant revision of goals. In: Fox, D., Gomes, C.P. (eds.) Proceedings of the Twenty-Third AAAI Conference on Artificial Intelligence, AAAI 2008, Chicago, Illinois, July 13-17, pp. 406–411. AAAI Press (2008)

[6] Bienvenu, M., Fritz, C., McIlraith, S.: Planning with qualitative temporal preferences. In: Proceedings of the 10th International Conference on Principles of Knowledge Representation and Reasoning (KR 2006), Lake District, UK, pp. 134–144 (June 2006), 200603101347_KR06BienvenuM.pdf

[7] Brewka, G., Eiter, T.: Prioritizing default logic. In: Intellectics and Computational Logic. Applied Logic Series, vol. 19, pp. 27–45. Kluwer (2000)

[8] Delgrande, J., Schaub, T.: Expressing preferences in default logic. Artificial Intelligence 123, 41–87 (2000)

[9] Emerson, E.A.: Temporal and modal logic. In: van Leeuwen, J. (ed.) Handbook of Theoretical Computer Science, vol. B, pp. 995–1072. MIT Press (1990)

[10] Fox, M., Long, D.: PDDL2.1: An Extension to PDDL for Expressing Temporal Planning Domains. Journal of Artificial Intelligence Research 20, 61–124 (2003)

[11] Pnueli, A.: The temporal logic of programs. In: Proceedings of the 18th IEEE Symposium on Foundations of Computer Science (FOCS), pp. 46–57 (1977)

[12] Reiter, R.: A logic for default reasoning. Artificial Intelligence 13(1,2), 81–132 (1980)

[13] Son, T.C., Pontelli, E.: Planning with Preferences using Logic Programming. Theory and Practice of Logic Programming 6, 559–607 (2006)

Explaining Preferences and Preferring Explanations[*]

Pedro Cabalar and Jorge Fandiño

Department of Computer Science
University of Corunna, Spain
{cabalar,jorge.fandino}@udc.es

Abstract. In this paper we study the possibility of providing causal explanations for preferred answer sets, such as those obtained from logic programs with ordered disjunction (LPODs). We use a recently defined multi-valued semantics for answer sets based on a causal algebra and consider its direct application to LPODs by several illustrating examples. We also explain the limitations of this simple approach and enumerate some open topics to be explored in the future.

1 Introduction

Although much work in problem solving has been devoted to problems with a small set of solutions that are hard to find, there are many other situations in which the number of solutions is astronomical, but not all of them are preferred in the same way. Think, for instance, on the configuration of a timetable for a university or a school: there exists a huge number of combinations with physically feasible timetables, but most of them do not have a *reasonable* distribution.

The definition of a suitable Knowledge Representation (KR) language for specifying preferences has proved to be a difficult endeavour. Apart from the long list of features usually expected from a KR formalism (simplicity, clear semantics, flexibility, elaboration tolerance, computability, complexity assessment, efficient inference methods, etc), the specification of preferences has an extra difficulty that has to do with their *subjective, ambiguous definition*. For instance, while any student or teacher could easily tell why a given random timetable is not reasonable, it is very difficult to formally encode all the preferences that capture the commonsense idea of "*reasonable timetable*" in the general case – furthermore, there would not be a complete agreement among different persons either and, in a multi-agent setting, taking into account everyone's preferences means seeking for a kind of compromise. But even when we have a single person, she may initially declare a list of preferences such as "*A is better than B.*" However, when this list grows, the results obtained by formal systems are usually far away from the expected outcomes that the person had in mind. To bridge the gap, several refinements can be applied, such as adding conditional preferences or including an ordering among them. Still, while the strict physical rules that govern a timetable assignment are objective and accurate, it is practically impossible to guarantee that the set of preferences is working *as expected* from a commonsense point of view.

Although there exist both qualitative and quantitative approaches for dealing with preferences in Artificial Intelligence, the interest in KR has been mostly focused on

[*] This research was partially supported by Spanish MEC project TIN2013-42149-P.

T. Eiter et al. (Eds.): Brewka Festschrift, LNAI 9060, pp. 218–232, 2015.

the qualitative orientation, probably because it is closer to commonsense reasoning, as humans rarely express their preferences in numerical terms[1].

As explained in [7], the relation between preferences and Non-Monotonic Reasoning (NMR) has been evident from the very beginning. On the one hand, the nature of preferences is clearly non-monotonic: the addition of new preferences may drastically change the obtained conclusions. On the other hand, we can also see a default as a kind of preference specification: a sentence like "birds normally fly" can be read as "if X is a bird, my *preferred belief* is that X flies." Indeed, many non-monotonic formalisms are defined in terms of a preference relation among logical models of a theory.

When one mentions research on preferences and NMR there is one researcher's name that immediately comes to mind: *Gerhard Brewka*. Being one of the pioneers in NMR, Gerd soon became interested in the topic of preferences, proposing extensions of Reiter's Default Logic [26] to include priorities among defaults [1,2]. He also got interested on an emerging problem solving paradigm, *Answer Set Programming* (ASP) [22,21] whose semantics (*stable models* [16] or *answer sets*) can also be seen as a particular case of Default Logic. ASP has become nowadays [5] a de facto standard for practical NMR and problem solving thanks to its clear semantics and the availability of efficient solvers together with a wide spectrum of applications running in real scenarios. In 1998, Gerd coauthored, together with Thomas Eiter, one of the first remarkable approaches of preferences in ASP [4]. Four years later, he introduced a different orientation called *Logic Programs with Ordered Disjunction* (LPODs) [3]. In LPODs, logic programs were extended with a new connective called *ordered disjunction* allowing the representation of ranked options for problem solutions in the heads of rules. As a result, LPODs provided a flexible and readable way for expressing (conditional) preferences combined with the expressiveness of default negation already embodied in ASP. Originally, the semantics of LPODs relied on an adapted definition of answer sets or, alternatively, resorted to program transformations (so-called "split programs"). However, in [8], it was shown how the ordered disjunction connective could be naturally captured in *Equilibrium Logic* [23], the most general logical characterisation of ASP. This actually allows seeing LPODs as a "regular" type of ASP programs extended with an additional preference relation on answer sets.

As we explained before, in a practical scenario, one can expect that the specification of preferences is obtained after several attempts and refinements, by repeatedly observing the obtained results and comparing them to the expected behaviour. In such a context, it seems clear that explanations play a fundamental role. There exist several approaches in the ASP literature focused on providing explanations for debugging [15,25,27,12] or obtaining justifications for the program outcome [24,13,29]. In a recent proposal [9], the idea of *causal justifications* for ASP programs was introduced. These causal justifications are embodied in ASP as a multi-valued extension where each true atom in a stable model is associated with an expression involving rule labels corresponding to the alternative proofs to derive the atom.

---

[1] An exception is, perhaps, when we consider optimization problems (minimizing cost, maximizing profit, etc) as an instance of preference specification. In any case, we mean here that, even though we are sometimes able to assign numerical weights to preferences, this is not usually present at our commonsense level, but a forced assignment *a posteriori*.

In this paper we study the possibility of providing explanations for LPODs. As a first direct attempt, we have considered the combination of LPODs with causal justifications, showing its behaviour on several examples. We also explain how it may seem sometimes reasonable to provide preferences, not only among program rules, but also on the explanations obtained. Finally, we discuss the obvious limitations of this first approach and foresee some interesting open topics to be explore in the future.

2   Logic Programs with Ordered Disjunction

In this section we begin providing some preliminary definitions and notation and then proceed to recall the definition of LPODs, both in its original formulation and in terms of a logical characterisation found in [8].

2.1   Preliminaries

We begin introducing some preliminary notation that will be useful later. Let $\mathbf{A}$ be a (possibly empty) sequence of (possibly repeated) formulas. We write $|\mathbf{A}|$ to stand for the length of $\mathbf{A}$. For any $k \in \{1, \ldots, |\mathbf{A}|\}$, by $\mathbf{A}[k]$ we mean the k-th expression in $\mathbf{A}$ and by $\mathbf{A}[1..k]$, the prefix of $\mathbf{A}$ of length k, that is, $(\mathbf{A}[1] \ldots \mathbf{A}[k])$. For a binary operator $\odot \in \{\vee, \wedge, \times\}$, by $(\odot \mathbf{A})$ we mean the formula resulting from the repeated application of $\odot$ to all formulas in $\mathbf{A}$ in the same ordering. As an example, given the sequence of atoms $\mathbf{A} = (a, b, c, d, e)$, the expression $(\times \mathbf{A}[1..3])$ represents the formula $a \times b \times c$. We write $not\ \mathbf{A}$ to stand for the sequence of formulas $(\ (not\ \mathbf{A}[1]) \ldots (not\ \mathbf{A}[k])\ )$ where $k = |\mathbf{A}|$. An empty conjunction is understood as $\top$ whereas an empty disjunction (both ordered $\times$ or regular $\vee$) is understood as $\bot$. The concatenation of two lists of formulas, $\mathbf{A}$ and $\mathbf{B}$, is simply written as $\mathbf{AB}$.

A *logic program* is a set of rules of the form:

$$(\vee \mathbf{A}) \vee (\vee not\ \mathbf{A}') \leftarrow (\wedge \mathbf{B}) \wedge (\wedge\ not\ \mathbf{B}') \tag{1}$$

where $\mathbf{A}, \mathbf{A}', \mathbf{B}$ and $\mathbf{B}'$ are lists of atoms. The consequent and antecedent of the implication above are respectively called the *head* and the *body* of the rule. In the examples, we will usually represent conjunctions in the body as commas, to follow the standard ASP notation. A rule with an empty head $\bot$ (that is, $|\mathbf{A}| + |\mathbf{A}'| = 0$) is called a *constraint*. A rule with an empty body $\top$ (that is, $|\mathbf{B}| + |\mathbf{B}'| = 0$) is called a *fact*, and we usually write the head F instead of $F \leftarrow \top$. A rule is said to be *normal* when $|\mathbf{A}| = 1$ and $|\mathbf{A}'| = 0$. A rule is *positive* when $|\mathbf{A}'| = |\mathbf{B}'| = 0$. We extend the use of these adjectives to a program, meaning that all its rules are of the same kind.

A rule head[2] of the form $p \vee \neg p$ behaves as a choice rule: we are free to include p or not. This kind of head is usually written as $\{p\}$ in ASP and we will sometimes use it too to increase readability.

---

[2] It can be noted that we allow the use of default negation in the head. This feature was first defined by [18]. The paper [20] explained how negation in the head could be expressed as double negation in the body. In [19], Janhunen proved that default negation in the head can be removed by a polynomial introduction of auxiliary atoms, showing that this feature does not introduce new expressiveness. However, it must be noted that this kind of programs may have non-minimal stable models, something that does not happen if default negation is not allowed in the head. As a final remark, [11] proved that rules of form (1) actually constitute a normal form for equilibrium logic [23] or, equivalently, for stable models for arbitrary propositional theories [14].

Answer sets of a program P are defined in terms of the classical Gelfond-Lifschitz reduct [16], that is extended as follows for the syntactic case we are considering (disjunctive heads with default negation [18]). The *reduct* of a program P with respect to a set of atoms I, written P^I, consists of a rule of the form $(\vee \mathbf{A}) \leftarrow (\wedge \mathbf{B})$ per each rule in P of the form (1) that satisfies $I \models (\wedge \mathbf{A}') \wedge (\wedge \textit{not } \mathbf{B}')$. We say that a set of atoms I is an *answer set* of a program P if I is a minimal model of P^I.

Answer sets differ from stable models in that they further allow a new negation (also called *classical*, *explicit*, or *strong* negation). For simplicity, we will understand strong negation of an atom p as a new atom "$\neg p$" and assume that each time one of these "negative" atoms is used, we implicitly further include the constraint:

$$\bot \leftarrow p, \neg p$$

2.2   LPODs: Original Definition

A *logic program with ordered disjunction* (LPOD) is a set of rules of the form:

$$(\times \mathbf{A}) \leftarrow (\wedge \mathbf{B}) \wedge (\wedge \textit{not } \mathbf{B}') \tag{2}$$

where $\mathbf{A}, \mathbf{B}$ and $\mathbf{B}'$ are lists of atoms. We say that a set of atoms I *satisfies* an LPOD rule r such as (2), written $I \models r$, when $I \models (\vee \mathbf{A}) \leftarrow (\wedge \mathbf{B}) \wedge (\wedge \textit{not } \mathbf{B}')$ in classical logic.

For each LPOD rule r of the form (2), we define its k-th *option*, written r_k, with $k \in \{1, \dots, |\mathbf{A}|\}$, as the normal rule:

$$\mathbf{A}[k] \leftarrow (\wedge \mathbf{B}) \wedge (\wedge \textit{not } \mathbf{B}') \wedge (\wedge \textit{not } \mathbf{A}[1..k{-}1])$$

A normal logic program P' is a *split program* of P if it is the result of replacing each LPOD rule $r \in P$ by one of its possible options r_k. A set of atoms I is an *answer set* of P if it is an answer set of some split program P' of P.

Example 1 (From [6]). Let P_1 be the LPOD:

$$a \times b \leftarrow \textit{not } c \qquad\qquad b \times c \leftarrow \textit{not } d$$

This LPOD has four split programs:

$$P_1 = \begin{cases} a \leftarrow \textit{not } c \\ b \leftarrow \textit{not } d \end{cases} \qquad P_2 = \begin{cases} a \leftarrow \textit{not } c \\ c \leftarrow \textit{not } d, \textit{not } b \end{cases}$$

$$P_3 = \begin{cases} b \leftarrow \textit{not } c, \textit{not } a \\ b \leftarrow \textit{not } d \end{cases} \qquad P_4 = \begin{cases} b \leftarrow \textit{not } c, \textit{not } a \\ c \leftarrow \textit{not } d, \textit{not } b \end{cases}$$

that yield three answer sets $\{a,b\}$ (from P_1), $\{c\}$ (from P_2 and P_4) and $\{b\}$ (from P_3 and P_4). $\qquad\qquad\square$

As explained in [6], answer sets of LPODs can also be described in terms of a program reduct, instead of using split programs.

Definition 1 (×**-reduct**). *The* ×*-reduct of an LPOD rule r such as* (2) *with respect to a set of atoms I denoted as* $r^I_\times$ *and defined as the set of rules:*

$$\mathbf{A}[i] \leftarrow (\wedge \mathbf{B}) \tag{3}$$

for all $i = 1, \ldots, |\mathbf{A}|$ *such that* $I \models (\wedge\ not\ \mathbf{B}') \wedge (\wedge\ not\ \mathbf{A}[1..i-1]) \wedge \mathbf{A}[i].$ □

As expected, the ×-*reduct* of an LPOD P with respect to I, written $P^I_\times$ is the union of all $r^I_\times$ for all LPOD rules $r \in P$. For instance, for $I = \{b,c\}$ and P:

$$a \times b \leftarrow c, not\ d \tag{4}$$

$$d \times a \leftarrow not\ b \tag{5}$$

$$d \times e \leftarrow not\ a \tag{6}$$

the reduct $P^I_\times$ would be the rule $\{b \leftarrow c\}$. Notice that $P^I_\times$ defined in this way is always a positive (non-disjunctive) logic program and so it has a least model [28].

Theorem 1 (**Brewka et al.** [6]). *A set of atoms I is an answer set of an LPOD P iff* $I \models P$ *and I is the least model of* $P^I_\times$. □

It is important to note that $I \models P^I_\times$ does not imply $I \models P$, and thus, the latter is also required in the above theorem. For instance, in the last example, the interpretation $\emptyset$ is the least model of $P^I_\times$ but does not satisfy the LPOD rule (6).

Three ordering relations can be used for selecting preferred answer sets. We say that an LPOD rule r of the form (2) is *satisfied to degree* $j \in \{1, \ldots, |\mathbf{A}|\}$ by a set of atoms I, written $I \models_j r$, when: I does not satisfy the body of r and $j = 1$; I satisfies the body of r and j is the minimum index for which $\mathbf{A}[j] \in I$. We define $deg_I(r) \overset{\text{def}}{=} j$ when $I \models_j r$ and define the set $I^j(P) \overset{\text{def}}{=} \{r \in P \mid I \models_j r\}$. Given two answer sets I, J of a given LPOD:

1. I is *cardinality-preferred* to J, written $I >_c J$, when for some truth degree k, $|I^k(P)| > |J^k(P)|$ whereas $|I^i(P)| = |J^i(P)|$ for all $i < k$.
2. I is *inclusion-preferred* to J, written $I >_i J$, when for some truth degree k, $J^k(P) \subset I^k(P)$ while $I^i(P) = J^i(P)$ for all $i < k$.
3. I is *Pareto-preferred* to J, written $I >_p J$, if for some rule $r \in P$, $deg_I(r) < deg_J(r)$ whereas for no rule $r' \in P$, $deg_I(r') > deg_J(r')$.

As an example, suppose we have a program with three preference rules r, s and t and that we get four answer sets I_1, I_2, I_3 and I_4 so that the degree of satisfaction for each rule in each interpretation is given by the table:

	r	s	t
I_1	1	2	1
I_2	1	1	2
I_3	1	3	2
I_4	1	3	4

Then, under cardinality preference we get that I_1 and I_2 are equally preferred, because they both have two rules with degree 1 and one rule with degree 2. $I_1 >_c I_3$ because I_3 only has one rule with degree 1, whereas $I_3 >_c I_4$ because they tie in 1's but I_3 has a 2 and I_4 no. As for the inclusion preference, I_1 and I_2 are now not comparable, since their sets of rules with degree 1 cannot be included one on another. However, we have $I_1 >_i I_3$ and $I_1 >_i I_4$ because the set of 1's in I_3 and I_4 are a subset of those in I_1. The same happens with $I_2 >_i I_3$ and $I_2 >_i I_4$. Finally, for Pareto preference, we get that I_1, I_2 and I_3 are all preferred to I_4 because the latter has equal or worse degree in all rules, one by one. Similarly, I_3 is less preferred than I_1 or I_2. However, I_1 is unrelated to I_2 because it has a better degree for rule t but worse degree for rule s.

2.3 Ordered Disjunction as an Operator

As explained in the introduction, in [8] it was shown how the original definition of answer sets for LPODs can be alternatively characterised by a logical encoding into Equilibrium Logic [23], and in particular, into its monotonic basis called the logic of *here-and-there* (HT) [17]. [8] showed that the expression $A \times B$ can be defined in HT as $A \vee (not\ A \wedge B)$. As a result of some simple transformations in the logic of HT, it was possible to prove that a rule of the form (2) can be seen as an abbreviation of the conjunction of the following rules:

$$\mathbf{A}[k] \vee not\ \mathbf{A}[k] \leftarrow (\wedge \mathbf{B}) \wedge (\wedge\ not\ \mathbf{B}') \wedge (\wedge\ not\ \mathbf{A}[1..k-1]) \tag{7}$$

$$\bot \leftarrow (\wedge \mathbf{B}) \wedge (\wedge\ not\ \mathbf{B}') \wedge (\wedge\ not\ \mathbf{A}) \tag{8}$$

for all $k = 1, \ldots, |\mathbf{A}|$. For a rule r like (2) we denote each rule (7) by $r[k]$. As an example, the HT translation of the LPOD rule $r : a \times b \times c \leftarrow p, not\ q$ consists of:

$$r[1]: \quad a \vee not\ a \leftarrow p, not\ q$$
$$r[2]: \quad b \vee not\ b \leftarrow p, not\ q, not\ a$$
$$r[3]: \quad c \vee not\ c \leftarrow p, not\ q, not\ a, not\ b$$
$$\bot \leftarrow p, not\ q, not\ a, not\ b, not\ c$$

Note that rule heads have the form of choice expressions: as explained before, we would usually write $a \vee \neg a$ as $\{a\}$. So, essentially, $r[1]$ says that when $p \wedge not\ q$, we have freedom to choose a or not. In its turn, $r[2]$ further says that if, additionally, a is false, then we can freely choose b or not, and so on. The constraint just checks that at least one choice is eventually chosen.

At a first sight, this definition may seem similar to the one based on split programs. Note that, in fact, $r[k]$ can be seen as a weaker version of the previously defined r_k where we have just added $not\ \mathbf{A}[k]$ with a disjunction in the head. However, it is important to note that the HT translation provides a unique ASP program and that the translation of each LPOD rule (2) is modular, so we can safely understand it as an abbreviation of all the rules (7) and (8).

3   Causal Justifications

In this section, we recall several definitions and notation from [9]. The intuitive idea is that atoms in a stable model will be assigned algebraic expressions instead of truth values 0, 1. These algebraic expressions are built with labels for the program rules plus three operations: a product '∗' meaning conjunction or joint causation; a concatenation '·' meaning ordered sequence of application of terms; and an addition '+' meaning different alternative proofs for a same atom.

A *signature* is a pair ⟨*At*, *Lb*⟩ of sets that respectively represent *atoms* (or *propositions*) and rule *labels*.

The syntax is defined as follows. As usual, a *literal* is defined as an atom p (positive literal) or its default negation *not* p (negative literal). In this paper, we will concentrate on programs without disjunction in the head (leaving its treatment for future work).

Definition 2 (Causal logic program). *Given a signature* ⟨*At*, *Lb*⟩, *a* (causal) *logic program P is a set of rules of the form*[3]:

$$t : H \vee (\vee \text{not } \mathbf{A}') \leftarrow (\wedge \mathbf{B}) \wedge (\wedge \text{ not } \mathbf{B}') \tag{9}$$

where $t \in Lb \cup \{1\}$ *where H is an atom and* $\mathbf{A}, \mathbf{B}, \mathbf{B}'$ *lists of atoms as before.*   □

For any rule R of the form (9) we define $label(R) \overset{\text{def}}{=} t$. When $t \in Lb$ we say that the rule is labelled; otherwise $t = 1$ and we omit both t and ':'. By these conventions, for instance, an unlabelled fact p is actually an abbreviation of $(1 : p \leftarrow)$. A logic program P is *positive* if it contains no default negation.

The semantics relies on assigning, to each atom, a causal term defined as follows.

Definition 3 (Causal term). *A* (causal) *term, t, over a set of labels Lb, is recursively defined as one of the following expressions* $t ::= l \mid \prod S \mid \sum S \mid t_1 \cdot t_2 \mid (t_1)$ *where* $l \in Lb$, t_1, t_2 *are in their turn causal terms and S is a (possibly empty and possible infinite) set of causal terms. When S is finite and non-empty,* $S = \{t_1, \ldots, t_n\}$ *we write* $\prod S$ *simply as* $t_1 * \cdots * t_n$ *and* $\sum S$ *as* $t_1 + \cdots + t_n$. *The set of causal terms is denoted by* $\mathbf{T}_{Lb}$.   □

We assume that '∗' has higher priority (lower precedence) than '+'. When $S = \emptyset$, we denote $\prod S$ by 1 and $\sum S$ by 0. These values are the indentities for the product and the addition, respectively. All three operations, '∗', '+' and '·' are associative. Furthermore, '∗' and '+' are commutative and they hold the usual absorption and distributive laws with respect to infinite sums and products of any completely distributive lattice, as shown[4] in Figure 1. The behaviour of the '·' operator is captured by the properties

---

[3] Note that disjunction of positive atoms are not allowed. In this paper, such a feature is unnecessary whereas its introduction in causal logic programs is still under study. The main difficulty for dealing with this extension has to do with the fact that the explanation for a disjunction $A \vee B$ can be, in principle, "divided" into the two disjuncts rather than alternatively assigned to one or another. This suggests that the right encoding of a rule $a \vee b \leftarrow c$ should actually correspond to a disjunction of rules $(a \leftarrow c) \vee (b \leftarrow c)$ which is not an equivalent formulation under this multi-valued framework.

[4] For the sake of readability, we only show the properties for finite sums and products, but they still hold in the infinite case.

shown in Figure 2. As we can see, distributivity with respect to the product is only applicable to terms c, d, e without sums (this means that the empty sum, 0, is not allowed either). We define the standard order relation $\leq$ as follows:

$$t \leq u \qquad \text{iff} \qquad (t * u = t) \qquad \text{iff} \qquad (t + u = u)$$

By the identity properties of $+$ and $*$, this immediately means that 1 is the top element and 0 the bottom element of this order relation.

Associativity	Commutativity	Absorption
$t + (u{+}w) = (t{+}u) + w$	$t + u = u + t$	$t = t + (t * u)$
$t * (u{*}w) = (t * u) * w$	$t * u = u * t$	$t = t * (t{+}u)$

Distributive	Identity	Idempotence	Annihilator
$t + (u{*}w) = (t{+}u) * (t{+}w)$	$t = t + 0$	$t = t + t$	$1 = 1 + t$
$t * (u{+}w) = (t * u) + (t * w)$	$t = t * 1$	$t = t * t$	$0 = 0 * t$

Fig. 1. Sum and product satisfy the properties of a completely distributive lattice

Absorption	Associativity	Identity	Annihilator
$t \quad = t + u \cdot t \cdot w$	$t \cdot (u{\cdot}w) = (t{\cdot}u) \cdot w$	$t = 1 \cdot t$	$0 = t \cdot 0$
$u \cdot t \cdot w = t * u \cdot t \cdot w$		$t = t \cdot 1$	$0 = 0 \cdot t$

Indempotence	Addition distributivity	Product distributivity
$t \cdot t = t$	$t \cdot (u{+}w) = (t{\cdot}u) + (t{\cdot}w)$	$c \cdot d \cdot e = (c \cdot d) * (d \cdot e) \quad \text{with } d \neq 1$
	$(t + u) \cdot w = (t{\cdot}w) + (u{\cdot}w)$	$c \cdot (d * e) = (c \cdot d) * (c \cdot e)$
		$(c * d) \cdot e = (c \cdot e) * (d \cdot e)$

Fig. 2. Properties of the '$\cdot$' operator (c, d, e are terms without '$+$')

As proved in [9], any causal term can be equivalently reduced to a disjunctive normal form with an addition of products of pairs $(l \cdot l')$ where l, l' are labels. In fact, each product of pairs can be seen as a syntactic representation of a graph whose nodes are labels and with an arc (l, l') per each pair $(l \cdot l')$.

Given a signature $\langle At, Lb \rangle$ a *causal interpretation* is a mapping $I : At \rightarrow \mathbf{T}_{Lb}$ assigning a causal term to each atom. We denote the set of causal interpretations by $\mathbf{I}$. For interpretations I and J we say that $I \leq J$ whether $I(p) \leq J(p)$ for each atom $p \in At$. Hence, there is a $\leq$-bottom interpretation $\mathbf{0}$ (resp. a $\leq$-top interpretation $\mathbf{1}$) that maps each atom p to 0 (resp. 1). Valuation of formulas is defined as follows:

$$I(not\ p) = \begin{cases} 1 \text{ if } I(p) = 0 \\ 0 \text{ otherwise} \end{cases} \qquad \begin{aligned} I(\alpha \wedge \beta) &= I(\alpha) * I(\beta) \\ I(\alpha \vee \beta) &= I(\alpha) + I(\beta) \end{aligned}$$

An interpretation I *satisfies* a positive rule $t : H \leftarrow (\wedge \mathbf{B})$ when:

$$I(\wedge \mathbf{B}) \cdot t \leq I(H)$$

As usual, I is a *model* of a positive program iff it satisfies all its rules. Positive programs have a $\leq$-least model that corresponds to the least fixpoint of a direct consequences operator (see [9] for further details).

The *reduct* of a program P with respect to a causal interpretation I, written P^I, is defined in a similar manner as before. Program P^I consists of all positive rules $t : H \leftarrow (\wedge \mathbf{B})$ such that there is a rule (9) in P for which $I\big((\wedge \mathbf{A}') \wedge (\wedge \textit{not } \mathbf{B}')\big) = 1$.

Definition 4 (Causal model). *Given a positive causal logic program P, a causal interpretation I is a* causal stable model *iff I is the $\leq$-least model of P^I.*   □

In [9], it was also shown that there exists a one-to-one correspondence between causal stable models of a program and its regular stable models (when labels are ignored). Furthermore, given the causal stable model I and its corresponding two-valued stable model J, the assignment $I(p)$ for an atom p precisely captures all the (non-redundant) proofs that can be built for deriving p in the positive program P^J.

Example 2 (From [9]). Some country has a law l that asserts that driving drunk is punishable with imprisonment. On the other hand, a second law m specifies that resisting arrest has the same effect. The execution e of a sentence establishes that a punishment implies imprisonment by default but there may be exceptional cases in which this punishment is not effective. In particular, some of such exceptions are a pardon, that the punishment was revoked, or that the person has diplomatic immunity. Suppose that some person drove drunk and resisted to be arrested.   □

We can capture this scenario with the following logic program P_1:

$l : punish \leftarrow drive, drunk$	$d : drive$	$a : abnormal \leftarrow pardon$
$m : punish \leftarrow resist$	$k : drunk$	$a : abnormal \leftarrow revoke$
$e : prison \leftarrow punish, not\, abnormal$	$r : resist$	$a : abnormal \leftarrow diplomat$

This program has a unique causal stable model I where $I(abnormal) = I(pardon) = I(revoke) = I(diplomat) = 0$ (false by default), $I(drive) = d$, $I(drunk) = k$, $I(resist) = r$, $I(punish) = (d*k) \cdot l + r \cdot m$ and $I(prison) = ((d*k) \cdot l + r \cdot m) \cdot e = (d*k) \cdot l \cdot e + r \cdot m \cdot e$. If we add one of the exceptions as a fact, like for instance *pardon*, we get a new unique stable model I' where the only differences with respect to I are $I'(pardon) = 1$, $I'(abnormal) = a$ and $I'(prison) = 0$. Note that default negation does not propagate causal information (the label a for *abnormal* has no effect on *prison*).

4 Causal Explanations for a Preferred Answer Set

In this section we directly combine both approaches (LPODs and causal logic programs) by extracting explanations of LPODs expressed as causal terms. Consider the following example from [3] about how to spend a free afternoon.

Example 3 (Brewka [3]). *You like to go to the beach, but also to the cinema. Normally you prefer the cinema over the beach, unless it is hot (which is the exception in the area where you live, except during the summer). If it is hot the beach is preferred over the cinema. In summer it is normally hot, but there are exceptions. If it rains the beach is out of question.*   □

This information can be captured by the following set of rules P_1:

$$c : cinema \times beach \leftarrow not\ hot$$
$$b : beach \times cinema \leftarrow hot$$
$$h : \qquad\qquad hot \leftarrow not\ \neg hot, summer$$
$$r : \qquad \neg beach \leftarrow rain$$

This program has two choices with ordered disjunction, c and b, that respectively correspond to preferring *cinema* or *beach* depending on the context. As explained before, these rules can be unfolded into:

$$c[1] : \{cinema\} \leftarrow not\ hot$$
$$c[2] : \quad \{beach\} \leftarrow not\ hot, not\ cinema$$
$$\bot \leftarrow not\ hot, not\ cinema, not\ beach$$
$$b[1] : \{beach\} \leftarrow hot$$
$$b[2] : \{cinema\} \leftarrow hot, not\ beach$$
$$\bot \leftarrow hot, not\ beach, not\ cinema$$

Assume now that we are given the fact *summer*. The answer sets for $P_1 \cup \{summer\}$ are $J_0 = \{summer, hot, beach\}$ and $J_1 = \{summer, hot, cinema\}$ but only J_1 is preferred (under all preference orderings) since it satisfies rule b to degree 1 while J_2 only satisfies b to degree 2, and coincides in the rest of rules. As explained before, there exists one causal stable model per each regular stable model for any program P. In particular, the causal stable model I_1 corresponding to J_1 assigns the causal values $I_1(summer) = 1$, $I_1(hot) = h$, $I_1(beach) = h \cdot b[1]$ while all false atoms in J_1 are assigned the value 0. On the other hand, the causal stable model I_2 corresponding to J_2 only differs in the assignments $I(cinema) = h \cdot b[2]$ and $I(beach) = 0$. It is interesting to note that, since fact *summer* was not labelled, the truth value for that atom becomes 1 ("completely" true), which is the top element of the lattice of causal values. A second observation is that the causal value of atoms can also be used to find out the degree of satisfaction of an ordered choice rule. For instance, in I_1 we can see that rule b is being satisfied to degree 1 because the head atom in that position, *beach*, is assigned a value in which $b[1]$ occurs. Similarly, in I_2, we know that b is satisfied to degree 2 because $I_2(cinema)$ contains a reference to $b[2]$. If an LPOD contains no repeated labels, it can be checked that, for any ordered choice rule r, we will never get two different occurrences $r[i]$ and $r[k]$ with $i \neq k$ in the values of atoms in a causal stable model.

Let us continue with the example as done in [3] and assume now that we add the information $\neg hot$. That is, we consider the program program $P_1 \cup \{summer, \neg hot\}$. Then, the new preferred answer set becomes $J_3 = \{summer, \neg hot, cinema\}$ and its corresponding causal version I_3 makes the assignments $I_3(summer) = 1$, $I_3(\neg hot) = 1$ and $I_3(cinema) = c[1]$. A second, non-preferred answer set, I_4, would vary in the assignments $I_4(cinema) = 0$ and $I_4(beach) = c[2]$. Notice that I_1 and I_3 are analogous in the sense that they switch their preference orders depending on whether we had *hot* or not, respectively. However, the causal values are not completely analogous: while in I_1 the explanation for *cinema* involves two labels, $h \cdot b[1]$, in I_3 the explanation for *beach* only refers to $c[1]$. This is because the meaning of default negation in causal justifications is understood as a default precondition, rather than an actual, effective cause. To generate a symmetric with respect to I_1 we should encode rule b as:

$$b : beach \times cinema \leftarrow \neg hot$$

and, if fact $\neg hot$ were labelled to trace its effects, say using:

$$g : \neg hot$$

then $I_3(beach)$ would become $g \cdot c[1]$.

It is not difficult to see that program $P_1 \cup \{summer, rain\}$ yields a unique preferred answer set whose causal version, I_5, yields the explanations $I_5(summer) = I_5(rain) = 1$, $I_5(\neg beach) = r$, $I_5(hot) = h$ and $I_5(cinema) = h \cdot c[2]$. Note how, in this case, $cinema$ is justified by h (the rule concluding hot) and, after that, $c[2]$ meaning that we were forced to select the second choice of rule c (since $beach$ was not possible[5]).

In all the previous variations of the example, we never had alternative proofs for an atom: all true atoms had a unique possible derivation in a given answer set. This is reflected by the fact that we did not get any instances of $+$ in algebraic expressions. To illustrate this effect, suppose that whenever we go windsurfing we always go to the beach whereas, normally, when the day is windy we are in the mood for windsurfing (if nothing prevents us from doing so). To capture this refinement, assume that P_2 is program P_1 plus rules:

$$s : \quad beach \leftarrow windsurf$$
$$w : windsurf \leftarrow wind, not \neg windsurf$$

and that we are in a windy day in the summer. The program $P_2 \cup \{wind, summer\}$ has one preferred answer set I_6 whose corresponding causal explanations are $I_6(summer) = I_6(wind) = 1$, $I_6(windsurf) = w$, $I_6(hot) = h$, $I_6(beach) = h \cdot b[1] + w \cdot s$. In other words, we get two explanations for $beach$: the previous one saying that, as it is hot h, we used the first choice of rule b; plus a second one saying that, as we want to make windsurf w, we applied rule s.

5   Preferred Explanations

In [10] it was shown how the number of alternative causal explanations for an atom in a positive program may grow exponentially in the worst case. The reason for that is related to the application of distributivity, something we need when we want to express the final atom value in disjunctive normal form (sum of alternative causes). So, as we explained in the introduction, this is another case in which we may have many potential "solutions" (the causal explanations) where we may be interested in showing preferences among them.

One straightforward manner to incorporate preferences among terms in the causal values lattice is adding *axioms* involving the order relation among terms. As an elementary expression, if we add an axiom $r \leq r'$ (that is $r + r' = r'$ or equivalently $r * r' = r$)

---

[5] Remember that we implicitly assume the existence of constraint $\perp \leftarrow beach, \neg beach$.

for a pair of rule labels r, r' we will be able to remove some less preferred explanations from causal terms. For instance, think about the last variation of the example, program P_2. We may be interested in preferring explanations that involve a non-preference rule like s or w over explanations that involve a preference like b. In our case, we could add the axioms:

$$b[1] \leq s \qquad b[2] \leq s \qquad b[1] \leq w \qquad b[2] \leq w$$

As a result, we would be able to prove that:

$$b[1] + w \cdot s = \underbrace{(b[1] + w)}_{=w} \cdot \underbrace{(b[1] + s)}_{=s} = w \cdot s$$

that is, $b[1] \leq w \cdot s$. Since $h \cdot b[1] \leq b[1]$ by absorption, we conclude $h \cdot b[1] \leq w \cdot s$ and, thus, $I_6(beach) = h \cdot b[1] + w \cdot s = w \cdot s$ removing, in this way, the less preferred explanation based on rule b.

Many different preference criteria can be thought for selecting the "best" explanations. For instance, it makes sense to prefer an explanation that uses the i-th choice of an ordered disjunction rather than the one that uses a j-th choice with $i < j$. To capture that behaviour, we could define the degree n of a causal term without sums as the maximum value k occurring in any label of the form $r[k]$ (0 if no label of that form occurs), and add axiom schemata to force that causal explanations with higher degree are smaller under the causal order relation. As an example, consider the following LPOD:

$$a : p \times q \times r$$
$$b : t \times h \times p \times q$$
$$c : h \times t \times q$$
$$\bot \leftarrow p$$
$$\bot \leftarrow h$$
$$\bot \leftarrow t$$

The preferred answer set makes q true with the explanation $I(q) = a[2] + b[4] + c[3]$ that, under the criterion mentioned above, would collapse to the explanation with smallest degree $I(q) = a[2]$. In other words, the "strongest" reason for q is that we took the second choice of rule a.

6   Conclusions and Open Topics

In this paper we have presented a first exploratory attempt to provide explanations or justifications for the preferred answer sets obtained from Logic Programs with Ordered Disjunction (LPODs). At a same time, we have also discussed the possibility of incorporating preferences when there exist alternative explanations for a same atom.

The current approach is a simple first step towards the final goal of providing explanations of preferred answer sets and helping the user to refine her formal representation. There are many open topics that are interesting for future work. As a first example, when explaining the outcome of an LPOD, the approach in this paper only provides the explanation of true atoms in a given preferred answer set. This may help us to find out where did the information contained in one preferred choice come from. However, in many cases, the question of why a given fact or literal, that we know that may be true in another solution to our problem (i.e., some answer set perhaps not preferred) has not been eventually true in some preferred answer set. Answering questions of the form "why-not" has been studied in [12] for a different algebraic approach and the incorporation of this type of queries to causal justifications is currently under study. Formally, this will involve the incorporation of a negation operator in the algebra of causal values. Still, even if we are eventually able of answering "why-not" questions, the case of LPODs introduces an additional difficulty since what we would probably want is to know how the set of preferences has prevented that a literal (possible in another answer set) became true in any preferred solution.

Regarding the topic on preferring explanations, the addition of a negation operator to the causal algebra could also be interesting to express preferences like, for instance, saying that any positive proof is preferred over a proof that depends on negation (a default). In the windsurfing variant of our running example, this would mean that adding a rule of the form:

$$m : beach \leftarrow romantic$$

together with the fact $t : romantic$ should provide a stronger explanation than $w \cdot s$ since $t \cdot m$ has not applied any default, whereas w was actually a default rule.

Acknowledgments. We want to thank Gerhard Brewka for his guidance role in the NMR community and encourage him to continue with his outstanding research for many years. It is also a pleasure to attend to his presentations full of enlightening ideas and sense of humor. We are very grateful to the anonymous reviewer for the suggestions and corrections that have helped to improve the paper.

References

1. Brewka, G.: Preferred subtheories: An extended logical framework for default reasoning. In: Proceedings of the 11th International Joint Conference on Artificial Intelligence, Detroit, MI, USA, pp. 1043–1048 (August 1989)
2. Brewka, G.: Reasoning about priorities in default logic. In: Proceedings of the 12th National Conference on Artificial Intelligence, Seattle, WA, USA, July 31-August 4, vol. 2, pp. 940–945 (1994)
3. Brewka, G.: Logic programming with ordered disjunction. In: Proceedings of the Eighteenth National Conference on Artificial Intelligence and Fourteenth Conference on Innovative Applications of Artificial Intelligence, Edmonton, Alberta, Canada, July 28-August 1, pp. 100–105 (2002)
4. Brewka, G., Eiter, T.: Preferred answer sets for extended logic programs. In: Proceedings of the Sixth International Conference on Principles of Knowledge Representation and Reasoning (KR 1998), Trento, Italy, June 2-5, pp. 86–97 (1998)
5. Brewka, G., Eiter, T., Truszczynski, M.: Answer set programming at a glance. Commun. ACM 54(12), 92–103 (2011)

6. Brewka, G., Niemelä, I., Syrjänen, T.: Logic programs with ordered disjunction. Computational Intelligence 20(2), 335–357 (2004)
7. Brewka, G., Niemelä, I., Truszczynski, M.: Preferences and nonmonotonic reasoning. AI Magazine 29(4), 69–78 (2008)
8. Cabalar, P.: A logical characterisation of ordered disjunction. AI Communications 24(2), 165–175 (2011)
9. Cabalar, P., Fandiño, J., Fink, M.: Causal graph justifications of logic programs. Theory and Practice of Logic Programming 14(4-5), 603–618 (2014), Special issue on ICLP 2014
10. Cabalar, P., Fandiño, J., Fink, M.: A Complexity Assessment for Queries Involving Sufficient and Necessary Causes. In: Fermé, E., Leite, J. (eds.) JELIA 2014. LNCS, vol. 8761, pp. 297–310. Springer, Heidelberg (2014)
11. Cabalar, P., Ferraris, P.: Propositional theories are strongly equivalent to logic programs. Theory and Practice of Logic Programming 7(6), 745–759 (2007)
12. Viegas Damásio, C., Analyti, A., Antoniou, G.: Justifications for logic programming. In: Cabalar, P., Son, T.C. (eds.) LPNMR 2013. LNCS, vol. 8148, pp. 530–542. Springer, Heidelberg (2013)
13. Denecker, M., De Schreye, D.: Justification semantics: A unifiying framework for the semantics of logic programs. In: Proc. of the Logic Programming and Nonmonotonic Reasoning Workshop, pp. 365–379 (1993)
14. Ferraris, P.: Answer sets for propositional theories. In: Baral, C., Greco, G., Leone, N., Terracina, G. (eds.) LPNMR 2005. LNCS (LNAI), vol. 3662, pp. 119–131. Springer, Heidelberg (2005)
15. Gebser, M., Pührer, J., Schaub, T., Tompits, H.: Meta-programming technique for debugging answer-set programs. In: Proc. of the 23rd Conf. on Artificial Inteligence (AAAI 2008), pp. 448–453 (2008)
16. Gelfond, M., Lifschitz, V.: The stable model semantics for logic programming. In: Kowalski, R.A., Bowen, K.A. (eds.) Logic Programming: Proc. of the Fifth International Conference and Symposium, vol. 2, pp. 1070–1080. MIT Press, Cambridge (1988)
17. Heyting, A.: Die formalen Regeln der intuitionistischen Logik. Sitzungsberichte der Preussischen Akademie der Wissenschaften, Physikalisch-mathematische Klasse, pp. 42–56 (1930)
18. Inoue, K., Sakama, C.: Negation as failure in the head. Journal of Logic Programming 35(1), 39–78 (1998)
19. Janhunen, T.: On the Effect of Default Negation on the Expressiveness of Disjunctive Rules. In: Eiter, T., Faber, W., Truszczyński, M. (eds.) LPNMR 2001. LNCS (LNAI), vol. 2173, pp. 93–106. Springer, Heidelberg (2001)
20. Lifschitz, V., Tang, L.R., Turner, H.: Nested expressions in logic programs. Annals of Mathematics in Artificial Intelligence 25(3-4), 369–389 (1999)
21. Marek, V., Truszczyński, M.: Stable models and an alternative logic programming paradigm, pp. 169–181. Springer (1999)
22. Niemelä, I.: Logic programs with stable model semantics as a constraint programming paradigm. Annals of Mathematics and Artificial Intelligence 25, 241–273 (1999)
23. Pearce, D.: A new logical characterisation of stable models and answer sets. In: Dix, J., Przymusinski, T.C., Moniz Pereira, L. (eds.) NMELP 1996. LNCS, vol. 1216, pp. 57–70. Springer, Heidelberg (1997)
24. Pereira, L.M., Aparício, J.N., Alferes, J.J.: Derivation procedures for extended stable models. In: Mylopoulos, J., Reiter, R. (eds.) Proceedings of the 12th International Joint Conference on Artificial Intelligence, pp. 863–869. Morgan Kaufmann (1991)

25. Pontelli, E., Son, T.C., El-Khatib, O.: Justifications for logic programs under answer set semantics. Theory and Practice of Logic Programming 9(1), 1–56 (2009)
26. Reiter, R.: A logic for default reasoning. Artif. Intell. 13(1-2), 81–132 (1980)
27. Schulz, C., Sergot, M., Toni, F.: Argumentation-based answer set justification. In: Proc. of the 11th Intl. Symposium on Logical Formalizations of Commonsense Reasoning, Commonsense 2013 (2013)
28. van Emden, M.H., Kowalski, R.A.: The semantics of predicate logic as a programming language. J. ACM 23(4), 733–742 (1976)
29. Vennekens, J.: Actual causation in cp-logic. TPLP 11(4-5), 647–662 (2011)

Preference-Based Diagnosis Selection
in Multi-Context Systems

Thomas Eiter, Michael Fink, and Antonius Weinzierl

Knowledge-based Systems Group
Institute of Information Systems
Vienna University of Technology, Austria
{eiter,fink,weinzierl}@kr.tuwien.ac.at

Abstract. Nonmonotonic Multi-Context Systems (MCS) provide a rigorous framework and flexible approach to represent and reason over interlinked, heterogeneous knowledge sources. Not least due to nonmonotonicity, however, an MCS may be inconsistent and resolving inconsistency is a major issue. Notions of diagnosis and inconsistency explanations have been developed for this purpose, considering the information exchange as the primary culprit. To discriminate between different possible solutions, we consider preference-based diagnosis selection. We develop a general meta-reasoning technique, i.e., an MCS transformation capable of full introspection on possible diagnoses, and we present a natural encoding of preferred diagnosis selection on top. Moreover, for the more involved notions of diagnosis utilized, we establish that the complexity does not increase. However, this does not carry over to selecting most preferred diagnoses as the encoding is not polynomial.

1 Introduction

Multi-Context Systems (MCS) provide a rigorous and flexible approach to represent and reason over multiple interlinked, possibly heterogeneous, knowledge sources. They thus address a highly important issue in contemporary knowledge representation and reasoning (KRR) as more and more bodies of knowledge, formalized in different representation languages, are shared, e.g., over the Web, and utilized in combination. The origins of MCS are rooted in the Trento School [10] and can be traced back to fundamental thoughts on contextualizing knowledge by McCarthy [11]. However, their significance for modern KRR is due to seminal advancements of the framework attributed to Gerd Brewka. His work on the topic was pioneering the incorporation of (i) *nonmonotonic reasoning* [6], thus allowing to reason from the *absence* of knowledge from a source (called *context*), further generalized by (ii) the accommodation of both *heterogeneous and nonmonotonic* contexts [4], thus paving the way to integrate predominant KR formalisms and logics as utilized today.

Our present contribution addresses the resulting framework of Nonmonotonic MCS [4], where a context is associated (in addition to a knowledge base) with a so-called *logic*, i.e., a formal abstraction of its particular representation language and semantics, and with a set of so-called *bridge rules* that intuitively represent its interlinking with other contexts. An MCS consists of a collection of contexts. Its semantics is defined in terms of

T. Eiter et al. (Eds.): Brewka Festschrift, LNAI 9060, pp. 233–248, 2015.

equilibria, i.e., a collection of belief sets (one for each context) compliant with the bridge rules and the semantics associated with each context. Not least due to nonmonotonicity, an MCS may be inconsistent (lack equilibria), which is undesired since it renders the system useless given that equilibria represent the meaning of an MCS.

In order to cope with this problem, notions of diagnosis and inconsistency explanations have been developed [7]. They aim at giving reasons for inconsistency and hinting at possible ways for resolution under the assumption that the information exchange is the culprit. For instance, given an inconsistent MCS the set of all diagnoses intuitively characterizes all possible ways to remove inconsistency by modifying its bridge rules (including deletion). Since this notion is purely technical, however, it is not amenable to a further distinction of unwanted diagnoses from preferred ones. Although a minimal diagnosis yields minimal modifications in order to ensure the existence of an equilibrium, this does not discriminate diagnoses whose modifications, e.g, yield serious consequences like wrongfully considering an ill patient as healthy and not giving her any medication.

Example 1. Let M be an MCS handling patient treatments and billing in a hospital; it contains the following contexts: a patient database C_1, a logic program C_2 suggesting proper medication, and a logic program C_3 handling the billing. Context C_1 provides information that the patient has severe hyperglycemia, that she is allergic to animal insulin, and that her health insurance is from a company classified B. Context C_2 suggests applying either human or animal insulin if the patient has hyperglycemia and requires that the applied insulin does not cause an allergic reaction. Context C_3 does the billing and encodes that insurance of class B only pays animal insulin. An overview of the MCS and its bridge rules is given in Figure 1 (cf. the next section for a more formal account). Bridge rule r_1 intuitively conveys the information regarding hyperglycemia; r_2 states that animal insulin can be applied if the patient is not allergic to it; bridge rules r_3 and r_4 encode that animal insulin, respectively human insulin, is billed if applied; and r_5 ensures that the insurance class of a patient is taken into account for billing.

As the patient has hyperglycemia and is allergic to animal insulin, a belief set would only be acceptable for C_2 if human insulin is given. As the insurance company doesn't cover human insulin, the billing context C_3 would not admit this; M is inconsistent.

Applying one of its (subset minimal) diagnoses would yield, respectively, that the illness of the patient is ignored, that the medication is not billed, that the insurance receives a bill it will not pay, or that the patient is given a medication she is allergic to.

It is thus not easy to identify a best minimal diagnosis among those available. If the health of the patient is most important, then diagnoses just causing wrong billing would be preferable. On the other hand, from an economic perspective, one might consider medication leading to wrong billing as unacceptable.

In this article we therefore address the problem of distinguishing and selecting most preferred diagnoses. Our goal is to realize corresponding reasoning tasks within the established MCS framework in a general way, in particular without confinement to a certain preference formalism. The core idea towards achievement is to use a context of an MCS for preference specification. This requires the ability of introspection or *meta-reasoning* regarding possible diagnoses of the MCS. Finding techniques that enable an MCS to achieve capabilities for meta-reasoning (about the diagnoses of itself) therefore

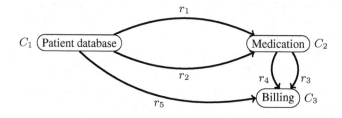

Fig. 1. Contexts and bridge rules of a hospital MCS $M = (C_1, C_2, C_3)$

is an important task. Our contribution in this respect is the definition of a general meta-reasoning technique as well as an investigation of some of its properties and a natural encoding for total preference orders.

Finally, we focus on computational complexity and present complexity results for decision problems associated with the more general notions of diagnosis applied. More specifically, we establish that both protecting bridge rules as well as prioritizing bridge rules, i.e., the techniques applied in our meta-reasoning encoding, do not incur additional cost. This does not carry over to the problem of selecting most preferred diagnosis though. Regarding the latter, the presented encoding, while intuitive, is not polynomial but exponential in the number of bridge rules used.

Compared to our previous work on the topic [8], which aimed at an encoding for CP-nets, we (i) address preference relations in general; (ii) advance the meta-reasoning approach regarding its introspective accuracy, enabling the distinct observation of all potential modifications that any diagnosis (candidate) may yield; and (iii) complement an intuitive discussion of computational complexity issues with formal results.

There are several close connections to the work of Gerd Brewka, to honor his 60th birthday which this collection set out for. For one, as already mentioned in the very beginning, the research area on MCS would probably lack most of its justification in terms of applicability to contemporary KRR practice without Gerd's significant achievements. Moreover, we are addressing preference issues over diagnoses for MCS, while Gerd Brewka has made numerous substantial contributions to preference handling in nonmonotonic logics; we refer to the article of the editors of this volume for a review and an appraisal of Gerd's eminent account of trend-setting contributions.

The remainder of this article is structured as follows. After some preliminaries, in Section 3 we introduce basic and general notions of preferred diagnoses under preference-based selection. In Section 4 we develop our approach to achieve meta-reasoning in MCS, and encode preference orders. In Section 5 we present and discuss computational complexity results of associated diagnostic reasoning tasks, before we conclude. Proofs of all results can be found in [14].

2   Preliminaries

We start by recalling MCS basics from [4] and the notion of diagnoses following [7].

Definition 1. *An* abstract logic *L, is a triple* $L = (\mathbf{KB}_L, \mathbf{BS}_L, \mathbf{ACC}_L)$ *where:*

- **KB**$_L$ *is the set of knowledge bases of L. We assume each element of* **KB**$_L$ *is a set.*
- **BS**$_L$ *is the set of possible belief sets, where the elements of a belief set are statements that possibly hold.*
- **ACC**$_L$: **KB**$_L$ → $2^{\mathbf{BS}_L}$ *is a function describing the semantics of the logic by assigning to each knowledge base a set of acceptable belief sets.*

Example 2 (Classical Propositional Logic). To capture classical (propositional) logic over a set Σ of propositional atoms, we may define:

- **KB**^{c} = $2^{\Sigma^{wff}}$ is the set of all subsets of Σ^{wff}, where Σ^{wff} is the set of well-formed formulas over Σ built using the connectives $\wedge, \vee, \neg, \rightarrow$;
- **BS**^{c} = $2^{\Sigma^{wff}}$, i.e., each set of formulas is a possible belief set; and
- **ACC**^{c} returns for each set $kb \in$ **KB**^{c} of well-formed formulas a singleton set that contains the set of formulas entailed by kb; if $\models_c$ denotes classical entailment, then **ACC**$^c(kb) = \{\{F \in \Sigma^{wff} \mid kb \models_c F\}\}$.

The resulting logic $L_\Sigma^c = (\mathbf{KB}^c, \mathbf{BS}^c, \mathbf{ACC}^c)$ captures entailment in classical logics.

Observe that any tautological formula is entailed by any knowledge base, hence any $bs \in \mathbf{ACC}^c(kb)$ for some $kb \in \mathbf{KB}^c$ is infinite (for $\Sigma \neq \emptyset$). In practice, therefore the formulas in knowledge bases and belief sets might be restricted to particular forms, e.g., to literals; we denote the logic where belief sets are restricted to literals by $L_\Sigma^{pl} = (\mathbf{KB}^{pl}, \mathbf{BS}^{pl}, \mathbf{ACC}^{pl})$, where $\mathbf{BS}^{pl} = \{bs \in \mathbf{BS}^c \mid bs \subseteq \{A, \neg A \mid A \in \Sigma\}\}$, $\mathbf{KB}^{pl} = \mathbf{KB}^c$, and $\mathbf{ACC}^{pl}(kb) = \{\{A \in \Sigma \mid kb \models_c A\} \cup \{\neg A \mid A \in \Sigma, kb \models_c \neg A\}\}$.

Example 3 (Disjunctive Answer Set Programming). For disjunctive logic programs under answer set semantics over a non-ground signature Σ (cf. [12] and [9]), we use the abstract logic $L_\Sigma^{asp} = (\mathbf{KB}, \mathbf{BS}, \mathbf{ACC})$, which is defined as follows:

- **KB** is the set of disjunctive logic programs over Σ, i.e., each $kb \in$ **KB** is a set of (safe) rules of the form

$$a_1 \vee \ldots \vee a_n \leftarrow b_1, \ldots, b_i, not\, b_{i+1}, \ldots, not\, b_m, \quad n + m > 0,$$

  where all a_i, b_j, are atoms over a first-order language Σ.
- **BS** is the set of Herbrand interpretations over Σ, i.e., each $bs \in$ **BS** is a set of ground atoms from Σ, and
- **ACC**(kb) returns the set of kb's answer sets: for $P \in$ **KB** and $T \in$ **BS**, let $P^T = \{r \in grnd(P) \mid T \models B(r)\}$ be the FLP-reduct of P w.r.t. T, where $grnd(P)$ returns the ground version of all rules in P. Then $bs \in$ **BS** is an answer set, i.e., $bs \in \mathbf{ACC}(kb)$, iff bs is a minimal model of kb^{bs}.

Definition 2. *Given a sequence* $L = (L_1, \ldots, L_n)$ *of abstract logics and* $1 \leq k \leq n$, *an* L^k *bridge rule over L is of the following form:*

$$(k:s) \leftarrow (c_1:p_1), \ldots, (c_i:p_j), \mathbf{not}\ (c_{j+1}:p_{j+1}), \ldots, \mathbf{not}\ (c_m:p_m). \tag{1}$$

where for each $1 \leq j \leq m$ *we have that* $c_j \in \{1, \ldots, n\}$, p_j *is an element of some belief set of the abstract logic* L_{c_j}, *and* $s \in \bigcup \mathbf{KB}_{L_k}$ *is a knowledge base formula of* L_k.

We denote by $\varphi(r)$ the formula s in the head of r and by $C_h(r)$ the context identifier k of the context where r belongs to. We refer to literals in the body of r as follows:

- $body^{\pm}(r) = \{(c_1 : p_1), \ldots, (c_m : p_m)\}$,
- $body^{+}(r) = \{(c_1 : p_1), \ldots, (c_j : p_j)\}$,
- $body^{-}(r) = \{(c_{j+1} : p_{j+1}), \ldots, (c_m : p_m)\}$, and
- $body(r) = \{(c_1 : p_1), \ldots, (c_j : p_j), \textbf{not } (c_{j+1} : p_{j+1}), \ldots, \textbf{not } (c_m : p_m)\}$.

Furthermore, $C_b(r)$ denotes the set of contexts referenced in r's body, i.e., $C_b(r) = \{c_i \mid (c_i : p_i) \in body^{\pm}(r)\}$. Note that different from [4], we explicitly state in the head of r the context k where r belongs to. This choice merely is syntactic sugar and allows for easier identification of the respective context. For technical use later, we denote by $cf(r)$ the *condition-free* bridge rule stemming from r by removing all elements in its body, i.e., $cf(r)$ is $(k : s) \leftarrow .$ and for any set of bridge rules R, we let $cf(R) = \bigcup_{r \in R} cf(r)$.

Definition 3. *A Multi-Context System* $M = (C_1, \ldots, C_n)$ *is a collection of contexts* $C_i = (L_i, kb_i, br_i)$, $1 \leq i \leq n$, *where*
- $L_i = (\textbf{KB}_i, \textbf{BS}_i, \textbf{ACC}_i)$ *is an abstract logic,*
- $kb_i \in \textbf{KB}_i$ *is a knowledge base, and*
- br_i *is a set of L^i-bridge rules over* $L = (L_1, \ldots, L_n)$.

Furthermore, for each $H \subseteq \{\varphi(r) \mid r \in br_i\}$ *it holds that* $(kb_i \cup H) \in \textbf{KB}_i$, *i.e., adding bridge rule heads to a knowledge base again yields a knowledge base.*

By $br(M) = \bigcup_{i=1}^{n} br_i$ and $C(M) = \{1, \ldots, n\}$ we denote the set of all bridge rules, respectively the set of all context identifiers of M. We write $br_i(M)$ to denote the set of bridge rules of context i of M, i.e., $br_i(M) = \{r \in br(M) \mid C_h(r) = i\}$.

Formally, given an MCS $M = (C_1, \ldots, C_n)$ with $C_i = (L_i, kb_i, br_i)$ and $L_i = (\textbf{KB}_i, \textbf{BS}_i, \textbf{ACC}_i)$, a *belief state* of M is a sequence $S = (S_1, \ldots, S_n)$ of belief sets $S_i \in \textbf{BS}_i$, $1 \leq i \leq n$.

Given a belief state S of M, one can evaluate for all bridge rules $r \in br(M)$ whether the body of r is satisfied in S, i.e., whether r is applicable in S. Formally, a bridge rule r of form (1) is *applicable* in a belief state S, denoted by $S \models r$, if for all $(j : p) \in body^{+}(r)$ it holds that $p \in S_j$, and for all $(j : p) \in body^{-}(r)$ it holds that $p \notin S_j$. For a set R of bridge rules and a belief state S, $app(R, S)$ denotes the set of bridge rules of R that are applicable in S, i.e., $app(R, S) = \{r \in R \mid S \models r\}$.

Equilibrium semantics designates some belief states as acceptable. Intuitively, equilibrium semantics selects a belief state $S = (S_1, \ldots, S_n)$ of an MCS M as acceptable, if each context C_i takes the heads of all its bridge rules that are applicable in S into account to enrich its knowledge base with, and accepts its designated belief set S_i under this enlarged knowledge base.

Definition 4. *A belief state* $S = (S_1, \ldots, S_n)$ *of an MCS M is an* equilibrium, *if for every belief set* S_i, $1 \leq i \leq n$, *it holds that*

$$S_i \in \textbf{ACC}_i\big(kb_i \cup \{\varphi(r) \mid r \in app(br_i, S)\}\big). \tag{2}$$

The set of all equilibria of M is denoted by $\text{EQ}(M)$.

To create bridge rules that are always resp. never applicable, we also allow bridge rules with body $\top$ resp. $\bot$; this is syntactic sugar for an empty body resp. a body containing $(\ell : p), \textbf{not } (\ell : p)$ where p is any belief of some context C_ℓ. For a bridge rule r of form $(k : s) \leftarrow \top.$ it therefore holds for all belief states S that $S \models r$, while for a bridge rule r' of form $(k : s) \leftarrow \bot.$ it holds for all belief states S that $S \not\models r'$.

In the following, we often consider modifications to the bridge rules of an MCS. We use the following notation to denote an MCS where bridge rules have been exchanged: given an MCS $M = (C_1, \ldots, C_n)$ over abstract logics $L = (L_1, \ldots, L_n)$ and a set R of bridge rules over L (compatible with M), we denote by $M[R]$ the MCS obtained from M by replacing its set of bridge rules $br(M)$ with R. For example, $M[br(M)] = M$ and $M[\emptyset]$ is M with no bridge rules at all.

Regarding equilibria, we write $M \models \bot$ to denote that M has no equilibrium, i.e., $EQ(M) = \emptyset$. Conversely, by $M \not\models \bot$ we denote the opposite, i.e., $EQ(M) \neq \emptyset$.

We say that an MCS is *inconsistent*, if it $EQ(M) = \emptyset$; equivalently, $M \models \bot$.

Example 4. Let us reconsider our introductory Example 1 more formally. In the MCS $M = (C_1, C_2, C_3)$ handling patient treatments and billing in a hospital, context C_1 uses the abstract logic L_Σ^{pl}, while both C_2 and C_3 use L_Σ^{asp}. We restrict our example to a single patient with the following knowledge bases for contexts:

$$kb_1 = \{hyperglycemia, allergic\_animal\_insulin, insurance\_class\_B\},$$

$$kb_2 = \left\{ \begin{array}{l} give\_human\_insulin \lor give\_animal\_insulin \leftarrow hyperglycemia. \\ \bot \leftarrow give\_animal\_insulin, not\ allow\_animal\_insulin \end{array} \right\},$$

$$kb_3 = \left\{ \begin{array}{l} bill \leftarrow bill\_animal\_insulin. \\ bill\_more \leftarrow bill\_human\_insulin. \\ \bot \leftarrow insurance\_class\_B, bill\_more.\} \end{array} \right\},$$

The bridge rules of M are:

r_1:	$(2 : hyperglycemia)$	$\leftarrow (1 : hyperglycemia).$
r_2:	$(2 : allow\_animal\_insulin)$	$\leftarrow \mathbf{not}\ (1 : allergic\_animal\_insulin).$
r_3:	$(3 : bill\_animal\_insulin)$	$\leftarrow (2 : give\_animal\_insulin).$
r_4:	$(3 : bill\_human\_insulin)$	$\leftarrow (2 : give\_human\_insulin).$
r_5:	$(3 : insurance\_class\_B)$	$\leftarrow (1 : insurance\_class\_B).$

As already argued intuitively in the introduction, M is inconsistent: Since the patient has hyperglycemia and is allergic to animal insulin, the only acceptable belief set at context C_2 contains *give_human_insulin*, i.e., the human insulin must be given. Since the insurance company does not cover human insulin, the billing context C_3 admits no acceptable belief set and the MCS M therefore is inconsistent.

Definition 5. *Given an MCS M, a diagnosis of M is a pair (D_1, D_2), $D_1, D_2 \subseteq br(M)$, such that $M[br(M) \setminus D_1 \cup cf(D_2)] \not\models \bot$. By notation, $D^\pm(M)$ is the set of all diagnoses.*

To obtain a more relevant set of diagnoses, by Occam's razor we prefer subset-minimal diagnoses, where for pairs $A = (A_1, A_2)$ and $B = (B_1, B_2)$ of sets, the pointwise subset relation $A \subseteq B$ holds iff $A_1 \subseteq B_1$ and $A_2 \subseteq B_2$.

Definition 6. *Given an MCS M, $D_m^\pm(M)$ is the set of all pointwise subset-minimal diagnoses of an MCS M, i.e.,*

$$D_m^\pm(M) = \{D \in D^\pm(M) \mid \forall D' \in D^\pm(M) : D' \subseteq D \Rightarrow D \subseteq D'\}.$$

Diagnoses correspond to potential repairs of an MCS as captured by the corresponding modification of bridge rules according to Definition 5. For instance, the minimal diagnoses of M in the previous example are the following:

$$D_m^\pm(M) = \{(\{r_1\}, \emptyset), (\{r_4\}, \emptyset), (\{r_5\}, \emptyset), (\emptyset, \{r_2\})\}$$

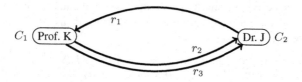

Fig. 2. Contexts and bridge rules of the MCS $M = (C_1, C_2)$ from Example 5

They respectively correspond to potential repairs, where the illness of the patient is ignored, where the medication is not billed, where the insurance receives a bill it will not pay, and where the patient is given a medication she is allergic to.

For another example, consider the following scenario.

Example 5. Prof. K and Dr. J plan to write a paper. We formalize their reasoning in an MCS M using two contexts C_1 and C_2, each employing L_{Σ}^{asp} for answer set semantics. Dr. J will write most of the paper and Prof. K will participate if she finds time or if Dr. J thinks the paper needs improvement (bridge rule r_1). Dr. J knows that participation of Prof. K results in a good paper (r_2 and kb_1) and he will name Prof. K as author if she participates (r_3). The knowledge bases of the contexts are:

$$kb_1 = \{\ contribute \leftarrow improve.; \quad contribute \leftarrow has\_time.\}$$
$$kb_2 = \{\ good \leftarrow coauthored.\}$$

The bridge rules of M are:

$$r_1: \qquad\qquad (1: improve) \leftarrow \textbf{not}\ (2: good). \qquad\qquad (3)$$
$$r_2: \qquad\qquad (2: coauthored) \leftarrow (1: contribute). \qquad\qquad (4)$$
$$r_3: \qquad\qquad (2: name\_K) \leftarrow (1: contribute). \qquad\qquad (5)$$

Figure 2 depicts the contexts and bridge rules of M. It appears that M is inconsistent, intuitively as the cycle through bridge rules r_1 and r_2 has an odd number of negations.

The set of minimal diagnoses of M is:

$$D_m^{\pm}(M) = \{\ (\{r_1\}, \emptyset),\ (\{r_2\}, \emptyset),\ (\emptyset, \{r_2\}),\ (\emptyset, \{r_1\})\ \}$$

The first two diagnoses break the cycle by removing a rule, the last two "stabilize" it.

In the remainder, we will allow for certain bridge rules to be exempt from modification in a diagnosis, i.e., they are protected. Protecting certain bridge rules from modification is essential for our meta-reasoning approach.

Definition 7 ([8]). *Let M be an MCS with* protected rules $br_P \subseteq br(M)$. *A diagnosis* excluding protected rules br_P *is a diagnosis* $(D_1, D_2) \in D^{\pm}(M)$, *where* $D_1, D_2 \subseteq br(M) \setminus br_P$; *by* $D_m^{\pm}(M, br_P)$ *we denote the set of all minimal such diagnoses.*

3   Preference-Based Diagnosis Selection

To compare diagnoses with each other and select the most appealing one(s), we use preferences. In the spirit of MCS, we also want this approach to be open to any kind of formalism for specifying preference. Taking a general stance, since any preference formalism essentially yields an order relation, preference is just an order relation (i.e. a transitive relation) on diagnoses.

Definition 8. *A preference order* over diagnoses for an MCS M *is a transitive binary relation* $\preceq$ *on* $2^{br(M)} \times 2^{br(M)}$; *we say that D is preferred to D' iff* $D \preceq D'$.

Given a preference order $\preceq$, we denote by $\prec$ its irreflexive version, i.e., $D \prec D'$ holds iff $D \preceq D'$ and $D \neq D'$ hold. Using a preference order $\preceq$, we can now define what constitutes a most preferred diagnosis. Again the intuition is that such a diagnosis is one which incurs the least amount of modifications and there exists no other diagnosis that is strictly more preferred. To do so, we first introduce $\preceq$-preferred diagnoses as diagnoses such that no other diagnosis is strictly more preferred; among them, we select then the subset-minimal ones. Formally,

Definition 9. *Let M be an inconsistent MCS. A diagnosis* $D \in D^{\pm}(M)$ *of M is* $\preceq$-*preferred , if for all* $D' \in 2^{br(M)} \times 2^{br(M)}$ *with* $D' \prec D \wedge D \npreceq D'$ *it holds that* $D' \notin D^{\pm}(M)$. *A diagnosis* $D \in D^{\pm}(M)$ *is minimal* $\preceq$-*preferred , if D is subset-minimal among all* $\preceq$-*preferred diagnoses. The set of* $\preceq$-*preferred (resp., minimal* $\preceq$-*preferred) diagnoses is denoted by* $D^{\pm}_{\preceq}(M)$ *(resp.,* $D^{\pm}_{m,\preceq}(M)$).

Observe that we do not require $\preceq$ to be acyclic and therefore we consider all diagnoses in a cycle to be equally preferred; this justifies the condition of $D' \prec D \wedge D \npreceq D'$ for defining $D^{\pm}_{\preceq}(M)$.

Example 6. Consider the hospital MCS M of Example 4 again, where bridge rules r_1 and r_2 transport information regarding the patient's health and bridge rules r_3, r_4, and r_5 cover the information flow for billing. If we consider it most important that information flow regarding health information is changed as little as possible, a preference order $\preceq$ as follows might be used:

$$(D_1, D_2) \preceq (D_1', D_2') \text{ iff } \{r_1, r_2\} \cap (D_1 \cup D_2) \subseteq (D_1' \cup D_2') \cap \{r_1, r_2\}.$$

Under this definition, the following preferences (and several more) hold:

$$(\{r_4, r_5\}, \emptyset) \preceq (\{r_1\}, \emptyset) \qquad (\{r_4\}, \emptyset) \preceq (\{r_1\}, \emptyset) \qquad (\{r_5\}, \emptyset) \preceq (\{r_1\}, \emptyset)$$
$$(\{r_4, r_5\}, \emptyset) \preceq (\emptyset, \{r_2\}) \qquad (\{r_4\}, \emptyset) \preceq (\emptyset, \{r_2\}) \qquad (\{r_5\}, \emptyset) \preceq (\emptyset, \{r_2\})$$
$$(\{r_4\}, \emptyset) \preceq (\{r_5\}, \emptyset) \qquad (\{r_5\}, \emptyset) \preceq (\{r_4\}, \emptyset)$$

Note that $\preceq$ indeed yields cyclic preferences among those diagnosis candidates that are incomparable, especially it holds that $(\{r_4\}, \emptyset) \prec (\{r_5\}, \emptyset)$ and $(\{r_5\}, \emptyset) \prec (\{r_4\}, \emptyset)$. The set of $\preceq$-preferred diagnoses of M then is:

$$D^{\pm}_{\preceq}(M) = \{(D_1, D_2) \mid D_1, D_2 \subseteq \{r_3, r_4, r_5\} \text{ and } r_4 \in D_1 \setminus D_2 \text{ or } r_5 \in D_1 \setminus D_2\}.$$

Note that $(\{r_5\}, \emptyset)$, $(\{r_4\}, \emptyset)$ and $(\{r_4, r_5\}, \emptyset)$ are all in $D^{\pm}_{\preceq}(M)$. Selecting from $D^{\pm}_{\preceq}(M)$ the subset-minimal ones, we obtain

$$D^{\pm}_{m,\preceq}(M) = \{(\{r_5\}, \emptyset), (\{r_4\}, \emptyset)\}$$

This agrees with our intuition that a minimum amount of modifications should be applied and we favor to modify bridge rules for billing information rather than modifying health-related bridge rules.

4   Meta-reasoning Encoding in MCS

A critical issue in realizing a meta-reasoning approach to select preferred diagnoses is accurate introspection: all potential modifications that some diagnosis may yield need to be distinctly observable. As we will show, one can encode the modifications of a diagnosis directly in an MCS such that observations are perfect, and the original system is no longer just observed but actively modified instead. Conceptually, given an MCS $M = (C_1, \ldots, C_n)$ all its bridge rules are rewritten and protected such that a diagnosis is applied only to the bridge rules of an additional context C_{n+1}. This context C_{n+1} then is able to definitely observe the modifications and to disclose this observation to all other contexts via its acceptable belief set.

The bridge rules of the original system are modified to consider the belief set of C_{n+1}. So they either behave like removed or like made unconditional, depending on what C_{n+1} beliefs. For these two modes of behavior, each bridge rule $r \in br(M)$ is replaced by two bridge rules in the meta-reasoning system: one bridge rule for becoming unconditional and one that behaves like r or like being removed (i.e., it simply does not fire when C_{n+1} believes r to be removed). The form of these two bridge rules is similar to the form of bridge rules in the HEX-encoding for computing diagnoses in [7] (rules (15), (21), and (22)).

While aiming at preferences, our meta-reasoning encoding is intended to be general enough to encompass further selection criteria such as, e.g., filters [8]. Therefore, we introduce a property θ that represents additional behavior of the context C_{n+1}. A preference encoding requires further bridge rules for mapping preferences to bridge rules; this set of additional bridge rules is called $\mathcal{K}$, so we obtain as meta-reasoning encoding of M an MCS $M^{mr(\theta, \mathcal{K})}$. In Section 4.1 we craft θ such that preferences on diagnoses map to the $\subseteq$-relation on $\mathcal{K}$. But first, we specify $M^{mr(\theta, \mathcal{K})}$ in general and show its suitability for meta-reasoning.

To encode (observe) diagnoses, the context C_{n+1} needs bridge rules where a diagnosis can be applied to and which can be observed reliably. To that end, for every $r \in br(M)$, we have the following two bridge rules to encode/observe whether r is removed or made unconditional.

$$d1(r): \qquad (n{+}1 : not\_removed_r) \leftarrow \top. \qquad (6)$$

$$d2(r): \qquad (n{+}1 : uncond_r) \leftarrow \bot. \qquad (7)$$

By $d1(r)$ (resp., $d2(r)$) we denote the bridge rule of form (6) (resp. (7)). Likewise, for a set $R \subseteq br(M)$, let $di(R) = \{di(r) \mid r \in R\}$, $i \in \{1, 2\}$. The meta-reasoning encoding $M^{mr(\theta, \mathcal{K})}$ is then as follows.

Definition 10. *Let $M = (C_1, \ldots, C_n)$ be an MCS and let $\mathcal{K}$ be a set of bridge rules r such that $body(r) = \{\bot\}$, $C_h(r) = n{+}1$, and $\varphi(r) \notin \{not\_removed_{r'}, uncond_{r'} \mid r' \in br(M)\}$. Let θ be a ternary property over $2^{br(M)} \times 2^{br(M)} \times 2^{\mathcal{K}}$. Then, the MCS $M^{mr(\theta, \mathcal{K})} = (C'_1, \ldots, C'_n, C_{n+1})$ is the meta-reasoning encoding wrt. θ and $\mathcal{K}$ if*

(i) *for every $C_i = (L_i, kb_i, br_i)$, $1 \leq i \leq n$, it holds that $C_i' = (L_i, kb_i, br_i')$ where br_i' contains for every $r \in br_i$ of form (1) the following two bridge rules:*

$$(i : s) \leftarrow (c_1 : p_1), \ldots, (c_j : p_j), \mathbf{not}\ (c_{j+1} : p_{j+1}), \ldots, \mathbf{not}\ (c_m : p_m),$$
$$\mathbf{not}\ (n+1 : removed_r). \tag{8}$$
$$(i : s) \leftarrow (n+1 : uncond_r). \tag{9}$$

and br_i' contains no other bridge rules.

(ii) $C_{n+1} = (L_{n+1}, kb_{n+1}, br_{n+1})$ *is any context such that:*

(a) $br_{n+1} = d1(br(M)) \cup d2(br(M)) \cup \mathcal{K}$ *and all rules with a head formula of form $not\_removed_r$ or $uncond_r$ are of form (6) or (7).*

(b) *for every $H \subseteq \{\varphi(r) \mid r \in br_{n+1}\}$, we have $S_{n+1} \in \mathbf{ACC}_{n+1}(kb_{n+1} \cup H)$ iff $\theta(R_1, R_2, R_3)$ holds for $R_1 = \{r \in br(M) \mid not\_removed_r \notin H\}$, $R_2 = \{r \in br(M) \mid uncond_r \in H\}$, $R_3 = \{r \in \mathcal{K} \mid \varphi(r) \in H\}$, and $S_{n+1} = \{removed_r \mid r \in R_1\} \cup \{uncond_r \mid r \in R_2\}$.*

The protected bridge rules br_P of $M^{mr(\theta, \mathcal{K})}$ are all rules of form (8) and (9).

The condition on acceptable belief sets at C_{n+1}, namely that $S_{n+1} = \{removed_r \mid r \in R_1\} \cup \{uncond_r \mid r \in R_2\}$ at first seems to be strong, as it disallows that any other belief occurs. On the other hand, however, the set of output-projected beliefs of context C_{n+1} is $OUT_{n+1} = \{removed_r, uncond_r \mid r \in br(M)\}$, i.e., no other belief of C_{n+1} is used by any bridge rule of $M^{mr(\theta, \mathcal{K})}$. We can therefore safely permit that C_{n+1} discloses other beliefs while the proofs of the results in this section go through. Note that the meta-reasoning encoding $M^{mr(\theta, \mathcal{K})}$ of some MCS M wrt. given θ and $\mathcal{K}$ is unique. If M, θ, and $\mathcal{K}$ are arbitrary but fixed, we call $M^{mr(\theta, \mathcal{K})}$ some meta-reasoning encoding.

Example 7. Recall the MCS $M = (C_1, C_2)$ in Example 5. Let $\mathcal{K} = \emptyset$ and $\theta(D_1, D_2, \emptyset)$ always hold; then $M^{mr(\theta, \mathcal{K})} = (C_1', C_2', C_3)$ is such that the contexts C_1 and C_2 equal modulo bridge rules the contexts C_1' and C_2', respectively. As M has the bridge rules r_1–r_3 in (3)–(5), the bridge rules of $M^{mr(\theta, \mathcal{K})}$ are as follows:

$$r_1' : \qquad (1 : improve) \leftarrow \mathbf{not}\ (2 : good), \mathbf{not}\ (3 : removed_{r_1}).$$
$$r_1'' : \qquad (1 : improve) \leftarrow (3 : uncond_{r_1}).$$
$$(2 : coauthored) \leftarrow (1 : contribute), \mathbf{not}\ (3 : removed_{r_2}).$$
$$(2 : coauthored) \leftarrow (3 : uncond_{r_2}).$$
$$(2 : name\_K) \leftarrow (1 : contribute), \mathbf{not}\ (3 : removed_{r_3}).$$
$$(2 : name\_K) \leftarrow (3 : uncond_{r_3}).$$

$d1(r_1) :$	$(3 : not\_removed_{r_1}) \leftarrow \top.$	$d2(r_1) :$	$(3 : uncond_{r_1}) \leftarrow \bot.$
$d1(r_2) :$	$(3 : not\_removed_{r_2}) \leftarrow \top.$	$d2(r_2) :$	$(3 : uncond_{r_2}) \leftarrow \bot.$
$d1(r_3) :$	$(3 : not\_removed_{r_3}) \leftarrow \top.$	$d2(r_3) :$	$(3 : uncond_{r_3}) \leftarrow \bot.$

Notice that only the latter half of the bridge rules of $M^{mr(\theta, \mathcal{K})}$ is not protected, i.e., the first six bridge rules are guaranteed not to be modified in a diagnosis with protected bridge rules. Figure 3 depicts the contexts and, for better visibility, it includes only the bridge rules of $M^{mr(\theta, \mathcal{K})}$ stemming from $r_1 \in br(M)$.

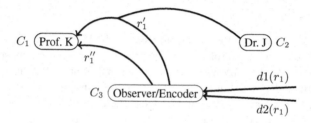

Fig. 3. Contexts of the meta-reasoning encoding $M^{mr(\theta,\mathcal{K})} = (C_1, C_2, C_3)$ from Example 7; only $r_1', r_1'', d1(r_1), d2(r_1)$ of $M^{mr(\theta,\mathcal{K})}$ stemming from $r_1 \in br(M)$ are shown

The remainder of this subsection is dedicated to prove that $M^{mr(\theta,\mathcal{K})}$ allows us to do meta-reasoning on diagnoses of M. For this purpose, we state fundamental properties essentially establishing a correspondence between minimal θ-satisfying diagnoses of M and minimal diagnoses of $M^{mr(\theta,\mathcal{K})}$. This result is central for our encoding of preferences which is addressed in the following subsection. Note that by $M[D_1, D_2]$ we denote the MCS M modified according to the diagnosis candidate (D_1, D_2), i.e., $M[D_1, D_2] = M[br(M) \setminus D_1 \cup cf(D_2)]$.

First of all, there is a one-to-one correspondence between diagnoses of M and diagnoses of $M^{mr(\theta,\mathcal{K})}$.

Proposition 1. *Let M be an MCS and $M^{mr(\theta,\mathcal{K})}$ be a meta-reasoning encoding with protected bridge rules br_P, and let $D_1, D_2 \subseteq br(M)$, $K \subseteq \mathcal{K}$.*

(1) Let $S = (S_1, \ldots, S_n)$ be a belief state of M and let $S' = (S_1, \ldots, S_n, S_{n+1})$ where $S_{n+1} = \{removed_r \mid r \in D_1\} \cup \{uncond_r \mid r \in D_2\}$. Then, $S \in$ EQ$(M[D_1, D_2])$ and $\theta(D_1, D_2, K)$ holds iff $S' \in$ EQ$(M^{mr(\theta,\mathcal{K})}[d1(D_1), d2(D_2) \cup K])$ holds.
(2) $(D_1, D_2) \in D^{\pm}(M)$ and $\theta(D_1, D_2, K)$ hold if and only if $(d1(D_1), d2(D_2) \cup K) \in D^{\pm}(M^{mr(\theta,\mathcal{K})}, br_P)$ holds.

Moreover, there are no diagnoses in $D_m^{\pm}(M^{mr(\theta,\mathcal{K})}, br_P)$ other than those which correspond to diagnoses of M.

Lemma 1. *Let M be an MCS and $M^{mr(\theta,\mathcal{K})}$ be some meta-reasoning encoding for M. For every $(R_1, R_2) \in D_m^{\pm}(M^{mr(\theta,\mathcal{K})}, br_P)$ there exist $D_1, D_2 \subseteq br(M)$ and $K \subseteq \mathcal{K}$ such that $R_1 = d1(D_1)$ and $R_2 = d2(D_2) \cup K$.*

We can now combine Lemma 1 with Proposition 1 to establish the correspondence between minimal θ-satisfying diagnoses of M and minimal diagnoses of $M^{mr(\theta,\mathcal{K})}$.

Proposition 2. *Let M be an MCS and $M^{mr(\theta,\mathcal{K})}$ be a meta-reasoning encoding, then the set of minimal θ-satisfying diagnoses with protected bridge rules br_P is*

$$D_m^{\pm}(M^{mr(\theta,\mathcal{K})}, br_P) = \Big\{ (d1(D_1), d2(D_2) \cup K) \mid$$
$$(D_1, D_2) \in D^{\pm}(M), \theta(D_1, D_2, K) \text{ holds}, [\nexists(D_1', D_2') \in D^{\pm}(M), K' \subseteq \mathcal{K} :$$
$$(D_1', D_2' \cup K') \subset (D_1, D_2 \cup K) \text{ and } \theta(D_1', D_2', K') holds] \Big\}.$$

4.1   Preference Encoding

We now show how to use the meta-reasoning encoding $M^{mr(\theta,\mathcal{K})}$ for realizing prefer-ences. The set $\mathcal{K}$ plays a crucial role, as a given preference order on diagnoses is mapped to the $\subseteq$ relation on $\mathcal{K}$. This allows us to select minimal $\preceq$-preferred diagnoses by con-sidering $\subseteq$-minimal diagnoses of $M^{mr(\theta,\mathcal{K})}$. Since the $\subseteq$-minimality on $\mathcal{K}$ should take precedence over the remaining modified bridge rules of $M^{mr(\theta,\mathcal{K})}$, we introduce a par-tial order on diagnosis candidates of $M^{mr(\theta,\mathcal{K})}$ such that D' occurs later than D if (1) D is a subset of D' wrt. $\mathcal{K}$ and (2) in case that both modify the same bridge rules of $\mathcal{K}$, then D is a subset of D' wrt. ordinary bridge rules of $M^{mr(\theta,\mathcal{K})}$ (i.e., the order is lexi-cographic wrt. set inclusion in (1) and (2)). Our encoding, called plain meta-reasoning encoding yields a one-to-one correspondence with minimal $\preceq$-preferred diagnoses for total preference orders.

In the following, we write $(D_1, D_2) \subseteq_{br_H} (D_1', D_2')$ for $(D_1 \cap br_H, D_2 \cap br_H) \subseteq (D_1' \cap br_H, D_2' \cap br_H)$, i.e., we denote by $\subseteq_{br_H}$ (resp. $=_{br_H}$) the restriction of $\subseteq$ (resp. $=$) to the set br_H. To realize a total preference order, the next definition is suitable which selects from the set of minimal diagnoses with protected bridge rules those that are minimal w.r.t. the prioritized bridge rules. The bridge rules that are marked as prioritized take precedence for minimality. A prioritized-minimal diagnosis is subset-minimal w.r.t. prioritized bridge rules (regardless of minimality of the remaining bridge rules).

Definition 11. *Let M be an MCS with protected rules $br_P \subseteq br(M)$ and prioritized rules $br_H \subseteq br(M)$. The set of* prioritized-minimal *diagnoses is*

$$D^{\pm}(M, br_P, br_H) =$$
$$\{D \in D_m^{\pm}(M, br_P) | \forall D' \in D_m^{\pm}(M, br_P) : D' \subseteq_{br_H} D \Rightarrow D' =_{br_H} D\}.$$

The letter H in br_H stands for higher importance. Before presenting the plain preference encoding, we illustrate how an arbitrary order relation over a pair of sets may be mapped to the $\subseteq$-relation on an exponentially larger set, i.e., we map $\preceq$ on diagnoses of an MCS M, to another set which is exponentially larger than the set of diagnoses of M.

Definition 12. *Let $\preceq$ be a preference relation on $2^{br(M)}$ and let $g : 2^{br(M)} \times 2^{br(M)} \to \mathcal{K}$ be an arbitrary bijective mapping. The* subset-mapping $map_{\preceq}^g : 2^{br(M)} \times 2^{br(M)} \to 2^{\mathcal{K}}$ *is for every $(D_1, D_2) \in 2^{br(M)} \times 2^{br(M)}$ given by*

$$map_{\preceq}^g(D_1, D_2) =$$
$$\{K \in \mathcal{K} \mid K = g(D_1', D_2') \text{ for some } (D_1', D_2') \preceq (D_1, D_2)\} \cup \{g(D_1, D_2)\}.$$

Observe that $map_{\preceq}^g(D_1, D_2)$ collects $g(D_1', D_2')$ of all (D_1', D_2') "below" (D_1, D_2). Furthermore, adding $g(D_1, D_2)$ mimics reflexivity regardless of the reflexivity of $\preceq$.

The next lemma shows that the subset-mapping correctly maps a preference relation on diagnoses to the subset-relation on an exponentially larger set. This allows to decide whether a diagnosis is more preferred than another solely based on set inclusion.

Lemma 2. *Let $\preceq$ be a preference on diagnosis candidates of an MCS M and g be any bijective mapping $g : 2^{br(M)} \times 2^{br(M)} \to \mathcal{K}$. Then, for any $(D_1, D_2) \neq (D_1', D_2') \in 2^{br(M)} \times 2^{br(M)}$, we have $(D_1, D_2) \preceq (D_1', D_2')$ iff $map_{\preceq}^g(D_1, D_2) \subseteq map_{\preceq}^g(D_1', D_2')$.*

We now use $map_{\preceq}^{g}$ to map the preference of a total order $\preceq$ to a set $\mathcal{K}$ which occurs in $M^{mr(\theta,\mathcal{K})}$. To this end, we choose $\theta(D_1, D_2, K)$ as $map_{\preceq}^{g}(D_1, D_2) = K$. Then every diagnosis with protected bridge rules $(d1(D_1), d2(D_2) \cup K)$ of $M^{mr(\theta,\mathcal{K})}$ contains the preference $\preceq$ encoded in K. Selecting a diagnosis of $M^{mr(\theta,\mathcal{K})}$ where K is minimal selects then a preferred diagnosis according to $\preceq$.

Definition 13. *Let M be an MCS and let $\preceq$ be a preference relation. Furthermore, let*

$$\mathcal{K} = \{(n+1 : diag_{D_1,D_2}) \leftarrow \bot. \mid D_1, D_2 \subseteq br(M)\}$$

and let g be a bijective function such that $g(D_1, D_2) = (n+1 : diag_{D_1,D_2}) \leftarrow \bot.$ for all $D_1, D_2 \subseteq br(M)$. Define $\theta(D_1, D_2, K)$ as $map_{\preceq}^{g}(D_1, D_2) = K$. Then the MCS $M^{mr(\theta,\mathcal{K})}$ is called the plain encoding *of M w.r.t. $\preceq$, which we also denote by $M^{pl\preceq}$; all bridge rules of $\mathcal{K}$ are prioritized, i.e., $br_H = \mathcal{K}$.*

Note that as $map_{\preceq}^{g}$ is a function, also θ amounts to a function $2^{br(M)} \times 2^{br(M)} \rightarrow \mathcal{K}$.

Example 8. We consider the hospital MCS M of Example 4 again using a preference order on diagnoses that is similar to the one of Example 6, i.e., we prefer diagnoses that change the bridge rules regarding health, r_1, r_2, as little as possible. To make the preference of the latter example total, we use cardinality-minimality, i.e., given $(D_1, D_2), (D_1', D_2') \in 2^{br(M)} \times 2^{br(M)}$ the preference order $\preceq$ is given by

$$(D_1, D_2) \preceq (D_1', D_2') \text{ iff } \left|\{r_1, r_2\} \cap (D_1 \cup D_2)\right| \leq \left|(D_1' \cup D_2') \cap \{r_1, r_2\}\right|.$$

Figure 4 shows the resulting MCS $M^{mr(\theta,\mathcal{K})}$, where only bridge rules stemming from $r_5 \in br(M)$ and some bridge rules of the observation context (i.e., from $\mathcal{K}$), are indicated. Note that $br_4(M^{mr(\theta,\mathcal{K})})$ has a bridge rule for every possible diagnosis of M.

As for the logic and knowledge base employed in $C_4 = (L_\Sigma^{asp}, kb_4, br_4)$, we use ASP again to demonstrate a possible realization, where kb_4 contains the following rules:

$$removed_r \leftarrow not\ not\_removed_r. \qquad\qquad \text{for all } r \in br(M)$$
$$\bot \leftarrow cur\_diag_{D_1,D_2}, not\ diag_{D_1,D_2}. \qquad \text{for all } D_1, D_2 \subseteq br(M)$$
$$cur\_diag_{D_1',D_2'} \leftarrow cur\_diag_{D_1,D_2}. \qquad \text{for all } (D_1', D_2') \preceq (D_1, D_2)$$
$$cur\_diag_{D_1,D_2} \leftarrow removed_{r_1}, \ldots, removed_{r_k}, \quad \text{for all } D_1 = \{r_1, \ldots, r_k\} \subseteq br(M),$$
$$uncond_{r_1'}, \ldots, uncond_{r_m'}. \qquad\qquad D_2 = \{r_1', \ldots, r_m'\} \subseteq br(M)$$

Intuitively, the first group of rule ensures that diagnosis observation is exposed correctly in an accepted belief set of C_4. The constraints ensure the presence of condition-free bridge rules (i.e., they map each diagnosis candidate to the corresponding bridge rule being condition-free); the next rules guarantee that all bridge rules corresponding to more-preferred diagnoses also must be condition-free (under ASP semantics, they effect $map_{\preceq}^{g}(D_1, D_2)$); the last group of rules recognizes one of the diagnosis candidates.

The set $D_m^{\pm}(M^{pl\preceq}, br_P)$ of minimal diagnoses with protected bridge rules of $M^{pl\preceq}$ corresponds to those diagnoses of M which are at the same time preferred according to $\preceq$ and $\subseteq$-minimal; they are not minimal $\preceq$-preferred in general.

For a total preference $\preceq$, however, the minimal $\preceq$-preferred diagnoses of M and the prioritized-minimal diagnoses of $M^{pl\preceq}$ coincide. As $map_{\preceq}^{g}$ is a function, this correspondence indeed is one-to-one. Intuitively, this shows that for a total preference order,

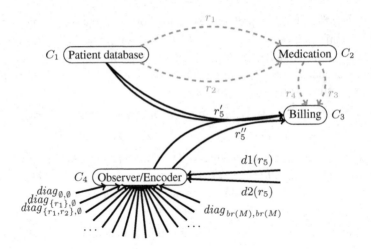

Fig. 4. Contexts and some bridge rules of $M^{pl\preceq} = (C_1, C_2, C_3, C_4)$ for the hospital MCS M from Example 8 w.r.t. $\preceq$. Only bridge rules stemming from r_5 and some from $\mathcal{K}$ are shown; dashed lines indicate bridge rules $r_1, \ldots, r_4$ from M (corresponding bridge rules in $M^{pl\preceq}$ are omitted).

the set of prioritized-minimal diagnoses of the plain encoding of M w.r.t. $\preceq$ can be used to select the minimal $\preceq$-preferred diagnoses of M w.r.t. $\preceq$.

Theorem 1. *For every MCS M and total preference $\preceq$ on its diagnoses, it holds that*

$$D^\pm(M^{pl\preceq}, br_P, br_H) =$$
$$\{(d1(D_1), d2(D_2) \cup map^g_{\preceq}(D_1, D_2)) \mid (D_1, D_2) \in D^\pm_{m,\preceq}(M)\}.$$

5 Computational Complexity

In this section we analyze the computational complexity of the more sophisticated notions of diagnoses for an MCS that have been utilized in the preceding sections. We formally establish that recognizing subset-minimal diagnoses with protected bridge rules is not harder than recognizing subset-minimal diagnoses, i.e., deciding $D \in D^\pm_m(M, br_P)$ is not harder than deciding $D \in D^\pm_m(M)$. Another result shows the same for prioritized-minimal diagnoses, i.e., deciding $D \in D^\pm(M, br_P, br_H)$ is as hard as deciding $D \in D^\pm_m(M)$. The latter notion of diagnosis is essentially applied by the plain encoding $M^{pl\preceq}$ and, given a total preference order $\preceq$, selects minimal $\preceq$-preferred diagnoses according to the preference. However, this does not mean that selecting minimal $\preceq$-preferred diagnoses according to a (total) preference order has the same complexity as the previous problems, as $M^{pl\preceq}$ uses exponentially many bridge rules (w.r.t. M).

Table 1 summarizes our results, where MCSD_m (resp., MCSDP_m, MCSDPH) denotes the problem of deciding whether for a given MCS M and $D \in 2^{br(M)} \times 2^{br(M)}$ it holds that $D \in D^\pm_m(M)$ (resp., $D \in D^\pm_m(M, br_P)$, $D \in D^\pm(M, br_P, br_H)$), where

Table 1. Membership results for deciding whether a diagnosis candidate is a protected, respectively prioritized-minimal, diagnosis; hardness holds if at least one context is hard for $CC(M)$

$(D_1, D_2) \in \mathcal{D}?$ Context complexity $CC(M)$	MCSD_m $\mathcal{D} = D_m^{\pm}(M)$	MCSDP_m $\mathcal{D} = D_m^{\pm}(M, br_P)$	MCSDPH $\mathcal{D} = D^{\pm}(M, br_P, br_H)$
P	$\mathbf{D_1^P}$	$\mathbf{D_1^P}$	$\mathbf{D_1^P}$
NP	$\mathbf{D_1^P}$	$\mathbf{D_1^P}$	$\mathbf{D_1^P}$
$\mathbf{\Sigma_i^P}, i \geq 1$	$\mathbf{D_i^P}$	$\mathbf{D_i^P}$	$\mathbf{D_i^P}$
Proposition	cf. [7]	3	4

$br_P, br_H \subseteq br(M)$). As for $CC(M)$, the context complexity $CC(C_i)$ of a context C_i (cf. [7] for formal details) is informally the complexity of deciding whether C_i has an acceptable belief set for a given interpretation of its bridge rules that is compliant with a given expected output (i.e., beliefs occurring in other bridge rules); $CC(M)$ is then an upper bound for all $CC(C_i)$, $1 \leq i \leq n$. More formally, we have:

Proposition 3. *The computational complexity (hardness and membership) of* MCSDP_m *is the same as for* MCSD_m.

Now consider the problem MCSDPH which amounts to deciding whether for all $T \in D_m^{\pm}(M, br_P)$ it holds that $T \subseteq_{br_H} D \Rightarrow T =_{br_H} D$, where D is a given diagnosis candidate. Again, we end up in the same complexity classes as for the previous problems.

Proposition 4. MCSDPH *is in* $\mathbf{D_i^P}$ *for context complexity* $CC(M)$ *in* $\mathbf{\Sigma_i^P}$ *and* $i \geq 1$; *if at least one context of* M *is hard for* $\mathbf{\Sigma_i^P}$, *then* MCSDPH *is* $\mathbf{D_i^P}$-*hard.*

6 Conclusion

We addressed the problem of discriminating between multiple diagnoses for an inconsistent MCS and selecting most preferred ones given additional preference information. Our method allows for the protection of certain bridge rules from modification and has been realized for total orders by means of a meta-reasoning approach, i.e., by an encoding into diagnostic reasoning on (ordinary) MCS that is capable of introspection regarding possible diagnoses. An investigation concerning computational complexity revealed that the generalized notions of diagnosis applied, i.e., protecting and prioritizing bridge rules, come at no additional cost. However, this is not the case for selecting most preferred diagnoses, where the encoding grows exponential in the number of bridge rules.

Concerning related work, most notably in a series of papers [1,2,3] an approach has been developed that guarantees the existence of an equilibrium (and thus consistency) in MCS. It is based on trust among contexts and provenance information. In contrast to that, we do not focus on a single formalism for preference, and in the spirit of MCS aim for a solution which is general and open to a wide variety of preference formalisms. Managed MCS [5] are a generalization of the MCS framework facilitating more complex operations on context knowledge bases rather than mere addition of information. This is achieved by means of so-called operational statements in bridge rule heads. This generalization paves the way to address potential inconsistency also at the knowledge sources, an issue complementary to inconsistency resolution at the bridge rule level. Another, however more specific, means to address inconsistency also on the source level is by resorting to supported equilibrium semantics [13]. It extends equilibrium semantics with notions for support and justification, which may be exploited for diagnoses that take modifications of the knowledge base for potential repair into account.

In additional work, we investigated a different, more succinct encoding on the basis of our general meta-reasoning approach, which extends to arbitrary preference orders. While succinctness expectedly leads to an increase in complexity, the encoding thus stays polynomial in size and can be shown to be worst-case optimal. Several problems in this context, however, remain as interesting topics for further research. For instance, the investigation of sufficient conditions to ensure locality/modularity properties, or the identification of classes of preference relations which do not yield a complexity increase are highly relevant issues. Eventually, also the practical realization of a succinct encoding in terms of meta-reasoning, e.g., as a front-end to the MCS-IE system (see [7]), may yield a working prototype implementation.

References

1. Bikakis, A., Antoniou, G.: Distributed defeasible contextual reasoning in ambient computing. In: Aarts, E., Crowley, J.L., de Ruyter, B., Gerhäuser, H., Pflaum, A., Schmidt, J., Wichert, R. (eds.) AmI 2008. LNCS, vol. 5355, pp. 308–325. Springer, Heidelberg (2008)
2. Bikakis, A., Antoniou, G.: Defeasible contextual reasoning with arguments in ambient intelligence. IEEE Trans. Knowl. Data Eng. 22(11), 1492–1506 (2010)
3. Bikakis, A., Antoniou, G., Hassapis, P.: Strategies for contextual reasoning with conflicts in ambient intelligence. Knowl. Inf. Syst. 27(1), 45–84 (2011)
4. Brewka, G., Eiter, T.: Equilibria in Heterogeneous Nonmonotonic Multi-Context Systems. In: Proc. 22nd Conf. Artificial Intelligence (AAAI 2007), pp. 385–390. AAAI Press (2007)
5. Brewka, G., Eiter, T., Fink, M., Weinzierl, A.: Managed multi-context systems. In: Walsh, T. (ed.) Proc. 22nd International Joint Conf. Artificial Intelligence (IJCAI 2011), pp. 786–791. AAAI Press/IJCAI (2011)
6. Brewka, G., Roelofsen, F., Serafini, L.: Contextual Default Reasoning. In: Veloso, M. (ed.) Proc. 20th International Joint Conf. Artificial Intelligence (IJCAI 2007), pp. 268–273. AAAI Press/IJCAI (2007)
7. Eiter, T., Fink, M., Schüller, P., Weinzierl, A.: Finding explanations of inconsistency in multi-context systems. Artif. Intell. 216, 233–274 (2014)
8. Eiter, T., Fink, M., Weinzierl, A.: Preference-based inconsistency assessment in multi-context systems. In: Janhunen, T., Niemelä, I. (eds.) JELIA 2010. LNCS, vol. 6341, pp. 143–155. Springer, Heidelberg (2010)
9. Faber, W., Leone, N., Pfeifer, G.: Recursive aggregates in disjunctive logic programs: Semantics and complexity. In: Alferes, J.J., Leite, J. (eds.) JELIA 2004. LNCS (LNAI), vol. 3229, pp. 200–212. Springer, Heidelberg (2004)
10. Giunchiglia, F.: Contextual reasoning. Epistemologia XVI, 345–364 (1993)
11. McCarthy, J.: Generality in artificial intelligence. Commun. ACM 30(12), 1029–1035 (1987)
12. Przymusinski, T.: Stable semantics for disjunctive programs. New Generation Computing 9(3), 401–424 (1991)
13. Tasharrofi, S., Ternovska, E.: Generalized multi-context systems. In: Baral, C., Giacomo, G.D., Eiter, T. (eds.) Proc. 14th International Conf. Principles of Knowledge Representation and Reasoning (KR 2014), pp. 368–377 (2014)
14. Weinzierl, A.: Inconsistency Management under Preferences for Multi-Context Systems and Extensions. PhD thesis, TU Vienna, A-1040 Vienna, Karlsplatz 13, Austria (October 2014)

Reduction-Based Approaches to Implement Modgil's Extended Argumentation Frameworks

Wolfgang Dvořák[1], Sarah Alice Gaggl[2], Thomas Linsbichler[3], and Johannes Peter Wallner[3]

[1] University of Vienna, Faculty of Computer Science, Austria
[2] Technische Universität Dresden, Computational Logic Group, Germany
[3] Vienna University of Technology, Institute of Information Systems, Austria

Abstract. This paper reconsiders Modgil's Extended Argumentation Frameworks (EAFs) that extend Dung's abstract argumentation frameworks by attacks on attacks. This allows to encode preferences directly in the framework and thus also to reason about the preferences themselves. As a first step to reduction-based approaches to implement EAFs, we give an alternative (but equivalent) characterization of acceptance in EAFs. Then we use this characterization to provide EAF encodings for answer set programming and propositional logic. Moreover, we address an open complexity question and the expressiveness of EAFs.

1 Introduction

Since the seminal paper of Dung in 1995 [9] argumentation has emerged to one of the major research fields in artificial intelligence and non-monotonic reasoning, with Dung's *abstract argumentation frameworks* (AFs) being one of the core formalisms. In this very simple yet expressive model, arguments and a binary *attack* relation between them, denoting conflicts, are the only components one needs for the representation of a wide range of problems and the reasoning therein. Nowadays numerous semantics exist to solve the inherent conflicts between the arguments by selecting sets of "acceptable" arguments.

In certain scenarios there are *preferences* about which arguments should go into the set of acceptable arguments, e.g. because the source of one argument is more trustworthy than the source of another [18]. Such preferences can have a significant impact on the evaluation of discussions. Consider for example a situation with two mutually conflicting arguments a and b. The only possibilities (under e.g. stable semantics of AFs) would be to accept either a or b. Thus, neither argument is skeptically justified, i.e. none of them appears in each solution, but given a preference of argument a over b one can resolve this situation such that a is skeptically justified. However, the basic Dung-style framework does not support the handling of preferences within the framework, neither on a syntactical nor on a semantical level. For example it is not possible to model a situation where one argument (resp. attack) is preferred over another one, or where some particular preference weakens an attack between two arguments.

T. Eiter et al. (Eds.): Brewka Festschrift, LNAI 9060, pp. 249–264, 2015.

Several approaches for incorporating preferences have been proposed in the literature. When *instantiating* an AF from a knowledge base one can deal with preferences in the underlying logical formalism and resolve them when building the framework (see e.g. [19]). Preferences can also be handled at the abstract level by generalizations of AFs. In *preference-based argumentation frameworks* (PAFs) [1] one has a partial ordering over the arguments, and an attack is only successful if the attacked argument is not preferred over the attacker with respect to the ordering. Thus the acceptability of an argument can be based either on defense or on preference with respect to the attacking arguments. *Value-based argumentation frameworks* (VAFs) [3] allow to assign values to the arguments. An additional ordering over the values can be used to evaluate preferences in a similar way as in PAFs. Brewka and Woltran introduced prioritized *bipolar abstract dialectical frameworks* (BADFs) [5] which allow to express for each statement a strict partial order on the links leading to it. Then, a statement is accepted unless its attackers are jointly preferred.

All these approaches have in common that they are tailored to *fixed* preferences. In some scenarios it might very well be the case that the assumed preference ordering is itself open to debate. Modgil's *extended argumentation frameworks* (EAFs) [18] are particularly appealing in this regard, as they allow to represent preferences as defeasible arguments themselves. More concretely, this approach is based on the idea that a preference for one argument a over another argument b can weaken an attack from b to a. Considering the example with mutually attacking arguments from above, in EAFs one can resolve this situation by introducing an argument c which stands for a preference of a over b by attacking the attack from b to a. Thereby, argument a is reinstated, while b cannot be accepted. However, if c is attacked by another argument d, the argument b can be reinstated again. Thus, EAFs can be used as a *meta-argumentation* approach to argue also about the preferences, where the acceptance of an argument depends on whether it can be *reinstated*. For instance one can encode VAFs as EAFs and then argue about the value ordering [18].

Although Modgil presented an extensive study of the new formalism and its extensions to VAFs and logic programs in [18], several computational properties of EAFs have been neglected therein. Dunne et al. [12] gave an exact *complexity* classification for reasoning in EAFs. They showed that whether an argument is acceptable w.r.t. a given set can be decided in polynomial time via a reduction to an AF. Hence the reasoning tasks in EAFs have the same complexity as in AFs. Later this reduction has also been turned into labeling-based algorithms [21]. In this work we will show the exact complexity of GROUNDED-SCEPTICISM, i.e. of deciding whether the grounded extension is contained in all preferred extensions, which was left open in [12]. Moreover we will show that, despite reasoning tasks having the same complexity, EAFs enjoy higher *expressiveness* in terms of realizability [11] compared to Dung-style AFs.

Recently the reduction-based approach for the implementation of argumentation related problems became very popular. In particular reductions to well established formalisms like answer set programming (ASP) [6,20] and propositional logic turned out to be suitable for the relevant reasoning problems [15,4,13]. So far, no such approach is known for EAFs. We believe this is partly due to fact that the given characterizations for the acceptance of an argument are not well suited for such encodings. Thus we will first present an alternative, but equivalent, characterization for the acceptance of an argument which then allows us to design succinct ASP encodings for all standard semantics of EAFs. These encodings have been incorporated in the web-interface *GERD - Genteel Extended argumentation Reasoning Device* and are freely accessible under http://gerd.dbai.tuwien.ac.at. Furthermore, the alternative characterization facilitates encodings in terms of propositional formulas which we will exemplify on the admissible semantics.

The organization of the remainder of the paper is as follows: In Section 2 we give the necessary background on argumentation and answer set programming. In Section 3 we first show an alternative characterization of acceptance and then exploit this characterization to encode the semantics in answer set programming and propositional logic. Further, in Section 4 we provide an exact complexity characterization of GROUNDED-SCEPTICISM, an open problem raised in [12] and show that all the EAF semantics from [18], except grounded, are more expressive than their counterparts in standard Dung AFs. Finally we conclude in Section 5.

2   Background

In this section we briefly introduce Dung's abstract argumentation frameworks (AFs) [9] (for an introduction to abstract argumentation see [2]) and Modgil's extended argumentation frameworks (EAFs) [18]. We first give the definition of AFs. In contrast to [9] we restrict ourselves to finite frameworks.

Definition 1. *An* Argumentation Framework (AF) *is a pair $F = (A, R)$ where A is a non-empty, finite set of arguments and $R \subseteq A \times A$ is the attack relation.*

The idea of EAFs is to express preferences of arguments over each other by allowing attacks on attacks. This allows one to argue about the preferences themselves. Attacks on attacks are implemented by an additional relation D which relates arguments to attacks in R.

Definition 2. *An* Extended Argumentation Framework (EAF) *is a triple $F = (A, R, D)$ where (A, R) is an AF and $D \subseteq A \times R$ a relation describing an argument x attacking an attack $(y, z) \in R$. Moreover, whenever $\{(x, (y, z)), (x', (z, y))\} \subseteq D$ then $\{(x, x'), (x', x)\} \subseteq R$.* [1]
Given a set of arguments $S \subseteq A$, an attack $(x, y) \in R$ succeeds w.r.t. S (we write $x \rightarrowtail^S y$) iff there is no $z \in S$ with $(z, (x, y)) \in D$. By R_S we denote the relation containing all attacks $(x, y) \in R$ that succeed w.r.t. S. A set $S \subseteq A$ is said to be conflict-free *in F, i.e. $S \in cf(F)$, if $x \not\rightarrowtail^S y$ and $\{(x, y), (y, x)\} \not\subseteq R$ for all $x, y \in S$.*

---

[1] Note that this property is essential for showing Dung's fundamental lemma for EAFs. However our implementations would still work for EAFs violating this property.

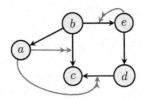

Fig. 1. The EAF F from Example 1

Now, as attacks can be defeated themselves, when defending an argument we have to make sure that also the used attacks are defended.

Definition 3. *Given an EAF $F = (A, R, D)$, $S \subseteq A$, and $v \rightarrowtail^S w$. Then $\mathcal{RS} \subseteq R_S$ is a* reinstatement set *for $v \rightarrowtail^S w$ if it satisfies the following conditions:*

R1 $v \rightarrowtail^S w \in \mathcal{RS}$.
R2 For each $(y, z) \in \mathcal{RS}$ it holds that $y \in S$.
R3 For every $(y, z) \in \mathcal{RS}$ and every $(x, (y, z)) \in D$ there is a $(y', x) \in \mathcal{RS}$.

An argument $a \in A$ is acceptable *w.r.t. (or defended by) a set $S \subseteq A$ if whenever $z \rightarrowtail^S a$ then there is a $y \in S$ with $y \rightarrowtail^S z$ and there is a reinstatement set for $y \rightarrowtail^S z$. For any $S \in cf(F)$ the* characteristic function $\mathcal{F}_F$ *is defined as $\mathcal{F}_F(S) = \{x \mid x$ is acceptable w.r.t. $S\}$.*

Example 1. Consider the EAF $F = (A, R, D)$ from Figure 1, and let $S = \{b, d\}$. Then, $R_S = \{(b, a), (b, c), (b, e), (d, c), (e, d)\}$, and there are the following reinstatement sets for the succeeding attacks:

- $\mathcal{RS}$ for $b \rightarrowtail^S a$: $\{(b, a)\}$;   – $\mathcal{RS}$ for $b \rightarrowtail^S c$: $\{(b, c), (b, a)\}$;
- $\mathcal{RS}$ for $b \rightarrowtail^S e$: $\{(b, e)\}$;   – $\mathcal{RS}$ for $d \rightarrowtail^S c$: $\{(d, c), (b, a)\}$.

There is no reinstatement set for $e \rightarrowtail^S d$, as $e \notin S$. Regarding acceptability, the argument d is acceptable w.r.t. S because for $e \rightarrowtail^S d$ we have $b \in S$ with $b \rightarrowtail^S e$ with $\mathcal{RS} = \{(b, e)\}$. Furthermore, b is acceptable w.r.t. S as well.   ◇

Definition 4. *Given an EAF $F = (A, R, D)$, a conflict-free set S is*

- *an* admissible set, *i.e. $S \in adm(F)$, if each $a \in S$ is acceptable w.r.t. S,*
- *a* preferred extension, *i.e. $S \in prf(F)$, if S is a $\subseteq$-maximal admissible set,*
- *a* stable extension, *i.e. $S \in stb(F)$, if for each $b \notin S$, there is some $a \in S$ with $a \rightarrowtail^S b$,*
- *a* complete extension, *i.e. $S \in com(F)$, if $a \in S$ iff a is acceptable w.r.t. S,*
- *and the* grounded extension $grd(F)$ *is given by $grd(F) = \bigcup_{k \geq 1} \mathcal{F}_F^k(\emptyset)$.*

Example 2. For the EAF F from Figure 1 we have the following extensions: $adm(F) = \{\emptyset, \{e\}, \{b\}, \{b, d\}, \{b, e\}\}$, $stb(F) = com(F) = prf(F) = \{\{b, d\}, \{b, e\}\}$, and $\{b, d\}$ is the unique grounded extension.   ◇

2.1 Answer Set Programming

In this section we recall the basics of logic programs under the answer set semantics [6,20].

We fix a countable set $\mathcal{U}$ of *(domain) elements*, also called *constants*. An *atom* is an expression $p(t_1, \ldots, t_n)$, where p is a *predicate* of arity $n \geq 0$ and each t_i is either a variable or an element from $\mathcal{U}$. An atom is *ground* if it is free of variables. $B_{\mathcal{U}}$ denotes the set of all ground atoms over $\mathcal{U}$. A *rule* r is of the form

$$a \leftarrow b_1, \ldots, b_k, \; not\, b_{k+1}, \ldots, \; not\, b_m.$$

with $m \geq k \geq 0$, where $a, b_1, \ldots, b_m$ are atoms, and *"not"* stands for *default negation*. The *head* of r is the set $H(r) = \{a\}$ and the *body* of r is $B(r) = \{b_1, \ldots, b_k, not\, b_{k+1}, \ldots, not\, b_m\}$. Furthermore, $B^+(r) = \{b_1, \ldots, b_k\}$ and $B^-(r) = \{b_{k+1}, \ldots, b_m\}$. A *constraint* is a rule with empty head. A rule r is *safe* if each variable in r occurs in $B^+(r)$. A rule r is *ground* if no variable occurs in r. A *fact* is a ground rule with empty body. An (input) database is a set of facts. A *program* is a finite set of rules. For a program π and an input database D, we often write $\pi(D)$ instead of $D \cup \pi$.

For any program π, let UP be the set of all constants in π. $Gr(\pi)$ is the set of rules $r\sigma$ obtained by applying, to each rule $r \in \pi$, all possible substitutions σ from the variables in r to elements of UP. An *interpretation* $I \subseteq B_{\mathcal{U}}$ *satisfies* a ground rule r iff $H(r) \cap I \neq \emptyset$ whenever $B^+(r) \subseteq I$ and $B^-(r) \cap I = \emptyset$. I satisfies a ground program π, if each $r \in \pi$ is satisfied by I. A non-ground rule r (resp., a program π) is satisfied by an interpretation I iff I satisfies all groundings of r (resp., $Gr(\pi)$). $I \subseteq B_{\mathcal{U}}$ is an *answer-set* of π iff it is a subset-minimal set satisfying the *Gelfond-Lifschitz reduct* $\pi^I = \{H(r) \leftarrow B^+(r) \mid I \cap B^-(r) = \emptyset, r \in Gr(\pi)\}$. We denote the set of answer-sets of π by $\mathcal{AS}(\pi)$.

3 Reduction-Based Approaches to EAFs

Towards reductions to answer set programming encodings and propositional logic we first give an alternative characterization of acceptance.

3.1 An Alternative Characterization of Acceptance

Reinstatement sets are defined for a single attack in an EAF $F = (A, R, D)$ and a set of arguments $S \subseteq A$. Here we show that we just need to consider one reinstatement set for all attacks in R_S.

Lemma 1. *If $\mathcal{RS}, \mathcal{RS}'$ are reinstatement sets for $y \rightarrowtail^S z$ and $y' \rightarrowtail^S z'$ respectively then $\mathcal{RS} \cup \mathcal{RS}'$ is a reinstatement set for both $y \rightarrowtail^S z$ and $y' \rightarrowtail^S z'$.*

Proof. We have to verify conditions R1-R3 from Definition 3.
R1) We have $y \rightarrowtail^S z \in \mathcal{RS} \cup \mathcal{RS}'$ and $y' \rightarrowtail^S z' \in \mathcal{RS} \cup \mathcal{RS}'$ as the former is contained in $\mathcal{RS}$ and the latter is in $\mathcal{RS}'$.

R2) Consider $(y, z) \in \mathcal{RS} \cup \mathcal{RS}'$ and w.l.o.g. assume that $(y, z) \in \mathcal{RS}$. As $\mathcal{RS}$ is a reinstatement set for $y \rightarrowtail^S z$ we have $y \in S$.

R3) Consider $(y, z) \in \mathcal{RS} \cup \mathcal{RS}'$ with $(x, (y, z)) \in D$ and again w.l.o.g. assume that $(y, z) \in \mathcal{RS}$. As $\mathcal{RS}$ is a reinstatement set for $y \rightarrowtail^S z$ we have that there is a $(y', x) \in \mathcal{RS}$ and thus also $(y', x) \in \mathcal{RS} \cup \mathcal{RS}'$.   □

As the union of two reinstatement sets for the same set S is again a reinstatement set there exists a unique maximal reinstatement set. This is by a standard argument: assume that there are two of them then the union of them would be a larger one contradicting the maximality of the original ones. This leads us to the definition of the *maximal reinstatement set* $\mathcal{RS}[S]$ of a set S.

Definition 5. *Given an EAF* (A, R, D) *and* $S \subseteq A$. *The (unique) maximal reinstatement set* $\mathcal{RS}[S]$ *of* S *is the maximal subset of* R_S *satisfying*

R2 For each $(y, z) \in \mathcal{RS}[S]$ *it holds that* $y \in S$.

R3 For every $(y, z) \in \mathcal{RS}[S]$ *and every* $(x, (y, z)) \in D$ *there is a* $(y', x) \in \mathcal{RS}[S]$.

We next show that when it comes to the verification of extensions S in EAFs we only have to consider the *maximal reinstatement set* $\mathcal{RS}[S]$ instead of all possible reinstatement sets for each attack $y \rightarrowtail^S z$.

Proposition 1. *Given an EAF* $F = (A, R, D)$, $S \subseteq A$, *and* $y \rightarrowtail^S z$. *There exists a reinstatement set for* $y \rightarrowtail^S z$ *iff* $\mathcal{RS}[S]$ *is a reinstatement set for* $y \rightarrowtail^S z$.

Proof. ⇒: Towards a contradiction assume that there is a reinstatement set $\mathcal{RS}$ for $y \rightarrowtail^S z$ but $y \rightarrowtail^S z \notin \mathcal{RS}[S]$. Then by Lemma 1 the set $\mathcal{RS} \cup \mathcal{RS}[S]$ would be a reinstatement set for $y \rightarrowtail^S z$. Thus $\mathcal{RS}[S] \subset \mathcal{RS} \cup \mathcal{RS}[S]$ and $\mathcal{RS} \cup \mathcal{RS}[S]$ satisfying R2 and R3 contradicting the maximality of $\mathcal{RS}[S]$.

⇐: By assumption $\mathcal{RS}[S]$ is a reinstatement set for $y \rightarrowtail^S z$.   □

Next we reformulate the condition for an argument to be acceptable.

Corollary 1. *Given an EAF* $F = (A, R, D)$, *an argument* $a \in A$ *is acceptable w.r.t.* $S \subseteq A$ *if whenever* $z \rightarrowtail^S a$ *then there is some* $y \in S$ *with* $(y, z) \in \mathcal{RS}[S]$.

Given S, the reinstatement set $\mathcal{RS}[S]$ can be computed in polynomial time.

Proposition 2. *Given an EAF* (A, R, D) *and* $S \subseteq A$. $\mathcal{RS}[S]$ *can be computed in polynomial time.*

Proof. The proof proceeds as follows. We first present a procedure to compute $\mathcal{RS}[S]$ and then show correctness and that it terminates in polynomial time.

Procedure:

- Start with $U = R_S \cap (S \times A)$.
- Repeat until fixed-point is reached:
  - For each $y \rightarrowtail^S z \in U$: if there is $(x, (y, z)) \in D$ such that there is no $(y', x) \in U$ then remove $y \rightarrowtail^S z$ from U.
- return $\mathcal{RS}[S] = U$

Correctness: To prove correctness we show (1) that the fixed-point satisfies R2 and R3. and (2) that in each iteration only attacks which are not in $\mathcal{RS}[S]$ are removed, i.e. $\mathcal{RS}[S] \subseteq U$ holds during the whole procedure.

(1) The property R2 is ensured by the initialization $U = R_S \cap (S \times A)$, that is at each time the set U only contains (y, z) with $y \in S$. Now consider property R3. As the algorithm terminated we have that for every $y \rightarrowtail^S z \in U$, if there is a $(x, (y, z)) \in D$ then there is also a $(y', x) \in U$. That is R3 holds.

(2) We prove this by induction on the number of iterations n. As base case we consider $n = 1$ meaning that the algorithm returns $U = R_S \cap (S \times A)$. As by definition $\mathcal{RS}[S] \subseteq R_S \cap (S \times A)$ we are fine. Now let U_i be the set after the i-th iteration. For the induction step we assume that $\mathcal{RS}[S] \subseteq U_{n-1}$ and show that then also $\mathcal{RS}[S] \subseteq U_n$. To this end consider a $(y, z) \in U_{n-1} \setminus U_n$. Then there is an $(x, (y, z)) \in D$ such that there is no $(y', x) \in U_{n-1}$. But this implies that there is an $(x, (y, z)) \in D$ such that there is no $(y', x) \in \mathcal{RS}[S]$ and thus, because of property R3, $(y, z) \notin \mathcal{RS}[S]$. Hence $\mathcal{RS}[S] \subseteq U_n$.

Polynomial-Time: For the initialization step notice that R_S can be computed in polynomial time and also checking whether an attack has its source in S is easy. As in each iteration of the loop, except the last one, at least one attack is removed from the set, there are at most as many iterations as attacks. Finally the condition in the loop can be tested in polynomial time.   □

3.2   Answer Set Programming Encodings

In this section we present ASP encodings based on our characterization of EAF acceptance of arguments. In our encodings we will use atoms **in**(a) to represent that an argument a is in an extension. The answer-sets of the combination of an encoding for a semantics σ with an ASP representation of an EAF F are in a 1-to-1 correspondence to $\sigma(F)$. More formally we have the following correspondence.

Definition 6. *Let I be an interpretation, $\mathcal{I}$ a set of interpretations, S a set and $\mathcal{S}$ a set of sets. We define $I \cong S$ iff $\{a \mid \mathbf{in}(a) \in I\} = S$. Further, $\mathcal{I} \cong \mathcal{S}$ iff there is a bijective function $f : \mathcal{I} \to \mathcal{S}$ such that for each $I \in \mathcal{I}$ we have $I \cong f(I)$.*

For readability we partition the encodings into several modules. We begin with the input database for a given EAF $F = (A, R, D)$, i.e. the facts representing the EAF.

$$\hat{F} := \{\mathbf{arg}(x). \mid x \in A\} \cup$$
$$\{\mathbf{att}(x, y). \mid (x, y) \in R\} \cup$$
$$\{\mathbf{d}(x, y, z). \mid (x, (y, z)) \in D\}$$

That is, **arg**(x) is a fact that represents that x is an argument in F. The binary predicate **att**(x, y) indicates that there is an attack from x to y and **d**(x, y, z) signifies that there is an attack from x to the attack from y to z.

Listing 1.1. Module π_{cf}

```
% guess  a  set  S
in (X)  ←  arg (X) , not out (X) .
out (X)  ←  arg (X) , not in (X) .

% mutually  attacking  arguments  are  forbidden  in  a  cf  set
←  att (X,Y) ,  att (Y,X) ,  in (X) ,  in (Y) .

% canceled  attacks  via  D
cancel (X,Y)  ←  att (X,Y) ,  in (Z) ,  d (Z,X,Y) .
succeed (X,Y)  ←  att (X,Y) , not cancel (X,Y) .
←  in (X) ,  in (Y) ,  succeed (X,Y) .
```

The first basic module π_{cf} is shown in Listing 1.1. Comments can be distinguished from rules by the preceding '%' symbol. The first two lines encode a typical ASP guess. The **in** and **out** predicates identify a subset S of the arguments in the given EAF. If $\mathbf{in}(x)$ is present in an answer-set then $x \in S$ and otherwise we have $\mathbf{out}(x)$ in the answer-set and $x \notin S$. The first constraint encodes that mutually attacking arguments cannot be in a conflict-free set of F. Using the predicates **succeed** and **cancel** we can derive all attacks (x, y) which are canceled by a $(z, (x, y)) \in D$, s.t. $z \in S$ for the guessed S. The last line encodes that no two conflicting arguments can be in S, if an attack in either direction succeeds.

Next we look at module π_{rs} in Listing 1.2, which computes $\mathcal{RS}[S]$ in the predicate **rs**. Intuitively the "procedure" is as in the proof of Proposition 2. We collect with **rsinit** all successful attacks coming from an argument in S. If for such an attack (y, z) there is an $x \in A$ s.t. $(x, (y, z)) \in D$, then we need to check if the attack (y, z) is reinstated by $\mathcal{RS}[S]$, in particular we need to check if there is an attack $(y', x) \in \mathcal{RS}[S]$. We mark such a case with $\mathbf{todef}(x, y, z)$. The procedure for computing the maximal reinstatement set now starts with the initial set of attacks and iteratively removes attacks until a fixed-point is reached. We remove (y, z) if there is an $(x, (y, z)) \in D$, s.t. in the set of the current iteration there is no (y', x).

The fixed-point computation is simulated by the predicate **unattacked_upto** and **remove**. The latter predicate marks attacks to be removed from **rsinit** in order to compute the unique maximal reinstatement set in **rs**. We iterate for each removal candidate marked by $\mathbf{todef}(x, y, z)$ over each argument n in the EAF. If $\mathbf{rsinit}(n, x)$ is not derivable or $\mathbf{remove}(n, x)$ was derived then (n, x) is not in the maximal reinstatement set and thus does not defend the attack (y, z) from $(x, (y, z))$. If this holds for all arguments in the EAF, then (y, z) is not defended and we mark it for removal by $\mathbf{remove}(y, z)$. For achieving this we use the module π_{order} to impose an order on the arguments. This is a standard module used in several ASP encodings of AF semantics, e.g. in [15]. We present here only the main predicates defined in this module. The predicate $\mathbf{lt}(x, y)$

Listing 1.2. Module π_{rs}

```
% rsinit represents all succeeding attacks coming from S
rsinit (Y,Z) ← in (Y), succeed (Y,Z).

% removal candidates
todef(X,Y,Z) ← rsinit (Y,Z), d(X,Y,Z).

% remove attacks
unattacked_upto (X,Y,Z,N) ← inf (N), todef(X,Y,Z),
                            not rsinit (N,X).
unattacked_upto (X,Y,Z,N) ← inf (N), todef(X,Y,Z), remove(N,X).
unattacked_upto (X,Y,Z,N) ← succ (M,N),
                            unattacked_upto (X,Y,Z,M),
                            not rsinit (N,X).
unattacked_upto (X,Y,Z,N) ← succ (M,N),
                            unattacked_upto (X,Y,Z,M),
                            remove (N,X).
unattacked (X,Y,Z) ← sup (N), unattacked_upto (X,Y,Z,N).
remove (Y,Z) ← unattacked (X,Y,Z).

% rs represents RS[S]
rs (X,Y) ← rsinit (X,Y), not remove (X,Y).
```

---

is used to relate x and y, s.t. x is ordered lower than y. Using $\mathbf{succ}(x, y)$ we derive that y is the immediate successor of x in this ordering and lastly **inf** and **sup** are the infimum and supremum elements. Now, we start with the infimum argument and go through the successor predicate **succ** to the next argument. If (y, z) is undefended up to the supremum then we have to remove it. Intuitively $\mathbf{unattacked\_upto}(x, y, z, n)$ states that $(x, (y, z))$ is not successfully attacked by an attack in $\mathcal{RS}[S]$ up to the argument n in the ordering. Lastly, in **rs** we simply derive all attacks from **rsinit**, for which we cannot derive that the attack should be removed. The attacks derived via **rs** correspond to $\mathcal{RS}[S]$.

In $\pi_{defense}$ (Listing 1.3) we simply state that each y is defeated if there is an attack in our reinstatement set given by **rs**. Note that we still refer to a guessed set S. Using this we derive which arguments are undefended. Now we present our ASP encoding for admissible sets. We combine the modules for the conflict-free property, reinstatement sets, order and defense and add an intuitive constraint ensuring that if an argument is in, then it has to be defended.

$$\pi_{adm} := \pi_{cf} \cup \pi_{rs} \cup \pi_{order} \cup \pi_{defense} \cup \{\leftarrow \mathbf{in}(X), \mathbf{undefended}(X).\}$$

It is straightforward to extend this encoding to complete semantics as follows.

$$\pi_{com} := \pi_{adm} \cup \{\leftarrow \mathbf{out}(X), not\ \mathbf{undefended}(X).\}$$

Listing 1.3. Module $\pi_{defense}$

```
% arguments which are defeated by RS[S]
defeated(Y) ← rs(X,Y).

% undefended arguments
undefended(A) ← arg(A), succeed(Z,A), not defeated(Z).
```

Listing 1.4. Module π_{range}

```
in_range(Z) ← in(Y), succeed(Y,Z).
```

For the stable semantics we compute for $S \subseteq A$ the set $\{a \mid b \rightarrowtail^S a, b \in S\}$. This is encoded in π_{range} in Listing 1.4. Stable semantics can be computed via

$$\pi_{stb} := \pi_{cf} \cup \pi_{range} \cup \{\leftarrow \mathbf{out}(Z), not\ \mathbf{in\_range}(Z).\}$$

The 1-to-1 correspondence between the answer-sets of our encodings and the σ-extensions is summarized in the following proposition.

Proposition 3. *For any EAF F: (i) $\mathcal{AS}(\pi_{cf}(\hat{F})) \cong cf(F)$; (ii) $\mathcal{AS}(\pi_{adm}(\hat{F})) \cong adm(F)$; (iii) $\mathcal{AS}(\pi_{com}(\hat{F})) \cong com(F)$; and (iv) $\mathcal{AS}(\pi_{stb}(\hat{F})) \cong stb(F)$.*

Encodings for grounded semantics of EAFs are straightforward to achieve via techniques used in [15]. Essentially by starting with the empty set we derive the grounded extension of a given EAF, by iteratively applying the characteristic function of EAFs [18]. The ASP encoding of the characteristic function is based on the module π_{rs}.

In spirit of promising approaches for computing reasoning tasks under preferred semantics [8,13] in AFs we can compute preferred extensions in EAFs by iteratively using simple adaptations of encodings for admissible semantics. The basic idea is to traverse the search space of admissible (or complete) extensions and iteratively compute larger admissible sets until we reach a maximal set. By restricting the future search space to admissible sets not contained in previously found preferred extensions, we can compute all preferred extensions in this way.

We implemented reasoning for EAFs under conflict-free, admissible, complete, grounded, preferred and stable semantics in the tool "GERD" available online[2]. Except for preferred semantics, we provide a single ASP encoding for download which computes all extensions of the desired semantics if augmented with an input database representing the given EAF. For solving one can use modern ASP solvers, like clingo [17]. For preferred semantics we provide a UNIX bash script, which calls clingo repeatedly to compute preferred extensions in the manner described above. In Fig. 2 one can see a screenshot of the web-interface.

---

[2] See http://gerd.dbai.tuwien.ac.at

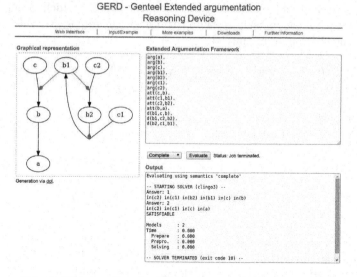

Fig. 2. Web-interface for ASP encodings of EAF semantics

3.3 Propositional Encoding

Our alternative characterization is not only useful in the context of ASP. To exemplify this we encode admissible semantics in terms of propositional logic. Notice that such encodings are the basis to generalize several (implementation) approaches studied for abstract argumentation, like for using SAT and QBF-solvers [4,16], monadic second order logic encodings [14], and approaches using iterative SAT-calls [8,13].

The idea of propositional logic encodings is to give a formula such that the models of the formula correspond to the extensions of the EAF. Given an EAF $F = (A, R, D)$ for each $x \in A$ we introduce a variable a_x encoding that x is in the extension S, i.e. x is in the extension iff a_x is true in the corresponding model. Then for each pair $(y, z) \in R$ we introduce variables $r_{y,z}$ encoding that $y \rightarrowtail^S z$. The truth-values of $r_{y,z}$ can be defined in terms of a_x.

$$\varphi_r = \bigwedge_{(x,(y,z))\in D} (\neg a_x \vee \neg r_{y,z}) \wedge \bigwedge_{(y,z)\in R} (r_{y,z} \vee (\bigvee_{(x,(y,z))\in D} a_x))$$

The first part saying that for each attack $(x, (y, z))$ either $x \notin S$ or $y \not\rightarrowtail^S z$. The second part is the reverse direction saying that either $y \rightarrowtail^S z$ or there is an attack $(x, (y, z))$ with $x \in S$. We are now ready to encode conflict-freeness.

$$\varphi_{cf} = \bigwedge_{(x,y)\in R} (\neg a_x \vee \neg a_y \vee \neg r_{x,y}) \wedge \bigwedge_{(x,y),(y,x)\in R} (\neg a_x \vee \neg a_y)$$

The first part says that for each $(x, y) \in R$ either $x \notin S$ or $y \notin S$ or the attack must be canceled by S. The second part encodes the condition that mutually conflicting arguments cannot be in the same conflict-free set.

To test admissibility we need a reinstatement set $\mathcal{RS}$ which is encoded by variables $rs_{y,z}$, i.e. the attack $(y,z) \in R$ is in the reinstatement set $\mathcal{RS}$ iff $rs_{y,z}$ is true in the corresponding model.

$$\varphi_{\mathcal{RS}} = \bigwedge_{(y,z)\in R} ((\neg rs_{y,z} \vee a_y) \wedge (\neg rs_{y,z} \vee r_{y,z})) \wedge \bigwedge_{(x,(y,z))\in D} (\neg rs_{y,z} \vee \bigvee_{(z',x)\in R} rs_{z',x})$$

The first part stating that if an attack (y,z) is in $\mathcal{RS}$ then $y \in S$ and $y \rightarrowtail^S z$. The second one says that for each $(x,(y,z))$ either there is an attack (z',x) in $\mathcal{RS}$ or (y,z) cannot be in $\mathcal{RS}$.

Finally we can encode the condition for a set S defending its arguments.

$$\varphi_{def} = \bigwedge_{(y,z)\in R} (\neg a_z \vee \neg r_{y,z} \vee \bigvee_{(x,y)\in R} rs_{x,y})$$

So for each attack (y,z) either $z \notin S$, the attack is canceled by S or y is counter attacked by an attack in $\mathcal{RS}$.

Now it is straight forward to show the following proposition.

Proposition 4. *Consider the function $Ext(M) = \{x \in A \mid a_x \in M\}$ mapping models to extensions. For any EAF F we have $adm(F) = \{Ext(M) \mid M$ is model of $\varphi_r \wedge \varphi_{cf} \wedge \varphi_{\mathcal{RS}} \wedge \varphi_{def}\}$.*

4   Complexity and Expressiveness of EAFs

In this section we first use our characterization of acceptance to answer an open complexity-question from [12]. Second, given that the complexity of the main reasoning tasks in EAFs and AFs coincide and complexity is often considered as an indicator for expressiveness one might expect that they have the same expressiveness. We answer this negatively by showing that for each semantics considered in this paper, except grounded, EAFs are more expressive than AFs.

4.1   Complexity of Grounded-Scepticism

Modgil [18] observed that in EAFs the grounded extension is not always contained in all the preferred extensions. This is in contrast to Dung's AFs where this is always the case and grounded semantics can be seen as strictly more skeptical than skeptical preferred reasoning, i.e. than considering the arguments that are contained in all preferred extensions. Dunne et al. [12] introduced the computational problem of GROUNDED-SCEPTICISM, i.e. deciding whether the grounded extension is contained in all the preferred extensions, and gave a coNP lower bound but left the exact complexity open.

Theorem 1. GROUNDED-SCEPTICISM *is Π_2^P-complete.*

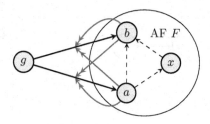

Fig. 3. The AF F' from the proof of Theorem 1, for $A = \{a, b, x\}$

Proof. We first show *membership in* Π_2^P. This is by a Σ_2^P algorithm for disproving that the grounded extension is contained in each preferred extension. This algorithm first computes the grounded extension G which is in P [12] and then guesses a preferred extension E. Then the NP-oracle is used to verify that E is a preferred extension and finally $G \subseteq E$ is tested.

To obtain *hardness* we give a reduction from the Π_2^P-hard problem $\mathsf{Skept}_{prf}^{AF}$, that is deciding whether an argument $x \in A$ is skeptically accepted w.r.t. *prf* in Dung AFs [10]. To this end consider an instance $F = (A, R), x \in A$ of $\mathsf{Skept}_{prf}^{AF}$. W.l.o.g. we can assume that $(x, x) \notin R$. We construct an EAF $F' = (A', R', D')$ with $A' = A \cup \{g\}$, $R' = R \cup \{(g, a) \mid a \in A \setminus \{x\}\}$ and $D' = \{(b, (g, a)) \mid a, b \in A \setminus \{x\}\}$ (see also Figure 3). Clearly F' can be constructed in polynomial time.

To complete the proof we next show that x is skeptically accepted in F iff $grd(F') \subseteq E$ for each $E \in prf(F')$. To this end we show that $com(F') = \{\{g, x\}\} \cup \{E \cup \{g\} \mid E \in com(F)\}$. First as g is not attacked at all it has to be contained in each complete extension. Considering $S = \{g\}$ we have that $\mathcal{RS}[S] = \{(g, a) \mid a \in A \setminus \{x\}\}$ and thus that g defends x and thus x must be in the grounded extension. Now consider $S = \{g, x\}$. Still $\mathcal{RS}[S] = \{(g, a) \mid a \in A \setminus \{x\}\}$ and none of the $a \in A \setminus \{x\}$ is acceptable as a is not defended against (g, a). Hence, $\{g, x\}$ is the grounded extension. Next consider an S with $S \cap (A \setminus x) \neq \emptyset$. Then $\rightarrowtail^S$ corresponds to R. As no attack in R is attacked by D' we have that $E \cup \{g\}$ is complete iff $E \in com(F)$.

By the above we have that either (i) $prf(F') = \{E \cup \{g\} \mid E \in prf(F)\}$ if there is an $E \in prf(F)$ with $x \in E$, or (ii) $prf(F') = \{\{g, x\}\} \cup \{E \cup \{g\} \mid E \in prf(F)\}$ otherwise. In the former $\{g, x\}$ is contained in all preferred extensions of F' iff x was skeptically accepted in F and in the latter $\{g, x\}$ is not contained in all preferred extensions but also x was not skeptically accepted in F. Hence, $\{g, x\}$ is contained in all preferred extensions of F' iff x is skeptically accepted in F. $\square$

4.2   Expressiveness of EAFs

Recently the expressiveness of the most prominent semantics of AFs was studied in terms of realizability [11]. A collection of sets of arguments $\mathbb{S}$, frequently called extension-set in the remainder of this section, is said to be realizable under a semantics σ, if there exists some AF F such that the σ-extensions of F coincide with $\mathbb{S}$, i.e. $\sigma(F) = \mathbb{S}$. In the following we show that the additional modelling

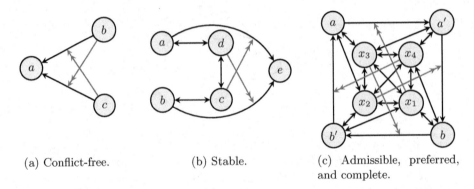

(a) Conflict-free.   (b) Stable.   (c) Admissible, preferred, and complete.

Fig. 4. EAFs witnessing the increased expressive power compared to AFs

power of EAFs also gives rise to increased expressiveness. This means that for every semantics under consideration, except grounded, there are extension-sets obtained by some EAF which do not have an AF as syntactic counterpart. We show EAFs with sets of extensions which cannot be realized under the corresponding AF-semantics in the following example (see also Figure 4).

Conflict-Free Sets: Given an arbitrary AF F, it holds that $cf(F)$ is downward closed, that is for every $E \in cf(F)$ also $E' \in cf(F)$ for each $E' \subseteq E$. This is, as already pointed out in [12], not necessarily true in EAFs. For example, the conflict-free sets of the EAF F_1 in Figure 4a coincide with $\{\emptyset, \{a\}, \{b\}, \{c\}, \{b,c\}, \{a,b,c\}\}$, which cannot be the collection of conflict-free sets of any AF. Observe that for $E = \{a,b,c\}$ both $\{a,b\} \subseteq E$ and $\{a,c\} \subseteq E$, but neither one of those sets is a conflict-free set of F_1. This comes by the fact that the success of attacks can be conditioned by the presence of arguments.

Stable Semantics: It was shown in [11] that for every AF $F = (A, R)$, the stable extensions of F, denoted by $\mathbb{S}$, form a tight set, i.e. the following holds: $\mathbb{S} \subseteq max_{\subseteq}\{S \subseteq A \mid \forall a, b \in S \; \exists T \in \mathbb{S} : \{a,b\} \subseteq T\}$. One can check that this condition does not hold for the extension-set $\mathbb{T} = \{\{a,b\}, \{a,c,e\}, \{b,d,e\}\}$. Hence there is no AF F with $stb(F) = \mathbb{T}$. On the other hand, the EAF F_2 depicted in Figure 4b has exactly $\mathbb{T}$ as stable extensions.

Preferred Semantics: The preferred semantics is among the most expressive semantics in AFs. For a collection of sets of arguments $\mathbb{S}$, the property called adm-closed is decisive for *prf*-realizability [11]: For each $A, B \in \mathbb{S}$ such that $A \cup B \notin \mathbb{S}$ (for *prf* just $A \neq B$) there have to be some $a, b \in (A \cup B)$ with $\nexists C \in \mathbb{S} : \{a,b\} \subseteq C$. Now consider the extension-set $\mathbb{U} = \{\{a,b\}, \{a',b'\}, \{a,a',x_1\}, \{a',b,x_2\}, \{b,b',x_3\}, \{a,b',x_4\}\}$ and observe that $A = \{a,b\}$ and $B = \{a',b'\}$ violate the condition. Each pair of arguments in $(A \cup B)$ occurs together in some element of $\mathbb{U}$ and is therefore necessarily without conflict in every AF trying to realize $\mathbb{U}$. On the other hand, we can again find an EAF realizing $\mathbb{U}$ under the preferred semantics, namely F_3 shown in Figure 4c, where conflicts are resolved by attacks from the x_i-arguments.

Admissible and Complete Semantics: Finally one can also show that $adm(F_3)$ (resp. $com(F_3)$) are not realizable by AFs under the admissible (resp. complete) semantics, indicating the increase in expressiveness for admissible and complete semantics. Towards a contradiction assume that $adm(F_3)$ (resp. $com(F_3)$) could be realized by an AF F under admissible (resp. complete) semantics. Then the preferred extensions $prf(F)$ of F are just the $\subseteq$-maximal sets in $adm(F_3)$ (resp. $com(F_3)$) and thus $prf(F) = \mathbb{U}$. However, this contradicts the observation from above that $\mathbb{U}$ is not prf-realizable in AFs.

5 Conclusion

In this work we revisited Modgil's extended argumentation frameworks [18], an appealing approach to incorporate preferences in abstract argumentation formalisms. We provided a different, yet equivalent, characterization of acceptance in EAFs, of which we made use of in reductions to two well-established formalisms. First we presented ASP encodings for all semantics together with an implementation in the online tool GERD. Second we encoded admissible semantics in terms of propositional logic as a basis for implementation approaches such as SAT- and QBF-solving. Moreover, we addressed a problem which was left open in the complexity analysis of EAFs [12] by showing that deciding whether the grounded extension is contained in all preferred extensions is Π_2^P-complete for EAFs. Finally we showed that the additional modelling capabilities within EAFs give rise to higher expressiveness for all but the grounded semantics.

Making use of the propositional encoding of admissible semantics in an (iterative) SAT-based implementation of EAF reasoning tasks is an obvious direction of future work. Moreover, the performance of our ASP-based implementation could be compared to labeling-based algorithms [21] in an empirical evaluation. Finally, the connection of EAFs to ADFs [7], a very recent and general argumentation formalism, should be explored, particularly by providing an efficient translation from EAFs to ADFs.

Acknowledgements. We express our gratitude to Gerd Brewka, to whom this Festschrift is dedicated. Each of the authors visited Gerd's group in Leipzig in the course of their work, which has led to many ongoing and fruitful collaborations and discussions. Insights gained through these visits have been, and continue to be, influential for our works.

We further thank Günther Charwat and Andreas Pfandler for their support for developing the web front-end GERD, Gerald Weidinger for his contributions to earlier versions of the ASP encodings and Pietro Baroni for his helpful comments on an earlier version of this paper.

This research has been supported by the Austrian Science Fund (FWF). Thomas Linsbichler's work has been funded by FWF project I1102 and Johannes Wallner's work has been funded by FWF project P25521.

References

1. Amgoud, L., Cayrol, C.: A reasoning model based on the production of acceptable arguments. Ann. Math. Artif. Intell. 34(1-3), 197–215 (2002)
2. Baroni, P., Caminada, M.W.A., Giacomin, M.: An introduction to argumentation semantics. Knowledge Eng. Review 26(4), 365–410 (2011)
3. Bench-Capon, T.J.M.: Persuasion in practical argument using value-based argumentation frameworks. J. Log. Comput. 13(3), 429–448 (2003)
4. Besnard, P., Doutre, S.: Checking the acceptability of a set of arguments. In: Proc. NMR, pp. 59–64 (2004)
5. Brewka, G., Woltran, S.: Abstract Dialectical Frameworks. In: Proc. KR 2010, pp. 102–111. AAAI Press (2010)
6. Brewka, G., Eiter, T., Truszczyński, M.: Answer set programming at a glance. Commun. ACM 54(12), 92–103 (2011)
7. Brewka, G., Ellmauthaler, S., Strass, H., Wallner, J.P., Woltran, S.: Abstract Dialectical Frameworks Revisited. In: Proc. IJCAI, pp. 803–809. AAAI Press / IJCAI (2013)
8. Cerutti, F., Dunne, P.E., Giacomin, M., Vallati, M.: Computing preferred extensions in abstract argumentation: A SAT-based approach. In: Black, E., Modgil, S., Oren, N. (eds.) TAFA 2013. LNCS, vol. 8306, pp. 176–193. Springer, Heidelberg (2014)
9. Dung, P.M.: On the acceptability of arguments and its fundamental role in non-monotonic reasoning, logic programming and n-person games. Artif. Intell. 77(2), 321–358 (1995)
10. Dunne, P.E., Bench-Capon, T.J.M.: Coherence in finite argument systems. Artif. Intell. 141(1/2), 187–203 (2002)
11. Dunne, P.E., Dvořák, W., Linsbichler, T., Woltran, S.: Characteristics of multiple viewpoints in abstract argumentation. In: Proc. KR, pp. 72–81. AAAI Press (2014)
12. Dunne, P.E., Modgil, S., Bench-Capon, T.J.M.: Computation in extended argumentation frameworks. In: Proc. ECAI, pp. 119–124. IOS Press (2010)
13. Dvořák, W., Järvisalo, M., Wallner, J.P., Woltran, S.: Complexity-sensitive decision procedures for abstract argumentation. Artif. Intell. 206, 53–78 (2014)
14. Dvořák, W., Szeider, S., Woltran, S.: Abstract argumentation via monadic second order logic. In: Hüllermeier, E., Link, S., Fober, T., Seeger, B. (eds.) SUM 2012. LNCS, vol. 7520, pp. 85–98. Springer, Heidelberg (2012)
15. Egly, U., Gaggl, S.A., Woltran, S.: Answer-Set Programming Encodings for Argumentation Frameworks. Argument and Computation 1(2), 147–177 (2010)
16. Egly, U., Woltran, S.: Reasoning in argumentation frameworks using Quantified Boolean Formulas. In: Proc. COMMA, pp. 133–144. IOS Press (2006)
17. Gebser, M., Kaminski, R., Kaufmann, B., Ostrowski, M., Schaub, T., Schneider, M.: Potassco: The Potsdam Answer Set Solving Collection. AI Communications 24(2), 105–124 (2011)
18. Modgil, S.: Reasoning about preferences in argumentation frameworks. Artif. Intell. 173(9-10), 901–934 (2009)
19. Modgil, S., Prakken, H.: A general account of argumentation with preferences. Artif. Intell. 195, 361–397 (2013)
20. Niemelä, I.: Logic Programming with Stable Model Semantics as a Constraint Programming Paradigm. Ann. Math. Artif. Intell. 25(3-4), 241–273 (1999)
21. Nofal, S., Dunne, P.E., Atkinson, K.: Towards experimental algorithms for abstract argumentation. In: Proc. COMMA, pp. 217–228. IOS Press (2012)

I don't care, I don't know ... I know too much! On Incompleteness and Undecidedness in Abstract Argumentation

Pietro Baroni[1], Massimiliano Giacomin[1], and Beishui Liao[2]

[1] Dip. Ingegneria dell'Informazione, Univ. of Brescia, Brescia, Italy
{pietro.baroni,massimiliano.giacomin}@unibs.it
[2] Center for the Study of Language and Cognition, Zhejiang Univ., Hangzhou, China
baiseliao@zju.edu.cn

Abstract. Incompleteness and undecidedness are pervasively present in human reasoning activities and make the definition of the relevant computational models challenging. In this discussion paper we focus on one such model, namely abstract argumentation frameworks, and examine several flavours of incompleteness and undecidedness thereof, by providing a conceptual analysis, a critical literature review, and some new ideas with pointers to future research.

Keywords: Argumentation frameworks, Argumentation semantics, Incompleteness, Undecidedness.

1 Introduction

In everyday life answering a question is not just a matter of choosing between "Yes" and "No". You may have no interest in giving a definite answer (whether you have it ready or not) or, for some justified reason, may be unable to produce it and prefer to take a less committed position. This variety of behaviors (and the reasoning underlying them) is a key feature of dialogues between human beings, and, in a sense, of human intelligence itself. Providing a formal counterpart to them is therefore a plus, if not a must, for any formal approach aiming at representing and/or supporting intelligent dialogical and/or inferential activities. This paper focuses on one such approach, namely *abstract argumentation*, and aims at providing a conceptual analysis, a critical literature review, and some new ideas with pointers to future research concerning the treatment of incompleteness and undecidedness in this context. In a nutshell, abstract argumentation focuses on the evaluation of the justification status of a set of (typically conflicting) arguments according to a given *argumentation semantics*. So it can be roughly regarded as a formal approach to answer, for every single argument, the question: "Is this argument acceptable?" Analyzing and discussing which answers are available beyond "Yes" and "No" is the subject of this work.

The paper is organized as follows. Section 2 recalls the necessary background concepts, Section 3 is devoted to partial evaluations in argumentation semantics, Section 4 deals with different forms of undecidedness, and Section 5 concludes.

T. Eiter et al. (Eds.): Brewka Festschrift, LNAI 9060, pp. 265–280, 2015.

2   Background

This work lies in the context of Dung's theory [15] of abstract argumentation frameworks (AFs), whose definition is recalled below.

Definition 1. *An argumentation framework (AF) is defined as a pair $\langle \mathcal{A}, \rightarrow \rangle$ in which $\mathcal{A}$ is a set of arguments and $\rightarrow \subseteq \mathcal{A} \times \mathcal{A}$ describes the attack relation between arguments in $\mathcal{A}$, so that $(\alpha, \beta) \in \rightarrow$ (also denoted as $\alpha \rightarrow \beta$) indicates that the argument α attacks the argument β. For a set $S \subseteq \mathcal{A}$, the attackers of S are defined as $S^{\leftarrow} = \{\alpha \in \mathcal{A} \mid \exists \beta \in S : \alpha \rightarrow \beta\}$ and the attackees of S are defined as $S^{\rightarrow} = \{\alpha \in \mathcal{A} \mid \exists \beta \in S : \beta \rightarrow \alpha\}$.*

In Dung's theory arguments are abstract entities, whose nature and structure are not specified, as the formalism is focused only on the representation of their conflicts. Given an *AF*, a basic problem consists in determining the conflict outcome, namely assigning a justification status to arguments. An *argumentation semantics* can be conceived, in broad terms, as a formal way to answer this question.

Two main approaches to semantics definitions have been adopted in the literature (see [5] for a review). In the *extension-based* approach the "outcome" of an argumentation semantics when applied to a given *AF* is a set of *extensions*, where each extension is a set of arguments considered to be jointly acceptable.

Definition 2. *Given an AF $\mathcal{F} = \langle \mathcal{A}, \rightarrow \rangle$, an extension-based semantics σ associates with $\mathcal{F}$ a subset of $2^{\mathcal{A}}$, denoted as $\mathcal{E}_\sigma(\mathcal{F})$.*

In the *labelling-based* approach the "outcome" is a set of labellings, where a labelling is the assignment to each argument of a label taken from a fixed set.

Definition 3. *Let $\mathcal{F} = \langle \mathcal{A}, \rightarrow \rangle$ be an AF and Λ a set of labels. A Λ-labelling of $\mathcal{F}$ is a total function $L : \mathcal{A} \longrightarrow \Lambda$. The set of all Λ-labellings of $\mathcal{F}$ is denoted as $\mathfrak{L}(\Lambda, \mathcal{F})$.*

Definition 4. *Given an AF $\mathcal{F} = \langle \mathcal{A}, \rightarrow \rangle$ and a set of labels Λ, a labelling-based semantics σ associates with $\mathcal{F}$ a subset of $\mathfrak{L}(\Lambda, \mathcal{F})$, denoted as $\mathcal{L}_\sigma(\mathcal{F})$.*

Some observations concerning the relationships between the labelling and extension-based approaches are worth making. First, as set membership can be expressed in terms of a binary labelling, e.g. with $\Lambda = \{\in, \notin\}$, the extension-based approach can be regarded as a special case of the general labelling-based approach. The latter is therefore potentially more expressive under a suitable choice of Λ. It has however to be noted that the almost universally adopted choice for Λ in the literature, namely the set $\Lambda^{iou} \triangleq \{\mathbf{in}, \mathbf{out}, \mathbf{und}\}$, has exactly the same expressiveness as the extension-based approach.

To see this, and also to introduce some concepts useful in the sequel, let us give some comments on the common intuitions underlying the two approaches.

First, coming back to the question about the justification status of arguments, each extension and each Λ^{iou}-labelling can be regarded as one of the possible (according to the semantics at hand) answers to the question. Indeed, an extension E identifies as justified arguments the members of E itself while a labelling identifies as justified arguments those that are labelled *in*. Further, arguments not included in E can be partitioned between those that are attacked by some member of E and those that are not. The former ones can be regarded as definitely rejected, and correspond to those labelled *out*, while the latter ones are in a sort of intermediate status between acceptance and rejection, and correspond to those labelled *und*. On this intuitive basis, a one-to-one formal correspondence between extensions and Λ^{iou}-labellings can be defined, which has been shown to hold for the main semantics in the literature [5].

As this paper deals mainly with general notions rather than with semantics-specific properties, we don't need to go through the various argumentation semantics considered in the literature and, for the sake of exemplification, we recall only the definition of *complete* semantics (denoted as $\mathcal{CO}$) in the two approaches. The two definitions are indeed equivalent (using the correspondence mentioned above) though they may appear rather different at first glance.

In the extension-based approach, basically a complete extension is a set of arguments which has no conflicts inside, defends all its elements against external attacks, and includes all the arguments it defends.

Definition 5. *Given an AF $\mathcal{F} = \langle \mathcal{A}, \rightarrow \rangle$, a set $S \subseteq \mathcal{A}$ is conflict-free iff $\nexists \alpha, \beta \in S : \alpha \rightarrow \beta$. S defends an argument α iff $\forall \beta$ s.t. $\beta \rightarrow \alpha$ $\exists \gamma \in S : \gamma \rightarrow \beta$. The set of arguments defended by S in $\mathcal{F}$ is denoted as $\mathcal{D}_{\mathcal{F}}(S)$. A set S is a complete extension of $\mathcal{F}$, i.e. $S \in \mathcal{E}_{\mathcal{CO}}(\mathcal{F})$, iff S is conflict-free and $S = \mathcal{D}_{\mathcal{F}}(S)$.*

In the labelling-based approach, a complete labelling is such that every argument label satisfies some legality constraints taking into account the labels assigned to the attackers of the argument.

Definition 6. *Let L be a Λ^{iou}-labelling of an AF $\mathcal{F} = \langle \mathcal{A}, \rightarrow \rangle$.*

- *An in-labelled argument is legally in iff all its attackers are labelled out.*
- *An out-labelled argument is legally out iff it has at least one attacker that is labelled in.*
- *An und-labelled argument is legally und iff not all its attackers are labelled out and it doesn't have an attacker that is labelled in.*

L is a complete labelling, i.e. $L \in \mathcal{L}_{\mathcal{CO}}(\mathcal{F})$ iff every argument is legally labelled.

Given that a semantics provides, in general, many[1] alternative answers (in form of extensions or labellings) to the "argument justification question", it has to be remarked that a further step consists in deriving a "synthetic" justification status for each argument considering the whole set of extensions or labellings.

---

[1] Most literature semantics provide at least one extension/labelling for every AF, with the exception of *stable* semantics [15] for which the set of extensions/labellings may be empty. To avoid detailed precisations, inessential to the subject of this paper, we assume non-empty sets of extensions/labellings in the following.

In the extension-based approach the two simplest ways to obtain this synthesis basically consist in the set-theoretical operations of intersection and union, leading respectively to the notions of *skeptical* and *credulous* justification, which have an obvious counterpart in the labelling-based approach.

Definition 7. *Given an extension-based semantics σ and an AF $\mathcal{F} = \langle \mathcal{A}, \rightarrow \rangle$, an argument α is* skeptically justified *iff $\forall E \in \mathcal{E}_\sigma(\mathcal{F})$ $\alpha \in E$; an argument α is* credulously justified *iff $\exists E \in \mathcal{E}_\sigma(\mathcal{F}) : \alpha \in E$. Given a labelling-based semantics σ and an AF $\mathcal{F} = \langle \mathcal{A}, \rightarrow \rangle$, an argument α is* skeptically justified *iff $\forall L \in \mathcal{L}_\sigma(\mathcal{F})$ $L(\alpha) = \mathbf{in}$; α is* credulously justified *iff $\exists L \in \mathcal{L}_\sigma(\mathcal{F}) : L(A) = \mathbf{in}$.*

On the basis of the quick review above, one may observe that traditional definitions in abstract argumentation are characterized by exhaustiveness (all the arguments in a framework are assigned a status by the semantics) and allow a unique form of undecidedness, corresponding to the **und** label. Both these constraints may turn out to be too rigid. On the one hand, exhaustiveness may be too demanding in practice, since it might be the case that providing an answer for all arguments is not always necessary. On the other hand, having a unique form of undecidedness may be regarded as poorly expressive, since the variety of cases where you don't have a definite answer may require a richer set of representation alternatives. We review and discuss approaches and ideas aiming at tackling these limitations in the next sections.

3   " I don't care! " Allowing for Incomplete Answers

Providing exhaustive answers is neither always a goal nor a necessity. In particular, there are several reasons why one may prefer not to evaluate the status of every argument. In the context of the reasoning or dialogical activity where the argumentation process is embedded, typically the actual goal is just assessing the status of a restricted subset of arguments, regarded as more important than the others[2], which are considered in the evaluation only if necessary for the main goal. Further, considering a dynamic context, where arguments and attacks may be modified on the fly, it may be the case that some parts of the framework are more subject to change than others and one may prefer, if possible, to restrict his/her evaluation to those parts of the framework which are regarded as "more stable", deferring the evaluation of other parts to a later moment and so avoiding to produce judgments probably needing a revision very soon. Two (not disjoint) motivations for partial evaluations emerge from these examples:

- saving computational resources by avoiding useless (i.e. unnecessary or too ephemeral) evaluations;
- even if computational resources are not an issue, avoiding to express positions beyond what is required (taking into account the goals and/or the dynamics of the process) according to a general criterion of *cautiousness* or *minimal commitment*.

---

[2] See, for instance, the notion of *desired set* introduced by Baumann and Brewka [10] in the context of the problem of argument enforcement.

Both motivations call for identifying some technically sound form of partial evaluation, though with different nuances that may have an effect on what kind of soundness is required. We review some literature approaches to *partial* argumentation semantics in the following subsections.

3.1   Using a *don't-care* Label

In [19] a labelling-based approach using the set of four labels $\Lambda^{JV} = \{+, -, \pm, \otimes\}$ is proposed. The first three labels correspond respectively to in, out, and und of the "traditional" Λ^{iou} set (the symbol $\pm$ indicating that both $+$ and $-$ are considered possible), while the fourth label[3] corresponds to a *don't-care* situation, namely to a non-assigned label. Indeed, a labelling L such that $L(\alpha) = \otimes$ for some argument α is called *partial* in [19], while a labelling L where $\nexists\alpha$ such that $L(\alpha) = \otimes$ will be called *total*.

In [19] the motivation for introducing a label corresponding to a *don't-care* situation is to have the possibility of not saying more than necessary, i.e. of not expressing any judgment concerning "arguments that are irrelevant or that do not interest the observer". This implies that, in principle, the choice of *don't-care* arguments is completely at the discretion of the agent carrying out the argumentation process. This freedom is however limited by the general legality constraints[4] on labellings based on the attack relation. In fact, according to [19, Definition 3] a (possibly partial) labelling L of an *AF* $\mathcal{F} = \langle \mathcal{A}, \rightarrow \rangle$ must satisfy the following conditions:

- $\forall \alpha \in \mathcal{A}$ if $L(\alpha) \in \{-, \pm\}$ then $\exists \beta \in \{\alpha\}^{\leftarrow}$ such that $L(\beta) \in \{+, \pm\}$;
- $\forall \alpha \in \mathcal{A}$ if $L(\alpha) \in \{+, \pm\}$ then $\forall \beta \in \{\alpha\}^{\leftarrow}$ $L(\beta) \in \{-, \pm\}$;
- $\forall \alpha \in \mathcal{A}$ if $L(\alpha) \in \{+, \pm\}$ then $\forall \beta \in \{\alpha\}^{\rightarrow}$ $L(\beta) \in \{-, \pm\}$.

While these rules do not mention explicitly the arguments labelled $\otimes$, they induce some constraints on them too. Intuitively, if you care about an argument, you should care also about some other arguments affecting or affected by it.

More precisely, $L(\alpha) = \otimes$ is possible only if the following conditions hold:

- $\forall \beta \in \{\alpha\}^{\leftarrow}$ $L(\beta) \in \{\otimes, -\}$;
- $\nexists \beta \in \{\alpha\}^{\rightarrow}$ such that $L(\beta) \in \{+, \pm\}$;
- $\forall \beta \in \{\alpha\}^{\rightarrow}$ if $L(\beta) = -$ then $\exists \gamma \in \{\beta\}^{\leftarrow} \setminus \{\alpha\}$ such that $L(\gamma) \in \{+, \pm\}$.

The first condition states that one can not abstain on an argument which has at least one attacker labelled $+$ or $\pm$. This evidences a sort of asymmetry in the approach of [19]: one can abstain on an argument that would otherwise be labelled $+$, but can not abstain on an argument that would otherwise be labelled $-$ or $\pm$. The second and third conditions concern the cases where one abstains on an argument α but not on (some of) the arguments attacked by α. More specifically, the second condition forbids any abstention on the attackers of an

---

[3] In [19] $\emptyset$ is used for the fourth label, we avoid the use of this overloaded symbol.

[4] Note that the legality constraints of [19] do not coincide with the "standard" legality constraints recalled in Definition 6.

argument labelled + or ±, while the third condition allows the abstention on an attacker of an argument β labelled − only if there is another attacker γ, labelled + or ±, justifying the label − of β.

The above rules imply in particular that "full carelessness" (i.e. a labelling L such that $L(\alpha) = \otimes$ for every argument α) is always possible, but partial carelessness is not arbitrary.

An additional observation concerns the relationship between abstention and the potential completions of a partial labelling L. A total labelling L' is a completion of a partial labelling L if $L(\alpha) \neq \otimes \Rightarrow L'(\alpha) = L(\alpha)$, i.e. if L' is obtained from L by replacing all and only the $\otimes$ labels with other labels (taking into account the legality constraints). In general, a legal partial labelling admits several different completions (and always admits at least one). It can be the case that a *don't-care* argument α gets the same label in all the possible completions of a partial labelling L, i.e. that the (only) legal label of α is univocally determined by the information carried by L. Still, according to [19], it is legal to abstain on α. This confirms that the $\otimes$ label does not correspond, *per se*, to any notion of indecision and is applicable to some arguments with an (implicitly) well determined label too.

While a further detailed discussion of the approach in [19] is beyond the scope of the present paper, the features discussed above will be enough to point out the basic differences with other notions of partial argumentation semantics reviewed in the next subsection.

3.2   Partial Semantics for Partial Computation

Given an AF $\mathcal{F} = \langle \mathcal{A}, \rightarrow \rangle$, let $S \subset \mathcal{A}$ be a set of arguments which are of some interest for an agent (in a sense, they are the complement of the *don't-care* arguments mentioned in the previous section). In order to derive the justification status of the interesting arguments one may wonder whether it is necessary to preliminarily carry out a computation involving the whole AF, i.e. to first compute $\mathcal{E}_\sigma(\mathcal{F})$ or $\mathcal{L}_\sigma(\mathcal{F})$, or it is sufficient to carry out a partial computation involving only S and those other parts of the framework affecting the evaluation of the arguments in S. Given that most computational problems in abstract argumentation are intractable, reducing the set of arguments and attacks considered in the derivation of the desired outcomes is of great interest, since it may yield significant savings of computational resources. This calls for a suitable notion of partial semantics applicable to the restrictions of a framework.

This notion is also crucial in the area of argumentation dynamics, namely in contexts where the considered AF is subject to modifications over time. If these modifications affect only a part of the whole framework, there is the opportunity to reuse previously computed results concerning the part of the framework unaffected by modifications, instead of reevaluating the whole framework from scratch. Similar issues also arise from related investigation lines in abstract argumentation, like the study of incremental algorithms for argumentation dynamics [22,8] and of multi-sorted reasoning [24].

Defining a partial semantics involves dealing with two interplaying notions: on the one hand, one has to devise suitable ways to restrict a framework to subframeworks which are appropriate for the definition of partial semantics, on the other hand, one has to identify suitable semantics properties ensuring that the relation between local and global semantics evaluation is sound.

As to defining restrictions, given an AF $\mathcal{F} = \langle \mathcal{A}, \rightarrow \rangle$ and a set of arguments $S \subset \mathcal{A}$ a straightforward way to define the restriction of $\mathcal{F}$ to S is to suppress all arguments in $\mathcal{A} \setminus S$ and all attacks involving at least one argument not in S. Accordingly, the restriction $\mathcal{F} \downarrow_S$ of $\mathcal{F}$ to S is defined as $\mathcal{F} \downarrow_S = \langle S, \rightarrow \cap (S \times S) \rangle$.

This definition appears rather rough as it "cuts" all the links between S and other arguments: indeed it ignores $S^{\leftarrow} \cap (\mathcal{A} \setminus S)$ and $S^{\rightarrow} \cap (\mathcal{A} \setminus S)$. In spite of this, such definition turns out to be very useful under a suitable choice of S and of the semantics σ to be "partialized". First, one can simply choose S such that it is *unattacked*, namely such that $S^{\leftarrow} \cap (\mathcal{A} \setminus S) = \emptyset$. Second, one may focus on semantics featuring the *directionality* property [6], namely such that the evaluation of an unattacked set is not affected by the remaining parts of the framework. The relevant formal definitions are recalled below.

Definition 8. *Given an AF* $\mathcal{F} = \langle \mathcal{A}, \rightarrow \rangle$, *a set* $S \subseteq \mathcal{A}$ *is* unattacked *iff* $S^{\leftarrow} \cap (\mathcal{A} \setminus S) = \emptyset$. *The set of unattacked sets of* $\mathcal{F}$ *is denoted as* $\mathcal{US}(\mathcal{F})$.

Definition 9. *An extension-based semantics* σ *satisfies the directionality criterion iff* $\forall \mathcal{F} = \langle \mathcal{A}, \rightarrow \rangle, \forall S \in \mathcal{US}(\mathcal{F}), \mathcal{AE}_\sigma(\mathcal{F}, S) = \mathcal{E}_\sigma(\mathcal{F} \downarrow_S)$, *where* $\mathcal{AE}_\sigma(\mathcal{F}, S) \triangleq \{(E \cap S) \mid E \in \mathcal{E}_\sigma(\mathcal{F})\} \subseteq 2^S$. *A labelling-based semantics* σ *with label set* Λ *satisfies the directionality criterion iff* $\forall \mathcal{F} = \langle \mathcal{A}, \rightarrow \rangle, \forall S \in \mathcal{US}(\mathcal{F}), \mathcal{AL}_\sigma(\mathcal{F}, S) = \mathcal{L}_\sigma(\mathcal{F} \downarrow_S)$, *where* $\mathcal{AL}_\sigma(\mathcal{F}, S) \triangleq \{L \cap (S \times \Lambda) \mid L \in \mathcal{L}_\sigma(\mathcal{F})\}$.

Under the above mentioned assumptions, a notion of partial semantics useful for partial and incremental computation has been introduced in [21]. Basically, given a set of arguments of interest S, the semantics evaluation is carried out on the restriction of $\mathcal{F}$ to the minimal unattacked set including S.

Definition 10. *Given an AF* $\mathcal{F} = \langle \mathcal{A}, \rightarrow \rangle$ *and a set of arguments* $S \subseteq \mathcal{A}$, *define* $rlvt_\mathcal{F}(S) = \min_\subseteq \{U \mid S \subseteq U \wedge U \in \mathcal{US}(\mathcal{F})\}$. *Given an extension-based (labelling-based) semantics* σ *satisfying the directionality criterion the partial semantics of* $\mathcal{F}$ *with respect to* S *is defined as* $\mathcal{E}_\sigma(\mathcal{F} \downarrow_{rlvt_\mathcal{F}(S)})$ $(\mathcal{L}_\sigma(\mathcal{F} \downarrow_{rlvt_\mathcal{F}(S)}))$.

The restriction to an unattacked set for a directional semantics has been (often implicitly) exploited as a starting point in works oriented towards incremental computation, like splitting argumentation frameworks [9], the division-based method [22] for argumentation dynamics and the decomposition-based approach [20]. In these contexts a further step towards a richer notion of partial semantics is made by considering the restriction to a set S which is not unattacked and receives some fixed influence from outside, formally this amounts to remove the assumption that $S^{\leftarrow} \cap (\mathcal{A} \setminus S) = \emptyset$, while still ignoring $S^{\rightarrow} \cap (\mathcal{A} \setminus S)$.

This has led to various notions of conditioned AF in the literature, where basically a conditioned AF is a framework receiving some attacks from a conditioning AF. In general, the conditioned and conditioning frameworks are obtained by partitioning a global framework according to some criterion. For instance, in a dynamic context, the conditioning framework corresponds to the part of the original framework which is not affected by a modification, so that previous computation results concerning this part can be reused for the new semantics evaluation concerning the affected part, corresponding to the conditioned framework. We recall here the relevant definitions from [22].

Definition 11. *Given an AF $\mathcal{F}_1 = \langle \mathcal{A}_1, \rightarrow_1 \rangle$, a conditioned AF with respect to $\mathcal{F}_1$ is a tuple $\mathcal{CAF} = (\langle \mathcal{A}_2, \rightarrow_2 \rangle, (\mathcal{C}(\mathcal{A}_1), \mathcal{I}_{(\mathcal{C}(\mathcal{A}_1), \mathcal{A}_2)}))$ in which*

- *$\mathcal{F}_2 = \langle \mathcal{A}_2, \rightarrow_2 \rangle$ is an AF that is conditioned by $\mathcal{C}(\mathcal{A}_1)$ in which $\mathcal{A}_2 \cap \mathcal{A}_1 = \emptyset$;*
- *$\mathcal{C}(\mathcal{A}_1) \subseteq \mathcal{A}_1$ is a nonempty set of arguments (called conditioning arguments) that have interactions with arguments in $\mathcal{A}_2$, i.e., $\forall \alpha \in \mathcal{C}(\mathcal{A}_1), \exists \beta \in \mathcal{A}_2$, such that $(\alpha, \beta) \in \mathcal{I}_{(\mathcal{C}(\mathcal{A}_1), \mathcal{A}_2)}$;*
- *$\mathcal{I}_{(\mathcal{C}(\mathcal{A}_1), \mathcal{A}_2)} \subseteq \mathcal{C}(\mathcal{A}_1) \times \mathcal{A}_2$ is the set of interactions from the arguments in $\mathcal{C}(\mathcal{A}_1)$ to the arguments in $\mathcal{A}_2$.*

Semantics directionality still plays a crucial role in this context: the idea is that extension (labelling) computation in $\mathcal{F}_2$ depends on $\mathcal{F}_1$ but not vice versa (since $\mathcal{F}_1$ does not receive attacks from $\mathcal{F}_2$), hence one can use the extensions (labellings) of $\mathcal{F}_1$ as fixed conditions to determine the extensions (labellings) of $\mathcal{F}_2$ (the reader is referred to [22] for details). It must however also be stressed that in this enriched context directionality alone is no more sufficient to ensure that local semantics definitions at the local level are coherent with those at the global level, i.e. that combining the results of local evaluations one obtains the same outcomes of global evaluation. In particular, the role of the SCC-recursiveness property [7] in this context has been pointed out in [8].

Recently, a further generalization in the study of partial argumentation semantics has been achieved [3,4] by considering arbitrary partitions of an *AF* into subframeworks that, differently from the cases reviewed above, can be in a relation of mutual dependence[5]. In this context, a partition induces a set of subframeworks, each of which can be regarded as an *AF* receiving inputs (through some attacks) from other subframeworks and in turn feeding inputs to other subframeworks through other attacks. Modeling each of these subframeworks as an *argumentation framework with input*, it has been possible to identify a *canonical local function* [4] representing the counterpart at the local level of the semantics definition at a global level, under very mild requirements satisfied by most argumentation semantics in the literature.

It turns out however that combining the outcomes of the canonical local function of a semantics σ applied to the subframeworks does not always yield the same results obtained by applying σ at the global level. In other words, not every semantics is *decomposable* with respect to arbitrary partitions of an *AF*: this result poses a theoretical limit to the possibility of defining a partial notion of semantics preserving the same meaning as a global one. Accordingly, an interesting issue consists in identifying some restricted classes of partitions (e.g.

---

[5] The use of arbitrary partitions is called parameterized splitting in [11].

those based on the graph-theoretical notion of strongly connected components) where decomposability is recovered (the reader is referred to [4] for some relevant results). A further research direction than can benefit from a generalized notion of local evaluation is *multi-sorted argumentation* [24], namely the study of the application of different semantics to different parts of a framework.

3.3   Discussion

While the approach in [19] represents explicitly the notion of *don't-care* arguments with a specific label, all the approaches reviewed in section 3.2 use some restriction of the framework to focus attention on some set of arguments which, for some reasons, deserves to be considered separately. Both *don't-care* arguments and (most of) the restriction mechanisms have to obey some constraints and, to the best of our knowledge, their relations have not been investigated yet in the literature. As a preliminary observation it can be noted that constraints on *don't-care* arguments take directly into account the effect that ignoring an argument has on other arguments, while the restriction mechanisms typically considered in the literature take this effect into account indirectly through some graph-theoretical properties (e.g. the one of being an unattacked set). It follows that contraints referred to restriction mechanisms can be more limiting than those expressed in terms of *don't-care* arguments. To exemplify this, consider the simple framework $\mathcal{F}_1 = \langle \{\alpha, \beta, \gamma\}, \{(\alpha, \gamma)(\beta, \gamma)\} \rangle$. Here the status of γ can be determined by considering only one of its attackers (indifferently α or β) and in fact the following labellings are legal according to [19]: $L_1 = \langle (\alpha, +), (\beta, \otimes), (\gamma, -) \rangle$, $L_2 = \langle (\alpha, \otimes), (\beta, +), (\gamma, -) \rangle$, which means (correctly) that one can focus on either $\mathcal{F}_1 \downarrow_{\{\alpha, \gamma\}}$ or $\mathcal{F}_1 \downarrow_{\{\beta, \gamma\}}$ without losing any information about the status of γ. However, $\{\alpha, \gamma\}$ and $\{\beta, \gamma\}$ are not unattacked sets in $\mathcal{F}_1$, thus none of the restriction mechanisms considered in subsection 3.2 would allow this: they would either force the inclusion of the missing argument or take into account it as an input, while (in this specific case) this is, in fact, unnecessary. It must be said however that constraints concerning *don't-care* arguments concern local attack relations only, while the restriction mechanisms provide a direct way to select suitable partitions of a framework at a global level.

This suggests that combining *don't-care* arguments with restriction mechanisms may yield more advanced notions of partial semantics with respect to the state of the art. This appears a very interesting direction of future research: in particular, this combined approach may gain additional efficiency improvements by providing better solutions to the problem of identifying the minimal amount of computation sufficient to ensure that the status of a given set of interesting arguments is the same as the one resulting from a computation over the whole framework. In this perspective interesting relations may be drawn with the notions of *argumentation multipoles* [4] and of *critical sets* [17].

As a final note, since partial semantics notions can be considered also in extensions of the traditional Dung's AFs (in particular in Abstract Dialectical Frameworks [14]), considering the use of *don't-care* arguments in these extended formalisms represents another interesting line of future work.

4   " I don't know ... I know too much " Variations of Undecidedness

4.1   Undecidedness Is Not All the Same

Even if you care about an argument, you may be unable to assign it a definite acceptance status (in or out using the Λ^{iou} label set, + or − using Λ^{JV}) and must be content with an intermediate status (und or ± respectively) representing some form of indecision. In both Λ^{iou} and Λ^{JV} the intermediate label is meant to represent every form of indecision, but one might observe that the reasons to be undecided can be rather different.

On the one hand, one may be undecided because s/he has no enough information to express a definite judgment and needs to wait for further information to arrive. For instance, if asked about whether it will rain tomorrow, you may have no hint at all, reply "I don't know", and then look for weather forecasts on the web. After surfing several weather web sites, however, you are not guaranteed to have gained a definite position, because some of them may promise a sunny day, while others presage thunderstorms. In this case, your indecision is still there but has changed nature since it is due to contradiction rather than to ignorance. Indeed, as suggested in [16], your reply should now be "I know too much", since you got an excess of (inconsistent) information.

Distinguishing these two kinds of indecision is the cornerstone of Belnap-Dunn (BD) four-valued logic [12]. BD-logic is based on the assumption that an information-providing agent has two basic moves available (namely asserting that a given statement is true or asserting that it is false) and that the status of a statement then results from the union of all the moves concerning it. So, if no move at all has been done, its status corresponds to indecision by ignorance (N: "neither told true nor told false"), if only positive or negative moves have been done the statement has a definite status (T: "told true" or F: "told false" respectively), if both positive and negative moves have been done, one gets indecision by contradiction (B: "both told true and told false"). The set of BD truth values is then $\Lambda^{BD} = \{\mathtt{N}, \mathtt{T}, \mathtt{F}, \mathtt{B}\}$.

The use in abstract argumentation of a set of labels $\Lambda^4 = \{\mathtt{none}, \mathtt{in}, \mathtt{out}, \mathtt{both}\}$ corresponding to the four truth values in Λ^{BD} has recently been proposed by Arieli [1], in the context of a conflict-tolerant approach to semantics definition, where the requirement of conflict-freeness for extensions/labellings is relaxed, in order to achieve non-conventional results in the handling of attack loops.

In this way a correspondence between extensions and Λ^4-labellings is obtained as follows. Given an extension E and an argument α:

− α is labelled in iff $\alpha \in E \land \alpha \notin E^{\rightarrow}$;
− α is labelled out iff $\alpha \notin E \land \alpha \in E^{\rightarrow}$;
− α is labelled none iff $\alpha \notin E \land \alpha \notin E^{\rightarrow}$;
− α is labelled both iff $\alpha \in E \land \alpha \in E^{\rightarrow}$.

Note that the fourth case is possible only if E is not conflict-free. While there is a formal correspondence and some intuitive analogy between the four labels in Λ^4 and the four truth values of BD-logic, it has to be remarked that they are conceptually different as they lie at different stages of the reasoning process.

The BD-model can be regarded as basically consisting of three phases:

1. *assertion production*: where agents make assertions by associating truth values to propositions;
2. *aggregation*: where different assertions concerning the same sentence are "put together" (by a simple union operation) yielding a four-valued labelling of propositions;
3. *use of aggregation outcomes*: where reasoning about labelled propositions is carried out (e.g. given two propositions p_1, labelled B, and p_2, labelled N, BD-logic specifies the truth value of $p_1 \vee p_2$, $p_1 \wedge p_2$, and so on ...).

To draw a comparison, also argumentation-based reasoning, called AB-model in the following, can be schematized in three phases:

1. *argument production*: where agents produce (possibly conflicting) arguments each supporting some conclusion;
2. *conflict management*: where semantics evaluation is applied to the set of arguments and attacks yielding a set of labellings of arguments;
3. *use of conflict outcomes*: where argument conclusions are evaluated on the basis of argument labels (note that the same conclusion can be supported by many arguments) and further reasoning is possibly carried out based on these evaluations.

The two models feature several structural similarities. Assertions in the BD-model can be regarded as a special kind of arguments following the generic scheme "If an agent tells that a given proposition p has a truth value v then there is a reason to believe that p has the truth value v." Hence the assertions correspond to the conclusions of the arguments. The aggregation in the BD-model can be regarded as a special kind of conflict management. The basic idea is that conflict arises when different truth values are asserted for the same proposition and that every conflict gives rise to "indecision by contradiction". In terms of Dung's theory, this amounts to consider the special case where only symmetric conflicts are present and to adopt a sceptical semantics (in particular the *grounded* semantics) for the evaluation of arguments. This in particular implies that only one labelling of arguments exists where all non conflicting arguments are accepted and all conflicting arguments are undecided. Then the conclusions of the accepted arguments get exactly the truth value that was asserted in the first phase, while the conclusions of conflicting arguments get the B value and the propositions not supported by any assertion/argument keep the N value. Due to its simplicity, conflict management is left implicit in the BD-model, which, in the aggregation phase, jumps directly to the assignment of truth values to propositions. Differently, conflict management between arguments is the focus of abstract argumentation theory, where semantics evaluation concerns assigning labels to *arguments* not to *conclusions*, while the step of evaluating conclusions and reasoning about the outcomes, namely the third process phase, is completely left out of the theory. Differently, this last phase is the main subject (not reviewed here) of the BD-model.

According to the analysis carried out above, we can identify three different "labelling" activities during the reasoning process.

First, *propositions* are labelled with *truth values*. This labelling is explicit in the assertion production phase of the BD-model, hence we will call these truth values *assertible values*. In the AB-model, this labelling corresponds to the contents of *argument conclusions* in the phase of argument production. These aspects are abstracted away and hence left implicit in abstract *AF*s.

Second, for the sake of conflict resolution, *arguments* are labelled with *acceptance values*. This activity is explicit in the conflict management phase of the AB-model (where acceptance values are called labels *tout court*), while it is left implicit in the BD-model.

Third, taking into account the results of conflict resolution, *argument conclusions*, i.e. *propositions*, are labelled with *aggregated conflict outcome values*. These values are produced in the aggregation phase in the BD-model, whose four-valued logic specifies then how to reason with them. On the other hand, in the AB-model they are regarded as a by-product of argument evaluation and, to the best of our knowledge, reasoning with them has received, by far, lesser attention in the literature.

The analysis carried out above evidences first of all the different nature of the uses of the "same" four values in the BD-model and in [1]. In the BD-model they are associated with *propositions/argument conclusions* and represent *aggregated conflict outcome values*, in [1] they are associated with *arguments* and represent *acceptance values*.

More interestingly, it points out some opportunities of cross-fertilization between these research areas.

On the one hand, the BD-model provides an advanced logic for reasoning about aggregated conflict outcomes which, to the best of our knowledge, has no parallel in the argumentation literature and could be used as a starting point to fill this significant gap in existing models of argumentation-based reasoning processes. Further, the use of a richer set of labels than Λ^{iou}, like Λ^4 in [1], promises a significant increase in the expressiveness (but also complexity) of labelling-based argumentation semantics, whose implications can be regarded as a largely unexplored research avenue. Moreover, since the notion of *don't-care* arguments encompassed in the Λ^{JV} set of labels is "orthogonal" to the distinction between none and both encompassed by the Λ^4 set, one might investigate the combination of the two ideas by considering a set of labels $\Lambda^5 = \{\text{none}, \text{in}, \text{out}, \text{both}, \otimes\}$.

On the other hand, the BD-model, initially conceived for the management of inconsistent inputs by a computer system [12] and recently considered as an approach to address the problem of inconsistent information on the Web [16], appears to rely on a very simple implicit argumentation model, using just one argumentation scheme for assertion production and an implicit skeptical semantics for argument acceptance evaluation. As a variety of more articulated models for argument construction [13] and evaluation [5] are available in the literature, using them to enrich the BD-model is a natural direction of investigation.

Leaving the development of these suggestions to future consideration, we focus in next subsection on another more fundamental issue concerning the modelling of undecidedness.

4.2   Epistemological Undecidedness

As discussed in the previous subsection, the BD-model assumes that the basic assertions an agent can make are binary: the set $\mathcal{AV}$ of *assertible values* is $\mathcal{AV} = \{T, F\}$ and the four labels in Λ^{BD} arise from the aggregation of multiple moves (or no move at all). In fact they correspond to all the possible subsets (including the empty one) of the set $\{T, F\}$. This model appears to be based on the assumption that the notion of a definite belief (corresponding to T and F) is more basic than the one of undecidedness, which is a derived concept: something which is undecided could (and, in a sense, should) be T or F in the end, but the lack of information or the presence of unresolved contradictory information prevents a more definite position.

It may be observed however that this modeling stance is somehow restricted and could be generalized. From a purely formal point of view, one may consider the case where the agents making the basic assertions adopt a richer set of assertible values. Following the BD-model scheme, this would give rise in turn to a richer set of *aggregated conflict outcome values*, since they correspond to the elements of $2^{\mathcal{AV}}$. To motivate this extension from a conceptual point of view, one may suggest the existence of an additional, more "fundamental", case of undecidedness, called *epistemological undecidedness* in the sequel. To provide a case for this, consider again the example of the weather forecast and suppose that the location you are interested in lies in a region with a specially complex geography, such that no existing weather forecast model is applicable. Then, you are undecided about whether tomorrow will be sunny (indeed you have good fundamental reasons to be so) and this indecision is rather different from the ones considered above. First, it clearly does not arise from contradictory information: you can not certainly say "I know too much". Second, even if it bears some superficial resemblance with the case "I don't know" represented by the truth value N in BD-logic, it is really different. The truth value N is meant to represent absence of information, i.e. no move at all by an agent, and can not conflict with a subsequent move: for instance if another agent makes a positive assertion then N is directly superseded by T. Epistemological undecidedness, instead, relies on some information and corresponds to a kind of move not encompassed by the models reviewed above: it may be represented by an additional assertible value U! corresponding to the intuitive answer: "I know that it is impossible to know". As a consequence, epistemological undecidedness can actually conflict with moves of other kinds. In the example, if one says that tomorrow will be sunny, your position will not be superseded and you may object to this assertion, even if you don't assert that it will be rainy.

One might think that objections based on epistemological undecidedness are analogous to the undercutting attacks exemplified by the famous Pollock's "red light" example [23]. In a nutshell, since an object looks red to you, you derive that it is red, but when you learn that the object is under a red light, your derivation is undercut and your reason to believe that the object is red is defeated, while still leaving open the possibility that it is actually red. In both epistemological undecidedness and Pollock's undercut, an objection is raised not by asserting the contrary of a given statement but providing reasons to leave it undecided. However there is a basic difference in the reasons of being undecided in the two cases. In Pollock's example the reason to be undecided is specific to the way the conclusion that the object is red has been derived. Knowing that the object is under a red light does not imply that you can not know whether the object is red, but only that you can not get to know it by looking at the object. For instance, if you have an old picture of the object under normal light, you get a new argument for which this specific undercut is no more effective (while, of course, other undercuts may arise). Thus Pollock's undercut is coherent with the view that indecision is due to the unability to definitely accept or reject a statement, while epistemological undecidedness means that you have reasons to regard a topic as unknowable independently of the way different positions can be derived. If you have reasons to believe that there is no way to forecast weather in a given location, then you are in conflict with any weather forecast, independently of the way it is derived. In this sense, an attack based on epistemological undecidedness can be seen as an additional form of rebut. The standard notion of rebut is based on the set of assertible values $\{T, F\}$ and a rebutting attack arises when different values are asserted for the same sentence, independently of the way they are derived. When extending the set of assertible values to $\mathcal{AV}^3 = \{T, F, U!\}$, the notion of rebut remains the same, i.e. that different values are asserted for the same sentence, independently of the way they are derived, but there is a larger variety of rebut situations: not just T vs. F but also, $U!$ vs. T, $U!$ vs. F, and possibly even a three-way duel[6] $U!$ vs. T vs. F.

A research agenda to encompass epistemological undecidedness into a BD-inspired AF model can then be drafted.

First, a suitable argument generation logic encompassing the extended set of assertible values $\mathcal{AV}^3 = \{T, F, U!\}$ has to be investigated. For the sake of exploring the implications of the adoption of $\mathcal{AV}^3$ at a more abstract level one could consider a simple BD-like model where agents can make three kinds of assertions about a sentence.

Second, an abstract framework to represent the attack relations between arguments has to be identified. Traditional AFs encompass a unique kind of binary attack relation, but its expressiveness is probably insufficient in the extended context. First, one may wonder whether attacks involving arguments based on $U!$ assertions against arguments involving arguments based on T or F assertions should be classified and treated differently from "traditional" attacks involving T vs. F assertions. Further, the distinction between rebutting and undercutting

---

[6] Like in the classic non-classical western movie *The Good, the Bad and the Ugly*.

attacks may need to be reassessed in this context. As a bottom ground for this representation, one may consider again a BD-like model where all attacks are symmetric and only unattacked arguments are accepted. A further research jump would be to consider the above issues in the contexts of abstract dialectical frameworks [14], where generic influence relations among arguments, rather than just attacks, are considered.

Finally, turning to reasoning about conflict outcomes for the propositions of interest, an extended logic would be needed for the *aggregated conflict outcome values*, which, following the line of the BD-model, might correspond to the element of $2^{A^{V^3}}$. To this purpose existing studies on bilattice-based generalizations of BD-logic could be taken as starting point [18,2].

5   Conclusions

We believe that sketching a few fluid research directions for the future is a suitable way to celebrate many solid research results achieved in the past. In this spirit, in this work we have analyzed and discussed some "non-mainstream" aspects of the treatment of incompleteness and undecidedness in argumentation, with the aim of posing questions rather than of giving answers. Whether these and similar matters represent just theoretical curiosities or will somehow contribute to narrow the gap between human reasoning and its formal models is an issue for next generations of researchers. For sure, their work will profit from the rich and still increasing conceptual and technical asset built by outstanding researchers like Gerhard Brewka, to whom the book including this chapter is dedicated.

Acknowledgments. The authors thank the anonymous reviewer for his/her helpful comments. This work was conceived and developed during a visit of prof. Beishui Liao to the University of Brescia supported partially by the National Natural Science Foundation of China under grant No. 61175058 and Zhejiang Provincial Natural Science Foundation of China under grant No. LY14F030014.

References

1. Arieli, O.: On the acceptance of loops in argumentation frameworks. J. of Logic and Computation (to appear, 2014)
2. Arieli, O., Avron, A.: The value of the four values. Artif. Intell. 102, 97–141 (1998)
3. Baroni, P., Boella, G., Cerutti, F., Giacomin, M., van der Torre, L.W.N., Villata, S.: On input/output argumentation frameworks. In: Proc. of the 4th Int. Conf. on Computational Models of Argument (COMMA 2012), pp. 358–365 (2012)
4. Baroni, P., Boella, G., Cerutti, F., Giacomin, M., Torre, L.W.N.v.d., Villata, S.: On the input/output behavior of argumentation frameworks. Artif. Intell. 217, 144–197 (2014)
5. Baroni, P., Caminada, M., Giacomin, M.: An introduction to argumentation semantics. Knowledge Engineering Review 26(4), 365–410 (2011)

6. Baroni, P., Giacomin, M.: On principle-based evaluation of extension-based argumentation semantics. Artif. Intell. 171(10/15), 675–700 (2007)
7. Baroni, P., Giacomin, M., Guida, G.: SCC-recursiveness: a general schema for argumentation semantics. Artif. Intell. 168(1-2), 165–210 (2005)
8. Baroni, P., Giacomin, M., Liao, B.: On topology-related properties of abstract argumentation semantics. A correction and extension to *Dynamics of argumentation systems: A division-based method*. Artif. Intell. 212, 104–115 (2014)
9. Baumann, R.: Splitting an argumentation framework. In: Delgrande, J.P., Faber, W. (eds.) LPNMR 2011. LNCS, vol. 6645, pp. 40–53. Springer, Heidelberg (2011)
10. Baumann, R., Brewka, G.: Expanding argumentation frameworks: Enforcing and monotonicity results. In: Proc. of the 3rd Int. Conf. on Computational Models of Argument (COMMA 2010), pp. 75–86 (2010)
11. Baumann, R., Brewka, G., Dvořák, W., Woltran, S.: Parameterized splitting: A simple modification-based approach. In: Erdem, E., Lee, J., Lierler, Y., Pearce, D. (eds.) Correct Reasoning. LNCS, vol. 7265, pp. 57–71. Springer, Heidelberg (2012)
12. Belnap, N.D.: How a computer should think. In: Ryle, G. (ed.) Contemporary aspects of philosophy, pp. 30–56. Oriel Press (1977)
13. Besnard, P., Garcia, A., Hunter, A., Modgil, S., Prakken, H., Simari, G., Toni, F.: Special issue: Tutorials on structured argumentation. Argument & Computation 5(1) (2014)
14. Brewka, G., Woltran, S.: Abstract dialectical frameworks. In: Proc. of the 12th Int. Conf. on Principles of Knowledge Representation and Reasoning (KR 2010), pp. 102–111 (2010)
15. Dung, P.M.: On the acceptability of arguments and its fundamental role in non-monotonic reasoning, logic programming, and n-person games. Artif. Intell. 77(2), 321–357 (1995)
16. Dunn, J.M.: Contradictory information: Too much of a good thing. J. of Philosophical Logic 39, 425–452 (2010)
17. Gabbay, D.M.: Fibring argumentation frames. Studia Logica 93(2-3), 231–295 (2009)
18. Ginsberg, M.L.: Multivalued logics: a uniform approach to reasoning in AI. Computer Intelligence 4, 256–316 (1988)
19. Jakobovits, H., Vermeir, D.: Robust semantics for argumentation frameworks. J. of Logic and Computation 9(2), 215–261 (1999)
20. Liao, B.: Toward incremental computation of argumentation semantics: A decomposition-based approach. Ann. Math. Artif. Intell. 67(3-4), 319–358 (2013)
21. Liao, B., Huang, H.: Partial semantics of argumentation: basic properties and empirical results. J. of Logic and Computation 23(3), 541–562 (2013)
22. Liao, B., Jin, L., Koons, R.C.: Dynamics of argumentation systems: A division-based method. Artif. Intell. 175(11), 1790–1814 (2011)
23. Pollock, J.: How to reason defeasibly. Artif. Intell. 57, 1–42 (1992)
24. Rienstra, T., Perotti, A., Villata, S., Gabbay, D.M., van der Torre, L.: Multi-sorted argumentation. In: Modgil, S., Oren, N., Toni, F. (eds.) TAFA 2011. LNCS, vol. 7132, pp. 215–231. Springer, Heidelberg (2012)

Infinite Argumentation Frameworks[*]
On the Existence and Uniqueness of Extensions

Ringo Baumann[1] and Christof Spanring[2,3]

[1] Computer Science Institute, Leipzig University, Germany
[2] Department of Computer Science, University of Liverpool, UK
[3] Institute of Information Systems, Vienna University of Technology, Austria

Abstract. Abstract properties satisfied for finite structures do not necessarily carry over to infinite structures. Two of the most basic properties are *existence* and *uniqueness* of something. In this work we study these properties for acceptable sets of arguments, so-called extensions, in the field of abstract argumentation. We review already known results, present new proofs or explain sketchy old ones in more detail. We also contribute new results and introduce as well as study the question of existence-(in)dependence between argumentation semantics.

1 Introduction

In the past two decades much effort has been spent on abstract argumentation, mainly with finite structures in mind. Be it in the context of non-monotonic reasoning, as an application of modal logic, or as a tool for structural text-analysis and data-mining (see [10] for an excellent summary). From a mathematicians point of view the infinite case has been widely neglected, although one should also highlight efforts of encoding infinite argumentation structures for efficient handling [3] as well as corresponding work in similar areas [1,11] and logical foundations of argumentation [16,9].

Clearly finite or countably infinite structures are an attractive and reasonable restriction, due to their computational nature. But the bigger picture in terms of fulfilled properties (such as existence and uniqueness) tends to hide behind bigger structures or certain subclasses of them. Which is why this work is to be seen as an effort of emphasizing arbitrary infinities for abstract argumentation.

In his seminal paper [14] Phan Minh Dung introduced a formal framework for argumentation, along with notions of acceptance, already including concepts of conflict-freeness, admissibility, completeness and stability (see [2] for an overview of acceptance conditions in argumentation). An argumentation framework (AF) consists of arguments and attacks, where attacks are presented by a directed binary relation on the arguments representing conflict between arguments. Dung and subsequent works use the term semantics to refer to acceptance conditions for sets of arguments. Whether such sets do exist at all is a main property of

[*] This research has been supported by DFG (project BR 1817/7-1) and FWF (project I1102).

T. Eiter et al. (Eds.): Brewka Festschrift, LNAI 9060, pp. 281–295, 2015.

interest. A (dis)proof in case of finite AFs appears to be mostly straightforward, in the general infinite case however conducting such proofs is more intricate. It usually involves the proper use of set theoretic axioms, like the *axiom of choice* or equivalent statements.

Dung already proposed the existence of preferred extensions in the case of infinite argumentation frameworks. It has later on (e.g. [13]) been pointed out that Dung has not been precise with respect to the use of principles. The existence of semi-stable extensions for finitary argumentation frameworks was first shown in [19], with the use of model-theoretic techniques, techniques that could also be extended to stage and other semantics. In this work we provide complete or alternative proofs. Furthermore, beside semi-stable and preferred semantics we consider a bunch of semantics considered in the literature. For instance, as a new result, we show that stage extensions are guaranteed as long as finitary AFs are considered. Finally, we shed light on the question of uniqueness of extensions.

Section 2 gives the necessary background information. We continue warming up with basic observations in Section 3. In Section 4 we present further results for preferred and lesser semantics. We proceed by giving insights into more advanced semantics (e.g. semi-stable) in Section 5. We conclude in Section 6.

2   Background

An *argumentation framework (AF)* $F = (A, R)$ is an ordered pair consisting of a possibly infinite set of arguments A and an attack relation $R \subseteq A \times A$. Instead of $(a, b) \in R$ we might write $a \rightarrowtail b$ and say that a *attacks* b. For sets $E_1, E_2 \subseteq A$ and arguments $a, b \in A$ we write $E_1 \rightarrowtail b$ if some $a \in E_1$ attacks b, $a \rightarrowtail E_2$ if a attacks some $b \in E_2$ and $E_1 \rightarrowtail E_2$ if some $a \in E_1$ attacks some $b \in E_2$. An argument $a \in A$ is *defended* by a set $E \subseteq A$ in F if for each $b \in A$ with $b \rightarrowtail a$, also $E \rightarrowtail b$. An AF $F = (A, R)$ is called *finite* if $|A| \in \mathbb{N}$. Furthermore, we say that F is *finitary* if every argument has only finitely many attackers, i.e. for any $a \in A$, we have $|\{b \in A \mid b \rightarrowtail a\}| \in \mathbb{N}$. The *range* E^+ of a set of arguments E is defined as extension with all the arguments attacked by E, i.e. $E^+ = E \cup \{a \in A \mid E \rightarrowtail a\}$.

A *semantics* σ is a function which assigns to any AF $F = (A, R)$ a set of sets of arguments denoted by $\sigma(F) \subseteq \wp(F)$. Each one of them, a so-called σ-*extension*, is considered to be acceptable with respect to F. For two semantics σ and τ we use $\sigma \subseteq \tau$ to indicate that for any AF F, $\sigma(F) \subseteq \tau(F)$. There is a huge number of commonly established semantics, motivations and intuitions for their use ranging from desired treatment of specific examples to fulfillment of a number of abstract principles. We consider ten prominent semantics, namely admissible, complete, preferred, semi-stable, stable, naive, stage, grounded, ideal and eager semantics (abbreviated by $cf, ad, co, pr, ss, stb, na, stg, gr, id$ and eg respectively). For recent overviews we refer the reader to [4,2].

Definition 1. *Given an AF $F = (A, R)$ and let $E \subseteq A$.*

1. $E \in cf(F)$ *iff for all $a, b \in E$ we have $a \not\rightarrowtail b$,*
2. $E \in ad(F)$ *iff $E \in cf(F)$ and for all $a \rightarrowtail E$ also $E \rightarrowtail a$,*

3. $E \in co(F)$ iff $E \in cf(F)$ and for any $a \in A$ defended by E in F, $a \in E$,
4. $E \in pr(F)$ iff $E \in ad(F)$ and there is no $E' \in ad(F)$ s.t. $E \subsetneq E'$,
5. $E \in ss(F)$ iff $E \in ad(F)$ and there is no $E' \in ad(F)$ s.t. $E^+ \subsetneq E'^+$,
6. $E \in stb(F)$ iff $E \in cf(F)$ and $E^+ = A$,
7. $E \in na(F)$ iff $E \in cf(F)$ and there is no $E' \in cf(F)$ s.t. $E \subsetneq E'$,
8. $E \in stg(F)$ iff $E \in cf(F)$ and there is no $E' \in cf(F)$ s.t. $E^+ \subsetneq E'^+$,
9. $E \in gr(F)$ iff $E \in co(F)$ and there is no $E' \in co(F)$ s.t. $E' \subsetneq E$,
10. $E \in id(F)$ iff $E \in ad(F)$, $E \subseteq \bigcap pr(F)$ and there is no $E' \in ad(F)$ satisfying $E' \subseteq \bigcap pr(F)$ s.t. $E \subsetneq E'$,
11. $E \in eg(F)$ iff $E \in ad(F)$, $E \subseteq \bigcap ss(F)$ and there is no $E' \in ad(F)$ satisfying $E' \subseteq \bigcap ss(F)$ s.t. $E \subsetneq E'$.

We recall that the intersection of an empty family of sets does not exist, as it would coincide with the *universal set* leading to the well known *Russel's paradox* (cf. [17] for more details). Consequently, functions like ideal or eager semantics may return *undefined* since their definitions include a subset-check with regard to an intersection.[1] The usual way to avoid undefined intersections is to fix a background set $\mathcal{U}$, a so-called *universe* (which is often explicitly stated or implicitely assumed in argumentation papers), and to define the intersection of a family of subsets $\mathcal{S}$ as $\bigcap \mathcal{S} = \{x \in \mathcal{U} \mid \forall S \in \mathcal{S} : x \in S\}$. Furthermore, in case of ideal and eager semantics one may equivalently replace $\mathcal{U}$ by A since the candidate sets E have to be admissible sets of the considered AF $F = (A, R)$. This means, $\bigcap \sigma(F) = \{x \in A \mid \forall E \in \sigma(F) : x \in E\}$.

The following proposition shows well known relations for the considered semantics.[2] In the interest of readability we present them graphically.

Proposition 1. *For semantics σ and τ, $\sigma \subseteq \tau$ iff there is a path from σ to τ in Figure 2, e.g. stb $\subseteq$ na for (stb, stg, na) is a path from stb to na.*

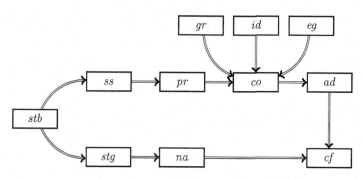

Fig. 2. Relations between Semantics

---

[1] We will see that $ss(F) = \emptyset$ may indeed be the case (Example 4) and thus, these considerations are essential for eager semantics.

[2] Note that the presented relations apply to both finite and infinite AFs. Detailed proofs can be found in [7, Proposition 2.7].

We call a semantics σ *universally defined* if for any AF F, $|\sigma(F)| \geq 1$. Whether a semantics warrants existence of extensions is of high interest. For instance, Dung already showed that AFs can be used to solve well known problems like the stable marriage problem [14]. If the considered problem is modeled correctly and the used semantics provides a positive answer with respect to universal definedness, then solutions of the problem are guaranteed. If a unique solution is guaranteed, i.e. $|\sigma(F)| = 1$ for any F we say that σ follows the *unique status* approach. We will see that existence as well as uniqueness depend on the considered structures. In the following section we start with a preliminary analysis.

3   Warming Up

As we have seen in Figure 2 the general subset relations for the considered semantics are fairly well known. Given two semantics σ, τ such that $\sigma \subseteq \tau$, then (obviously) universal definedness of σ carries over to τ. We start with the investigation of finite AFs.

3.1   Finite AFs

It is well known that stable semantics does not warrant the existence of extensions even in the case of finite AFs. The following minimalistic AFs demonstrate this assertion.

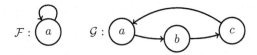

Fig. 3. Non-existence of Stable Extension

Both AFs represent odd-cycles and indeed this is a decisive property. It can be shown that being odd-cycle free is sufficient for warranting at least one stable extension.[3] The universal definedness of complete semantics is a well-investigated result from [14].

What about the other semantics considered in this paper? If we take a closer look at Definition 1 we observe that they always possess at least one extension in case of finite AFs.[4] This can be seen as follows: Firstly, the empty set is always admissible and conflict-free. Furthermore, the definitions of the semantics are looking for conflict-free or admissible sets maximal in range or maximal/minimal

---

[3] This is due to the fact that firstly, *limited controversial* AFs always possess a stable extension [14, Theorem 33] and secondly, in case of finite AFs being odd-cycle free coincides with being limited controversial.

[4] In Sections 4 and 5 we prove this assertion in a rigorous manner for finitary or even arbitrary AFs. The existence of extensions for finite AFs is implied.

with respect to subset relation. Finally, since we are dealing with finite AFs there are only finitely many subsets that have to be considered and thus, the existence of maximal and minimal elements is guaranteed.

3.2 Infinite AFs

It is an important observation that warranting the existence of σ-extensions in case of finite AFs does not necessarily carry over to the infinite case, i.e. the semantics σ does not need to be universally defined. Take for instance semi-stable and stage semantics. To the best of our knowledge the first example showing that semi-stable as well as stage semantics does not guarantee extensions in case of infinite AFs was given in [18, Example 5.8.] and is picked up in the following example.

Example 1. Consider the AF $F = (A \cup B \cup C, R)$ as illustrated in Figure 4 where

- $A = (a_i)_{i \in \mathbb{N}}$, $B = (b_i)_{i \in \mathbb{N}}$, $C = (c_i)_{i \in \mathbb{N}}$ and
- $R = \{a_i \rightarrowtail b_i, b_i \rightarrowtail a_i, b_i \rightarrowtail c_i, c_i \rightarrowtail c_i \mid i \in \mathbb{N}\} \cup$
  $\{b_i \rightarrowtail b_j, b_i \rightarrowtail c_j \mid i, j \in \mathbb{N}, j < i\}$

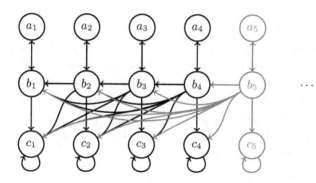

Fig. 4. An illustration of the AF from Example 1

The set of preferred and naive extensions coincide, in particular $pr(F) = na(F) = \{A\} \cup \{E_i \mid i \in \mathbb{N}\}$ where $E_i = (A \setminus \{a_i\}) \cup \{b_i\}$. Furthermore, none of these extensions is maximal with respect to range since $A^+ \subsetneq E_i^+ \subsetneq E_{i+1}^+$ for any $i \in \mathbb{N}$. In consideration of $ss \subseteq pr$ and $stg \subseteq na$ (cf. Figure 2) we conclude that this framework does have neither semi-stable nor stage extensions.

There are two questions which arise naturally. Firstly, do stage or semi-stable extensions exist in case of finitary AFs. A positive answer in case of semi-stable semantics was conjectured in [13, Conjecture 1] and firstly proved with substantial effort by Emil Weydert in [19, Theorem 5.1]. Weydert proved his result in a first order logic setup using generalized argumentation frameworks. In this paper we provide an alternative proof using transfinite induction. Moreover, as a new result, we present a proof for the existence of stage semantics in case of finitary AFs.

The second interesting question is whether there is some kind of existence-dependency between semi-stable and stage semantics in case of infinite AFs. The following two examples show that this is not the case. More precisely, it is possible that some AF does have semi-stable but no stage extensions and it is also possible that there are stage but no semi-stable extensions.

Example 2 (No Stage but Semi-stable Extensions). Taking into account the AF $F = (A \cup B \cup C, R)$ from Example 1. Consider a so-called *normal deletion* [6] F' of F as illustrated in Figure 5 where $F' = F|_B$.

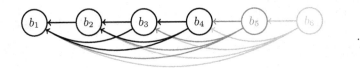

Fig. 5. An illustration of the AF from Example 2

We observe that the empty set is the unique admissible extension of F'. Consequently, by definition of semi-stable semantics, $ss(F') = \{\emptyset\}$. On the other hand, $stg(F') = \emptyset$. This can be seen as follows: for any $i \in \mathbb{N}$, $B_i = \{b_i\}$ is a naive extension in F' and there are no other naive extensions. Obviously, there is no range maximal naive set since $B_i^+ \subsetneq B_{i+1}^+$ for any $i \in \mathbb{N}$.

Example 3 (No Semi-Stable but Stage Extensions). Consider again Example 1. We define a so-called *normal expansion* [8] $F' = (A \cup B \cup C \cup D \cup E, R \cup R')$ of F as illustrated in Figure 6, where

- $D = (d_i)_{i \in \mathbb{N}}$, $E = (e_i)_{i \in \mathbb{N}}$ and
- $R' = \{a_i \rightarrowtail d_i, d_i \rightarrowtail a_i, b_i \rightarrowtail d_i, d_i \rightarrowtail b_i, d_i \rightarrowtail c_i, e_i \rightarrowtail d_i, e_i \rightarrowtail e_i \mid i \in \mathbb{N}\}$

In comparison to Example 1 we do not observe any changes as far as preferred and semi-stable semantics are concerned. In particular, $pr(F') = \{A\} \cup \{E_i \mid i \in \mathbb{N}\}$ where $E_i = (A \setminus \{a_i\}) \cup \{b_i\}$ and again, none of these extensions is maximal with respect to range. Hence, $ss(F') = \emptyset$. Observe that we do have additional conflict-free as well as naive sets, especially the set D. Since any $e \in E$ is self-defeating and unattacked and furthermore, $D^+ = A \cup B \cup C \cup D$ we conclude, $stg(F') = \{D\}$.

4   Minor Results

4.1   Universal Definedness of Preferred and Naive Semantics

We start with proving that preferred as well as naive semantics are universally defined. We mention that the case of preferred semantics was already considered

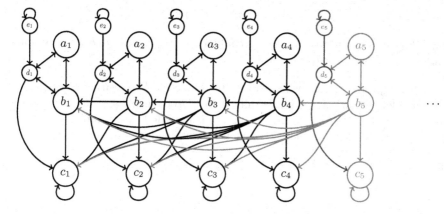

Fig. 6. An illustration of the AF from Example 3

in [14, Corollary 12]. The proof is mainly due to *Zorn's lemma*. In order to keep the paper self-contained we recapitulate the famous lemma below.

Lemma 1 ([20]). *Given a partially ordered set $(P, \leq)$. If any $\leq$-chain possesses an upper bound, then $(P, \leq)$ has a maximal element.*

One may easily show that the following "strengthened" version is equivalent to Zorn's lemma.

Lemma 2. *Given a partially ordered set $(P, \leq)$. If any $\leq$-chain possesses an upper bound, then for any $p \in P$ there exists a maximal element $m \in P$, s.t. $p \leq m$.*

The following lemma paves the way for showing the universal definedness of naive and preferred semantics.

Lemma 3. *Given $F = (A, R)$ and $E \subseteq A$,*

1. *if $E \in cf(F)$, then there exists $E' \in na(F)$ s.t. $E \subseteq E'$ and*
2. *if $E \in ad(F)$, then there exists $E' \in pr(F)$ s.t. $E \subseteq E'$.*

Proof. For any $F = (A, R)$ we have the associated powerset lattice $(\wp(A), \subseteq)$. Consider now the partially ordered fragments $\mathcal{C} = (cf(F), \subseteq)$ and $\mathcal{A} = (ad(F), \subseteq)$. In accordance with Lemma 2 the existence of naive and preferred supersets is guaranteed if any $\subseteq$-chain possesses an upper bound in $\mathcal{C}$ or $\mathcal{A}$, respectively. Given a $\subseteq$-chain $(E_i)_{i \in I}$ in $\mathcal{C}$ or $\mathcal{A}$, respectively.[5] Consider now $E = \bigcup_{i \in I} E_i$. Obviously, E is an upper bound of $(E_i)_{i \in I}$, i.e. $E_i \subseteq E$ for any $i \in I$. It remains to show that E is conflict-free or admissible, respectively. Conflict-freeness is a finite condition. This means, if there were conflicting arguments $a, b \in E$ there would have to be some $i \in I$ with $a, b \in E_i$. Assume now E is not admissible. Consequently, there is some $a \in E$ that is not defended by E. Hence, for some $i \in I$ we have $a \in E_i$ contradicting the admissibility of E_i.

---

[5] Remember that any set can be written as an indexed family. This can be done via using the set itself as index set.

Theorem 7. *For any F, $pr(F) \neq \emptyset$ and $na(F) \neq \emptyset$.*

Proof. Since the empty set is always conflict-free and admissible we may apply Lemma 3 and the assertion is shown.

Since any preferred extension is a complete one (cf. Proposition 1) we deduce that complete semantics is universally defined too. The following proposition shows even more, namely any admissible set is bounded by a complete extension and furthermore, any complete extension is contained in a preferred one.

Proposition 2. *Given $F = (A, R)$ and $E \subseteq A$,*

1. *if $E \in ad(F)$, then there exists $E' \in co(F)$ s.t. $E \subseteq E'$ and*
2. *if $E \in co(F)$, then there exists $E' \in pr(F)$ s.t. $E \subseteq E'$.*

Proof. Given $E \in ad(F)$. Thus, there exists $E' \in pr(F)$ s.t. $E \subseteq E'$ (Lemma 3). Since $pr \subseteq co$ (Proposition 1) the first statement is shown. Consider $E \in co(F)$. Hence, $E \in ad(F)$ (Proposition 1). Consequently, there exists $E' \in pr(F)$ s.t. $E \subseteq E'$ (Lemma 3) and we are done.

4.2   Uniqueness of Grounded and Ideal Semantics

We now turn to grounded as well as the more credulous ideal semantics. The universal definedness in case of grounded semantics was already implicitly given in [14]. Unfortunately, this result was not explicitly stated in the paper. Nevertheless, in [14, Theorem 25] it was shown that firstly, the set of all complete extensions form a complete semi-lattice, i.e. the existence of a greatest lower bound for any non-empty subset S is implied. Secondly, it was proven that the grounded extension is the least complete extension. Consequently, for any AF F we may set $S = co(F)$ and the assertion is shown. The following theorem shows that the same applies to ideal semantics.

Theorem 8. *For any F, $id(F) \neq \emptyset$.*

Proof. Given an arbitrary AF $F = (A, R)$. We define $ad_{\cap pr}(F) = \{E \in ad(F) \mid E \subseteq \bigcap_{P \in pr(F)} P\}$. Now consider $\mathcal{A} = (ad_{\cap pr}(F), \subseteq)$. Obviously, $ad_{\cap pr}(F) \neq \emptyset$ since for any F, $\emptyset \in ad(F)$ and furthermore, $\emptyset \subseteq S$ for any set S. In order to show that $id(F) \neq \emptyset$ it suffices to prove that there is a $\subseteq$-maximal set in $\mathcal{A}$. Again we use Zorn's lemma. Given a $\subseteq$-chain $(E_i)_{i \in I}$ in $\mathcal{A}$. Consider $E = \bigcup_{i \in I} E_i$. Obviously, E is an upper bound of $(E_i)_{i \in I}$ and furthermore, conflict-freeness and even admissibility is given because $E_i \in ad(F)$ for any $i \in I$ (cf. proof of Lemma 3 for more details). Moreover, since $E_i \subseteq \bigcap_{P \in pr(F)} P$ for any $i \in I$ we deduce $E \subseteq \bigcap_{P \in pr(F)} P$ guarenteeing $E \in \mathcal{A}$. Consequently, by Lemma 1 $\mathcal{A} = (ad_{\cap pr}(F), \subseteq)$ possesses $\subseteq$-maximal elements concluding the proof.

The uniqueness of grounded semantics was shown already by Dung [14, Theorem 25, statement 2]. We present a proof for ideal semantics.

Theorem 9. *For any F, $|id(F)| = 1$.*

Proof. $|id(F)| \geq 1$ is already given by Theorem 8. Hence, it suffices to show $|id(F)| \leq 1$. Suppose, to derive a contradiction, that for some $I_1 \neq I_2$ we have $I_1, I_2 \in id(F)$. Consequently, by Definition 1, $I_1, I_2 \in ad(F)$ and $I_1, I_2 \subseteq \bigcap_{P \in pr(F)} P$ as well as neither $I_1 \subseteq I_2$, nor $I_2 \subseteq I_1$. Obviously, $I_1 \cup I_2 \subseteq \bigcap_{P \in pr(F)} P$ and since preferred extensions are conflict-free we obtain $I_1 \cup I_2 \in cf(F)$. Since both sets are assumed to be admissible we derive $I_1 \cup I_2 \in ad(F)$ contradicting the $\subseteq$-maximality of I_1 and I_2. $\qquad \square$

5   Main Results

When dealing with range-maximal extensions in infinite AFs as seen in the previous examples we might deal with sets of sets of arguments that keep growing in size with respect to their range. For being able to handle constructions of this kind we introduce the following two definitions. The intuition for the first definition is that we want to be able to say something about arguments and sets occuring (un)restricted in collections of extensions. For the second definition we focus on the idea of infinitely range-growing sets of extensions.

Definition 10 (Keepers, Outsiders, Keeping Sets and Compatibility).
Consider some AF F. For $\mathcal{E}$ a set of sets of arguments we call $\mathcal{E}^+ = \bigcup_{E \in \mathcal{E}} E^+$ the range of $\mathcal{E}$ and for some argument $a \in \mathcal{E}^+$ we say that:

- *a is a keeper of $\mathcal{E}$ if it occurs range-unbounded in $\mathcal{E}$, i.e. for any $E_1 \in \mathcal{E}$ with $a \notin E_1$ there is some $E_2 \in \mathcal{E}$ such that $a \in E_2$ and $E_1^+ \subseteq E_2^+$;*
- *a is an outsider of $\mathcal{E}$ if it is not a keeper of it, i.e. there is some $E_1 \in \mathcal{E}$ with $a \notin E_1$ such that there is no $E_2 \in \mathcal{E}$ with $a \in E_2$ and $E_1^+ \subseteq E_2^+$.*

Furthermore for a set $A \subseteq \mathcal{E}^+$ we say that:

- *A is a keeping set of $\mathcal{E}$, or kept in $\mathcal{E}$, if it occurs range-unbounded in $\mathcal{E}$, i.e. for every $E_1 \in \mathcal{E}$ with $A \not\subseteq E_1$ there is some $E_2 \in \mathcal{E}$ such that $A \subseteq E_2$ and $E_1^+ \subseteq E_2^+$.*
- *A is called compatible with $\mathcal{E}$ if every finite subset of A is kept in $\mathcal{E}$, i.e. for every finite $A_{<\omega} \subseteq^{<\omega} A$ we have that $A_{<\omega}$ is a keeping set of $\mathcal{E}$.*

Definition 11 (Range Chain, Chain Range, Induced AF). *Consider some AF F. A set of sets of arguments $\mathcal{E}$ is called a range chain if for any $E_1, E_2 \in \mathcal{E}$ we have $E_1^+ \subseteq E_2^+$ or $E_2^+ \subseteq E_1^+$, again the range of $\mathcal{E}$ (the chain range $\mathcal{E}^+$) is defined as $\mathcal{E}^+ = \bigcup_{E \in \mathcal{E}} E^+$.*
Now for a given range chain $\mathcal{E}$ we will consider the by $\mathcal{E}$ induced AF $F|_{\mathcal{E}}$:

$$F|_{\mathcal{E}} = (\mathcal{E}^+, \{(a,b) \mid a, b \in \mathcal{E}^+, (a,b) \in R_F\} \cup \{(b,b) \mid b \text{ outsider of } \mathcal{E}\})$$

Observe that naturally finite range chains or chains that have a maximum will not be of interest to us. Also observe the implicit transitivity, i.e. for $E_1, E_2, E_3 \in \mathcal{E}$ from $E_1^+ \subsetneq E_2^+$ and $E_2^+ \subsetneq E_3^+$ it follows that also $E_1^+ \subsetneq E_3^+$. Thus a range chain by definition gives a well-ordering on the equivalence class of elements with equal range. We might need the axiom of choice though, to select one specific extension for every equivalence class.

Lemma 4 (Axiom of Choice). *For every set of non-empty sets $\mathcal{E}$ there is a choice function, i.e. a function f selecting one member of each set, for all $E \in \mathcal{E}$ we have $f(E) \in E$.*

One may show that the axiom of choice is equivalent to Zorn's lemma. It is nowadays widely accepted, but the concept has been shown to be independent from other axioms of set theory. Uses of choice often appear to be implicit, in the following we explicitly mark when the axiom of choice is necessary.

5.1   Semi-stable and Stage Extensions in Case of Finitary AFs

In the case of semi-stable and stage extensions we deal with semantics that sometimes are seen as weaker forms of stable semantics. In this sense we think of range chains that range-cover the whole framework, or in other words we will reduce frameworks to arguments being relevant (Definition 11) to some range chain only. The following definition deals with the question whether some argument or sets of arguments might be part of some stable extension. The intuition being that we can recursively try to cover the full range of some AF, the following definition helps in defining the recursion step.

Definition 12 (Unresolved Range). *Given some AF F, a range chain $\mathcal{E}$ such that $F|_{\mathcal{E}} = F$, and a set $A \subseteq \mathcal{E}^+$. We define the unresolved range of A as the set A^* that as a next step has to be resolved if A is to be subset of a stable extension. A^* thus consists of arguments endangering A without defense, as well as arguments attacked by A^+ but not by A. Also see Figure 13 for an illustration.*

$$A^* = \{b \notin A^+ \mid b \rightarrowtail A\} \cup \{a \notin A^+ \mid A^+ \rightarrowtail a\}$$

Lemma 5. *Given some finitary AF F, some range chain $\mathcal{E}$, such that $F|_{\mathcal{E}} = F$, and some with $\mathcal{E}$ compatible set $A \subseteq \mathcal{E}^+$. Then there is some with $\mathcal{E}$ compatible set $B \subseteq \mathcal{E}^+$ such that $A \subseteq B$ and $A^* \subseteq B^+$, we have $A^+ \cup A^* \subseteq B^+$.*

Proof. First observe that for every finite set $A_{<\omega} \subseteq A^+ \cup A^*$ there has to be a finite set $B_{<\omega}$ such that $A_{<\omega} \cap A \subseteq B_{<\omega}$ and $A_{<\omega} \cap A^* \subseteq B_{<\omega}^+$. This is due to the finitary condition and the definitions, for every finite set of arguments there are only a finite number of sets that have at most this range, but since the chain $\mathcal{E}$ is unbounded in F there is at least one. Furthermore if B resolves $A_1 \cup A_2$ then B resolves A_1 and A_2. By transfinite induction on the size of B we can show that there is a set with the desired properties. Observe that the axiom of choice might be necessary though.

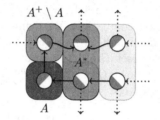

Fig. 13. An illustration of unresolved range A^* (Definition 12). Observe that the right-most area characterizes all arguments that can resolve A^*, when incorporating A.

Theorem 14. *For any finitary F, $|ss(F)| \geq 1$ and $|stg(F)| \geq 1$.*

Proof. Take some finitary AF F, and $\sigma = pr$ or $\sigma = na$, and $\sigma^+ = ss$ or $\sigma^+ = stg$ respectively. We will show that for any range chain $\mathcal{E} \subseteq \sigma(F)$ there is some σ-extension E that covers the full chain range, i.e. $\mathcal{E}^+ \subseteq E^+ \in \sigma(F)$. By then applying Zorn's Lemma it follows that $\mathcal{E}$ also contains at least one range-maximum, i.e. a range-maximal set or in other words a σ^+-extension.

To this end for any range chain $\mathcal{E} \subseteq \sigma(F)$, we proceed with the following steps using transfinite recursion to find an upper bound A with $\mathcal{E}^+ \subseteq A^+$ such that there is some $E \in \sigma(F)$ with $A \subseteq E$.

1. Consider only relevant arguments of F
2. Recursion Start, motivation and intuition
3. Successor Step, augment by resolving keeper sets or compatible keepers
4. Limit Step, collect successor steps
5. Remarks, conflict-freeness and range-completeness

1. Consider Only Relevant Arguments of F: As presented in Definition 11 we will make use of some AF $F|_{\mathcal{E}}$ that contains only arguments from the range of $\mathcal{E}$, plus all outsiders are self-attacking. If we retrieve a conflict-free (admissible) set A such that A contains only keepers of $\mathcal{E}$ and spans the whole range, $A^+ = \mathcal{E}^+$, we can as stated in Lemma 2 retrieve a σ-extension that covers the whole chain range. Clearly every stable extension of $F|_{\mathcal{E}}$ serves this purpose. In the following we will thus construct a stable extension and consider some AF F where $F|_{\mathcal{E}} = F$.

2. Define the Recursion Start: As recursion start we will use the set $A_0 = \{a\}$ for some keeper a of $\mathcal{E}$. In each step we will augment this set in a clever way, by choosing compatible sets that either cover the unresolved range or some arbitrary compatible keeper.

3. Successor Steps, $\alpha = \beta + 1$: Given some compatible set A_β. If A_β has some unresolved range $A_\beta^* \neq \emptyset$ we choose a compatible set $A_\alpha \supset A_\beta$ such that $A_\beta^* \subset A_\alpha^+$. As stated in Lemma 5 such a set exists, but we might need the axiom of choice to find one. If on the other hand $A_\beta^* = \emptyset$ we pick some compatible keeper $a \notin A_\beta$ such that $A_\alpha = A_\beta \cup \{a\}$ is compatible with $\mathcal{E}$.

4. Limit Steps, α*:* Given a range chain $\{A_i\}_{i<\alpha}$ where for any $i < j$ we have $A_i \subseteq A_j$ and all A_i are finitely compatible. We define $A_\alpha = \bigcup_{i<\alpha} A_i$, implicitly using the axiom of choice. By definition A_α is compatible with $\mathcal{E}$ for otherwise there would be some finite subset $B \subseteq^{<\omega} A_\alpha$ that is not kept in $\mathcal{E}$, but then due to the construction it follows that already $B \subseteq A_i$ for some $i < \alpha$, in contradiction to the successor step.

5. Conflict-Freeness and Range-Completeness: Conflict-freeness follows from compatibility, range-completeness follows from definition of unresolved range and successor/limit steps resolving this issue. Latest at each limit step, A_α becomes admissible and independent from arguments that are not member of A_α^+, i.e. if $a \rightarrowtail A_\alpha$ then $A_\alpha \rightarrowtail a$, and if $A_\alpha^+ \rightarrowtail a$ then $A_\alpha \rightarrowtail a$, and if $a \rightarrowtail b$ where $b \in A_\alpha^+$ then $A_\alpha \rightarrowtail b$.

Having showed that every range chain of σ-extensions has an upper bound in $\sigma(F)$ using Zorn's lemma we now conclude that there is a range-maximal σ-extension, in other words a σ^+-extension.

5.2   The Special Case of Eager Semantics

One may have wondered why we did not consider eager semantics in Section 4.2. The reason for this simply is that eager semantics does not follow the unique status approach.[6] More precisely, if there are no semi-stable extensions then eager semantics equals preferred semantics. Moreover, in this case we have infinitely many eager extensions. If the set of semi-stable extensions is nonempty then eager semantics is uniquely determined.

Theorem 15. *For any F, we have:*

1. $ss(F) \neq \emptyset \Rightarrow |eg(F)| = 1$,
2. $ss(F) = \emptyset \Rightarrow eg(F) = pr(F)$ *and*
3. $ss(F) = \emptyset \Rightarrow |eg(F)| \geq |\mathbb{N}|$.

Proof. ad 1.) The proof is almost identical with the one presented for Theorem 8. Simply replace preferred by semi-stable semantics.

ad 2.) Let $F = (A, R)$ and assume $ss(F) = \emptyset$. Remember that $\bigcap_{P \in ss(F)} P = \{x \in A \mid \forall P \in ss(F) : x \in P\}$. Given that $ss(F) = \emptyset$ we deduce $\bigcap_{P \in ss(F)} P = A$ since $\forall P \in ss(F) : x \in P$ becomes a vacuous truth. Hence, eager semantics calls for subset-maximal admissible sets. This means, $eg(F) = pr(F)$.

ad 3.) Assume $|eg(F)| = n$ for some finite cardinal $n \in \mathbb{N}$. Due to statement 2 we derive, $|pr(F)| = n$. Remember that $ss \subseteq pr$ (cf. Proposition 1). Consequently, among the finitely many preferred extensions there has to be a range-maximal one. This means, $ss(F) \neq \emptyset$.

Since finitary AFs do always possess semi-stable extensions we state the following corollary.

Corollary 1. *For any finitary F,* $|eg(F)| = 1$.

---

[6] Observe that our assertion does not contradict the claimed uniqueness in [12] since the author considered the restricted case of finite AFs only.

5.3   A Note on *cf2* and *stg2* Semantics

Two semantics which have defied any attempt of solving w.r.t. the problem of existence in case of finitary AFs are *cf2* and *stg2* semantics [5,15]. Both are defined via a general recursive schema which is based on decomposing AFs along their *strongly connected components (SCCs)*. Roughly speaking,[7] the schema takes a base semantics σ and proceeds along the induced partial ordering and evaluates the SCCs according to σ while propagating relevant results to subsequent SCCs. This procedure defines a $\sigma2$ semantics.[8]

Given SCC-recursiveness we have to face some difficulties in drawing conclusions with respect to infinite or finitary AFs. If every subframework does have an initial SCC (which is guarenteed for finite AFs), i.e. some strongly connected subframework that is not attacked from the outside, then obviously this AF provides a $\sigma2$-extension as soon as every single component provides a σ-extension. If on the other hand there is no initial SCC things become more complicated and in particular especially due to the recursive definitions not that easy to handle. So for now we go with the following conjecture.

Conjecture 1. For any finitary F, $|cf2(F)| \geq 1$ and $|stg2(F)| \geq 1$.

A noteworthy observation is that both semantics are not universally defined. Consider therefore the following example.

Example 4 (Example 2 continued). Let $\sigma \in \{cf2, stg2\}$. Consider the AF F' depicted in Figure 5. Here, for a sequence $(b_i)_{i \in \mathbb{N}}$ of arguments we have that $b_i \rightarrowtail b_j$ iff $i > j$. This means, any argument b_i constitutes a SCC $\{b_i\}$ which is evaluated as $\{b_i\}$ by the base semantics of σ. Consequently, $\emptyset$ cannot be a σ-extension. Furthermore, a singleton $\{b_j\}$ cannot be a σ-extension either. The b_i's for $i > j$ are not affected by b_j and thus, the evaluation of $\{b_i\}$ do not return $\emptyset$ as required. Finally, any set containing more than two arguments would rule out at least one of them and thus, cannot be a σ-extension.

5.4   Summary of Results

The following table gives a comprehensive overview over results presented in this paper. The entry $\exists$ ($\exists!$) in row *certain* and column σ indicates that the existence of σ-extension is guaranteed (and uniquely determined) given that *certain* frameworks are considered. The question mark represents an open problem.

---

[7] Due to the limited space we have to refer the reader to [5] for more details.

[8] Following this terminology we have to rename *cf2* semantics to *na2* semantics since its base semantics is the naive semantics and not conflict-free sets.

	stb	ss	stg	cf2	stg2	pr	ad	co	gr	id	eg	na	cf
finite		∃	∃	∃	∃	∃	∃	∃	∃!	∃!	∃!	∃	∃
finitary		∃	∃	?	?	∃	∃	∃	∃!	∃!	∃!	∃	∃
arbitrary						∃	∃	∃	∃!	∃!	∃	∃	∃

Fig. 16. Existence and Uniqueness of Extension

6   Conclusions and Related Work

In this paper we gave an overview on the question whether certain semantics guarantee the existence or even unique determination of extensions. Whereas most of the literature concentrated on finite AFs we stick to the arbitrary infinite case as well as the subclass of finitary AFs. We present full or alternative proofs for already known results like universal definedness of preferred semantics and existence of semi-stable extensions in case of finitary frameworks. Furthermore, we completed the picture for the remaining semantics in case of non-finite structures. To mention two results: Firstly, stage semantics behaves similarly to semi-stable, i.e. extensions are guaranteed as long as finitary AFs are considered. Secondly, eager semantics is universally defined but either there is exactly one or there are infinitely many eager extensions. The former case is ensured for finitary structures. In the latter case eager semantics coincide with preferred semantics. To sum up, eager semantics does not generally follow the unique status approach.

It is a non-trivial problem to decide whether certain abstract properties satisfied for finite AFs carry over to infinite structures. In [2, Section 4.4] the authors wrote "As a matter of fact, we are not aware of any systematic literature analysis of argumentation semantics properties in the infinite case.". This paper can be seen as a first step in this direction.

Acknowledgements. We are grateful to Thomas Linsbichler for detailed and valuable comments on the overall manuscript. Furthermore, we thank Sarah Alice Gaggl, Paul Dunne, Wolfgang Dvořák, Davide Grossi, Frank Loebe, Hannes Strass and Emil Weydert for discussing certain examples as well as details.

The paper is dedicated to Gerhard Brewka on the occasion of his 60th birthday. It is great honour to us to contribute this paper to the *Festschrift*.

References

1. Bárány, V., Grädel, E., Rubin, S.: Automata-based presentations of infinite structures. In: Finite and Algorithmic Model Theory, pp. 1–76. Cambridge University Press (2011)

2. Baroni, P., Caminada, M., Giacomin, M.: An introduction to argumentation semantics. Knowledge Engineering Review 26(4), 365–410 (2011)
3. Baroni, P., Cerutti, F., Dunne, P.E., Giacomin, M.: Automata for infinite argumentation structures. Artificial Intelligence 203, 104–150 (2013)
4. Baroni, P., Giacomin, M.: Semantics of abstract argument systems. In: Rahwan, I., Simari, G.R. (eds.) Argumentation in Artificial Intelligence, pp. 25–44. Springer (2009)
5. Baroni, P., Giacomin, M., Guida, G.: SCC-recursiveness: A general schema for argumentation semantics. Artificial Intelligence 168(1-2), 162–210 (2005)
6. Baumann, R.: Context-free and context-sensitive kernels: Update and deletion equivalence in abstract argumentation. In: ECAI, pp. 63–68 (2014)
7. Baumann, R.: Metalogical Contributions to the Nonmonotonic Theory of Abstract Argumentation. College Publications (2014)
8. Baumann, R., Brewka, G.: Expanding argumentation frameworks: Enforcing and monotonicity results. In: COMMA. FAIA, vol. 216, pp. 75–86. IOS Press (2010)
9. Trevor, J.M.: Bench-Capon and Paul E. Dunne. Argumentation in AI and law: Editors' introduction. Artificial Intelligence and Law 13(1), 1–8 (2005)
10. Trevor, J.M.: Bench-Capon and Paul E. Dunne. Argumentation in artificial intelligence. Artificial Intelligence 171(10-15), 619–641 (2007)
11. Blumensath, A., Grädel, E.: Finite presentations of infinite structures: Automata and interpretations. Theory of Computing Systems 37(6), 641–674 (2004)
12. Caminada, M.W.A.: Comparing two unique extension semantics for formal argumentation: Ideal and eager. In: BNAIC, pp. 81–87 (2007)
13. Martin, W.A.: Caminada and Bart Verheij. On the existence of semi-stable extensions. In: BNAIC (2010)
14. Dung, P.M.: On the acceptability of arguments and its fundamental role in nonmonotonic reasoning, logic programming and n-person games. Artificial Intelligence 77(2), 321–357 (1995)
15. Dvořák, W., Gaggl, S.A.: Stage semantics and the SCC-recursive schema for argumentation semantics. Journal of Logic and Computation (2014)
16. Grossi, D.: On the logic of argumentation theory. In: AAMAS, pp. 409–416. International Foundation for Autonomous Agents and Multiagent Systems (2010)
17. Halmos, P.R.: Naive Set Theory. In: Undergraduate Texts in Mathematics. Springer (1960)
18. Verheij, B.: Deflog: on the logical interpretation of prima facie justified assumptions. Journal of Logic and Computation 13(3), 319–346 (2003)
19. Weydert, E.: Semi-stable extensions for infinite frameworks. In: BNAIC, pp. 336–343 (2011)
20. Zorn, M.: A remark on method in transfinite algebra. Bulletin of the American Mathematical Society 41, 667–670 (1935)

Judgment Aggregation
in Abstract Dialectical Frameworks

Richard Booth

Université du Luxembourg
6 rue Richard Coudenhove-Kalergi, Luxembourg
ribooth@gmail.com

Abstract. Abstract dialectical frameworks (ADFs) are a knowledge representation formalism introduced as a generalisation of Dung's abstract argumentation frameworks (AFs) by Gerhard Brewka and co-authors. We look at a judgment aggregation problem in ADFs, namely the problem of aggregating a profile of complete interpretations. We generalise the family of *interval aggregation methods*, studied in the AF case in our previous work, to the ADF case. Along the way we define the notions of *down-admissible* and *up-complete* interpretations, that were already previously defined for the AF case by Caminada and Pigozzi. These aggregation methods may open the way to define interesting new semantics for ADFs, such as a generalisation to the ADF case of the *ideal* semantics for AFs.

Keywords: Abstract dialectical frameworks, argumentation frameworks, judgment aggregation, interval methods.

1   Introduction

Abstract Dialectical Frameworks (ADFs) [5,4] have recently been introduced by Gerhard Brewka and colleagues as a knowledge representation formalism that generalises the popular Abstract Argumentation Frameworks (AFs) introduced by Dung [9]. Several different *semantics* for ADFs have been defined which each provide a way to map any ADF to its set of *models* or *interpretations*. Usually these different semantics are defined so as to generalise an existing semantics of AFs, such as *admissible* and *complete* semantics. In this paper we likewise seek to explore within the wider setting of ADFs a problem that has recently received attention in the more confined setting of AFs. Namely we are interested in the problem of *aggregation opinions* in ADFs.

Our aggregation problem can be described as follows. Suppose we have a group of agents who share a given ADF D. Each agent has a particular opinion about the truth-value of the statements in D, and we assume each agent is *rational* in the sense that their interpretation is a model of D according to some commonly agreed semantics (which, in this paper, will be the complete semantics). The question is, can we aggregate these opinions into a single group interpretation that represents the opinion of the group as a whole? In the AF

T. Eiter et al. (Eds.): Brewka Festschrift, LNAI 9060, pp. 296–308, 2015.
© Springer International Publishing Switzerland 2015

setting, this question (which can be thought of as a special case of the problem of *judgment aggregation* [11,12]) has been investigated in [3]. There, a general family of methods for aggregating complete AF labellings called *interval methods* was defined and studied. In this paper we will show how this family can be extended to cover the case of aggregation in ADFs.

Although simple to define and understand, the interval methods of [3] suffered from the rather severe drawback that they were not guaranteed to output a rational (i.e., complete) labelling for every possible AF. To remedy this, it was suggested to add a post-processing *repair* step to the output. This step consisted of two sub-procedures, the *down-admissible* followed by the *up-complete* procedures, which were first introduced in [7]. We will see that these procedures, that were so far only defined in the AF setting, can be generalised to the ADF case, thus yielding a family of ADF aggregation operators - the *DAUC interval methods* - that guarantee a rational outcome.

The plan of this paper is as follows. We start in the next section by giving preliminary background on ADFs. Then in Section 3 we formally introduce the ADF aggregation problem and give some postulates for aggregation methods. In Section 4 we define interval aggregation methods and axiomatically characterise them. Then in Section 5 we present the down-admissible and up-complete procedures for ADFs and define the DAUC interval methods. Lastly we conclude, including a discussion about possible applications for defining new semantics for ADFs, in particular a counterpart of ideal semantics from AFs.

2   Abstract Dialectical Frameworks

Abstract dialectical frameworks were first introduced by Brewka and Woltran [5] and then further developed by Brewka et al [4] as a useful generalisation of Dung's abstract argumentation frameworks [9]. The idea is that we have a collection S of atomic *statements* (essentially just propositional atoms), and each $s \in S$ has a propositional formula φ_s associated to it that intuitively represents the *justification* for accepting s. Roughly, if we have enough grounds for holding φ_s to be true, then that gives us license to hold s to be true. The following setup of ADFs is based on [4] (which was, in turn, inspired by the algebraic approach to non-monotonic reasoning from [8] - see also [13] for a comprehensive study of algebraic semantics for ADFs).

To begin, we assume a countable universal set U of possible *statements* from which all ADFs are formed. Then an ADF may be defined as follows:

Definition 1. *An* abstract dialectical framework *is a pair $D = (S, C)$ where*
 − *$S \subseteq U$ is a finite set of statements.*
 − *C is a collection $\{\varphi_s\}_{s \in S}$ of propositional formulas built from S. Formula φ_s is called the* condition *of s.*
We will sometimes (if D is not clear from the context) denote the sets of statements and conditions of an ADF D by S_D and C_D respectively.

For simplicity we assume for each $s \in S$ that φ_s doesn't contain redundant statements, that is, for each statement t appearing in φ_s, the set of (2-valued) interpretations satisfying $\varphi_s(t/\mathbf{t})$ differs from the set of (2-valued) interpretations satisfying $\varphi_s(t/\mathbf{f})$, where $\varphi_s(t/\mathbf{t})$ denotes the formula resulting from substituting t everywhere by $\mathbf{t}$, and similarly for $\varphi_s(t/\mathbf{f})$, where $\mathbf{t}$ and $\mathbf{f}$ denote propositional truth and falsity respectively. That is, the truth or falsity of t can make a difference to the truth value of φ_s.

An ADF comes with an implicit graph structure, with S as the nodes, reflecting the dependencies between statements. To each ADF D we associate the set of links L_D by setting $(t, s) \in L_D$ iff $s, t \in S_D$ and t appears in φ_s. We denote the set of parents of s by $\mathrm{Par}_D(s)$, i.e., $\mathrm{Par}_D(s) = \{t \in S_D \mid (t, s) \in L_D\}$. Dung argumentation frameworks (AFs) form a subclass of the class of ADFs. Indeed an ADF D is an AF iff each φ_s is equivalent to $\bigwedge_{t \in \mathrm{Par}_D(s)} \neg t$.

Example 1. Following [4], we may represent an ADF by listing its statements, with the condition of each statement written in square brackets immediately after it. For example one possible ADF D_0 with $S_{D_0} = \{a, b, c\}$ may be written as follows.

$$a\ [\mathbf{t}], \qquad b\ [b], \qquad c\ [\neg a \vee b].$$

A D-interpretation is just a function $v : S \rightarrow \{\mathbf{t}, \mathbf{f}, \mathbf{u}\}$ assigning one of the truth-values $\mathbf{t}$ (true), $\mathbf{f}$ (false) or $\mathbf{u}$ (unknown) to each statement in S. For notational convenience we define a negation operator on the set of truth-values by setting $\neg\mathbf{t} = \mathbf{f}$, $\neg\mathbf{f} = \mathbf{t}$ and $\neg\mathbf{u} = \mathbf{u}$. The ordering $\sqsubseteq$ between D-interpretations is defined by $v_1 \sqsubseteq v_2$ iff for all $s \in S$, $v_1(s) \leqslant v_2(s)$, where $\leqslant$ is the (reflexive) information ordering between truth-values given by $\mathbf{u} \leqslant \mathbf{t}$ and $\mathbf{u} \leqslant \mathbf{f}$ (and no other pair $(\mathbf{x}, \mathbf{y})$ for $\mathbf{x} \neq \mathbf{y}$ is in $\leqslant$). The set of truth-values forms a complete meet-semi-lattice[1] under $\leqslant$, with meet operation $\sqcap$ behaving as a "consensus" operator, i.e., $\mathbf{t} \sqcap \mathbf{t} = \mathbf{t}$, $\mathbf{f} \sqcap \mathbf{f} = \mathbf{f}$, and the meet of all other pairs returning $\mathbf{u}$. The set of all D-interpretations, equipped with ordering $\sqsubseteq$, inherits this semi-lattice structure with meet operation $\sqcap$ defined by $(v_1 \sqcap v_2)(s) = v_1(s) \sqcap v_2(s)$.

We say a D-interpretation is *2-valued* if it assigns only values in $\{\mathbf{t}, \mathbf{f}\}$. Given a D-interpretation v, the set of 2-valued interpretations $\sqsubseteq$-extending v is denoted by $[v]_2$. Then we define a function Γ_D taking D-interpretations to D-interpretations as follows by setting, for all $s \in S_D$:

$$[\Gamma_D(v)](s) = \bigsqcap\{w(\varphi_s) \mid w \in [v]_2\}.$$

That is, to determine $[\Gamma_D(v)](s)$ we look at all possible ways the 3-valued interpretation v may be completed to a 2-valued one. If there is consensus on the value of the condition φ_s among all of these then $[\Gamma_D(v)](s)$ is set to that value. Otherwise $[\Gamma_D(v)](s) = \mathbf{u}$. An alternative formulation of Γ_D can be given as follows. For each D-interpretation v let $v^\wedge$ denote the conjunction

---

[1] A complete meet-semi-lattice is such that *(i)* every non-empty finite subset has a greatest lower bound, and *(ii)* every non-empty directed subset has a least upper bound, where a subset X is directed if any two elements of X have an upper bound in X.

$\bigwedge\{s \mid v(s) = \mathbf{t}\} \wedge \bigwedge\{\neg s \mid v(s) = \mathbf{f}\}$. Then, for each $s \in S_D$

$$[\Gamma_D(v)](s) = \begin{cases} \mathbf{t} & \text{if } v^\wedge \models \varphi_s \\ \mathbf{f} & \text{if } v^\wedge \models \neg\varphi_s \\ \mathbf{u} & \text{otherwise} \end{cases}$$

where $\models$ denotes entailment in classical propositional logic. It is shown in [5] that Γ_D is monotonic in $\sqsubseteq$, i.e., if $v_1 \sqsubseteq v_2$ then $\Gamma_D(v_1) \sqsubseteq \Gamma_D(v_2)$.

The notions of *admissible* and *complete* D-interpretations can then be defined in terms of the Γ_D-function as follows.

Definition 2. *A D-interpretation is* admissible *iff* $v \sqsubseteq \Gamma_D(v)$. *It is* complete *iff* $v = \Gamma_D(v)$.

Intuitively, a D-interpretation is admissible if it doesn't assign $\mathbf{t}$ or $\mathbf{f}$ to any statement s without *justification* for doing so. An admissible D-interpretation is complete if it assigns $\mathbf{t}$ or $\mathbf{f}$ to every statement for which justification is at hand. As a fixed point of Γ_D, a complete D-interpretation can be thought of a *rational, internally coherent* belief state regarding the truth or falsity of the statements in S_D. For the special case in which D is an AF, these notions coincide with the notions of admissible and complete *argument labellings* of [6] (see also [1]).

Example 2. Consider ADF D_0 from Example 1. We can write D_0-interpretations as triples (p, q, r) of truth-values expressing the values of a, b, c in that order. There are three possible complete D_0-interpretations: $v_1 = (\mathbf{t}, \mathbf{t}, \mathbf{t})$, $v_2 = (\mathbf{t}, \mathbf{u}, \mathbf{u})$ and $v_3 = (\mathbf{t}, \mathbf{f}, \mathbf{f})$. An example of an interpretation which is admissible but not complete is $v_4 = (\mathbf{u}, \mathbf{t}, \mathbf{t})$. The all-unknown interpretation - in this case $v_5 = (\mathbf{u}, \mathbf{u}, \mathbf{u})$ - is always admissible.

The notions of admissible or complete D-interpretations provide just two possible *semantics* for ADFs. Others are possible (see [4,13]) but for this paper we will focus on only these.

3   Aggregating Complete Interpretations: Postulates

The aggregation setting we have in mind is as follows. We assume a fixed set $Ag = \{1, \ldots, n\}$ of *agents* (for some fixed $n \geqslant 2$). The idea is that, given some arbitrary ADF D, each agent forms some opinion over the truth or falsity of each statement, subject to the constraints encoded in D. Each agent i's opinion is expressed as a complete D-interpretation v_i, and they are collected in a D-*profile* $\mathbf{v} = (v_1, \ldots, v_n)$. For any $T \subseteq S_D$ and D-interpretation v we denote by $v[T]$ the projection of v to just the statements in T, and we denote by $\mathbf{v}[T]$ the n-tuple $(v_1[T], \ldots, v_n[T])$. We would like to determine a *single* D-interpretation that reflects the opinion of the group as a whole.

Definition 3. *An ADF* aggregation method *(hereafter* aggregation method *for short) is a function $\mathcal{F}$ that assigns, to each ADF D and each profile $\mathbf{v}$ of complete D-interpretations, a D-interpretation $\mathcal{F}_D(\mathbf{v})$.*

How should we define a good aggregation method? Before describing some concrete families of such methods in the next sections, we take a look at a few desirable postulates for aggregation methods. These are inspired by and appropriately modified from postulates studied in the AF case in [3] (which, in turn, have been mostly inspired by postulates from the judgment aggregation literature [11,12]). Free variables in these postulates, e.g., D, $\mathbf{v}$ in the first three postulates below, are implicitly universally quantified.

The first, basic, group of postulates is as follows:

Collective Completeness $\mathcal{F}_D(\mathbf{v})$ is a complete D-interpretation.

Anonymity If $\mathbf{v}'$ is a permutation of $\mathbf{v}$ then $\mathcal{F}_D(\mathbf{v}') = \mathcal{F}_D(\mathbf{v})$.

Unanimity If $v_i = v$ for all $i \in Ag$ then $\mathcal{F}_D(\mathbf{v}) = v$.

Collective Completeness requires that the output of the aggregation should be a rational interpretation. For *Anonymity* we say "$\mathbf{v}'$ is a permutation of $\mathbf{v}$" to mean that $\mathbf{v} = (v_1, \ldots, v_n)$ and $\mathbf{v}' = (v_{\sigma(1)}, \ldots, v_{\sigma(n)})$ for some permutation σ on Ag. Thus this postulate says the identity of the agents does not matter in the aggregation process. *Unanimity* says that if all agents agree on the same D-interpretation then this should be the output.

Although a basic requirement, *Collective Completeness* will turn out not to be satisfied by the family of aggregation methods we present in the next section. However, restricting it to a particularly simple kind of ADF - in fact a kind of AF - brings it to within much easier reach. We say an AF D is a *2-loop AF* iff $S_D = \{s, t\}$ and $L_D = \{(s,t), (t,s)\}$ for some distinct $s, t \in U$.

Minimal Collective Completeness If D is a 2-loop AF, then $\mathcal{F}_D(\mathbf{v})$ is a complete D-interpretation.

The next two postulates try to ensure minimum levels of *satisfaction* for the agents with the collective outcome. Given a tuple $(\mathbf{x}_i)_{i \in Ag}$ of truth-values the **t/f**-*winner* (resp. **t/f**-*loser*) in $(\mathbf{x}_i)_{i \in Ag}$ is that value among $\{\mathbf{t}, \mathbf{f}\}$ which appears more (resp. less) often in $(\mathbf{x}_i)_{i \in Ag}$. For example the **t/f**-loser in $(\mathbf{t}, \mathbf{u}, \mathbf{u}, \mathbf{f}, \mathbf{t})$ is **f**.

t/f-Plurality If $\mathbf{x}$ is the **t/f**-loser in $(v_i(s))_{i \in Ag}$ then $[\mathcal{F}_D(\mathbf{v})](s) \neq \mathbf{x}$.

Compatibility $v_i(s) = \neg[\mathcal{F}_D(\mathbf{v})](s)$ implies $v_i(s) = \mathbf{u}$.

t/f-*Plurality* thus says the collective value assigned to s cannot be $\mathbf{x} \in \{\mathbf{t}, \mathbf{f}\}$ if strictly more agents voted for it to be $\neg \mathbf{x}$. *Compatibility* is a stronger property that says the collective value cannot be $\mathbf{x} \in \{\mathbf{t}, \mathbf{f}\}$ if *at least one agent* voted for it to be $\neg \mathbf{x}$. The postulate is so-called because it says that the collective interpretation $\mathcal{F}_D(\mathbf{v})$ must be *compatible* with the interpretation of *every* agent i.

Definition 4. *Two D-interpretations u, v are compatible iff there is no statement s such that $u(s) = \neg v(s) \neq \mathbf{u}$.*

This notion of compatibility plays a leading role in the AF aggregation setting of Caminada and Pigozzi [7]. The following lemma regarding the interplay between the notions of compatibility and completeness will be used in the proof of Proposition 5 in Section 5.

Lemma 1. *Let u be a complete D-interpretation. Then, for any D-interpretation v, if v is compatible with u then so is $\Gamma_D(v)$.*

Proof. Suppose u is complete but $\Gamma_D(v)$ is not compatible with u. Then there must be some $s \in S_D$ such that $[\Gamma_D(v)](s) = \neg u(s) \neq \mathbf{u}$. By completeness of u this gives $[\Gamma_D(v)](s) = \neg[\Gamma_D(u)](s) \neq \mathbf{u}$, which implies $v^\wedge \wedge u^\wedge \models \bot$. But this can only happen if $v(t) = \neg u(t) \neq \mathbf{u}$ for some $t \in S_D$, i.e., if v is not compatible with u. □

For the next aggregation postulate, we say that a given truth-value $\mathbf{y}$ is *between* truth-values $\mathbf{x}$ and $\mathbf{z}$ iff $\mathbf{y} = \mathbf{x}$ or $\mathbf{y} = \mathbf{z}$ or $[\mathbf{y} = \mathbf{u}$ and $\mathbf{x} = \neg \mathbf{z}]$. The next postulate implies that if a particular collective outcome $\mathbf{x} \in \{\mathbf{t}, \mathbf{f}\}$ is obtained for statement s, and if some of the agents then change the truth-value they assign to s so that they move *closer* to this collective outcome, then the collective outcome does not change.

> **Monotonicity** Let $\mathbf{v}, \mathbf{v}'$ be D-profiles such that for all $s \in S_D$ and all $i \in Ag$, if $v_i(s) \neq v_i'(s)$ then $([\mathcal{F}_D(\mathbf{v})](s) \in \{\mathbf{t}, \mathbf{f}\}$ and $v_i'(s)$ is between $v_i(s)$ and $[\mathcal{F}_D(\mathbf{v})](s))$. Then $\mathcal{F}_D(\mathbf{v}') = \mathcal{F}_D(\mathbf{v})$.

All the postulates until now referred to only a single ADF D. The remaining postulates deal with restricting the behaviour of $\mathcal{F}$ across different, but related, ADFs. The first enforces a certain *neutrality* over the *names* of the statements used in an ADF. Given two ADFs $D = (S, C)$ and $D' = (S', C')$ a *renaming* from D to D' is a bijection $\tau : S \to S'$ such that $\varphi_{\tau(s)} = \tau(\varphi_s)$ for each $s \in S$, where $\tau(\varphi_s)$ is obtained from φ_s by replacing every occurrence of each statement t with $\tau(t)$. A renaming lifts to a function taking D-interpretations v to D'-interpretations $\tau(v)$ by taking $[\tau(v)](s) = v(\tau^{-1}(s))$ for each $s \in S'$. As the following result shows, both the admissible and complete semantics for ADFs are invariant under renaming.[2]

Proposition 1. *Let τ be a renaming from D to D'. If v is an admissible, resp. complete, D-interpretation then $\tau(v)$ is an admissible, resp. complete, D'-interpretation.*

Proof. (Outline) Follows mainly from that fact that, for each $s \in S_D$ and any D-interpretation v we have $v^\wedge \models \varphi_s$ iff $\tau(v)^\wedge \models \varphi_{\tau(s)}$, and $v^\wedge \models \neg\varphi_s$ iff $\tau(v)^\wedge \models \neg\varphi_{\tau(s)}$. □

A renaming τ further extends naturally to a mapping from D-profiles $\mathbf{v}$ to D'-profiles $\tau(\mathbf{v}) = (\tau(v_1), \ldots, \tau(v_n))$. The *Renaming* postulate for aggregation methods can then be formalised as follows:

---

[2] In the AF setting, this is known as the *language independence* property of AF semantics [2].

Renaming If τ is a renaming from D to D' then $\tau(\mathcal{F}_D(\mathbf{v})) = \mathcal{F}_{D'}(\tau(\mathbf{v}))$.

We remark that in the restricted case of AFs this postulate can be simplified so that it talks about graph isomorphisms rather than renamings (see the *Isomorphism* postulate in [3]).

The next postulate is a strong version of the *Independence* postulate which forms the basis of several important results (especially impossibility results) in judgment aggregation. It says that the collective truth-value of s depends at most on the tuple of individual truth-values assigned to s by the agents, regardless of which other statements may or may not be present in D.

ADF-Independence If $\mathbf{v}$ is a D-profile and $\mathbf{v}'$ is a D'-profile and $s \in S_D \cap S_{D'}$, then $\mathbf{v}[s] = \mathbf{v}'[s]$ implies $[\mathcal{F}_D(\mathbf{v})](s) = [\mathcal{F}_{D'}(\mathbf{v}')](s)$.

As expected, this postulate turns out to be too strong, and anyway could be argued against on the basis that it asks us to disregard dependency information between statements (in the form of the set L_D) that is explicitly submitted as part of the input to the problem. We thus formulate a weaker version, inspired by the *Directionality* property for AF semantics [2]. Given an ADF $D = (S, \{\varphi_s\}_{s \in S})$ and $T \subseteq S$, we say T is *primary in* D if for no $t \in T, s \in S\backslash T$ do we have $(s,t) \in L_D$, i.e., each statement in T depends only on statements within T. We denote by $D \downarrow T$ the ADF $(T, \{\varphi_s\}_{s \in T})$, with the φ_s "inherited" from D. Then the *Directionality* postulate for ADF aggregation can be formulated as follows:

Directionality If $T \subseteq S_D$ is primary in D then $\mathcal{F}_{D \downarrow T}(\mathbf{v}[T]) = \mathcal{F}_D(\mathbf{v})[T]$.

(Note one can straightforwardly show that if v is admissible, resp. complete, in D and T is primary in D, then $v[T]$ is admissible, resp. complete, in $D \downarrow T$.) This property says that the outcome of aggregation for a primary set T of statements is independent of statements outside the set.

4   Interval Aggregation Methods

We now describe a family of ADF aggregation methods, generalised from the family of AF aggregation methods from [3] known as *interval methods*.

Let Int_n denote the set of non-zero *intervals* over $\{0, 1, \ldots, n\}$, i.e., $Int_n = \{(k,l) \mid k,l \in \{0,1,\ldots,n\}$ and $k < l\}$. Then to define a member of this family, we just choose some distinguished set $Y \subseteq Int_n$. We say Y is *widening*[3] if $(a,b) \in Y$ whenever $(k,l) \in Y$ and $a \leq k, l \leq b$, and is *zero-based* if $k = 0$ whenever $(k,l) \in Y$. Each possible choice of Y yields an aggregation method $\mathcal{F}^Y$ by setting, for each ADF D, D-profile $\mathbf{v}$ and $s \in S_D$:

$$[\mathcal{F}_D^Y(\mathbf{v})](s) = \begin{cases} \mathbf{x} \text{ if } \mathbf{x} \in \{\mathbf{t}, \mathbf{f}\} \text{ and } (|N_{s:\neg\mathbf{x}}^{\mathbf{v}}|, |N_{s:\mathbf{x}}^{\mathbf{v}}|) \in Y. \\ \mathbf{u} \text{ otherwise} \end{cases}$$

---

[3] The widening interval methods are very closely related to *quota systems* studied in voting theory by Young et al [14].

Here, $N_{s:\mathbf{x}}^{\mathbf{v}}$ denotes the set of agents who assign value $\mathbf{x}$ to s in $\mathbf{v}$, i.e., $N_{s:\mathbf{x}}^{\mathbf{v}} = \{i \in Ag \mid v_i(s) = \mathbf{x}\}$. Thus $\mathcal{F}_D^Y(\mathbf{v})$ sets the collective truth-value of s to be the t/f-winner $\mathbf{x}$ in $(v_i(s))_{i \in Ag}$ provided such a winner exists and $(|N_{s:\neg\mathbf{x}}^{\mathbf{v}}|, |N_{s:\mathbf{x}}^{\mathbf{v}}|) \in Y$. Otherwise the collective value is set to $\mathbf{u}$.

Definition 5. *An aggregation method $\mathcal{F}$ will be called an* interval method *iff $\mathcal{F} = \mathcal{F}^Y$ for some $Y \subseteq Int_n$ such that $(0, n) \in Y$. If, furthermore, Y is widening, resp. zero-based, then we say $\mathcal{F}$ is a* widening, *resp.* zero-based, *interval method.*

The restriction $(0, n) \in Y$ is essentially made to ensure $\mathcal{F}^Y$ satisfies the *Unanimity* postulate.

The family of interval methods contains a number of interesting special cases. We mention three here, the first two of which were first studied in the AF case in [7]:

- Sceptical: $Y^{\text{Scep}} = \{(0, n)\}$. Take the collective value of a statement s to be $\mathbf{x}$ if *all* agents voted for $\mathbf{x}$, otherwise take $\mathbf{u}$. We use $\mathcal{F}^{\text{Scep}}$ to denote $\mathcal{F}^{Y^{\text{Scep}}}$. Note that $\mathcal{F}^{\text{Scep}}(\mathbf{v}) = \bigsqcap_{i \in Ag} v_i$.

- Credulous: $Y^{\text{Cred}} = \{(0, l) \mid l \geq 1\}$. Take the collective value to be $\mathbf{x} \in \{\mathbf{t}, \mathbf{f}\}$ if at least one agent voted for $\mathbf{x}$ and none voted for the opposite $\neg\mathbf{x}$. Otherwise take $\mathbf{u}$. We use $\mathcal{F}^{\text{Cred}}$ to denote $\mathcal{F}^{Y^{\text{Cred}}}$.

- Simple majority: $Y^{\text{SMaj}} = Int_n$. Here we just take the t/f-winner whenever it exists, and take $\mathbf{u}$ otherwise. We use $\mathcal{F}^{\text{SMaj}}$ to denote $\mathcal{F}^{Y^{\text{SMaj}}}$.

Notice that all three of Y^{Scep}, Y^{Cred} and Y^{SMaj} are widening, and all except Y^{SMaj} are zero-based.

Example 3. Consider the following ADF D_1 with $S_{D_1} = \{a, b, c, d\}$.

$$a\ [a], \qquad b\ [b], \qquad c\ [c], \qquad d\ [\neg a \wedge \neg b \wedge \neg c].$$

Assume $n = 4$ and that $\mathbf{v} = (v_1, v_2, v_3, v_4)$ with $v_1 = (\mathbf{t}, \mathbf{t}, \mathbf{t}, \mathbf{f})$, $v_2 = (\mathbf{f}, \mathbf{t}, \mathbf{u}, \mathbf{f})$, $v_3 = (\mathbf{t}, \mathbf{t}, \mathbf{u}, \mathbf{f})$, $v_4 = (\mathbf{u}, \mathbf{f}, \mathbf{u}, \mathbf{u})$. Then $\mathcal{F}^{\text{Scep}}(\mathbf{v}) = (\mathbf{u}, \mathbf{u}, \mathbf{u}, \mathbf{u})$, $\mathcal{F}^{\text{Cred}}(\mathbf{v}) = (\mathbf{u}, \mathbf{u}, \mathbf{t}, \mathbf{f})$ and $\mathcal{F}^{\text{SMaj}}(\mathbf{v}) = (\mathbf{t}, \mathbf{t}, \mathbf{t}, \mathbf{f})$.

We can characterise the family of interval methods in terms of postulates as follows.

Theorem 1. *Let $\mathcal{F}$ be an aggregation method. Then $\mathcal{F}$ is an interval method iff it satisfies Anonymity, Unanimity, Minimal Collective Completeness, t/f-Plurality, Renaming and ADF-Independence.*

Proof. (Outline). Soundness is relatively straightforward. The completeness part largely follows the same pattern as the proof of the corresponding theorem for the restricted AF case in [3]. We first show how to construct, from any given aggregation method $\mathcal{F}$, a subset $Y(\mathcal{F}) \subseteq Int_n$: Let D_0 be a 2-loop AF such that $S_{D_0} = \{a_0, b_0\}$. There are three complete D_0-interpretations, which we denote by $v_{\mathbf{t}}$, $v_{\mathbf{f}}$ and $v_{\mathbf{u}}$, where the subscript represents the value of a_0 (with the label of b_0 of course being always $\neg v(a_0)$). Then we define $Y(\mathcal{F})$ by setting

$Y(\mathcal{F}) = \{(k,l) \in Int_n \mid [\mathcal{F}_{D_0}(\mathbf{v}_{k,l})](a_0) = \mathbf{t}\}$, where $\mathbf{v}_{k,l}$ is any D_0-profile such that precisely k agents provide labelling $v_{\mathbf{f}}$ and l agents provide $v_{\mathbf{t}}$. Note by *Anonymity* that the precise distribution of labellings among $\mathbf{v}_{k,l}$ doesn't matter. $Y(\mathcal{F})$ is well-defined, i.e., it doesn't matter which 2-loop AF we take to define it (by *Renaming*) and $(0,n) \in Y(\mathcal{F})$ (by *Unanimity*). One can then show that $\mathcal{F}$ and $\mathcal{F}^{Y(\mathcal{F})}$ agree on the 2-loop AF D_0, i.e., that for every D_0-profile $\mathbf{v}$ we have $\mathcal{F}_{D_0}(\mathbf{v}) = \mathcal{F}_{D_0}^{Y(\mathcal{F})}(\mathbf{v})$. This part depends on *Anonymity*, *Renaming*, *Minimal Collective Completeness* and $\mathbf{t}/\mathbf{f}$-*Plurality*. Then finally we extend this to hold for *any* ADF D using *ADF-Independence* and *Renaming*.   □

Regarding the other postulates mentioned in the previous section, *Directionality* is satisfied by every interval method, since it is a direct weakening of *ADF-Independence*, but it can be shown that none of the remaining three, i.e., *Collective Completeness*, *Compatibility* and *Monotonicity* is satisfied in general. The last two, however, can be obtained by adding restrictions on Y.

Proposition 2. *Let $\mathcal{F}^Y$ be an interval method.*
(i) *$\mathcal{F}^Y$ satisfies* Monotonicity *iff Y is widening.*
(ii) *$\mathcal{F}^Y$ satisfies* Compatibility *iff Y is zero-based.*

(The proof of this is straightforward. We remark that the "only if" directions of these two results are essentially already covered by the analogous results proved for the AF case in [3].) As a corollary we see that all three of our example interval methods $\mathcal{F}^{Scep}$, $\mathcal{F}^{Cred}$ and $\mathcal{F}^{SMaj}$ satisfy *Monotonicity*, while all except $\mathcal{F}^{SMaj}$ satisfy *Compatibility*.

What about *Collective Completeness*? Readers familiar with the judgment aggregation literature will not be surprised to learn that there is *no* interval method satisfying *Collective Completeness*, even if we restrict to AFs, as shown in [3].

Theorem 2 ([3]). *There is no aggregation method (for any $n > 1$) satisfying all of* Anonymity, Unanimity, Renaming, ADF-Independence *and* Collective Completeness.

One response to this result in the AF case which was followed in [3] (thereby generalising the approach of [7] who focussed only on the special cases $\mathcal{F}^{Scep}$ and $\mathcal{F}^{Cred}$) was to give up *ADF-Independence* by applying the *down-admissible* and *up-complete* procedures to the outcome of aggregation. We will follow this route here.

5   Down-admissible and Up-complete Procedures

The purpose of the down-admissible procedure in [7] was to take any AF-labelling and to revise it *downwards* (along the ordering $\sqsubseteq$), just enough so that it becomes an admissible labelling. It turns out that this procedure quite easily generalises to the ADF setting. Suppose we start from any given D-interpretation v.

We then iteratively construct a sequence $v_0, v_1, \ldots$ of D-interpretations by setting $v_0 = v$ and $v_{i+1} = v_i \sqcap \Gamma_D(v_i)$ for $i \geqslant 0$. Clearly $v_{i+1} \sqsubseteq v_i$ for each i. Let $a = \min\{i \mid v_{i+1} = v_i\}$. By the finiteness of S_D a is guaranteed to exist.

Definition 6. *Let D be an ADF and v a D-interpretation. The* down-admissible *interpretation of v, denoted by $\downarrow v$ is defined by $\downarrow v = v_a$, where the sequence $v_0, v_1, \ldots, v_a$ is defined as above.*

Since $v_a = v_a \sqcap \Gamma_D(v_a)$ we have $v_a \sqsubseteq \Gamma_D(v_a)$ and so $\downarrow v$ is admissible. In fact it is the largest admissible D-interpretation that is $\sqsubseteq$-smaller than v, as the next result confirms.

Proposition 3. *Let v' be an admissible D-interpretation such that $v' \sqsubseteq v$. Then $v' \sqsubseteq \downarrow v$.*

Proof. We show by induction on i that $v' \sqsubseteq v_i$ for all $i = 0, 1, \ldots, a$ in the above procedure. Since $v_0 = v$ the base case $i = 0$ holds by assumption. So now assume $v' \sqsubseteq v_i$. We will show also $v' \sqsubseteq v_{i+1}$, i.e., $v' \sqsubseteq (v_i \sqcap \Gamma_D(v_i))$. To show this it is enough to show both $v' \sqsubseteq v_i$ and $v' \sqsubseteq \Gamma_D(v_i)$. The first of these holds by inductive hypothesis. For the second, we know $v' \sqsubseteq \Gamma_D(v')$ from the assumption that v' is admissible. We also know $\Gamma_D(v') \sqsubseteq \Gamma_D(v_i)$ from $v' \sqsubseteq v_i$ and the monotonicity of Γ_D. From these two we conclude $v' \sqsubseteq \Gamma_D(v_i)$ as required. □

Example 4. Let D_2 be the following ADF, with $S_{D_2} = \{a, b, c, d\}$.

$$a\ [a], \qquad b\ [b], \qquad c\ [\neg a \vee b], \qquad d\ [c],$$

and consider the D_2-interpretation $v = v_0 = (\mathbf{t, f, t, t})$. We have $\Gamma_{D_2}(v_0) = (\mathbf{t, f, f, t})$, so $v_1 = v_0 \sqcap \Gamma_{D_2}(v_0) = (\mathbf{t, f, u, t})$. Now $\Gamma_{D_2}(v_1) = (\mathbf{t, f, f, u})$, so $v_2 = (\mathbf{t, f, u, u})$. Since v_2 is admissible, the procedure stops here with $\downarrow v = v_2 = (\mathbf{t, f, u, u})$.

As the previous example shows, the down-admissible interpretation of v need not be a complete D-interpretation. In [7] the purpose of the up-complete procedure was to take any admissible AF-labelling and to revise it *upwards* (along $\sqsubseteq$), just enough so that it becomes a complete labelling. As with the down-admissible procedure, it is relatively straightforward to generalise this procedure to the ADF case. Starting with an admissible D-interpretation v we can construct a sequence $v = v_0, v_1, v_2, \ldots$ of D-interpretations by setting $v_{i+1} = \Gamma_D(v_i)$ for $i \geqslant 0$. From the assumption that v is admissible (so $v_0 \sqsubseteq v_1$) and the monotonicity of Γ_D we have $v_i \sqsubseteq v_{i+1}$ for $i \geqslant 0$. Let $c = \min\{i \mid v_{i+1} = v_i\}$. Again, by finiteness c is guaranteed to exist.

Definition 7. *Let D be an ADF and v an admissible D-interpretation. The* up-complete *interpretation of v, denoted by $\uparrow v$ is defined by $\uparrow v = v_c$, where the sequence $v = v_0, v_1, \ldots, v_c$ is defined as above.*

Clearly v_c is complete, and the next result confirms it to be the smallest complete D-interpretation that is $\sqsubseteq$-larger than v.

Proposition 4. *Let v' be a complete D-interpretation such that $v \sqsubseteq v'$. Then $\uparrow v \sqsubseteq v'$.*

Proof. We show by induction on i that $v_i \sqsubseteq v'$. Since $v_0 = v$ the base case $i = 0$ holds by assumption. So now assume $v_i \sqsubseteq v'$. Then, by monotonicity of Γ_D we know $\Gamma_D(v_i) \sqsubseteq \Gamma_D(v')$, i.e., $v_{i+1} \sqsubseteq \Gamma_D(v')$. But since $v' = \Gamma_D(v')$ by the assumption that v' is complete, this gives us $v_{i+1} \sqsubseteq v_i$ as required.   □

Example 5. Let us continue Example 4. Let $v_0 = \downarrow v = (\mathbf{t}, \mathbf{f}, \mathbf{u}, \mathbf{u})$. Then $v_1 = \Gamma_{D_2}(v_0) = (\mathbf{t}, \mathbf{f}, \mathbf{f}, \mathbf{u})$, $v_2 = \Gamma_{D_2}(v_1) = (\mathbf{t}, \mathbf{f}, \mathbf{f}, \mathbf{f}) = \Gamma_{D_2}(v_2)$. Thus $\uparrow(\downarrow v) = (\mathbf{t}, \mathbf{f}, \mathbf{f}, \mathbf{f})$.

We denote the composite operation $\uparrow(\downarrow v)$ of taking the down-admissible followed by the up-complete interpretations of v by $\Updownarrow v$. Taken in combination, these procedures provide a way of transforming any aggregation method into one that is guaranteed to satisfy *Collective Completeness*.

Definition 8. *Let $\mathcal{F}$ be an aggregation method. The DAUC version of $\mathcal{F}$, denoted by $\hat{\mathcal{F}}$, is defined by setting, for any ADF D and D-profile $\mathbf{v}$, $\hat{\mathcal{F}}_D(\mathbf{v}) = \Updownarrow(\mathcal{F}_D(\mathbf{v}))$.*

What can we say about the properties of $\hat{\mathcal{F}}$, other than *Collective Completeness*? The next proposition gives us some other properties of $\hat{\mathcal{F}}$, provided that $\mathcal{F}$ satisfies them.

Proposition 5. *Let $\mathcal{F}$ be an aggregation method. For each of the following postulates, if $\mathcal{F}$ satisfies that postulate then so does $\hat{\mathcal{F}}$: Anonymity, Unanimity, Renaming, Compatibility and Directionality.*

Proof. (Outline) The proofs for *Anonymity* and *Unanimity* are straightforward. *Renaming* is preserved mainly due to the fact that, for any D-interpretation v and renaming τ (to some D') we have $v^\wedge \models \varphi_s$ iff $\tau(v)^\wedge \models \varphi_{\tau(s)}$, and $v^\wedge \models \neg\varphi_s$ iff $\tau(v)^\wedge \models \neg\varphi_{\tau(s)}$. For *Compatibility* suppose $\mathcal{F}$ satisfies that postulate. Then for every $D, \mathbf{v}$, $\mathcal{F}_D(\mathbf{v})$ is compatible with every agent's interpretation v_i. Since $\downarrow\mathcal{F}_D(\mathbf{v}) \sqsubseteq \mathcal{F}_D(\mathbf{v})$ we know $\downarrow\mathcal{F}_D(\mathbf{v})$ must also be compatible with every v_i. By Lemma 1 this compatibility is then preserved at each step of the up-complete procedure for $\uparrow(\downarrow\mathcal{F}_D(\mathbf{v}))$ and so finally $\hat{\mathcal{F}}_D(\mathbf{v})$ is also compatible. Finally, *Directionality* is preserved due to that fact that if t is a statement not appearing in φ_s, then $v^\wedge \models \varphi_s$ iff $v^\wedge_- \models \varphi_s$ (and similarly for $\neg\varphi_s$), where $v^\wedge_-$ is the same as $v^\wedge$ but with any literal t or $\neg t$ removed.   □

Combined with the results of the previous section, this gives us a list of sound postulates for the DAUC versions of the interval methods.

Corollary 1. *Let $\mathcal{F}$ be an interval method. Then $\hat{\mathcal{F}}$ satisfies Collective Completeness, Anonymity, Unanimity, Renaming and Directionality.*

Of course the DAUC interval methods do not satisfy *ADF-Independence* by Theorem 2. Regarding t/f-*plurality*, we know from Propositions 2 and 5 that if Y is zero-based then $\widehat{\mathcal{F}}^Y$ satisfies *Compatibility* and hence also t/f-*plurality*. In fact it turns out that being zero-based is a *necessary* condition for $\widehat{\mathcal{F}}^Y$ to satisfy t/f-*plurality*. This follows already from the analogous result proved for the AF case in [3].

Proposition 6 ([3]). *Let* $\mathcal{F}^Y$ *be an interval method. Then* $\widehat{\mathcal{F}}^Y$ *satisfies* t/f-plurality *iff* Y *is zero-based.*

Regarding *Monotonicity*, in view of Proposition 2 one might expect that a necessary and sufficient condition for $\widehat{\mathcal{F}}^Y$ to satisfy that postulate is that Y is widening. However we have thus far been unable to prove or disprove this, and so it remains an open question for now.

6 Conclusion

We looked at the problem of defining methods for aggregation that take any profile of complete D-interpretations, over any given ADF D, and return a group D-interpretation. We showed that much of the same machinery used in the more specialised case of aggregating complete labellings of AFs can be applied to this problem. In particular we were able to define and axiomatically characterise a generalised version of the interval methods of [3], and to apply the down-admissible and up-complete procedures to transform the output of any interval method into a complete D-interpretation.

As noted in [7] for the AF case, one imaginative use for aggregation methods is as a route to define a (single-status) *semantics* for AFs. The role of an AF semantics is to prescribe, for every possible AF and for each argument a in the AF, which label represents the "common sense" label that a should be assigned in the context of that AF. One way to obtain this common sense labelling is to *aggregate* all possible rational labellings. In [7] this manoeuvre was carried out using both $\widehat{\mathcal{F}}^{\text{Scep}}$ and $\widehat{\mathcal{F}}^{\text{Cred}}$, and both were shown to correspond to some already existing semantics. Specifically, the result of aggregating all possible complete labellings[4] using $\widehat{\mathcal{F}}^{\text{Scep}}$ coincides with the *grounded labelling* [6,9], while aggregating all possible complete labellings using $\widehat{\mathcal{F}}^{\text{Cred}}$ results in the *ideal labelling* [7,10]. This latter result is interesting, since until now there has been no generalised version of ideal semantics proposed for ADFs. The above discussion suggests that we can obtain such an ADF semantics by taking the output of the result of aggregating *all* complete D-interpretations using $\widehat{\mathcal{F}}^{\text{Cred}}$. A related question is: what happens when we aggregate all complete D-interpretations using *other* members of the family of DAUC interval methods, such as $\widehat{\mathcal{F}}^{\text{SMaj}}$. Does this give rise to other meaningful ADF semantics? These questions will be left for further study.

---

[4] [7] also considered the results of aggregating other sets of labellings, such as all possible *preferred* labellings.

Another open question regards the axiomatic characterisation of the DAUC versions of the interval methods. In this paper we have managed to give a list of sound postulates for this family (Corollary 1). It remains to be proved that this list is complete. Finally, in this paper we have restricted ourselves to the problem of aggregating *complete* interpretations. It would be interesting to look at aggregation using other ADF semantics, such as those described in [4].

Acknowledgments. This work is supported by Fonds National de Recherche (DYNGBaT project). Thanks are due to Edmond Awad and Iyad Rahwan for earlier helping to develop some of the ideas for the restricted case of AFs, and to Johannes Wallner for some helpful comments.

References

1. Baroni, P., Caminada, M., Giacomin, M.: An introduction to argumentation semantics. Knowledge Engineering Review 26(4), 365–410 (2011)
2. Baroni, P., Giacomin, M.: On principle-based evaluation of extension-based argumentation semantics. Artificial Intelligence 171(10), 675–700 (2007)
3. Booth, R., Awad, E., Rahwan, I.: Interval methods for judgment aggregation in argumentation. In: Proceedings of the 14th International Conference on Principles of Knowledge Representation and Reasoning (KR 2014), pp. 594–597 (2014)
4. Brewka, G., Ellmauthaler, S., Strass, H., Wallner, J.P., Woltran, S.: Abstract dialectical frameworks revisited. In: Proceedings of the 23rd International Joint Conference on Artificial Intelligence (IJCAI 2013), pp. 803–809 (2013)
5. Brewka, G., Woltran, S.: Abstract dialectical frameworks. In: Proceedings of the 12th International Conference on Principles of Knowledge Representation and Reasoning (KR 2010), pp. 102–111 (2010)
6. Caminada, M., Gabbay, D.: A logical account of formal argumentation. Studia Logica 93(2-3), 109–145 (2009)
7. Caminada, M., Pigozzi, G.: On judgment aggregation in abstract argumentation. Autonomous Agents and Multi-Agent Systems 22(1), 64–102 (2011)
8. Denecker, M., Marek, V.W., Truszczyński, M.: Ultimate approximation and its application in nonmonotonic knowledge representation systems. Information and Computation 192(1), 84–121 (2004)
9. Dung, P.M.: On the acceptability of arguments and its fundamental role in nonmonotonic reasoning, logic programming and n-person games. Artificial Intelligence 77(2), 321–357 (1995)
10. Dung, P.M., Mancarella, P., Toni, F.: Computing ideal sceptical argumentation. Artificial Intelligence 171(10), 642–674 (2007)
11. Grossi, D., Pigozzi, G.: Judgment Aggregation: A Primer. Morgan and Claypool (2014)
12. List, C., Puppe, C.: Judgment aggregation: A survey. In: Handbook of Rational and Social Choice. Oxford University Press (2009)
13. Strass, H.: Approximating operators and semantics for abstract dialectical frameworks. Artificial Intelligence 205, 39–70 (2013)
14. Young, S.C., Taylor, A.D., Zwicker, W.S.: Counting quota systems: A combinatorial question from social choice theory. Mathematics Magazine, 331–342 (1995)

What Is a Reasonable Argumentation Semantics?

Sarah Alice Gaggl, Sebastian Rudolph, and Michaël Thomazo*

Technische Universität Dresden, Computational Logic Group, Germany

Abstract. In view of the plethora of different argumentation semantics, we consider the question what the essential properties of a "reasonable" semantics are. We discuss three attempts of such a characterization, based on computational complexity, logical expressivity and invariance under partial duplication, which are satisfied by most, if not all, known semantics. We then challenge each of these proposals by exhibiting plausible semantics which still not satisfy our criteria, demonstrating the difficulty of our endeavor.

Keywords: abstract argumentation, complexity, expressiveness, invariance under modifications.

1 Introduction

Since initiated by Dung's seminal paper [12], the field of abstract argumentation has attracted a lot of interest from researchers all over the world. One striking phenomenon in the community that sets it apart from other fields related to logic and knowledge representation is the past and ongoing proliferation of the proposed different semantics [3,15].

Typically, new argumentation semantics are motivated by providing scenarios where existing semantics do not exhibit the wanted behavior. This phenomenological and case-based approach is certainly worthwhile in a "pioneering phase", where the space of possibilities needs to be explored. However, with the field advancing and becoming more mature, it becomes more and more important to categorize and compare the different proposals for argumentation semantics as well as to identify common principles.

There is a lot of ongoing work on this along different lines. Most notably, argumentation semantics can be distinguished and classified according to the computational complexities of the associated reasoning tasks [14]. Note that evaluation criteria and rationality postulates have been discussed for abstract argumentation and its many variations and extensions [4,9].

With the wide range of existing argumentation semantics and many criteria around that help distinguishing them, it seems interesting to ask for commonalities shared by all semantics that are considered "reasonable". Is it possible to

---

* The third author is supported by the Alexander von Humboldt Foundation.

T. Eiter et al. (Eds.): Brewka Festschrift, LNAI 9060, pp. 309–324, 2015.

identify a "common core" of criteria that would characterize minimal requirements to an argumentation semantics? This paper discusses three properties shared by most, if not all, current semantics:

- Computational complexity. Reasoning tasks associated with argumentation semantics seem to be situated at a rather low (mostly the first, not more than the second) level of the polynomial hierarchy.
- Expressibility in monadic second-order logic (MSO). This logic has been propagated as an appropriate language for defining argumentation semantics [17]. This proposal insinuates that any "reasonable" semantics should be MSO-expressible.
- Invariance under duplication of parts of the framework. To the best of our knowledge, this criterion has not been proposed in the literature, but we found it intuitive and indeed, widely applicable.

For each of the three criteria, we show that they are satisfied by a majority of argumentation semantics. On the other hand, we critically scrutinize their universal validity and succeed in coming up with semantics which violate them while still being intuitively reasonable.

The paper is organized as follows. In Section 2 we recall the background on abstract argumentation frameworks and computational complexity. In Section 3 we introduce a semantics based on a game-theoretic approach and show that its computational complexity is higher than for the standard semantics. Then, in Section 4 we consider MSO-expressibility and exhibit a seemingly natural semantics which is not expressible in MSO logic. Section 5 is dedicated to the study of the behavior of semantics when an AF contains "structural duplicates". Finally, in Section 6 we conclude the article and point out possible future directions.

2   Preliminaries

In this section we introduce the basics of abstract argumentation, the semantics we need for further investigations and recall necessary notions from complexity theory.

Abstract Argumentation. We start with a definition of abstract argumentation frameworks following [12].

Definition 1. *An* argumentation framework *(AF) is a pair* $F = (A, R)$, *where* A *is a finite set of arguments and* $R \subseteq A \times A$. *The pair* $(a, b) \in R$ *means that* a attacks b. *A set* $S \subseteq A$ defeats b *(in* F*) in symbols* $S \rightarrowtail b$, *if* $\exists a \in S$, *s.t.* $(a, b) \in R$. *An* $a \in A$ *is* defended *by* $S \subseteq A$ *(in* F*) iff,* $\forall b \in A$, *it holds that, if* $(b, a) \in R$, *then* S *defeats* b *(in* F*). An* $a \in A$ *is in* conflict *with* $b \in A$, *if either* $(a, b) \in R$ *or* $(b, a) \in R$.

The inherent conflicts between the arguments are solved by selecting subsets of arguments, where a semantics σ assigns a collection of sets of arguments to an AF F. The basic requirement for all semantics is that the sets are conflict-free.

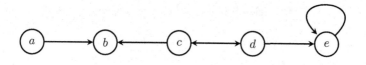

Fig. 1. AF F from Example 1

Definition 2. *Let $F = (A, R)$ be an AF. A set $S \subseteq A$ is said to be* conflict-free *(in F), if there are no $a, b \in S$, such that $(a, b) \in R$. We denote the collection of sets which are conflict-free (in F) by $cf(F)$. A set $S \subseteq A$ is maximal conflict-free or* naive, *if $S \in cf(F)$ and for each $T \in cf(F)$, $S \not\subset T$. We denote the collection of all naive sets of F by $naive(F)$. For the empty AF $F_0 = (\emptyset, \emptyset)$, we set $naive(F_0) = \{\emptyset\}$.*

Towards definitions of the semantics we introduce the following formal concepts [12].

Definition 3. *Given an AF $F = (A, R)$ and some $S \subseteq A$, the* characteristic function *$\mathcal{F}_F : 2^A \to 2^A$ of F is defined as $\mathcal{F}_F(S) = \{x \in A \mid x \text{ is defended by } S\}$.*

We consider the following semantics.

Definition 4. *Let $F = (A, R)$ be an AF. A set $S \in cf(F)$ is said to be*

- *a* stable *extension (of F), i.e. $S \in stable(F)$, if $S_R^+ = A$ where $S_R^+ = S \cup \{a \mid \exists b \in S : (b, a) \in R\}$ is the* range *of S;*
- *an* admissible *extension, i.e. $S \in adm(F)$ if each $a \in S$ is defended by S;*
- *a* complete *extension (of F), i.e. $S \in comp(F)$, if each $S \in adm$ and for each $a \in A$ defended by S (in F), $a \in S$ holds;*
- *a* preferred *extension, i.e. $S \in prf(F)$ if $S \in adm(F)$ and for each $T \in adm(F)$, $S \not\subset T$;*
- *the* grounded *extension (of F), i.e. the unique set $S \in grd(F)$, is the least fixed point of the characteristic function $\mathcal{F}_F$.*

AFs are typically represented as directed graphs where the nodes correspond to the arguments and the edges to the attacks.

Example 1. Let $F = (A, R)$ be an AF with arguments $A = \{a, b, c, d, e\}$ and attacks $R = \{(a, b), (c, b), (c, d), (d, c), (d, e), (e, e)\}$. The corresponding graph is depicted in Figure 1. F has the following sets of extensions for the introduced semantics, $stable(F) = \{\{a, d\}\}$, $prf(F) = \{\{a, c\}, \{a, d\}\}$, $comp(F) = \{\{a\}, \{a, c\}, \{a, d\}\}$, $grd(F) = \{\{a\}\}$ and $adm(F) = \{\{\}, \{a\}, \{c\}, \{d\}, \{a, c\}, \{a, d\}\}$.

Computational Complexity. We assume the reader to be familiar with standard complexity classes, i.e. P, NP, coNP and PSPACE (polynomial space). Nevertheless, we briefly recapitulate the concept of oracle machines and some related

Table 1. Complexity of decision problems ($\mathcal{C}$-c denotes completeness for class $\mathcal{C}$)

	Ver_σ	$Cred_\sigma$	$Skept_\sigma$	$Exists_\sigma^{\neg\emptyset}$
naive	in P	in P	in P	in P
stable	in P	NP-c	coNP-c	NP-c
adm	in P	NP-c	trivial	NP-c
comp	in P	NP-c	P-c	NP-c
prf	coNP-c	NP-c	Π_2^P-c	NP-c

complexity classes. Let $\mathcal{C}$ notate some complexity class. By a $\mathcal{C}$-oracle machine we mean a (polynomial time) Turing machine which can access an oracle that decides a given (sub)-problem in $\mathcal{C}$ within one step. We denote the class of decision problems, that can be solved by such machines, as $P^\mathcal{C}$ if the underlying Turing machine is deterministic and $NP^\mathcal{C}$ if the underlying Turing machine is non-deterministic. The class $\Sigma_2^P = NP^{NP}$, denotes the problems which can be decided by a non-deterministic polynomial time algorithm that has access to an NP-oracle. The class $\Pi_2^P = coNP^{NP}$ is defined as the complementary class of Σ_2^P, i.e. $\Pi_2^P = co\Sigma_2^P$. The relations between the complexity classes used in this work are $P \subseteq NP\ (coNP) \subseteq \Sigma_2^P\ (\Pi_2^P) \subseteq PSPACE$.

We are interested in the following decision problems (for a semantics σ).

- $Cred_\sigma$: Given AF $F = (A, R)$ and $a \in A$. Is a contained in *some* $S \in \sigma(F)$?
- $Skept_\sigma$: Given AF $F = (A, R)$ and $a \in A$. Is a contained in *each* $S \in \sigma(F)$?
- Ver_σ: Given AF $F = (A, R)$ and $S \subseteq A$. Is $S \in \sigma(F)$?
- $Exists_\sigma^{\neg\emptyset}$: Given AF $F = (A, R)$. Does there exist a set $S \subseteq A, S \neq \emptyset$ such that $S \in \sigma(F)$?

The complexity landscape for the semantics considered in this article is given in Table 1 (see [10,11,13]).

3   About Computational Requirements

The decision problems associated with most of the classical Dung semantics have relatively low computational complexity. Indeed, most of the problems belong to the first level of the polynomial hierarchy, with the exception of the skeptical acceptance for preferred semantics, which is complete for the second level of the polynomial hierarchy (see Table 1). This is an appreciable feature, since it allows one to use efficient solvers developed in other communities, such as satisfiability solvers or answer-set programming solvers, either directly or used as oracles in a more complex algorithm [18,16].

In our task of compiling a set of properties that reasonable semantics should fulfill, should we include an upper-bound on the complexity of classical reasoning problems? To tackle this question, we adopt a game-oriented approach, as in [19].

As already argued in the literature, games are a natural approach to argumentation, since they fit with the intuition of an iterative process. Their main use with respect to abstract argumentation frameworks has been to provide alternative characterizations of credulously and skeptically accepted arguments according to a variety of known semantics. We adopt a dual approach here, using games to define novel semantics. We then explore the complexity of reasoning under such semantics.

This section is organized as follows:

- first, we argue that shifting the focus from the extension to the way it has been built may allow to distinguish between extensions that would otherwise be similar; in particular, we present a way to structurally (and partially) rank preferred extensions;
- second, we explore semantics that can be expressed thanks to games. In particular, we introduce a semantics whose credulous acceptance problem is PSPACE-complete. While this semantics is maybe not immediate, we believe that it demonstrates a still unexplored space of game-based semantics of high complexity.

Dynamics of Preferred Extensions. In the argumentation semantics that we have presented so far, all arguments are chosen simultaneously. That is, an acceptance condition is checked on a potential extension, but the way this extension has been created is ignored. In [19], this is indicated as not fully intuitive, as argumentation often refers to an iterative process, where arguments are given one at a time. We provide another reason to pay attention to the generation process and not only to its result: it provides further structural insights on how to distinguish extensions.

To illustrate our point, let us consider the argumentation framework F_d drawn in Figure 2. This framework has two preferred extensions, which are $\{1, 2\}$ and $\{3, 4\}$. By looking only at these two sets, there is no reason to distinguish one from the other: both are preferred, both are of the same size, and we assume not to have any preference information on the arguments. However, let us assume that arguments are added one at a time. There are two ways to generate the first extension: either choose 1 then 2, or choose 2 and then 1. Similarly, there are two ways to generate the second extension. By looking at these sequences, the two extensions can then be distinguished: at any step, the set built towards the second extension is admissible. Indeed, $\{3\}$ is admissible, as well as $\{3, 4\}$. This is the case neither for $\{1\}$ nor for $\{2\}$. This means that the extension $\{3, 4\}$ can be generated by constructing only admissible sets, whereas $\{1, 2\}$ cannot. Let us define formally a malus function on preferred extensions.

Definition 5 (Malus of a preferred extension). *Let F be an argumentation framework, and let S be a preferred extension of F. Let $(s_1, \ldots, s_n)$ be a sequence of elements of S where each element of S appears exactly once. The malus of $(s_1, \ldots, s_n)$ is the number of indices i such that $1 \leq i \leq n$ and $\{s_1, \ldots, s_i\}$ is not an admissible set. The malus of S is the minimal malus of any such a sequence $(s_1, \ldots, s_n)$.*

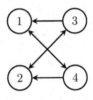

Fig. 2. The argumentation framework F_d

Equipped with this notion of malus, we can now define a notion of preference on preferred extensions.

Definition 6. *Let F be an argumentation framework, S_1 and S_2 be two preferred extensions of F. S_1 is preferred to S_2 if the malus of S_1 is smaller than the malus of S_2.*

The intuition behind this notion of preference is that a (linear) argumentation, where at each step the obtained set of arguments is admissible, is more solid than one for which this is not the case.

From Semantics to Games and Back. A natural way to use information on how an extension has been generated is to look at it as the result of a game. We already mentioned that games have been used to characterize credulous and skeptical acceptance for a variety of semantics. Let us give some more details about this approach, as presented in [19]. Two player games are used, where both players, "PRO" and "CON", play alternately. PRO aims at proving credulous acceptance of an argument, while CON tries to disprove this. The set of moves allowed is defined in order to capture a given semantics. Credulous acceptance is then defined with respect to *winning strategies* of PRO. Hence, games have been used to shed a new light on already existing semantics. We adopt here a dual approach, where we start from a family of games, and explore which semantics may be defined in this way.

In the literature, an extension is defined from the arguments that PRO uses. We adopt a slightly different approach: both players "collaborate" to create an extension, but their contributions are chosen with the goal to maximize their own satisfaction. By collaborating, we mean that both players are adding arguments to what will become an extension. At each step, the arguments they can add depends on the structure of the graph and on the already played arguments. This is specified thanks to the definition of *legal sequences*. However, both players may have different objectives: this is represented by a payoff function, that associates each outcome of the game with a payoff for each player. An extension is then the set of arguments that have been played during an *optimal* play of both players.

Let us now formally define the three ingredients of an *argumentation game* $\mathcal{G}$ which we introduced informally above: legal sequences, payoff function and optimal play.

Definition 7 (Legal sequences). *A set of* legal sequences $\mathcal{S}$ *on an argumentation framework F is a finite set of tuples of arguments of F that is prefix-closed, that is, if $(a_1, \ldots, a_n) \in \mathcal{S}$, then $(a_1, \ldots, a_{n-1})$ also belongs to $\mathcal{S}$. The outcomes $\mathcal{O}$ of the game are sequences that are not a strict prefix of any other sequence in $\mathcal{S}$.*

A move of the game is the transition from a legal sequence to another legal sequence by adding an argument at the end. Moves resulting in a sequence of odd size are played by Player 1, while other moves are played by player 2.

Note that we could also define infinite games, but we stick to the finite case for simplicity. We now introduce payoff functions, that describe the "satisfaction" of each player after playing a given sequence.

Definition 8 (Payoff function). *Let $\mathcal{S}$ be a set of sequences, $\mathcal{O}$ be the set of outcomes. A payoff function is a function from O to $\mathbb{N} \times \mathbb{N}$. The first component is the payoff for Player 1, while the second is for Player 2.*

Players aim at maximizing their payoff, and use *strategies* in order to do so. Strategies define what to play in each given situation.

Definition 9 (Strategy). *A strategy for Player 1 (resp. Player 2) is a function that associates to each legal sequence of even length (resp. odd length) another legal sequence that can be reached by a move of Player 1 (resp. Player 2).*

Strategies of particular interest are the so-called optimal strategies.

Definition 10 (Optimal strategy). *A strategy is optimal if it maximizes the minimal payoff a player may get by playing it, whatever the opponent's strategy is.*

We now have all the tool to define the semantics associated with a game.

Definition 11 (Game semantics). *Let $\mathcal{G}$ be an argumentation game. Let $F = (A, R)$ be an argumentation framework. The extensions of F according to $\mathcal{G}$ are the set of arguments E that can be played when both players are following an optimal strategy.*

Thus, the choices of a set of legal sequences and a payoff function define a semantics for argumentation frameworks. Let us notice that some choices may violate even the most widely accepted properties of a semantic, such as language independence [4]. It is however possible to regain such a property by adequately restricting the set of legal sequences and the set of payoff functions one may use.

We now instantiate the previous definitions to define the *last-word game* and its associated semantics. The aim of each player is the following: either he/she wants to ensure that he/she will choose the last argument, or, if that cannot be ensured, he/she wants the extension to be as large as possible. At each time, they can choose any argument that maintain conflict-freeness, and that is attacked by at least one argument that was attacked by the previously chosen argument.

Definition 12 (Legal sequence for the last-word game). *Let* $F = (A, R)$ *be an argumentation framework. A legal sequence for the last word game is defined inductively as follows:*

- *the empty sequence is a legal sequence;*
- (a_1) *is a legal sequence for any* $a_1 \in A$ *such that* $(a_1, a_1) \notin R$;
- *if* $(a_1, \ldots, a_n)$ *is a legal sequence, and there exists* $b, a_{n+1} \in A$ *such that* $(a_n, b) \in R$ *and* $(b, a_{n+1}) \in R$, *and* $(a_i, a_{n+1}) \notin R$ *for any* i *with* $1 \leq i \leq n + 1$, *then* $(a_1, \ldots, a_n, a_{n+1})$ *is a legal sequence.*

Definition 13 (Payoff for the last-word game). *Let* $(a_1, \ldots, a_n)$ *be an outcome for the last word game. The last-word payoff* f_{lw} *is defined as follows:*

- *if* n *is odd, then* $f_{lw} = (|A| + n, n)$;
- *if* n *is even,* $f_{lw} = (n, |A| + n)$.

Theorem 1. *Credulous acceptance for the last-word semantics is* PSPACE-*complete.*

Proof. (Sketch) Membership is direct. For hardness, we reduce the problem of the existence of a winning strategy for the first player in GENERALIZEDGEOGRAPHY to credulous acceptance under the last-word semantics. Let us first recall that GENERALIZEDGEOGRAPHY is a two player game played on a directed graph. At each step, a player chooses a non-visited vertex that is a successor of the last played vertex. The last player who can play wins. An example of instance is given in Example 2. We first create an instance G^* of GENERALIZEDGEOGRAPHY such that the first player has a winning strategy starting from one of two special moves depending on the existence of a winning strategy in the original instance G. We thus create an argumentation framework by replacing each edge in G^* by two attacks. □

Example 2. Figure 3 presents an example of instance for GENERALIZEDGEOGRAPHY. Player 1 could play 1. Player 2 has two choices: either 2 or 3. If Player 2 plays 2, Player 1 plays 3 and wins. If Player 2 plays 3, Player 2 wins. A winning strategy for Player 1 is to play 3 from the beginning.

Figure 4 is the argumentation framework obtained from the instance of Figure 3 by the reduction used in the proof of Theorem 1. a_1, a_2 and a_3 correspond to vertices of the original instance. a_{v_1} and a_{v_2} correspond to vertices added to ensure that Player 1 has a winning strategy, starting either with a_{v_1} or a_{v_2}. Other vertices corresponds to edges in the original instance.

While possibly not overly intuitive, we believe that this semantics helps making a case for interesting semantics that incorporate information on how an extension may have been created, and such semantics are likely to have a higher computational complexity than the classical ones.

Fig. 3. An instance of GENERALIZEDGEOGRAPHY

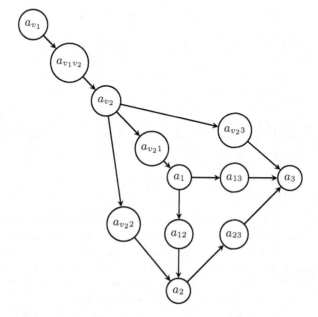

Fig. 4. The argumentation framework obtained from the instance of Example 2

4 Expressiveness of Argumentation Semantics

Another angle from which one can investigate argumentation semantics is the logical expressivity needed to define them. Note that each argumentation framework $F = (A, R)$ can be seen as a relational structure with one binary relation and therefore as a logical interpretation for a signature containing one binary predicate symbol. This perspective allows for characterizing argumentation semantics in terms of the logical expressiveness needed for defining them.

It has been argued before [17] that a significant number of semantics can be expressed by monadic second-order (MSO) logic formulae. MSO logic is an extension of first-order predicate logic by *set variables* (usually denoted by upper case letters like X) which are used to represent sets of domain elements. They can be quantified over and used in *membership atoms* of the form $x \in X$ which are interpreted in the intuitive way.

Now, an MSO formulae $\varphi[X]$ with one free set variable X can be seen as a formal definition of some semantics σ as follows: for any AF $F = (A, R)$ and $S \subseteq A$ the following holds: $S \in \sigma(F)$ iff F satisfies $\varphi[X]$ under the variable assignment $X \mapsto S$. Finally, a semantics σ is called MSO-expressible if such a defining MSO formula exists for it.

As stated above, virtually all mainstream argumentation semantics are MSO-expressible. As an example, the admissible semantics can be expressed by the following formula:

$$\forall x, y \, \big(R(x,y) \wedge (y \in X) \; \rightarrow \; \neg (x \in X) \wedge \exists z. (R(z,x) \wedge z \in X) \big)$$

Note that MSO-expressibility guarantees certain properties: the computational complexity of all the reasoning tasks described in Section 2 will be on some fixed level of the polynomial hierarchy. By contraposition, we can infer that any semantics with a complexity of PSPACE or above cannot be expressed in MSO logic. While we saw an example of this in Section 3, we focus here on the question if there is a reasonable semantics with comparably low reasoning complexity which is nevertheless not MSO-expressible. Indeed, the following semantics satisfies these properties.

Definition 14. A set $S \in cf(F)$ is said to be a multi-admissible extension if $|\{b \in S \mid (a,b) \in R\}| \leq |\{c \in S \mid (c,a) \in R\}|$ holds for every $a \in A \setminus S$.

In words, a multi-admissible extension S must attack each argument a outside S at least as often as a attacks S. We deem this a rather reasonable semantics, as it is very close to the admissible semantics (in fact, every multi-admissible extension is also admissible), but additionally takes the multiplicity of the attacks carried out by an external argument into account by requiring them to be compensated by an according number of counter-attacks.

It is straightforward to check that verifying if some set S is a multi-admissible extension can be done in polynomial time, which immediately ensures that the complexity of all other reasoning tasks is not worse than on the first level of the polynomial hierarchy.

We will next show that despite this comparably low complexities, this semantics cannot be expressed in MSO logic.

Theorem 2. There is no MSO formula that expresses the multi-admissible semantics.

For the proof of this theorem, we use a well known result of Büchi linking regular word languages and MSO logic.

Definition 15. Let Σ be a finite alphabet. The word interpretation $\mathcal{I}_w$ of some word $w = \alpha_1 \ldots \alpha_n \in \Sigma^*$ is the relational structure with base set $\{1, \ldots, n\}$ the binary relation $<$ defined in the usual way, and unary relations P_α for all $\alpha \in \Sigma$ with $i \in P_\alpha^{\mathcal{I}_w}$ iff $\alpha = \alpha_i$ for every $i \in \{1, \ldots, n\}$.

Theorem 3 (Büchi [8]). A word language $L \subseteq \Sigma^*$ is regular if and only if there exists an MSO sentence φ satisfying $L = \{w \mid \mathcal{I}_w \models \varphi\}$.

This result is now leveraged for an indirect proof: we argue that a hypothetical MSO formula expressing multi-admissible semantics could be used to come up with an MSO formula characterizing a non-regular language.

Proof. (Sketch) Assume there is an MSO formula $\varphi[X]$ characterizing multi-admissible extensions. Let $\varphi'[X]$ be the MSO formula obtained from $\varphi[X]$ by replacing every atom $R(x, y)$ by the subformula $(P_b(x) \wedge P_c(y)) \vee (P_c(x) \wedge P_a(y))$. Thereby, we assume an abstract framework where every node is labeled by a, b or c; then we let each b-labeled node attack every c-labeled node and have each c-labeled node attack every a-labeled node.

Finally, for checking if the set of all nodes labeled with a or b can be an extension, let $\psi[X] = \forall x.(x \in X \leftrightarrow P_a(x) \vee P_b(x))$. By construction this is the case, if more nodes are labeled with b than with a.

Then, every word interpretation $\mathcal{I}_w$ corresponding to some word w over $\{a, b, c\}$ satisfies that it is a model of $\exists X.(\varphi'[X] \wedge \psi[X])$ if and only if w contains more bs than as. However, the language of all words with these properties is not regular as can be easily shown using the well-known pumping lemma for regular languages.   □

From a more general perspective, MSO logic is known to be incapable of comparing cardinalities of sets of unbounded size. Thus, it will be difficult to cast any semantics relying on such a comparison into MSO logic.

5   Invariant Behavior under Modification of the Framework

The evaluation of AFs is solely based on syntactic properties. For example checking whether a set of arguments is accepted under stable semantics requires that there are no two arguments in the set which attack each other and all arguments not contained in the set are attacked by the set.

Due to the non-monotonic behavior of AFs, modifications, i.e. adding or deleting arguments or attacks, may change the outcome of a semantics in a way that arguments which have been accepted before are not acceptable afterwards. In the literature, most of the work was focused on studying equivalences, where one identifies a kernel of an AF, and if two different AFs posses the same kernel they are strongly equivalent to each other [20].

In this section we study what happens to the extensions if some part of the framework is duplicated. A duplicate will be a set of arguments which has internally and externally the same relations as its original. However, there is no connection i.e. no attacks between the original and the duplicate.

Definition 16. *Let $F = (A, R)$ be an AF. A set $D \subset A$ is a duplicate in F, with its original set $\hat{D} = \{\hat{a} \in A \mid a \in D\}$ satisfying $\hat{D} \cap D = \emptyset$ and $|\hat{D}| = |D|$ if there are only the following four types of attacks between arguments $d', e' \in D$, their originals $\hat{d}, \hat{e} \in \hat{D}$ and $x, y \in A \setminus (D \cup \hat{D})$.*

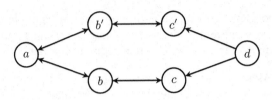

Fig. 5. AF F from Example 3

R1) $(d', e') \in R$ *iff* $(\hat{d}, \hat{e}) \in R$;
R2) $(d', x) \in R$ *iff* $(\hat{d}, x) \in R$;
R3) $(x, d') \in R$ *iff* $(x, \hat{d}) \in R$;
R4) $(x, y) \in R$.

In the following we will denote the duplicate of an argument a with a' and the original of a duplicate b with $\hat{b}$. For an AF $F = (A, R)$ and a set $D \subseteq A$ we can add a set of duplicate A' such that $A' = \{a' \mid a \in D\}$, then the obtained AF with duplicates will be denoted by $F' = (A \cup A', R \cup R')$, where R' is as in $R1 - R3$ in Definition 16.

Example 3. Consider AF from Figure 5. There, the set $A' = \{b', c'\}$ is a duplicate in F with its original set $\hat{A} = \{b, c\}$.

We say a semantics σ is *weakly duplicate invariant* if for any AF F and its related AF F' with duplicates, each σ-extension S of F is related to a σ-extension S' of F' in such a way that all arguments from S are accepted as well as those duplicates from A' if their original argument was contained in S.

Definition 17. *A semantics σ is* weakly duplicate invariant *if for any AF $F = (A, R)$ and $F' = (A \cup A', R \cup R')$ such that the set A' is a duplicate in F', R' are the attacks related to duplicates and for any $S \subseteq A$ the following holds*

$$S \in \sigma(F) \Rightarrow S' \in \sigma(F'),$$

where $S' = S \cup \{a' \in A' \mid a \in S\}$.

Lemma 1. *Conflict-free sets are weakly duplicate invariant.*

Proof. Let $F = (A, R)$ and $F' = (A \cup A', R \cup R')$ be AFs such that the set A' is a duplicate in F', R' are the attacks related to duplicates in F'. Towards a contradiction assume there is a set $S \in cf(F)$ but $S' \notin cf(F')$, where $S' = S \cup \{a' \in A' \mid a \in S\}$, thus $S \subseteq S'$ and we can have the four following cases.

R1: $a, b \in A'$ then it follows that $(\hat{a}, \hat{b}) \in R$ with $\hat{a}, \hat{b} \in S$, a contradiction;
R2: $a \in A'$, it follows that $(\hat{a}, b) \in R$ with $\hat{a} \in S$, a contradiction;
R3: $b \in A'$, it follows that $(a, \hat{b}) \in R$ with $\hat{b} \in S$, a contradiction;
R4: (a, b) is an ordinary attack, thus $a, b \in S$, a contradiction.

$\square$

Theorem 4. *Stable, admissible, preferred, complete and naive semantics are weakly duplicate invariant.*

Proof. Let $F = (A, R)$ and $F' = (A \cup A', R \cup R')$ be AFs such that the set A' is a duplicate in F', R' are the attacks related to duplicates in F'.

For stable semantics: Towards a contradiction assume there is a set $S \in stable(F)$ but $S' \notin stable(F')$, where $S' = S \cup \{a' \in A' \mid a \in S\}$. As $S \in stable(F)$ clearly $S \in cf(F)$, and from Lemma 1 we thus know that $S' \in cf(F')$. Hence, there is an argument $a \notin S'^+_R$ and due to the definition of the range, $a \notin S'$ and clearly $a \notin S$. Hence, for each $b \in S'$ we have $(b, a) \notin R \cup R'$. We need to consider the following four cases.

R1: $a, b \in A'$ then it follows that $(\hat{b}, \hat{a}) \notin R$, thus $\hat{a} \notin S^+_R$, a contradiction;
R2: $b \in A'$, it follows that $(\hat{b}, a) \notin R$ and $a \notin S^+_R$, a contradiction;
R3: $a \in A'$, it follows that $(b, \hat{a}) \notin R$ and $\hat{a} \notin S^+_R$, a contradiction;
R4: $a, b \in A \setminus A' \cup \hat{A}$ thus $a \notin S^+_R$, a contradiction.

For admissible semantics: Towards a contradiction assume there is a set $S \in adm(F)$ but $S' \notin adm(F')$, where $S' = S \cup \{a' \in A' \mid a \in S\}$. As $S \in adm(F)$ clearly $S \in cf(F)$, and from Lemma 1 we thus know that $S' \in cf(F')$. Hence, there is an argument $a \in S'$ which is not defended by S'. This means, there is an argument $b \in A \cup A'$ s.t. $(b, a) \in R \cup R'$ but for each $c \in S'$ we have $(c, b) \notin R \cup R'$. We can have the following eight cases.

C1: $(c', b') \notin R'$ and $(b', a') \in R'$, then $(\hat{c}, \hat{b}) \notin R$ and $(\hat{b}, \hat{a}) \in R$, thus $\hat{a} \in S$ is not defended by S, a contradiction;
C2: $(c', b') \notin R'$ and $(b', a) \in R'$, then $(\hat{c}, \hat{b}) \notin R$ and $(\hat{b}, a) \in R$, with $a \in A \setminus (A' \cup \hat{A})$, thus, $a \in S$ is not defended by S, a contradiction;
C3: $(c', b) \notin R'$ and $(b, a') \in R'$, then $(\hat{c}, b) \notin R$ and $(b, \hat{a}) \in R$, with $b \in A \setminus (A' \cup \hat{A})$, thus, $\hat{a} \in S$ is not defended by S, a contradiction;
C4: $(c', b) \notin R'$ and $(b, a) \in R$, then $(\hat{c}, b) \notin R$, with $a, b \in A \setminus (A' \cup \hat{A})$, thus, $a \in S$ is not defended by S, a contradiction;
C5: $(c, b') \notin R'$ and $(b', a') \in R'$, then $(c, \hat{b}) \notin R$ and $(\hat{b}, \hat{a}) \in R$, with $c \in A \setminus (A' \cup \hat{A})$, thus, $\hat{a} \in S$ is not defended by S, a contradiction;
C6: $(c, b') \notin R'$ and $(b', a) \in R'$, then $(c, \hat{b}) \notin R$ and $(\hat{b}, a) \in R$, with $a, c \in A \setminus (A' \cup \hat{A})$, thus, $a \in S$ is not defended by S, a contradiction;
C7: $(c, b) \notin R$ and $(b, a') \in R'$, then $(\hat{b}, a) \in R$, with $b, c \in A \setminus A' \cup \hat{A}$, thus, $a \in S$ is not defended by S, a contradiction;
C8: $(c, b) \notin R$ and $(b, a) \in R$, with $a, b, c \in A \setminus A' \cup \hat{A}$, thus, $a \in S$ is not defended by S, a contradiction;

For preferred semantics: We show that for each $S \in prf(F)$ it holds that $S' \in prf(F')$ for $S' = S \cup \{a' \in A' \mid a \in S\}$. We know that $S \in adm(F)$ and from above that also $S' \in adm(F')$. Moreover, for each $T \in adm(F)$ we have $T \subseteq S$. As in the primed version of the extension we only add arguments if their originals are contained in the non-primed version, one can easily see that for each $T' \in adm(F)$, $T' \subseteq S$ as well, where $T' = T \cup \{a' \in A' \mid a \in T\}$. It follows that $S \in prf(F')$.

The proofs of other semantics rely on similar arguments. $\square$

We find that all standard semantics are weakly duplicate invariant. So one can see this as a preference on argumentation semantics. Interestingly, this means that all these semantics have a monotonic behavior when duplicates are added to the framework.

Still, weak duplicate invariance is not a criterion to be taken for granted for all reasonable argumentation semantics: indeed, it is not too hard to see that the multi-admissible semantics introduced in the previous section violates this criterion.

Theorem 5. *The multi-admissible semantics is not weakly duplicate invariant.*

Proof. Consider the AF $F = (A, R)$ with $A = \{a, b, c\}$ and $R = \{(c, a), (b, c)\}$. Obviously $S = \{a, b\}$ is a multi-admissible extension of (A, R). Now consider the AF $F' = (\{a, a', b, c\}, \{(c, a), (c, a'), (b, c)\})$. Clearly, $S' = \{a, a', b\}$ is not a multi-admissible extension of F', thus we have shown our claim.   □

What happens if one considers the other direction of duplicate invariance? In the following we define that a semantics σ is *strongly duplicate invariant* if for each σ-extension S' of the AF F' with the duplicate A', the extension S obtained by deleting the duplicate arguments from S' is a σ-extension of the respective AF F without duplicates.

Definition 18. *A weakly duplicate invariant semantics σ is* strongly duplicate invariant *if for any AFs $F = (A, R)$ and $F' = (A \cup A', R \cup R')$ such that the set A' is a duplicate in F', R' are the attacks related to duplicates and $S' \subseteq A \cup A'$, the following holds*

$$S' \in \sigma(F') \Rightarrow S \in \sigma(F)$$

where $S = S' \cap A$.

Theorem 6. *Stable, preferred, complete, admissible and naive semantics are not strongly duplicate invariant.*

Proof. Consider the AF $F' = (A \cup A', R \cup R')$ with arguments $A = \{a, b, c, d\}$ and $A' = \{b', c'\}$, and attacks $R = \{(a, b), (b, a), (b, c), (c, b), (c, d)\}$ and $R' = \{(a, b'), (b', a), (b', c'), (c', b'), (c', d)\}$ as depicted in Figure 6. Let $F = (A, R)$ be an AF obtained from F' without the duplicate A'. Consider the set $S' = \{b, c'\}$ which is a stable (resp. preferred, complete, admissible, naive) extension of F' but the set $S = \{b\}$ obtained from S' by deleting the duplicate argument c' is not a stable (resp. preferred, complete, admissible, naive) extension of F.   □

Theorem 7. *The grounded semantics is strongly duplicate invariant.*

Proof. (Sketch) Let F be an argumentation framework, and let F' be obtained by F by duplicating some of its arguments. Let us denote $E_0 = E'_0 = \emptyset$. Let us also define $E_{i+1} = \mathcal{F}_F(E_i)$ as well as $E'_{i+1} = \mathcal{F}_{F'}(E'_i)$, where we recall that $\mathcal{F}_F$ denotes the characteristic function. We prove by induction on i that $E'_i = E_i \cup \{y' \mid \exists y \in E_i : y'$ is a duplicate of $y\}$. This proves in particular the result for the grounded extensions of F and F'. Weak and strong duplicate invariance are clear from this equality.   □

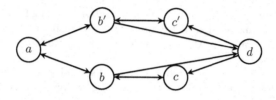

Fig. 6. AF F'

6 Conclusion

On our quest for a better understanding of the gist of argumentation semantics, we have been investigating three characteristics we found to be shared by
the mainstream argumentation semantics. These characteristics were based on
three general classification schemes typically encountered in theoretical computer science: computational complexity, expressibility in some logical language
and invariance under certain transformations.

While this endeavor certainly enhanced our understanding of the matter, we
found that for each of the criteria, counterexamples can be constructed which,
arguably, still have the "look and feel" of a typical argumentation semantics. In
our view, this demonstrates the nontrivial philosophical dimension of an area
that tries to capture the essence of "argumentation" on an abstract and formal
level.

While our studies focused on the traditional Dung-style setting, a plethora of
generalizations and extensions have been proposed, such as abstract dialectical
frameworks [7,6], bipolar AFs [1], preference-based AFs [2], and value-based AFs
[5]. All of these new approaches would certainly benefit from a thorough study
of commonalities and differences in terms of general formal properties of the
diverse semantics.

Acknowledgements. As this Festschrift is dedicated to Gerd Brewka's 60 th
birthday, we want to congratulate him as well as thank him for his inspiring
work and the fruitful and enjoyable discussions.

References

1. Amgoud, L., Cayrol, C., Lagasquie, M.-C., Livet, P.: On bipolarity in argumentation frameworks. Int. Journal of Intelligent Systems 23, 1–32 (2008)
2. Amgoud, L., Vesic, S.: Repairing preference-based argumentation frameworks. In:
Proc. IJCAI 2009, pp. 665–670 (2009)
3. Baroni, P., Caminada, M., Giacomin, M.: An introduction to argumentation semantics. Knowledge Eng. Review 26(4), 365–410 (2011)
4. Baroni, P., Giacomin, M.: On principle-based evaluation of extension-based argumentation semantics. Artif. Intell. 171(10-15), 675–700 (2007)
5. Bench-Capon, T.J.M.: Persuasion in practical argument using value-based argumentation frameworks. J. Log. Comput. 13(3), 429–448 (2003)

6. Brewka, G., Polberg, S., Woltran, S.: Generalizations of dung frameworks and their role in formal argumentation. IEEE Intel. Sys. 29(1), 30–38 (2014)
7. Brewka, G., Woltran, S.: Abstract Dialectical Frameworks. In: Proc. KR 2010, pp. 102–111 (2010)
8. Büchi, R.J.: On a decision method in restricted second order arithmetic. In: Proc. Logic, Methodology and Philosophy of Science 1960, pp. 1–11 (1962)
9. Caminada, M., Amgoud, L.: On the evaluation of argumentation formalisms. Artif. Intell. 171(5-6), 286–310 (2007)
10. Coste-Marquis, S., Devred, C., Marquis, P.: Symmetric argumentation frameworks. In: Godo, L. (ed.) ECSQARU 2005. LNCS (LNAI), vol. 3571, pp. 317–328. Springer, Heidelberg (2005)
11. Dimopoulos, Y., Torres, A.: Graph theoretical structures in logic programs and default theories. Theor. Comput. Sci. 170(1-2), 209–244 (1996)
12. Dung, P.M.: On the acceptability of arguments and its fundamental role in non-monotonic reasoning, logic programming and n-person games. Artif. Intell. 77(2), 321–358 (1995)
13. Dunne, P.E., Bench-Capon, T.J.M.: Coherence in finite argument systems. Artif. Intell. 141(1/2), 187–203 (2002)
14. Dunne, P.E., Wooldridge, M.: Complexity of abstract argumentation. In: Simari, G., Rahwan, I. (eds.) Argumentation in Artificial Intelligence, pp. 85–104. Springer, US (2009)
15. Dvořák, W., Gaggl, S.A.: Stage semantics and the scc-recursive schema for argumentation semantics. J. Log. Comput. 2014 (2014)
16. Dvořák, W., Järvisalo, M., Wallner, J.P., Woltran, S.: Complexity-sensitive decision procedures for abstract argumentation. Artif. Intell. 206, 53–78 (2014)
17. Dvořák, W., Szeider, S., Woltran, S.: Abstract argumentation via monadic second order logic. In: Hüllermeier, E., Link, S., Fober, T., Seeger, B. (eds.) SUM 2012. LNCS, vol. 7520, pp. 85–98. Springer, Heidelberg (2012)
18. Egly, U., Gaggl, S., Woltran, S.: Answer-set programming encodings for argumentation frameworks. In Argument and Computation 1(2), 147–177 (2010)
19. Modgil, S., Caminada, M.: Proof theories and algorithms for abstract argumentation frameworks. In: Rahwan, I., Simari, G. (eds.) Argumentation in Artificial Intelligence, pp. 105–132. Springer (2009)
20. Oikarinen, E., Woltran, S.: Characterizing strong equivalence for argumentation frameworks. Artif. Intell. 175(14-15), 1985–2009 (2011)

Open Problems in Abstract Argumentation

Ringo Baumann and Hannes Strass

Computer Science Institute, Leipzig University, Germany

Abstract We give a list of currently unsolved problems in abstract argumentation. For each of the problems, we motivate why it is interesting and what makes it (apparently) hard to solve.

1 Introduction

Formal argumentation has established itself as an active subfield of artificial intelligence [16]. Argumentation is concerned with how conflicts between different pieces of knowledge, possibly involving preferences among them, can be resolved in a principled manner. The further subfield of *abstract argumentation* ignores the potential internal structure of arguments, and instead concentrates on the interaction between different arguments. The predominantly used approach is that by Dung [20], where argumentation scenarios are represented using *argumentation frameworks (AFs)* $F = (A, R)$ consisting of a set A of abstract arguments and a relation R of attacks between these arguments.

This seemingly lightweight formalism has led to a large amount of research around it. Gerd Brewka is among those who had a lasting impact on the field. With this paper, we want to honor his contributions and take the opportunity to point out some avenues for future work.

We do this by collecting together various open problems from different areas and presenting them all in one place.[1] The list we give here is not necessarily complete, nor is it representative. However, we think that it nicely illustrates the breadth of abstract argumentation research, and the various connections to other fields of mathematics and logic that have been discovered. For presentation purposes, we keep the common background to a minimum, and rather introduce the necessary background that is needed for each problem individually.

2 Background

In the following we consider a fixed countably infinite set $\mathcal{U}$ of arguments, called *universe*. Furthermore, we define $\mathcal{A} = \{F \mid F = (A, R), A \subseteq \mathcal{U}, R \subseteq A \times A\}$ containing all AFs w.r.t. $\mathcal{U}$. Instead of $(a, b) \in R$ we write $a \rightarrowtail b$ and say that

---

[1] Independently, Stefan Woltran had the same idea for his invited talk "Abstract Argumentation: All Problems Solved?" at ECAI 2014 (as part of the *Frontiers of Artificial Intelligence* series). We took up several suggestions for open problems from that talk and subsequent personal communication with Stefan.

T. Eiter et al. (Eds.): Brewka Festschrift, LNAI 9060, pp. 325–339, 2015.

a attacks b. For sets $E_1, E_2 \subseteq A$ and arguments $a, b \in A$ we say that $E_1 \rightarrowtail b$ if some $a \in E_1$ attacks b, $a \rightarrowtail E_2$ if a attacks some $b \in E_2$ and $E_1 \rightarrowtail E_2$ if some $a \in E_1$ attacks some $b \in E_2$. An argument $a \in A$ is defended by a set $E \subseteq A$ in F if for each $b \in A$ with $b \rightarrowtail a$, $E \rightarrowtail b$. The range E^+ of a set of arguments E is defined by the extension of E with all arguments attacked by E, i.e. $E^+ = E \cup \{a \in A \mid E \rightarrowtail a\}$.

A semantics σ is a function which assigns to any F a set of sets of arguments denoted by $\sigma(F)$. Each one of them, a so-called σ-extension, is considered to be acceptable with respect to F (for a recent overview see [1]). In the following we define conflict-free and admissible sets as well as complete, preferred, semi-stable, stable, naive, stage, grounded, ideal and eager semantics which will be frequently considered throughout the paper (abbreviated by $cf, adm, com, pr, ss, st, nai, stg, grd, id, eg$). Semantics that are used only once will be defined in the corresponding sections.

Definition 1. *Given an AF $F = (A, R)$. We call a set $E \subseteq A$*

1. *$E \in cf(F)$ if for all $a, b \in E$ we have $a \not\rightarrowtail b$,*
2. *$E \in adm(F)$ if $E \in cf(F)$ and for all $a \rightarrowtail E$ also $E \rightarrowtail a$,*
3. *$E \in com(F)$ if $E \in adm(F)$ and for any $a \in A$ defended by E in F, $a \in E$,*
4. *$E \in pr(F)$ if $E \in adm(F)$ and there is no $E' \in adm(F)$ s.t. $E \subsetneq E'$,*
5. *$E \in ss(F)$ if $E \in adm(F)$ and there is no $E' \in adm(F)$ s.t. $E^+ \subsetneq E'^+$,*
6. *$E \in st(F)$ if $E \in cf(F)$ and $E^+ = A$,*
7. *$E \in nai(F)$ if $E \in cf(F)$ and there is no $E' \in cf(F)$ s.t. $E \subsetneq E'$,*
8. *$E \in stg(F)$ if $E \in cf(F)$ and there is no $E' \in cf(F)$ s.t. $E^+ \subsetneq E'^+$,*
9. *$E \in grd(F)$ if $E \in com(F)$ and there is no $E' \in com(F)$ s.t. $E' \subsetneq E$.*
10. *$E \in id(F)$ if $E \in adm(F)$, $E \subseteq \bigcap_{P \in pr(F)} P$ and there is no $E' \in adm(F)$ satisfying $E' \subseteq \bigcap_{P \in pr(F)} P$ s.t. $E \subsetneq E'$,*
11. *$E \in eg(F)$ if $E \in adm(F)$, $E \subseteq \bigcap_{P \in ss(F)} P$ and there is no $E' \in adm(F)$ satisfying $E' \subseteq \bigcap_{P \in ss(F)} P$ s.t. $E \subsetneq E'$.*

3 Open Problems

1. Given an AF, can all implicit conflicts (pairs of arguments that do not occur jointly in any extension) be made explicit (by adding one or two attacks between them)?
2. What are the signatures (sets of extension-sets that can be realized by AFs under a semantics) of complete, cf2 and resolution-based grounded semantics?
3. What is the precise computational complexity of credulous acceptance with respect to ideal semantics?
4. What is the maximal number of complete extensions in an AF with n arguments?
5. Is there a closed-form expression for the average number of stable extensions of AFs with n arguments and x attacks?
6. What is the (σ, Φ)-characteristic of semi-stable semantics?
7. What is the (stable, semi-stable, preferred)-spectrum?
8. How can normal deletion equivalence in case of stage, semi-stable, eager, preferred, ideal and naive semantics be characterized?

3.1 Explicit-Conflict Conjecture

The fundamental building blocks of Dung's AFs are arguments. The fundamental means of *expression*, however, are attacks between arguments, as these ultimately influence which arguments can be accepted together. An attack between two arguments a and b is an explicit manifestation of a conflict between the two. But in addition to such syntactic, *explicit* conflicts, incompatibilities between arguments may also arise on the semantical level, that is, whenever two arguments never occur in an extension together. In such a case, we will speak about an *implicit* conflict. Clearly, for semantics based on conflict-freeness, each explicit conflict leads to an implicit conflict. But it is also possible to have implicit conflicts that are not explicit, as we show below in Figure 1. To make matters more formal, consider the following definition. Roughly, for a set X of sets of arguments (say, extensions), $Pairs_X$ captures which arguments co-occur in at least one of the elements of X. This relation directly yields implicit conflicts, and can be used to figure out whether there are implicit conflicts that are not explicit.

Definition 2. *Let $X \subseteq 2^{\mathcal{U}}$ and $Pairs_X = \{(a,b) \mid exists\ E \in X\ s.t.\ \{a,b\} \subseteq E\}$. An AF $F = (A, R)$ is conflict-explicit under semantics σ iff for each $a, b \in A$ such that $(a,b) \notin Pairs_{\sigma(F)}$, we find $(a,b) \in R$ or $(b,a) \in R$ (or both).*

In words, a framework is conflict-explicit under σ if any two arguments of the framework that do not occur jointly in a σ-extension are explicitly conflicting, that is, there is an attack one way or the other.

Fig. 1. An argumentation framework that is not conflict-explicit under stable semantics. Observe that $st(F) = \{\{a,d\},\{b,c\}\}$ and $(c,d) \notin Pairs_{\mathsf{s}}$ but $(c,d) \notin R$ as well as $(d,c) \notin R$. If we add attacks (c,d) or (d,c) we obtain an equivalent (under stable semantics) conflict-explicit (under stable semantics) AF.

The open problem now consists of proving or disproving whether every AF F has a conflict-explicit AF F' over the same arguments with the same stable extensions.

Conjecture 1. *For each AF $F = (A, R)$ there exists an AF $F' = (A, R')$ which is conflict-explicit under the stable semantics such that $st(F) = st(F')$.*

While formulating this conjecture is reasonably straightforward (it is perhaps the "easiest" conjecture of this paper, in terms of required background), Baumann et al. [13] have illustrated in a series of examples that the problem itself is far from easy. Clearly, given an argumentation framework F that is not conflict-explicit, our first try at making it conflict-explicit would be to add, for each conflict that is implicit but not explicit, an attack (or two). However, as Figure 2 shows, we cannot choose attacks to add at random. This creates a combinatorial

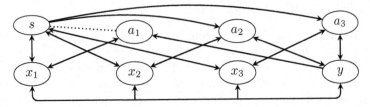

Fig. 2. Orientation of attacks due to previously non-explicit conflicts matters: First observe that $st(F) = \{\{a_1, a_2, x_3\}, \{a_1, a_3, x_2\}, \{a_2, a_3, x_1\}, \{s, y\}\}$. Next, $Pairs_{st(F)}$ yields one pair of arguments a_1 and s whose conflict is not explicit by F, that is, $(a_1, s) \notin Pairs_{st(F)}$, but $(a_1, s), (s, a_1) \notin R_F$. Now adding the attack (a_1, s) to F would create the additional stable extension $\{a_1, a_2, a_3\} \notin st(F)$. On the other hand, by adding the attack (s, a_1), we get the conflict-explicit AF F' with $st(F) = st(F')$.

problem, since for each of k non-explicit implicit conflicts, we have three possibilities of how to deal with it, thus 3^k possibilities in total. Even worse, just adding attacks does not suffice in the general case. In an example that is too large to reproduce here, Baumann et al. [13] show that there are cases where one has to modify parts of the framework that are not directly involved in the implicit conflicts.

3.2 Signatures of Complete, cf2 and Resolution-Based Grounded Semantics

Given an argumentation semantics σ, the *signature of* σ is the set

$$\Sigma_\sigma = \{\sigma(F) \mid F \text{ is an AF }\}.$$

That is, the signature of a semantics collects all sets of sets of arguments that can possibly arise as extension-set of some argumentation framework. This is a quite fundamental concept, since it provides a bird's eye view on capabilities and limitations of the semantics. For example, the signature of the grounded semantics clearly contains only (and all) singleton sets, since the grounded semantics is unique for any given AF, but an arbitrary singleton $\{E\}$ is realized by the AF $(E, \emptyset)$.

The notion of signature has been defined and studied by Dunne et al. [24,25], who also provide characterizations of the signatures for conflict-free, naive, stage, admissible, preferred and stable semantics. A characterization of Σ_σ consists of necessary and sufficient conditions that allow to decide (in a more sophisticated way than using brute force), given a set X of desired extensions, whether there exists an AF F such that $\sigma(F) = X$. For example, for the grounded semantics, the property of X being a singleton is both necessary and sufficient; therefore, the easily checkable singleton property precisely characterizes Σ_{grd}. For stable semantics, it is a necessary condition that X is a $\subseteq$-antichain, but this condition is not sufficient as the extension-set $X = \{\{a, b\}, \{a, c\}, \{b, c\}\}$ is not stable-realizable [25] (while being a $\subseteq$-antichain).

However, for several semantics, precise characterizations of their signatures are as yet unknown. Among these are the complete, cf2 and resolution-based grounded semantics. We will first recall some additional necessary technical prerequisites to formulate the open problems. However, for a lack of space, we have to refer the reader to [4] for details on the *cf2* semantics.[2] The resolution-based family of semantics is defined as follows [2]: for an AF $F = (A, R)$, a *resolution* of F is any AF $F' = (A, R')$ such that $R' \subseteq R$, $(a, a) \in R$ implies $(a, a) \in R'$, $(a, b) \in R$ with $a \neq b$ implies either $(a, b) \in R'$ or $(b, a) \in R'$ (but not both). Denoting the set of all resolutions of F by $\gamma(F)$, for a semantics σ, its resolution-based version σ^* is defined by

$$\sigma^*(F) = \min_{\subseteq} \left(\bigcup_{G \in \gamma(F)} \sigma(G) \right)$$

The resolution-based grounded semantics is then the grounded instance of this general scheme, that is, $rbg = grd^*$.

Now we can sketch the current state of knowledge and formulate the open problems: For complete semantics, we have $\Sigma_{adm} \subsetneq \Sigma_{com}$ [25]. For cf2, the current knowledge only says that $\Sigma_{nai} \subsetneq \Sigma_{cf2} \subsetneq \Sigma_{stg}$.[3] For the resolution-based grounded semantics, we know that $\Sigma_{rbg} \subsetneq \Sigma_{pr}$ and that Σ_{rbg} is incomparable to the signatures of naive, stage and stable semantics [26]. Thus the open problem is this:

Open Problem 2. *What are exact characterizations of Σ_{com}, Σ_{cf2}, Σ_{rbg}?*

3.3 Computational Complexity of Ideal Semantics

The ideal semantics was introduced by Dung, Mancarella and Toni [21]. It covers an important middle ground between the grounded semantics (that is sometimes too restrictive) and sceptical reasoning over the preferred semantics (that is sometimes too permissive). As an illustration, consider Figure 3, an example taken from [22]. Recall that formally, for an argumentation framework $F = (A, R)$, a set $S \subseteq A$ is an *ideal set* if it is admissible and a subset of each preferred extension. Furthermore, S is the *ideal extension* if it is the $\subseteq$-maximal ideal set. Thus arises the question of the computational complexity of ideal semantics, that is, whether its attractive properties (from a semantical standpoint) are (somewhat negatively) reflected in a high computational cost.

As a quick recapitulation [31], recall that the complexity class NP contains all problems L that have polytime-computable witness relation; that is, $L \in$ NP iff there are $W_L \in$ P and $k \in \mathbb{N}$ such that: $x \in L$ iff there is a y such that

---

[2] Roughly, the computation of *cf2* semantics proceeds along the strongly connected components of AFs. Naive extensions are determined in all components in the order of their dependence on one another, and statuses of arguments in previous SCCs are propagated to subsequent SCCs.

[3] Stefan Woltran, personal communication.

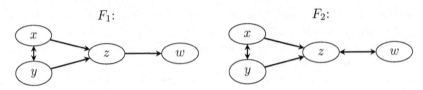

Fig. 3. Two argumentation frameworks F_1, F_2. In both, the grounded extension is empty, and argument w is contained in every preferred extension. The ideal semantics can distinguish between the two, since in F_1 argument w cannot defend itself (ideal extension $\emptyset$) while in F_2 it can (ideal extension $\{w\}$).

$(x, y) \in W_L$ and $|y| \leq |x|^k$. (Intuitively y is the polynomial-size witness proving that $x \in L$.) The class coNP contains all languages L whose complement $\overline{L}$ is in NP. The complexity class $\Theta_2^P = \mathsf{P}_\parallel^{\mathsf{NP}}$ contains all problems that are decidable in deterministic polynomial time using polynomially many non-adaptive calls to an NP oracle. An NP oracle call can be understood as having a constant-time decision subroutine for NP problems. Non-adaptive means that the oracle calls are independent of each other, that is, the answer to one oracle call may not influence a latter query to the oracle. (In the class Δ_2^P, on the other hand, oracle calls can build upon one another.) There is a special subclass of Θ_2^P, the class $\mathsf{DP} = \mathsf{D}_2^P$, where the number of oracle calls is exactly two. We clearly find that $\mathsf{NP} \subseteq \mathsf{D}_2^P \subseteq \Theta_2^P = \mathsf{P}_\parallel^{\mathsf{NP}} \subseteq \mathsf{P}^{\mathsf{NP}} = \Delta_2^P$.

Dunne [22] studies the following decision problems for ideal semantics:[4]

CAI Given $F = (A, R)$ and $a \in A$, is a contained in the ideal extension of F?
INE Given $F = (A, R)$, is its ideal extension non-empty?
VIE Given $F = (A, R)$ and $S \subseteq A$, is S the ideal extension?

Theorem 1 ([22, Theorem 1]). **CAI** *is* coNP-*hard;* **INE** *is* NP-*hard;* **VIE** *is* DP-*hard.*

Dunne [22] later provides conditional completeness results, dependent on knowing the exact complexity of **CAI**:

Theorem 2 ([22, Theorem 6])

- *If* **CAI** *is* NP-*hard, then* **CAI** *is* $\mathsf{P}_\parallel^{\mathsf{NP}}$-*complete.*
- *If* **CAI** *is in* coNP, *then* **INE** *is* NP-*complete.*
- *If* **CAI** *is in* coNP, *then* **VIE** *is* DP-*complete.*

Thus many of the open problems rest on resolving whether **CAI** is NP-hard or **CAI** is in coNP. Currently, there is strong evidence that **CAI** is not in coNP. This evidence rests on the (open) complexity of the unique satisfiability problem (given a propositional formula φ, is there *exactly one* model for φ?), and randomised reductions [22]. Dunne [22] shows that with high probability:

---

[4] The paper contains many more results, but for the purpose of this paper we are only interested in the open problems.

Conjecture 1. **CAI**, **INE** and **VIE** are $P_\parallel^{NP}$-complete.

Dunne et al. [23] observed that the ideal semantics can be parameterized with respect to base semantics. They also conjecture the gap between the complexity of credulous and skeptical acceptance for preferred extensions to be a major influence on the difficulty in determining the precise complexity of ideal semantics.

3.4   Maximal Number of Complete Extensions

In [14] the authors presented a first analytical and empirical study of the maximal and average numbers of extensions in case of abstract argumentation frameworks. The study was restricted to the case of stable semantics. In particular, it was shown that for any AF possessing n arguments the maximal number of stable extensions does not exceed $3^{\frac{n}{3}}$. Interestingly, the authors reduced the problem of determining the maximal number of stable extensions in argumentation frameworks to the problem of determining the maximal number of maximal independent sets in undirected graphs. The latter was already solved by John W. Moon and Leo Moser in 1965 [29].

We recapitulate the main theorem. The upper bound is presented as a function in the number of arguments denoted by $\sigma_{max}(n)$.

Theorem 3 ([14, Theorem 1]). *In the case of stable sematics, the function $\sigma_{max} : \mathbb{N} \to \mathbb{N}$ is given by*

$$\sigma_{max}(n) = \begin{cases} 1, & \text{if } n = 0 \text{ or } n = 1, \\ 3^s, & \text{if } n \geq 2 \text{ and } n = 3s, \\ 4 \cdot 3^{s-1}, & \text{if } n \geq 2 \text{ and } n = 3s + 1, \\ 2 \cdot 3^s, & \text{if } n \geq 2 \text{ and } n = 3s + 2. \end{cases}$$

Recently, it was shown that $\sigma_{max}(n)$ also serves as the maximal number of semi-stable, preferred, stage as well as naive extensions [25].

Why is it interesting to study the maximal number of extensions? The obtained results can be used to provide lower bounds for the minimal realizability of certain sets of extensions (cf. [13] for a detailed analysis). Furthermore, the results may yield upper bounds for algorithms computing extensions. Last but not least, the maximal number of extensions is simply a further criterion (or better, fundamental property) which helps to classify the plethora of argumentation semantics. This line of research was motivated and initiated by Pietro Baroni and Massimiliano Giacomin [3].

In case of admissible and conflict-free sets we may only state the naive bound 2^n in case of n arguments. This is due to the fact that for any set A and its associated AF $F_A = (A, \emptyset)$ we have $cf(F) = adm(F) = 2^A$. Up to now we were not able to find a proof for the maximal number of complete extensions.

Open Problem 3. *What is σ_{max} in case of complete semantics?*

We as well as our colleagues from Vienna, Thomas Linsbichler and Stefan Woltran, conjecture the following.

Conjecture 4. *In case of complete semantics* $\sigma_{\max} : \mathbb{N} \to \mathbb{N}$ *is given by*

$$\sigma_{\max}(n) = \begin{cases} 1, & \text{if } n = 0 \text{ or } n = 1, \\ 3^{\frac{n}{2}}, & \text{if } n \geq 2 \text{ and } n \text{ even}, \\ 4 \cdot 3^{\frac{n-3}{2}}, & \text{otherwise.} \end{cases}$$

To see that the maximal number is at least as large as conjectured consider the AFs $\mathcal{E}_n$ and $\mathcal{O}_n$ for even or odd n, respectively:

$$\mathcal{E}_n = \left(\left\{ a_i, b_i \mid 1 \leq i \leq \frac{n}{2} \right\}, \left\{ (a_i, b_i), (b_i, a_i) \mid 1 \leq i \leq \frac{n}{2} \right\} \right)$$

$$\mathcal{C}_3 = (\{a, b, c\}, \{(a, b), (b, a), (a, c), (c, a), (b, c), (c, b)\})$$

$$\mathcal{O}_n = \mathcal{C}_3 \cup \left(\left\{ a_i, b_i \mid 1 \leq i \leq \frac{n-3}{2} \right\}, \left\{ (a_i, b_i), (b_i, a_i) \mid 1 \leq i \leq \frac{n}{2} \right\} \right)$$

Obviously, for even n, $com(\mathcal{E}_n) = 3^{\frac{n}{2}}$ and for odd $n \geq 3$, $com(\mathcal{O}_n) = 4 \cdot 3^{\frac{n-3}{2}}$. To prove Conjecture 4, it would thus suffice to show that the given values are also upper bounds for the maximal number of complete extensions.

3.5   Average Number of Stable Extensions

What is the average number of extensions for an AF possessing n arguments and k attacks? This means, we are interested in an expectation value *without actually inspecting* the AF except for determining the parameters n and k, which can be done in linear time. This problem was firstly tackled in [14] for the case of stable semantics. The authors presented some precise values, denoted by $\bar{\sigma}(n, k)$, given that the number of attacks k is close to 0 or close to n^2.

Proposition 1 ([14, Proposition 3]). *For any suitable[5] $n \in \mathbb{N}$, we have*

$$\bar{\sigma}(n, 0) = 1 \qquad\qquad \bar{\sigma}(n, n^2 - 3) = \frac{3 \cdot (n^2 - n - 1)}{(n+1) \cdot (n^2 - 2)}$$

$$\bar{\sigma}(n, 1) = 1 - \frac{1}{n} \qquad\qquad \bar{\sigma}(n, n^2 - 2) = \frac{2}{n+1}$$

$$\bar{\sigma}(n, 2) = 1 - \frac{2n - 2}{n^2 + n} \qquad\qquad \bar{\sigma}(n, n^2 - 1) = \frac{1}{n}$$

The reason why the authors did not present a closed-form function is the enormus combinatorial blowup which has to be handled efficently. Nevertheless, the achieved results can be used to show that the average number of stable extensions in the case of very small numbers of attacks approaches from below to 1. In the case of very large numbers of attacks we have a convergence to 0 from above. What happens in the middle ground? With an increasing number of attacks, does the average number of stable extensions just decrease in a monotone

---

[5] Note that AFs do not possess negative numbers of attacks. Consequently, the considered n's have to ensure that the second argument of $\bar{\sigma}$ is non-negative.

fashion? It turns out that while the number of attacks linearly increases, the average number of extensions first decreases, then increases and then decreases again. This observation is not restricted to a specific number of arguments (cf. [14, Figures 1 and 2, Table 1]). The main open problem of this section is a sufficiently precise specification of the function $\overline{\sigma}(n, k)$.

Open Problem 5. *What is $\overline{\sigma}(n, k)$?*

In this regard we present two conjectures supported by the analytical and empirical results in [14]. The first conjecture claims that the average number of stable extensions of AFs is always located in between 0 and 1.

Conjecture 6. *For any natural numbers n and k with $0 < k < n^2$ we have:*

$$0 < \overline{\sigma}(n, k) < 1.$$

The second conjecture claims that the local maximum always coincides with $n^2 - n$. This conjecture is precisely verified for AFs possessing at most 10 arguments (cf. [14, Table 1]).

Conjecture 7. *Let $n \in \mathbb{N}$ and define $\overline{\sigma}^n(k) : \mathbb{N} \to \mathbb{R}$ where $\overline{\sigma}^n(k) = \overline{\sigma}(n, k)$. Then,*

$$\overline{\sigma}^n(k) \text{ possesses a local maximum at } k_{max} = n^2 - n.$$

3.6   Minimal Change Problem for Semi-stable Semantics

More recently several problems regarding *dynamic* aspects of abstract argumentation have been addressed in the literature [18,19,17,27]. One much cited problem among these concerns the acceptability of certain arguments and is called *enforcing problem* [10]. This is, in brief, the question whether it is possible, given a specific set of allowed operations, to modify a given AF such that a desired set of arguments becomes an extension or a subset of an extension of the modified AF. Several sufficient conditions under which enforcements are (im)possible were identified.

Consider the following snapshot of a dialogue among agents A and B depicted in Figure 4. Assume it is A's turn and her desired set of arguments is $E = \{a_1, a_2, a_3\}$. Furthermore, A and B are discussing under preferred semantics.

In order to enforce E agent A may come up with new arguments (for example through introducing an argument which attacks b_2 and b_3) and/or question old arguments or attacks between them, respectively (for example through questioning the self-attack of c). Please note that firstly, in this scenario enforcing is possible and secondly, there are at least two different possibilities to achieve that. This observation leads to the more general problem of *minimal change* [7]. That is, in brief, i) is it possible to enforce a desired set of arguments, and if so, ii) what is the minimal number of modifications (additions or removals of attacks) to reach such an enforcement. This value, called (σ, Φ)-characteristic, depends on the underlying semantics σ and type of allowed modifications Φ. Here is the precise definition taken from [7].

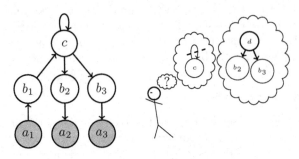

Fig. 4. Snapshot of a Dialogue

Definition 3. *Given a semantics σ, an AF $F = (A, R)$ and a relation $\Phi \subseteq A \times A$. The (σ, Φ)-characteristic of a set $C \subseteq A$ is a natural number or infinity defined by the following function*

$$N_{\sigma,\Phi}^F : 2^A \to \mathbb{N}_\infty$$

$$C \mapsto \begin{cases} 0, & \exists C' : C \subseteq C' \text{ and } C' \in \sigma(F) \\ k, & k = \min\{d(F, G) \mid (F, G) \in \Phi, N_{\sigma,\Phi}^G(C) = 0\} \\ \infty, & \text{otherwise.} \end{cases}$$

The distance function $d(F, G)$ is defined as the number of added or removed attacks needed to transform F to G.

Quite surprisingly, it was shown that, in case of stable, preferred, complete and admissible semantics there are local criteria to determine the characteristic, although infinitely many possibilities to modify a given AF exist (see [9] for detailled explanations including all proofs). Let us consider again the dialouge depicted in Figure 4. Using the results in [7] one may show that the characteristic equals 1 if we allow arbitrary modifications, 2 if the deletion of former attacks is forbidden and ∞ (i.e. it is impossible to enforce $\{a_1, a_2, a_3\}$) if A only can come up with weaker arguments. These are fresh arguments which do not attack previous arguments.

Let F be an AF and Φ be a certain modification type. Due to the fact that any stable extension is a semi-stable one and furthermore, any semi-stable extension is preferred we have, $N_{st,\Phi}^F \geq N_{ss,\Phi}^F \geq N_{pr,\Phi}^F$ ([7, Corollary 3]). Whereas $N_{st,\Phi}^F$ and $N_{pr,\Phi}^F$ are already computable a characterization in case of semi-stable semantics remains an open problem.

Open Problem 8. *Are there local criteria determining $N_{ss,\Phi}^F$?*

The main reason why semi-stable semantics has defied any attempt of solving is the requirement of range-maximization which cannot be decided by looking at the candidate set only. On a final note, we want to mention that neither $N_{st,\Phi}^F$ nor $N_{pr,\Phi}^F$ coincide with $N_{ss,\Phi}^F$ in general (cf. examples at the end of Sections 4.1, 4.2 and 4.3 in [7]).

3.7   Spectra and Fibres

An at first glance more theoretical problem is the so-called *spectrum problem* [11]. The name was chosen because of its similarity with the famous *Spektralproblem* in model theory [32].[6] Given a certain semantics σ and a modification type Φ, the question is whether there is, for a given natural number n, an AF F and a set of arguments E such that n is the (σ, Φ)-characteristic of E with respect to F. In other words, we ask for the set of natural numbers which may occur as (σ, Φ)-characteristics, the so-called (σ, Φ)-*spectrum*. More generally, one may ask for n-tuples of characteristics representing several semantics simultaneously. Here is the definition of the (st, ss, pr, Φ)-spectrum.[7]

Definition 4. *Let $\Phi \subseteq A \times A$. The (st, ss, pr, Φ)-spectrum is a set of triples (so-called fibres) defined as follows:*

$$\mathcal{S}_{(st,ss,pr,\Phi)} = \{(k,l,m) \mid \exists\ AF\ F = (A, R)\ \exists\ C \subseteq A,\ s.t.$$
$$N_{st,\Phi}^{F} = k, N_{ss,\Phi}^{F} = l\ and\ N_{pr,\Phi}^{F} = m\}.$$

The first open problem is related to the spectrum w.r.t. to weak expansions, denoted by $\mathcal{S}_{(st,ss,pr,W)}$. In case of weak expansion the addition of weaker arguments, i.e. arguments which do not attack previous arguments, is allowed. In case of stable and preferred semantics it is already shown [7, Theorem 6] that there are only two possibilities, namely either a desired set is already contained in an extension, i.e. the characteristic equals zero, or the set is unenforceable, i.e. the characteristic equals infinity. Interestingly, semi-stable semantics does possess values between zero and infinity. Here is an example.

$F:$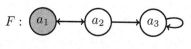

Fig. 5. $N_{ss,W}^{F}(\{a_1\}) = 2$

In [11, Section 3.2] it is formally shown that $N_{ss,W}^{F}(\{a_1\}) = 2$ holds, indeed. Morever, the AF F and the set $\{a_1\}$ justify $(\infty, 2, 0) \in \mathcal{S}_{(st,ss,pr,W)}$. Unfortunately, up to now, there are no characterization theorems for semi-stable semantics (see Problem 8). Nevertheless, several results are already achieved and it turns out that a complete classification of $\mathcal{S}_{(st,ss,pr,W)}$ can be given provided that the following problem is solved.

Open Problem 9. *For any natural number $n \geq 2$, $(\infty, n, 0) \in \mathcal{S}_{(st,ss,pr,W)}$?*

Conjecture 10. *Yes!*

---

[6] Roughly speaking, Scholz investigated the possible sizes finite models of a first-order sentence may have.

[7] A more general definition including arbitrary n-tuples is given in [11, Definition 2].

The reason why we believe *Yes!* is the following proposition stating that there are infinitely many numbers n between 2 and ∞, i.e. $(\infty, n, 0)$ is a fibre of the (st, ss, pr, W)-*spectrum*.

Proposition 2 ([11, Proposition 6]). *For any natural number $n \in \mathbb{N}$ there exists $k \in \mathbb{N}$, such that $n \leq k \leq 2n$ and $(\infty, k, 0) \in \mathcal{S}_{(st,ss,pr,W)}$.*

The second open problem regarding spectra and fibres is with respect to arbitrary modifications, so-called *updates* [8, Definition 5]. More precisely, what are the fibres of the corresponding (st, ss, pr)-spectrum, denoted by $\mathcal{S}_{(st,ss,pr,U)}$.

Open Problem 11. *What is $\mathcal{S}_{(st,ss,pr,U)}$?*

It is already shown that $(k, l, m) \in \mathcal{S}_{(st,ss,pr,U)}$ implies $k \geq l \geq m$ [11, Proposition 7]. This property is called *m.d.s.* – standing for "monotonic decreasing sequence". We conjecture that the considered spectrum is even *m.d.s.-complete*, i.e. for any $k \geq l \geq m$ we have $(k, l, m) \in \mathcal{S}_{(st,ss,pr,U)}$.

Conjecture 12. $\mathcal{S}_{(st,ss,pr,U)}$ *is m.d.s.-complete.*

To verify this conjecture one has to present witnessing AFs $F_{k,l,m}$ together with a certain set of arguments C, s.t. $N_{st,U}^{F_{k,l,m}}(C) = k$, $N_{ss,U}^{F_{k,l,m}}(C) = l$ and $N_{pr,U}^{F_{k,l,m}}(C) = m$. Due to the multitude of possibilities to modify a certain argumentation scenario together with the lack of local criteria to determine the semi-stable characteristic (Problem 8) we were unable to find a proof so far.

The determination of spectra yields interesting insights into how particular semantics are related. For instance, the fact that $\mathcal{S}_{(st,ss,pr,U)}$ is m.d.s. simply means that whenever enforcing is possible for all of them it is at least as difficult using stable (semi-stable) semantics as it is using semi-stable (preferred) semantics. If it is indeed m.d.s.-complete we know in addition that it can in fact be arbitrarily more difficult.

3.8 Characterizing Normal Deletion Equivalence

Notions of equivalence which guarantee intersubstitutability w.r.t. further modifications have received considerable interest in nonmonotonic reasoning (see [28,34,33] among others). Quite recently this topic emerged in abstract argumentation. In the following we list the notions considered in the literature in chronological order (see [15,12] for recent overviews).

1. expansion and local expansion equivalence [30][8]
2. weak expansion equivalence [5]
3. normal and strong expansion equivalence [6]
4. minimal change equivalence [7]
5. update, deletion, local deletion and normal deletion equivalence [8]

---

[8] In [30] the authors used the term *strong equivalence* instead of expansion equivalence. Due to the different notions defined later, expansion equivalence became similarly popular since the term precisely characterizes the considered modifications.

Much work has been done to characterize the mentioned equivalence notions. Many characterization theorems rely on *kernels* which are purely syntactical concepts. Quite surprisingly, so-called *context-sensitive* kernels originally introduced to characterize strong expansion equivalence even serve as parts of the characterizations of normal deletion equivalence w.r.t. admissible, complete and grounded semantics [8, Theorem 16]. Unfortunalety, further standard semantics have defied any characterization attempts.

Open Problem 13. *How to characterize normal deletion equivalence in case of stage, semi-stable, eager, preferred, ideal and naive semantics?*

We proceed with the precise definition togehter with an example.

Definition 5. *Two AFs $F = (A, R)$ and $G = (B, S)$ are normal deletion equivalent w.r.t. σ (denoted by $F \equiv_{ND}^{\sigma} G$) iff for any set of argumens C, $\sigma(F \setminus C) = \sigma(G \setminus C)$. Hereby $F \setminus C \overset{\text{def}}{=} \big((A, R)|_{A \setminus C}\big).$*

Roughly speaking, normal deletion equivalent frameworks cannot be semantically distinguished by forgetting arguments together with their corresponding attacks.

Example 1. Consider the following two AFs F and G.

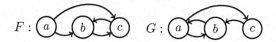

Although both possess the unique preferred extension $\{a\}$ the AFs are not normal deletion equivalent w.r.t. preferred semantics. This can be seen as follows. If we retract the argument c, then $\{b\}$ becomes preferred in $G \setminus \{c\}$ but still not in $F \setminus \{c\}$. Consequently, $F \not\equiv_{ND}^{pr} G$.

$$F \setminus \{c\} : \quad \boxed{a} \quad \boxed{b} \qquad G \setminus \{c\} : \quad \boxed{a} \quad \boxed{b}$$

As a final note we mention that it is already checked that none of the existing kernels can contribute anything to solving Open Problem 13. This means, if kernels play a decisive role, then new kernel definitions are required.

4   Conclusion

We presented eight open problems in abstract argumentation, one of Gerd's major research areas in the last decade. For each of the problems, we tried to motivate why the problem is important, gave a formal problem statement and explained why the problem is (or at least seems to be) hard to solve. Some of the problems stem directly from work that Gerd was personally involved in, while others are inspired by his work.

Acknowledgements. We dedicate this paper to Gerhard Brewka, whose support and guidance was of substantial importance in our academic careers. *All the best, Gerd, and thank you for everything!* The authors are also grateful to Stefan Woltran for adding several open problems and acting as a second reader, thus suggesting numerous improvements of the text.

References

1. Baroni, P., Caminada, M., Giacomin, M.: An introduction to argumentation semantics. Knowledge Engineering Review 26(4), 365–410 (2011)
2. Baroni, P., Dunne, P.E., Giacomin, M.: On the resolution-based family of abstract argumentation semantics and its grounded instance. Artificial Intelligence 175(3), 791–813 (2011)
3. Baroni, P., Giacomin, M.: On principle-based evaluation of extension-based argumentation semantics. Artificial Intelligence 171(10-15), 675–700 (2007)
4. Baroni, P., Giacomin, M., Guida, G.: SCC-recursiveness: A general schema for argumentation semantics. Artificial Intelligence 168(1-2), 162–210 (2005)
5. Baumann, R.: Splitting an argumentation framework. In: Delgrande, J.P., Faber, W. (eds.) LPNMR 2011. LNCS, vol. 6645, pp. 40–53. Springer, Heidelberg (2011)
6. Baumann, R.: Normal and strong expansion equivalence for argumentation frameworks. Artificial Intelligence 193, 18–44 (2012)
7. Baumann, R.: What does it take to enforce an argument? Minimal change in abstract argumentation. In: ECAI, pp. 127–132 (2012)
8. Baumann, R.: Context-free and context-sensitive kernels: Update and deletion equivalence in abstract argumentation. In: ECAI, pp. 63–68 (2014)
9. Baumann, R.: Metalogical Contributions to the Nonmonotonic Theory of Abstract Argumentation. College Publications (2014)
10. Baumann, R., Brewka, G.: Expanding argumentation frameworks: Enforcing and monotonicity results. In: COMMA. FAIA, vol. 216, pp. 75–86. IOS Press (2010)
11. Baumann, R., Brewka, G.: Spectra in abstract argumentation: An analysis of minimal change. In: Cabalar, P., Son, T.C. (eds.) LPNMR 2013. LNCS, vol. 8148, pp. 174–186. Springer, Heidelberg (2013)
12. Baumann, R., Brewka, G.: The equivalence zoo for dung-style semantics. Journal of Logic and Computation: Special Issue (2014)
13. Baumann, R., Dvořák, W., Linsbichler, T., Strass, H., Woltran, S.: Compact Argumentation Frameworks. In: ECAI, pp. 69–74 (2014)
14. Baumann, R., Strass, H.: On the Maximal and Average Numbers of Stable Extensions. In: Black, E., Modgil, S., Oren, N. (eds.) TAFA 2013. LNCS, vol. 8306, pp. 111–126. Springer, Heidelberg (2014)
15. Baumann, R., Woltran, S.: The role of self-attacking arguments in characterizations of equivalence notions. Journal of Logic and Computation: Special Issue (2014)
16. Bench-Capon, T.J.M., Dunne, P.E.: Argumentation in artificial intelligence. Artificial Intelligence 171(10-15), 619–641 (2007)
17. Bisquert, P., Cayrol, C., de Saint-Cyr, F.D., Lagasquie-Schiex, M.-C.: Change in argumentation systems: Exploring the interest of removing an argument. In: Benferhat, S., Grant, J. (eds.) SUM 2011. LNCS, vol. 6929, pp. 275–288. Springer, Heidelberg (2011)
18. Boella, G., Kaci, S., van der Torre, L.W.N.: Dynamics in argumentation with single extensions: Abstraction principles and the grounded extension. In: ECSQARU, pp. 107–118 (2009)

19. Cayrol, C., de Saint-Cyr, F.D., Lagasquie-Schiex, M.-C.: Change in abstract argumentation frameworks: Adding an argument. Journal of Artificial Intelligence Research, 49–84 (2010)
20. Dung, P.M.: On the acceptability of arguments and its fundamental role in nonmonotonic reasoning, logic programming and n-person games. Artificial Intelligence 77(2), 321 (1995)
21. Dung, P.M., Mancarella, P., Toni, F.: Computing ideal sceptical argumentation. Artificial Intelligence 171(10), 642–674 (2007)
22. Dunne, P.E.: The computational complexity of ideal semantics. Artificial Intelligence 173(18), 1559–1591 (2009)
23. Dunne, P.E., Dvořák, W., Woltran, S.: Parametric properties of ideal semantics. Artificial Intelligence 202, 1–28 (2013)
24. Dunne, P.E., Dvořák, W., Linsbichler, T., Woltran, S.: Characteristics of multiple viewpoints in abstract argumentation. In: Proceedings of DKB, pp. 16–30 (2013)
25. Dunne, P.E., Dvořák, W., Linsbichler, T., Woltran, S.: Characteristics of multiple viewpoints in abstract argumentation. In: KR, pp. 72–81 (2014)
26. Dvořák, W., Linsbichler, T., Oikarinen, E., Woltran, S.: Resolution-based grounded semantics revisited. In: COMMA. IOS Press (2014)
27. Liao, B.S., Jin, L., Koons, R.C.: Dynamics of argumentation systems: A division-based method. Artificial Intelligence, 1790–1814 (2011)
28. Lifschitz, V., Pearce, D., Valverde, A.: Strongly equivalent logic programs. ACM Transactions on Computational Logic, 526–541 (2001)
29. Moon, J.W., Moser, L.: On cliques in graphs. Israel Journal of Mathematics, 23–28 (1965)
30. Oikarinen, E., Woltran, S.: Characterizing strong equivalence for argumentation frameworks. Artificial Intelligence 175(14-15), 1985–2009 (2011)
31. Papadimitriou, C.H.: Computational complexity. John Wiley and Sons Ltd (2003)
32. Scholz, H.: Ein ungelöstes Problem in der symbolischen Logik. Journal of Symbolic Logic 17, 160 (1952)
33. Truszczyński, M.: Strong and uniform equivalence of nonmonotonic theories – an algebraic approach. In: Annals of Mathematics and Artificial Intelligence, pp. 245–265 (2006)
34. Turner, H.: Strong equivalence for causal theories. In: LPNMR, pp. 289–301 (2004)

Mind the Divide Surrounding Knowledge Representation

Wolfgang Bibel

Abstract. The paper identifies the so-called belief sets mediation problem as one of those important issues which tend to fall into the cracks between KR and its neighboring areas and thus do not receive the deserved attention by KR. It also questions the exclusive restriction of KR on the traditional linguistic (or symbolic) representation of knowledge and argues for a widening of the research agenda in this respect in collaboration with neighboring fields. These specific issues are embedded in a general view of knowledge and its representation.

1 Introduction

This contribution is written in order to honor and congratulate Gerhard (Gerd) Brewka who is about to become sixty. Due to our joint interest in logic-based reasoning our respective paths crossed for the first time in the eighties of the last century. In the course of our interactions then Gerd asked Bernd Neumann, Hamburg, and me to supervise his PhD thesis which, in essence and in detail, he worked out more or less on his own with an excellent result. Since then it has always been a great pleasure for me to interact with him in a variety of ways.

Over the course of our careers both of us have taken for granted the basic assumptions underlying logic as well as the area of knowledge representation and reasoning (KR). In this note I try to alert our community to the general issue whether some of these basic assumptions should still be held undisputed. In particular I point to two specific issues which in my view today might call for a revision of some of those assumptions. One (discussed in Section 5) concerns the aggregation of belief and knowledge sets if more than one person is involved. More specifically it concerns what I call the *belief sets mediation problem*, an issue which seems to be largely ignored in KR on the assumption that this is a topic beyond KR, ie. beyond the divide which separates KR from neighboring areas. But the neighboring areas have their own assumptions so that in fact no seamless approach between KR and those areas is possible. In consequence serious cracks remain, rather than co-evolving results which might inform each other.

The other issue I point out in Section 6 of this note concerns the exclusive focus of KR on the traditional linguistic (or symbolic) representation of knowledge in systems. As we all experience, knowledge means much more to humans with a conscious mind than some symbolic formula. I argue that the time might have come to extend the focus in KR on aspects of knowledge which go beyond the pure symbolism of the kind considered so far. This means that, in collaboration

T. Eiter et al. (Eds.): Brewka Festschrift, LNAI 9060, pp. 340–355, 2015.

with cognitive neuroscientists and cognitive scientists, KR scientists should step back and query the basic assumptions underlying our field in that basic aspect and possibly explore some new terrain in it.

These two specific issues are embedded in a broader view of the concept of knowledge and its representation, expanded in Sections 2 through 4 in order to present a somewhat holistic perspective as might be appropriate for a senior scientist. Concerning my views on the reasoning part in KR I refer, for instance, to my earlier articles [5,6].

2   The Role of Knowledge and Inference in Society and IT

Knowledge is an essential component of any individual as well as of any society as a whole. Its importance is emphasized by the fact that modern societies are often even tagged as "knowledge societies".[1] It is also a commonplace that different pieces of knowledge can be combined to yield a further piece of knowledge, a process termed reasoning. Reasoning is omnipresent in human thinking. For instance, without reasoning, communication via natural language would simply not be possible. In short, knowledge and reasoning (K&R) without the slightest doubt are of utmost importance.

Due to the eminent role of K&R their modeling in computers was attempted shortly after these new devices became more generally available in the early fifties of the last century. Since that time a huge amount of work has been done in modeling K&R in computers with varying success and many ups and downs. For instance, we experienced the "expert systems" hype of the eighties in the last century focusing on the explicit representation of knowledge and involving inferencing. A renewed interest in these knowledge-based methods came up under the label of "semantic web" in the last decade. Independently, dealing with knowledge in a less hard-coded form than in the expert systems approach and involving learning techniques in a substantial way the new paradigm of cognitive computing[2] has been coined. Also, a discipline termed KR (for knowledge representation and reasoning) evolved in the past decades.

Yet the fact is that the role of K&R has remained stuck in a relatively small niche within the whole of information technology (IT).[3] In other words, there is a huge discrepancy between the importance of K&R in IT and the one in society, discussed already in [6] (under a perspective different from the one in the present article). What explains this wide gap? Is the tiger still in the cage [13]? Or, might it be that we are not on the right track in this area, in formal or technological

---

[1] As we will notice later in the text our societies are actually rather contradictory in the appreciation of knowledge, eg. when democratic voting on knowledge-intensive issues is concerned.

[2] See eg. http://www.research.ibm.com/cognitive-computing, last access 11 Aug. 2014.

[3] Note that the processing of text as done, for instance, in search machines like Google or in so-called knowledge management systems in a strict sense use the techniques of K&R only in a marginal way.

terms? Is what we call knowledge adequately formalized and represented in IT? Or is something substantial still missing? Might Wolfram have a point when he writes in [31, p. 627]: *"But it is my strong suspicion that in fact logic is very far from fundamental, particularly in human thinking."*[4]

It is these kinds of questions which motivate the analysis in the present paper.

3   Embedding Knowledge in the Cosmic Evolution

In order to set the stage for our analysis of the role of knowledge let us start with the well-known model of the cosmic evolution as it is currently held by science. This model on the basis of numerous data, in brief, assumes that the cosmos started out some 14 billion years ago with an event called the "big bang". A consequence of the model is that there was nothing "preceding" this event.[5]

There are numerous theories about how the cosmos evolved from this beginning. In [31, ch. 9] many of these are discussed in some detail and a new theory is added therein. Wolfram assumes that the physical evolution of the cosmos might follow a simple set of rules comparable perhaps to those in the cellular automata studied in his book. In this view at any state the entire cosmos would consist of an (astronomically huge) number of cells. To each of these a mechanism set up by a fixed set of rules applies, this way transforming any cell to another one quasi in a computational manner. The accumulation of all these transformations at any state amounts to the steady evolution of the entire cosmos. Altogether this view of the *universe as a computational system* is meant to explain how the cosmos (including space and time and everything else) continues to evolve in a discrete way.[6]

To take such an alternative view of the universe seems to be consistent with all the scientific knowledge we up to this point have accumulated. But like with the issue concerning some precedence of the big bang we have no firm knowledge about the evolution of the universe, just a huge amount of data, knowledge of details and many theories with underlying but unconfirmed assumptions. This shakiness of even our knowledge about the physical world is an important feature of all our knowledge, let alone the one about knowledge as a phenomenon in our minds. In formal terms and in a first approximation, all our knowledge is

---

[4] See also [31, p. 809].

[5] Since according to the model time and space originated with the event, strictly speaking it makes not even sense to use a term like "preceding". But the point here is rather to be aware that the model and its consequences are based on assumptions which could still turn out false (cf. eg. [21] for some discussion). Recent theories assume even that the cosmos might consist of billions of universes, ie. multiverses rather than a single universe.

[6] Konrad Zuse already in the 1940s was perhaps the first to come up with this idea under the term "Rechnender Raum", published much later, eg. in [32] to cite an English text. Wolfram acknowledges this [31, p. 1026], claiming however that Zuse had in mind a continuous rather than something like a discrete cellular automaton, which presumably misinterprets Zuse's view.

therefore of the logical form $A \rightarrow K$, whereby A summarizes all the basing assumptions and K the scientifically established facts. Let us keep this in mind for our analysis of KR and work out some of the assumptions underlying it in the following sections.

In Section 3 of [7] two major steps in the evolution of the universe were pointed out. The first one is characterized by the evolutionary discovery of *information coding and inheriting* which appeared with life through DNA encoding. In the computational view of the universe this discovery amounts to the linguistic – or rather chemical – specification of a kind of a subroutine in the form of a DNA which is copied, possibly with modifications, and called again and again through the course of billions of years.

The second major step occurred when creatures such as humans obtained access to some of the information processed within their bodies by way of conscious thinking. That is, we humans are able to be aware of some of the input into our senses which by our brains is somehow transformed into a model of the perceived world. We can consciously store and memorize it and in this way extend our model of the environment and accumulate knowledge about it. Any such acquired knowledge can be passed on to later generations. Also, with such knowledge (along with assumptions or beliefs) we can explain observed phenomena and even make predictions. Perhaps most importantly, we can imagine whole processes in anticipation as well as in recollection. This way sort of a virtual world has come into existence — or rather billions of such virtual worlds, one for each conscious creature —, in a sense besides the real one, whereby this virtual world may play the roles of a representation or a simulation of parts of the real one. Since this virtual world itself to some extent is under our conscious observation, this observation insofar takes place at a meta-knowledge level, which means that we know about our knowing and thinking. It is exactly this meta-level feature and everything related to it which historically appears to be a completely novel feature and which we therefore consider as an outstanding (second) step in the cosmic evolution.

This novel feature endows humans with unprecedented capabilities. For instance, we are able to ask and pursue fundamental questions such as ones about the course of the cosmic evolution, its origin and destination, about the possibility of some purpose behind this evolution, about human's free will and reasonable goals, and many others. None of those has found a scientifically convincing answer so far, but due to this feature we now already have under certain assumptions found answers to myriads of less fundamental, but practically relevant questions.[7]

---

[7] The preceding description of the second step has reminded Ulrich Furbach of Plato's Allegory of the Cave in his work "The Republic" or "Politeia" (514–521) [24]. Indeed, the allegory describes the potential of human *Erkenntnis* which I summarize in the notion of the second step in a similar way. Given our current state of scientific knowledge, Plato's understanding of the allegory might nevertheless have been somewhat different from ours of the second step.

4   On the Notion of Knowledge

Humans are so familiar with their thinking and knowing that in everyday life it rarely is a topic for consideration. For philosophers however it has been a fiercely debated topic for thousands of years, establishing a discipline called *epistemology*. For human thinking it seems to be a rather hard discipline as the endless debates over the centuries demonstrate. With the advent of Intellectics, ie. of AI (including KR), Cognitive Science and Cognitive Neuroscience, some precision entered into this discipline. I therefore begin with the illustration of the various aspects around the concept of knowledge in a detail which might be clear to specialists but may often be ignored thus occasionally leading to confusions.

The illustration will be done with a simple example of a knowledge fact, say the fact in the real world that Mr. Gauck is (currently our German) president, formally $is\_president(Gauck)$, or shortly $p(G)$. Now consider any person, say *Marie*, or shortly M, who knows about this fact. In detail this means a lot of things at the same time. Namely, in M's brain there is some representation of the person G, say G^M, as well as of the property p of being president, say p^M. In addition, Marie's brain associates G^M with p^M, say $[p(G)]^M$, in whatever way this might physiologically be achieved.[8] So $[p(G)]^M$ is a representation in the brain's virtual world of the $p(G)$ in the real world and similarly for its constituents.

When we refer to $p(G)$ in this example we actually refer to the denoted actual fact in the real world rather than to the linguistic term $'['p'('G')]'$ (in the real world) which is still something different to be noted. Moreover, this linguistic term has yet again a representation in Marie's brain, say $'['p'('G')]'^M$, which again is somehow related by Marie's brain to $[p(G)]^M$.[9]

This kind of a terminological description of the various aspects underlying the concept of knowledge which is illustrated here was in essence already introduced in [2]. Logicians like W.V.O. Quine have pointed out such distinctions under terms such as "de re" for $p(G)$ and "de dictu" for $[p(G)]^M$ (see eg. [22, p. 268ff]), to mention just one example. For neuroscientists the distinction is obvious anyway.[10] If these different aspects are precisely kept apart and formally introduced,

---

[8] For readers familiar with the philosophical literature it will be clear from this wording that we stay away from the debate about "qualia" in this manner. In the author's opinion such a discussion will become of substance not before science gets some clues on whatever level of abstraction how consciousness might be realized in the brain.

[9] $'['p'('G')]'^M$ might be seen as the term denoting an expression in what is called the mental language. In the philosophical literature one can find numerous further distinctions such as whether M's consciousness is focused on, say, G^M or not. This particular distinction is made because we may indeed consciously concentrate on something like a person or a color, or this object or property may just be taken into account in our reasoning more or less unconsciously. We regard this and any other distinction not relevant for the present purpose and therefore do not take account of them here.

[10] Graciano illustrates the distinction for the example of white light. He speaks of *item I* for the phyical thing in the real world (cf. $p(G)$) and distinguishes three (resp. four) items (IIa,b-IV) in the brain which refer to the real world thing (and which we summarize here as $[p(G)]^M$) [14, p. 48].

several of the (pseudo-) problems from the philosophical literature evaporate. As one out of several examples for this observation I mention the philosophical debate about F. Jackson's "knowledge argument" to which, for instance, the whole part 4 in [22] is devoted. Given the precise distinctions presented here this part becomes trivially obvious and thus more or less superfluous along with the extended literature on which it is based.[11]

The question now is in which context any of these aspects comes to bear. Human thinking obviously takes place on the level illustrated for Marie by $[p(G)]^M$. Since our thinking to an important part is associated with language, this association means that $'['p'('G')]'^M$ somehow goes along with $[p(G)]^M$ within the brain. Section 2 (entitled "Knowledge and Language") in [6] analyses this association in more details.

But what then is common knowledge? It is a social fabric: Only if any member i of a social group agrees that $[p(G)]^i$ holds then the group as a whole will accept $p(G)$ as common knowledge communicated as $'['p'('G')]'$.[12] The constructs and phrases in some natural language are common knowledge of this kind. For this reason no distinction is usually made between a language construct in the real world (like $'['p'('G')]'$ or its natural language counterpart) and its mental representation $'['p'('G')]'^M$. Above we spoke of the "actual fact in the real world" in the context of $p(G)$. Actually, the property p is socially attributed to the person G rather than one of his intrinsic properties. In other words, the "real world" in some respect is human-imagined as well. But we nevertheless take it as the real world in the common understanding.

The systems based on the techniques from KR are known as knowledge systems (see eg. [6]). In such a system $p(G)$ is represented and processed linguistically, ie. by way of $'['p'('G')]'$. In contrast to human knowledge processing, the processed symbols have no associated meanings, ie. they are not "grounded" as this association is usually called. Before we discuss these important statements in Section 6 in more detail, let us have a look on further aspects of knowledge which will lead to the first of the two issues announced in Section 1.

---

[11] To give an example, in thought experiments Jackson considers, for instance, a person Mary, a brilliant and omniscient scientist but constrained in a black-white world, and poses the question whether she would learn something new when freed from this constraint and seeing blue sky for the first time. Of course, the blueness of sky gives rise to a literal exactly like $[p(G)]^M$ which could not be present in the former black-white scenario. This illustrates that, once such precise notations were used throughout the entire debate, the posed questions became trivial and the answers obvious.

[12] This characterisation of common knowledge is admittedly insufficient. In the given version it covers what [12] call "group knowledge". In their view common knowledge C means that not only everyone knows C (as with group knowledge), but also everyone knows that everyone knows C, and everyone knows that everyone knows that everyone knows C, and so on to infinity. Such an infinite construction seems unsatisfactory either in this case. [14, p. 202ff] points out the direction how we could reach a more satisfactory definition: everone is aware type A of C and everyone attributes awareness type B of C to everyone in the group (for details see there).

5 Knowledge and Belief

There is no firm knowledge available for humans. As we already pointed out in Section 3 even the physical theories concerning our universe are ultimately based on a number of assumptions which may or may not turn out true. All the more the same holds for the aspects of knowledge discussed in Section 4. The heated debates among scientists on these and any other topics are ample proof for these evident facts. In order to cope with these uncertainties in our knowledge we need make precise the differing degrees of certainty for any pieces of knowledge.

In a first rough distinction concerning these uncertainties there is knowledge on the one side and beliefs on the other. Assumptions, like those of which we talked before, thus belong to the beliefs rather than to the knowledge. And we already pointed out that all of our knowledge K should actually be written as $A \to K$ whereby A summarizes the assumptions (or beliefs).[13] If this advice were carefully followed many disputes would dissolve.

Let us have a look at such a situation in which for simplicity just two persons, say Marie and Peter, are involved. Both have a certain amount of knowledge at their disposal, say K_1^M and K_2^P. Similarly, they have a set of beliefs, say B_1^M and B_2^P. Assume $B_1^M = B_2^P$ and that M and P have the justification for their knowledge on the basis of their beliefs available then they could share their respective knowledge with each other leading to $(K_1 \cup K_2)^M = (K_1 \cup K_2)^P$.

This case just described is a typical one for scientific disciplines. Their scientists share common beliefs underlying their work and they use rational methods for justifying their results. Also science has established procedures for scrutinizing and then publishing the results. Due to the authority established for science as a whole through the successes experienced in the past by the society at large, knowledge accumulated this way by individuals becomes sanctioned as common knowledge (see Section 4).[14]

However, the case just described nevertheless is a rare one. Typically, we are faced with the situation characterized by $B_1^M \neq B_2^P$. In words, any two persons hold different beliefs. As long as $B_1^M \to K_1^M$, $B_1^M \to K_2^P$, $B_2^P \to K_1^M$, and $B_2^P \to K_2^P$ all hold then M and P could still share their respective knowledge with each other leading to $(K_1 \cup K_2)^M = (K_1 \cup K_2)^P$ as before.

Again, it is a rare case that $B_i^X \to K_j^Y$ hold for all the noted combinations. Except for these two special cases in all remaining cases we run into difficulties in any straightforward attempt to aggregate the respective belief and knowledge sets. Namely, such an aggregation requires sort of a mediation of the belief sets beforehand. Let us, hence, talk of the *belief sets mediation* in the context of the problem just described. Although we are obviously talking here of a rather fundamental issue in the context of knowledge and belief, I am not aware of any work that has addressed it explicitly within KR. Only if you surpass the divide

---

[13] In Computer Science (CS) scientists have for a long time been careful to note their assumptions explicitly like in theorems of the kind: "If P$\neq$NP then ..."; similarly, of course, for mathematicians.

[14] In former times other authorities (like the church, the ruling celebrities etc.) tried to sanction common knowledge.

in the landscape made up by respective scientific areas you get again ground under your feet in the sense that problems of the kind of belief sets mediation have been addressed there at least in an implicit way. This is, for instance, the case in the area of multiagent systems. In other words, because of this divide there is no seamless extension of the theories from KR to cover other than the generally preferred issues in this field.

What we have illustrated here for the knowledge and beliefs approach, notably for the belief sets mediation problem, holds for other approaches in a similar way. For instance, the entire part V on "Uncertain knowledge and reasoning" (chapters 13–17) in the standard AI text [27] with only a minor exception is exclusively focused on the single-agent case, the minor exception being a few pages on game theory as an entirely new theory with no connection to the rest of the part.

What we experience here in KR seems to be a general phenomenon in our current science structure. This is made up of numerous areas which are very specialized and in which each is based on its own assumptions. In other words, each of these areas is surrounded by numerous cracks which separate it from otherwise closely related areas. As a consequence the potential synergy between such closely related areas does not come to bear. Often the wheel is rediscovered in each of them.

As already indicated above, in the present case of the belief sets mediation problem beyond the divide we would reach areas such as, for instance, multiagent systems, computational social choice, etc. (see eg. [30], [26], [15]). The emphasis in those areas however is on "multi". But how can you deeply understand the mechanisms effective in a collective of many agents concerning the belief sets mediation problem, if you have not first come to a grip of the mechanisms effective among just two agents based on those of a single agent? What mechanism — to illustrate the point made here with a nice example from [9] – prevented Aristotle from acknowledging and supporting Aristarch's early idea that the earth revolves around the sun?[15]

In general words, I am pleading here for taking into our research focus important topics which lie in the cracks surrounding our core area KR as illustrated with the particular problem of aggregating the beliefs and the knowledge of two persons. In the particular case in quest, this would, for instance, mean that we start out from the results in KR on preferences within belief sets of a single agent, for instance those nicely presented in [8]. Then we study the mechanisms which would seem most useful, rational and fair to aggregate two such belief sets of two different agents into a common one and this way solve the belief sets mediation problem.

A number of questions would arise in such a study. For instance, different belief sets tend to be inconsistent; how could consistency be established thereby respecting the individual preferences? Should there be some "objective" background knowledge base for judging arguments? And how could one agree on

---

[15] A similarly revealing example is Newton's discovery of the physical nature of white light (discussed in [14, p. 47]).

such background knowledge base? How can beliefs be supported by arguments? Is this a way to weight beliefs by the strength of the arguments supporting it? Is this a way for a more objective measurement of beliefs in comparison with just individual preferences? What other ways for this purpose could one think of? What would voting mean in the two-agent case, thus possibly revealing further fundamental flaws in the naïve use of this widely used mechanism? Namely, if the knowledge status of two individuals is differing wrt. the knowledge relevant for the issue over which the vote is taken, then the principle of the equality of all citizens and in consequence the one-vote-per-person principle becomes extremely questionable in view of a rational solution for knowledge-intensive problems. In this respect our democratic societies intentionally ignore the knowledge status and thus fail to appreciate the relevance of knowledge, in an extreme way in fact, rendering our societies contradictory in their general attitude towards knowledge (and in many other respects at that).

Once the two-agent case has been studied to a certain extent and those and many more questions have satisfactorily been answered, then – and only then –– one would be in a position to generalize the results to the case of more than two agents resp. belief sets. It is to be expected that by way of these insights results in multiagent systems under the topics of preference aggregation, negotiation, argumentation, etc. might appear in a new light. Similarly, a deeper understanding of the mechanisms might evolve which underlie what Thomas Kuhn coarsely described as "paradigm shifts" in science [19].

The research strategy which we just illustrated might similarly be applied to other issues as well. Of particular importance in our context would be the integration or mediation of individual and general goals, of interests, of values, and so forth. Knowledge and reasoning derive their importance especially in their roles within planning ahead in time in order to achieve aspired goals to the benefit of individuals, groups, societies or humankind. Hence again the step from planning in the one-agent case, extensively studied in KR, to that of more agents again requires a careful study.

As we see our analysis has identified research areas which fall into the cracks between well-established areas. As already indicated these in-between-areas are by no means of a purely academic character. Rather we are addressing here practical problems which are truly omnipresent and extremely important in everyday scenarios. They loom in any discussion among two or more people, in any scientific, commercial, political or religious dispute and thus in any situation where differing beliefs need become harmonized. Had KR worked out some kind of solution, it could be readily applied to a realization of the outline of a truly democratic society given in [4] at a high level of abstraction (see especially Section 4.6 there). It is therefore amazing that the kind of problems posed here have been neglected so far to a large extent within KR. Rather humanity continues to stick to the general human attitude to defend a belief the more the less generally accessible and provable evidence is available for backing it. In other words, humans compensate the lack of generally defendable evidence for some belief by intolerance with those holding different respective beliefs. The millions of people killed, for instance, for religious beliefs in the course of history are proof to these statements. KR could help to improve this sad situation.

Perhaps the negligence of these kinds of practical problems in KR might be one important reason why knowledge and reasoning is not as dominant in IT as one would expect, as discussed in Section 2. I would therefore like to urge science, especially researchers in KR to focus not only on knowledge (based on fixed sets of assumptions) but to a similar extent also on the sets of beliefs which determine our reasoning in various applications. It is obvious from every day experience that much can be gained from progress in this so far largely neglected area.

There is a lot which could then be done in this respect in numerous applications. Imagine, for instance, if politics would begin to involve operations like those mentioned above (such as the aggregation of belief sets) – in order to appreciate the extreme importance of the sort of problem that I am addressing here. As the recent successes of systems such as Eugene Goostman[16] or Watson[17] demonstrate, systems dealing with knowledge in some way or another have reached a level of performance which seems sufficient and appropriate for attacking problems of the kind addressed here.

Before we end this section, we briefly sketch some of the areas (within or outside of KR) of relevance for the issues discussed above, in order to take the wind out of the sails of potential superficial critics of our analysis. This survey is by no means meant to be exhaustive. We already mentioned above the relevance for the belief sets mediation problem introduced in this section of the areas of multiagent systems and computational social choice with representative references, but pointed out also the different focus of these areas. Similarly, we already mentioned game theory [28] which is related to the issue raised here, especially if one takes information exchange in game trees and cooperative game theory into consideration. But how could game theory help Aristotle and Aristarch in their imagined dispute on a heliocentric universe, mentioned above? As far as I can judge it, the tools in game theory are not readily applicable to the belief sets mediation problem for two or more individuals.

At first sight the "highly abstract" argumentation frameworks introduced in [11] might seem tuned to address problems like our mediation problem. Unfortunately, the research initiated by this framework up to this day has remained too abstract and thus has not become of any relevance for practical problems. In particular, these frameworks ignore the contents of the knowledge contained in the arguments; as the name says, they are frameworks, which is not enough for solving our problem.

The mediation of belief sets might remind of the area of merging (or amalgamating) ontologies, knowledge bases, or theories within KR (eg. [10], [18]). Indeed, part of the problem with differing beliefs might be related to eg. conceptually diverging ontologies, merging operators and such. But on the whole the work in these related areas does not cover the core of the belief sets mediation

---

[16] See http://en.wikipedia.org/wiki/Eugene_Goostman, accessed 9 June 2014.

[17] See http://en.wikipedia.org/wiki/Watson_%28computer%29, accessed 9 June 2014.

problem. Similarly with the area of belief revision [1] which covers, for instance, changing the assumption of yoghurt being in my fridge, but not beliefs such as scientific, political or religious ones and the problems these cause if they differ between two or more agents. The area which perhaps comes closest to dealing with the belief sets mediation problem is the one of judgment aggregation. But again, work such as [23] is too abstract to be really helpful in our context.

6   Conscious Knowledge

In Section 2 we have emphasized the importance of knowledge for individuals as well as for the society. Is knowledge truly important for humans? In what sense – or under what common goal for humanity as a whole – does knowledge improve the human condition in a wide sense? We are not going to discuss these questions in any detail here. They are rather meant to point to the fact that even the "knowledge" of the importance of knowledge is rather a belief in the sense of the previous section, if a strong belief at that. Its strength derives from the fact that in comparison with the conditions of our ancestors, say those around 200 years ago, our present conditions are much preferable. This improvement is almost exclusively due to accumulated knowledge and its application. Also, numerous psychological studies support the view that the use of knowledge is greatly advantageous.[18] Even in your personal life you can experience every day that knowing helps a lot in any circumstances. So we continue to assume as a strong hypothesis that knowledge is of a great value.

In Section 4 we have pointed out that there are several different aspects of knowledge in dependence of the particular representation we envisage. Basically, we have distinguished four different such aspects, illustrated with our Gauck example by $p(G)$, the fact in the real world, $[p(G)]^M$, its representation in Mary's brain, $'['p'('G')]'$, the (real world) linguistic description of the real world fact, and finally $'['p'('G')]'^M$, the representation in the brain of this linguistic artifact.

The field KR has restricted its attention exclusively to the linguistic representation $'['p'('G')]'$. In this respect, it follows the long tradition of (mathematical) logic which for more than two thousand years has abstracted from the meanings of the symbols it is manipulating. There is no doubt that this logical approach has brought us an enormous progress and many impressive results. But will it be sufficient, in order to bring about intelligence at the level of human intelligence in the long run, if we are dealing exclusively with the linguistic representation?

In this final section I will argue that we should extend our focus to include in some way or another the information represented by $[p(G)]^M$.[19] This of course

---

[18] See eg. [17], [29], etc.

[19] The author has brought up this issue in earlier publications. For instance, in [6, p. 95] the basis for logic-based KR is presented in the form of a thesis (termed "Sprachbedeutungsthese", or "thesis about the meaning of language") and it is stated "that this thesis holds only in a first approximation and cannot be maintained under a more precise analysis" (translated by the present author). Further details concerning this issue can be found on the pp. 100f of that publication.

is much easier said than done, since I am asking here to deal with our conscious knowledge. As we all know consciousness has remained one of the great mysteries and so far has withstood any attempts to be unveiled. My point is that KR should all the more vigorously participate in those attempts.

Consciousness has attracted the interest of philosophers for many hundreds of years since Aristotle (see eg. [22, p. 397f]). A famous early definition can be found in the works of John Locke: "Consciousness is the perception of what passes in a man's own mind" (see [20], vol. 1, book II, ch. 1, §19, p. 95). From our viewpoint the sentence does not pass as an acceptable definition at all.[20] Rather consciousness is such a complex phenomenon that as yet no such definition, let alone a generally accepted scientific theory, of consciousness exists despite the many volumes filled with discussions – or should we rather say stories – on the topic.

On the other hand, the evolution of certain aspects of consciousness lies at the heart of the dominance of the human species in this world. In other words, the underlying phenomena must somehow play a crucial role in our intellectual capabilities. Indeed, if Mary thinks of Gauck being president, this seems to anyone with the same thought so much more than what is indicated by the two symbols p and G in $[p(G)]^M$.[21] Yet, logic – and with it KR – are based on the assumption that in a sense we can dispense with these additional ingredients of a thought like "Gauck being president" and nevertheless achieve human-level intelligence just by manipulating symbols like p and G instead.[22]

With these remarks I am not criticizing the path of logic and KR up to this point in our history. The progress achieved on this formal basis has been impressive. In fact, the present author has spent his entire career to support it, although we always have known (or rather believed) that this formal basis will most likely not be the end of the story. It is now felt, however, that we have reached the point in time where one should dare taking a revolutionary further step in which the ingredients involved in consciousness will play a role in knowledge representation.

I am not alone in pleading for such a step. Support also comes from cognitive-psychological studies of human reasoning. For instance, Johnson-Laird quite early established a whole line of research on deduction as experienced by hu-

---

[20] The underlying view of consciousness is also strongly disputed, eg. by G. Güzeldere in [22, pp. 397ff]. As long as we don't have a precise computational model for the realization of consciousness in the brain or in some artifact, in the author's opinion these disputes are anyway bound to lack substance.

[21] "Each word has so much meaning behind it that it is like a flag that stands for an entire country." [14, p. 109]

[22] There are first steps within KR to account for such "additional ingredients". For instance, in a symbol-oriented representation all formal knowledge around any such symbol like G (ie. containing G) might be attached to it (and similarly with p) which might be a first naïve approximation of what the brain achieves during such a thought (see paragraph at the end of this section). But what about the picture I have in mind of Gauck along with $p(G)$, to mention one of the further possibilities?

mans and in some contrast with deductive formalisms in KR [16].[23] This approach does not yet take conscious ingredients explicitly into account, of course; yet, its "mental models" are a step towards conscious experiences in human thinking and reasoning. So, definitely cognitive scientists of such a genre should get involved in the endeavor I am proposing.

Another one whom I would like to mention in support of my proposal is Alan Robinson, a pioneer of KR and famous for his work on resolution. One of his works [25] starts with the following sentences:

> Twenty years ago I wrote the following: "Logic deals with what follows from what. ... The correctness of a piece ... does not depend on what the reasoning is about." (Robinson, 1979, p. 1) I believed then that this explanation of logic is enough to account also for real proofs. I have now come to appreciate the shortcomings of this point of view.

Again, he does not yet take conscious ingredients into account in his analysis. But what he proposes in the cited text and in related publications[24] is nothing else than a step in exactly that direction, restricted to the context of mathematical proofs.[25] If logic and KR under its present paradigms seem not sufficient for mathematics and proofs, how much more will this insufficiency be felt in less formalized areas of knowledge processing.

The discipline which in our days has the say about consciousness is cognitive neuroscience. Here is certainly not the place to give an overview of the state of the art in this discipline concerning this particular topic. A remarkable recent book on the topic is [14]. In our context one should simply take note that it is a truly hot topic within this discipline with a huge amount of literature available. Cognitive neuroscientists do however encourage the collaboration of other disciplines involved.[26] But KR stays apart as if it had nothing to say on this topic? Why?

An obvious explanation is the complexity of the problem one is facing, a good reason for shying away rather than delving into it. But neuroscientists like

---

[23] The theory of mental models, developed in that book and refined in several publications following it, aims at capturing the difference between human and formal reasoning.

[24] Concretely, he for instance argues for "*much careful empirical study of the assimilation of real proofs by real recipients.*" [25, p. 294]

[25] Wolfram in [31, p. 1156] on the other hand points out that there are a number of practical proofs done with the aid of computers which "*can be quite devoid of what might be considered meaningful structure.*" But this does of course not devaluate the importance of "meaningful structure" in creative mathematical thinking.

[26] An example is [9, Sect. I] in which the author writes on the topic of revealing the mechanisms subserving psychological functions: "*... it would be wisest to conduct research on many levels simultaneously ...*". As long as AI (and KR) are committed to pursue their original goals they represent one of those levels. In fact Churchland speaks of the consciousness problem as of a "constraint problem", a term borrowed from KR. And Graziano explicitly says: "*... awareness is a description, a representation, constructed in the brain* [14, p. 36], whereby in his terminology awareness is an essential part of consciousness.

Graziano take on the challenge – why not joined and supported by KR scientists? Perhaps we are still too much influenced by Frege's view which made us believe that natural language (NL) itself is just a syntactic language like that of formal logic. However, it is very likely that NL texts potentially carry more information for conscious human minds than is visible at the syntactic level. If so, how could this information be represented and activated in a computational way?

We in the logic community have all been proud to stay in a tradition which has lasted for more than two thousand years. The tradition — like all traditions — is based on assumptions (like those mentioned by Robinson above). Such assumptions are useful for making progress for a while, sometimes even for two thousand years. But as we discussed in Section 5 assumptions are beliefs which may turn out false. I believe that it is time to query the truth of some of the beliefs behind traditional logic and KR.[27]

Unfortunately, I have to disappoint those readers who now might expect a detailed roadmap for attacking the problem of activating knowledge which might be associated with the conscious $[p(G)]^M$ and its relation with $'['p'('G')]'^M$, whereby I continue to illustrate the general case with our example. This would amount to the outline of a major project in the field, far beyond the limits given for the present paper. Due to age I take it as my privilege to encourage the younger generations of KR researchers in collaboration with cognitive neuroscientists and cognitive scientists to take up the problem which we raised in this section and design a work plan for it. I just note that $[p(G)]^M$ refers to some kind of a mental simulation of the person Gauck and its attribute or, in general, to a model of the world and the conscious self. Something similar would have to be realized in a system in order to bring knowledge representation and reasoning closer to the human model both in terms of performance and of similarity with the original.

At the very least, the traditional representation of knowledge by way of the exclusively linguistic approach discussed above, should take serious well-known insights mostly ignored so far. Namely, think of a knowledge base (KB) involving G for Gauck and p for being president. Imagine that the entire KB were represented as a directed acyclic graph (DAG) with each occurring symbol represented only once in the KB.[28] Then this representation would already model an important feature out of all those of conscious knowledge. Namely, a symbol like the G would assemble as its direct next neighbors all the knowledge about the person Gauck available in the KB – exactly like with the conscious thought of Gauck which immediately triggers all kinds of knowledge about this person present in our brains. Or, perhaps a novel computer architecture such as the recent chip

---

[27] [9, Sect. I] talks of "eliminative materialism" to emphasize that a materialistic approach to consciousness might eventually force us to eliminate previously held assumptions (like those underlying KR).

[28] An explanation and illustration of this kind of representation of KB (already alluded to in Footnote 22 above) can eg. be found in [3, pp. 26f].

built by IBM[29] might lend itself to a representation of knowledge closer to the one in our brains?

Acknowledgements. I thank Ulrich Furbach and Alan Robinson for helpful comments and suggestions on a preliminary version of this text. Thanks are also due to an anonymous referee whom I owe a number of helpful suggestions for improvements, to Jim Delgrande, Joe Halpern, Vladimir Lifschitz and Torsten Schaub for inspiring discussions on the topics of the paper, the editors for the invitation to this contribution, and Hannes Straß for his support in coping with the Springer style.

References

1. Alchourrón, C.A., Gärdenfors, P., Makinson, D.: On the logic of theory change: Partial meet contraction and revision functions. Journal of Symbolic Logic 50, 510–530 (1985)
2. Bibel, W.: On first-order reasoning about knowledge and belief. In: Plander, I. (ed.) Proceedings of the 3rd International Conference on Artificial Intelligence and Information-Control Systems of Robots, pp. 9–16. North Holland, Amsterdam (1984)
3. Bibel, W.: Wissensrepräsentation und Inferenz – Eine grundlegende Einführung. Vieweg, Braunschweig (1993)
4. Bibel, W.: Lehren vom Leben – Essays über Mensch und Gesellschaft. Deutscher Universitäts-Verlag, Wiesbaden (2003)
5. Bibel, W.: Research perspectives for logic and deduction. In: Stock, O., Schaerf, M. (eds.) Reasoning, Action and Interaction in AI Theories and Systems. LNCS (LNAI), vol. 4155, pp. 25–43. Springer, Heidelberg (2006)
6. Bibel, W.: Wissenssysteme und Komplexitätsbewältigung. In: Leiber, T. (ed.) Dynamisches Denken und Handeln – Philosophie und Wissenschaft in einer komplexen Welt – Festschrift für Klaus Mainzer zum 60. Geburtstag, pp. 91–109. Hirzel Verlag, Stuttgart (2007)
7. Bibel, W.: Artificial Intelligence in a historical perspective. AI Communications 27(1), 87–102 (2014)
8. Brewka, G., Niemelä, I., Truszczyński, M.: Preferences and nonmonotonic reasoning. AI Magazine 29(4), 69–78 (2008)
9. Churchland, P.S.: Can neuroscience teach us anything about consciousness? Proceedings and Addresses of the American Philosophical Society 67(4), 23–40 (1994)
10. Delgrande, J., Schaub, T.: A consistency-based framework for merging knowledge bases. Journal of Applied Logics 5(3), 459–477 (2007)
11. Dung, P.M.: On the acceptability of arguments and its fundamental role in nonmonotonic reasoning, logic programming and n-person games. Artificial Intelligence 77(2), 321–357 (1995)
12. Fagin, R., Halpern, J.Y., Moses, Y., Yardi, M.Y.: Reasoning About Knowledge. MIT Press, Cambridge (1995)

---

[29] See http://www.forbes.com/sites/alexknapp/2014/08/07/ibm-builds-a-scalable-computer-chip-inspired-by-the-brain/, last access 11 Aug. 2014.

13. Feigenbaum, E.: The tiger in the cage: The applications of knowledge-based systems. In: Klahr, P., Byrnes, E. (eds.) Proceedings of the Fifth Innovative Applications of AI Conference. The AAAI Press, Menlo Park (1993) Special Invited Talk
14. Graziano, M.S.A.: Consciousness and the Social Brain. Oxford University Press, Oxford (2013)
15. Hunter, A., Parsons, S., Wooldridge, M.: Measuring inconsistency in multi-agent systems. Künstliche Intelligenz 28(3), 169–178 (2014)
16. Johnson-Laird, P.N., Byrne, R.M.J.: Deduction. Lawrence Erlbaum Associates, Hove and London (1991)
17. Kahneman, D.: Thinking, Fast and Slow. Farrar, Straus and Giroux, New York (2011)
18. Konieczny, S., Lang, J., Marquis, P.: DA^2 merging operators. Artificial Intelligence 157(1-2), 49–79 (2004)
19. Kuhn, T.S.: The Structure of Scientific Revolutions, 3rd edn. University of Chicago Press, Chicago (1996)
20. Locke, J.: The Works of John Locke. London (1823)
21. McGinn, C.: Consciousness and space. Journal of Consciousness Studies 2(3), 220–230 (1995)
22. Metzinger, T.: Bewußtsein: Beiträge aus der Gegenwartsphilosophie, 5th edn. Mentis Verlag, Paderborn(2005)
23. Pigozzi, G.: Belief merging and the discursive dilemma: an argument-based account to paradoxes of judgment aggregation. Synthese 152(2), 285–298 (2006)
24. Platon: Sämtliche Werke, Band II. Rowohlt Taschenbuch Verlag, Reinbek, 29th edn. (2002)
25. Robinson, J.A.: PROOF = GUARANTEE + EXPLANATION. In: Hölldobler, S. (ed.) Intellectics and Computational Logic, pp. 277–294. Kluwer Acad. Publ., Dordrecht (2000)
26. Rossi, F., Venable, K.B., Walsh, T.: A Short Introduction to Preferences – Between Artificial Intelligence and Social Choice. Morgan & Claypool, San Rafael (2011)
27. Russell, S.J., Norvig, P.: Artificial Intelligence: A Modern Approach, 2nd edn. Pearson Education, Upper Saddle River (2003)
28. Tadelis, S.: Game Theory: An Introduction. Princeton Univ. Press, Princeton (2013)
29. Treisman, A., Souther, J.: Illusory words: The roles of attention and of top-down constraints in conjoining letters to form words. Journal of Experimental Psychology: Human Perception and Performance 12(1), 3–17 (1986)
30. Weiss, G. (ed.): Multiagent Systems, 2nd edn. MIT Press, Cambridge (2013)
31. Wolfram, S.: A new kind of science. Wolfram Media Inc., Champaign (2002)
32. Zuse, K.: The computing universe. International Journal of Theoretical Physics 21(6-7), 589–600 (1982)

Still Craving a Porsche

Thomas F. Gordon

Fraunhofer FOKUS
Berlin, Germany

Abstract. Reminiscence of my private and professional experiences with
Gerd.

Gerd and I were colleagues at the Institute for Applied Information Technology
(FIT) of the Gesellschaft für Mathematik and Datenverarbeitung (GMD) at
Schloß Birlinghoven in Sankt Augustin, near Bonn. Gerd joined the new Expert
Systems group, soon to be led by Thomas Christaller, in 1984, at about the time
he completed his diploma in Computer Science at the University of Bonn. I had
started working at GMD a bit earlier, in the Spring of 1983, as a member of
the Research Center for Information Law headed by Herbert Fiedler, one of the
founders of legal informatics in Germany. As luck would have it, the two groups
were located on the same floor of the same building. Gerd's office was located
almost directly across from mine on the other side of the building. All of us had
private offices back then, which seems like a luxury today. But thanks to a coffee
room and twice a day coffee breaks, when just about everyone took the time to
chat and socialize, another luxury, we weren't at all isolated and got to know
each other well.

As it happens, I had been hired by Herbert Fiedler to conduct research on legal
expert systems, so the founding of an expert systems research group on the same
floor was a happy coincidence, one of many in my career. I had just completed a
law degree at the University of California, Davis, and was in Germany to be with
my future wife, Ines. (At that time, I still believed this would be a temporary
visit, just long enough for Ines to finish her doctorate, but here I am, still in
Germany, more than 30 years later.) Herbert Fielder was nearing retirement
and his research group was moving to a location nearer to the law school of the
University of Bonn, where he held his professorship. I made the wise decision to
take the opportunity offered to me to switch to the Expert Systems group. Due
to our shared research interests we had been working together closely anyway,
so this just formalized the status quo.

Gerd and I, along with Ulrich Junker, shared an interest in nonmonotonic
logic. Gerd had already done some research on the topic for his diploma thesis.
I had been trying to model legislation using Horn clause logic in Prolog and
struggling to find ways to handle legal rules with exceptions and priority relations among conflicting rules, which became the subject of some of my first
publications [7,8]. I remember the three of us spending hours at the chalk board
exchanging ideas and helping each other with our research. And I would like to

T. Eiter et al. (Eds.): Brewka Festschrift, LNAI 9060, pp. 356–359, 2015.

think the legal examples I introduced helped to shape our common understanding of some of the problems, such as the insufficiency of specificity as a principle for prioritising default rules. The law recognizes a variety of principles for prioritizing conflicing rules, such as preferring rules from a higher authority (Lex Superior) and preferring newer rules (Lex Posterior), in addition to preferring more specific rules (Lex Specialis).

Later Gerd and I had an opportunity to intensify our collaboration, by working together in the TASSO project [5] funded by the German Federal Ministry for Research and Technology and headed by Wolfgang Bibel at the Technical University of Darmstadt. Other members of the project included Josef Schneeberger and Torsten Schaub, in Darmstadt, along with Dieter Bolz, Hans-Werner Güsgen, Peter Henne, Joachim Hertzberg, Ulrich Junker, Rüdiger Kolb, Gerhard Paaß, Franco di Primio, Erich Rome, Günther Schmitgen and Karl-Heinz Wittur at GMD. During this time, Gerd, Josef, Torsten and I all were or became PhD students with Wolfgang Bibel, our "doctor father", which makes us I suppose "doctor brothers". I have fond memories of this period as being especially productive and enjoyable, with a great, harmonious team and nearly perfect research conditions. It seems that back then it was easier to obtain funding for large, long research projects.[1]

Gerd was a guest researcher at the International Computer Science Institute (ICSI), in Berkeley, California, from 1991 to 1992. Since I lived in California for many years and had family there, I flew over regularly and remember visiting Gerd and his family at their home in Berkeley.

It wasn't until 1994, both of us still at GMD, that Gerd and I wrote our first article together, "How to Buy a Porsche" [1], for the AAAI-94 Workshop on Computational Dialectics in Seattle, Washington [11], which Ron Loui and I organized. The paper presented a new logic for decision-making, called Qualitative Value Logic, as part of our work in the Zeno project [9] on developing methods and tools for supporting argumentation about the pros and cons of alternative options in deliberation dialogues. The leading example in the paper was about a deliberation between a husband and wife, purely fictional of course, about whether to buy a Volvo or Porsche. Our wives and children were with us in Seattle, and I remember a nice day trip after the conference with our families to visit a nearby forest, where we were astonished by the tame deer.

In 1996, Gerd and I organized a second computational dialectics workshop [2], which took place in Bonn as part of the Fundamentals of Applied and Practical Reasoning (FAPR) conference. It was there that Douglas Walton and I met for the first time. Doug became my principal collaborator in the Carneades project several years later.

---

[1] I am deeply grateful to Wolfgang Bibel for pulling strings to have me accepted as a PhD student, despite my lack of computer science degree and my inability to write German. And also for his guidance and continued encouragement, also many years later. And while I am thanking people, let me also acknowledge Torsten Schaub for helping me to obtain an honorary professorship at the computer science department of the University of Potsdam.

Gerd and I remained in contact over the years. I remember visting him in Vienna during his first professorship there. And also visiting him several times in Leipzig, which after all is not so far from Berlin, where I now work, including a very enjoyable workshop in 2009 on computational models of argument that Gerd hosted. Other participants I remember include Leila Amgoud, Tony Hunter, Henry Prakken, and Stefan Woltran.

The original Carneades model of argument and burden of proof [10] was limited to cycle-free argument graphs and not based on Dung's work on abstract argumentation frameworks [6], the leading model of argument in the computational models of argument community. I asked Gerd if he would be interested in helping me to overcome the cycle-free limitation by finding some mapping from Carneades argument graphs to Dung abstract argumentation frameworks, and thus also bring Carneades in line with the mainstream of the field. A short time later he contacted me to tell me he had found another way to overcome the limitation, based on a new model he had developed with Stefan Woltran, to be called "Abstract Deliberation Frameworks". I hope I remember this story correctly, but my recollection is that I suggested calling them Abstract *Dialectical* Frameworks (ADFs) instead, to avoid confusion with deliberation in argumentation theory, where it is a kind of dialogue, but also to resonate with our prior work on computational dialectics. This suggestion was adopted in their KR 2010 paper presenting the system [4]. It was noted that the work on ADFs had started as an attempt to add proof standards of the kind modeled in Carneades to Dung frameworks, but the paper stopped short of showing how to reconstruct Carneades, without the cycle limitation, using ADFs. This was done shortly thereafter in a paper Gerd was invited to present at the 2010 Computational Models of Argument (COMMA) conference [3].

I consider Gerd a good friend, perhaps I should say old friend by now, if that is appropriate on this occasion. I have always enjoyed his company and good humor. We share several interests, including being hobby musicians. I remember Gerd accompaning me on bass when I played a few songs at the party to celebrate the completion of my PhD. Perhaps we will find further opportunities to collaborate professionally. Certainly work remains to be done on relations between computational models of argument and practical decision-making. Perhaps the time will come to continue our work on "How to Buy a Porsche". Neither of us has one yet.

References

1. Brewka, G., Gordon, T.F.: How to Buy a Porsche: An Approach to Defeasible Decision Making. In: Working Notes of the AAAI-94 Workshop on Computational Dialectics, Seattle, Washington, pp. 28–38 (1994)
2. Brewka, G., Gordon, T.F. (eds.): Proceedings of the FAPR-96 Workshop on Computational Dialectics (1996)
3. Brewka, G., Gordon, T.F.: Carneades and Abstract Dialectical Frameworks: A Reconstruction. In: Proceedings of the Third International Conference on Computational Models of Argument (COMMA), pp. 3–12. IOS Press, Amsterdam (2010)

4. Brewka, G., Woltran, S.: Abstract Dialectical Frameworks. In: Proceedings of the Twelfth International Conference on the Principles of Knowledge Representation and Reasoning, pp. 102–111. AAAI Press (2010)
5. di Primio, F. (ed.): Methoden der Künstlichen Intelligenz für Grafikanwendungen. Addison-Wesley (1995)
6. Dung, P.M.: On the acceptability of arguments and its fundamental role in non-monotonic reasoning, logic programming and n-person games. Artificial Intelligence 77(2), 321–357 (1995)
7. Gordon, T.F.: The Role of Exceptions in Models of the Law. In: Fiedler, H., Traunmüller, R. (eds.) Formalisierung im Recht und Ansätze juristischer Expertensysteme, pp. 52–59. J. Schweitzer Verlag, Munich (1986)
8. Gordon, T.F.: Some Problems with Prolog as a Knowledge Representation Language for Legal Expert Systems. In: Arnold, C. (ed.) Yearbook of Law, Computers and Technology, pp. 52–67. Leicester Polytechnic Press, Leicester (1987)
9. Gordon, T.F., Karacapilidis, N.: The Zeno argumentation framework. In: Proceedings of the Sixth International Conference on Artificial Intelligence and Law, Melbourne, Australia, pp. 10–18. ACM Press (1997)
10. Gordon, T.F., Prakken, H., Walton, D.: The Carneades Model of Argument and Burden of Proof. Artificial Intelligence 171(10-11), 875–896 (2007)
11. Loui, R.P.: The Workshop on Computational Dialectics. AI Magazine 16(4), 101–104 (1995)

Author Index